France

Vintage	Red Bordeaux		White Bordeaux		Alsace
	Médoc/Graves	Pom/St-Ém	Sauternes & sw	Graves & dry	
2017	6–8	6–7	8–9	7–8	9–10
2016	8–9	8–9	8–10	7–9	7–8
2015	7–9	8–10	8–10	7–9	7–9
2014	7–8	6–8	8–9	8–9	7–8
2013	4–7	4–7	8–9	7–8	8–9
2012	6–8	6–8	5–6	7–9	8–9
2011	7–8	7–8	8–10	7–8	5–7
2010	8–10	7–10	7–8	7–9	8–9
2009	7–10	7–10	8–10	7–9	8–9
2008	6–8	6–9	6–7	7–8	7–8
2007	5–7	6–7	8–9	8–9	6–8
2006	7–8	7–8	7–8	8–9	6–8
2005	9–10	8–9	7–9	8–10	8–9
2004	7–8	7–9	5–7	6–7	6–8
2003	5–9	5–8	7–8	6–7	6–7
2002	6–8	5–8	7–8	7–8	7–8
2001	6–8	7–8	8–10	7–9	6–8
2000	8–10	7–9	6–8	6–8	8–10
1999	5–7	5–8	6–9	7–10	6–8

France continued

Vintage	Burgundy			Rhône	
	Côte d'Or red	Côte d'Or white	Chablis	North	South
2017	6–8	8–9	6–8	7–9	7–9
2016	7–8	7–8	7–8	7–9	7–9
2015	7–9	7–8	7–8	8–9	8–9
2014	6–8	7–9	7–9	7–8	6–8
2013	5–7	7–8	6–8	7–9	7–8
2012	8–9	7–8	7–8	7–9	7–9
2011	7–8	7–8	7–8	7–8	6–8
2010	8–10	8–10	8–10	8–10	8–9
2009	7–10	7–9	7–8	7–9	7–8
2008	7–9	7–9	7–9	6–7	5–7
2007	7–8	8–9	8–9	6–8	7–8
2006	7–8	8–10	8–9	7–8	7–9
2005	7–9	7–9	7–9	7–8	6–8
2004	6–7	7–8	7–8	6–7	6–7

Beaujolais 2017, 15, 14, 11. Crus will keep. **Mâcon-Villages** (white). Drink 17, 15, 14. **Loire** (sweet Anjou and Touraine) best recent vintages: 15, 10, 09, 07, 05, 02, 97, 96, 93, 90, 89; Bourgueil, Chinon, Saumur-Champigny: 17, 15, 14, 10, 09, 06, 05, 04, 02. **Upper Loire** (Sancerre, Pouilly-Fumé): 17, 15, 14, 12. **Muscadet**: DYA.

HUGH
JOHNSON'S
POCKET
WINE BOOK
2019

MITCHELL BEAZLEY

Hugh Johnson's Pocket Wine Book 2019

Edited and designed by Mitchell Beazley,
an imprint of Octopus Publishing Group Limited,
Carmelite House, 50 Victoria Embankment
London EC4Y 0DZ
www.octopusbooks.co.uk

An Hachette UK Company
www.hachette.co.uk

Distributed in the US by Hachette Book Group
1290 Avenue of the Americas
4th and 5th Floors
New York, NY 10020
www.octopusbooksusa.com

ISBN (UK): 978-1-78472-482-5
ISBN (US): 978-1-78472-528-0

General Editor **Margaret Rand**
Commissioning Editor **Hilary Lumsden**
Senior Editor **Pauline Bache**
Proofreader **Jamie Ambrose**
Art Director **Yasia Williams-Leedham**
Designer **Jeremy Tilston**
Picture Library Manager **Jennifer Veall**
Senior Production Manager **Katherine Hockley**

Printed and bound in China

Mitchell Beazley would like to acknowledge and thank the following
for supplying photographs for use in this book:

Alamy Stock Photo Bon Appétit 323; Jon Arnold Images Ltd. 325.
Cephas Picture Library © Herbert Lehmann 331; © Jean-Bernard Nadeau
326. **Dreamstime.com** Photozeko7 16; Rosshelen 336; Sergey Kravchenko 321.
Getty Images James Braund 13; Peter Zelei Images 4. **iStock** ClaudioStocco
14; igorr1 7; Magone 334; MarkSwallow 1; Travellerboy 11; ValentynVolkov 332;
Veronika Roosimaa 6. **StockFood** Herbert Lehmann 335.
www.rawwine.com 328.

HUGH
JOHNSON'S
POCKET
WINE BOOK
2019

GENERAL EDITOR
MARGARET RAND

Acknowledgements

This store of detailed recommendations comes partly from my own notes and mainly from those of a great number of kind friends. Without the generous help and cooperation of innumerable winemakers, merchants and critics, I could not attempt it. I particularly want to thank the following for help with research or in the areas of their special knowledge:

Ian D'Agata, Helena Baker, Amanda Barnes, Lana Bortolot, Jim Budd, Michael Cooper, Michael Edwards, Sarah Jane Evans MW, Rosemary George MW, Caroline Gilby MW, Anthony Gismondi, Paul Gregutt, Anne Krebiehl MW, James Lawther MW, Tim Teichgraeber, Konstantinos Lazarakis MW, John Livingstone-Learmonth, Michele Longo, Campbell Mattinson, Adam Montefiore, Jasper Morris MW, Ch'ng Poh Tiong, André Ribeirinho, Margaret Rand, Ulrich Sautter, Eleonora Scholes, Paul Strang, Sean Sullivan, Marguerite Thomas, Gal Zohar, Philip van Zyl.

Contents

How to use this book

The top line of most entries consists of the following information:

1. Aglianico del Vulture Bas

2. r dr (s/sw sp)

3. ★★★

4. 10' 11 12 13 14' 15 (16)

1. Aglianico del Vulture Bas

Wine name and the region the wine comes from, abbreviations of regions are listed in each section.

2. r dr (s/sw sp)

Whether it is red, rosé or white (or brown), dry, sweet or sparkling, or several of these (and which is most important):

r	red
p	rosé
w	white
br	brown
dr	dry*
sw	sweet
s/sw	semi-sweet
sp	sparkling

( ) brackets here denote a less important wine
* assume wine is dry when dr or sw are not indicated

3. ★★★

Its general standing as to quality: a necessarily rough-and-ready guide based on its current reputation as reflected in its prices:

★	plain, everyday quality
★★	above average
★★★	well known, highly reputed
★★★★	grand, prestigious, expensive

So much is more or less objective. Additionally there is a subjective rating:

★ etc.   Stars are coloured for any wine that, in my experience, is usually especially good within its price range. There are good everyday wines as well as good luxury wines. This system helps you find them.

4. 10' 11 12 13 14' 15 (16)

Vintage information: those recent vintages that can be
recommended, and of these, which are ready to drink this year, and
which will probably improve with keeping. Your choice for current
drinking should be one of the vintage years printed in **bold** type.
Buy light-type years for further maturing.

16 etc.   recommended years that may be currently available
14' etc.   vintage regarded as particularly successful for the property
          in question
11 etc.   years in bold should be ready for drinking (those not in bold
          will benefit from keeping)
13 etc.   vintages in colour are those recommended as first choice
          for drinking in 2019. (*See also* Bordeaux introduction, p.100.)
(17) etc.   provisional rating

The German vintages work on a different principle again: *see* p.158.

Other abbreviations & styles

DYA   drink the youngest available
NV   vintage not normally shown on label;
            in Champagne this means a blend of several
            vintages for continuity
CHABLIS   properties, areas or terms cross-referred within
            the section; all grapes cross-ref to Grape
            Varieties chapter on pp.16–26
Foradori   entries styled this way indicate wine especially
            enjoyed by Hugh Johnson (mid-2017–18)

At first I called it fitting angels onto a pinhead. Then the image changed to taking a census in a rabbit warren. I was talking, of course, about the compression needed to justify the title of this book. Pockets, alas, can't expand the way SUVs have done recently. But the number of wines worth recording does – exponentially. Not just the number (of wines, wineries, wine regions...) but the complexity of what they are offering. I've tried the image of weaving – the vineyard is the warp, the grape variety the weft. But embroidery is more like it: the million little stitches that make up a tapestry.

In a tapestry, of course, they form into patterns to make the big picture. In wine? Is there a big picture? Only when you get down to drinking. Wine-drinkers polarize (like sports buffs, or buffs of any persuasion) into geeks, nerds or however you term the ultra-keen with fine-print memories, and the sort whose enthusiasm comes and goes. I hear it twice a week: "I don't know anything about wine, but I know what I like." "But I've forgotten its name" often comes next. I sympathize. I sympathize, too, with the majority whose eyes flick first to the right-hand column: the prices. There is plenty there these days to send eyebrows into orbit. You don't have time to read another diatribe from me on restaurant mark-ups. Auction prices, also, can affect your blood pressure.

What everyone wants to know is what will taste familiar, only better than they remembered. Preferably with a memorable name. I have the answer, of course. It's printed on every page of this book. The choice you have to make is where to start looking.

Commentators (I am one) can have an exaggerated respect (even affection) for their subjects – the suffering souls they have seen in a hail-smitten vineyard or sitting up all night with a fermentation that's going sideways. Sommeliers are sometimes the worst, positively hugging their personal discoveries. Personal feelings can easily sway opinion – and you can argue that if feelings aren't personal they are not feelings at all. Is an objective measure of wine possible? Of its "quality", maybe. By taking an average of enough expert opinions you certainly get close, however flawed some of the opinions may be. For most people, though, the subjective view is simply more important. I love certain wines/people/places because I love them. And, by the way, I'll try to get you to love them too.

Let me reassure you: it's all better than it was. Of course there's room for wobble. Vintages vary (too much rain, not enough).

Even bottles vary. Vintners can have off-vintages if they make mistakes or wrong decisions. Many employ consultants as an insurance policy. Even they can blow it.

It's experience, research and rivalry that push standards steadily upwards. "Agenda" – it means things to be done. By you: follow the guidebook. By wine producers: taste, taste, taste. Find the key to what makes your wine yours. Look for the USP that comes from your corner of the earth and what you have done with it. It is not easy to be recognizable among 50 Mendoza Malbecs or Kiwi Sauvignons. It's not cheating to blend in a bit of Merlot or Semillon to make it more "yours". Some have a clear idea of the wine they're aiming to make. (Some, sadly, get their idea from a marketing department.) Others strain their senses to find or identify what Nature has doled out to them. "Sense of place" is what critics want (even if they can't define it). Not just place, I would say, but purpose.

The fun, these days, is in discovery – self-discovery (see above) if you're a winemaker. If you're a mere drinker, it's shaking off prejudice. I admit, for all my curiosity (and, I hope, open-mindedness) I have only recently drunk the "orange" wines that came into fashion a couple of years ago. But if you'll go along with a fashionable chef's wacky combination of flavours (the alternative is starvation) you have no reason to refuse wine made in a clay pot in the ground or in a concrete egg. You want your wine brilliant, no prickle, harmonious, diamond-bright, its tannins and acidity polished, mellowed, under control? You don't know what thrills you're missing.

I've noticed a tendency to smugness recently. We've grown out of the unfortunate phase of oak and alcohol being mistaken for quality, haven't we? We've all sworn fealty to terroir, to the vineyard being more important than the cellar. We drive, so we'll try "low alcohol". All those Greek and Italian grapes we've never heard of? We give them a try. Canada? Why not? Turkey, sure. Brazil, no problem. Now here comes China: suddenly, I'm told, the biggest wine country of all. We're only seeing the beginning.

For years I have been a referee at the annual Oxford and Cambridge winetasting match. These days I can tell you which way to bet: the team with more Chinese players. Astute? I've never seen people learn the rules so quickly.

I've slowly ticked off items on my agenda over the years. I've dealt with 100-point scoring (it's wounded, but still kicking) red wines puffed up with colourants and oak at excessive levels of alcohol. Too much is still over 15%, even if it says 14% on the label. I haven't talked much about fakes. It's more prevalent than ever among luxury wines. If you're not quite sure, don't buy the super-rareties (though any international brand could be subject to fakery).

The final "too much" is money. The secondary market is (like, I suppose, all markets) out of control. There is a global lust after maybe a hundred famous labels. Their prices regularly beat stock markets – and (in the UK) gains are untaxed. Most are in extremely limited supply; the word "cult" fits them nicely. I considered having a symbol for these speculators' wines in addition to the four stars they would earn just be being famous and expensive, but they don't need my help. "Fine wine," said a San Franciscan wine sage a few years ago, "used to be for the worthy." He meant people who had taken the time and trouble to study and appreciate it. "Now," he said sadly, "it's for the wealthy." Prices are easier to understand.

Other bees in my bonnet: the size of wine glasses. There is an argument (the gospel according to Riedel) for huge, thin-walled bowls for prestigious tastings, where only a smidgen of a sample will be poured. They add glamour to the occasion – and the wine. But for regular use, when they are routinely filled nearly half full, the portion size is simply excessive; 175ml of wine is almost a quarter of a bottle – and more than you can drink if you're driving home. It is the essence of fine wines to satisfy with a generous sip, followed by a moment's reflection. I've seen people guzzle them, and it makes me sick.

Bee number two: corks. Why do we need them? I'm longing for the day when I can throw away my corkscrew. Screwcaps may not be aesthetically perfect, but they work. I've often opened white wines that have been screwcapped for ten years and never yet found one prematurely aged. Whereas corks, despite every precaution, can still let you down. It may be a generation before First Growths change their minds. But I've changed mine. I want to see every wine available with a screwcap, and if someone can design one that looks glamorous it won't take too long to happen.

In order to clear up a few misunderstandings about the stars system in this book, please refresh your memory of the rubric on page 6 and the front jacket flap. Do note they are not quality judgements, except indirectly, inasmuch as consensus about quality builds reputations. There are a few wineries that charge high prices to attract attention; should they then earn four stars? The colour of the stars is indicative: red stars mean well-earned merit, including value for money, however much.

For Europe, 2017 was the year of the frost. For California, it was the year of forest fires. Both were catastrophic for those affected. But as is the way with wine, for those who escaped it was a good vintage – though not one of the greats, anywhere.

Europe first. Frost struck on a wide front on the morning of April 27, and because the spring had been warm the vines were well advanced. It could hardly have happened at a worse moment.

In **Bordeaux**, the further you were from the river, and the lower-lying you were, the more likely you were to be hit. Langoa-Barton, Léoville-Barton and Léoville-Poyferré, on their gravelly dunes, escaped, but Camensac lost 90 per cent, and Chasse-Spleen 50. Classed Growths often escape frosts that hit less fortunate vineyards. At Domaine de Chevalier in Pessac-Léognan, some parcels were 100 per cent frosted while others, just 3m (10ft) higher, were untouched. At Château Brown they found that a frosted vine might be next to an unfrosted one – it was patchy and inconsistent. In Pomerol the plateau escaped, but the lower parts (and the difference in altitude looks trivial) lost 75–80 per cent.

The vines then produced a second crop of clusters, and sometimes a third as well; and because it was still early in the year these had often ripened sufficiently to look almost indistinguishable from first-crop clusters by the time of picking. But because the flavours would never be ripe enough they had to be removed – not an easy task. It was a year when expensive optical sorting machines, which can check 10,000 berries per minute, came into their own.

In **Champagne**, after a frosty start, the Chardonnay was pretty successful everywhere; the Pinot Noir patchy, with good results on the Montagne de Reims; the Pinot Meunier less good. What there is of it: Drappier lost 70 per cent, having been hit last year as well. The last time they were frosted two years in a row, says Hugo Drappier, was 1956 and 1957.

In **Burgundy**, almost perversely, they're celebrating the biggest vintage for a couple of years, and one which they badly needed. Indeed, some reports suggest unusually high yields, with vines compensating for the previous year. Growers managed to ward off frost by getting together to burn straw bales among the vines. Chablis, where the frost went on for 15 days, was less

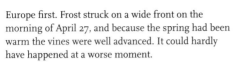

fortunate, and after five days everybody simply ran out of burners. Not everything was hit, but quantities of Chablis will be well down. After the frost came heat and sometimes hail. Morey-St-Denis had hail, and everywhere had heat, and there was some shrivelling and some problems with physiological ripeness. Rain in late August came as a relief. There was more rain around harvest time, so uneven ripeness combined with some dilution. Not a great year – but at least there's plenty of it.

In the **Rhône**, frost in Crozes-Hermitage and St-Joseph took the edge off, though the North in general had a good year. In the South a heatwave hurt the fruit-set of the all-important Grenache after flowering – which means less wine. What there is is very concentrated, but volumes are about 40 per cent down.

Germany had frost, **Austria** had less, but in both countries after that it was a story of heat and rain – sometimes too much heat and too little rain, but always just enough rain to keep the vines going. Hail hit various spots – Baden and Württemburg, and parts of the Mosel, Rheingau and Rheinhessen, as well as much of **Switzerland** – in August. And rain around harvest proved a problem in both countries. At Meyer-Näkel in Germany's Ahr, it looked like the best year ever until three weeks before harvest, when the rain arrived. In much of Austria, rain set the seal on an uneven year, and quality will be uneven too. Selection in the vineyard will be the key to making good wines.

Italy had a mixed year, In Friuli whites did best, but 20 days of rain at harvest was a problem for reds. Piedmont was hotter, with Barbera regularly hitting 15% alcohol. **Spain** suffered frost, drought and sometimes hail as well: Ribera del Duero had all three, and Rioja Alta the first two. Regions near the sea (Priorat and Galicia) survived best, though forest fires hit parts of Rías Baixas post-harvest. **Portugal** escaped frost but certainly had drought and high temperatures, and forest fires in the north. Reds are probably a better bet than whites.

And then there was **California**. The whole world watched the terrifying film footage of out-of-control fires: ironically, it had been a near-perfect summer until then. At the moment it's not clear how much smoke damage there is to the new wine: but luckily about 90 per cent of the grapes were already picked. There were wildfires in parts of **Oregon**, too, but the Willamette Valley was untouched and seems to have made good Pinot Noir and Chardonnay. **Washington State** was relatively cool and one of the few spots to have enjoyed a calm, uneventful 2017.

The story of 2016 is of a return to freshness after the opulence of 2015: plenty of good stuff in Bordeaux, but in Burgundy not much to go round.

There are no real surprises in the development of wines in any region. Italian wine-growers are happy; Spaniards/Germans/Austrians/Californians: all happy (the latter as happy as they can be given the drought, and more recent fires and mudslides.) Across Europe 2016 is seen as a sort of coming home; a reassuring success in the face of often difficult conditions, and a display of modern winemaking at its best: balanced, fresh and expressing the character of the year.

Bordeaux, not yet in bottle at time of writing, is looking very good indeed: a vintage to buy. The northern Médoc generally is both ripe and fresh, with tannins of real finesse, and more consistent than 2015. Margaux is slightly more mixed. Pessac-Léognan has some real stars, and St-Émilion/Pomerol are both looking very good, the former continuing its move away from overoaking, and the latter helped by its clay soils to survive the summer drought. Alcohol is generally down on 2015. Winemakers (and writers) love to find parallel vintages in the past, but with 2016 they're struggling. This combination of really silky tannins with intense, ripe fruit and great freshness has them flummoxed. Maybe 2010 is the closest comparison, but the 2016s are less massive. It's a modern classic and so will need time to show off all its paces. Curiously, the frost that reduced the volume of the 2017 vintage helped to inflate the 2016s en-primeur price, and also reduce the quantity offered en primeur. The 2017 frost hit on April 26–7, at the start of the 2016 primeur campaign. It wasn't long before prices started to creep up (prices are set by the châteaux at this stage, not by the market, though the châteaux pride themselves on being able to read the market. Well, they would). The châteaux also started to hold more back for the future. So if you didn't buy anything en primeur don't worry – there'll be no shortage once the wines are in bottle.

In **Burgundy**, the quantities of 2016 are tiny, but the wines are often very delicious. Whites have the right amount of tension combined with ripe fruit; reds are aromatic and fresh with fine tannins. Some of the reds look a little austere in youth, but will evolve. Both reds and whites are for medium-term drinking: much less opulent than the 2015s but more classically burgundian. It's a very good year, incidentally, for buying Bourgogne Blanc or Bourgogne Rouge.

A closer look at 2016

If you like Champagne, try Champagne with some oak-ageing

No, we haven't been converted to the flavour of vanilla. Oak is being used in Champagne to add creaminess and weight, not oaky flavours, and certainly not tannin: tannin in Champagne is horrible. "Creamy" is the usual adjective for the extra dimension given by carefully handled oak. Krug and Bollinger are the obvious examples, but producers of the calibre of Vilmart, Jacques Selosses, Jacquesson, Claude Giraud, Jérôme Prevost, Lenoble and Larmandier-Bernier are fermenting in oak. The final wine should have no less precision and freshness, but should gain richness, and an ability to match with food.

If you like white burgundy, try Sonoma Coast Chardonnay

The attraction of white burgundy, to those who love it, is that it doesn't really taste of Chardonnay. What it should do is transmit a sense of the terroir – of the chalk and clay, the stoniness and freshness of a particular hillside. It should also never be fat or too opulent – 2015 is a difficult vintage for lovers of white burgundy. Over in California, the cool, high, windswept and foggy Sonoma Coast can't reproduce the geology of the Côte d'Or – why should it? – but it can offer Chardonnay grown at the climatic margin, with verticality, acidity and depth, from geologically complex soils. This is pretty close to the San Andreas Fault, and the earth has been moving for a long time.

If you like Fino Sherry, try Retsina

These are both, admittedly, minority interests. But Fino is finding a new following among people hooked on its pungent freshness, its refusal to taste of grapes. Good Retsina (and that's not a contradiction in terms) does have some grapiness about it, but it's a muted, ethereal grapiness, because it's balanced by an equally ethereal beeswax-and-turpentine note of resin. It shouldn't be oily or heavy, but it should be clean as a whistle, linear and fresh. Try it, honestly (*see* p.238).

If you like young Pinot Noir, try Refosco

Young Pinot is wonderfully appealing: juicy red fruit, crunchy acidity, a bit of grip and that transparency of texture that makes you want another glass. Friuli's most widely grown indigenous red grape, Refosco dal Peduncolo Rosso, has all that. Granted, it's intrinsically a more rustic grape than Pinot, but because it doesn't gain sugar that easily it can be left on the vine until the tannins are ripe, and still have just 13% alcohol. It has high acidity and lovely juiciness, and sometimes a savoury, almost meaty character. It's a perfect match for all the game dishes you'd match with Pinot, plus goose, duck or just a plate of salami.

If you like Beaujolais, try Schioppetino

Schioppetino is another Friuli grape – you can see where we've been this year. Paradoxically it's more refined, less rustic than Refosco, but when you taste it, particularly the simpler examples, really good Beaujolais is what comes to mind. It has a fresh, green-peppercorn note, and was hardly known until it was rediscovered in just one small region; now it's planted all over Friuli. It has a natural grace and a touch of blueberry fruit, along with floral notes and really good freshness. It's not that well known outside Friuli, though, or we might be saying, if you like Schioppetino, try Beaujolais. Good Beaujolais is something that also merits rediscovery.

If you like red burgundy, try Mornington Peninsula Pinot Noir

Red burgundy gets more and more expensive as the world learns more and more about its charms – and its risks. Australia's Mornington Peninsula has been growing and making Pinot Noir for several decades now, and the wines are thoroughly convincing. This being Australia, there are plenty of growers making wild-ferment wines (that's without commercial yeast) and offering Pinots of purity and elegance. The other region to look for is Yarra Valley, which is overflowing with Pinot expertise: look for wines of slightly more weight, with perfume and crunchy, savoury fruit.

If you like wines with aroma, try different glasssses

Different glasses really do affect how wines smell and taste. Riedel takes it to extremes, with umpteen glass shapes; you don't have to go that far. You want a big enough bowl that tapers in at the top – and the Riedel Riesling/Zinfandel glass is a perfect all-purpose shape for everything from Champagne to rich reds. (Nobody in Champagne uses flutes any more; they don't flatter the wine.) Whites are good in this shape, too, and can be lost in a bigger glass. Wine is at its most aromatic, however, in Zalto glasses. They have an angular shape and are so light they're hardly there – until they break, when you remember how much they cost. Other companies are now copying that shape in cheaper ranges, and these are worth hunting down.

Grape varieties

In the past two decades a radical change has come about in all except the most long-established wine countries: the names of a handful of grape varieties have become the ready-reference to wine. In senior wine countries, above all France and Italy, more complex traditions prevail. All wine of old prestige is known by its origin, more or less narrowly defined – not just by the particular fruit juice that fermented. For the present the two notions are in rivalry. Eventually the primacy of place over fruit will become obvious, at least for wines of quality. But for now, for most people, grape tastes are the easy reference point – despite the fact that they are often confused by the added taste of oak. If grape flavours were really all that mattered, this would be a very short book. But of course they *do* matter, and a knowledge of them both guides you to flavours you enjoy and helps comparisons between regions. Hence the originally Californian term "varietal wine", meaning, in principle, made from one grape variety. At least seven varieties – Cabernet Sauvignon, Pinot Noir, Riesling, Sauvignon Blanc, Chardonnay, Gewurztraminer and Muscat – taste and smell distinct and memorable enough to form international wine categories. To these add Merlot, Malbec, Syrah, Sémillon, Chenin Blanc, Pinots Blanc and Gris, Sylvaner, Viognier, Nebbiolo, Sangiovese, Tempranillo. The following are the best and/or most popular wine grapes.

All grapes and synonyms are cross-referenced in small capitals throughout every section of this book.

Grapes for red wine

Agiorgitiko Greek; the grape of Nemea, now planted almost everywhere. Versatile and delicious, from soft and charming to dense and age-worthy. A must-try.

Aglianico S Italian, the grape of Taurasi; dark, deep and fashionable.

Alicante Bouschet Used to be beyond pale, now stylish in Alentejo, Chile esp old vines.

Aragonez *See* TEMPRANILLO.

Auxerrois *See* MALBEC, if red. White Auxerrois has its own entry in White Grapes.

Băbească Neagră Traditional "black grandmother grape" of Moldova; light body and ruby-red colour.

Babić Dark grape from Dalmatia, grown in stony seaside v'yds round Šibenik. Exceptional quality potential.

Baga Portugal. Bairrada grape. Dark and tannic. Great potential but hard to grow.

Barbera Widely grown in Italy, best in Piedmont: high acidity, low tannin, cherry fruit. Ranges from barriqued and serious to semi-sweet and frothy. Fashionable in California and Australia; promising in Argentina.

Blauburger Austrian cross between BLAUER PORTUGIESER and BLAUFRÄNKISCH. Makes simple wines.

Blauburgunder *See* PINOT N.

Blauer Portugieser Central European esp Germany (Rheinhessen, Pfalz, mostly for rosé), Austria, Hungary. Light, fruity reds: drink young, slightly chilled.

Blaufränkisch (Kékfrankos, Lemberger, Modra Frankinja) Widely planted in Austria's Mittelburgenland: medium-bodied, peppery acidity, a characteristic salty note, berry aromas and eucalyptus. Often blended with CAB SAUV or ZWEIGELT. Lemberger in Germany (speciality of Württemberg), Kékfrankos in Hungary, Modra Frankinja in Slovenia.

Boğazkere Tannic and Turkish. Produces full-bodied wines.

Bonarda Ambiguous name. In Oltrepò Pavese, an alias for Croatina, soft fresh *frizzante* and still red. In Lombardy and Emilia-Romagna an alias for Uva Rara. Different in Piedmont. Argentina's Bonarda can be any of these, or something else. None are great.

Bouchet St-Émilion alias for CAB FR.

Brunello SANGIOVESE, splendid at Montalcino.

Cabernet Franc [Cab Fr] The lesser of two sorts of Cab grown in B'x, but dominant in St-Émilion. Outperforms CAB SAUV in Loire (Chinon, Saumur-Champigny, rosé), in Hungary (depth and complexity in Villány and Szekszárd) and often in Italy. Much of ne Italy's Cab Fr turned out to be CARMENÈRE. Used in B'x blends of Cab Sauv/MERLOT across the world.

Cabernet Sauvignon [Cab Sauv] Grape of great character: slow-ripening, spicy, herby, tannic, with blackcurrant aroma. Main grape of the Médoc; also makes some of the best California, S American, East European reds. Vies with SHIRAZ in Australia. Grown almost everywhere, and led vinous renaissance in eg. Italy. Top wines need ageing; usually benefits from blending with eg. MERLOT, CAB FR, SYRAH, TEMPRANILLO, SANGIOVESE etc. Makes aromatic rosé.

Cannonau GRENACHE in its Sardinian manifestation; can be v. fine, potent.

Carignan (Carignane, Carignano, Cariñena) Low-yielding old vines now v. fashionable everywhere from s of France to Chile; best: Corbières. Lots of depth and vibrancy. Overcropped Carignan is wine-lake fodder. Common in North Africa, Spain (as Cariñena) and California.

Carignano *See* CARIGNAN.

Cariñena *See* CARIGNAN.

Carmenère Old B'x variety now a star – rich and deep – in Chile (pronounced *carmeneary*). B'x is looking at it again.

Castelão *See* PERIQUITA.

Cencibel *See* TEMPRANILLO.

Chiavennasca *See* NEBBIOLO.

Cinsault (Cinsaut) A staple of s France, v.gd if low-yielding, wine-lake stuff if not. Makes gd rosé. One of parents of PINOTAGE.

Cornalin du Valais Swiss speciality with high potential esp in Valais.

Corvina Dark and spicy; one of best grapes in Valpolicella blend. Corvinone, even darker, is a separate variety.

Côt *See* MALBEC.

Dolcetto Source of soft, seductive dry red in Piedmont. Now high fashion.

Dornfelder Deliciously light reds, straightforward, often rustic, well-coloured in Germany, parts of US, England. German plantings have doubled since 2000.

Duras Spicy, peppery, structured; exclusive to Gaillac and parts of Tarn Valley, Southwest France.

Fer Servadou Exclusive to Southwest France, aka Mansois in Marcillac, Braucol in Gaillac and Pinenc in St-Mont. Redolent of red summer fruits and spice.

Fetească Neagră Romania: "black maiden grape" with potential as showpiece variety; can give deep, full-bodied wines with character. Acreage increasing.

Frühburgunder An ancient German mutation of PINOT N, mostly in Ahr but also in Franken and Württemberg, where it is confusingly known as Clevner. Lower acidity than Pinot N.

Gamay The Beaujolais grape: v. light, fragrant wines, best young, except in Beaujolais crus (*see* France) where quality can be high, wines for 2–10 yrs. Grown in the Loire Valley, in central France, in Switzerland and Savoie. California's Napa Gamay is Valdiguié.

Gamza *See* KADARKA.

Garnacha (Cannonau, Garnatxa, Grenache) Widespread pale, potent grape fashionable with *terroiristes*, because it expresses its site. Also gd for rosé and *vin doux naturel* – esp in s of France, Spain, California – but also mainstay of beefy Priorat. Old-vine versions prized in S Australia. Usually blended with other varieties. Cannonau in Sardinia, Grenache in France.

Garnatxa *See* GARNACHA.

Graciano Spanish; part of Rioja blend. Aroma of violets, tannic, lean structure, a bit like PETIT VERDOT. Difficult to grow but increasingly fashionable.

Grenache *See* GARNACHA.

Grignolino Italy: gd everyday table wine in Piedmont.

Kadarka (Gamza) Spicy, light East Europe reds. In Hungary revived esp for Bikavér.

Kalecik Karasi Turkish: sour-cherry fruit, fresh, supple. A bit like GAMAY. Drink young.

Kékfrankos Hungarian BLAUFRÄNKISCH.

Lagrein N Italian, dark, bitter finish, rich, plummy. DOC in Alto Adige (*see* Italy).

Lambrusco Productive grape of the lower Po Valley; quintessentially Italian, cheerful, sweet and fizzy red.

Lefkada Rediscovered Cypriot variety, higher quality than MAVRO. Usually blended as tannins can be aggressive.

Lemberger *See* BLAUFRÄNKISCH.

Malbec (Auxerrois, Côt) Minor in B'x, major in Cahors (alias Auxerrois), star in Argentina. Dark, dense, tannic but fleshy wine capable of real quality. High-altitude versions in Argentina are bee's knees. Bringing Cahors back into fashion.

Maratheftiko Deep-coloured Cypriot grape with quality potential.

Mataro *See* MOURVÈDRE.

Mavro Most planted black grape of Cyprus but only moderate quality. Best for rosé.

Mavrodaphne Greek; the name means "black laurel". Used for sweet fortifieds; speciality of Patras, but also found in Cephalonia. Dry versions on the increase, show great promise.

Mavrotragano Greek, almost extinct but now revived; on Santorini. Top quality.

Mavrud Probably Bulgaria's best. Spicy, dark, plummy late-ripener native to Thrace. Ages well.

Melnik Bulgarian grape from the region of the same name. Dark colour and a nice dense, tart-cherry character. Ages well.

Mencía Making waves in Bierzo, Spain. Aromatic, steely tannins and lots of acidity.

Merlot The grape behind the great fragrant and plummy wines of Pomerol and (with CAB FR) St-Émilion, a vital element in the Médoc, soft and strong (and *à la mode*) in California, Washington, Chile, Australia. Lighter, often gd in n Italy (can be world-class in Tuscany), Italian Switzerland, Slovenia, Argentina, S Africa, NZ, etc. Perhaps too adaptable for own gd: can be v. dull; less than ripe it tastes green. Much planted in Eastern Europe esp Romania.

Modra Frankinja *See* BLAUFRÄNKISCH.

Modri Pinot *See* PINOT N.

Monastrell *See* MOURVÈDRE.

Mondeuse Found in Savoie; deep coloured, gd acidity. Related to SYRAH.

Montepulciano Deep-coloured grape dominant in Italy's Abruzzo and important along Adriatic coast: Marches to s Puglia. Also name of a Tuscan town, unrelated.

Morellino SANGIOVESE in Maremma, s Tuscany. Esp Scansano.

Mourvèdre (Mataro, Monastrell) A star of s France (eg. Bandol), Australia (aka Mataro) and Spain (aka Monastrell). Excellent dark, aromatic, tannic grape, gd for blending. Enjoying new interest in eg. S Australia and California.

Napa Gamay Identical to Valdiguié (s of France). Nothing to get excited about.

Nebbiolo (Chiavennasca, Spanna) One of Italy's best red grapes; makes Barolo, Barbaresco, Gattinara and Valtellina. Intense, nobly fruity, perfumed wine with steely tannin: improves for yrs.

Negroamaro Puglian "black bitter" red grape with potential for either high quality or high volume.

Nerello Mascalese Characterful Sicilian red grape; potential for elegance.

Nero d'Avola Dark-red grape of Sicily, quality levels from sublime to industrial.

Nielluccio Corsican; plenty of acidity and tannin. Gd for rosé.

Öküzgözü Soft, fruity Turkish grape, usually blended with BOĞAZKERE, rather as MERLOT in B'x is blended with CAB SAUV.

País Pioneer Spanish grape in Americas. Rustic; some producers now trying harder.

Pamid Bulgarian: light, soft, everyday red.

Periquita (Castelão) Common in Portugal esp round Setúbal. Originally nicknamed Periquita after Fonseca's popular (trademarked) brand. Firm-flavoured, raspberryish reds develop a figgish, tar-like quality.

Petite Sirah Nothing to do with SYRAH; gives rustic, tannic, dark wine. Brilliant blended with ZIN in California; also found in S America, Mexico, Australia.

Petit Verdot Excellent but awkward Médoc grape, now increasingly planted in CAB areas worldwide for extra fragrance. Mostly blended but some gd varietals esp in Virginia.

Pinotage Singular S African cross (PINOT N X CINSAULT). Has had a rocky ride, getting better from top producers. Gd rosé too. "Coffee Pinotage" is espresso-flavoured, sweetish, aimed at youth.

Pinot Crni *See* PINOT N.

Pinot Meunier (Schwarzriesling) [Pinot M] The 3rd grape of Champagne, scorned by some, used by most. Less acid than PINOT N; invaluable for blending. Found in many places, either vinified as a white for fizz, or occasionally as still red. Samtrot is a local variant in Württemberg.

Pinot Noir (Blauburgunder, Modri Pinot, Pinot Crni, Spätburgunder) [Pinot N] The glory of Burgundy's Côte d'Or, with scent, flavour and texture unmatched anywhere. Recent German efforts have been excellent. V.gd in Austria esp in Kamptal, Burgenland, Thermenregion. Light wines in Hungary; mainstream, light to weightier in Switzerland (aka Clevner). Splendid results in Sonoma, Carneros, Central Coast, as well as Oregon, Ontario, Yarra Valley, Adelaide Hills, Tasmania, NZ's South Island (Central Otago) and S Africa's Walker Bay. Some v. pretty Chileans. New French clones promise improvement in Romania. Modri Pinot in Slovenia; probably country's best red. In Italy, best in ne and gets worse as you go s. PINOTS BL and GR are mutations of Pinot N.

Plavac Mali (Crljenak) Croatian, and related to ZIN, like so much round there. Lots of quality potential, can age well, though can also be alcoholic and dull.

Primitivo S Italian grape, originally from Croatia, making big, dark, rustic wines, now fashionable because genetically identical to ZIN. Early ripening, hence the name. The original name for both seems to be Tribidrag.

Refosco (Refošk) Various DOCs in Italy esp Colli Orientali. Deep, flavoursome and age-worthy wines, particularly in warmer climates. Dark, high acidity. Refošk in Slovenia and points e, genetically different, tastes similar.

Refošk *See* REFOSCO.

Roter Veltliner Austrian; unrelated to GRÜNER V. There is also a Frühroter and a Brauner Veltliner.

Rubin Bulgarian cross, NEBBIOLO X SYRAH. Peppery, full-bodied.

Sagrantino Italian grape grown in Umbria for powerful, cherry-flavoured wines.

St-Laurent Dark, smooth, full-flavoured Austrian speciality. Can be light and juicy or deep and structured. Also in Pfalz.

Sangiovese (Brunello, Morellino, Sangioveto) Principal red grape of Tuscany and central Italy. Hard to get right, but sublime and long-lasting when it is. Dominant in Chianti, Vino Nobile, Brunello di Montalcino, Morellino di Scansano and various fine IGT offerings. Also in Umbria (eg. Montefalco and Torgiano) and across the Apennines in Romagna and Marches. Not so clever in the warmer, lower-altitude v'yds of the Tuscan coast, nor in other parts of Italy despite its nr-ubiquity. Interesting in Australia.

Sangioveto *See* SANGIOVESE.

Saperavi The main red of Georgia, Ukraine, etc. Blends well with CAB SAUV (eg. in Moldova). Huge potential, seldom gd winemaking.

Schiava *See* TROLLINGER.

Schioppetino NE Italian, high acidity, high quality. Elegant, refined, can age.

Schwarzriesling PINOT M in Württemberg.

Sciacarello Corsican, herby and peppery. Not v. tannic.

Shiraz *See* SYRAH.

Spanna *See* NEBBIOLO.

Spätburgunder German for PINOT N.

Syrah (Shiraz) The great Rhône red grape: tannic, purple, peppery wine that matures superbly. Important as Shiraz in Australia, increasingly gd under either name in Chile, S Africa, terrific in NZ (esp Hawke's Bay). Widely grown.

Tannat Raspberry-perfumed, highly tannic force behind Madiran, Tursan and other firm reds from Southwest France. Also rosé. Now the star of Uruguay.

Tempranillo (Aragonez, Cecibel, Tinto Fino, Tinta del País, Tinta Roriz, Ull de Llebre) Aromatic, fine Rioja grape, called Ull de Llebre in Catalonia, Cencibel in La Mancha, Tinto Fino in Ribera del Duero, Tinta Roriz in Douro, Tinta del País in Castile, Aragonez in s Portugal. Now Australia too. V. fashionable; elegant in cool climates, beefy in warm. Early ripening, long maturing.

Teran (Terrano) Close cousin of REFOSCO esp on limestone (karst) in Slovenia.

Teroldego Rotaliano Trentino's best indigenous variety; serious, full-flavoured wine esp on flat Campo Rotaliano.

Tinta Amarela *See* TRINCADEIRA.

Tinta del País *See* TEMPRANILLO.

Tinta Negra (Negramoll) Until recently called Tinta Negra Mole. Easily Madeira's most planted grape and the mainstay of cheaper Madeira. Now coming into its own in Colheita wines (*see* Portugal).

Tinta Roriz *See* TEMPRANILLO.

Tinto Fino *See* TEMPRANILLO.

Touriga Nacional [Touriga N] The top Port grape, now widely used in the Douro for floral, stylish table wines. Australian Touriga is usually this; California's Touriga can be either this or Touriga Franca.

Trincadeira (Tinta Amarela) Portuguese; v.gd in Alentejo for spicy wines. Tinta Amarela in the Douro.

Trollinger (Schiava, Vernatsch) Popular pale red in Germany's Württemberg; aka Vernatsch and Schiava. Covers a group of vines, not necessarily related. In Italy, snappy and brisk.

Vernatsch *See* TROLLINGER.

Xinomavro Greece's answer to NEBBIOLO. "Sharp-black"; the basis for Naoussa, Rapsani, Goumenissa, Amindeo. Some rosé, still or sparkling. Top quality, can age for decades. Being tried in China.

Zinfandel [Zin] Fruity, adaptable grape of California with blackberry-like, and sometimes metallic, flavour. Can be structured and gloriously lush, ageing for decades, but also makes "blush" pink, usually sweet, jammy. Genetically the same as s Italian PRIMITIVO.

Zweigelt (Blauer Zweigelt) BLAUFRÄNKISCH X ST-LAURENT, popular in Austria for aromatic, dark, supple, velvety wines. Also found in Hungary, Germany.

Grapes for white wine

Airén Bland workhorse of La Mancha, Spain: fresh if made well.

Albariño (Alvarinho) Fashionable, expensive in Spain: apricot scented, gd acidity. Superb in Rías Baixas; shaping up elsewhere, but not all live up to the hype. Alvarinho in Portugal just as gd: aromatic Vinho Verde esp in Monção, Melgaço.

Aligoté Burgundy's 2nd-rank white grape. Sharp wine for young drinking, perfect for mixing with cassis (blackcurrant liqueur) to make Kir. Widely planted in East Europe, and esp Russia.

Alvarinho *See* ALBARIÑO.

Amigne One of Switzerland's speciality grapes, traditional in Valais esp Vétroz. Total planted: 43 ha. Full-bodied, tasty, often sweet but also bone-dry.

Ansonica *See* INSOLIA.

Arinto Portuguese; the mainstay of aromatic, citrus wines in Bucelas; also adds welcome zip to blends esp in Alentejo.

Arneis Nw Italian. Fine, aromatic, appley-peachy, high-priced grape, DOCG in Roero, DOC in Langhe, Piedmont.

Arvine Rare but excellent Swiss *spécialité*, from Valais. Also Petite Arvine. Dry or sweet, fresh, long-lasting wines with salty finish.

Assyrtiko From Santorini; one of the best grapes of the Mediterranean, balancing power, minerality, extract and high acid. Built to age. Could conquer the world....

Auxerrois Red Auxerrois is a synonym for MALBEC, but white Auxerrois is like a fatter, spicier PINOT BL. Found in Alsace and much used in Crémant; also Germany.

Beli Pinot *See* PINOT BL.

Blanc Fumé *See* SAUV BL.

Boal *See* BUAL.

Bourboulenc This and the rare Rolle make some of the Midi's best wines.

Bouvier Indigenous aromatic Austrian grape esp gd for Beerenauslese and Trockenbeerenauslese, rarely for dry wines.

Bual (Boal) Makes top-quality sweet Madeira wines, not quite so rich as MALMSEY.

Carricante Italian. Principal grape of Etna Bianco, regaining ground.

Catarratto Prolific white grape found all over Sicily esp in w in DOC Alcamo.

Cerceal *See* SERCIAL.

Chardonnay (Morillon) [Chard] The white grape of Burgundy and Champagne, now ubiquitous worldwide, partly because it is one of the easiest to grow and vinify. Also the name of a Mâcon-Villages commune. The fashion for overoaked butterscotch versions now thankfully over. Morillon in Styria, Austria.

Chasselas (Fendant, Gutedel) Swiss (originated in Vaud). Neutral flavour, takes on local character: elegant (Geneva); refined, full (Vaud); exotic, racy (Valais). Fendant in Valais. Makes almost 3rd of Swiss wines but giving way esp to red. Gutedel in Germany; grown esp in s Baden. Elsewhere usually a table grape.

Chenin Blanc [Chenin Bl] Wonderful white grape of the middle Loire (Vouvray, Layon, etc). Wine can be dry or sweet (or v. sweet), but with plenty of acidity. Formerly called Steen in S Africa; many ordinary but best noble. California can do it well but doesn't bother.

Cirfandl *See* ZIERFANDLER.

Clairette Important Midi grape, low-acid, part of many blends. Improved winemaking helps.

Colombard Slightly fruity, nicely sharp grape, makes everyday wine in S Africa, California and Southwest France. Often blended.

Dimiat Perfumed Bulgarian grape, made dry or off-dry, or distilled. Far more synonyms than any grape needs.

Ermitage Swiss for MARSANNE.

Ezerjó Hungarian, with sharp acidity. Name means "thousand blessings".

Falanghina Italian: ancient grape of Campanian hills. Gd dense, aromatic dry whites.

Fendant *See* CHASSELAS.

Fernão Pires *See* MARIA GOMES.

Fetească Albă / Regală Romania has two Fetească grapes, both with slight MUSCAT aroma. F. Regală is a cross of F. Albă and GRASĂ; more finesse, gd for late-harvest wines. F. NEAGRĂ is dark-skinned.

Fiano High-quality grape giving peachy, spicy wine in Campania, s Italy.

Folle Blanche (Gros Plant) High acid/little flavour make this ideal for brandy. Gros Plant in Brittany, Picpoul in Armagnac, but unrelated to true PICPOUL. Also respectable in California.

Friulano (Sauvignonasse, Sauvignon Vert) N Italian: fresh, pungent, subtly floral. Used to be called Tocai Friulano. Best in Collio, Isonzo, Colli Orientali. Found in nearby Slovenia as Sauvignonasse; also in Chile, where it was long confused with SAUV BL. Ex-Tocai in Veneto now known as Tai.

Fumé Blanc *See* SAUV BL.

Furmint (Šipon) Superb, characterful. The trademark of Hungary, both as the principal grape in Tokaji and as vivid, vigorous table wine, sometimes mineral, sometimes apricot-flavoured, sometimes both. Šipon in Slovenia. Some grown in Rust, Austria for sweet and dry.

Garganega Best grape in Soave blend; also in Gambellara. Top esp sweet, age well.

Garnacha Blanca (Grenache Blanc) The white version of GARNACHA/Grenache, much used in Spain and s France. Low acidity. Can be innocuous, or surprisingly gd.

Gewurztraminer (Traminac, Traminec, Traminer, Tramini) [Gewurz] One of the most pungent grapes, spicy with aromas of rose petals, face cream, lychees, grapefruit. Wines are often rich and soft, even when fully dry. Best in Alsace; also gd in Germany (Baden, Pfalz, Sachsen), Eastern Europe, Australia, California,

Pacific Northwest and NZ. Can be relatively unaromatic if just labelled Traminer (or variants). Italy uses the name Traminer Aromatico for its (dry) "Gewurz" versions. (The name takes an Umlaut in German.) Identical to SAVAGNIN.

Glera Uncharismatic new name for Prosecco vine: Prosecco is now wine only.

Godello Top quality (intense, mineral) in nw Spain. Called Verdelho in Dão, Portugal, but unrelated to true VERDELHO.

Grasă (Kövérszölö) Romanian; name means "fat". Prone to botrytis; important in Cotnari, potentially superb sweet wines. Kövérszölö in Hungary's Tokaj region.

Graševina *See* WELSCHRIESLING.

Grauburgunder *See* PINOT GR.

Grechetto Ancient grape of central and s Italy noted for the vitality and stylishness of its wine. Blended, or used solo in Orvieto.

Greco S Italian: there are various Grecos, probably unrelated, perhaps of Greek origin. Brisk, peachy flavour, most famous as Greco di Tufo. Greco di Bianco is from semi-dried grapes. Greco Nero is a black version.

Grenache Blanc *See* GARNACHA BLANCA.

Grillo Italy: main grape of Marsala. Also v.gd full-bodied dry table wine.

Gros Plant *See* FOLLE BLANCHE.

Grüner Veltliner [Grüner V] Austria's fashionable flagship white grape. Remarkably diverse: from simple, peppery everyday wines to others of great complexity and ageing potential. A little elsewhere in Central Europe, and now showing potential in NZ.

Gutedel *See* CHASSELAS.

Hárslevelű Other main grape of Tokaji, but softer, peachier than FURMINT. Name means "linden-leaved". Gd in Somló, Eger as well.

Heida Swiss for SAVAGNIN.

Humagne Swiss speciality, older than CHASSELAS. Fresh, plump, not v. aromatic. Humagne Rouge, also common in Valais, is not related but increasingly popular. Humagne Rouge is the same as Cornalin du Aosta; Cornalin du Valais is different. (Keep up at the back, there.)

Insolia (Ansonica, Inzolia) Sicilian; Ansonica on Tuscan coast. Fresh, racy wine at best. May be semi-dried for sweet wine.

Irsai Olivér Hungarian cross of two table varieties, makes aromatic, MUSCAT-like wine for drinking young.

Johannisberg Swiss for SILVANER.

Kéknyelű Low-yielding, flavourful grape giving one of Hungary's best whites. Has the potential for fieriness and spice. To be watched.

Kerner Quite successful German cross. Early ripening, flowery (but often too blatant) wine with gd acidity.

Királyleanyka Hungarian; gentle, fresh wines (eg. in Eger).

Koshu Supposedly indigenous Japanese grape/wine, much hyped. Fresh, harmless.

Kövérszölö *See* GRASĂ.

Laski Rizling *See* WELSCHRIESLING.

Leányka Hungarian. Soft, floral wines.

Listán *See* PALOMINO.

Loureiro Best Vinho Verde grape variety after ALVARINHO: delicate floral whites. Also found in Spain.

Macabeo *See* VIURA.

Malagousia Rediscovered Greek grape for gloriously perfumed wines.

Malmsey *See* MALVASIA. The sweetest style of Madeira.

Malvasia (Malmsey, Malvazija, Malvoisie, Marastina) Italy, France and Iberia. Not a single variety but a whole stable, not necessarily related or even alike. Can be white or red, sparkling or still, strong or mild, sweet or dry, aromatic or neutral.

Slovenia's and Croatia's version is Malvazija Istarka, crisp and light, or rich, oak-aged. Sometimes called Marastina in Croatia. "Malmsey" (as in the sweetest style of Madeira) is a corruption of Malvasia.

Malvoisie *See* MALVASIA. A name used for several varieties in France, incl BOURBOULENC, Torbato, VERMENTINO. Also PINOT GR in Switzerland's Valais.

Manseng, Gros / Petit Gloriously spicy, floral whites from Southwest France. The key to Jurançon. Superb late-harvest and sweet wines too.

Maria Gomes (Fernão Pires) Portuguese; aromatic, ripe-flavoured, slightly spicy whites in Barraida and Tejo.

Marsanne (Ermitage) Principal white grape (with ROUSSANNE) of the Northern Rhône (Hermitage, St-Joseph, St-Péray). Also gd in Australia, California and (as Ermitage Blanc) the Valais. Soft, full wines that age v. well.

Melon de Bourgogne *See* MUSCADET.

Misket Bulgarian. Mildly aromatic; the basis of most country whites.

Morillon CHARD in parts of Austria.

Moscatel *See* MUSCAT.

Moscato *See* MUSCAT.

Moschofilero Pink-skinned, rose-scented, high-quality, high-acid, low-alcohol Greek grape. Makes white, some pink, some sparkling.

Müller-Thurgau [Müller-T] Aromatic wines to drink young. Makes gd sweet wines but usually dull, often coarse, dry ones. In Germany, most common in Pfalz, Rheinhessen, Nahe, Baden, Franken. Has some merit in Italy's Trentino-Alto Adige, Friuli. Sometimes called Ries x Sylvaner (incorrectly) in Switzerland.

Muscadelle Adds aroma to white B'x esp Sauternes. In Victoria used (with MUSCAT, to which it is unrelated) for Rutherglen Muscat.

Muscadet (Melon de Bourgogne) Makes light, refreshing, v. dry wines with a seaside tang around Nantes in Brittany. Also found (as Melon) in parts of Burgundy.

Muscat (Moscatel, Moscato, Muskateller) Many varieties; the best is Muscat Blanc à Petits Grains (alias Gelber Muskateller, Rumeni Muškat, Sarga Muskotály, Yellow Muscat). Widely grown, easily recognized, pungent grapes, mostly made into perfumed sweet wines, often fortified, as in France's *vin doux naturel*. Superb, dark and sweet in Australia. Sweet, sometimes v.gd in Spain. Most Hungarian Muskotály is Muscat Ottonel except in Tokaj, where Sarga Muskotály rules, adding perfume (in small amounts) to blends. Occasionally (eg. Alsace, Austria, parts of s Germany) made dry. Sweet Cap Corse Muscats often superb. Light Moscato fizz in n Italy.

Muskateller *See* MUSCAT.

Narince Turkish; fresh and fruity wines.

Neuburger Austrian, rather neglected; mainly in the Wachau (elegant, flowery), Thermenregion (mellow, ample-bodied) and n Burgenland (strong, full).

Olaszriesling *See* WELSCHRIESLING.

Païen *See* SAVAGNIN.

Palomino (Listán) The great grape of Sherry; with little intrinsic character, it gains all from production method. As Listán, makes dry white in Canaries.

Pansa Blanca *See* XAREL·LO.

Pecorino Italian: not a cheese but alluring dry white from a recently nr-extinct variety. IGT in Colli Pescaresi.

Pedro Ximénez [PX] Makes sweet brown Sherry under its own name, and used in Montilla and Málaga. Also grown in Argentina, the Canaries, Australia, California and S Africa.

Picpoul (Piquepoul) Southern French, best known in Picpoul de Pinet. Should have high acidity. Picpoul Noir is black-skinned.

Pinela Local to Slovenia. Subtle, lowish acidity; drink young.

Pinot Bianco See PINOT BL.

Pinot Blanc (Beli Pinot, Pinot Bianco, Weißburgunder) [Pinot Bl] A cousin of PINOT N, similar to but milder than CHARD. Light, fresh, fruity, not aromatic, to drink young. Gd for Italian *spumante*, and potentially excellent in the ne esp high sites in Alto Adige. Widely grown. Weißburgunder in Germany and best in s: often racier than Chard.

Pinot Gris (Pinot Grigio, Grauburgunder, Ruländer, Sivi Pinot, Szürkebarát) [Pinot Gr] Ultra-popular as Pinot Grigio in n Italy, even for rosé, but top, characterful versions can be excellent (from Alto Adige, Friuli). Cheap versions are just that. Terrific in Alsace for full-bodied, spicy whites. Once important in Champagne. In Germany can be alias Ruländer (sw) or Grauburgunder (dr): best in Baden (esp Kaiserstuhl) and s Pfalz. Szürkebarát in Hungary, Sivi P in Slovenia (characterful, aromatic).

Pošip Croatian; mostly on island of Korčula. Quite characterful, citrus; high yielding.

Prosecco Old name for grape that makes Prosecco. Now you have to call it GLERA.

Renski Rizling Rhine RIES.

Rèze Super-rare ancestral Valais grape used for *vin de glacier*.

Ribolla Gialla / Rebula Acidic but characterful. In Italy, best in Collio. In Slovenia, traditional in Brda. Can be v.gd, even made in eccentric ways.

Rieslaner German cross (SILVANER X RIES); low yields, difficult ripening, now v. rare (less than 50 ha). Makes fine Auslesen in Franken and Pfalz.

Riesling Italico See WELSCHRIESLING.

Riesling (Renski Rizling, Rhine Riesling) [Ries] Greatest, most versatile white grape, diametrically opposite in style to CHARD. Offers range from steely to voluptuous, always positively perfumed, with far more ageing potential than Chard. Great in all styles in Germany; forceful and steely in Austria; lime-cordial and toast fruit in S Australia; rich and spicy in Alsace; Germanic and promising in NZ, NY State, Pacific Northwest; has potential in Ontario, S Africa.

Rkatsiteli Found widely in Eastern Europe, Russia, Georgia. Can stand cold winters and has high acidity, which protects it to some degree from poor winemaking. Also grown in ne US.

Robola In Greece (Cephalonia) a top-quality, floral grape, unrelated to RIBOLLA GIALLA.

Roditis Pink grape grown all over Greece, mostly makes whites. Gd when yields low.

Roter Veltliner Austrian; unrelated to GRÜNER V. There is also a Frühroter and an (unrelated) Brauner Veltliner.

Rotgipfler Austrian; indigenous to Thermenregion. With ZIERFANDLER, makes lively, lush, aromatic blend.

Roussanne Rhône grape of real finesse, now popping up in California and Australia. Can age many yrs.

Ruländer See PINOT GR.

Sauvignonasse See FRIULANO.

Sauvignon Blanc [Sauv Bl] Makes distinctive aromatic, grassy-to-tropical wines, pungent in NZ, often minerally in Sancerre, riper in Australia. V.gd in Rueda, Austria, n Italy (Isonzo, Piedmont, Alto Adige), Chile's Casablanca Valley and S Africa. Blended with SÉM in B'x. Can be austere or buxom (or indeed nauseating). Sauv Gris is a pink-skinned, less aromatic version of Sauv Bl with untapped potential.

Sauvignon Vert See FRIULANO.

Savagnin (Heida, Païen) Grape for *vin jaune* from Jura: aromatic form is GEWURZ. In Switzerland known as Heida, Païen or Traminer. Full-bodied, high acidity.

Scheurebe (Sämling) Grapefruit-scented German RIES X SILVANER (possibly), v. successful in Pfalz esp for Auslese and upwards. Can be weedy: must be v. ripe to be gd.

Sémillon [Sém] Contributes lusciousness to Sauternes but decreasingly important for Graves and other dry white B'x. Grassy if not fully ripe, but can make soft dry wine of great ageing potential. Superb in Australia; NZ, S Africa promising.

Sercial (Cerceal) Portuguese: makes the driest Madeira. Cerceal, also Portuguese, seems to be this plus any of several others.

Seyval Blanc [Seyval Bl] French-made hybrid of French and American vines. V. hardy and attractively fruity. Popular and reasonably successful in e US and England but dogmatically banned by EU from "quality" wines.

Silvaner (Johannisberg, Sylvaner) Can be excellent in Germany's Rheinhessen, Pfalz, esp Franken; plant/earth flavours and mineral notes. V.gd (and powerful) as Johannisberg in the Valais, Switzerland. The lightest of the Alsace grapes.

Šipon *See* FURMINT.

Sivi Pinot *See* PINOT GR.

Spätrot *See* ZIERFANDLER.

Sylvaner *See* SILVANER.

Tămâioasă Românească Romanian: "frankincense" grape, with exotic aroma and taste. Belongs to MUSCAT family.

Torrontés Name given to a number of grapes, mostly with an aromatic, floral character, sometimes soapy. A speciality of Argentina; also in Spain. DYA.

Traminac Or Traminec. *See* GEWURZ.

Traminer Or Tramini (Hungary). *See* GEWURZ.

Trebbiano (Ugni Blanc) Principal white grape of Tuscany, found all over Italy in many different guises. Rarely rises above the plebeian except in Tuscany's Vin Santo. Some gd dry whites under DOCs Romagna or Abruzzo. Trebbiano di Soave or di Lugana, aka VERDICCHIO, is only distantly related. Grown in southern France as Ugni Blanc, and Cognac as St-Émilion. Mostly thin, bland wine; needs blending (and more careful growing).

Ugni Blanc [Ugni Bl] *See* TREBBIANO.

Ull de Llebre *See* TEMPRANILLO.

Verdejo The grape of Rueda in Castile, potentially fine and long-lived.

Verdelho Great quality in Australia (pungent, full-bodied); rare but gd (and medium-sweet) in Madeira.

Verdicchio Potentially gd, muscular, dry; central-e Italy. Wine of same name.

Vermentino Italian, sprightly with satisfying texture, ageing capacity. Potential here.

Vernaccia Name given to many unrelated grapes in Italy. Vernaccia di San Gimignano is crisp, lively; Vernaccia di Oristano is Sherry-like.

Vidal French hybrid much grown in Canada for Icewine.

Vidiano Most Cretan producers are in love with this. Powerful, stylish. Lime/apricot fruit, gd acidity.

Viognier Ultra-fashionable Rhône grape, finest in Condrieu, less fine but still aromatic in the Midi. Gd examples from California, Virginia, Uruguay, Australia.

Viura (Macabeo, Maccabéo, Maccabeu) Workhorse white grape of n Spain, widespread in Rioja, Catalan Cava country. Also Southwest France. Gd quality potential.

Weißburgunder PINOT BL in Germany.

Welschriesling (Graševina, Laski Rizling, Olaszriesling, Riesling Italico) Not related to RIES. Light and fresh to sweet and rich in Austria; ubiquitous in Central Europe, where it can be remarkably gd for dry and sweet wines.

Xarel·lo (Pansa Blanca) Traditional Catalan grape, used for Cava, with Parellada, MACABEO. Neutral but clean. More character (lime cordial) in Alella: Pansa Blanca.

Xynisteri Cyprus's most planted white grape. Can be simple and is usually DYA, but when grown at altitude makes appealing, minerally whites.

Zéta Hungarian; BOUVIER X FURMINT used by some in Tokaji Aszú production.

Zierfandler (Spätrot, Cirfandl) Found in Austria's Thermenregion; often blended with ROTGIPFLER for aromatic, orange-peel-scented, weighty wines.

Wine & food

Fashions change and food and wine evolve. The menu is frequently just a list of ingredients. Is the cumin the big feature, or is it the kale? The on-trend wines are equally unpredictable. Luckily if you are moved to try something orange, or made in an amphora, or a "Pét-Nat" – which means short-cut bubbly – the odds are it will forgive whatever you choose. If you want to be original, almost futuristically on-trend, and yet enjoy your dinner, choose Sherry.

Before the meal – apéritifs

Cocktail-addicts can look away now. The conventional and most effective appetite-creating apéritif wines are either sparkling (epitomized by Champagne) or fortified (epitomized by Sherry in Britain, Holland and Scandinavia, or Port in France, vermouth in Italy, etc.) A glass of a light table wine before eating is the easy choice, but why not do better? **Warning** Avoid peanuts; they destroy wine flavours. Olives are too piquant for many wines. Don't serve them with Champagne; they need Sherry or a Martini. With Champagne, nibble almonds, pistachios, cashews, cheese straws or succulent gougères straight from the oven.

First courses

Aïoli Its garlic heat demands a thirst-quencher. Cold young Rhône white, Picpoul, Provence rosé, VERDICCHIO, Loire SAUV BL. Beer, marc or grappa... you'll hardly notice.

Antipasti With the classic ham, olives and pickled bits: dry or medium white, Italian (ARNEIS, Soave, PINOT GRIGIO, VERMENTINO, GRECHETTO); light but gutsy red, eg. Valpolicella. Or Fino Sherry; sadly Italy doesn't know this.

Artichokes Not great for wine. An incisive dry white: NZ SAUV BL; Côtes de Gascogne or a modern Greek (precisely, 4-yr-old MALAGOUSIA, but easy on the vinaigrette); maybe Côtes du Rhône. **With hollandaise** Full-bodied crisp dry white: Pouilly-Fuissé, German Erstes Gewächs.

Asparagus Green or white are both difficult for wine, being slightly bitter (white is worse), so wine needs plenty of flavour. VIOGNIER has many adherents. Rheingau RIES is a classic (they have *Spargelfests* in those parts), but Ries generally gd to try. SAUV BL echoes the flavour. SÉM beats CHARD esp Australian, but Chard works well with melted butter or hollandaise. Alsace PINOT GR, even dry MUSCAT can work, or Jurançon Sec. Argument for trying a really sweet wine too, maybe not Yquem.

Aubergine (Melitzanosalata or Imam Bayaldi) Crisp New World SAUV BL, eg. from S Africa or NZ; or modern Greek or Sicilian dry white. Baked aubergine dishes (eg. *Imam Bayaldi*) need sturdy reds: SHIRAZ, ZIN, or indeed Turkish. Or Mediterranean whites (incl Fino).

Avocado Not a wine natural. Dry to medium slightly sweet white with gd acidity: Rheingau or Pfalz Kabinett, GRÜNER V, Wachau RIES, Sancerre, PINOT GR; Australian CHARD (unoaked), or a dry rosé. **With prawns** Premier Cru Chablis.

with mozzarella and tomato Crisp but ripe white: Soave, Sancerre, Greek white.

Burrata Forget mozzarella; this is the crème de la crème. So a top Italian white, FIANO or Cusumano's Grillo. I'll try Sauternes one day.

Carpaccio, beef or fish The beef version works well with most wines, incl reds. Tuscan is appropriate, but fine CHARDS are gd. So are vintage and pink Champagnes. Give Amontillado a try. **Salmon** Chard or Champagne. **Tuna** VIOGNIER, California Chard or NZ SAUV BL.

Caviar Iced vodka (and) full-bodied Champagne (eg. Bollinger, Krug). Don't (ever) add raw onion.

Ceviche Australian RIES or VERDELHO, Chilean SAUV BL, TORRONTÉS. Manzanilla.

Charcuterie / salami High-acid, unoaked red works better than white. Try Italian native reds: simple Valpolicella, REFOSCO, SCHIOPPETINO, TEROLDEGO, young Nebbiolo. If you must have white, it needs acidity. Chorizo presents problems, making wines taste metallic. Don't waste anything fine on it.

Dim sum Classically, China tea. PINOT GR or classic German dry RIES; light PINOT N. For reds, soft tannins are key. Bardolino, Rioja; Côtes du Rhône. Also NV Champagne or English fizz.

Eggs *See also* SOUFFLÉS. Not easy: eggs have a way of coating your palate. Omelettes: follow the other ingredients; mushrooms suggest red. With a truffle omelette, vintage Champagne. As a last resort I can bring myself to drink Champagne with scrambled eggs or eggs Benedict. Florentine, with spinach, is not a winey dish.

quails' eggs Blanc de blancs Champagne; Viognier.

gulls' eggs Push the luxury: mature white burgundy or vintage Champagne.

oeufs en meurette Burgundian genius: eggs in red wine with a glass of the same.

Escargots (or frogs' legs) A comfort dish calling for Rhône reds (Gigondas, Vacqueyras). In Burgundy, white: St-Véran or Rully. In the Midi *petits-gris* go with local white, rosé or red. In Alsace, PINOT BL or dry MUSCAT. On the Loire, frogs' legs and semi-dry CHENIN BL.

Fish terrine or fish salad (incl crab) Calls for something fine. Pfalz RIES Spätlese Trocken, GRÜNER V, Premier Cru Chablis, Clare Valley RIES, Sonoma CHARD; or Manzanilla.

Foie gras Sweet white: Sauternes, Tokaji Aszú 5 Puttonyos, late-harvest PINOT GR or RIES, Vouvray, Montlouis, Jurançon *moelleux*, GEWURZ. Old dry Amontillado can be sublime. With hot foie gras, mature vintage Champagne. But never CHARD, SAUV BL, or (shudder) red.

Haddock, smoked, mousse, soufflé or brandade Wonderful for stylish, full-bodied white: Grand Cru Chablis or Pessac-Léognan; Sonoma, S African or NZ CHARD.

Herrings, raw or pickled Dutch gin (young, not aged) or Scandinavian akvavit, and cold beer. If you must, try MUSCADET, but it's a waste (of the wine).

Mezze A selection of hot and cold vegetable dishes. Fino Sherry is in its element. So are Greek whites.

Mozzarella with tomatoes, basil Fresh Italian white, eg. Soave, Alto Adige. VERMENTINO from Liguria or Rolle from the Midi. *See also* AVOCADO.

Oysters, raw NV Champagne, Chablis, MUSCADET, white Graves, Sancerre, or Guinness. Experiment with Sauternes. Manzanilla is excellent. Flat oysters are worth good wine; Pacific ones drown it.

stewed, grilled or otherwise cooked Puligny-Montrachet or gd New World CHARD. Champagne gd with either.

Pasta Red or white according to the sauce:

cream sauce (eg. carbonara) Orvieto, GRECO di Tufo. Young SANGIOVESE.

meat sauce MONTEPULCIANO d'Abruzzo, Salice Salentino, MALBEC.

pesto (basil) sauce BARBERA, Ligurian VERMENTINO, NZ SAUV BL, Hungarian FURMINT.

seafood sauce (eg. vongole) VERDICCHIO, Soave, Grillo, Cirò, unoaked CHARD.

tomato sauce Chianti, Barbera, Sicilian red, ZIN, S Australian GRENACHE.

Pastrami Alsace RIES, young SANGIOVESE or St-Émilion.

Pâté, chicken liver Calls for pungent white (Alsace PINOT GR or MARSANNE), a smooth red eg. light Pomerol, Volnay or NZ PINOT N. More strongly flavoured pâté (duck, etc.) needs Gigondas, Moulin-à-Vent, Chianti Classico or gd white Graves. Amontillado can be a marvellous match.

Pipérade Navarra rosado, Provence or Midi rosé, dry Australian RIES. Or red: Corbières or La Clape.

Prosciutto (also with melon, pears or figs) Full, dry or medium white: Orvieto,

GRECHETTO, FIANO, GRÜNER V, Tokaji FURMINT, Australian SEM or Jurançon Sec. SERCIAL Madeira. Manzanilla.

Risotto Follow the flavour.

with vegetables (eg. Primavera) PINOT GR from Friuli, Gavi, youngish SÉM, DOLCETTO or BARBERA d'Alba.

with fungi porcini Finest mature Barolo or Barbaresco.

nero A rich dry white: VIOGNIER or even Corton-Charlemagne.

seafood A favourite dry white.

Salads Any dry and appetizing white or rosé wine.

NB Vinegar in salad dressings *destroys* the flavour of wine. Why don't the French know this? If you want salad at a meal with fine wine, dress it (gingerly) with wine or lemon juice instead of vinegar. Sea salt and good oil are the key.

Salmon, smoked Dry but pungent white: Fino (esp Manzanilla), Condrieu, Alsace PINOT GR, Grand Cru Chablis, Pouilly-Fumé, Pfalz RIES Spätlese, vintage Champagne. Vodka, schnapps or akvavit.

Soufflés As show dishes these deserve ★★★ wines.

cheese Mature red burgundy or B'x, CAB SAUV (not Chilean or Australian), etc. Or fine mature white burgundy.

fish (esp smoked haddock with chive cream sauce) Dry white: ★★★Burgundy, B'x, Alsace, CHARD, etc.

spinach (tough on wine) Mâcon-Villages, St-Véran or Valpolicella. Champagne (esp vintage) can also spark things with the texture of a soufflé.

Tapas Perfect with cold fresh Fino Sherry, which can cope with the wide range of flavours, hot and cold. Or sake.

Tapenade Manzanilla or Fino Sherry, or any sharpish dry white or rosé.

Taramasalata A Mediterranean white with personality, Greek if possible. Fino Sherry works well. Try Rhône MARSANNE.

Trout, smoked More delicate than smoked salmon. Mosel RIES Kabinett or Spätlese. Chablis or Champagne Blanc de Blancs.

Whitebait Crisp dry whites, eg. FURMINT, Greek, Touraine SAUV BL, VERDICCHIO, white Dão, Fino Sherry. Or beer.

Fish

Abalone Dry or medium white: SAUV BL, Meursault, PINOT GR, GRÜNER V. In Hong Kong: Dom Pérignon (at least).

Anchovies, marinated It scarcely matters. In eg. salade Niçoise: Provence rosé.

Bass, sea V.gd for any fine/delicate white: Clare dry RIES, Chablis, white Châteauneuf-du-Pape, WEISSBURGUNDER from Baden, Pfalz. But rev the wine up for more seasoning, eg. ginger, spring onions; more powerful Ries, not necessarily dry.

***Beurre blanc*, fish with** A top-notch MUSCADET *sur lie*, a SAUV BL/SÉM blend, Premier Cru Chablis, Vouvray, ALBARIÑO or Rheingau RIES.

Brandade Premier Cru Chablis, Sancerre Rouge or NZ PINOT N.

Brill More delicate than turbot: hence a top fish for fine old Puligny and the like. With the richness of hollandaise you could go up to Montrachet.

Cod, roast Gd neutral background for fine dry/medium whites: Chablis, Meursault, Corton-Charlemagne, Cru Classé Graves, GRÜNER V, German Kabinett or Grosses Gewächs, or gd lightish PINOT N. Persuade the chef not to add chorizo.

black cod with miso sauce NZ or Oregon Pinot N, Meursault Premier Cru or Rheingau RIES Spätlese. Vintage Champagne.

Crab Crab (esp Dungeness) and RIES together are part of the Creator's plan. But He also created Champagne.

Chinese, with ginger and onion German RIES Kabinett or Spätlese Halbtrocken. Tokaji FURMINT, GEWURZ.

cioppino SAUV BL; but West Coast friends say ZIN. Also California sparkling.

cold, dressed Top Mosel Ries, dry Alsace or Australian Ries or Condrieu.

softshell Unoaked CHARD, ALBARIÑO or top-quality German Ries Spätlese.

Thai crabcakes Pungent Sauv Bl (Loire, S Africa, Australia, NZ) or Ries (German Spätlese or Australian).

with black bean sauce A big Barossa SHIRAZ or SYRAH. Even a tumbler of Cognac.

with chilli and garlic Quite powerful Ries, German Grosses Gewächs or Wachau.

Curry A generic term for a multitude of flavours. Chilli emphasizes tannin, so reds need to be supple or silky ones. Any fruity, low-acid rosé can be a gd bet. Hot-and-sour flavours (with tamarind, tomato, eg.) need acidity (perhaps SAUV BL); mild, creamy dishes need richness of texture (dry Alsace RIES). Orange wine could work. But best of all is Sherry: Fino with fish, Palo Cortado or dry Amontillado with meat. It's revelatory.

Eel, smoked First choice is Fino Sherry. RIES, Alsace, or Austrian, or GRÜNER V. Vintage Champagne. Schnapps.

Fish and chips, *fritto misto*, tempura Anything white goes, as long as there's no vinegar. Chablis, white B'x, SAUV BL, PINOT BL, Gavi, Fino, white Dão, Koshu, sake, or NV Champagne or Cava.

Fish pie (with creamy sauce) ALBARIÑO, GODELLO, Soave Classico, RIES Erstes Gewächs.

Gravadlax SERCIAL Madeira (eg. 10-yr-old Henriques), Amontillado, Tokaji FURMINT, orange wine. Or NV Champagne.

Haddock Rich, dry whites: Meursault, California CHARD, MARSANNE or GRÜNER V.

smoked as for KIPPERS, but see under EGGS, SOUFFLÉS.

Hake SAUV BL or any fresh fruity white: Pacherenc, Tursan.

cold with mayonnaise fine CHARD.

Halibut As for TURBOT.

Herrings, fried / grilled Need a sharp white to cut their richness. Rully, Chablis, MUSCADET, Bourgogne ALIGOTÉ, Greek, dry SAUV BL. Or Indian tea. Or cider.

Ikan bakar This classic Indonesian/Malay dish works well with GRÜNER V.

Kedgeree Full white, still or sparkling: Mâcon-Villages, S African CHARD, GRÜNER V, German Grosses Gewächs or (at breakfast) Champagne.

Kippers A gd cup of tea, preferably Ceylon (milk, no sugar). Scotch? Dry Oloroso Sherry is surprisingly gd.

Lamproie à la Bordelaise Glorious with 5-yr-old St-Émilion or Fronsac. Or Douro reds with Portuguese lampreys.

Lobster with a rich sauce, eg. Thermidor: Vintage Champagne, fine white burgundy, Cru Classé Graves. Alternatively, for its inherent sweetness, Sauternes, Pfalz Spätlese, even Auslese.

plain grilled, or cold with mayonnaise NV Champagne, Alsace RIES, Premier Cru Chablis, Condrieu, Mosel Spätlese or a local fizz.

Mackerel, grilled Hard or sharp white to cut the oil: SAUV BL from Touraine, Gaillac, Vinho Verde, white Rioja or English white. Or Guinness.

smoked An oily wine-destroyer. Manzanilla, Vinho Verde or Schnapps, peppered or bison-grass vodka.

Monkfish A succulent but neutral dish; depends on the sauce. Full-flavoured white or red, depending.

Mullet, grey VERDICCHIO, Rully or unoaked CHARD. **Red** a chameleon, tasty and delicate, adaptable to gd white or a delicate red esp PINOT N.

Mussels, marinières MUSCADET *sur lie*, Premier Cru Chablis, unoaked CHARD. **Curried** Something semi-sweet; Alsace RIES. **Garlic/parsley** See ESCARGOTS.

Paella, shellfish Full-bodied white or rosé, unoaked CHARD, ALBARIÑO or GODELLO. Or local Spanish red.

Perch, sandre Exquisite fish for finest wines: top white burgundy, Grand Cru Alsace

RIES or noble Mosels. Or try top Swiss CHASSELAS (eg. Dézaley, St-Saphorin).

Prawns, with mayonnaise Menetou-Salon.

with garlic Keep the wine light, white or rosé, and dry.

with spices Up to and incl chilli, go for a bit more body, but not oak: dry RIES or Italian, eg. FIANO.

Salmon, seared or grilled PINOT N is fashionable option, but CHARD is better. MERLOT, light claret not bad. Fine white burgundy best: Puligny-/Chassagne-Montrachet, Meursault, Corton-Charlemagne, Grand Cru Chablis; GRÜNER V, Condrieu, California, Idaho or NZ CHARD, Rheingau Kabinett/Spätlese, Australian RIES.

fishcakes Call for similar, but less grand, wines.

Sardines, fresh grilled V. dry white: Vinho Verde, MUSCADET or modern Greek.

Sashimi Japanese preference is for a white with body (Chablis Premier Cru, Alsace RIES) with white fish, PINOT N with red. Both need acidity: low-acidity wines don't work. Simple Chablis can be too thin. If soy is involved, then low-tannin red (again, Pinot). Remember sake (or Fino). As though you'd forget Champagne.

Scallops An inherently slightly sweet dish, best with medium-dry whites.

in cream sauces German Spätlese, Montrachets or top Australian CHARD.

grilled or seared Hermitage Blanc, GRÜNER V, Pessac-Léognan Blanc, vintage Champagne or PINOT N.

with Asian seasoning NZ Chard, CHENIN BL, GODELLO, Grüner V, GEWURZ.

Scandi food Scandinavian dishes often have flavours of dill, caraway, cardamom and combine sweet and sharp flavours. Go for acidity and some weight: GODELLO, FALANGHINA, VERDELHO, Australian, Alsace or Austrian RIES. Pickled/fermented/raw fish is more challenging: beer or akvavit. *See also* entries for smoked fish, etc.

Shellfish Dry white with plain boiled shellfish, richer wines with richer sauces. RIES is the grape.

with *plateaux de fruits de mer* Chablis, MUSCADET de Sèvre et Maine, PICPOUL de Pinet, Alto Adige PINOT BL.

Skate / raie with brown butter White with some pungency (eg. PINOT GR d'Alsace or ROUSSANNE) or a clean, straightforward wine ie. MUSCADET or VERDICCHIO.

Snapper SAUV BL if cooked with oriental flavours; white Rhône or Provence rosé with Mediterranean flavours.

Sole, plaice, etc., plain, grilled or fried Perfect with fine wines: white burgundy or its equivalent.

with sauce According to the ingredients: sharp, dry wine for tomato sauce, fairly rich for creamy preparations.

Sushi Hot wasabi is usually hidden in every piece. German QbA Trocken wines, simple Chablis, ALVARINHO or NV Brut Champagne. Obvious fruit doesn't work. Or, of course, sake or beer.

Swordfish Full-bodied, dry white (or why not red?) of the country. Nothing grand.

Tagine, with couscous North African flavours need substantial whites to balance – Austrian, Rhône – or crisp, neutral whites that won't compete. Go easy on the oak. VIOGNIER or ALBARIÑO can work well.

Teriyaki A way of cooking, and a sauce, used for meat as well as fish. Germans favour off-dry RIES with weight: Kabinett can be too light.

Trout, grilled or fried Delicate white wine, eg. Mosel (esp Saar or Ruwer), Alsace PINOT BL, FENDANT.

Tuna, grilled or seared Best served rare (or raw) with light red wine: young Loire CAB FR or red burg. Young Rioja is a possibility.

Turbot The king of fishes (or "ambitious brill" in *HMS Pinafore*). Serve with your best rich, dry white: Meursault or Chassagne-Montrachet, Corton-Charlemagne, mature Chablis or its California, Australian or NZ equivalent. Condrieu. Mature Rheingau, Mosel or Nahe Spätlese or Auslese (not Trocken).

Meat, poultry, game

Barbecues The local wine: Australian, S African, Chilean, Argentina are right in spirit. Reds need tannin and vigour. Or the freshness of cru Beaujolais.

Beef (see also STEAK) Boiled Red: B'x (eg. Fronsac), Roussillon, Gevrey-Chambertin or Côte-Rôtie. Medium-ranking white burgundy is gd, eg. Auxey-Duresses. In Austria you may be offered skin-fermented TRAMINER. Mustard softens tannic reds, horseradish kills your taste: can be worth the sacrifice.

    roast An ideal partner for any fine red. Even Amarone. *See* above for mustard. The silkier the texture of the beef (eg. wagyu, Galician), the silkier the wine.

    stew, daube Sturdy red: Pomerol or St-Émilion, Hermitage, Cornas, BARBERA, SHIRAZ, Napa CAB SAUV, Ribera del Duero and Douro red.

Beef stroganoff Dramatic red: Barolo, Valpolicella Amarone, Priorat, Hermitage, late-harvest ZIN. Georgian SAPERAVI or Moldovan Negru de Purkar.

Boudin blanc **(white pork sausage)** Loire CHENIN BL esp when served with apples: dry Vouvray, Saumur, Savennières; mature red Côte de Beaune if without.

Boudin noir **(blood sausage)** Local SAUV BL or CHENIN BL (esp in Loire). Or Beaujolais cru esp Morgon. Or light TEMPRANILLO. Or Fino.

Brazilian dishes Pungent flavours that blend several culinary traditions. Sherry would add another. Rhônish grapes work for red, or white with weight: VERDICCHIO, Californian CHARD. Or Caipirinhas. And a ten-mile run afterwards..

Cabbage, stuffed Hungarian KADARKA; village Rhône; Salice Salentino, PRIMITIVO and other spicy s Italian reds. Or Argentine MALBEC (no oak, if you can find one).

Cajun food Fleurie, Brouilly or New World SAUV BL. **With gumbo** Amontillado.

Cassoulet Red from Southwest France (Gaillac, Minervois, Corbières, St-Chinian or Fitou) or SHIRAZ. But best of all Fronton, Beaujolais cru or young TEMPRANILLO.

Chicken Kiev Alsace RIES, Collio, CHARD, Bergerac rouge.

Chicken / turkey / guinea fowl, roast Virtually any wine, incl v. best bottles of dry to medium white and finest old reds (esp burgundy). The meat of fowl (guinea fowl is stronger, drier) can be adapted with sauces to match almost any fine wine (eg. coq au vin; the burgundy can be red or white, or *vin jaune* for that matter). **Fried** Sparkling works well.

Chilli con carne Young red: Beaujolais, TEMPRANILLO, ZIN, Argentine MALBEC, Chilean CARMENÈRE. Many drink beer.

Chinese food To the purist there's no such thing: food in China is regional – like Italian, only more confusing. I often serve both whites and reds concurrently during Chinese meals; no one wine goes with the whole affair. Peking duck is pretty forgiving. Champagne becomes a thirst quencher. Beer, too.

    Cantonese Rosé or dry to dryish white – Mosel RIES Kabinett or Spätlese Trocken. Ries should not be too dry; GEWURZ is often suggested but rarely works; GRÜNER V is a better bet. You need wine with acidity. Dry sparkling (esp Cava) works with textures. Reds can work, but should have worked off young tannins and not be too dry, or overtly oaky. PINOT N 1st choice; ★★St-Émilion or Châteauneuf.

    Shanghai Richer and oilier than Cantonese, not one of wine's natural partners. Shanghai tends to be low on chilli but high on vinegar of various sorts. German and Alsace whites can be a bit sweeter than for Cantonese. For reds, try MERLOT – goes with the salt. Or mature Pinot N, but a bit of a waste.

    Szechuan style VERDICCHIO, Alsace PINOT BL or v. cold beer. Mature Pinot N can also work; but see above. The Creator intended tea.

    Taiwanese LAMBRUSCO works with trad Taiwan dishes if you're tired of beer.

Choucroute garni Alsace PINOT BL, PINOT GR, RIES or lager.

Cold roast meat Generally better with full-flavoured white than red. Mosel Spätlese or Hochheimer and Côte Chalonnaise are v.gd, as is Beaujolais. Leftover cold beef with leftover vintage Champagne is bliss.

Confit d'oie / de canard Young, tannic red B'x, California CAB SAUV and MERLOT, Priorat cut richness. Alsace PINOT GR or GEWURZ match it.

Coq au vin Red burgundy. Ideal: one bottle of Chambertin in the dish, two on the table. *See also* under chicken.

Dirty (Creole) rice Rich, supple red: NZ PINOT N, GARNACHA, BAIRRADA, MALBEC.

Duck or goose Rather rich white, esp for the strong flavour of goose: Pfalz Spätlese or off-dry Grand Cru Alsace. Or mature, gamey red: Morey-St-Denis, Côte-Rôtie, Pauillac, Bairrada. With oranges or peaches, the Sauternais propose drinking Sauternes, others Monbazillac or RIES Auslese. Mature, weighty vintage Champagne is gd too, and handles accompanying red cabbage surprisingly well. **Peking** *See* CHINESE FOOD.

    wild duck Big-scale red: Hermitage, Bandol, California or S African CAB SAUV, Australian SHIRAZ – Grange if you can afford it.

    with olives Top-notch Chianti or other Tuscans.

    roast breast & confit leg with Puy lentils Madiran (best), St-Émilion, Fronsac.

Game birds, young, roast The best red wine you can afford, but not too heavy.

    older birds in casseroles Red (Gevrey-Chambertin, Pommard, Châteauneuf-du-Pape, Dão, or Grand Cru Classé St-Émilion, Rhône). Don't forget game birds can be even better cold the next day esp with fine German wines.

    well-hung game Vega Sicilia, great red Rhône, Château Musar.

    cold game Best German RIES; or mature vintage Champagne.

Game pie, hot Red: Oregon PINOT N, St-Émilion Grand Cru Classé. **Cold** Gd-quality white burgundy, German Erstes Gewächs, cru Beaujolais, Champagne.

Goulash Flavoursome young red: Hungarian Kékoportó, ZIN, Uruguayan TANNAT, Douro red, MENCÍA, young Australian SHIRAZ. Or dry white from Tokaj.

Grouse *See* GAME BIRDS; but push the boat right out. Top burgundy or Châteauneuf.

Haggis Fruity red, eg. young claret, young Portuguese red, New World CAB SAUV or MALBEC or Châteauneuf-du-Pape. Or, of course, malt whisky.

Ham, cooked Softer red burgundies: Volnay, Savigny, Beaune; Chinon or Bourgueil; sweetish German white (RIES Spätlese); lightish CAB SAUV (eg. Chilean), New World PINOT N. Don't forget heavenly match of ham and Sherry.

Hamburger Young red: Australian CAB SAUV, Chianti, ZIN, Argentine MALBEC, Chilean CARMENÈRE or SYRAH, TEMPRANILLO. Or full-strength cola (not diet). If you add cheese, and stuff, heaven help you; you're on your own.

Hare Jugged hare calls for flavourful red: not-too-old burgundy or B'x (eg. Gigondas), Bandol, Barbaresco, Ribera del Duero, Rioja Res; same for saddle or for hare sauce with pappardelle.

Indian dishes Dry Sherry is brilliant. A fairly weighty Fino with fish; Palo Cortado, Amontillado, Oloroso with meat, according to weight of dish; heat's not a problem. Texture works too. Or, medium-sweet white, v. cold: Orvieto *abboccato*, S African CHENIN BL, Alsace PINOT BL, TORRONTÉS, Indian sparkling, Cava or NV Champagne. Rosé is gd all-rounder. For tannic impact Barolo or Barbaresco, or deep-flavoured reds: Châteauneuf, Cornas, Australian GRENACHE or MOURVÈDRE, or Valpolicella Amarone (will emphasize heat). Hot-and-sour flavours need acidity. **Sri Lankan** More extreme flavours, coconut. Sherry, rich red, rosé, mild white.

Japanese dishes A different set of senses come into play. Texture and balance are key; flavours are subtle. Gd mature fizz works well, as does mature dry RIES; you need acidity, a bit of body, and complexity. Dry FURMINT can work well. Umami-filled meat dishes favour light, supple, bright reds: Beaujolais perhaps, or mature PINOT N. Full-flavoured *yakitori* needs lively, fruity, younger versions of the same reds. *See also* SUSHI, SASHIMI, TERIYAKI.

Kebabs Vigorous red: modern Greek, Corbières, Chilean CAB SAUV, ZIN or Barossa SHIRAZ. SAUV BL, if lots of garlic.

Korean dishes Fruit-forward wines seem to work best with strong, pungent Korean flavours. PINOT N, Beaujolais, Valpolicella can all work: acidity is needed. Non-aromatic whites: GRÜNER V, SILVANER, VERNACCIA. But I drink beer.

Lamb, roast One of the traditional and best partners for v.gd red B'x, or its CAB SAUV equivalents from the New World. In Spain, finest old Rioja and Ribera del Duero Res or Priorat, in Italy ditto SANGIOVESE.

　slow-cooked roast Flatters top reds, but needs less tannin than pink lamb.

Liver Young red: Beaujolais-Villages, St-Joseph, Médoc, Italian MERLOT, Breganze CAB SAUV, ZIN, Priorat, Bairrada.

　calf's Red: Rioja Crianza, Fleurie. Or a big Pfalz RIES Spätlese.

Meat as a garnish Self-explanatory term. Light cool-climate PINOT N, SAUV BL.

Mexican food Californians favour RIES: Calavera restaurant in Oakland lists 33 RIES, mostly German.

Moussaka Red or rosé: Naoussa, SANGIOVESE, Corbières, Côtes de Provence, Ajaccio, young ZIN, TEMPRANILLO.

Mutton A stronger flavour than lamb, and not usually served pink. Needs a strong sauce. Robust red; top-notch, mature CAB SAUV, SYRAH. Sweetness of fruit (eg. Barossa) suits it.

Osso bucco Low-tannin, supple red: DOLCETTO d'Alba, PINOT N. Dry Italian white: Soave.

Ox cheek, braised Superbly tender and flavoursome, this flatters the best reds: Vega Sicilia, St-Émilion. Best with substantial wines.

Oxtail Rather rich red: St-Émilion, Pomerol, Pommard, Nuits-St-Georges, Barolo, or Rioja Res, Priorat or Ribera del Duero, California or Coonawarra CAB SAUV, Châteauneuf-du-Pape, mid-weight SHIRAZ, Amarone.

Paella Young Spanish: red, dry white, rosé: Penedès, Somontano, Navarra or Rioja.

Pigeon or squab PINOT N perfect; young Rhône, Argentine MALBEC, young SANGIOVESE. Try Franken SILVANER Spätlese. With luxurious squab, top quite tannic red.

Pork, roast A perfect rich background to a fairly light red or rich white. It deserves ★★★ treatment: Médoc is fine. Portugal's suckling pig is eaten with Bairrada Garrafeira; S America's with CARIGNAN; Chinese is gd with PINOT N.

　pork belly Slow-cooked and meltingly tender, needs red with some tannin or acidity. Italian gd: Barolo, DOLCETTO, BARBERA. Or Loire red, lightish Argentine MALBEC.

Pot au feu, bollito misto, cocido Rustic reds from region of origin: SANGIOVESE di Romagna, Chusclan, Lirac, Rasteau, Portugal's Alentejo, Spain's Yecla, Jumilla.

Quail Succulent little chick deserves tasty red or white. Rioja Res, mature claret, PINOT N. Or a mellow white: Vouvray or St-Péray.

Quiche Egg and bacon are not great wine matches, but one must drink something. Alsace RIES or PINOT GR, even GEWURZ, is classical. Beaujolais could be gd too.

Rabbit Lively, medium-bodied young Italian red, eg. AGLIANICO del Vulture, REFOSCO; Chiroubles, Chinon, Saumur-Champigny or Rhône rosé.

　with prunes Bigger, richer, fruitier red.

　with mustard Cahors.

　as ragu Medium-bodied red with acidity.

Satay McLaren Vale SHIRAZ, Alsace, NZ GEWURZ. Peanut sauce: problem for any wine.

Sauerkraut (German) Franken SILVANER, lager or Pils. (But *see also* CHOUCROUTE GARNI.)

Sausages See also CHARCUTERIE, FRANKFURTERS. The British banger requires a young MALBEC from Argentina (a red wine, anyway).

Singaporean dishes Part Indian, part Malay and part Chinese, Singaporean food has big, bold flavours that don't match easily with wine – not that that bothers the country's many wine-lovers. Off-dry RIES is as gd as anything. With meat dishes, ripe, supple reds: Valpolicella, PINOT N, DORNFELDER, unoaked MERLOT or CARMENÈRE.

Steak *au poivre* A fairly young Rhône red or CAB SAUV.

　filet, ribeye or tournedos Any gd red esp burgundy (but not old wines with

Béarnaise sauce: top New World PINOT N is better).

Fiorentina (bistecca) Chianti Classico Riserva or BRUNELLO. Rarer the meat, more classic the wine; the more cooked, the more you need New World, sweet/strong wines. Argentine MALBEC is perfect for steak Argentine-style, ie. cooked to death.

Korean *yuk whe* (world's best steak tartare) Sake.

tartare Vodka or light young red: Beaujolais, Bergerac, Valpolicella. Aussies drink GAMAY with kangaroo tartare, charred plums, Szechuan pepper.

T-bone Reds of similar bone structure: Barolo, Hermitage, Australian CAB SAUV or SHIRAZ, Chilean SYRAH, Douro.

Steak-and-kidney pie or pudding Red Rioja Res or mature B'x. Pudding (with suet) wants vigorous young wine.

Stews and casseroles Burgundy such as Nuits-St-Georges or Pommard if fairly simple; otherwise lusty, full-flavoured red: young Côtes du Rhône, Toro, Corbières, BARBERA, SHIRAZ, ZIN, etc.

Sweetbreads A rich dish, so grand white wine: Rheingau RIES or Franken SILVANER Spätlese, Grand Cru Alsace PINOT GR or Condrieu, depending on sauce.

Tagines Depends on what's under the lid, but fruity young reds are a gd bet: Beaujolais, TEMPRANILLO, SANGIOVESE, MERLOT, SHIRAZ. Amontillado is great.
    chicken with preserved lemon, olives VIOGNIER.

Tandoori chicken RIES or SAUV BL, young red B'x or light n Italian red served cool. Also Cava and NV Champagne, or of course Palo Cortado or Amontillado Sherry.

Thai dishes Ginger and lemon grass call for pungent SAUV BL (Loire, Australia, NZ, S Africa) or RIES (Spätlese or Australian). Most curries suit aromatic whites with a touch of sweetness: GEWURZ is also gd.

Tongue Gd for any red or white of abundant character esp Italian. Also Beaujolais, Loire reds, TEMPRANILLO and full, dry rosés.

Veal, roast A friend of fine wine. Gd for any fine old red that may be fading with age (eg. Rioja Res, old Médoc) or German or Austrian RIES, Vouvray, Alsace PINOT GR.

Venison Big-scale reds, incl MOURVÈDRE, solo as in Bandol or in blends. Rhône, B'x, NZ Gimblett Gravels or California CAB SAUV of a mature vintage; or rather rich white (Pfalz Spätlese or Alsace PINOT GR). With a sweet and sharp berry sauce, try a German Grosses Gewächs RIES, or a Chilean CARMENÈRE or SYRAH.

Vietnamese food Slanted Door, famous San Fran Vietnamese restaurant, favours RIES, dry or up to Spätlese, German, Austrian, NZ. Also GRÜNER V, SEM; for reds, PINOT N, CAB FR, BLAUFRÄNKISCH.

Vitello tonnato Full-bodied whites: CHARD; light reds (eg. Valpolicella) served cool. Or a southern rosé.

Wild boar Serious red: top Tuscan or Priorat. NZ SYRAH. I've even drunk Port.

Vegetarian dishes (*See also* FIRST COURSES)

Baked pasta dishes *Pasticcio*, lasagne and cannelloni with elaborate vegetarian fillings and sauces: an occasion to show off a grand wine esp finest Tuscan red, but also claret and burgundy.

Beetroot Mimics a flavour found in red burgundy. You could return the compliment.
    and goat's cheese gratin Sancerre, B'x SAUV BL.

Cauliflower, roast, etc. go by other (usually bold) flavours. Try Austrian GRÜNER V, Valpolicella, NZ PINOT N.
    cauliflower cheese Crisp, aromatic white: Sancerre, RIES Spätlese, MUSCAT, ALBARIÑO, GODELLO. Beaujolais-Villages. No, go on; comfort wine with comfort food.

Couscous with vegetables Young red with a bite: SHIRAZ, Corbières, Minervois; rosé; orange wine; Italian REFOSCO or SCHIOPPETTINO.

Fennel-based dishes SAUV BL: Pouilly-Fumé or NZ; SYLVANER or English SEYVAL BL; or young TEMPRANILLO.

Fermented foods *See also* SAUERKRAUT, CHOUCROUTE, KOREAN. *Kimchi* and *miso* are being worked into many dishes. Fruit and acidity are generally needed. If in sweetish veg dishes, try Alsace.

Grilled Mediterranean vegetables Italian whites; reds: Brouilly, BARBERA, TEMPRANILLO or SHIRAZ.

Lentil dishes Sturdy reds such as Corbières, ZIN or SHIRAZ.

    dhal, with spinach Tricky. Soft light red or rosé is best, and not top-flight.

Macaroni cheese As for CAULIFLOWER CHEESE.

Mushrooms (in most contexts) A boon to most reds and some whites. Context matters as much as species. Pomerol, California MERLOT, Rioja Res, top burgundy or Vega Sicilia. Button or Paris mushrooms with cream: fine whites, even vintage Champagne. On toast: best claret – even Port. Ceps/porcini: Ribera del Duero, Barolo, Chianti Rufina, Pauillac or St-Estèphe, NZ Gimblett Gravels.

Onion / leek tart/ *flamiche* Fruity, off-dry or dry white: Alsace PINOT GR or GEWURZ is classic; Canadian, Australian or NZ RIES; Jurançon. Or Loire CAB FR.

Peppers or aubergines (eggplant), stuffed Vigorous red: Nemea, Chianti, DOLCETTO, ZIN, Bandol, Vacqueyras.

Pumpkin / squash ravioli or risotto Full-bodied, fruity dry or off-dry white: VIOGNIER or MARSANNE, demi-sec Vouvray, Gavi or S African CHENIN.

Ratatouille Vigorous young red: Chianti, NZ CAB SAUV, MERLOT, MALBEC, TEMPRANILLO; young red B'x, Gigondas or Coteaux du Languedoc. Fino Sherry can work too.

Root vegetables Sweet potatoes, carrots, etc., often mixed with eg. beetroot, garlic, onions have plenty of sweetness. Rosé esp with some weight, or orange wine.

Seaweed Depends on context. *See also* SUSHI. Iodine notes with Austrian GRÜNER V, RIES.

Spiced vegetarian dishes *See* INDIAN DISHES, THAI DISHES (MEAT, POULTRY, GAME).

Truffles Black truffles are a match for finest Right Bank B'x, but even better with mature white Hermitage or Châteauneuf. White truffles call for best Barolo or Barbaresco of their native Piedmont. Or at breakfast, on fried eggs, BARBERA.

Watercress, raw Makes every wine on earth taste revolting. Soup is slightly easier, but doesn't need wine.

Wild garlic leaves, wilted Tricky: a fairly neutral white with acidity will cope best.

Desserts

Apple pie, strudel, or tarts Sweet German, Austrian or Loire white, Tokaji Aszú, or Canadian Icewine.

Apples, Cox's Orange Pippins Vintage Port (and sweetmeal biscuits) is the Saintsbury [wine] Club plan.

Bread-&-butter pud Fine 10-yr-old Barsac, Tokaji Aszú, Australian botrytized SEM.

Cakes & gâteaux *See also* CHOCOLATE, COFFEE, GINGER, RUM. BUAL or MALMSEY Madeira, Oloroso or Cream Sherry. Asti, sweet Prosecco.

Cheesecake Sweet white: Vouvray, Anjou, or Vin Santo – nothing too special.

Chocolate A talking point. Generally only powerful flavours can compete. Texture matters. BUAL, California Orange MUSCAT, Tokaji Aszú, Australian Liqueur Muscat, 10-yr-old Tawny or even young Vintage Port; Asti for light, fluffy mousses. Experiment with rich, ripe reds: SYRAH, ZIN, even sparkling SHIRAZ. Banyuls for a weightier partnership. Médoc can match bitter black chocolate, though it's a bit of a waste, and Amarone is more fun. Armagnac, or a tot of gd rum.

    and olive oil mousse 10-yr-old Tawny Port or as for black chocolate, above.

Christmas pudding, mince pies Tawny Port, Cream Sherry or that liquid Christmas pudding itself, PEDRO XIMÉNEZ Sherry. Tokaji Aszú. Asti, or Banyuls.

Coffee desserts Sweet MUSCAT, Australia Liqueur Muscats, or Tokaji Aszú.

Creams, custards, fools, syllabubs *See also* CHOCOLATE, COFFEE, RUM. Sauternes, Loupiac, Ste-Croix-du-Mont or Monbazillac.

Crème brûlée Sauternes or Rhine Beerenauslese, best Madeira, or Tokaji Aszú. (With concealed fruit, a more modest sweet wine.)

Ice cream & sorbets Give wine a break.

Lemon flavours For dishes like tarte au citron, try sweet RIES from Germany or Austria or Tokaji Aszú; v. sweet if lemon is v. tart.

Meringues (eg. Eton Mess) Recioto di Soave, Asti or top vintage Champagne that's well-aged.

Nuts (incl praliné) Finest Oloroso Sherry, Madeira, Vintage or Tawny Port (nature's match for walnuts), Tokaji Aszú, Vin Santo, or Setúbal MOSCATEL. Cashews and Champagne are wickedy gd. Pistachios go better with Fino.

 salted nut parfait Tokaji Aszú, Vinsanto.

Orange flavours Try with old Sauternes, Tokaji Aszú or California Orange MUSCAT.

Panettone Vinsanto. Jurançon *moelleux*, late-harvest RIES, Barsac, Tokaji Aszú.

Pears in red wine Rivesaltes, Banyuls, or RIES Beerenauslese.

Pecan pie Orange MUSCAT or Liqueur Muscat.

Raspberries (no cream, little sugar) Excellent with fine reds which themselves taste of raspberries: young Juliénas, Regnié.

Rum flavours (baba, mousses, ice cream) MUSCAT – from Asti to Australian Liqueur, according to weight of dish.

Strawberries, wild (no cream) With red B'x (most exquisitely Margaux) poured over.

 with cream Sauternes, sweet B'x, Vouvray *moelleux*; Vendange Tardive Jurançon.

Summer pudding Fairly young Sauternes of a gd vintage.

Sweet soufflés Sauternes or Vouvray *moelleux*. Sweet (or rich) Champagne.

Tiramisú Vin Santo, young Tawny Port, MUSCAT de Beaumes-de-Venise, Sauternes, or Australian Liqueur Muscat. Better idea: skip the wine.

Trifle Should be sufficiently vibrant with its internal Sherry (Oloroso for choice).

Zabaglione Light-gold Marsala or Australian botrytized SEM, or Asti.

Wine & cheese

The notion that wine and cheese were married in heaven is not borne out by experience. Fine red wines are slaughtered by strong cheeses; only sharp or sweet white wines survive. Principles to remember (despite exceptions): first, the harder the cheese, the more tannin the wine can have; second, the creamier the cheese, the more acidity is needed in the wine – and don't be shy of sweetness. Cheese is classified by its texture and the nature of its rind, so its appearance is a guide to the type of wine to match it. Below are examples. I always try to keep a glass of white wine for my cheese.

Bloomy rind soft cheeses, pure-white rind if pasteurized, or dotted with red: Brie, Camembert, Chaource, Bougon (goats milk "Camembert") Full, dry white burgundy or Rhône if the cheese is white and immature; powerful, fruity St-Émilion, young Australian (or Rhône) SHIRAZ/SYRAH or GRENACHE if it's mature.

Blue cheeses The extreme saltiness of Roquefort or most blue cheeses needs the sweetness of Sauternes (or Tokaji), esp old Stilton, and Port, (youngish) Vintage or Tawny, is a classic. Intensely flavoured old Oloroso, Amontillado, Madeira, Marsala and other fortifieds go with most blues. Never gd claret, please.

Cooked cheese dishes, *Frico* Traditional in Friuli. Cheese baked or fried with potatoes or onions; high-acid local REFOSCO (r), or RIBOLLA GIALLA (w).

 Mont d'Or Delicious baked, and served with potatoes. Fairly neutral white with freshness: GRÜNER V, Savoie.

 fondue Trendy again. Light, fresh white as above.

 macaroni or cauliflower cheese Easy-drinking red or dry white.

Fresh, no rind: cream cheese, crème fraîche, mozzarella Light crisp white: Chablis,

Bergerac, Entre-Deux-Mers; rosé: Anjou, Rhône; v. light, young, fresh red: B'x, Bardolino, Beaujolais.

Hard cheeses, waxed or oiled, often showing marks from cheesecloth: Gruyère family, Manchego and other Spanish cheeses, Parmesan, Cantal, Comté, old Gouda, Cheddar and most "traditional" English cheeses Hard to generalize; Gouda, Gruyère, some Spanish, and a few English cheeses complement fine claret or CAB SAUV and great SHIRAZ/SYRAH. But strong cheeses need less refined wines, preferably local ones. Sugary, granular old Dutch red Mimolette, Comté or Beaufort gd for finest mature B'x. Also for Tokaji Aszú. But try whites too.

Natural rind (mostly goats cheese) with bluish-grey mould (the rind becomes wrinkled when mature), sometimes dusted with ash: St-Marcellin Sancerre, light SAUV BL, Jurançon, Savoie, Soave, Italian CHARD; or young Vintage Port.

Semi-soft cheeses, thickish grey-pink rind: Livarot, Pont l'Evêque, Reblochon, Tomme de Savoie, St-Nectaire Powerful white B'x, even Sauternes, CHARD, Alsace PINOT GR, dryish RIES, s Italian and Sicilian whites, aged white Rioja, dry Oloroso Sherry. The strongest of these cheeses kill almost any wines. Try marc or Calvados.

Washed-rind soft cheeses, with rather sticky, orange-red rind: Langres, mature Époisses, Maroilles, Carré de l'Est, Milleens, Münster Local reds esp for Burgundian cheeses; vigorous Languedoc, Cahors, Côtes du Frontonnais, Corsican, s Italian, Sicilian, Bairrada. Also powerful whites esp Alsace GEWURZ, MUSCAT.

Food & your finest wines

With v. special bottles, the wine guides the choice of food rather than vice versa. The following is based largely on gastronomic conventions, some bold experiments and much diligent and on-going research. They should help bring out the best in your best wines.

Red wines

Amarone Classically, in Verona, *risotto all'Amarone* or *pastissada*. But if your butcher doesn't run to horse, then shin of beef, slow-cooked in more Amarone.

Barolo, Barbaresco Risotto with white truffles; pasta with game sauce (eg. *pappardelle alla lepre*); porcini mushrooms; Parmesan.

Great Syrahs: Hermitage, Côte-Rôtie, Grange; Vega Sicilia Beef (such as the super-rich, super-tender, super-slow-cooked ox cheek I had at Vega Sicilia), venison, well-hung game; bone marrow on toast; English cheese (esp best farm Cheddar) but also hard goats milk and ewes milk cheeses such as England's Berkswell or Ticklemore. I treat Côte-Rôtie like top red burgundy.

Great Vintage Port or Madeira Walnuts or pecans. A Cox's Orange Pippin and a digestive biscuit is a classic English accompaniment.

Red Bordeaux v. old, light, delicate wines, (eg. pre-59) Leg or rack of young lamb, roast with a hint of herbs (not garlic); *entrecôte*; simply roasted (and not too well-hung) partridge; roast chicken.

fully mature great vintages (eg. 59 61 82 85) Shoulder or saddle of lamb, roast with a touch of garlic; roast ribs or grilled rump of beef.

mature but still vigorous (eg. 89 90) Shoulder or saddle of lamb (incl kidneys) with rich sauce. Fillet of beef *marchand de vin* (with wine and bone marrow). Grouse. Avoid beef Wellington: pastry dulls the palate.

Merlot-based Beef as above (fillet is richest) or well-hung venison. In St-Émilion, lampreys.

Red burgundy Consider weight and texture, which grow lighter/more velvety with age. Also character of the wine: Nuits is earthy, Musigny flowery, great Romanées can be exotic, Pommard is renowned for its four-squareness. Roast chicken or (better) capon is a safe standard with red burgundy; guinea fowl for slightly stronger wines, then partridge, grouse or woodcock for those progressively more rich and pungent. Hare and venison (*chevreuil*) are alternatives.

great old burgundy The Burgundian formula is cheese: Époisses (unfermented); a fine cheese but a terrible waste of fine old wines. *See above.*

vigorous younger burgundy Duck or goose roasted to minimize fat. Or *faisinjan* (pheasant cooked in pomegranate juice). Or lightly smoked gammon.

Rioja Gran Reserva, Top Duero reds Richly flavoured roasts: wild boar, mutton, saddle of hare, whole suckling pig.

White wines

Beerenauslese / Trockenbeerenauslese Biscuits, peaches, greengages. Desserts made from rhubarb, gooseberries, quince, apples. But TBAs don't need food.

Condrieu, Château-Grillet, Hermitage Blanc V. light pasta scented with herbs and tiny peas or broad beans. Or v. mild tender ham. Old white Hermitage loves truffles.

Grand Cru Alsace: Ries *Truite au bleu*, smoked salmon, or *choucroute garni*.

Pinot Gr Roast or grilled veal. Or truffle sandwich (slice a whole truffle, make a sandwich with salted butter and gd country bread – not sourdough or rye – wrap and refrigerate overnight. Then toast it in the oven).

Gewurztraminer Cheese soufflé (Münster cheese).

Vendange Tardive Foie gras or tarte tatin.

Old vintage Champagne (not Blanc de Blancs) As an apéritif, or with cold partridge, grouse, woodcock. The evolved flavours of old Champagne make it far easier to match with food than the tightness of young wine. Hot foie gras can be sensational. Don't be afraid of garlic or even Indian spices, but omit the chilli.

late-disgorged old wines have extra freshness plus tertiary flavours. Try with truffles, lobster, scallops, crab, sweetbreads, pork belly, roast veal, chicken.

Sauternes Simple crisp buttery biscuits (eg. *langues de chat*), white peaches, nectarines, strawberries (without cream). Not tropical fruit. Pan-seared foie gras. Lobster or chicken with Sauternes sauce. Château d'Yquem recommends oysters (and indeed lobster). Experiment with blue cheeses. Rocquefort is classic, but needs a powerful wine.

Tokaji Aszú (5–6 puttonyos) Foie gras recommended. Fruit desserts, cream desserts, even chocolate can be wonderful. Roquefort. It even works with some Chinese, though not with chilli – the spice has to be adjusted to meet the sweetness. Szechuan pepper is gd. Havana cigars are splendid. So is the naked sip.

Top Chablis White fish simply grilled or *meunière*. Dover sole, turbot, halibut are best; brill, drenched in butter, can be excellent. (Sea bass is too delicate; salmon passes but does little for the finest wine.)

Top white burgundy, top Graves, top aged Riesling Roast veal, farm chicken stuffed with truffles or herbs under skin, or sweetbreads; richly sauced white fish (turbot for choice) or scallops, white fish as above. Or lobster or poached wild salmon.

Vouvray moelleux, etc. Buttery biscuits, apples, apple tart.

Fail-safe face-savers

Some wines are more useful than others – more versatile, more forgiving. If you're choosing restaurant wine to please several people, or just stocking the cellar with basics, these wines will go with a wide range of dishes: red – Alentejo, BARBERA d'Asti/d'Alba, BLAUFRÄNKISCH, Beaujolais, Chianti, GRENACHE/GARNACHA if not overextracted/overoaked, MALBEC (easy on the oak), PINOT N, Valpolicella; white – Alsace PINOT BL, ASSYRTIKO, unoaked or v. lightly oaked CHARD, Fino Sherry, GRÜNER V, RIES from Alsace and Germany (dry and fruity), Sancerre, gd Soave, VERDICCHIO.

France

More heavily shaded areas are
the wine-growing regions.

Abbreviations used in the text:

Al	Alsace
Beauj	Beaujolais
Burg	Burgundy
B'x	Bordeaux
Cas	Castillon-Côtes de Bordeaux
Chab	Chablis
Champ	Champagne
Cors	Corsica
C d'O	Côte d'Or
Fron	Fronsac
L'doc	Languedoc
Lo	Loire
Mass C	Massif Central
Prov	Provence
N/S Rh	Northern/Southern Rhône
Rouss	Roussillon
Sav	Savoie
SW	Southwest
AC	appellation contrôlée
ch, chx	château(x)
dom, doms	domaine(s)

Funnily enough nobody argues about which country comes first or
gets most pages in this or any other world wine guide. France simply
invented the whole performance: finding local differences of style and
quality, defining, improving, building on, perfecting them until they have
become a currency of their own. How your yokel farmers, busy, hungry,
shivering in winter (and of course paying taxes) found time to select their
vines, propagate the good ones, then nurse their wine in its barrel, is one
of history's great puzzles. They didn't know they were interpreting their
landscape, anywhere between Alsace and Brittany, the Alps and Pyrénées,
for posterity. We, lucky posterity, have the pick of the dazzling results. Not
everyone agrees that the government should barge in to regulate such
a glorious diversity. Personally I think appellations are a vital consumer
aid. What they can't catch, though, is the constant flood of new ideas and
techniques that keep pushing quality up – or in some cases sideways.

The subject of this year's supplement, Organic, Biodynamic and
Natural Wines sheds light on how unexpected France can be. You wouldn't
think that a nation so keen on reason and logic would give biodynamics

France entries also cross-reference to Châteaux of Bordeaux

the time of day, but it has been the driving force in Burgundy for years now. No better argument for biodynamics could be found than the pure, crystal-line detail of modern burgundy. You could argue (and we do; *see* pp.321–36) that the logic of biodynamics isn't always logic at all. But the point is that something is working, and something is causing biodynamic growers in the Loire, Rhône, Alsace, the South, Bordeaux, to make astonishing wines.

Why is Bordeaux so much less keen on organics and biodynamics than Burgundy? Partly it's differences of climate (Burgundy being drier), but it's also differences of scale, and attitude. These differences help to make France the varied place it is. Bordeaux has its super-grand estates, but others may struggle to make a living. Most of the rest of vinous France is still small-scale and family-owned. Younger generations come in like whirlwinds, wanting to try everything. Their grandparents, who were delighted to adopt chemicals and abandon horses, think it funny that their grandchildren want to return to the old ways.

Recent vintages of the French classics

Red Bordeaux

Médoc / Red Graves For many wines, bottle age is optional: for these it is indispensable. Minor châteaux from light vintages need only two or three years, but even modest wines of great years can improve for 15 or so, and the great châteaux of these years can profit from double that time.

2017 Worst frost since 1991 (and hail in Graves). Some attractive Cab Sauv in north Médoc communes but volumes down everywhere. Be selective.

2016 Quality and quantity. Late harvest but healthy grapes. Cab Sauv with colour, depth, structure. Close to 2010.

2015 Excellent year for Cab Sauv but not the structure of 2005, 2010. Some variation. More rain at harvest in north Médoc than south.

2014 Saved by an Indian summer. Cab Sauv bright and resonant. Good to very good in terms of quality and quantity. Classic in style.

2013 Worst vintage since 1992. Patchy success at Classed Growth level. A vintage for early drinking.

2012 Erratic weather. Small crop. Difficulties ripening Cab Sauv. Some ready.

2011 Mixed quality but better than its reputation. Classic freshness with moderate alcohol. Modest crus ready to drink.

2010 Outstanding. Magnificent Cab Sauv, deep -coloured, concentrated, firmly structured. At a price. To keep for years.

2009 Outstanding year, touted as "The Greatest". Structured wines with an exuberance of fruit. Don't miss this. Accessible or to keep.

2008 Much better than expected; fresh, classic flavours. Ageing potential.

2007 A difficult year. Some quite stylish but some are wearying. Be selective.

Fine vintages: 06 05 00 98 96 95 90 89 88 86 85 82 75 70 66 62 61 59 55 53 49 48 47 45 29 28.

St-Émilion / Pomerol

2017 Badly hit by frost. St-Émilion/Pomerol plateaus fared best. Decent Cab Fr.

2016 Conditions same as Médoc. Some young vines suffered in drought but overall excellent.

2015 Great year for Merlot. Perfect conditions. Colour, concentration, balance.

2014 More rain than the Médoc so Merlot variable. Very good Cab Fr. Satisfactory.

2013 Difficult flowering (so tiny crop) and rot in Merlot. Modest year; take care.

2012 Conditions as Médoc. Earlier harvested Merlot marginally more successful.

2011 Complicated, as Médoc. Good Cab Fr. Pomerol best overall? Don't shun it.

2010 Outstanding. Powerful wines again with high alcohol. Concentrated.

2009 Again, outstanding. Powerful wines (high alcohol) but seemingly balanced. Hail in St-Émilion cut production at certain estates.

2008 Similar conditions to the Médoc. Tiny yields, quality surprisingly good. Starting to drink, but best will age.

2007 Same pattern as Médoc. Extremely variable, but nothing to keep for long.

Fine vintages: 05 01 00 98 95 90 89 88 85 82 71 70 67 66 64 61 59 53 52 49 47 45.

Red burgundy

Côte d'Or Côte de Beaune reds generally mature sooner than grander wines of Côte de Nuits. Earliest drinking dates are for lighter commune wines – eg. Volnay, Beaune; latest for Grands Crus, eg. Chambertin, Musigny. Even the best burgundies are more attractive young than equivalent red Bordeaux. It can seem magical when they really blossom years later.

2017 Survived the frosts! Big crop of attractive wines, mostly ripe enough, should be good except where overproduced.

2016 What was made (frost) looks great – healthy, ripe fruit with desirable freshness.

2015 Dense, concentrated wines, as 2005, but with the additional juiciness of 2010. Earning a stellar reputation; don't miss them.

2014 Beaune, Volnay, Pommard hailed once again. Attractive fresh reds of medium density but lovely fragrance. Take a look soon.

2013 Côte de Beaune hailed again. Small crop for Nuits, delicious perfumed wines for those who waited, with crunchy energy. Lesser wines ready.

2012 Côte de Beaune lost crop to hail. Small crop of fine wines in Côte de Nuits, exuberant yet classy. Still to be kept, though.

2011 Some parallels with 2007. Early harvest, lighter wines, now accessible.

2010 Turning into a great classic, pure, fine-boned yet also with impressive density. Village wines and some 1ers crus open for business.

2009 Beautiful, ripe, plump reds. Still adolescent, but some already accessible. Beware overripe examples. Now to 2030?

2008 Lean but lively, appeal more to Burgundy devotees than more general wine-lovers. Best wines show Pinot purity, opening up nicely. Now to early 2020s.

2007 Small crop of attractive, perfumed wines. Don't expect real density. Rather good in Côte de Beaune. Start drinking up.

Fine vintages: 05 03 02 99 96 (drink or keep) 95 93 90 88 85 78 71 69 66 64 62 61 59 (mature).

White burgundy

Côte d'Or White wines are now rarely made for ageing as long as they did 20 years ago, but top wines should still improve for ten years or more. Most Mâconnais and Chalonnais (St-Véran, Mâcon-Villages, Montagny) usually best drunk early (two to three years).

2017 Large but manageable crop of extremely promising wines, ripe but with good grip.

2016 Frost damage widespread but vineyards that survived produced good crop of juicily attractive wines.

2015 Rich, concentrated, from warm, dry summer. Most had sense to pick early and have done well, later wines may be too heavy. Similar to 2009 but more successes.

2014 Finest, most consistent vintage for a generation. White fruit flavours, ripe but fresh, elegant and balanced. Successful whites throughout Burgundy. Start drinking.

2013 Those who picked early made lively wines but late-picked examples flabby. Drink soon and be careful.

2012 Tiny production, poor flowering and repeated hailstorms. Decent weather later; wines full of energy, showing well.

2011 Fine potential for conscientious producers, some flesh and good balance, but it was easy to overcrop. Attractive early, drinking well now.

2010 Exciting wines with good fruit-acid balance, some damaged by September storms. Starting to develop exotic aromatics. Now to 2020.

2009 Full crop, healthy grapes, two styles: first-rate wines to keep from early pickers, otherwise can be flabbily unbalanced.

Fine vintages (all ready): 05 02 99 96 93 92 85 79 73 59.

Chablis

Grand Cru Chablis of vintages with both strength and acidity really need
at least five years, can age superbly for 15 years or more; Premiers Crus
proportionately less, but give them three years at least. Then, for the full effect,
decant them. Yes, really.

2017 Another frost disaster. Despairing vignerons, prices rising.

2016 Hail, frost, more hail, hardly any wine.

2015 Hot, dry summer; rich, ripe wines with a concentrated core.

2014 Excellent early crop, happy vignerons. Saline, fresh, well worth keeping.

2013 Small crop, late harvest, rot issues. Mixed bag, mostly drink up.

2012 Small crop, mostly very fine. Early pickers ultra-concentrated, classically
austere; late pickers soft, low acid, after rain. Good to drink.

Beaujolais

2017 Large crop but hideous hail especially in Fleurie and Moulin-à-Vent.

16 Large crop of juicy wines, unless hailed (Fleurie). 15 Massive wines,
best outstanding, others alcoholic monsters. 14 Fine crop, enjoyable now.
13 Late vintage with mixed results. 12 Tiny crop, economic misery, vineyards
abandoned. 11 Refined, classy wines, drinking well.

Southwest France

2017 Warm winter, disastrous April frosts reduced yield 25–100 per cent. Later
heatwave brought picking forward. Rain intervened but October glorious.
What was made will be very good.

2016 Crop small, but long, hot, dry summer a tonic.

2015 Year of outstanding promise, overshadowing even 2014.

2014 Started with a cool winter, ended gloriously. Sweet whites outstanding.

2013 Initially thought to be disastrous, some good wines made by top growers.

2012 Good, though crop reduced by poor weather early on.

2011 Good, some Cahors, Madiran rather overstated. Excellent whites.

The Midi

2017 Small quantity, but excellent quality: frost, unusual here; bad flowering,
summer drought. Rain at right moment would have made a great vintage.

2016 Very dry; ripe, healthy grapes, low quantity. Developing beautifully.

2015 Ripe fruit, balanced with elegant tannins, continuing to develop well.

2014 Tricky year: hail in La Clape, Minervois; best have turned out very well,
but rain spoilt others.

2013 Some lovely wines, developing nicely, some areas better than others.

2012 Quantity down, quality good; wines drinking well.

Northern Rhône

Depending on site and style, these can be as long-lived as burgundies. White
Hermitage can keep for as long as red. Impossible to generalize, but don't be
in a hurry with red or white.

2017 Very good. Full, thorough reds, deeper than 16, show sunshine, packed-in
tannins. Whites for hearty food.

2016 Good to very good, reds pure, harmonious, classic at Côte-Rôtie. Note
Cornas, Crozes-Hermitage reds. Marvellous Hermitage whites, other
whites good, clean.

2015 Excellent reds everywhere, wonderful, very long-lived Hermitage,
Côte-Rôtie. Full whites, can be heady.

2014 Plump reds, gain depth over time. Excellent whites: style and freshness.

2013 Very good reds, with tight body, crisp tannin and freshness. 15–20 years life. Exceptional whites (Hermitage, St-Joseph, St-Péray).
2012 Very good Hermitage, open-book Côte-Rôtie. Fresh reds come together well, will last 15 years+. Whites have style, freshness (Condrieu).
2011 Good Hermitage, Cornas. Côte-Rôtie more body recently. Whites okay.
2010 Top-notch. Reds: marvellous depth, balance, freshness. Long-lived. Côte-Rôtie as good as 78. Very good Condrieu, rich whites elsewhere.
2009 Excellent, sun-packed wines. Some rich Hermitage, very full Côte-Rôtie. Best Crozes, St-Joseph have aged well. Rather big whites: can live.
2008 Rain. Top names best. Good, clear whites. Reds: 8–12 years.

Southern Rhône

2017 Very good. Small yield. Rich, bold reds, tannins ripe despite drought. Most strict top domaines did best. Full, true southern whites.
2016 Excellent for all (Châteauneuf, old vines Grenache triumph). Rich, sensuous, long reds, a fruit bonanza. Sun-filled whites, plenty of body; keep some to mature.
2015 Very good: rich, dark, good body, firm tannins, often enticing flair. Quality high across board (Gigondas); cheap reds value. Very good, full whites.
2014 Good in places, aromatic finesse returns to Châteauneuf. Stick to best names; dilution issue. NB Gigondas, Rasteau, Cairanne. Fresh whites.
2013 Tiny crop. Sparky, vibrant, slow-burn reds, very low Grenache yields: atypical wines. Châteauneuf best from old vines. Gd-value Côtes du Rhône. Very good whites.
2012 Full reds, lively, good tannins. Open-book vintage. Food-friendly whites.
2011 Sunny, supple, can be fat, drink quite early. Alcohol issue. Decent whites.
2010 Outstanding. Full-bodied, balanced reds. Tiptop Châteauneuf. Clear-fruited, well-packed tannins. Whites deep, long.
2009 Dense reds. Drought: some baked features, grainy tannins. Good Rasteau. Sound whites.
2008 Dodgy; life 12–15 years (top names). Very good, lively whites, to drink.

Champagne

2017 Spring frost then rot after August rains. Early-picked Chardonnay (Krug, Roederer) will be very good, fine Pinot N in Aube (missed August rain).
2016 Interesting Pinot N; Chard variable. Very small crop. Reserve wines will be in demand.
2015 Warm, dry summer: great Pinot N, refined Meunier, some overripe Chard; other Chards sumptuous.
2014 Chard best. Unlikely to be vintage year, but maybe for Blanc de Blancs.
2013 Potentially brilliant for classic cool Chard of Côte des Blancs. Pinot N hit and miss – glorious in Äy.
2012 Exquisite Pinot Noir, best since 1952, fine Meunier, Chard less brilliant.
2011 Lack of proper maturity, structure; some fine growers, the daring did well.
2010 Difficult for Pinots N/M. Chard initially firm, tastes better and better, good base for NV cuvées; growers and bijou maisons made good Vintage Blanc de Blancs.
Fine vintages: 08' 07 06' 04 02' 00 98 96' 95 92 90 89 88' 82 76.

The Loire

2017 Good quality with quantity slightly up on 2016 but April frosts again (Muscadet, Savennières, parts of Touraine). Bourgueil and Menetou-Salon spared.

2016 April frost, then floods, mildew, sunburn; low quantity but quality good. Sancerre spared.

2015 Good to very good across range. Fine sweet wines in Layon and l'Aubance.

2014 Well-balanced dry whites, ripe reds to age. Outstanding Muscadet.

2013 Low sugar, high acidity. Some attractive, early drinking. A little Anjou sweet.

2012 Melon de Bourgogne, Sauv Bl high quality plus some reds; avoid sweet.

2011 Topsy-turvy. Rot in Muscadet. Quality very variable. Top sweet Anjou.

Alsace

2017 Savage spring frosts, so small crop. But in quality, one of best since World War Two, with 1947, 1971, 2008.

2016 Classic finely balanced vintage and plenty of it, unlike 2013, 2014, 2015.

2015 Rich vintage, one of driest ever. Great Pinot N, if not much of it.

2014 Gewurz and Pinot Gr attacked by Suzuki fruit fly. Ries wonderful, generous, great acidity.

2013 Becoming a classic vintage, now opening up. Great potential (Ries).

2012 Small crop of concentrated wines, in dry style of 2010.

Abymes Sav w ★→★★ Hilly area nr Chambéry, next to APREMONT. Fresh DYA Vin de SAV AC cru (300 ha). Jacquère grape (80% min) Try: des Anges, Ducret, Giachino, Labbe, Perrier, Ravier, Sabots de Venus.

Ackerman Lo r p w (dr) (sw) sp ★→★★★ Leading Lo NÉGOCIANT. SAUMUR sparkling house (1811). Ackerman incl: Celliers du Prieuré, Varière (ANJOU), Donatien-Bahuaud and Drouet (Pays Nantais), Monmousseau, Perruche, Rémy-Pannier. CH de SANCERRE bought 2017.

AC or AOC (Appellation Contrôlée) / AOP Government control of origin and production (but not quality) of most top French wines; around 45 per cent of total. Now being converted to AOP (Appellation d'Origine Protegée – which is much nearer the truth than Contrôlée).

Agenais SW Fr r p w ★ DYA IGP of Lot-et-Garonne. Famous for prunes: better bet than grapes, though a few DOMS (Boiron, Campet, Lou Gaillot) make fair wine. Co-ops boring.

Alain Chabanon, Dom L'doc ★★★ Once-pioneering MONTPEYROUX producer keeps up with Campredon, Esprit de Font Caude, MERLOT-based Merle aux Alouettes. Delicious whites Le Petit Trélans, pure VERMENTINO, age-worthy Trélans Vermentino/CHENIN BL.

Allemand, Thiérry N Rh r ★★★ 90' 91' 95' 98' 99' 00' 01' 02 03 04 05' 06' 07' 08' 09' 10' 11' 12' 13' 14' 15' 16' 17' Magnificent CORNAS 5-ha DOM, low sulphur, organic. Two v. deep, smoky wines. Top is Reynard (profound, complex; 20 yrs+), Chaillot (v.gd fruit) drinks earlier.

Alliet, Philippe Lo r w ★★★ →★★★★ 05' 08 09' 10' 11 12 14' 15' 16 (17) One of CHINON's (17 ha) CAB FR stars. Tradition, VIEILLES VIGNES 50-yr-old+ vines on gravel. Two steep s-facing v'yds e of Chinon: L'Huisserie, Coteau de Noire. Now with son Pierre.

Aloxe-Corton Burg r w ★★→★★★ 99' 02' 03 05' 08 09' 10' 11 12' 14 15' 16 (17) The n end of CÔTE DE BEAUNE, famous for GRANDS CRUS CORTON, CORTON-CHARLEMAGNE, but less interesting at village or PREMIER CRU level. Reds attractive if not overextracted. Best DOMS: Follin-Arbelet, Rapet, Senard, Terregelesses, TOLLOT-BEAUT.

AOP and IGP: what's happening in France

The Europe-wide introduction of AOP (Appellation d'Origine Protegée) and IGP (Indication Géographique Protegée) means that these terms may now appear on labels. AC/AOC will continue to be used, but for simplicity and brevity this book now uses IGP for all former VDP.

Alquier, Jean-Michel L'doc r w ★★★ Stellar FAUGÈRES producer. MARSANNE/ROUSSANNE/ GRENACHE Des Vignes au Puits; SAUV Pierres Blanches. Reds; Les Premières (young vines); Maison Jaune, only in gd Grenache yrs; Les Bastides (old higher-altitude SYRAH); Syrah-based Les Grandes Bastides d'Alquier longer in new oak.

Alsace (r) w (sw) (sp) ★★ ⇢★★★★ Sheltered e slope of Vosges and 1800 sun hrs make France's Rhine wines: aromatic, fruity, full-strength, drier styles back in vogue (thank goodness). Still much sold by variety (PINOT BL, RIES, GEWURZ). Yet rich diversity of 13 geological formations (incl granite, gneiss, limestone) shapes best terroir wines for ageing. Ries, up to 20 yrs for GRAND CRU. Once fragile **Pinot N improving fast** (esp 10 12 15 16 17). See VENDANGE TARDIVE, SÉLECTION DES GRAINS NOBLES.

Alsace Grand Cru Al ★★★ ⇢★★★★ 06 07 08' 10 12 13 (esp Ries) ★★★15 17' AC. Restricted to 51 of best named v'yds (approx 1600 ha, 800 in production) and four noble grapes (PINOT GR, RIES, GEWURZ, MUSCAT). Production rules require higher min ripeness. Concept of local management allows extra rules specific to each cru. PINOT N's GC status still pending – such is French bureaucracy.

Amiel, Mas Rouss r w sw ★★★ Leading MAURY estate. Exemplary CÔTES DU ROUSS, MAURY, IGP. Look for Vol de Nuit from v. old CARIGNAN, GRENACHE-based Vers le Nord, Origine, Altaïr, others. Plus young *grenat* (Maury version of RIMAGE), venerable RANCIO VDN 20- to 40-yr-old Maury.

Amirault, Yannick Lo ★★★ ⇢★★★★ 05' 06 08' 09' 10' 11 12 14' 15' 16 (17) Organic. Top grower in BOURGUEIL (20 ha)/ST-NICOLAS-DE-BOURGUEIL (10 ha). Best CUVÉES: La Mine (St-Nicolas), La Petite CAVE, Le Grand Clos, Les Quartiers (Bourgueil).

Angerville, Marquis d' C d'O r w ★★★★ Bio superstar in VOLNAY, not just classy but classical too esp legendary CLOS des Ducs (MONOPOLE). Enjoy Champans, Taillepieds as well. See also DOM DU PÉLICAN for Jura interests.

Anglès, Ch d' L'doc ★★★ Stellar LA CLAPE estate renovated by Eric Fabre, ex-technical director of CH LAFITE, captivated by MOURVÈDRE. Unoaked Classique (r p w), age-worthy oaked *grand vin* (r w).

Anjou Lo r p w (dr) (sw) (sp) ★ ⇢★★★★ Both region and AC encompassing ANJOU, SAUMUR. Poor reputation holds region back. CHENIN BL dry whites: wide range of styles from light quaffers to complex – looking to create crus; juicy reds, incl GAMAY; fruity CAB FR-based Anjou Rouge; age-worthy but tannic ANJOU-VILLAGES, incl CAB SAUV. Mainly dry SAVENNIÈRES; lightly sweet to rich COTEAUX DU LAYON Chenin Bl; rosé (dr s/sw), sp mainly CRÉMANT. Sweets: buy 10 11 14 15. Avoid 12. Hotbed of natural wines.

Anjou-Coteaux de la Loire Lo w sw s/sw ★★ ⇢★★★ 05' 07' 09 10' 11' 14 15' 16 (17) Small (32 ha, 15 producers) AC for sweet CHENIN BL w of Angers; more racy than COTEAUX DU LAYON. Esp CH de Putille, Delaunay, Fresche, Musset-Roullier (v.gd).

Anjou-Villages Lo r ★ ⇢★★★ 05' 08 09' 10' 11 12 14' 15' 16 (17) Structured red AC (CAB FR/CAB SAUV, a few pure Cab Sauv). Grippy tannins can be a problem; best given some bottle age. Top wines gd value esp Bergerie, Brancherau, Brizé, CADY, CH Pierre-Bise, CLOS de Coulaine, Delesvaux, Ogereau, Sauveroy, Soucherie. Sub-AC Anjou-Villages-Brissac same zone as COTEAUX DE L'AUBANCE; look for Bablut, CH de Varière (part of ACKERMAN), Haute Perche, Montigilet, Princé, Richou, Rochelles. 2017 early vintage.

Apremont Sav w ★★ Keep up to 5 yrs. Biggest cru of SAV (400 ha, 28 per cent of production) just s of Chambéry. Jacquère only grape. Producers: Aphyllantes, Blard, Boniface, Dacquin, Masson, Perrier, Rouzan.

Arbin Sav r ★★ 30 ha. Deep-coloured, lively spicy red from MONDEUSE grapes, ideal après-ski. Drink at 1–2 yrs. Try: l'Idylle, Magnin.

Arbois Jura r p w (sp) ★★ ⇢★★★ 10' 12 14' 15' 16 (17) AC of n Jura, great spot for wine, cheese, chocolates, walking and Louis Pasteur museum. CHARD, and/or SAVAGNIN whites, VIN JAUNE, reds from Poulsard, Trousseau or PINOT N. Try terroirtrue Stephane TISSOT, fresh *ouillé* styles from DOM DU PÉLICAN, oxidative whites from Overnoy/Houillon, plus all-rounders AVIET, Pinte, Renardières, Rolet.

Ariège SW Fr r p w ★ **14 15** (16) Small, hard-to-find IGP between Toulouse and Pyrénées. Try bio DOM des Coteaux d'Engravies (esp varietal SYRAH) and Swiss winemaker Dominik Benz.

Arjolle, Dom de l' L'doc ★★★ Large CÔTES DE THONGUE family-run estate. Range incl Equilibre, Equinoxe, Paradoxe, varietals and blends, and two original Vins de France: Z for ZIN, K for CARMENÈRE.

Arlaud C d'O r ★★★→★★★★ Leading MOREY-ST-DENIS estate energized by Cyprien A and siblings. Beautifully poised, modern wines with depth and class from exceptional BOURGOGNE Roncevie up to GRANDS CRUS. Fine range of Morey PRÈMIERS CRUS esp Ruchots.

Arlay, Ch d' Jura r p w sw ★★ Ancient, aristocratic Jura estate based in imposing CH: Sound all-round offer of all colours incl VIN JAUNE.

Arlot, Dom de l' C d'O r w ★★→★★★ AXA-owned NUITS-ST-GEORGES estate, interesting Nuits whites and classy, fragrant reds esp CLOS des Forêts St Georges, ROMANÉE-ST-VIVANT, VOSNE-ROMANÉE Suchots. Now less dogmatically whole-bunch vinification.

Armand, Comte C d'O r ★★★★ Sole owner of exceptional CLOS des Epeneaux, most graceful wine of POMMARD and other v'yds in AUXEY, VOLNAY. Great wines esp since 1999, poise, longevity, but tiny crops 2012–16.

Only AOP wines can be called Ch X; IGP wines must settle for Dom X.

Aube Champ Southern v'yds of CHAMP, aka Côte des Bar. V.gd PINOT N **12 14 15' 17**. Impressive new MOËT winery at Gyé-sur-Seine wholly devoted to rosé Champ. Harvest 17 luckier than in Marne – less rain.

Aupilhac, Dom d' L'doc ★★★ Pioneer in MONTPEYROUX, now followed by several others. Sylvain Fadat favours old-vine Le CARIGNAN (his 1st wine in 1989) as well as L'DOC classics, and higher-altitude Les Cocalières.

Auxey-Duresses C d'O r w ★★→★★★ (r) **03 05' 09' 10' 11 12 14 15' 16** (17) (w) 14' **15' 16** (17) CÔTE DE BEAUNE village in valley behind MEURSAULT. Fresh light-tasting *whites offer value*, reds less rustic now they ripen in most yrs. Best: (r) COMTE ARMAND, COCHE-DURY, Gras, MAISON LEROY (Les Boutonniers), Moulin aux Moines, Prunier; (w) Lafouge, LEROUX, ROULOT.

Aveyron SW Fr r p w ★ IGP DYA. ★★Nicolas Carmarans, fan of rare grapes (Négret de Banyars), emerges as star of these country wines. More orthodox ★DOMS Bertau, Bias (PINOT N), Pleyjean (new owner). *See* AOPS ENTRAYGUES, ESTAING, MARCILLAC.

Aviet, Lucien Jura ★★ Fine ARBOIS grower, nicknamed Bacchus. Gd-value, eg. attractive light Poulsard and tangy SAVAGNIN.

Avize Champ ★★★★ Côte des Blancs GRAND CRU CHARD village sets a v. high standard in top grower/DOM Champ: Agrapart, Corbon, De Sousa, Selosse and great co-op Union Champagne.

Aÿ Champ Revered PINOT N village, home of BOLLINGER, DEUTZ. Mix of merchants and growers' wines, either made in barrel, eg. Claude Giraud, master of Argonne oak, or in tanks. *Gosset-Brabant* Noirs d'Aÿ excels. Aÿ Rouge (Coteaux Champenois) now excellent in ripe yrs (esp 15').

Ayala Champ Reborn Aÿ house, owned by BOLLINGER. Fine Brut Zéro, BLANC DE BLANCS. Ace Prestige Perle d'Ayala **08' 09 12' 13 15' 16**. Precision, purity. Energy under Caroline Latrine, chef de CAVE.

Bachelet Burg r w ★★→★★★★ Widespread family name in C D'O. Best for whites: B-Monnot (esp PULIGNY, BÂTARD-MONTRACHET), Jean-Claude B (CHASSAGNE, St-Aubin, etc). Related to Madame President Bachelet of Chile but not to Denis B who makes great GEVREY-CHAMBERTIN and unrelated to other Bs. Don't forget.

Bandol Prov r p (w) ★★★ **98 99 00 01 02 03 04 05 06 07 08 09 10 11 12 13 14 15 16 17**

FRANCE

Compact coastal AC; PROV's finest. Superb barrel-aged reds; huge ageing potential. MOURVÈDRE key, with GRENACHE, CINSAULT; elegantly structured rosé from young vines, drop of white from CLAIRETTE, UGNI BLANC, occasionally SAUV BL. Several stars: DOMS de la Bégude, Gros'Noré, La Bastide Blanche, Lafran Veyrolles, La Suffrène, Mas de la Rouvière, *Pibarnon*, Pradeaux, TEMPIER, Terrebrune, Vannières.

Banyuls Rouss r br sw ★★→★★★ Deliciously original and underappreciated VDN, based on old GRENACHES NOIR, BLANC, Gris. Young vintage RIMAGE is fresh, fruity. Traditional RANCIOS, aged for many yrs, much more rewarding. Serious alternative to fine old Tawny Port. Best: DOMS du Mas Blanc (★★★), la Rectorie (★★★), la Tour Vieille (★★★), Les CLOS de Paulilles, Coume del Mas (★★), Madeloc, Vial Magnères. *See also* MAURY.

Baronne, Ch La L'doc ★★★ Bio family estate in CORBIÈRES; min intervention in cellar. Barrels, amphoras, eggs... Corbières Alaric, Les Chemins, Les Lanes and (CARIGNAN planted 1892) Pièce de Roche. IGP Hauterive. Sulphur-free Les Chemins de Traverse, and VIN DE FRANCE VERMENTINO/Grenache Gris (w).

Barrique B'X (and Cognac) term for oak barrel holding 225 litres. Used globally, but global mania for excessive new oak now fading. Average price €750/barrel.

Barsac Saut w sw ★★ →★★★★ 89' 90' 95 96 97' 98 99' 01' 02 03' 05' 07' 09' 10' 11' 12 13 14 15 16 Neighbour of SAUT with similar botrytized wines from lower-lying limestone soil; fresher, less powerful. Frost damage in 2017. Top: CAILLOU, CLIMENS, COUTET, DOISY-DAËNE, DOISY-VÉDRINES, NAIRAC.

Barthod, Ghislaine C d'O r ★★★★ →★★★★ Reason to fall in love with CHAMBOLLE-MUSIGNY, if you haven't already. Wines of perfume, delicacy, yet depth, concentration. Impressive range of nine PREMIER CRUS incl Charmes, Cras, Fuées, Les Baudes.

Bâtard-Montrachet C d'O w ★★★★ 99' 00 02' 04' 05' 06 07' 08' 09' 10 11 12 13 14' 15 (17) 12-ha GRAND CRU downslope from LE MONTRACHET itself. Grand, hefty whites that should need time; more power than neighbours BIENVENUES-B-M and CRIOTS B-M. Seek: BACHELET-Monnot, CARILLON, DOM LEFLAIVE, FAIVELEY, GAGNARD, H BOILLOT, LATOUR, LEROUX, MOREY, OLIVIER LEFLAIVE, Pernot, Ramonet, SAUZET, VOUGERAIE.

Baudry, Dom Bernard Lo r p w ★★→★★★ 05 08 09' 10' 11 12 14' 15' 16' (17) 32 ha Cravant-les-Coteaux, gravel and limestone; Mathieu Baudry in charge. V.gd CHINONS, from CHENIN BL whites to CAB FR (r p); drink Les Granges early; Les Grézeaux, CLOS Guillot, Croix Boissée more complex. Organic; hand-harvested.

Baudry-Dutour Lo r p w (sp) ★★→★★★ 05' 08 09' 10' 11 14' 15' 16 (17) CHINON's largest producer, incl CHX de St Louans (r w), La Grille, La Perrière, La Roncée. Created 2003 by J-M Dutour and Christophe Baudry. Functional winery in Panzoult. Reliable: light, early-drinking to age-worthy reds/whites. IGP SAUV BL.

Baumard, Dom des Lo r p w sw sp ★★→★★★ 03 05' 07' (sw) 08 09 10 11 14 15 16 (17) 40 ha ANJOU domaine esp CHENIN BL whites, incl SAVENNIÈRES (CLOS St Yves, Clos du Papillon), Clos Ste Catherine. Apostle of cryoextraction for QUARTS DE CHAUME – illegal from 2020.

Baux-en-Provence, Les Prov r p w ★★ →★★★ 10 11 12 13 14 15 16 17 V'yds of tourist village on dramatic bauxite outcrop of Alpilles: sadly tourism can breed complacency. White from CLAIRETTE, GRENACHE BLANC, Rolle, ROUSSANNE. Reds CAB SAUV, SYRAH, GRENACHE. Most v'yds organic. Best estate remains *Trévallon*: IGP Cab/Syrah blend. Also Ch Romanin, Dom Hauvette, Estoublon, Mas de la Dame, Milan, Ste Berthe, Terres Blanches, Valdition.

Béarn SW Fr r p w ★ →★★ (r) 15 (17) (p w) AOP DYA. Co-op at ★Bellocq for thirst-quenching pink. Reds from ★DOMS de la Callabère, Lapeyre/Guilhémas. Whites from rare Ruffiat de Moncade grape.

Beaucastel, Ch de S Rh r w ★★★★ 90' 95' 96' 97 98 99' 00' 01' 03' 04 05' 06' 07' 08 09' 10' 11' 12' 13' 14' 15' 16' 17' Large, organic CHÂTEAUNEUF estate: old MOURVÈDRE, 100-yr-old ROUSSANNE. Darkly fruited, recently smoother wines, drink at 2 yrs or

> **New on the Beaujolais block**
>
> BEAUJ is one of greater Burg's most dynamic regions, where prices remain relatively affordable: so much so that many C D'O producers are investing in land here: JADOT, Louis BOILLOT, Thibault LIGER-BELAIR in MOULIN À VENT; BOUCHARD, DROUHIN, LAFARGE-Vial in FLEURIE. Others sniffing around.... Alternatively look to hungry "new kid in town" producers: Julie Balagny or Julien Sunier in FLEURIE, P-H Thillardon in CHÉNAS, Richard Rottiers in MOULIN À VENT. It's GAMAY, though; you may still prefer PINOT N.

from 7–8. Intense, top-quality 60% Mourvèdre Hommage à Jacques Perrin (r). *Wonderful old-vine Roussanne*: enjoy over 5–25 yrs. Genuine, serious own-vines CÔTES DU RH Coudoulet de Beaucastel (r, v.gd 16'), lives 8 yrs+. Famille Perrin GIGONDAS (v.gd), RASTEAU, VINSOBRES (best) all gd, authentic. Note organic Perrin Nature Côtes du Rh (r w). Growing N Rh merchant venture, Nicolas Perrin (stylish). (*See also* Tablas Creek, California.)

Beaujolais r (p) (w) ★ DYA. Basic appellation of the huge Beauj region. Often dull but doesn't need to be – try those from hills around Bois d'Oingt. Can now be sold as COTEAUX BOURGUIGNONS.

Beaujolais Primeur / Nouveau Beauj More of an event than a drink. The BEAUJ of the new vintage, hurriedly made for release at midnight on the 3rd Wednesday in Nov. Enjoy juicy fruit but don't let it put you off real thing.

Beaujolais-Villages Beauj r ★★ 14 15' 16 17 Next best v'yds after the ten named crus, eg. MOULIN-À-VENT. Look for top growers Burgaud, Chemarin, Lacarelle and local sub-divisions such as Lantigné.

Beaumes-de-Venise S Rh r (p) (w) br ★★ (r) 09' 10' 12' **13' 15'** 16' 17' (MUSCAT) DYA. Village nr GIGONDAS, high v'yds, popular for VDN Muscat apéritif/dessert. Serve v. cold: grapey, honeyed, can be stylish, eg. DOMS Beaumalric, Bernardins (musky, traditional), Coyeux, Durban (rich, long life), Fenouillet (brisk), JABOULET, Pigeade (fresh, v.gd), VIDAL-FLEURY, co-op Rhonéa. Also punchy, grainy reds. CH Redortier, de Fenouillet, Doms Cassan, Durban, Ferme St Martin (organic), St-Amant (gd w). Leave for 2–3 yrs. Simple whites (some dry MUSCAT, VIOGNIER).

Beaumont des Crayères Champ Côte d'Epernay co-op making model PINOT M-based Grande Rés NV. Vintage Fleur de Prestige top value **04 06 08' 10** 12' 13 14 15'. Great CHARD-led CUVÉE Nostalgie 02' **06** 09 13. New Fleur de Meunier BRUT Nature **09** 12' 15'.

Beaune C d'O r (w) ★★★ 02' **03** 05' **07 08** 09' 10' **11 12 14** 15' 16 (17) Centre of Burg wine trade, classic merchants: BOUCHARD, CHAMPY, CHANSON, DROUHIN, JADOT, LATOUR, Remoissenet and young pretenders Gambal, Lemoine, LEROUX, Roche de Bellène; top DOMS Croix, LAFARGE, MONTILLE, plus iconic HOSPICES DE BEAUNE. No GRANDS CRUS but some graceful, perfumed PREMIER CRU reds, eg. Bressandes, Cras, Vignes Franches; more power from Grèves. Try Aigrots, CLOS St Landry and esp *Clos des Mouches (Drouhin)* for whites.

Becker, Caves J Al r w ★→★★★ Organic estate since 99, now certified bio. Stylish wines, incl poised, taut GRAND CRU Froehn in GEWURZ, RIES **10'** 13 14' 15'. Fine Ries GC Mandelberg 10 13 14 15 17.

Bellet Prov r p w ★★ Minute AC; c.70 ha within city of Nice; rarely seen elsewhere. Rewarding white from Rolle surprisingly age-worthy. Braquet, Folle Noire for light red (DYA). 15 valiant producers: CH de Bellet, oldest, has new owner. Also CLOS St Vincent, Collet de Bovis, DOM de la Source, Les Coteaux de Bellet, Toasc.

Bellivière, Dom de Lo r w sw (sp) ★★→★★★ **10' 11'** 13 14' **15'** 16 (17) 15-ha, bio; Christine, Eric and son Clément. Brilliantly balanced CHENIN BL: JASNIÈRES, COTEAUX DU LOIR, peppery red Pineau d'Aunis.

Bergerac SW Fr r p w dr sw ★→★★★ **12 14** 15 16 **(17)** AOP adjoining B'x, same grapes, much cheaper. ★★CHX de la Jaubertie, Tour de Grangemont, ★★★CLOS des Verdots, DOMS du Cantonnet, Fleur de Thénac, Jonc-Blanc, *Tour des Gendres*, Vari. Growers in sub-AOPS MONBAZILLAC, MONTRAVEL, PÉCHARMANT, ROSETTE, SAUSSIGNAC also make some of best Bergerac AOP. Disparate styles, huge quality variation.

Berlioz, Gilles Sav V.gd boutique bio DOM (3.5 ha) in CHIGNIN. Four small parcels planted: Altesse, MONDEUSE, Jacquère, Persan. Wines: Chez l'Odette (Jacquère), El Hem, Le Jaja, Les Filles, Les Fripons.

Berthet-Bondet, Jean Jura r w ★★ Leading light for CH-CHALON VIN JAUNE but covers all bases for Jura red, white and CRÉMANT reliably. COTES DU JURA tradition v.gd value.

Bertrand, Gérard L'doc r p w ★★ Ambitious grower and NÉGOCIANT, now one of biggest in Midi: Villemajou (CORBIÈRES cru Boutenac), Laville-Bertou (MINERVOIS-La Livinière), l'Aigle (LIMOUX), IGP Hauterive Cigalus, la Sauvageonne (Terrasses du Larzac), recently bought CH de la Soujeole (Malepère), DOM du Temple and Deux Roc in Cabrières. Flagship: *l'Hospitalet* (LA CLAPE) with top wine Hospitalis. Aspirational, expensive CLOS d'Ora (Minervois-La Livinière). Also Prima Nature: zero sulphur. Converting to bio.

Besserat de Bellefon Champ ★★ Épernay house specializing in gently sparkling CHAMP (old CRÉMANT style). Part of LANSON-BCC group. Respectable rising quality, always gd value, esp 13 14 15, tiny but excellent 17'.

Beyer, Léon Al r w ★★ ·★★★ Blue-chip house of remarkable consistency. Intense, dry wines esp superb RIES Comtes d'Eguisheim 10 13 14' 15 17 actually GRAND CRU PFERSIGBERG (not mentioned on label). Ideal gastronomic, mature wines found in many Michelin-starred restaurants. Serious PINOT N 10' 12 14 15 17.

Bichot, Maison Albert Burg r w ★★ ·★★★ Major BEAUNE merchant/grower. Impressive wines: sturdy style, more concentrated than perfumed. Best wines from own DOMS, CLOS Frantin (NUITS), du Pavillon (Beaune), LONG-DEPAQUIT (CHAB).

Bienvenues-Bâtard-Montrachet C d'O ★★★ ·★★★★ 02' 04 05 06 07 08 09 10 11 12 14' 15 (17) Fractionally lighter, earlier-maturing version of BÂTARD, with tempting creamy texture. Best: BACHELET, CARILLON, LEFLAIVE, Ramonet, VOUGERAIE.

Billecart-Salmon Champ ★★★ Discreet icon now with modern profile; 200th anniversary 2018. Immaculate quality across board. New CUVÉE Louis BLANC DE BLANCS debuts in delicate, supremely elegant 06. Superb CLOS St-Hilaire BLANC DE NOIRS 98 02', NF Billecart 02' 06, BRUT 07 great value and powerful expression of PINOT N. Subtly oaked Cuvée Sous Bois. Exquisite ★★★★ *Elizabeth Salmon Rosé* 02 06 a fine follow-on.

Bize, Simon C d'O r w ★★★ Savigny grower, also go to for quality PREMIERS CRUS (r w).

Blagny C d'O r w ★★ ·★★★ 99' 02' 03' 05' 08 09' 10' 11 12 14 15' 16' (17) Hamlet on hillside above MEURSAULT and PULIGNY. Own AC for austere yet fragrant reds, sadly in retreat as growers replant with CHARD, sold as Meursault-Blagny PREMIER CRU. Best v'yds: La Jeunelotte, Pièce Sous le Bois, Sous le Dos d'Ane. Best growers (r) DE CHERISEY, LEROUX, Matrot; (w) Cherisey, LATOUR, MATROT.

Blanc de Blancs Any white wine made from white grapes only esp CHAMP. Indication of style, not of quality.

Blanc de Noirs White (or slightly pink or "blush") wine from red grapes, esp CHAMP: generally rich, even blunt, in style. But many now more refined; better PINOT N and new techniques.

Blanck, Paul & Fils Al r w ★★ ·★★★ Grower at Kientzheim. Finest from 6-ha GRAND CRU Furstentum (RIES, GEWURZ, PINOT GR), Grand Cru SCHLOSSBERG (great Ries 08' 10 12 13' 14 15' 17'). Excellent quality Classique generic range: tiptop, great value.

Blanquette de Limoux L'doc w sp ★★ Great-value bubbles from cool hills sw of Carcassonne; older history than CHAMP. 90% Mauzac with a little CHARD, CHENIN BL. AC CRÉMANT de Limoux, more elegant with Chard, Chenin Bl, PINOT N, and less Mauzac. Large Sieur d'Arques co-op. Also Antech, Delmas, Laurens,

RIVES-BLANQUES, Robert and several newcomers: DOMS La Coume-Lumet, Les Hautes Terres, Jo Riu, Monsieur S.

Blaye B'x r ★→★★ 09' 10' 11 12 14 15 16 Designation for better reds (lower yields, higher v'yd density, longer maturation) from AC BLAYE-CÔTES DE B'X.

Blaye-Côtes de Bordeaux B'x r w ★→★★ 10' 12 14 15 16' Mainly MERLOT-led red AC on right bank of Gironde. A little dry white (mainly SAUV BL). Best CHX: Bel Air la Royère, Bourdieu, Cantinot, des Tourtes, Gigault (CUVÉE Viva), Haut-Bertinerie, Haut-Colombier, Haut-Grelot, Jonqueyres, Monconseil-Gazin, Mondésir-Gazin, Montfollet, Roland la Garde, Segonzac. Also Charron and CAVE des Hauts de Gironde (Tutiac) co-op for whites.

Boeckel, Dom Al ★★★ Long-estab estate in fairytale Mittelbergheim, now expanded to 23 ha in best marl and sandstone sites of Bas Rhin. Great RIES esp Wibbelsberg, Clos Eugenie 10 13 14 15' 17. GRAND CRU Zotzenberg unique site for top *Sylvaner*. Exemplary CRÉMANT D'AL.

Boillot C d'O r w Leading Burg family. Look for ★★★Jean-Marc (POMMARD) esp for fine, long-lived whites; ★★→★★★★★Henri (MEURSAULT), potent whites and modern reds; ★★★Louis (CHAMBOLLE, married to GHISLAINE BARTHOD) for ever-improving reds, and his brother Pierre ★★→★★★ (GEVREY).

Boisset, Jean-Claude Burg Ultra-successful merchant/grower group created over last 50 yrs. Boisset label and esp own v'yds DOM DE LA VOUGERAIE excellent. Recent additions to empire are the brands VINCENT GIRARDIN (Burg) and HENRI MAIRE (JURA). Also projects in California (Gallo connection), Canada, Chile, Uruguay.

Boizel Champ ★★★ Exceptional aged BLANC DE BLANCS NV and prestige Joyau de France 02' 08 09 12' 15', Joyau Rosé 04 06 08' 09 12' 15. Also Grand Vintage BRUT 04 06 09 12 15. CUVÉE Sous Bois. Fine quality, great value.

Bollinger Champ ★★★★ Great classic house, ever-better quality, much fresher than it was. BRUT Special NV top form since 2012; Grande Année 00 02' 04 05 07 08'. PINOT N-led, innovative Vintage Rosé 06, lush, powerful, high 30 per cent of Côte aux Enfants rouge, brilliant with game. Excavated secret cellar La Gallerie 1829 must-visit: display of bottles back to 1830s, res wines to 1892. *See* LANGLOIS-CH.

Bonneau du Martray, Dom C d'O (r) ★★★ (w) ★★★★ Reference producer for CORTON-CHARLEMAGNE, bought 2016 by Stanley Kroenke, owner of Screaming Eagle (California) and Arsenal football club (UK). Intense wines designed for long (c.10 yrs) ageing, glorious mix of intense fruit, underlying minerals. Small amount of fine red CORTON.

Bonnes-Mares C d'O r ★★★★ 90' 93 95 96' 98 99' 00 02' 03 05' 06 07 08 09' 10' 11 12' 13 14 15' 16' (17) GRAND CRU between CHAMBOLLE-MUSIGNY and MOREY-ST-DENIS with some of latter's wilder character. Sturdy, long-lived wines, less fragrant than MUSIGNY. Best: Bernstein, BRUNO CLAIR, Drouhin-Laroze, DE VOGÜÉ, Dujac, Groffier, JADOT, MUGNIER, ROUMIER, VOUGERAIE.

Bonnezeaux Lo w sw ★★★ →★★★★ 89' 90' 95' 96' 97' 03' 05' 09 10' 11' 14 15' 16 (17) 80 ha; 40 producers. Rich, almost immortal CHENIN BL from three sw-facing slopes in COTEAUX DU LAYON. Esp: CHX de Fesles, La Varière (ACKERMAN) and DOMS de Mihoudy, du Petit Val, Les Grandes Vignes.

Bordeaux r (p) w ★→★★ 15 16 Catch-all AC for generic B'x (represents nearly half region's production). Most brands (DOURTHE, Michel Lynch, MOUTON CADET, SICHEL) are in this category. *See also* CHX Bauduc, BONNET, Reignac, Ronan by Clinet, Tour de Mirambeau. Quality, quantity severely hit by frost in 2017.

Bordeaux Supérieur B'x r ★→★★ 09' 10' 12 14 15 16 Superior denomination to above. Higher min alc, lower yield, longer ageing. Mainly bottled at property. Frost damage in 2017. Consistent CHX: Camarsac, Grand Verdus, Grand Village, Grée-Laroque, Jean Faux, Landereau, Parenchère (CUVÉE Raphaël), Penin, PEY LA TOUR (Rés), Reignac, THIEULEY, Turcaud (Cuvée Majeure).

Borie-Manoux B'x Admirable B'x shipper, CH-owner: BATAILLEY, BEAU-SITE, DOM DE L'EGLISE, LYNCH-MOUSSAS, TROTTEVIEILLE. On-line wine sales.

Bouchard Père & Fils Burg r w ★★ →★★★★ Top BEAUNE merchant, quality v. sound all round. Whites best in MEURSAULT and GRANDS CRUS esp CHEVALIER-MONTRACHET. Flagship reds: Beaune Vigne de L'Enfant Jésus, CORTON, *Volnay Caillerets Ancienne Cuvée Carnot*. Part of HENRIOT Burg interests with WILLIAM FÈVRE (CHAB), CH de Poncié (BEAUJ).

Bouches-du-Rhône Prov r p w ★ IGP from Marseille environs. Simple, hopefully fruity, reds from s varieties, plus CAB SAUV, SYRAH, MERLOT.

Bourgeois, Henri Lo r p w ★★ →★★★ 05 07 08 10 11 12 14' 15 16 17 Model SANCERRE grower/merchant in Chavignol. Dynamic, close-knit family always looking to improve. V.gd: CHÂTEAUMEILLANT, COTEAUX DU GIENNOIS, MENETOU-SALON, POUILLY-FUMÉ, QUINCY, IGP Petit Bourgeois. Best: Jadis, La Bourgeoise (r w), MD de Bourgeois, Sancerre d'Antan. Can age beautifully. Also Clos Henri in Marlborough, NZ.

Bourgogne Burg r (p) w ★ →★★ (r) 05' 09' 10' 12' 14 15' 16 (17) (w) 14' 15 16 (17) Ground-floor AC for Burg, ranging from mass-produced to bargain beauties. Sometimes comes with subregion attached, eg. CÔTE CHALONNAISE, HAUTES CÔTES and latest addition, C D'O. From PINOT N (r) or CHARD (w) but can be declassified BEAUJ crus (sold as Bourgogne GAMAY).

Bourgogne Passe-Tout-Grains Burg r (p) ★ Age 1–2 yrs. Burg blend of PINOT N (more than 30%), GAMAY. Fresh, sometimes funky. Can keep longer from top C D'O DOMS, eg. Castagnier, CHEVILLON, LAFARGE, ROUGET.

Bourgueil Lo r (p) ★★ →★★★ 05' 08 09' 10' 11 12 14 15' 16 (17) Dynamic AC, 1400 ha, full-bodied TOURAINE reds, rosés based on CAB FR. Gd vintages age 50 yrs+. Inc AMIRAULT, Ansodelles, Audebert, Chevalerie, Courant, de la Butte, Gambier, Herlin, Lamé Delisle Boucard, Ménard, Minière, Nau Frères, Omasson, Revillot, Rochouard. Largely fought off frost in 2017.

Bouscassé, Dom SW Fr r w ★★★ 10' 11' 12 14 15' (17') BRUMONT's Napa-style base. Reds require just as much patience as his MONTUS. Petit Courbu-based dry PACHERENC (little or no oak) gorgeous.

Bouvet-Ladubay Lo (r) p w sp ★★ →★★★ Mainly SAUMUR sparkling and CRÉMANT DE LO returned in 2015 to Monmousseau family control. Patrice M (president), daughter Juliette (CEO). CUVÉE Trésor (p w) and BRUT Extra Zéro best.

Bouzereau C d'O r w ★★ →★★★ The B family infest MEURSAULT, in a gd way. Try whites from Jean-Baptiste (DOM Michel B), Vincent B or B-Gruère & Filles.

Bouzeron Burg (r) w ★★ 15' 16 (17) CÔTE CHALONNAISE village with unique AC for ALIGOTÉ; stricter rules and greater potential than straight BOURGOGNE Aligoté. BOUCHARD PÈRE, Briday, FAIVELEY, Jacqueson gd; A & P DE VILLAINE outstanding.

Bouzy Rouge Champ r ★★ 96 97 99 02 09 12 15' Still red of famous PINOT N village. Formerly like v. light burg, now with more intensity (climate change, better viticulture), also refinement. CLOS, Colin and Paul Bara best producers, last with star winemaker from 2018.

Boxler, Albert Al Bijou DOM making supreme ★★★★AL GRAND CRU Sommerberg RIES 13 15, excellent PINOTS GR, BL, top CRÉMANT. Restrained oak usage and eco v'yd care.

Brocard, J-M Chab w ★★ →★★★ Successful quality grower/merchant. Julien B has

---

Bio Burgundy

Burg is a leading light in the bio movement. Great DOMS have persuaded others to follow: BONNEAU DU MARTRAY, COMTE ARMAND, Clavelier, DAUVISSAT, DRC, DROUHIN, Lafarge, LAFON, LEFLAIVE, LEROY, LIGER-BELAIR, ROSSIGNOL-TRAPET, TRAPET, VOUGERAIE. Question to Dominique Lafon: "Aren't you worried about non-bio contamination from your neighbours?" Answer: "Actually I have contaminated them into turning biodynamic…"

added bio methods to father Jean-Marc's flair. Sustainable mix of volume CHAB lines and high-class individual bottlings. Try GRAND CRU Les Preuses.

Brouilly Beauj r ★★ 09′ 14′ 15′ 16 17 Largest of ten BEAUJ crus: solid, rounded wines with some depth of fruit, approachable early but can age 3–5 yrs. Top growers: CH de la Chaize, Ch Thivin, Chermette, Dubost, Lapalu, Michaud, Piron.

Brumont, Alain SW Fr r w ★★★ Leader in MADIRAN. Trend to easier-drinking wines reflected by ★Torus and range of quaffable IGPS. ★★★PACHERENCS (dr sw) outstanding. Super-growths BOUSCASSÉ, Le Tyre, MONTUS still dominate area.

Brut Champ Term for dry classic wines of CHAMP. Most houses have reduced dosage (adjustment of sweetness) in recent yrs. But great Champ can still be made at 8–9g residual sugar.

Brut Ultra / Zéro Term for bone-dry wines (no dosage) in CHAMP (also known as Brut Nature); back in fashion, quality generally improving. Needs ripe yr, old vines, max care, eg. ROEDERER Brut Nature, Veuve Fourny Nature.

Bugey Sav r p w sp ★→★★ AC 2009 (490 ha) for sparkling, *pétillant*, still. Three sectors: Belley, Cerdon, Montagnieu. Eight associated Bugey ACs. Whites mainly CHARD also incl ALIGOTÉ, Jacquère, Roussette. Reds: GAMAY, MONDEUSE, PINOT N. Growers: Angelot, Lingot-Martin, Monin, Peillot, Pellerin.

Buxy, Caves de Burg r (p) w ★→★★ Leading CÔTE CHALONNAISE co-op for decent CHARD, PINOT N, source of many merchants' own-label ranges. Easily largest supplier of AC MONTAGNY.

Buzet SW Fr r (p) (w) ★★ 14 15′ (17) ★B'X with Gascon touch. The AOP is led by nonconformist bio/natural ★★★DOM du Pech. ★Ambitious co-op, CHX du Frandat, bio Dom Salisquet.

Stone walls in a v'yd hold heat: tomatoes (and grapes) will ripen 200m higher.

Cabernet d'Anjou Lo p s/sw ★→★★ DYA. DEMI-SEC to sweet rosé. Locally popular style, pre-siesta summer quaffing, remarkable old vintages 47 49 (★★★) v. rare. Bablut, CADY, CH PIERRE-BISE, Chauvin, Clau de Nell, de Sauveroy, Grandes Vignes, Montgilet, Ogereau, Varière.

Cadillac-Côtes de Bordeaux B'X r ★→★★ 10′ 12 14 15 16 Long, narrow, hilly zone on right bank of Garonne. Mainly MERLOT with CABS SAUV, FR. Medium-bodied, fresh reds; quality extremely varied. Best: Alios de Ste-Marie, Biac, Carignan, *Carsin*, CLOS Chaumont, Clos Ste-Anne, de Ricaud, Grand-Mouëys, Le Doyenné, Les Guyonnets, Mont-Pérat, Plaisance, Puy Bardens, Réaut (Carat), *Reynon*, Suau.

Cady, Dom Lo r p w sw sp ★★→★★★ 09 10′ 11′ 14′ 15′ 16′ (17) V.gd family in St Aubin de Luigné. Full range of ANJOU with accent on CHENIN, incl COTEAUX DU LAYON esp Chaume, Les Varennes. 2017 v. promising.

Cahors SW Fr r ★★→★★★★ 09′ 10 11 12 14 15′ (17) AOP based on min 70% MALBEC. Battle between authentic typicity and Argentinian flirtation. All red (some white IGPS). Bad frost 2017. Early-drinking from ★★CHX Paillas, Chx Croze de Pys, CLOS Coutale, Des Ifs. Wait longer for ★★★Ch Chambert, DOM de la Bérengeraie, Lo Domeni; ★★Chx Armandière, Clos Troteligotte, Gaudou, La Coustarelle, Nozières, Ponzac, Vincens. Longer still for ★★★*Clos de Gamot*, Clos Triguedina. Modern: ★★★CH DU CÈDRE, Clos d'Un Jour, Dom du Prince, Lamartine, La Périé, La Reyne, Les Croisille; ★★Eugénie, La Caminade. Cult ★★★★Dom Cosse-Maisonneuve straddles range. Influential Vigouroux family empire incl ★★Chx Hautes-Serres, Mercuès and Léret-Monpézat.

Cailloux, Les S Rh r (w) ★★★78′ 79′ 81′ 85′ 89′ 90′ 95′ 96′ 98′ 99 00′ 01 03′ 04′ 05′ 06′ 07′ 09′ 10′ 11′ 12′ 13′ 14 15′ 16′ 17′ 18-ha CHÂTEAUNEUF DOM; elegant, profound, typical, handmade reds, v.gd value. Special wine Centenaire, oldest GRENACHE 1889 noble, costly. Also DOM André Brunel (esp gd-value CÔTES DU RH red Est-Ouest), decent Féraud-Brunel Côtes du Rh merchant range.

FRANCE

Cairanne S Rh r p w ★★ →★★★ 07' 09' 10' 11 12' 13' 14 15' 16' 17' Now a cru, above Villages category. Gd range DOMS, wines of character, dark fruits, mixed herbs, some finesse esp CLOS Romane, Doms Alary (stylish), Amadieu (pure, bio), Boisson (traditional), Brusset (deep), Cros de Romet, Escaravailles (flair), Féraud-Brunel, Grands Bois (organic), Grosset, Hautes Cances (traditional), Jubain, **Oratoire St Martin** (detail, classy), Présidente, Rabasse-Charavin (punchy), *Richaud* (great fruit). Food-friendly, 3D *whites*.

Cal Demoura, Dom L'doc r p w ★★★ Estate to follow in TERRASSES DU LARZAC. Meticulous winemaking by Vincent Goumard: Paroles de Pierre, L'Etincelle with six different grape varieties (w); L'DOC blends (r) Combariolles, predominantly GRENACHE Feu Sacré, Terres de Jonquières and new Fragments, mainly old SYRAH.

Canard-Duchêne Champ House owned by ALAIN THIÉNOT. BRUT Vintage 08 09 12', Charles VII Prestige multi-vintage. ★★CUVÉE Léonie. Improved Authentique Cuvée (organic) 09 12'. Single-v'yd Avize Gamin 12 13 15.

Canon-Fronsac B'x r ★★ →★★★ 05' 06 08 09' 10' 11 12 14 15 16 Small enclave within FRON, otherwise same wines. 47 growers. Best: rich, full, finely structured. Try CHX Barrabaque, Canon Pécresse, Cassagne Haut-Canon la Truffière, DU GABY, Grand-Renouil, La Fleur Cailleau, MOULIN PEY-LABRIE, Pavillon, Vrai Canon Bouché.

Carillon C d'O w ★★★ Classic PULIGNY producer, now separated between brothers. Jacques in old tradition; more ambitious François has new v'yds. Top sources for PREMIERS CRUS, eg. Combettes, Perrières, Referts. Reds less interesting.

Cassis Prov (r) (p) w ★★ DYA. Pleasure port in hills e of Marseille best-known for savoury dry whites based on CLAIRETTE, MARSANNE, eg. CLOS Ste Magdeleine, DOM de la Ferme Blanche, Fontcreuse, Paternel. Growers fight with property developers, so prices high, but quality interesting.

Castelnau, De Champ Est 1916, marque named for World War One general. Sleeping giant co-op: 900 ha on Montagne de Reims and Marne Valley. Longer lees-ageing since 2012. V.gd 02 Hors Categorie.

Castillon-Côtes de Bordeaux B'x r ★★ →★★★ 08 09' 10' 12 14 15 16 Appealing e neighbour of ST-ÉM becoming a boom-town; similar wines, usually less plump. Plenty of new investors from POMEROL and St-Ém. Top: Alcée, Ampélia, Cap de FAUGÈRES, CLOS Les Lunelles, Clos Louie, Clos Puy Arnaud, Côte Montpezat, D'AIGUILHE, Joanin Bécot, l'Aurage, La Clarière-Laithwaite, Montlandrie, Poupille, Robin, Veyry, Vieux CH Champs de Mars.

Cathiard, Dom Sylvain C d'O r ★★★★ Sylvain's son Sébastien makes wines of astonishing quality from VOSNE-ROMANÉE esp Malconsorts, Orveaux, Reignots, and NUITS-ST-GEORGES Aux Thorey, Murgers, which will develop well over time, if less immediately seductive than his dad's wines.

Cave Cellar, or any wine establishment.

Cave coopérative Wine-growers' co-op winery; over half of all French production. Often well-run, -equipped, wines gd value for money, but many closing down.

Cazes, Dom Rouss r p w sw ★★ →★★★ Largest bio producer in ROUSS. Pioneered B'X varieties, now favours Midi: Le Canon du Maréchal GRENACHE/SYRAH; Crédo CÔTES DU ROUSS-VILLAGES with Ego, Alter. Sensational aged RIVESALTES CUVÉE Aimé Cazes. CLOS de Paulilles for BANYULS, COLLIOURE. New sulphur-free Hommage; MAURY SEC. Now part of Advini, but still family-run. Great value.

Cédre, Ch du SW Fr r w ★★ →★★★ 09' 10 11' 12' 14 15' (17) Well-known leader of modern CAHORS school. For many ★★★Le Prestige easier and of same quality as hefty top growths. Delicious ★★VIOGNIER IGP. Substantial NÉGOCIANT business.

Cépage Grape variety. See pp.16–26 for all.

Cérons B'x w sw ★★ 10' 11 13 14 15 16 Tiny 23-ha sweet AC next to SAUT. Less intense wines, eg. CHX de Cérons, Grand Enclos, Haura, Seuil.

Chablis w ★★ →★★★ 10' 12' 14' 15 16 (17) Scintillating CHARD from n Burg, infused

Chablis

There is no better expression of the all-conquering CHARD than the full but tense, limpid but stony wines it makes on the heavy limestone soils of CHAB. Best makers use little or no new oak to mask the precise definition of variety and terroir: Barat, B Defaix, ★Bessin, ★Billaud-Simon, ★Boudin, ★c MOREAU, ★Dampt family, DOM des Malandes, ★Droin, ★DROUHIN, Duplessis, E Vocoret, G Robin, ★J Collet, J DURUP, J-M BROCARD, ★J-P Grossot, LAROCHE, LONG-DEPAQUIT, ★L Michel, MOREAU-NAUDET, N Fèvre, ★Picq, ★Pinson, Piuze, ★RAVENEAU, ★Samuel Billaud, Servin, Temps Perdu, Tribut, ★V DAUVISSAT, ★W FÈVRE. Simple, unqualified "Chab" may be thin, and PETIT CHAB thinner; well worth premiums for PREMIER CRU or GRAND CRU. Co-op, LA CHABLISIENNE, has high standards (esp ★Grenouille) and many different labels. (★ = outstanding.)

with marine minerality. My default white, when not overcropped or overoaked (happily rare now). Supply problems: major frosts in 16, 17 raising prices.

Chablis Grand Cru Chab w ★★★ →★★★★ 00' 02' 05' 07' 08' 09 10' 11 12' 14' 15 16 (17) Contiguous block overlooking River Serein, most conc CHAB, needs age to show detail. Seven v'yds: Blanchots (floral), Bougros (incl Côte Bouguerots), CLOS (usually best), Grenouilles (spicy), Preuses (cashmere), Valmur (structure), Vaudésir (plus brand La Moutonne). Many gd growers.

Chablisienne, La Chab r w ★★-★★★ Exemplary co-op responsible for huge slice of CHAB production esp supermarket-own labels. Gd individual CUVÉES too, eg. GRAND CRU Grenouilles.

Chablis Premier Cru Chab w ★★★ 02' 05' 08' 09 10' 11 12' 14' 15 16 (17) Well worth small premium over straight CHAB: better sites on rolling hillsides; Five favourites in rising order of richness: Forêts, Mont de Milieu, Montée de Tonnerre, Vaillons, Vaulorent.

Chambertin C d'O r ★★★★ 90' 93 96' 98 99' 01 02' 03 05' 06 07 08 09' 10' 11 12' 13 14 15' 16 (17) Candidate for Burg's most imperious wine; amazingly dense, sumptuous, long-lived, expensive. Producers who match potential incl: Bernstein, BOUCHARD PÈRE & FILS, Charlopin, Damoy, DUGAT-Py, DROUHIN, DOM LEROY, MORTET, PRIEUR, ROSSIGNOL-TRAPET, ROUSSEAU, TRAPET.

Chambertin-Clos de Bèze C d'O r ★★★★ 90' 93 96' 98 99' 01 02' 03 05' 06 08 09' 10' 11 12' 13 14 15 16 (17) Splendid neighbour to CHAMBERTIN, slightly more accessible in youth, velvet texture, deeply graceful. Best Bart, CLAIR, Damoy, DROUHIN, Drouhin-Laroze, Duroché, FAIVELEY (incl super-CUVÉE Les Ouvrées Rodin), Groffier, JADOT, Prieuré-Roch, ROUSSEAU.

Chambolle-Musigny C d'O r ★★★-★★★★ 90' 93 95' 96' 99' 02' 03 05' 07 08 09' 10' 11 12' 13 14 15' 16 (17) Silky, velvety wines from CÔTE DE NUITS: CHARMES for substance, more chiselled from Cras, Fuées, and majesty from Amoureuses, plus GRANDS CRUS BONNES MARES, MUSIGNY. Superstars: BARTHOD, CATHIARD, DE VOGÜÉ, Groffier, MUGNIER, ROUMIER; but try Amiot-Servelle, DROUHIN, Felletig, HUDELOT-Baillet, Pousse d'Or, RION, Sigaut.

Champagne Sparkling wines of PINOTS N/M and/or CHARD, and region (33,805 ha in production, c.90 miles e of Paris); made by *méthode traditionnelle*. Bubbles from elsewhere, however gd, cannot be Champ.

Champagne le Mesnil Champ ★★★ Top-flight co-op in greatest GRAND CRU CHARD village. Exceptional CUVÉE Sublime 08' 09 13 15 17 from finest sites. Impressive Cuvée Prestige 05 08 09 13 17'. Real value.

Champy Père & Cie Burg r w ★★→★★★ BEAUNE-based NÉGOCIANT with ancient origins (1720). Sound rather than scintillating, strongest around hill of CORTON.

Chandon de Briailles, Dom C d'O r w ★★★ DOM known for fine, lighter style yet perfumed reds, esp PERNAND-VERGELESSES, Île de Vergelesses, CORTON Bressandes. Bio farming, lots of stems, no new oak define style. Some wines sulphur-free.

Chanson Père & Fils Burg r w ★→★★★ Resurgent BEAUNE merchant, quality whites and fine if idiosyncratic reds (whole-cluster aromatics). Try Beaunes esp CLOS des Fèves (r), CLOS DES MOUCHES (w). Great CORTON-Vergennes (w).

Chapelle-Chambertin C d'O r ★★★ 90' 93 96' 99' 02' 03 05' 08 09' 10' 11 12' 13 14' 15' 16 17 Lighter neighbour of CHAMBERTIN, thin soil does better in cooler, damper yrs. Fine-boned wine, less meaty. Top: Damoy, Drouhin-Laroze, JADOT, ROSSIGNOL-TRAPET, TRAPET, Tremblay.

Chapoutier N Rh ★★→★★★★ Vocal bio grower/merchant based at HERMITAGE. Generally stylish reds via low-yield, plot-specific, expensive CUVÉES. Thick GRENACHE CHÂTEAUNEUF – Barbe Rac, Croix de Bois (r), CÔTE-RÔTIE La Mordorée; Hermitage – L'Ermite (outstanding r w), Le Pavillon (deep, crunchy r), Cuvée de l'Orée, Le Méal (w). Also ST-JOSEPH Les Granits (r w). Hermitage whites outstanding, 100% MARSANNE. Gd-value *Meysonniers Crozes*. V'yds in COTEAUX D'AIX-EN-PROV, CÔTES DU ROUSS-VILLAGES (gd DOM Bila-Haut), RIVESALTES. Michel Chapoutier bought BEAUJ house Trenel in 2015, CH des Ferrages (PROV) in 2016, has AL v'yds and Australian joint ventures esp Doms Tournon and Terlato & Chapoutier (fragrant, fine); also Portuguese Lisboa project.

Charbonnière, Dom de la S Rh r (w) ★★★ 98 99' 00 01' 03 04 05' 06' 07' 09' 10' 11' 12' 13' 14 15' 16' 17' Progressive 17-ha CHÂTEAUNEUF estate run by sisters. Sound Tradition wine, distinguished, authentic Mourre des Perdrix, also Hautes Brusquières, new L'Envol, VIEILLES VIGNES. Stylish, tasty white. Also peppery, small-quantity VACQUEYRAS red.

Chardonnay As well as a white wine grape, also the name of a MÂCON-VILLAGES commune, hence Mâcon-Chardonnay.

Charlemagne C d'O w ★★★★ 13 14' 15' 16 (17) Almost extinct sister appellation to CORTON-CHARLEMAGNE, revived by DOM DE LA VOUGERAIE (2013). Same style and rules as sibling.

Charmes-Chambertin C d'O r ★★★★ 90' 93 96' 99' 01 02' 03 05' 06 07 08 09' 10' 11 12' 13 14 15' 16 (17) GEVREY GRAND CRU 31 ha, incl neighbour MAZOYÈRES-CHAMBERTIN. Raspberries and cream plus dark-cherry fruit, sumptuous texture, fragrant finish at best. Try ARLAUD, BACHELET, DUGAT, DUJAC, Duroché, Jouan, LEROY, MORTET (from 2016), Perrot-Minot, Roty, ROUSSEAU, Taupenot-Merme, VOUGERAIE.

Chartogne-Taillet Champ A disciple of SELOSSE, Alexandre Chartogne is a new star in CHAMP. Exceptional BRUT Ste Anne NV and single-v'yds Le Chemin de Reims and Les Barres; striking energy.

Charvin, Dom S Rh ★★★ 99' 01' 06' 07' 08 09' 10' 11' 12' 13' 14 15' 16' 17' Terroir-focused 8-ha CHÂTEAUNEUF estate, 85% GRENACHE, no oak, only one CUVÉE. Spiced, mineral, high-energy red, with vintage accuracy. V.gd-value CÔTES DU RH red.

Chassagne-Montrachet C d'O r w ★★→★★★★ (w) 02' 04 05' 06' 07 08' 09' 10 11 12' 13 14' 15 16 (17) Large village at s end of CÔTE DE BEAUNE. Great whites from eg. Blanchot, Cailleret, La Romanée GRANDS CRUS. Best reds: CLOS St Jean, Morgeot, others more rustic. Try: Coffinet, COLIN, GAGNARD, MOREY, Pillot families plus DOMS Heitz-Lochardet, MOREAU, Niellon, Ramonet (reds too). But too much indifferent village white grown on land better suited to red.

Château (Ch) Means an estate, big or small, gd or indifferent, particularly in B'X (*see* pp.100–23). Means, literally, castle or great house. In Burg, DOM is usual term.

Champagne domaines to watch in 2019
ANSELME SELOSSE, Armand (Arnaud) Margaine, Didier Doué, Lancelot-Pienne, Lilbert et Fils, Nathalie Falmet, Nicolas Maillart, Paul Bara, Veuve Fourny, Vilmart.

Château-Chalon Jura w ★★★★ 96 99' 00 05' **08 09 10'** Not a CH but AC and village, the summit of VIN JAUNE style from SAVAGNIN grape. Min 6 yrs barrel age, not cheap. A more winey version of Sherry, not fortified. Ready to drink (or cook a chicken in) when bottled, but gains with further age. Fervent admirers search out BERTHET-BONDET, MACLE, Mossu, or Bourdy for old vintages.

Château-Grillet N Rh w ★★★★ 95' 98' 00' 01' 04' 05 06' 07' 08 09' 10' 11 12' 13 14' 15' 16' 17' France's smallest AC. 3.7-ha curved amphitheatre v'yd nr CONDRIEU, sandy granite terraces. Bought by F Pinault of CH LATOUR in 2011, prices up, wine *en finesse*, albeit less deep than in past. Smooth, restrained VIOGNIER: drink at cellar temp, decanted, with new-wave food.

Châteaumeillant Lo r p ★→★★ Dynamic 58-ha AC sw Bourges. 23 producers. GAMAY, PINOT N for light reds (75%), VIN GRIS (25%). Pinot N potentially best red but pure versions stupidly banned. BOURGEOIS, Chaillot, Gabrielle, Goyer, Joffre, Joseph Mellot, Lecomte, Nairaud-Suberville, Roux, Rouzé, Siret-Courtaud. Frost in 2017.

Châteauneuf-du-Pape S Rh (w) ★★★→★★★★ 78' 81' 85 88 89' 90' 95' 96 98' 99' 00' 01' 03' 04' 05' 06' 07' 08 **09'** 10' **11 12' 13' 14** 15' 16' 17' Nr Avignon, about 50 gd DOMS (remaining 85 inconsistent to poor). Up to 13 grapes (r w), headed by GRENACHE, plus SYRAH, MOURVÈDRE, Counoise. Warm, aromatic, textured, long-lived; can be fine, pure, magical, but till mid-2010s too many heavy, sip-only Parker-esque wines. Small, traditional names can be gd value, while prestige old-vine wines (v.gd GRENACHE 16') to avoid are late-vintage, new oak, 16% alc, too pricey. Whites fresh, fruity, or sturdy, best can age 15 yrs. Top names: CHX DE BEAUCASTEL, Fortia, Gardine (lovely modern, also w), Mont-Redon, RAYAS (unique, marvellous), Sixtine, Vaudieu; DOMS du Banneret (trad), Beaurenard, Bois de Boursan (value), Bosquet des Papes (value), Chante Cigale, Chante Perdrix, CHARBONNIÈRE, Charvin (terroir), CLOS du Caillou, Clos du Mont-Olivet, CLOS DES PAPES (ace), Clos St-Jean (sip), Cristia, de la Janasse, de Barroche, de la Vieille Julienne, Font-de-Michelle (stylish), Grand Veneur (oak), Henri Bonneau, LES CAILLOUX, Marcoux (fantastic VIEILLES VIGNES), Pegaü (de Capo is cult), Pierre André (traditional), P Usseglio, R Usseglio (bio), Roger Sabon, Sénéchaux (modern), CH Sixtine, St-Préfert (sleek), Vieux Donjon, VIEUX TÉLÉGRAPHE.

Chave, Dom Jean-Louis N Rh r w ★★★★ 85' 88' 89' 90' 91' 94 95' 96 97 98' 99' 00 01' 03' 04 05' 06' 07' 08 09' 10' 11' 12' 13' 14' 15' 16' 17' Excellent family DOM at heart of HERMITAGE. Classy, silken, long-lived reds (more plush recently), incl expensive, occasional Cathelin. V.gd white (mainly MARSANNE); marvellous, occasional VIN DE PAILLE. Deep, grainy, copious ST-JOSEPH red (incl Dom Florentin 2009 and new v'yds), fruity J-L Chave brand St-Joseph Offerus, jolly CÔTES DU RH Mon Coeur, sound merchant Hermitage Farconnet (r w).

Chavignol Lo r p w Leading SANCERRE village, v. steep v'yds Cul de Beaujeu (largely white), Les Monts Damnés dominate enclosed village + Grande Côte. Clay-limestone soil gives full-bodied, mineral whites and reds that age 15 yrs+. V. fine young producers: Matthieu Delaporte (Vincent Delaporte), Pierre Martin. Others with vines: ALPHONSE MELLOT, Boulay (v.gd), BOURGEOIS, Cotat, DAGUENEAU, Paul Thomas, Thomas Laballe.

Châteauneuf as it should be

CHÂTEAUNEUF-DU-PAPE should be a seductive wine of finesse, pedigree, suave tannins, floral wisps with notes of cedar, Provençal herbs. The shape should be spherical. Praise be that in the fabulous 2016 vintage, some (often younger) growers knew not to overextract, and instead go with nature's flow: DOMS Chante Cigale Vieilles Vignes, de la Solitude Cornelia Constanza, Font de Michelle Étienne Gonnet, Marcoux Vieilles Vignes, Raymond Usseglio Impériale.

FRANCE

Chénas Beauj r ★★★ 09′ 11′ 12 14′ 15′ **16** 17 Smallest BEAUJ cru, between MOULIN-À-VENT and JULIÉNAS, gd-value, meaty, age-worthy, merits more interest. Try: CH Bonnet, DUBOEUF, LAPIERRE, Pacalet, Piron, Thillardon (rising star), Trichard, co-op.

Chêne Bleu S Rh ★★★ Ambitious part-bio DOM high in hills of SÉGURET. Extravagant.

Chevalier-Montrachet C d'O w ★★★★★ 99′ 00′ 02′ 04 05′ **06 07′** 08 09′ 10 11 12 13 14′ 15 16 (17) Just above MONTRACHET on hill, just below in quality, yet makes brilliant crystalline wines. Long-lived but can be accessible early. Special CUVÉES Les Demoiselles from JADOT, LOUIS LATOUR and La Cabotte from BOUCHARD; top example is LEFLAIVE. Try: CH de Puligny, Dancer, Niellon, SAUZET.

Cheverny Lo r p w ★ ★★★ 10 14 15 16 (17) LO AC (532 ha) nr Blois. White from SAUV BL/Chard blend. Light reds mainly GAMAY, PINOT N (also CAB FR, CÔT). *Cour-Cheverny* (48 ha): Romorantin v. age-worthy. Esp CLOS Tue-Boeuf, de Montcy, Gendrier, Huards, Philippe Tessier; DOMS de la Desoucherie, du Moulin, Veilloux, Villemade. Frost in 2016 and esp 2017.

Chevillon, R C d'O r ★★★ Fabulous range of accessible but age-worthy NUITS-ST-GEORGES PREMIERS CRUS: Les St-Georges, Vaucrains for power, but try Pruliers, Chaignots, etc. too.

Chidaine, François Lo (r) w dr sw sp ★★★ 08′ 09 10′ 11 14 15 16 (17) Bio champion. Brilliant MONTLOUIS (20 ha) single v'yds, VIN DE FRANCE, VOUVRAY (10 ha), like JACKY BLOT stupidly barred from using AC Vouvray. Owns historic CLOS Baudoin (Vouvray). Focus on dry, DEMI-SEC. AC TOURAINE (7 ha) at Chissay (Cher Valley).

Chignin Sav w ★ DYA. AC 1973. Light, soft white from Jacquère grapes for Alpine summers. Chignin-Bergeron (with ROUSSANNE grapes) is best and liveliest.

Chinon Lo r p (w) ★★ ★★★★ 05′ 08 09′ 10′ 11 12 14′ 15′ **16′** (17) 2300 ha (10% p, 2% w); 200 producers. Sand, gravel, limestone: light to rich TOURAINE CAB FR. Best age 30 yrs+. Parts frosted 2016, 17. A little dry CHENIN BL (some wood). Best: ALLIET, BAUDRY, BAUDRY-DUTOUR, Couly-Dutheil, Dozon, Grosbois, JM Raffault, Jourdan-Pichard, Landry, L'R, Noblaie, Pain, Pierre & Bertrand Couly; CHX de Coulaine.

Chiroubles Beauj r ★★ 14 15′ 17 BEAUJ cru in hills above FLEURIE: fresh, fruity, savoury wines. Growers: Ch de Javernand, Cheysson, Lafarge-Vial, Métrat, Passot, Raousset, or merchants DUBOEUF, Trenel.

Chorey-lès-Beaune C d'O r (w) ★★ 05′ 09′ 10′ 12 14 15′ 16 (17) How many people have discovered joy of red burg through TOLLOT-BEAUT's Chorey? Pleasurable, affordable, accessible mini-BEAUNE. Also: Arnoux, DROUHIN, Guyon, JADOT, Rapet.

Chusclan S Rh r p w ★ ★★ 15′ 16′ **17′** CÔTES DU RH-VILLAGES with above-average Laudun-Chusclan co-op, incl gd crisp whites. Soft reds, cool rosés. Best co-op labels (r) Chusclan DOM de l'Olivette, CÔTES DU RH Femme de Gicon (r), Enfant Terrible (w), Excellence, LIRAC DOM St Nicolas. Also full CH Signac (best Chusclan, can age), Dom La Romance (fresh, organic), special CUVÉES from *André Roux*.

Clair, Bruno C d'O r p w ★★★ ★★★★★ Top-class CÔTE DE NUITS estate for supple, subtle, savoury wines. Gd-value MARSANNAY, old-vine SAVIGNY La Dominode, GEVREY-CHAMBERTIN (CLOS ST-JACQUES, Cazetiers) and standout CHAMBERTIN-CLOS DE BÈZE. Best whites from MOREY-ST-DENIS, CORTON-CHARLEMAGNE.

Clairet B'x Between rosé/red. B'x Clairet is AC. Try CHX Fontenille, Penin, Turcaud.

Clairette de Die N Rh w dr s/sw sp ★★ NV Rh/low Alpine bubbles: flinty or (better) semi-sweet MUSCAT sparkling, beautiful setting. Underrated, muskily fruited, gd value; or dry CLAIRETTE, can age 3–4 yrs. NB: Achard-Vincent, Carod, Jaillance (value), Poulet et Fils (terroir), J-C Raspail (organic, gd IGP SYRAH).

Clape, Auguste, Pierre, Olivier N Rh r (w) ★★★ ★★★★★ 89′ 90′ 95′ 97 98′ 99′ 00 01′ 02 03′ 04′ 05′ 06′ 07′ 08 09′ 10′ 11′ 12′ 13′ 14′ 15′ 16′ 17′ The kings of CORNAS. Supreme SYRAH v'yds, many old vines, gd soil work. Profound, lingering reds, great vintage accuracy, need 6 yrs+, live 25+. Clear fruit in youngish-vines Renaissance. Superior CÔTES DU RH, VIN DE FRANCE (r), ST-PÉRAY (improved).

Clape, La L'doc r p w ★★→★★★ Dramatic limestone massif twixt Narbonne and Mediterranean; once an island. High sunshine hours for warm, spicy reds, esp MOURVÈDRE. Sea air gives deliciously salty, herbal whites, based on BOURBOULENC, with ageing potential. New appellation and also Cru du L'doc. CHX ANGLÈS, Camplazens, La Négly, *l'Hospitalet*, Mire l'Etang, Pech-Céleyran, Pech-Redon, Ricardelle, *Rouquette-sur-Mer* and Mas du Soleila, Sarrat de Goundy.

Climat Burg Refers to individual named v'yd at any level esp in CÔTE D'OR, eg. MEURSAULT Tesson, MAZOYÈRES-CHAMBERTIN. UNESCO World Heritage status.

Clos A term carrying some prestige, reserved for distinct (walled) v'yds, often in one ownership (esp AL, Burg, CHAMP).

Clos de Gamot SW Fr r ★★★ '05' '08' 09' 10 11 12 15' (17) Textbook eg. of traditional CAHORS before outsiders started messing about with it. ★★★★Low-yield CUVÉE Vignes Centenaires (best yrs only) miraculously survives recent Cahors fashions, deer and wild boar, but vines sadly facing retirement. Needs keeping.

Clos de Tart C d'O r ★★★★ 99' 00 01' 02' 03 05' 06 07 08' 09 10' 11 12 13' 14 15' 16' (17) Hugely expensive MOREY-ST-DENIS GRAND CRU. Sylvain Pitiot (director 1996–2014) made a powerful, late-picked style. From 2017 part of Artemis empire (CH LATOUR, CH GRILLET, etc.).

Clos de Vougeot C d'O r ★★★→★★★★ 90' 93' 96' 99' 01 02' 03' 05' 06 07 08 09' 10' 11 12' 13' 14 15' 16 (17) Celebrated CÔTE DE NUITS GRAND CRU with many owners. Occasionally sublime, needs 10 yrs+ to show real class. Style, quality depend on producer's philosophy, technique and position. Top: BOUCHARD, Castagnier, CH de la Tour (stems), DROUHIN, EUGÉNIE (intensity), *Faiveley*, Forey, GRIVOT, *Gros*, HUDELOT-Noëllat, JADOT, LEROY, LIGER-BELAIR, MÉO-CAMUZET, MONTILLE, MORTET, MUGNERET, *Vougeraie.*

Clos de la Roche C d'O r ★★★★ 90' 93' 95 96' 98 99' 01 02' 03 05' 06 07 08 09' 10' 11 12' 13 14 15' 16' (17) Maybe finest GRAND CRU of MOREY-ST-DENIS, as much grace as power, more savoury than sumptuous, blueberries. Needs time. DUJAC, PONSOT references but try Amiot, ARLAUD, Bernstein, Castagnier, Coquard, H LIGNIER, LEROY, LIGNIER-Michelot, Pousse d'Or, Remy, ROUSSEAU.

Clos des Lambrays C d'O r ★★★ 99' 02 03 05' 06 09' 10' 11 12' 13 14 15' 16' (17) All but MONOPOLE GRAND CRU v'yd at MOREY-ST-DENIS, now belongs to LVMH. Early-picked, spicy, stemmy style may change with new winemaker from 2018.

Clos des Mouches C d'O r w ★★★ (w) 02 05' 09' 10' 11 14' 15 16' (17) PREMIER CRU v'yd in several BURG ACS. Mouches = honeybees; see label of DROUHIN's iconic BEAUNE bottling. Also BICHOT, CHANSON (Beaune), plus Clair, Moreau, Muzard (SANTENAY), Germain (MEURSAULT).

Clos des Papes S Rh r w ★★★★ 89' 90' 95 98' 99' 00 01' 03' 04' 05' 06' 07' 08 09' 10' 11 12' 13' 14' 15' 16' 17' Always classy CHÂTEAUNEUF DOM of Avril family, small yields. Rich, intricate, textured red, more succulent recently (mainly GRENACHE, MOURVÈDRE, drink at 2–3 yrs or from 8+); *great white* (six varieties, complex, allow time, merits rich cuisine; 2–3 yrs, then 10–20).

Clos du Mesnil Champ ★★★★ KRUG's famous walled v'yd in GRAND CRU Le Mesnil. Long-lived, pure CHARD vintage, great mature yrs like 95 *à point* till 2020+; 00 02 03 08' 13' 15' will be classics, as will 17'.

Clos du Roi C d'O r ★★→★★★ Frequent Burg v'yd name. The king usually chose well. Best v'yd in GRAND CRU CORTON (Camille Giroud, DE MONTILLE, Pousse d'Or, VOUGERAIE); top PREMIER CRU v'yd in MERCUREY, future Premier Cru (?) in MARSANNAY. Less classy in BEAUNE.

Clos Rougeard Lo r w (sw) ★★★★ 03 05' 06 07 08 09' 10' 11 12 14 15 16 (17) Legendary/ICONIC small DOM of Nady and late Charly Foucault. Great finesse, age brilliantly: SAUMUR Blanc, SAUMUR-CHAMPIGNY, COTEAUX DE SAUMUR. Sold 2017 to Martin and Olivier Bouygues (CH MONTROSE; *see* B'x chapter).

Clos St-Denis C d'O r ★★★ 90' 93' 95 96' 99' 01 02' 03 05' 06 07 08 09' 10' 11 12' 13 14 15' 16' (17) GRAND CRU at MOREY-ST-DENIS. Sumptuous wine in youth, growing silky with age: ARLAUD, Bertagna, Castagnier, DUJAC, JADOT, Jouan, Leroux, PONSOT.

Clos Ste-Hune Al w ★★★★ Top TRIMBACH bottling from GRAND CRU ROSACKER. Greatest RIES in AL? Super 10 13 15' 17. Initially austere, needing 10–15 yrs+ ageing; complex mineral subtleties for great fish cuisine. GRAND CRU SCHLOSSBERG 13' 16 17' a riveting contrast with CLOS Ste-Hune.

Clos St-Jacques C d'O r ★★★★ 90' 93 95 96' 98 99' 01 02' 03 05' 06 07 08 09' 10' 11 12' 13 14 15' 16 (17) Hillside PREMIER CRU in GEVREY-CHAMBERTIN with perfect se exposure. Excellent producers: CLAIR, ESMONIN, FOURRIER, JADOT, ROUSSEAU; powerful, velvety reds often ranked and priced above many GRANDS CRUS.

Clovallon, Dom de L'doc r w ★★ Haute Vallée de l'Orb. Catherine Roque made name with elegant PINOT N Pomarèdes, original white blend Aurièges. Now run by daughter Alix; new CUVÉE Les Indigènes. Mother at Mas d'Alezon, FAUGÈRES for ★★★Presbytère, Montfallette, (w) Cabretta.

Coche-Dury C d'O r w ★★★★ Superb MEURSAULT DOM led by Jean-François Coche and son Raphaël. Exceptional whites from ALIGOTÉ to CORTON-CHARLEMAGNE; v. pretty reds too. Hard to find at sensible prices. Gd-value cousin Coche-Bizouard is sound, but not same style.

Colin C d'O (r) w ★★★ →★★★★ Leading CHASSAGNE-MONTRACHET and ST-AUBIN family; new generation turning heads with brilliant whites esp Pierre-Yves C-MOREY and Philippe C. DOM Marc C remains classic source.

Colin-Morey ★★★ Pierre-Yves C-M has struck a chord with his vibrant tingling whites esp from ST-AUBIN and CHASSAGNE-MONTRACHET PREMIER CRU, with their characteristic gun-flint bouquets. Great wines in youth and for ageing.

Sky-high v'yd values in Burg could finish family doms: unaffordable taxes.

Collines Rhodaniennes N Rh r w ★★ N Rh IGP has character, quality, incl v.gd Seyssuel, sparky granite hillside reds v.gd value, often from top estates. Can contain young-vine CÔTE-RÔTIE. Mostly SYRAH (best), plus MERLOT, GAMAY, mini-CONDRIEU VIOGNIER (best), CHARD. Reds: A Paret, A Perret, Bonnefond, E Barou, *Jamet* (v.gd), Jasmin, J-M Gérin, L Chèze, Monier-Pérreol, N Champagneux, S Ogier (v.gd), S Pichat, Rostaing. Whites: Alexandrins, A Perret (v.gd), Barou, F Merlin, *G Vernay (v.gd)*, P Marthouret, X Gérard, Y Cuilleron.

Collioure Rouss r p w ★★ Table-wine twin of BANYULS from same terraced coastal v'yds. Charcterful reds, mainly GRENACHE, enjoy maritime influence. Gd whites based on GRENACHE BLANC and better Gris. Top: DOMS Bila-Haut, de la Rectorie, du Mas Blanc, La Tour Vieille, Madeloc, Vial-Magnères; Coume del Mas; Les CLOS de Paulilles. Co-ops Cellier des Templiers, l'Etoile.

Comté Tolosan SW Fr r p w ★→★★ Mostly DYA IGP covering most of sw and multitude of sins. *See* PYRÉNÉES-ATLANTIQUES. Otherwise ★★DOM de Ribonnet (all colours, huge variety of CÉPAGES) stands out.

Condrieu N Rh w ★★★ →★★★★ 10' 12' 13 14' 15 16' 17' Home of VIOGNIER; floral, musky airs, pear, apricot flavours from sandy granite slopes. Best: cool, pure, precise (2016 over 15); but danger of excess oak, sweetness, alc, price. Rare white match for asparagus. 75 growers; quality varies. Best: A Paret, A Perret (all three wines gd), Boissonnet, CHAPOUTIER, C Pichon, DELAS, Faury (esp La Berne), F Merlin, F Villard (lighter recently), Gangloff (great style), GUIGAL (big), *G Vernay* (fine, classy), Niéro, ROSTAING, St Cosme, X Gérard (value), Y Cuilleron.

Corbières L'doc r (p) (w) ★★→★★★ 09 10 11 12 13 14 15 16 17 Largest AC of L'DOC, with cru of Boutenac. Others in pipeline, but nothing definite. Wines as varied as scenery: coastal lagoons, hot dry hills. Enormous choice. Try: CHX

Aiguilloux, *Aussières*, Borde-Rouge, LA BARONNE, Lastours, la Voulte Gasparets, Les CLOS Perdus, Les Palais, *Ollieux Romanis*, Pech-Latt; DOMS de Fontsainte, de Villemajou, du Grand Crès, du Vieux Parc, Trillol, Villerouge; Clos de l'Anhel, Grand Arc, Serres-Mazard. Castelmaure an outstanding co-op.

Cornas N Rh r ★★★ →★★★★ 78' 83' 85' 88' 89' 90' 91' 94' 95' 96 97' 98' 99' 00' 01' 02 03' 04 05' 06' 07' 08 09' 10' 11' 12' 13' 14 15' 16' 17' Top-quality N Rhô SYRAH, *très à la mode* (incl crazed thirst for wines of departed growers). Deep, strongly fruited, always mineral-tinted. Can drink some for vibrant early fruit, really need 5 yrs+. Stunning 2010, also 2015. Top: ALLEMAND (top 2), Balthazar (traditional), *Clape* (benchmark), Colombo (new oak), Courbis (modern), *Delas*, *Dom du Tunnel*, J&E Durand (racy fruit), G Gilles, JABOULET (St-Pierre CUVÉE), P&V Jaboulet, Lemenicier, M Barret (bio, improved), Tardieu-Laurent (deep, oak), Voge (oak), V Paris.

Corsica / Corse r p w ★ →★★★ ACS Ajaccio, PATRIMONIO; plus crus Calvi, Coteaux du Cap Corse, Sartène. IGP: Île de Beauté. Lots of variety. Elegant spicy reds from SCIACARELLO; structured reds from NIELLUCCIO; gd rosés; *tangy, herbal Vermentino whites*. Sweet MUSCATS. Top: Abbatucci, Alzipratu, Canarelli, CLOS Capitoro, Clos d'Alzeto, Clos Poggiale, Fiumicicoli, *Peraldi*, Pieretti, *Nicrosi*, Saperale, *Torraccia*, Vaccelli. Hard to find, but fit today's passion for the rare and indigenous.

Corton C d'O r (w) ★★★ →★★★★ 90' 95 96' 99' 01 02' 03' 05' 06 07 08 09' 10' 11 12' 13 14 15' 16 (17) Over-large GRAND CRU. Most of hill should not be, but gives decent wines at price nonetheless. Don't expect all to be brooding monsters. CLOS DU ROI v'yd tops bill but seek out Bressandes for suavity, characterful Renardes, supple VIGNE au Saint. Try BONNEAU DU MARTRAY, BOUCHARD, Camille Giroud, CHANDON DE BRIAILLES, DOM des Croix, DRC, Dubreuil-Fontaine, FAIVELEY (CLOS DES CORTONS), Follin-Arbelet, MÉO-CAMUZET, Senard, TOLLOT-BEAUT. Occasional whites, eg. HOSPICES DE BEAUNE, CHANSON from Vergennes v'yd.

Corton-Charlemagne C d'O w ★★★ →★★★★ 99' 00' 02' 03 04 05' 06' 07' 08 09' 10' 11 12' 13' 14' 15' 16 (17) Potentially scintillating GRAND CRU, invites mineral descriptors, should age well. Sw- and w-facing limestone slopes, plus band round top of hill. Top: *Bonneau du Martray*, BOUCHARD, *Coche-Dury*, FAIVELEY, HOSPICES DE BEAUNE, JADOT, LATOUR, MONTILLE, P Javillier, Rapet, Rollin, *Vougeraie*.

Costières de Nîmes S Rh r p w ★ →★★ 15' 16' 17' Region sw of CHÂTEAUNEUF, similar stony soils, gd quality. Red (GRENACHE, SYRAH) is robust, spicy, ages well, gd value. Best: CHX de Grande Cassagne, de Valcombe, d'Or et des Gueules, L'Ermitage, Mas Carlot (gd fruit), Mas des Bressades (top fruit), Mas Neuf, Montfrin (organic), Mourgues-du-Grès, Nages, Roubaud, Tour de Béraud Vessière (w); DOMS de la Patience (organic), du Vieux Relais, Galus, M KREYDENWEISS, Petit Romain. Gd, *lively rosés, stylish whites* (ROUSSANNE).

Côte Chalonnaise Burg r w sp ★★ Region immediately s of C D'O; always threatening to be rediscovered. Lighter wines, lower prices. BOUZERON for ALIGOTÉ, *Rully* for accessible, juicy wines in both colours; *Mercurey* and GIVRY have more structure and can age; MONTAGNY for leaner CHARD.

Côte d'Or Burg Département name applied to central and principal Burg v'yd slopes: CÔTE DE BEAUNE and CÔTE DE NUITS. Not used on labels except for long-delayed BOURGOGNE C d'O AC, introduced for 2017 vintage.

Côte de Beaune C d'O r w ★★ →★★★★ S half of C D'O. Also a little-seen AC in its own right applying to top of hill above BEAUNE itself. Try from DROUHIN: largely declassified Beaune PREMIER CRU. Also VOUGERAIE.

Côte de Beaune-Villages C d'O r ★★ 09' 10' 12 14 15' 16 (17) Reds from lesser villages of s half of C D'O. Nowadays usually NÉGOCIANT blends.

Côte de Brouilly Beauj r ★★ 09' 11' 13' 14 15' 16 (17) Variety of styles as soils vary on different flanks of Mont Brouilly. Merits a premium over straight BROUILLY. Try J-P Brun, Léonis, Pacalet, Thivin.

Côte de Nuits C d'O r (w) ★★→★★★★ The n half of c d'o. Nearly all red wines, from CHAMBOLLE-MUSIGNY, MARSANNAY, FIXIN, GEVREY-CHAMBERTIN, MOREY-ST DENIS, NUITS-ST GEORGES, VOSNE-ROMANÉE, VOUGEOT.

Côte de Nuits-Villages C d'O r (w) ★★ 05′ 09′ 10′ 12′ 13 14 15′ 16 (17) Junior AC for extreme n/s ends of CÔTE DE NUITS; can be bargains. Top: Chopin, Gachot-Monot, Jourdan. Also gd: Ardhuy, Arlot, D BACHELET. Single-v'yd versions now appearing.

Côte Roannaise Lo r p ★★ 12 14′ 15′ 16′ 17′ Dynamic, exciting AC, lower slopes of granite hills w of Roanne. Excellent GAMAY. Try: Désormière, Fontenay, Giraudon, Paroisse, Plasse, Pothiers, Sérol, Vial. Excellent white IGP Urfé from ALIGOTÉ, CHARD, ROUSSANNE, VIOGNIER. Fine 2017.

Côte-Rôtie N Rh r ★★★ →★★★★ 78′ 85′ 89′ 90′ 91′ 95′ 98′ 99′ 00 03′ 04 05′ 06′ 07′ 08 09′ 10′ 11 12′ 13′ 14 15′ 16′ 17′ Finest Rh red, mainly SYRAH, some VIOGNIER, style links to Burg. Violet airs, pure (esp 2016), complex, v. fine with age (5–10 yrs+). Exceptional, v. long-lived 2010, 2015. Top: *Barge* (traditional), B Chambeyron, Billon, Bonnefond (oak), Bonserine (esp La Garde), Burgaud, CHAPOUTIER, Clusel-Roch (organic), DELAS, DOM de Rosiers, Duclaux, Gaillard (oak), Garon, GUIGAL (long oaking), *Jamet* (wonderful), Jasmin, J-M Gérin, J-M Stéphan (organic), Lafoy, Levet (traditional), *Rostaing* (fine), S Ogier (racy, oak), VIDAL-FLEURY (La Chatillonne).

Côtes Catalanes Rouss r p w ★★→★★★ IGP; quality belies humble status. Some of ROUSS's best. Innovative growers working with venerable bush vines esp GRENACHE, CARIGNAN (r w and Gris). Best: DOMS *Casenove*, *Dom of the Bee*, GÉRARD GAUBY, *Jones*, L'Horizon, La Préceptorie Centernach, Le Soula, Matassa, Olivier Pithon, Padié, Roc des Anges, Soulanes, Treloar, Vaquer.

Côtes d'Auvergne Mass C r p (w) ★→★★ AC (410 ha). Widely spread AC. GAMAY, some PINOT N, CHARD. Best reds improve 2–3 yrs. Villages: Boudes, Chanturgue, Châteaugay, Corent (p), Madargues (r). Producers: Bernard, CAVE St-Verny, Goigoux, Maupertuis, Montel, Pradier, Sauvat.

Côtes de Bordeaux B'x r ✦ AC launched in 2008 for reds. Embraces and permits cross-blending between CAS, FRANCS, BLAYE, CADILLAC and Ste-Foy (from 2016). Growers who want to maintain *the identity of a single terroir* have stiffer controls (NB) but can put Cas, Cadillac, etc. before Côtes de B'x. BLAYE-CÔTES DE B'X, FRANCS-CÔTES DE B'X also produce a little dry white. Around 1000 growers in group (represents ten per cent of B'x production). Try CHX Dudon, Lamothe de Haux, Malagar.

Côtes de Bourg B'x r w ✦→★★★ 08 09′ 10′ 12 14 15 16 Solid, savoury reds, a little white from e bank of Gironde. Mainly MERLOT but 10% MALBEC. 400 growers. Top CHX: Brûlesécaille, Bujan, Civrac, *Falfas*, Fougas-Maldoror, Grand-Maison, Grave (Nectar VIEILLES VIGNES), Haut-Guiraud, Haut-Macô, Haut Mondésir, Macay, Mercier, Nodoz, *Roc de Cambes*, Rousset, Sociondo.

Côtes de Duras SW Fr r p w ★→★★★ 15′ 16 (17) Gd-value AOP, s of BERGERAC, not esp distinctive but famous for nest of passionate organic growers like ★★★DOMS Mont Ramé, Mouthes-les-Bihan, Nadine Lusseau, Petit Malromé; ★★La Fon Longue, La Tuilerie la Brille, Les Cours, Les Hauts de Riquet, Mauro Guicheney. ch Condom's ★★★sweet still outstanding. Other gd growers: ★★DOMS Chater, de Laulan, Grand Mayne.

Côtes de Gascogne SW Fr (r) (p) w ★★ DYA IGP. ★★Giants PRODUCTEURS PLAIMONT, and esp 900-ha+ DOM Tariquet have most market share for these bar-style wines, light, often aromatic, fun. ★★Doms Chiroulet, d'Arton, d'Espérance, de l'Herré, Horgelus, Ménard, Millet, Miselle, Pellehaut and CH des Cassagnoles. Or ★Chx de Laballe, de Lauroux, de Magnaut, Papolle, St Lannes manage to survive the pressure. NB ✦Sédouprat red CUVÉE Sanglier.

Côtes de Millau SW Fr r p w IGP ★ from upper Tarn Valley. DYA. Lord Foster's Millau viaduct celebrated in wines from worthy co-op. There are worthy independents too, eg. ★DOM du Vieux Noyer.

Côtes de Montravel SW Fr w sw ★★ 12 14′ 15′ **16** 17′ Sub-AOP of BERGERAC; squeezed between dr and sw. Attractive, unfashionable wines usually SÉM-based. Better with foie gras than most stickies.

Côtes de Provence Prov r p w ★→★★★ 10 11 12 13 14 15 16 17 (p w) DYA. Huge AC concentrating on rosé, 89 per cent, with research improving quality; sets trend for palest of rosés elsewhere. Satisfying reds, mainly SYRAH, GRENACHE, CINSAULT, plus CAB. Fruity whites. Fréjus, La Londe, Pierrefeu, STE-VICTOIRE are subzones. Leaders: Commanderie de Peyrassol; DOMS de la Courtade, des Planes, *Gavoty* (superb), la Bernarde, Rabiega, *Richeaume*, Rimauresq, Roubine, Ste Rosaline; CHX d'Esclans, de Selle, Léoube; CLOS Mireille. Bubbly still in pipeline. *See* BANDOL, COTEAUX D'AIX, COTEAUX VAROIS.

Côtes de Thongue L'doc r p w ★★ (p w) DYA. Best IGP of HÉRAULT, in Thongue Valley. Original blends and single varietals. Best reds age. DOMS ARJOLLE, Condamine l'Evèque, l'Horte, La Croix Belle.

Côtes de Toul Al r p w ★ DYA. V. light wines from Lorraine; mainly VIN GRIS.

Côtes du Brulhois SW Fr r p (w) ★→★★ 14′ 15′ 16 (17) Lively AOP nr Agen; borrows its "black wine" tag from CAHORS. Dark, brooding reds (some TANNAT obligatory). Handful of independents ★★DOM Bois de Simon, des Thermes, du Pountet, ★CHX Coujétou-Peyret, la Bastide enjoy support from gd co-op.

Côtes du Forez Lo r p (sp) ★→★★ DYA. Most s Lo AC (147 ha), level with CÔTE-RÔTIE. GAMAY (r p). Bonnefoy, CLOS de Chozieux, Guillot, Mondon & Demeure, Real, Verdier/Logel. Excellent AC plus expanding IGP: CHARD, CHENIN BL, PINOT GR, ROUSSANNE, VIOGNIER. Gd 2017.

Côtes du Jura Jura r p w (sp) ★★→★★★★ 99′ 00 03′ 05′ 06 09 10 11 12 14 15 16 (17) Revitalized region, big on natural wines and trendy with sommeliers, so pricey. Light perfumed reds from PINOT N, Poulsard, Trousseau. Try PIGNIER, Puffeney. Whites from fresh, fruity CHARD to deliberately oxidative SAVAGNIN or blends. NB: BERTHET-BONDET, Bourdy, CH D'ARLAY, DOM DU PÉLICAN, DOM LABET, Ganevat, LUCIEN AVIET, STÉPHANE TISSOT. *See also* ARBOIS, CH CHALON, L'ÉTOILE ACS.

Côtes du Rhône S Rh r p w ★→★★ 15′ 16′ 17′ The wide base of S Rh, 170 communes. Incl gd SYRAH from Brézème & St-Julien-en-St-Alban (N Rh). Split between enjoyable, handmade quality (incl CHÂTEAUNEUF estates, numbers rising) and dull, mass-produced. Lively fruit more emphasized; 2016 ace. Mainly GRENACHE, also SYRAH, CARIGNAN. Best drunk young. Vaucluse top, then GARD (Syrah).

Côtes du Rhône-Villages S Rh r p w ★→★★ 10′ 15′ 16′ 17′ Full-bodied, forthright reds from 7700 ha, incl 19 named S Rh villages. Best are generous, spicy, gd

---

Top Côtes du Rhône producers

Put on your specs and study this: CHX Fonsalette (beauty), Gigognan, Hugues, La Borie, La Courançonne, Montfaucon (w also), Rochecolombe (organic) St Cosme, St-Estève, Trignon (incl VIOGNIER); DOMS André Brunel (stylish), Bastide St Dominique, Bramadou, Carabiniers (bio), Charvin (terroir, v.gd), Chaume-Arnaud (organic), Combebelle, Coudoulet de BEAUCASTEL (classy red), Corinne Depeyre (organic), Cros de la Mûre (great value), Espigouette, Ferrand (full), Gramenon (bio), Grand Nicolet (genuine), Haut-Musiel, Janasse (old GRENACHE), Jaume, M-F Laurent (organic), Manarine, M Dumarcher (organic), Réméjeanne (w also), Romarins, Soumade, Vieille Julienne (classy); CAVE Estézargues, CLOS des Cîmes (v. high v'yds), DELAS, E GUIGAL (great value), Famille Perrin, GEORGES DUBOEUF, Maison Bouachon, Mas Poupéras; co-ops CAIRANNE, RASTEAU.

value. Red heart is GRENACHE, plus SYRAH, MOURVÈDRE. Improving *whites*, often incl VIOGNIER, ROUSSANNE added to rich base CLAIRETTE, GRENACHE BLANC – *gd with food*. *See* CHUSCLAN, LAUDUN, PLAN DE DIEU, ST-GERVAIS, SABLET, SÉGURET (QUALITY), VALRÉAS, VISAN (improving). New villages from 2016 vintage: Ste-Cécile (gd range DOMS), Suze-la-Rousse, Vaison la Romaine. NB: Gadagne (robust), MASSIF D'UCHAUX (gd), PLAN DE DIEU (robust), PUYMÉRAS, SIGNARGUES. Try: CHX Fontségune, Signac; Doms Aphillantes (character), Aure, Bastide St Dominique, *Biscarelle* (flair), Cabotte (bio), Coulange, Coste Chaude, Crève Coeur, Grand Veneur, Grands Bois (organic), Gravennes, *Janasse*, Jean David (organic), Jérome, Mas de Libian (bio), Montbayon, Montmartel, *Mourchon*, Pasquiers, Pique-Basse, Rabasse-Charavin, Rémejeanne, Renjarde, Romarins, Saladin, St-Siffrein, Ste-Anne, Valériane, Viret (cosmopolitan); CAVE DE RASTEAU, LES VIGNERONS d'Estézargues.

Côtes du Roussillon-Villages Rouss r ★ ★★★ 11 12 13 14 15 16 17 32 villages in n part of ROUSS with Caramany, Latour de France, Lesquerde, Tauravel, Les Aspres singled out on label. Co-ops inevitably important, but quality and character from independent estates: Boucabeille, *Cazes*, CLOS des Fées, Clot de l'Oum, des Chênes, *Gauby*, Les VIGNES de Bila-Haut, Mas Becha, *Mas Crémat*, Modat, Piquemal, Rancy, Roc des Anges, Thunevin-Calvet. Côtes du Rouss to s for simple warming reds. *See also* CÔTES CATALANES.

Côtes du Tarn SW Fr r p w ★ DYA. IGP used by some GAILLAC growers seeking escape from AOP rules. Off-dry SAUV BL from ★★DOM d'en Segur and Lou Bio range from DOM VIGNES de Garbasses outstanding.

Côtes du Vivarais S Rh r p w ★ 15' 16' 17' Mostly DYA. Across hilly Ardèche country w of Montélimar. Marked improvement: quaffable, based on GRENACHE, SYRAH; some more sturdy, oak-aged reds. NB: Gallety (best, depth, lives well), Mas de Bagnols, *Vignerons de Ruoms* (v.gd value).

Coteaux Bourguignons Burg ★ DYA. Mostly reds, GAMAY, PINOT N. New AC since 2011 to replace BOURGOGNE Grand Ordinaire and to sex up basic BEAUJ. Rare whites ALIGOTÉ, CHARD, MELON, PINOTS BL, GR.

Coteaux Champenois r (p) w ★★★ (w) DYA. AC for still wines of CHAMP, eg. BOUZY. Vintages as for Champ. Better reds with climate change, and viticulture (09 12').

Coteaux d'Aix-en-Provence Prov r p w ★★ Extensive AC with Aix at centre, from Durance River to Mediterranean, from Rhône to STE-VICTOIRE mtn. Diversity of terroirs, grape varieties, both B'X, Midi. Stylish wines. CHX Beaupré, Calissanne, La Réaltière, Les Bastides, Les Béates, Revelette, *Vignelaure* and DOM du Ch Bas. *See also* LES BAUX-EN-PROV, PALETTE.

Coteaux d'Ancenis Lo r p w (sw) ★ ★★ 14 15 16 (17) Generally DYA. AOP (150 ha e of Nantais). Dry, DEMI-SEC, sweet CHENIN BL whites, age-worthy *Malvoisie* (PINOT GR); light reds, rosés mainly GAMAY, plus CABS SAUV, FR, esp Pierre Guindon, Landron Chartier, Pléiade, Quarteron.

Coteaux de Chalosse SW Fr r p w ★ DYA. Local IGP from Les Landes, from local grape varieties eg. Arriloba, Baroque, Egiodola. Local co-op now merged with Tursan. ★DOMS de Labaigt, Tastet.

Coteaux de Glanes SW Fr r p ★★ DYA IGP from Upper Dordogne. Locals can't get enough of these ever-improving wines from small co-op. Ségalin grape distinguishes from other mainstream blends.

Coteaux de l'Ardèche S Rh r p w ★ ★★ 15' 16' 17' Rocky hills w of Rh, wide selection, quality inching up, often gd value. New DOMS; fresh reds, some oaked (unnecessary); VIOGNIER (eg. CHAPOUTIER, Mas de Libian), MARSANNE. Best from SYRAH, also GAMAY (often old vines), CAB SAUV (Serret). Restrained, burg-style Ardèche CHARD by LOUIS LATOUR (Grand Ardèche v. oaky). Ferraton, DOMS du Colombier, Flacher, Grangeon, Jacouton, Mazel, Vigier, CH de la Selve.

Coteaux de l'Aubance Lo sw ★★ ★★★ 89' 90' 05' 07' 09 10' 11' 13 14' 15' 16 (17)

Small AC (160 ha) for long-ageing sweet CHENIN BL. Nervier, less rich than COTEAUX DU LAYON except SÉLECTION DES GRAINS NOBLES. S of LO nr Angers, less steep than Layon. Esp Bablut, CH Princé, Haute-Perche, Montgilet, Richou, Rochelles, Varière. Lower slopes esp hit by 2017 frost.

Coteaux de Saumur Lo w sw ★★→★★★ 09 10' 11' **14' 15'** 16 (17) Late-harvest CHENIN BL (just 12 ha). Like COTEAUX DU LAYON, less rich, more delicate, citrus. Esp Champs Fleuris, Nerleux, St Just, Targé, Vatan. Better with cheese than desserts.

Coteaux des Baronnies S Rh r p w ★→★★ DYA. Rh IGP in high hills e of VINSOBRES. SYRAH (best), CAB SAUV, MERLOT, CHARD (for once gd value), plus GRENACHE, CINSAULT, etc. Genuine, fresh country wines: improving simple reds, also clear VIOGNIER. NB: DOMS du Rieu-Frais, Le Mas Sylvia, Rosière.

Coteaux du Giennois Lo r p w ★→★★ DYA. Small AC (204 ha), spread-out v'yds along LO, Cosne to Gien. 2016, 17 badly frosted. Bright, lemony SAUV BL (103 ha) lighter style of SANCERRE or POUILLY-FUMÉ; can be v.gd. Light reds blend GAMAY/ PINOT N. Best: BOURGEOIS, Charrier, Catherine & Michel Langlois, Émile Balland, Jean Marie Berthier (esp L'Inédit), Paulat, Treuillet, Villargeau.

Coteaux du Languedoc See LANGUEDOC.

Coteaux du Layon Lo w sw ★★→★★★★ **89 90** 03 05' 07' 09 10' 11' **14' 15'** 16 (17) Heart of ANJOU: long-lived sweet CHENIN BL. Seven villages can add name to AC. Chaume now PREMIER CRU. Top ACs: BONNEZEAUX, QUARTS DE CHAUME. Growers: Baudouin, BAUMARD, Breuil, *Ch Pierre-Bise*, Chauvin, Delesvaux, Forges, Gueugniard, Juchepie, Ogereau, *Pithon-Paillé*, Soucherie. Frost again in 2017. Sadly difficult to sell: not a dessert wine.

Coteaux du Loir Lo r p w d r sw ★→★★★ 09' 10' **14' 15'** 16 (17) N tributary of Loire, Le Loir; picturesque, dynamic region with Coteaux du Loir (80 ha), *Jasnières* (65 ha). Steely, fine, precise, long-lived CHENIN BL, GAMAY, peppery Pineau d'Aunis, some fizz, plus Grolleau (rosé), CAB, CÔT. Top: Ange Vin, Breton, DOM DE BELLIVIÈRE, Fresneau, Gigou, Janvier, Le Briseau, Les Maisons Rouges, Roche Bleue.

Coteaux du Lyonnais Beauj r p (w) ★ DYA Junior BEAUJ. Best en PRIMEUR.

Coteaux du Quercy SW Fr r p ★ **15'** 17 AOP S of CAHORS. CAB FR basis of everyday winter warmers gd with stews and game. Will keep. Worthy co-op challenged by ★★DOMS du Guillau, Merchien (IGP) and ★Doms d'Ariès, Mystère d'Éléna (Dom de Revel).

Coteaux du Vendômois Lo r p w ★→★★ **14 15** 16 (17) AC, 28 communes, c.150 ha: Vendôme to Montoire in Le Loir Valley. Mostly VIN GRIS from Pineau d'Aunis (Chenin Noir) reds typically peppery, also blends of CAB FR, PINOT N, GAMAY. Whites: CHENIN BL, CHARD. Producers: Brazilier, Four à Chaux, J Martellière, Montrieux (Emile Heredia), Patrice Colin; CAVE du Vendômois (200 ha total).

Coteaux et Terrasses de Montauban SW Fr r p w ★→★★ DYA IGP created, dominated by highly successful DOM de Montels, which has spread to CAHORS (DOM Serre de Bovila). Huge range gd-value wines. Don't forget ★Dom Biarnès, Mas des Anges.

Coteaux Varois-en-Provence Prov r p w ★→★★ **12 13 14 15** 16 17 Small AC sandwiched between bigger COTEAUX D'AIX and CÔTES DE PROV. Warming reds, fresh rosés from usual s varieties. Potential being realized esp SYRAH. Try CHX la Calisse, Miraval, Trians; DOMS des Alysses, *des Aspras*, des Chaberts, du Deffends, du Loou, *Routas*.

Coulée de Serrant Lo w dr sw ★★★ 95 96 97 99 02 03 05 07 08 10' 11 12 13 14 15 16 Historic, steep CHENIN BL monopole 7-ha bio v'yd overlooking LO in heart of AC SAVENNIÈRES. Virginie Joly in charge. V. oxidative style sharply divides opinions. Severe frost 2017.

Courcel, Dom de C d'Or r ★★★ Leading POMMARD estate, fine floral wines using ripe grapes and whole bunches. Top, age-worthy, PREMIERS CRUS Rugiens and Epenots, plus interesting Croix Noires.

Crémant In CHAMP, used to mean "creaming" (half-sparkling): now called *demi-*

mousse/perle. Since 1975, AC for quality classic-method sparkling from AL, B'X, BOURGOGNE, Die, Jura, LIMOUX, Lo and Luxembourg.

Crépy Sav w ★★ AC since 1948. Light, soft white from s shore of Lake Geneva. 80% min CHASSELAS. Largest producer: Grande CAVE de Crèpy Mercier (part bio).

Criots-Bâtard-Montrachet C d'O ★★★ 02' 04 05 06 07 08 09 10 11 12 14' 15 (17) Tiny MONTRACHET satellite, 1.57 ha. Less concentrated than BÂTARD. Try Belland, Blain-GAGNARD, Fontaine G, Lamy, or d'Auvenay if you're v. rich.

Cros Parantoux Burg ★★★★ Cult PREMIER CRU in VOSNE-ROMANÉE made famous by the late Henri Jayer. Now made to great acclaim and greater price by Doms ROUGET and MÉO-CAMUZET. But Brûlée better?

Crozes-Hermitage N Rh r w ★★→★★★★ 09' 10' 12' 13' 14 15' 16' 17' SYRAH from mainly flat valley nr River Isère: dark-berry fruit, liquorice, tar; mostly early-drinking (2–5 yrs). Often more stylish from granite hills nr HERMITAGE: fine, red-fruited, can age; 2016 fun wines. Best (simple CUVÉES) ideal for grills, parties. Some oaked, older-vine wines cost more. Top: *A Graillot*, Aléofane (r w), Belle (organic), *Chapoutier*, Dard & Ribo (organic), *Delas* (Le CLOS v.gd, DOM des Grands Chemins), E Darnaud, G Robin; Doms Combier (organic), de *Thalabert* of JABOULET, des Entrefaux (oak), des Hauts-Châssis, des Lises (fine), *du Colombier*, Dumaine (organic), Fayolle Fils & Fille (stylish), Les Bruyères (organic, big fruit), Melody, Mucyn, Remizières (oak), Rousset, Ville Rouge, Y Chave. Drink *white* (MARSANNE) early, v.gd vintages recently. Value.

Cuve close Quicker method of making sparkling wine in a tank. Bubbles die away in glass much quicker than with *méthode traditionnelle*.

Champ in bottle loses one bar of pressure every 10 yrs.

Cuvée Wine contained in a *cuve* or vat. A word of many uses, incl synonym for "blend" and 1st-press wines (as in CHAMP). Often just refers to a "lot" of wine.

Dagueneau, Didier Lo w ★★★→★★★★ 03 05' 07 08' 09' 10' 11 12' 13 14' 15' 16' (17) Best producer of POUILLY-FUMÉ (12 ha): precise, age-worthy SAUV BL. Run by Didier's son Louis-Benjamin and daughter Charlotte. Hand-picking, immaculate winery, indigenous yeasts. Top CUVÉES: Pur Sang, Silex. Also SANCERRE (Les Monts Damnés, CHAVIGNOL), JURANÇON.

Dauvissat, Vincent Chab ★★★★ Imperturbable bio producer of CHAB using old barrels and local 132-litre *feuillettes*. Grand, age-worthy wines similar to RAVENEAU cousins. Best: La Forest, Les CLOS, Preuses, Séchet. Try also Fabien D.

Deiss, Dom Marcel Al r w ★★★ Bio grower at Bergheim. Favours blended wines from individual v'yds, often different varieties co-planted, mixed success. Best wine RIES Schoenenbourg 10 11 12 13 15'.

Delamotte Champ BRUT; *Blanc de Blancs* 04 06 07 08'; CUVÉE Nicholas Delamotte. Fine, small, CHARD-dominated house at LE MESNIL. V.gd *saignée* rosé. Managed with SALON by LAURENT-PERRIER. Called "the poor man's Salon" but sometimes surpasses it, as in 85' 02 04, delightful ready 07.

Delas Frères N Rh r p w ★★→★★★★ Consistent N Rh v'yd owner/merchant, with CONDRIEU, CROZES-HERMITAGE, CÔTE-RÔTIE, HERMITAGE v'yds. Best: *Côte-Rôtie Landonne*, Hermitage DOM des Tourettes (r w), Les Bessards (r, terroir, v. fine, smoky, long life), ST-JOSEPH Ste-Épine (r). S Rh: esp CÔTES DU RH St-Esprit (r), Grignan-les-Adhémar (r). Whites lighter recently. Owned by ROEDERER.

Demi-sec Half-dry: in practice more like half-sweet (eg. CHAMP typically 45g/l dosage).

Derenoncourt, Stéphane B'x Leading international consultant; self-taught, focused on terroir, fruit, balance. Own property, *Dom de l'A* in CAS.

Deutz Champ Always v.gd balance of freshness and wininess. BRUT Classic NV; Brut 06 08 lovely harmonious 12 (from 2019). Top-flight CHARD CUVÉE Amour de Deutz 06 08 09 12; Amour de Deutz Rosé 06. One of top small CHAMP houses,

ROEDERER-owned. **_Superb Cuvée William Deutz_ 95 88.** New Parcelles d'Ay 2010, powerful, tight, austere.

Dirler-Cadé, Dom Al Excellent estate in Bergholtz. Exceptional old-vines MUSCAT GRAND CRU Saering, depth and sculpted elegance 09 **12 13 14** in riper style of S AL. Fine RIES GC Saering 08 13 14 15' 17'.

Domaine (Dom) Property. *See* under name, eg. TEMPIER, DOM.

Dom Pérignon Champ Luxury CUVÉE of MOËT & CHANDON. Ultra-**_consistent quality in incredible quantities_**, creamy character esp, with 10–15 yrs bottle age; v. tight in youth. 96 superb at 20 yrs. Oenotèque (long bottle age, recent disgorgement, boosted price) renamed Plénitude; 7, 16, 30 yrs+ (P1, P2, P3); superb P2 98; excellent P2 93. Superb **02** on release now in transition to 2nd Plenitude, exotic **03,** great **04** 06. More PINOT N focus in DP Rosé 04 05.

Dopff au Moulin Al w ★★★ Ancient, top-class family producer. Class act in GEWURZ GRANDS CRUS Brand, Sporen 08 **10 12 13 14** 15' 16 17'; lovely RIES SCHOENENBOURG 10' 13 exceptional come 2020; *Sylvaner de Riquewihr 14.* Pioneer of AL CRÉMANT; v.gd CUVÉES: Bartholdi, Julien, Bio. Specialist in classic dry wines.

Dourthe B'x Sizeable merchant/grower; wide range, quality emphasis. CHX: BELGRAVE, LA GARDE, LE BOSCQ, Grand Barrail Lamarzelle Figeac, PEY LA TOUR, RAHOUL. *Dourthe No 1* (esp white) well-made generic B'x. Now on-line sales.

Drappier, André Champ Great family-run AUBE house. DOM of fine PINOT N, now 60 ha+, 15 certified bio; **_Pinot-led NV_,** ★★BRUT ZÉRO, Brut *sans souffre* (no sulphur), ★★★Millésime d'Exception **06** 08 09 12 esp of great potential; ace Prestige CUVÉE Grande Sendrée 08' 12 17'. Cuvée Quatuor (four *cépages*). Superb older vintages 95' **85** 82 (magnums).

DRC (Dom de la Romanée-Conti) C d'O r w ★★★★ Grandest estate in Burg. MONOPOLES ROMANÉE-CONTI and LA TÂCHE, major parts of ÉCHÉZEAUX, GRANDS-ÉCHÉZEAUX, RICHEBOURG, ROMANÉE-ST-VIVANT and a tiny part of MONTRACHET. Also CORTON from 2009. Crown-jewel prices. Keep top vintages for decades.

Drouhin, Joseph & Cie Burg r w ★★★ →★★★★ Fine family-owned grower/NÉGOCIANT in BEAUNE; v'yds (all bio) incl (w) Beaune *Clos des Mouches,* MONTRACHET (Marquis de LAGUICHE) and large CHAB holdings. Stylish, fragrant reds from pretty CHOREY-LÈS-BEAUNE to majestic *Musigny,* GRANDS-ÉCHÉZEAUX, etc. Also DDO (Domaine Drouhin Oregon), *see* US.

Duboeuf, Georges Beauj r w ★★ →★★★ "Mr BEAUJ", architect of Nouveau craze. Huge range of CUVÉES, all the crus, varying quality levels, plus gd range of MÂCON whites.

Dugat C d'O r ★★★ Cousins Claude and Bernard (Dugat-Py) make excellent, deep-coloured GEVREY-CHAMBERTIN, respective labels. Both flourishing with new generation. Tiny volumes esp GRANDS CRUS, huge prices esp Dugat-Py.

Dujac, Dom C d'O r w ★★★ →★★★★ MOREY-ST-DENIS grower famed for use of stems to make sensual, smoky reds, from village Morey to oustanding GRANDS CRUS esp CLOS DE LA ROCHE, CLOS ST-DENIS, ÉCHÉZEAUX. These days darker, denser than pre-2001. Lighter merchant wines as D Fils & Père and DOM Triennes in COTEAUX VAROIS.

Dureuil-Janthial Burg r w ★★ Top DOM in RULLY in capable hands of Vincent D-J, with *fresh, punchy whites* and cheerful, juicy reds. Try Maizières (r w) or PREMIER CRU Meix Cadot (w).

Durup, Jean Chab w ★★ Volume CHAB producer as DOM de l'Eglantière and CH de Maligny, allied by marriage to Dom Colinot in IRANCY.

Duval-Leroy Champ Dynamic Vertus CHAMP house, family-owned. 200 ha of mainly fine CHARD crus. New shift to vegan-friendly Champ, ie. natural clarification and settling, avoiding milk-protein fining agents. V.gd Fleur de Champagne NV. Top Blanc de Prestige *Femme* 04 **08 13** 15' 17.

Échézeaux C d'O r ★★★ **90' 93 96'** 99' 02' 03 05' **06** 08 09' **10' 11** 12' 13 14 15' 16 (17) GRAND CRU next to CLOS DE VOUGEOT, but totally different style: lacy, ethereal, scintillating. Can vary depending on exact location. Best: Arnoux, Berthaut, DRC, DUJAC, EUGÉNIE, GRIVOT, GROS, Guyon, Lamarche, LIGER-BELAIR, Mongeard-MUGNERET, Mugneret-Gibourg, ROUGET, Tremblay.

Ecu, Dom de l' Lo (r) w dr (sp) ★★★ 10' 11 12 14' 15' Bio MUSCADET-SÈVRE-ET-MAINE (Granite, Taurus). Dynamic Fred Niger took over from Guy Bossard in 2010. Gd CAB FR, PINOT N. Many different CUVÉES, Loire's largest park of amphorae. Severe frost 2016, 17.

Edelzwicker Al w ★ DYA. Blended light white. CH d'Ittenwiller, HUGEL Gentil gd.

Eguisheim, Cave Vinicole d' Al r w ★★ Impeccable co-op. Excellent value: fine GRANDS CRUS Hatschbourg, HENGST, Ollwiller, Spiegel. Owns Willm. Top label: WOLFBERGER. Best: Grande Rés 09 10 11 12, Sigillé, Armorié. Gd CRÉMANT, PINOT N (esp 10' 11 12 15).

Entraygues et du Fel and Estaing SW Fr r p w ★→★★ DYA. Two tiny AOP neighbours in terraces above Lot Valley. Tingling CHENIN BL for whites esp ★★DOMS Méjanassère, Laurent Mousset (gd reds esp ★★La Pauca, excellent rosé). ★★Nicolas Carmarans now making AOP reds as well as AVEYRON IGPS.

Entre-Deux-Mers B'x w ★→★★ DYA. Often gd-value dry white B'x (drink *entre deux huitres*) from between the rivers Garonne and Dordogne. Best: CHX BONNET, Chantelouve, Fontenille, Haut Rian, Landereau, Les Arromans, Les Tuileries, Marjosse, Moulin de Launay, Nardique-la-Gravière, Sainte-Marie, *Tour de Mirambeau*, Turcaud.

Esmonin, Dom Sylvie C d'O r ★★★ Rich, dark wines from fully ripe grapes esp since 2000. Lots of oak and lots of stems. Notable GEVREY-CHAMBERTIN VIEILLES VIGNES, CLOS ST-JACQUES. Cousin Frédéric has Estournelles St-Jacques.

Etoile, L' Jura w ★★ AC of Jura best-known for elegant CHARD grown on limestone and marl. VIN JAUNE and VIN DE PAILLE also allowed but not reds. Top tips: Cartaux-Bougaud, DOM de Montbourgeau, Philippe Vandelle.

Eugénie, Dom C d'O r (w) ★★★→★★★★ Former DOM Engel in VOSNE, first Burg acquisition by François Pinault of CH LATOUR in 2006. Powerful, dark-coloured wines. CLOS VOUGEOT, GRANDS-ÉCHÉZEAUX best, but try village Clos d'Eugénie.

Faiveley, J Burg r w ★★→★★★★ More grower than merchant, making succulent, richly fruity wines since sea-change in 2007. Gd-value from CÔTE CHALONNAISE, but save up for top wines from CHAMBERTIN-CLOS DE BÈZE, CHAMBOLLE-MUSIGNY, CORTON *Clos des Cortons*, NUITS. Ambitious recent acquisitions throughout C D'O and now DOM Billaud-Simon (CHAB).

Faller, Théo / Weinbach, Dom Al w ★★★→★★★★ Founded by Capuchin monks in 1612. Late Laurence Faller made wines of great complexity: often drier style esp GRANDS CRUS SCHLOSSBERG (RIES esp 08 10' 13 new L'Inédit 15' 17). Wines of great *character and elegance*. Esp CUVÉE Ste Catherine SÉLECTION DES GRAINS NOBLE GEWURZ 71 90 09'. Older sister Catherine now at helm, brother in vyds.

Faugères L'doc r (p) (w) ★ →★★★ 12 13 14 15 16 17 Early AC, 1982, and now Cru du L'doc. Compact, seven villages, defined by schist, for fresh and spicy, age-worthy reds. Elegant whites from MARSANNE, ROUSSANNE, VERMENTINO and GRENACHE BLANC. Est families as well as newcomers. Look for DOMS Cébène, Chaberts, Chenaie, des Trinités, JEAN-MICHEL ALQUIER, Léon Barral, Mas d'Alezon, OLLIER-TAILLEFER, St Antonin, *Sarabande* and many others. High proportion of organic growers.

Fèvre, William Chab w ★★★→★★★★ Biggest owner of CHAB GRANDS CRUS; Côte Bougerots and Les CLOS outstanding. Small yields, no expense spared, priced accordingly, a top source for concentrated, age-worthy wines. Owned by HENRIOT.

Fiefs Vendéens Lo r p w ★→★★★ 09 10 14' 15' 16 (17) Mainly DYA AC. From the Vendée nr Sables d'Olonne, both tourist wines and serious age-worthy ones. CHARD, CHENIN BL, MELON, SAUV BL (w), CAB FR, CAB SAUV, GAMAY, Grolleau Gris,

Négrette, PINOT N (r p). Esp: Coirier, DOM St-Nicolas (bio – top producer), Mourat (122 ha), Prieuré-la-Chaume (bio). Frost in 2016, 17.

Fitou L'doc r ★★ 12 13 14 15 16 17 Characterful rugged red from inland hills s of Narbonne as well as tamer coastal v'yds. Midi's oldest AC for table wine, created in 1948. 11 mths' ageing, benefits from bottle-age. Seek out CH de Nouvelles, Champs des Soeurs, DOM Bergé-Bertrand, Jones, Lérys, Rolland.

Fixin C d'O r (w) ★★★ 99′ 02′ 03 05′ 06 09′ 10′ 11 12′ 13 14 15′ 16 (17) Worthy and undervalued n neighbour of GEVREY-CHAMBERTIN. Sturdy, sometimes splendid reds but can be rustic. Best v'yds: CLOS de la Perrière, Clos du Chapitre, Clos Napoléon. Rising star is Amélie Berthaut, plus established DOMS Bart, CLAIR, FAIVELEY, Gelin, Guyard, Joliet, MORTET.

Fleurie Beauj r ★★★ 13 14 15′ (17) Top BEAUJ cru for perfumed, strawberry fruit, silky texture. Racier from La Madone hillside, richer below. Horribly hailed on in 16, 17, sadly. Classic names: CH de Poncié, Chignard, CLOS de la Roilette, Depardon, DUBOEUF, Métrat, co-op. Naturalists: Balagny, Dutraive, Métras, Sunier. Newcomers: Graillot (DOM de Fa), Lafarge-Vial.

Fourrier, Domaine C d'O r ★★★★ Jean-Marie F has taken a sound GEVREY-CHAMBERTIN DOM to new levels, with cult prices to match. Sensual vibrant reds at all levels. Best CLOS ST-JACQUES, Combe aux Moines, GRIOTTE-CHAMBERTIN.

Francs-Côtes de Bordeaux B'x r w ★★ 09′ 10′ 12 14 15 16 Tiny B'X AC next to CAS. Fief of Thienpont (PAVIE-MACQUIN) family. Mainly red from MERLOT but some gd white (eg. Charmes-Godard). Reds can age a little. Top CHX: Francs, Laclaverie, La Prade, Le Puy (Emilien), Marsau, Puyanché, *Puygueraud*.

Fronsac B'x r ★★→★★★ 05′ 06 08 09′ 10′ 11 12 14 15 16 Underrated hilly AC w of ST-ÉM; great-value MERLOT-dominated red, some ageing potential. Top CH: Arnauton, DALEM, Fontenil, *la Dauphine*, la Grave, la Rivière, la Rousselle, LA VIEILLE CURE, LES TROIS CROIX, Haut-Carles, Mayne-Vieil, *Moulin-Haut-Laroque*, Richelieu, Tour du Moulin, Villars. *See also* CANON-FRON.

Fronton SW Fr r p ★★ 15′ 16′ 17 AOP n of Toulouse. Virtual exclusivity of Négrette (sometimes unblended). Suggests violets, cherries, liquorice. Best at 3 yrs. Try ★★CHX Baudare, best-known *Bellevue-la-Forêt*, *Bouissel*, Boujac, Caze, du Roc, Flotis, Plaisance (esp sulphur-free Alabets), DOMS des Pradelles, Viguerie de Belaygues. No AOP for whites as yet.

Fuissé, Ch Burg w ★★→★★★ Both commercial and quality leader in POUILLY-FUISSÉ. Top terroirs Le CLOS, Combettes. Also BEAUJ CRUS, eg. JULIÉNAS.

Gagnard C d'O (r) w ★★★ →★★★★ Well-known clan in CHASSAGNE-MONTRACHET. Long-lasting wines esp Caillerets, BÂTARD from Jean-Noël G; while Blain-G, Fontaine G have full range incl rare CRIOTS-BÂTARD, MONTRACHET itself. Gd value offered by all Gagnards.

Gaillac SW Fr r p w dr sw sp ★→★★ (r) 15′ 16′ 17′ (w sw) 14′ 15′ 16 17′ (p w dr sp) DYA. Ever-improving AOP w of Albi. Distinguished by eclectic grapes eg. Braucol, DURAS, Len de l'El, Mauzac and growing number of bio producers. ★★★Causse-Marines, La Ramaye, Laurent Cazottes, Le Champ d'Orphée, Peyres-Roses, *Plageoles*, ★★L'Enclos des Braves, L'Enclos des Roses, La Ferme du Vert; DOMS Brin, d'Escausses, du Moullin, Mayragues, Rotier; CHX Bourguet (w sw), Larroque, Palvié (r). Bargains from ★★Doms Labarthe, La Chanade, Mas Pignou.

Ganevat Jura w ★★★→★★★★ CÔTES du JURA superstar. Single-v'yd CHARD (eg. Chalasses, Grand Teppes), pricey but fabulous. Also innovative reds.

Gauby, Dom Gérard Rouss r w ★★★ Exemplary ROUSS producer, attracted several others to village of Calce. Bio. Both IGP CÔTES CATALANES, CÔTES DU ROUSS-VILLAGES Muntada; Les Calcinaires VIEILLES VIGNES. Associated with DOM Le Soula. Dessert wine Le Pain du Sucre.

Gers SW Fr r p w ★ DYA IGP usually sold as CÔTES DE GASCOGNE; indistinguishable.

Gevrey-Chambertin C d'O r ★★★ 90' 96' 99' 02' 03 05' **06 07 08** 09' 10' 11 12' 13 14 15' 16 (17) Major AC for interesting savoury reds at all levels up to great CHAMBERTIN and GRAND CRU cousins. Top PREMIERS CRUS Cazetiers, Combe aux Moines, Combottes, CLOS ST-JACQUES. Value from single-v'yd village wines (En Champs, La Justice) and VIEILLES VIGNES bottlings. Top: BACHELET, BOILLOT, BURGUET, Damoy, DROUHIN, Drouhin-Laroze, DUGAT, Dugat-Py, Duroché, ESMONIN, FAIVELEY, FOURRIER, Géantet-Pansiot, Harmand-Geoffroy, JADOT, LEROY, MORTET, ROSSIGNOL-TRAPET, Roty, ROUSSEAU, Roy, SÉRAFIN, TRAPET.

Gigondas S Rh r p ★★ →★★★ 78' 89' 90' 95' 98' 99' 00' 01' 03' 04' 05' 06' 07' 08 09' 10' 11 12' 13' 14' 15' 16' 17' Top S Rh red. Striking v'yds on stony clay-sand plain rise to Alpine limestone hills e of Avignon; GRENACHE, plus SYRAH, MOURVÈDRE. Robust, smoky, wines; best offer fine, clear, dark-red fruit. Ace 2010, 15, 16. More oak recently, higher prices, but genuine local feel in many. Top: Boissan, Bosquets (gd modern), Bouïssière (punchy), Brusset, Cayron, CH de Montmirail, *Clos des Cazaux* (value), CLOS du Joncuas (organic, traditional), *Famille Perrin*, Goubert, Gour de Chaulé (fine), Grapillon d'Or, Longue Toque, Moulin de la Gardette (stylish), Notre Dame des Pallières, *Les Pallières*, P Amadieu, Pesquier, Pourra (robust), *Raspail-Ay*, Roubine, Santa Duc (now stylish), Semelles de Vent, St-Cosme (swish), St Gayan (long-lived), Teyssonnières. Heady rosés.

Gimonnet, Pierre Champ ★★→★★★ 28 ha of GRAND and PREMIER CRUS on n Côte des Blancs. New v'yd in Oger. Enviably consistent CHARD. Ace CUVÉE Gastronome for seafood (10 13 15).

Girardin, Vincent C d'O r w ★★ →★★★ White-specialist MEURSAULT-based grower/ NÉGOCIANT, now under BOISSET ownership.

Givry Burg r (w) ★★ 09' 10' 12 13 14 15' 16 (17) Top tip in CÔTE CHALONNAISE for tasty reds that can age. Better value than MERCUREY. Rare whites nutty in style. Best (r): JOBLOT, CLOS Salomon, *Faiveley*, F Lumpp, Masse, Thénard.

Goisot Burg r w ★★★ Jean-Hugues G, outstanding producer for single-v'yd bottlings of ST-BRIS (SAUV) and Côtes d'Auxerre for CHARD, PINOT N. Consistent quality at fair price, so now scarce.

Gosset Champ Old AŸ house merging tradition and modernity. New Grand BLANC DE NOIRS, v. elegant, aged on CHARD lees; Grande Rés NV. Prestige CUVÉE Celebris Chard-driven in Extra-BRUT style, v. fine in **04** 05, great 98, sublime **95**; straight vintage Grande Millésime 06 a model of delicate precision and detail.

Gouges, Henri C d'O r w ★★★ Grégory G at helm for rich, meaty, long-lasting NUITS-ST-GEORGES from several PREMIER CRU v'yds. Some find them too tannic in youth. Try Vaucrains, Les St-Georges or Chaignots. Interesting *white Nuits* incl PINOT BL.

Grand Cru Official term neaning different things in different areas. One of top Burg v'yds with its own AC. In AL, one of 51 top v'yds, each now with its own rules. In ST-ÉM, 60 per cent of production is St-Ém Grand Cru, often run-of-the-mill. In MÉD there are five tiers of Grands Crus Classés. In CHAMP top 17 villages are Grands Crus. New now designation in Lo for QUARTS DE CHAUME, and emerging system in L'DOC. Take with pinch of salt in PROV.

Grande Rue, La C d'O r ★★★ 90' 95 96' 98 02' 03 05' 06 07 08 09' 10' 11 12' 13 14 15' 16 (17) Starting to see best of this narrow strip of GRAND CRU between LA TÂCHE and ROMANÉE-CONTI. Not quite in same league, certainly not same price. MONOPOLE of DOM Lamarche.

Grands-Échézeaux C d'O r ★★★★ 90' 93 95 96' 99' 00 02' 03 05' 06 07 08 09' 10' 11 12' 13 14 15' 17 Superlative GRAND CRU next to CLOS DE VOUGEOT, but with a MUSIGNY silkiness. More weight than most ÉCHÉZEAUX. Top: BICHOT (CLOS Frantin), DRC, DROUHIN, EUGÉNIE, G Noëllat, GROS, Lamarche, Mongeard-MUGNERET.

Grange des Pères, Dom de la L'doc r w ★★★ IGP Pays l'Hérault. Cult estate neighbouring MAS DE DAUMAS GASSAC, created by reclusive Laurent Vaillé for 1st vintage (1992). Red from SYRAH, MOURVÈDRE, CAB SAUV; white 80% ROUSSANNE, plus MARSANNE, CHARD. Stylish wines with ageing potential.

Gratien, Alfred and Gratien & Meyer Champ ★★★ BRUT 83' 02 04 08' 09 12 13 15' 17' Small but beautiful; Brut NV. CHARD-led Prestige CUVÉE Paradis Brut, Rosé (multi-vintage). Excellent quirky CHAMP and Lo house, now German-owned. Fine, v. dry, lasting, oak-fermented wines, incl *The Wine Society's house Champagne*. Careful buyer of top crus from favourite growers. Gratien & Meyer counterpart at SAUMUR.

Graves B'x r w ★→★★ 08 09' 10' 12 14 15 16 Gravel soils provide the name. Juicy, appetizing reds, fresh SAUV/SÉM dry whites (will age). One of best values in B'x today. Frost, hail in 2017. Top CHX: ARCHAMBEAU, Brondelle, de Cérons, CHANTEGRIVE, CLOS Bourgelat, *Clos Floridène*, CRABITEY, Ferrande, Fougères, Grand Enclos du CH de Cérons, Haura, Magneau, Pont de Brion, Rahoul, *Respide Médeville*, Roquetaillade La Grange, St-Robert CUVÉE Poncet Deville, Vieux CH Gaubert, Villa Bel Air.

Graves de Vayres B'x r w ★ DYA. Tiny AC within E-2-M zone. Red, white, *moelleux*.

Grignan-les-Adhémar S Rh r (p) w ★→★★ 15' 16' 17' Mid-Rh AC; best reds hearty, tangy, herbal. Leaders: Baron d'Escalin, DELAS, La Suzienne (value); DOMS de Bonetto-Fabrol, de Montine (stylish r, gd p w, also r CÔTES DU RH), Grangeneuve best (esp VIEILLES VIGNES), St-Luc; CHX Bizard, La Décelle (incl w Côtes du Rh).

Griotte-Chambertin C d'O r ★★★★ 90' 95 96' 99' 02' 03 05' 06 07 08 09' 10' 11 12' 13 14 15' 16 (17) Small GRAND CRU next to CHAMBERTIN; nobody has much volume. Brisk red fruit, with depth and ageing potential, from DROUHIN, DUGAT, FOURRIER, *Ponsot*, R Leclerc.

Grivot, Jean C d'O r w ★★★→★★★★ Huge improvements at this VOSNE-ROMANÉE DOM in past decade, reflected in higher prices. Superb range topped by GRANDS CRUS CLOS DE VOUGEOT, ÉCHÉZEAUX, RICHEBOURG.

Gros, Doms C d'O r w ★★★→★★★★ Family of VIGNERONS in VOSNE-ROMANÉE with stylish wines from Anne (sumptuous RICHEBOURG), succulent reds from Michel (CLOS de Réas), Anne-Françoise (now in BEAUNE) and Gros Frère & Soeur (CLOS VOUGEOT En Musigni). Not just GRANDS CRUS; try value HAUTES-CÔTES DE NUITS. Also Anne's DOM Gros-Tollot in MINERVOIS.

Gros Plant du Pays Nantais Lo w (sp) ★→★★ DYA. Much-improved AC from GROS PLANT (FOLLE BLANCHE), best racy, saline, delicious with oysters. Try: Basse Ville, ECU, Haut-Bourg, Luneau-Papin, Poiron-Dabin, Preuille. Sparkling: either pure or blended. 2017 April frost.

Guigal, Ets E N Rh r w ★★→★★★★ Famous grower-merchant: CÔTE-RÔTIE mainly, plus CONDRIEU, CROZES-HERMITAGE, HERMITAGE, ST-JOSEPH; from 2017, 53-ha CHÂTEAUNEUF DOM de Nalys v'yds. Merchant: Condrieu, Côte-Rôtie, Crozes-Hermitage, Hermitage, S Rh. Owns Dom de Bonserine (deep Côte-Rôtie), VIDAL-FLEURY (fruit, quality up). Top, v. expensive Côte-Rôties La Mouline, La Landonne, La Turque (ultra rich, new oak for 42 mths, so atypical), also v.gd Hermitage, St-Joseph Vignes de l'Hospice; all reds dense. Standard wines: gd esp *top-value Côtes du Rh* (r p w). Best whites: Condrieu, Condrieu La Doriane (oaky), Hermitage.

Hautes-Côtes de Beaune / Nuits C d'O r w ★★ (r) 12 13 14 15' 16 (17) (w) 14' 15' 16 (17) ACS for villages in hills behind CÔTE DE BEAUNE/NUITS. Attractive lighter reds, whites for early drinking. Best whites: Devevey, MÉO-CAMUZET, Montchovet, Thevenot-le-Brun. Top reds: Carré, Duband, Féry, GROS, Jacob, Jouan, Magnien, Mazilly, Naudin-Ferrand, Parigot, Verdet. Also useful large co-op nr BEAUNE.

Haut-Médoc B'x r ★★→★★★ 05' 06 08 09' 10' 11 12 14 15 16 Prime source of dry, digestible CAB/MERLOT reds. Usually gd value. Some variation in soils and wines: sand and gravel in s; heavier clay and gravel in n; sturdier wines. Five Classed Growths (BELGRAVE, CAMENSAC, *Cantemerle*, LA LAGUNE, LA TOUR-CARNET). Other top CHX: D'AGASSAC, Aurilhac, BELLE-VUE, CAMBON LA PELOUSE, Charmail, CISSAC, CITRAN,

Clément-Pichon, COUFRAN, *de Lamarque*, Gironville, LANESSAN, Larose Perganson, *Malescasse*, SÉNÉJAC, SOCIANDO-MALLET.

Haut-Montravel SW Fr w sw ★★ 12 14' 15' 16 17' Sweetest of the three MONTRAVEL white AOPS, best (★★★CH Puy-Servain-Terrement, bargain ★★DOMS Moulin Caresse, Libarde) worthy rivals to better-known MONBAZILLAC, SAUSSIGNAC.

Haut-Poitou Lo r p w sp ★ →★★ 14 15 16 (17) Best age 5–6+ yrs. AC (around 750 ha) n of Poitiers from CAB SAUV, CAB Fr, GAMAY, CHARD, PINOT N, SAUV BL. Dynamic *Ampelidae* (Frédéric Brochet) dominates. IGP wines 120 ha. Also La Tour Beaumont, Morgeau La Tour.

Heidsieck, Charles Champ Iconic house, smaller than before, wines more brilliant than ever. BRUT Ré all purity and subtle mature complexity. Peerless Blanc des Millénaires 04. Brut Vintage in prime form esp 83; CHAMP Charlie Prestige CUVÉE likely to be reintroduced from 2023/25.

Heidsieck Monopole Champ Once-great CHAMP house. Fair quality, gd price. Gold Top 07 09. Part of Vranken group.

Hengst Al GRAND CRU. Gives powerful wines. Excels with top GEWURZ from JOSMEYER, ZIND-HUMBRECHT; also AUXERROIS, CHASSELAS, PINOT N.

Henri Abelé Champ New name for Abel Lepitre, now focusing on exports. Best CUVÉE Sourire de Reims 07 08 09, new Sourire Rosé 06 09 from Les Riceys (Aube), expansive burg style. Gd value.

Henriot Champ BRUT Souverain NV much improved; ace BLANC DE BLANCS de CHARD NV; Brut 98' 02' 04; Brut Rosé 06 09. Fine family CHAMP house. New long-aged *Cuve 38*, a solera of GRAND CRU Chard since 1990. Outstanding long-lived Prestige CUVÉE Les Enchanteleurs 59★★★ 88 96' 02 04 08' 13 15'. Also owns BOUCHARD PÈRE & FILS, FÈVRE.

Terroir wins in Champ: all grapes in Aÿ, even Chard, taste of Pinot N.

Hermitage N Rh r w ★★★ →★★★★ 61' 66' 78' 83' 85' 88 89' 90' 91' 95' 96 97' 98' 99' 00 01' 03' 04 05' 06' 07' **09**' 10' **11**' 12' 13' 14' 15' 16' 17' (2010, 15 both brilliant) Part granite hill on e Rhône bank with grandest, deepest, most stylish SYRAH and complex, nutty/white-fruited, fascinating, v. long-lived white (MARSANNE, some ROUSSANNE) best left for 6–7yrs+. Best: Belle, *Chapoutier*, Colombier, DELAS, Faurie (pure), GUIGAL, Habrard (w), *J-L Chave* (rich, elegant), M Sorrel (mighty Le Gréal r), Nicolas Perrin, *Paul Jaboulet*, Philippe & Vincent Jaboulet (r w), Tardieu-Laurent (oak). TAIN co-op gd (esp Gambert de Loche).

Hortus, Dom de l' L'doc r w ★★★ Next generation taking over at this PIC ST-LOUP producer. Intriguing Bergerie IGP Val de Montferrand (w) with seven grape varieties; elegant Bergerie and oak-aged Grande CUVÉE (r). Also CLOS du Prieur (r) in cooler TERRASSES du LARZAC.

Hospices de Beaune C d'O Spectacular medieval foundation with grand charity auction of CUVÉES from its 61 ha for Beaune's hospital, 3rd Sunday in Nov, run since 2005 by Christie's. Individuals can buy as well as trade. Standards more consistent under Roland Masse (retired 2015); another step forward with Ludivine Griveau taking over. Try BEAUNE cuvées, VOLNAYS or expensive GRANDS CRUS, (r) CORTON, ÉCHÉZEAUX, MAZIS-CHAMBERTIN, (w) BÂTARD-MONTRACHET. Bargains unlikely.

Hudelot C d'O r w ★★★ VIGNERON family in CÔTE DE NUITS. New life breathed into H-NOËLLAT (VOUGEOT), while H-Baillet (CHAMBOLLE) challenging hard. Former more stylish, latter more punchy.

Huet Lo w ★★★★ 89' 90' 95' 96' 97' 02' 03' 05' 06 08' 09' 10' 11' **14 15' 16'** (17) Top VOUVRAY, bio; CHENIN BL benchmark. Anthony Hwang also owns Királyudvar in Tokaji (*see* Hungary). Winemaker: Jean-Bernard Berthomé. Single v'yds: CLOS du Bourg, Le Haut Lieu, Le Mont. Almost immortal esp sweet: 19 21 24 47 59 89 90. Also *pétillant*. Well worth decanting.

Hugel & Fils Al r w sw ★★→★★★ Top AL house (yellow labels) at Riquewihr famed for late-harvest wines esp RIES, GEWURZ VENDANGE TARDIVE, SÉLECTION DE GRAINS NOBLES. Jubilee range discontinued; new release of superb Ries Schoelhammer 07 10 13 17 from GRAND CRU site.

IGP (Indication Géographique Protegée) Potentially most dynamic category in France (with over 150 regions), allowing scope for experimentation. Successor to VDP, from 2009 vintage, but position unchanged and new terminology still not accepted by every area. Zonal names most individual: eg. CÔTES DE GASCOGNE, CÔTES DE THONGUE, Pays des Cévennes, Haute Vallée de l'Orb, among others. Enormous variety in taste and quality but never ceases to surprise.

Irancy Burg r (p) ★★ 05' 09' 10 12 14' 15' 16 (17) Light though structured red made nr CHAB from PINOT N and more rustic local César. Elbows-on-table stuff. Best v'yds: Palotte, Mazelots. Best: Cantin, *Colinot*, *Dauvissat*, Goisot, Renaud, Richoux.

Irouléguy SW Fr r p (w) ★→★★★ 12' 14 15 16 17 Basque AOP. Reds based on TANNAT and CAB FR (echoes of MADIRAN). ★★★Ameztia, Arretxea, Mourguy; ★★Abotia, Bordathio, Bordaxuria, Brana, Etchegaraya, Gutizia, Ilarria. Gd whites based on Petit Courbu grape esp excellent co-op (★★★Xuri d'Ansa), DOM Xubialdea. Rosés make perfect summer drinking.

Jaboulet Aîné, Paul N Rh r w Grower-merchant at Tain. Wines polished, modern. Once-leading producer of HERMITAGE esp ★★★★ La Chapelle (fabulous 78, 90), quality varied since 90s, revival since 2010 on reds. Also CORNAS St-Pierre, CROZES Thalabert (can be stylish), Roure (sound); owns DOM de Terre Ferme CHÂTEAUNEUF, merchant of other Rh, notably CÔTES DU RH *Parallèle 45*, CONDRIEU, VACQUEYRAS, VENTOUX (r, quality/value). Whites lack true Rh body, drink most young, range incl new v. expensive La Chapelle white (not made every yr).

Jacquart Champ Simplified range from co-op-turned-brand, concentrating on what it does best: PREMIERS CRUS Côte des Blancs CHARD from member growers. Fine range of Vintage BLANC DE BLANCS 10 08 07 06 05 04 targeted at restaurants. V.gd Vintage Rosé 02 04 06. Globetrotting new winemaker. 17' looks v.gd for Chard.

Jacquesson Champ Bijou Dizy house, precise, v. dry wines. Top single-v'yd Avize CHAMP Caïn 02 04 05 08'. Corne Bautray, all CHARD. Dizy 04 08 09, excellent *numbered NV cuvées* 730' 731 732 733 734 735 738 739 740 (12 base: best yet) 741.

Jadot, Louis Burg r p w ★★→★★★★ Dynamic BEAUNE merchant making powerful whites (DIAM closures) and well-constructed age-worthy reds with significant v'yd holdings in BEAUJ, C D'O, MÂCON; esp POUILLY-FUISSÉ (DOM Ferret), MOULIN-À-VENT (CH des Jacques, *Clos du Grand Carquelin*).

Jasnières Lo w dr (sw) ★★→★★★ 08' 09' 10' 11 14' 15' 16 (17) CHENIN BL, lively, sharp, dry to sweet, AC (65 ha), s-facing slopes Loir Valley. Esp Breton, DE BELLIVIÈRE, Gigou, Janvier, J-B Métais, L'Ange Vin (also VIN DE FRANCE), Le Briseau, Les Maisons Rouges, Roche Bleue, Ryke. V. age-worthy. 2017 promising.

Jobard C d'O r w ★★★ VIGNERON family in MEURSAULT. Top DOMS are Antoine J esp long-lived Poruzots, Genevrières, CHARMES; and Rémi Jobard for immediately classy Meursaults plus reds from MONTHÉLIE, VOLNAY.

Joblot Burg r w ★★ Reference DOM for GIVRY; new CUVÉES Empreinte, Mademoiselle from 2016, plus classics La Servoisine and CLOS du Cellier Aux Moines.

Joseph Perrier Champ Fine family-run CHAMP house with v.gd PINOTS N, M v'yds esp in own Cumières DOM. Ace Prestige CUVÉE Joséphine 89 02 04 08' 09 12'. Excellent BRUT Royale NV, as generous as ever but more precise with less dosage. Distinctive, tangy BLANC DE BLANCS 02 04 06 09 08 13' 15', fine food wine. 15'; now drier, finer Cuvée Royale Brut NV.

Josmeyer Al w ★★→★★★ Fine and long-lived wines. Superb RIES *Grand Cru Hengst* 10 12 13' 14 15'. Also v.gd Auxerrois, and entry-level Ries Le Dragon. Smart biodynamist, rigorous but realistic.

FRANCE

Juliénas Beauj r ★★★ 09' 13 14 15' 16 17 Rich, hearty; juicy, structured from surprisingly unfashionable CRU: Aufranc, Burrier, CH FUISSÉ, Michel Tête, Trenel.

Jurançon SW Fr w dr sw ★→★★★ (sw) 11' 12 13 14 15 16' 17 (dr) 15' 16 17 Separate AOPS (sw and dr w), both styles balancing richness and acidity. DAGUENEAU's tiny ★★★★Jardins de Babylon sets the benchmark for ★★★DOMS *Cauhapé*, de Sarros, de Souch, Lapeyre, Larrédya, Thou; ★★CHX Jolys, Lapuyade; and Doms Bellauc, Bellegarde, Bordenave, Capdevielle, Castéra, Guirardel, Haugarot, Nigri, Uroulat and CLOS Benguères; ★Gan co-op gd value.

Kaefferkopf Al w dr (sw) ★★★ The 51st GRAND CRU of AL at Ammerschwihr. Permitted to make blends as well as varietal wines, possibly not top-drawer.

Kientzler, Andre Al w sw ★★→★★★ Small, v. fine grower at Ribeauvillé. V.gd RIES from GRANDS CRUS Osterberg, Geisberg 09 12 11 13 14 15', small but exceptional 17. Lush GEWURZ from Grand Cru Kirchberg 09 11 12 15. Rich, classic sweet wines. Model v'yd care, without faith in isms or fads.

Kreydenweiss, Marc Al w sw ★★→★★★★ Fine bio AL DOM around Andlau, now run by Antoine Kreydenweiss and sisters, children of Marc. Subtler oak now. Diversity of soils: v.gd PINOT GR GRAND CRU Moenchberg (marly limestone) and top-flight RIES Kastelberg (black schist), ages 10–20 yrs+; 90 08 13 14 15. Also in COSTIÈRES DE NÎMES, S Rh.

Krug Champ Grande CUVÉE ★★★★ esp 160th Edition based on 04; 164th Edition (08 base) still young. Vintage 95' 98 00 02 04; Rosé; CLOS DU MESNIL 00' 02 03; CLOS D'AMBONNAY 95' 98' 00; Krug Collection 69 76' 81 85. Supremely prestigious house. Rich and nutty wines, oak-fermented; highest quality, ditto price. Vintage 03 a fine surprise, 02 magnificent in 2020. No vintage in 12, pity as great PINOT N yr.

Kuentz-Bas Al w sw ★★→★★★ Great improvements since Jean-Baptiste Adam bought DOM in 2004. Among highest AL v'yds, organic/bio methods result in serious yet accessible wines: drier RIES 13 15' 16 17', Fine PINOT GR, GEWURZ VENDANGE TARDIVE 08 09 15 17.

Labet, Dom Jura ★★★ Key CÔTES DU JURA estate in s part of region (Rotalier). Best-known for range of single-v'yd CHARD whites, eg. En Billat, En Chalasse, La Bardette; gd PINOT N, VIN JAUNE.

Ladoix C d'O r w ★★ (r) 05' 08 09' 10' 11 12 14 15' 16 (17) (w) 12 14' 15 16 (17) Explore here for fresh, exuberant whites, eg. Grechons, and juicy reds esp Les Joyeuses from local DOMS Chevalier, Loichet, Mallard, Ravaut. Those with more cash try Le Cloud from Prieuré-Roch.

Ladoucette, de Lo (r) (p) w ★★★ 10 12 14 15 16 (17) Largest individual POUILLY-FUMÉ producer at CH du Nozet (165ha). Expensive prestige brand Baron de L. SANCERRE

Jura jewels

What other region has so many styles? They seem to like confusing customers – sommeliers love the game. **Dry whites** from CHARD, many single-v'yd versions now. Also tangy blends with SAVAGNIN. Fresh or deliberately **oxidative** pure Savagnin exciting too; many made in natural style can be pretty gamey. See CÔTES DU JURA, ARBOIS, L'ÉTOILE. *Vin typé* on labels means heading towards Sherry. *Vin ouillé* means "ullaged": the barrel has been topped-up to avoid oxidation. **Light reds** from PINOT N, Poulsard, Trousseau, or blends. Some more rosé than red. Côtes du Jura, Arbois. Aged **sherrified whites** known as VIN JAUNE. See CH-CHALON. Intensely sweet **vin de paille** made fom red and white grapes. Fortified **Macvin**, local version of ratafia. Classic producers: Bourdy, MACLE, Overnoy, Puffeney. Avant garde: A&M TISSOT, GANEVAT, PIGNIER. Volume/value: co-ops (known here as CAVES Fruitières), Boilley, J Tissot, LABET, HENRI MAIRE.

Comte Lafond, owns La Poussie (Bué's most impressive site) and also Marc Brédif: CHINON, VOUVRAY, Albert Pic.

Lafarge, Michel C d'O r ★★★★ Classic VOLNAY bio estate run by Frédéric L, son of ever-present Michel, over 100 vintages between them. Outstanding, long-lived PREMIERS CRUS *Clos des Chênes*, Caillerets, CLOS du CH des Ducs. Also fine BEAUNE esp Grèves and some whites. New FLEURIE project, Lafarge-Vial.

Lafon, Dom des Comtes Burg r w ★★★→★★★★ Fabulous bio MEURSAULT DOM, back to reliable best with long-lasting red VOLNAY *Santenots* equally outstanding. Value from excellent Mâconnais wines under Heritiers L label, while Dominique L makes his own COTE DE BEAUNE wines separately.

Laguiche, Marquis de C d'O w ★★★★ Largest owner of Le MONTRACHET and a fine PREMIER CRU CHASSAGNE, both excellently made by DROUHIN.

Lalande de Pomerol B'x r ★★ 05' 06 08 09' 10' 11 12 14 15 16 Improving satellite neighbour of POM. Similar style but less density. Hit by frost in 2017. Top CHX: Ame de Musset, Bertineau St-Vincent, Chambrun, La Chenade, LA FLEUR DE BOÜARD, La Sergue, Les Cruzelles, Garraud, Grand Ormeau, Haut-Chaigneau, Jean de Gué, Laborderie-Mondésir, *Les Hauts Conseillants*, Pavillon Beauregard, Perron (La Fleur), Sabines, Siaurac, TOURNEFEUILLE.

Landron, Doms Lo w dr sp ★★→★★★ 10 13 14' 15 16 (17) V.gd producer (48 ha) of bio MUSCADET-SÈVRE-ET-MAINE: Amphibolite, Fief du Breil.

Langlois-Château Lo (r) (w) sp ★★→★★★ SAUMUR, BOLLINGER-owned (incl 89 ha). Gd CRÉMANT de Lo esp Quadrille, Rés. Still wines, v.gd Saumur Blanc VIEILLES VIGNES 05 09 13 14 15.

Languedoc r p w General term for the Midi. Also AC incl CORBIÈRES, MINERVOIS, ROUSS from Cabardès to Sommières, but not Malepère. In theory AC Coteaux du L'doc no longer exists. Rules the same. Bottom of pyramid of Midi ACs. Hierarchy of superior crus is work in progress. Subregions incl Cabrières, Grès de Montpellier, Pézenas, Quatourze, St Saturnin: usual L'doc grapes. Tiny Cabardès and Malepère where B'x meets Midi. CLAIRETTE du L'doc tiny, once-fashionable white. Not all ACs have much specific identity: go by grower.

Lanson Champ Black Label NV; Rosé NV; Vintage BRUT on a roll esp 02 08 12' 15. Renewed house, part of LANSON-BCC group. Ace prestige NV Lanson Père et Fils Noble CUVÉE BLANC DE BLANCS, rosé and vintage; new Brut vintage single-vyd CLOS Lanson 06 08 09 12. Extra Age multi-vintage, Blanc de Blancs esp gd. Experienced new winemaker Hervé Dantan (since 15) starting to allow some malo (*see* A Little Learning) for a rounder style.

Lapierre, Marcel Beauj r ★★★ Mathieu, son of pioneer Marcel L, runs cult DOM making sulphur-free MORGON. Try CUVÉE Camille from best plots or fresh, juicy Raisins Gaulois.

Laplace, Dom SW Fr Oldest of all MADIRAN growers but modern-style ★★★*Ch d'Aydie*, needs time. Odie d'Aydie less so. Try lighter all-TANNAT IGPS ★★Les Deux Vaches, ★Aramis. Excellent ★★★PACHERENCS (dr sw). Sweet fortified Maydie with chocolate.

Laroche Chab w ★★ Major player in CHAB with range from special CUVÉE *Res de*

Languedoc rising stars

Keen drinkers now scan L'DOC with rising expectations. We haven't seen the half yet. NB: all founded since 2008, and looking gd: **Cabardès** Guilhem Barré; **Corbières** L'Espérou, Olivier Mavit; **Faugères** Grain Sauvage, Mas Lou, Les Serrals; **Fitou** Sarrat d'en Sol; **La Clape** La Combe de St Paul; **Limoux** Cathare, Monsieur S; **St-Chinian** La Lauzeta, Les Païssels, Lanye Barrac; **Pézenas** La Grange des Bouys, Ste Cécile du Parc; **Terrasses du Larzac** Clos Maïa, Les Chemins de Carabote, Mas Combarèla; **Pic St Loup** CH Fontanès, Mas Gourdou, Mas Peyrolle.

l'Obediencerie named for historic HQ (worth a visit), up to GRANDS CRUS. Also Mas La Chevalière in L'DOC.

Latour, Louis Burg r w ★★→★★★★ Famous traditional family grower/merchant making full-bodied whites from C D'O v'yds (esp CORTON-CHARLEMAGNE), Mâconnais, Ardèche (all CHARD) while reds are looking classier – CORTON, ROMANÉE-ST-VIVANT. Also owns Henry Fessy in BEAUJ.

Latricières-Chambertin C d'O r ★★★★ 90' 93 96' 99' 02' 03 05' 06 07 08 09' 10' 11 12' 13 14 15' 16 (17) GRAND CRU next to CHAMBERTIN, rich if not quite as intense. Does well in warm dry yrs. Best: Arnoux, BIZE, Drouhin-Laroze, Duband, FAIVELEY, LEROY, Remy, ROSSIGNOL-TRAPET, TRAPET.

Laudun S Rh r p w ★ →★★ 15 16' 17' Sound CÔTES DU RH-VILLAGE, w bank. Excellent, fresh, dashing whites. Early, red fruit/peppery reds (lots of SYRAH), lively rosés. Immediate flavours from CHUSCLAN-Laudun co-op. *Dom Pelaquié* best esp elegant white. Also CHX Courac, de Bord, Juliette, St-Maurice; DOMS B Duseigneur (bio), Carmélisa, Maravilhas (bio, r w), Olibrius.

Laurent-Perrier Champ Important house; family presence less obvious, ripe for a change of ownership? BRUT NV (CHARD-led) still perfect apéritif. V.gd skin-contact Rosé. Fine vintages: 02 04 06 08 12. Grand Siècle CUVÉE multi-vintage on form, peerless Grand Siècle Alexandra Rosé 09. Ultra-Brut still needs improvement.

Leflaive, Dom Burg w ★★★★ Appointment of Pierre Vincent as winemaker will restore this cult PULIGNY-MONTRACHET DOM to v. top after slight wobble on death of Anne-Claude L. Steps being taken to restore longevity of great wines from GRANDS CRUS, incl LE MONTRACHET, CHEVALIER and *fabulous premiers crus*: Pucelles, Combettes, Folatières etc. MÂCON Verzé for value.

Leflaive, Olivier C d'O r w ★★ →★★★ White specialist NÉGOCIANT at PULIGNY-MONTRACHET. Smart wines of late, spot on with BOURGOGNE Les Setilles as with own GRAND CRU v'yds. Also La Maison d'Olivier, hotel, restaurant, tasting room.

Leroux, Benjamin C d'O r w ★★★ Former manager of COMTE ARMAND, now building reputation as BEAUNE-based NÉGOCIANT equally at home in red or white. Poised, honest wines. Try PREMIERS CRUS from CHASSAGNE, GEVREY, VOLNAY.

Leroy, Dom C d'O r w ★★★★ Lalou Bize Leroy, bio pioneer, delivers extraordinary quality from tiny yields ex-dom in VOSNE-ROMANÉE and from DOM d'Auvenay. Both fiendishly expensive even ex-dom. Amazing treasure house of mature wines from family NÉGOCIANT, Maison Leroy.

Liger-Belair, Comte C d'O r ★★★★ Comte Louis-Michel L-B makes brilliantly ethereal wines in VOSNE-ROMANÉE, an ever-increasing stable headed by monumental LA ROMANÉE. Try also village La Colombière, PREMIER CRU Reignots and NUITS-ST-GEORGES crus.

Liger-Belair, Thibault C d'O r ★★★→★★★★ New winery in NUITS-ST-GEORGES, for succulent bio burg from generics up to Les St-Georges and GRAND CRU RICHEBOURG. Also range of stellar old-vine single-v'yd MOULIN-À-VENT.

Lignier C d'O r w ★★★ Family in MOREY-ST-DENIS. Best is Hubert (eg. CLOS DE LA ROCHE), now managed by son Laurent. Class also from Virgile Lignier-Michelot, but still awaiting return to form at DOM Georges L.

Limoux L'doc r w ★★ Still wine AC to complement bubbly BLANQUETTE, CRÉMANT de Limoux. Obligatory oak-ageing for white, from CHARD, CHENIN, Mauzac, as varietal or blend. Red AC based on MERLOT, plus SYRAH, GRENACHE, CABS. PINOT N, illogically for a cool climate, only allowed in CRÉMANT and for IGP Haute Vallée de l'Aude. Growers: DOMS de Baronarques, de Fourn, Mouscaillo, RIVES-BLANQUES and Cathare, *Jean-Louis Denois*.

Lirac S Rh r p w ★★ 10' 12' 13 15' 16' 17' Four villages nr TAVEL, stony, quality soils. Spicy red (can live 5 yrs+), recent drive from new CHÂTEAUNEUF owners achieving clearer fruit, more flair. Reds best, esp DOMS *de la Mordorée* (best, r w), Carabiniers (bio), Duseigneur (bio), Giraud, Joncier (bio, character), Lafond Roc-Epine, La Lôyane, La Rocalière (gd fruit), Maby (Fermade, gd w), Marcoux (stylish), Plateau des Chênes; CHX de Bouchassy (gd w), de Manissy, de Montfaucon (v.gd w CÔTES DU RH), de Ségriès, Mont-Redon, St-Roch; Mas Isabelle (handmade), Rocca Maura, R Sabon. Whites project freshness, body, go 5 yrs.

Listrac-Médoc H-Méd r ★★→★★★ 05′ 06 08 09′ 10′ 11 12 14 **15** 16 Highest point in MÉD (43m)! Much-improved AC for savoury red B'x; now more fruit, depth and MERLOT. Growing number of gd whites under AC B'x. Best CHX: Cap Léon Veyrin, CLARKE, Ducluzeau, FONRÉAUD, Fourcas-Borie, FOURCAS-DUPRÉ, FOURCAS-HOSTEN, l'Ermitage, Mayne-Lalande, Reverdi, SARANSOT-DUPRÉ.

Long-Depaquit Chab w ★★★ Sound CHAB DOM with famous flagship brand, La Moutonne. Part of BICHOT empire.

Lorentz, Gustave Al w ★★→★★★ Grower/merchant at Bergheim. RIES is strength in GRANDS CRUS Altenberg de Bergheim, Kanzlerberg, age-worthy 10′ **12** 13 15 16 17. Young volume wines (esp GEWURZ) are well made. Fine organic Evidence Gewurz 09 11 16 17.

Lot SW Fr ★→★★ DYA. IGP of Lot département useful largely to growers (eg. CLOS DE GAMOT, DU CÈDRE) who make rosé and whites but whose AOP is limited to red. Also ★★DOMS Belmont, Sully, Tour de Belfort esp ★★CLOS d'Auxonne (nr Montcuq).

Loupiac B'x w SW ★★ 07 09′ 10′ 11 13 14 **15** 16 Minor SÉM-dominant *liquoreux*. Lighter, fresher than SAUT across River Garonne. Top CHX: CLOS Jean, Dauphiné-Rondillon, *de Ricaud*, Les Roques, Loupiac-Gaudiet, Noble.

Lubéron S Rh r p w ★→★★ 15′ 16′ **17′** Modish hilly appendix to S Rh; terroir is dry, no more than okay. Too many technical wines, low on soul. SYRAH lead role. Bright star: CH de la Canorgue. Also gd: DOM de la Citadelle, Fontenille, Le Novi (terroir); Chx Clapier, Edem, Fontvert (bio, gd w), O Ravoire, St-Estève de Neri (improving), Tardieu-Laurent (rich, oak), Marrenon, Val-Joanis and *La Vieille Ferme* (can be VIN DE FRANCE).

Lussac-St-Émilion B'x r ★★ 08 09′ 10′ 12 14 **15** 16 Lightest of the ST-ÉM satellites; variable quality, fair prices. Top CHX: Barbe Blanche, Bel Air, Bellevue, Courlat, DE LUSSAC, La Grenière, La Rose-Perrière, Le Rival, LYONNAT, Mayne-Blanc.

Macération carbonique Traditional fermentation technique: whole bunches of unbroken grapes in a closed vat. Fermentation inside each grape eventually bursts it, giving vivid, fruity, mild wine, not for ageing. Esp in BEAUJ, though not for best wines; now much used in the Midi and elsewhere, even CHÂTEAUNEUF.

Macle, Dom Jura ★★★ Legendary producer of CH-Chalon VIN JAUNE for long ageing.

Mâcon Burg r (p) w DYA. Simple, juicy GAMAY reds and most basic rendition of Mâconnais whites from CHARD.

Mâcon-Villages Burg w ★★ **14′** 15 16 (17) Chief appellation for Mâconnais whites. Individual villages may also use their own names eg. Mâcon-Lugny. Co-ops at Lugny, TERRES SECRETES, Viré for best prices, plus quality growers Guffens-Heynen, Guillot, Guillot-Broux, LAFON, LEFLAIVE, Maillet, Merlin.

Macvin Jura From se France, not Scotland. Grape juice is fortified by local marc to make a sweet apéritif between 16–22% alc. Most Jura producers make one.

Organics in the Languedoc wind

Climatic conditions in L'DOC, esp the drying winds, favour organic viticulture, making it the biggest area in France for organics: 21,910 ha, or 9.4 per cent of total v'yd, is organic, with 1301 growers. Some ACS more organic than others: TERRASSES DU LARZAC boasts 65 per cent of producers, FAUGÈRES 50, ST-CHINIAN 21. Some growers work organically but do not register, finding it too expensive to pay an annual fee/ha, or want freedom to spray if necessary.

FRANCE

Madiran SW Fr r ★★→★★★ 12' **13** 14 15' 16 17 Gascon AOP. Mainspring of TANNAT grape. Growers face two ways: dark, traditional tannic style, and fruitier, easier-to-sell. Worth confronting the tannins. ★★★DOMS Berthoumieu (recently sold), Capmartin, CLOS Basté, Damiens, Dou Bernés, Labranche-Laffont, Laffont, Laffitte-Teston, *Laplace*, Pichard (improving) and CH de Gayon are giving front-runners Chx BOUSCASSÉ, *Montus*, gd marks for money. ★★Barréjat, ★★Crampilh, Maouries not far behind.

Madura, Dom la L'doc r w ★★★ Ex-*régisseur* of B'X CH FIEUZAL created own estate in ST-CHINIAN. Stylish Classique, Grand Vin. White an original blend of SAUV BL/PICPOUL.

Mailly Grand Cru Champ Top co-op, all GRAND CRU grapes in multiple orientations. Prestige CUVÉE des *Echansons* 02 04 08' 12 for long ageing. Sumptuous Echansons Rosé 09, refined, classy L'Intemporelle 02 04 06 08' 12'. Sébastien Moncuit, cellarmaster since 2014, a rising star.

Maire, Henri Jura r w sw ★ Former legend, creator of Vin Fou, still a huge producer, mostly from own v'yds, sometimes using DOM names eg. Sobief, Bregand, or supermarket brand Auguste Pirou. At best sound.

Mann, Albert Al r w ★★→★★★ Top grower at Wettolsheim: rich, elegant. V.gd AUXERROIS, ace range of GRANDS CRUS: HENGST, SCHLOSSBERG, Steingrubler. Great red PINOT N Les Stes Claires in 15. Immaculate bio v'yds.

Maranges C d'O r (w) ★★ 05' 09' 10' 12 **13 14** 15' 16 (17) Robust well-priced reds from s end of CÔTE DE BEAUNE. Try PREMIERS CRUS Boutière, Croix Moines, Fussière. Best: BACHELET-Monnot, Chevrot, Contat-Grangé, Giroud, MOREAU.

Marcillac SW Fr r p ★★ AOP known for vivid sharpish reds. Nr-varietals (Mansois, aka FER SERVADOU) from AVEYRON. Best at 3 yrs. For fans, as gd with strawberries as with charcuterie or bangers and mash. ★★Co-op (eg. single DOM de Ladrecht) works alongside ★★DOMS Costes, du Cros, largest independent grower (gd w IGPS too), Vieux Porche; ★de l'Albinie (adds CAB SAUV), Mioula.

Margaux H-Méd r ★★→★★★★ 04 05' 06 08 09' **10' 11** 12 14 15 16 MÉD communal AC famous for elegant, fragrant wines. Reality is diversity of style. Top CHX: BOYD-CANTENAC, BRANE-CANTENAC, DAUZAC, DU TERTRE, FERRIÈRE, GISCOURS, ISSAN, KIRWAN, LASCOMBES, MALESCOT-ST-EXUPÉRY, MARGAUX, PALMER, RAUZAN-SÉGLA. Gd-value chx: ANGLUDET, Haut Breton Larigaudière, LABÉGORCE, Paveil de Luze, SIRAN.

Marionnet, Henry Lo r w ★★★ 14' 15' 16 17 Adventurous, original e-TOURAINE 60-ha DOM incl ungrafted v'yds, now run by son Jean-Sebastién. SAUV BL (top CUVÉE L'Origine), GAMAY, Provignage (Romorantin planted 1850), La Pucelle de Romorantin, Renaissance. Managing historic v'yd at CH de Chambord (1st vintage 2018).

Marmande SW Fr r p (w) ★ →★★ (r) 14' 15' 16 17 Fashionable ★★★Elian da Ros leads way at this improving Gascon AOP, where rare Abouriou grape a virtual exclusivity. ★★CH de Beaulieu SYRAH-based. ★★DOMS Beyssac, Bonnet, Cavenac and Ch Lassolle blend Abouriou with B'x grapes. Merged co-ops still dull.

Marsannay C d'O r p (w) ★★→★★★ (r) 09' 10' 12' **13** 14 15' (17) Most n AOC of CÔTE DE NUITS, hoping to get PREMIERS CRUS (eg. CLOS du Roy, Longeroies, Champ Salomon). Accessible, crunchy, fruit-laden reds, eg. Audoin, Bart, Bouvier, Charlopin, CLAIR, Fournier, *Pataille*, TRAPET. V.**gd** rosé needs 1–2 yrs; whites less exciting.

Mas, Doms Paul L'doc r p w ★★★ Highly ambitious big player; 650 ha of own estates, controls 1312 ha from Grès de Montpellier to ROUSS. Based nr Pézenas. Mainly IGP. Innovative marketing. Esp known for Arrogant Frog range; also La Forge, Les Tannes, Les VIGNES de Nicole and DOMS Ferrandière, Crès Ricards in TERRASSES DU LARZAC, Martinolles in LIMOUX and CH Lauriga in ROUSS. Côté Mas brand from Pézenas. Working on organics and low sulphur.

Mas Bruguière L'doc ★★★ Successful family estate in PIC ST-LOUP; Xavier talented 7th generation. L'Arbouse, La Grenadière and Le Septième.

Mas de Daumas Gassac L'doc r p w ★★★ 05 06 07 **08 09 10 11 12** 13 14 15 16 17 Set new standards in Midi with CAB-based age-worthy reds from apparently unique soil. Quality now surpassed by others. Also *perfumed white* from CHENIN and several others; super-*cuvée Émile Peynaud* (r); rosé Frizant. Delicious sweet Vin de Laurence (MUSCAT/SERCIAL). Now competent 2nd generation.

Mas Jullien L'doc ★★★ Early TERRASSES DU LARZAC leader maintaining reputation. Focus on Carignan Bl, CHENIN BL for white. Red: Autour de Jonquières, Carlan, Etats d'Ame, Lous Rougeos from L'DOC varieties.

Massif d'Uchaux S Rh r ★★ 15' 16' **17'** Gd Rh village, brightly fruited, spiced reds, not easy to sell, but best true, stylish. NB: CH St Estève (incl gd VIOGNIER), DOMS **Cros de la Mûre** (character, gd value), de la Guicharde, La Cabotte (bio, on top form), Renjarde (polished fruit).

Maury Rouss r sw ★★→★★★ Reputation est on sweet VDN GRENACHES Noir, BLANC, Gris, grown on island of schist. Now characterful dry red, AC Maury SEC prompted by recent improvements, led by **Mas Amiel**. New estates incl **Dom of the Bee**; Jones. Sound co-op. **Venerable old Rancios** v. rewarding esp with chocolate.

Mazis- (or Mazy-) Chambertin C d'O r ★★★★ 90' **93 96'** 99' 02' **03** 05' 06 07 08 09' 10' **11** 12' 13 14 15' 16' (17) GRAND CRU of GEVREY-CHAMBERTIN, top class in upper part; intense, *heavenly wines*. Best: Bernstein, DUGAT-Py, FAIVELEY, HOSPICES DE BEAUNE, LEROY, Maume-Tawse, MORTET, ROUSSEAU.

Mazoyères-Chambertin C d'O ★★★★ Can be sold as CHARMES-CHAMBERTIN, but more growers now labelling M as such. Try DUGAT-Py, LEROUX, Perrot-Minot, Taupenot-Merme.

Médoc B'x r ★★ **05' 06 08** 09' 10' **11** 14 15 **16** AC for reds in nr-flat n part of MÉD peninsula (aka Bas-Méd). Often more guts than grace. Many growers, so be selective. Top CHX: Bournac, CLOS Manou, d'Escurac, Fontis, **Goulée**, GREYSAC, **La Tour-de-By**, LES ORMES-SORBET, LOUDENNE, Lousteauneuf, PATACHE D'AUX, POITEVIN, **Potensac**, PREUILLAC, Ramafort, Rollan-de-By (HAUT-CONDISSAS), TOUR HAUT-CAUSSAN, TOUR ST-BONNET, Vieux Robin.

Meffre, Gabriel S Rh r w ★★→★★★ Consistent S Rh merchant, owns gd GIGONDAS DOM Longue Toque. Fruit quality up, less oak. Also CHÂTEAUNEUF (gd St-Théodoric, also small doms), VACQUEYRAS St Barthélemy. Reliable to gd S/N Rh Laurus (new oak, gd 15) range esp CONDRIEU, HERMITAGE (w), ST-JOSEPH.

Mellot, Alphonse L'doc r w ★★→★★★★★ 05 08' 09' 10' 12' 14' **15' 16'** (17) Impeccable SANCERRE (r w), bio, incl La Moussière (r w), CUVÉE Edmond, Génération XIX (r w); gd single v'yds incl **Satellite** (r): Demoiselle, En Champs; Les Pénitents (Côtes de La Charité IGP) CHARD, PINOT N. Alphonse Jnr now fully in charge.

Menetou-Salon Lo r p w ★★→★★★ 10' 11 12 14' **15'** (17') AOP 561 ha (376 w, 185 r) Nr SANCERRE; similar SAUV BL from e/w v'yds. 2017 gd quality and volume. Some fine reds (PINOT N). Best: BOURGEOIS, **Clement** (Chatenoy), Gilbert (bio, gd r), **Henry Pellé** (gd r), Jacolin, Jean-Max Roger, Teiller, Tour St-Martin.

Méo-Camuzet C d'O r w ★★★★ Noted DOM in VOSNE-ROMANÉE: icons Brûlée, Cros Parantoux, RICHEBOURG. Value from M-C Frère et Soeur (NÉGOCIANT branch) and plenty of choice in between. Sturdy, oaky wines that age well.

Merande, Ch de Sav r ★★ Top producer delivers lasting MONDEUSE red (**12'**): violets, spices, black fruits, saline finish of a great v'yd. Value.

Mercurey Burg r (w) ★★→★★★ 09' 10' 12 **13 14 15'** 16 (17) Leading village of CÔTE CHALONNAISE, mostly muscular reds, improving whites, value. Try CH de Chamirey, de Suremain, FAIVELEY, Juillot-Theulot, Lorenzon, M Juillot, Raquillet.

Mesnil-sur-Oger, Le Champ ★★★★ Top Côte des Blancs village, v. long-lived CHARD. Best: André Jacquart-Doyard, Pierre Péters, JL Vergnon (till 17), KRUG CLOS du Mesnil. Needs 10 yrs ageing.

Méthode Champenoise Champ Traditional method of putting bubbles into CHAMP

FRANCE

by refermenting wine in its bottle. Outside Champ region, makers must use terms "classic method" or *méthode traditionnelle*.

Meursault C d'O (r) w ★★★ →★★★★ 02' 04 05' 07' 08 09' 10' 11 **12 13** 14' 15 16 (17) Potentially great full-bodied whites from PREMIERS CRUS: Charmes, Genevrières, Perrières, more nervy from hillside v'yds *Narvaux*, Tesson, *Tillets*. Producers: Boisson-Vadot, M BOUZEREAU, V Bouzereau, Boyer-Martenot, CH DE MEURSAULT, COCHE-DURY, de Cherisey, Ente, Fichet, GIRARDIN, *Javillier*, JOBARD, *Lafon*, Latour-Labille, Matrot, Mikulski, *P Morey*, Potinet-Ampeau, PRIEUR, *Roulot*. *See also* BLAGNY.

Meursault, Ch de C d'O r w ★★★ Huge strides lately at this 61-ha estate of big-biz Halley family: decent red from BEAUNE, POMMARD, VOLNAY. Now world-class white, mostly MEURSAULT, also v.gd BOURGOGNE BLANC, PULIGNY PREMIER CRU.

Minervois L'doc r (p) (w) ★★ **10 11 12 13** 14 15 16 17 Hilly AC region, one of L'DOC's best. CRU La Livinière (potential AC) has stricter selection, lower yield, longer ageing. Characterful, savoury reds esp CHX Coupe-Roses, La Grave, La Tour Boisée, Oupia, St-Jacques d'Albas, Villerembert-Julien; *Abbaye de Tholomiès*, Borie-de-Maurel, *Ch de Gourgazaud*, CLOS Centeilles, Combe Blanche, DOM l'Ostal Cazes, Laville-Bertrou, Maris, *Ste Eulalie*. *Gros and Tollot* (from Burg) raising bar. Potential new crus Cazelles, Laure.

Miquel, Laurent L'doc ★★ 200 ha v'yds in CORBIÈRES (Les Auzines) and ST-CHINIAN (Cazal Viel). Unusual in specializing in aromatic whites, IGP VIOGNIER, now adventurous ALBARIÑO too. Own v'yds plus NÉGOCIANT activity, with Solas, Vendanges Nocturnes, Nord Sud.

Mis en bouteille au château / domaine Bottled at CH, property, or estate. NB: *dans nos* CAVES (in our cellars) or *dans la région de production* (in the area of production) often used but mean little.

Riquewihr in Al can boast 90 per cent of soil types found in the world.

Moët & Chandon Champ By far largest CHAMP house, impressive quality for such a giant. New mega-winery at Gyé-sur-Seine devoted to rosé in volume to meet world demand (*see* AUBE). Fresher, less sweet BRUT Imperial NV continues to improve. New rare prestige CUVÉE MCIII "solera" concept aimed at rich technophiles, addicts of exclusiveness. Better value in run of Grand Vintages Collection, long lees-aged: 90 **02**, new sumptuous, elegant 09 08 a little severe. Branches across Europe and New World. *See also* DOM PÉRIGNON.

Monbazillac SW Fr w sw ★★ →★★★ 09 **10 11'** 12 14' 15 BERGERAC sub-AOP: ★★★★*Tirecul-la-Gravière* worthy challenge to best SAUTERNES. Well up there too ★★★CLOS des Verdots, L'Ancienne Cure, Les Hauts de Caillavel and co-op's *Ch de Monbazillac*. ★★CHX de Belingard-Chayne, Grande Maison, Haut-Theulet, Pécoula, de Rayre, Theulet will not disappoint.

Mondeuse Sav r w ★★ SAVOIE grape and wine. Both white and red varieties. Red in Arbin, BUGEY, Chignin, etc. Best can age.

Monopole A v'yd that is under single ownership.

Montagne-St-Émilion B'x r ★★ **08** 09' 10' 12 14 15 **16** Largest satellite of ST-ÉM. Solid reputation. Top CHX: Beauséjour, Calon, Croix Beauséjour, Faizeau, La Couronne, Maison Blanche, Montaiguillon, Roudier, Teyssier, Tour Bayard, Vieux Bonneau, *Vieux Ch St-André*.

Montagny Burg w ★★ 14' 15 16 (17) CÔTE CHALONNAISE village with crisp whites, mostly in hands of CAVE de BUXY but gd NÉGOCIANTS too, incl JM BOILLOT, JM PILLOT, O LEFLAIVE. Best local growers incl Feuillat-Juillot, S Aladame.

Montcalmès, Dom L'doc ★★★ Talented brother/sister team in TERRASSES DU LARZAC. White AC from MARSANNE/ROUSSANNE, plus pure CHARD and intriguing blend VIN DE FRANCE. Stylish blends of SYRAH/GRENACHE/MOURVÈDRE, plus varietal Grenache and AC L'DOC Le Geai based on Grenache.

Monthélie C d'O r (w) ★★→★★★ 05' 09' 10' **11** 12 14 15' 16 (17) Pretty reds, grown uphill from VOLNAY, but a touch more rustic. Les Duresses is best PREMIER CRU. Try BOUCHARD PÈRE & FILS, *Ch de Monthélie* (Suremain), *Coche-Dury*, Darviot-Perrin, Florent Garaudet, LAFON.

Montille, de C d'O r w ★★★ Dense, spicy, whole-bunch reds from BEAUNE, VOLNAY (esp Taillepieds), POMMARD (Rugiens), CÔTE DE NUITS (Malconsorts) and exceptional whites from MEURSAULT plus outstanding PULIGNY-MONTRACHET Caillerets. Also runs mini-NÉGOCIANT Deux Montille (w) and improving CH de Puligny.

Montlouis sur Loire Lo w dr sw sp ★★→★★★ 89' 02 05' 08' 09 10' 11 14' 15 **16** (17) Dynamic sister AC (450 ha) to VOUVRAY, S side of Lo, CHENIN BL; 55 per cent sparkling incl Pétillant Originel. 2016/17 (frost) helicopters to combat (17). Top: Berger, BLOT, CHANSON, CHIDAINE, Delecheneau, Jousset, Merias, Moyer, Saumon, *Taille-aux-Loups*, Vallée Moray, Weisskopf.

Montpeyroux L'doc ★★→★★★ Lively village within TERRASSES DU LARZAC with growing number of talented growers. Aspiring to cru status. Try: CHABANON, DOM D'AUPILHAC, Villa Dondona. Newcomers: Joncas, Mas d'Amile. Serious co-op.

Montrachet (or Le Montrachet) C d'O w ★★★★ 92' 93 96' 99 00' 01 02' 04 05' 06 07 08 09' **10 11** 12 13 14' 15 (17) GRAND CRU v'yd in both PULIGNY- and CHASSAGNE-MONTRACHET. Potentially much the greatest white burg: perfumed, intense, dry yet luscious. Top: BOUCHARD, DRC, LAFON, LAGUICHE (DROUHIN), LEFLAIVE, Ramonet.

Montravel SW Fr p w dr ★★ (r) 12' **14** 15' 16 17 (p w) DYA. Sub-AOP of BERGERAC. Oaked MERLOT obligatory for modern reds from ★★★DOMS de Bloy, de Krevel; ★★CHX Jonc Blanc, Laulerie, Masburel, Masmontet, Moulin-Caresse; ★★dry white and rosé from same and other growers. *See also* CÔTES DE MONTRAVEL for off-dry, HAUT-MONTRAVEL for stickies.

Montus, Ch SW Fr r w ★★★ 04 05' 09' 10' 11 12' 14 15' 17 Patient MADIRAN-lovers happy to wait 7 yrs or more for ALAIN BRUMONT's all-TANNAT well-oaked red. Classy sweet and dry white barrel-raised PACHERENCS DU VIC-BILH (drink at 4 yrs+) on same level.

Moreau Burg r w ★★→★★★ Widespread family in CHAB esp *Dom Christian M* (try CLOS des Hospices) and DOM M-Naudet. Other Moreau families in CÔTE DE BEAUNE esp Bernard M for vigorous CHASSAGNE and David M in SANTENAY.

Morey, Doms C d'O r w ★★★ VIGNERON family in CHASSAGNE-MONTRACHET esp Caroline and husband Pierre-Yves, Colin-M, Jean-Marc (Chenevottes), Marc (Virondot), Thomas (fine, stony Baudines), Vincent (Embrazées, plumper style), Michel M-Coffinet (LA ROMANÉE). Also Pierre M in MEURSAULT for Perrières and BÂTARD-MONTRACHET.

Morey-St-Denis C d'O (w) ★★★→★★★★ 90' 93 96' 99' 02' 03 05' 06 07 08 09' 10' 11 12' 13 14 15' 16' (17) Terrific source of quality red burg, to rival neighbours GEVREY-CHAMBERTIN, CHAMBOLLE-MUSIGNY. GRANDS CRUS CLOS DE LA ROCHE, CLOS DE LAMBRAYS, CLOS DE TART, CLOS ST DENIS. And many gd producers: Amiot, ARLAUD, Castagnier, CLOS DE TART, *Clos des Lambrays*, Dujac, Jeanniard, H LIGNIER, LIGNIER-Michelot, Perrot-Minot, PONSOT, Remy, *Roumier*, Taupenot-Merme.

Morgon Beauj r ★★★ 09' 11' 12 13 14 15' 16 (17) Powerful BEAUJ cru, volcanic slate of Côte du Py makes meaty, age-worthy wine, clay of Les Charmes for earlier, smoother drinking. Javernières v'yd combines both. Try Burgaud, CH de Pizay, *Ch des Lumières* (JADOT), Desvignes, Foillard, Gaget, Goddard, LAPIERRE, Piron, Sunier.

Mortet, Denis C d'O r ★★★→★★★★ Arnaud Mortet on song with powerful yet refined reds from BOURGOGNE Rouge to CHAMBERTIN. Key wines GEVREY-CHAMBERTIN Mes Cinq Terroirs, PREMIERS CRUS Lavaut St-Jacques, Champeaux. From 2016 separate range under Arnaud M label.

Moueix, J-P et Cie B'x Libourne-based NÉGOCIANT and proprietor named after legendary founder. Son Christian runs company with his son Edouard. CHX: BELAIR-MONANGE, CLOS La Madeleine (from 2017), HOSANNA, LA FLEUR-PÉTRUS, LATOUR-À-POMEROL, TROTANOY. Distributes PETRUS. Also in California (*see* DOMINUS ESTATE).

Moulin-à-Vent Beauj r ★★★ 05′ 09′ 10′ 11′ 12 14 15′ 16 (17) Grandest BEAUJ cru, transcending the GAMAY grape. Weight, spiciness of Rh but matures towards rich, gamey PINOT flavours. Increasing interest in single-v'yd bottlings from eg. CH du Moulin-à-Vent, DOM La Bruyère, JADOT's Ch *des Jacques*, Janin (CLOS Tremblay), Janodet, LIGER-BELAIR (Les Rouchaux), Louis BOILLOT, Merlin (La Rochelle).

Moulis H-Méd r ★★→★★★ 04 05′ 06 08 09′ 10′ 11 12 14 15 16 Tiny inland AC w of MARGAUX, with some honest, gd-value wines. Top CHX: Anthonic, Biston-Brillette, BRANAS GRAND POUJEAUX, BRILLETTE, *Chasse-Spleen*, Dutruch Grand Poujeaux, Garricq, *Gressier Grand Poujeaux*, MAUCAILLOU, Maucamps Barton, *Poujeaux*.

Moutard Champ Quirky Aubois CHAMP house attached to old local grapes, incl PINOT BL and esp boudoirish Arban(n)e. Quality greatly improved by current Moutard, François. Fine CUVÉE des Six CÉPAGES 02 04 06 09 10 12 14′ 15 17.

Mugneret C d'O r w ★★★→★★★★ VIGNERON family in VOSNE-ROMANÉE. Sublime, stylish wines from Georges M-Gibourg (esp ÉCHÉZEAUX), also Gérard M, Dominique M and DOM Mongeard-M.

Mugnier, J-F C d'O r w ★★★★ Outstanding grower of CHAMBOLLE-MUSIGNY *Les Amoureuses* and *Musigny*. Finesse not muscle equally at home with MONOPOLE NUITS-ST-GEORGES CLOS de la Maréchale.

Mumm, GH & Cie Champ Cordon Rouge NV; fine BRUT Sélection; Mumm de Cramant reborn as BLANC DE BLANCS NV (just as gd); Cordon Rouge 02 04 06′ 08 09 12′ 15′; Rosé NV. Major house of Pernod-Ricard. Ongoing rise in quality, esp terroir CUVÉES called Mumm RSVR: Mumm de Verzenay BLANC DE NOIRS 08 12′, RSVR Blanc de Blancs 12. *See also* California.

Muscadet Lo w ★★ 14′ 15′ 16 17 Popular, bone-dry wine from nr Nantes. 8200 ha in total. Ideal with fish, seafood. Still often great value. Best SUR LIE. Choose zonal ACS: *see* following entries. Growers' woes continue in 2017: severe frost in parts, others barely touched. Small crops since 2012. Impressive MUSCADET CRUS COMMUNAUX.

Muscadet-Coteaux de la Loire Lo w ★→★★ 15 16 17 Small (150 ha, 40 growers), MUSCADET zone e of Nantes. Esp Guindon, Landron-Chartier, La Pléiade, Ponceau, Quarteron, VIGNERONS de la Noëlle.

Muscadet Côtes de Grand Lieu Lo ★→★★★ 14′ 15 16 17 MUSCADET zonal AOP (230 ha, 30 growers) by Atlantic. Best SUR LIE: Eric Chevalier, Herbauges (107 ha), Haut-Bourg, Malidain. Frost: 2016, 17 (quarter lost).

Muscadet Crus Communaux Lo ★★→★★★ MUSCADET's new top category. Long lees ageing from specified sites, startlingly gd, complex wines. 1st three communes ratified (2011): Clisson, Gorges, Le Pallet. 2018 (?) Goulaine, Monnières-St Fiacre, Mouzillon-Tillières. Later: Champtoceaux, La Haye Fouassière, Vallet.

Muscadet-Sèvre-et-Maine Lo ★→★★★ 05′ 06 09′ 10 12 14′ 15 16 (17) Largest (5890 ha) and best MUSCADET zone. Increasingly gd and great value. Top: Bonnet-Huteau, CH Briacé, Caillé, *Chereau Carré*, Cormerais, Delhommeau, Douillard, DOM DE L'ECU, Dom de la Haute Fevrie, *Gadais*, Gunther-Chereau, Huchet, Landron, Lieubeau, Luneau-Papin, Métaireau, Olivier, *Sauvion*. Can age a decade. Try CRUS COMMUNAUX. Parts badly frosted 2016, 17.

Muscat de Frontignan L'doc sw ★★ NV Small AC outside Sète for MUSCAT VDN. Also late-harvest, unfortified, oak-aged IGP wines. Leader remains CH la Peyrade. Delicious with blue cheese. Nearby Muscat de Lunel (DOM du CLOS de Bellevue) and Muscat de Mireval (Dom de la Rencontre) v. similar.

Muscat de Rivesaltes Rouss w sw ★★ Sweet grapey fortified MUSCAT VDN AC from large area centred on town of Rivesaltes. Muscat SEC IGP increasing as demand

> Muscadet grows old gracefully
> Everyone looks for latest vintage of MUSCADET, but top Muscadets (top producers, gd vintages esp with long lees-ageing) can last and improve 20 yrs+, ending up not unlike old CHAB. Look for newly coined CRU COMMUNAUX: Clisson, Gorges, Le Pallet, with Goulaine, CH-Thébaud, Monnières-St-Fiacre, Mouzillon-Tillières waiting in wings (long lees-ageing, greater complexity). Plus: Bonnet-Huteau, Bruno Cormerais, CH de la Gravelle (Gunther Chereau), Daniel Rineau, DOM DE L'ECU (Frédéric Niger van Herck/Guy Bossard), DOM Michel Brégeon, Jérémie Huchet, Jérémie Mourat, Jo Landron, Les VIGNERONS du Pallet, Luneau-Papin, Marc Ollivier (Dom de la Pépière), Vincent Caillé (Le Faye d'Homme).

for sweet VDN declines. Look for Corneilla for DOM CAZES, Treloar; Baixas co-op.

Muscat de St-Jean de Minervois L'doc w sw ★★ Tiny AC for fresh, honeyed VDN MUSCAT. Try DOM de Barroubio, CLOS du Gravillas, Clos Bagatelle. Village co-op prefers dry Muscat.

Musigny C d'O r (w) ★★★★ 90' 91 93 95 96' 98 99' 01 02' 03 05' 06 08 09' 10' 11 12' 13 14 15' 16 (17) GRAND CRU in CHAMBOLLE-MUSIGNY. Can be most beautiful, if not most powerful, of all red burgs. Best: DE VOGÜÉ, DROUHIN, JADOT, LEROY, MUGNIER, PRIEUR, ROUMIER, VOUGERAIE.

Nature Unsweetened, esp for CHAMP: no dosage. Fine if v. ripe grapes, raw otherwise.

Négociant-éleveur Merchant who "brings up" (ie. matures) the wine.

Nerthe, Ch la S Rh r w ★★★ 89' 90' 95' 96' 98' 99' 00 01 03 04' 05' 06' 07' 09' 10' 11 12' 13 15 16 CHÂTEAUNEUF estate. Somewhat uninspiring these days. New winemaker has yet to make an impact. Hope springs eternal.

Noëllat C d'O r ★★★ Noted VOSNE-ROMANÉE family. Georges N making waves since 2010 and expanding fast, Michel N offers sound range. *See also* v. stylish HUDELOT-N in VOUGEOT.

Nuits-St-Georges C d'O r ★★→★★★★ 90' 93 96' 99' 02' 03 05' 06' 07 08 09' 10' 11 12' 13 14 15' 16 (17) Three parts to this major AC: Premeaux v'yds for elegance (various CLOS: de la Maréchale, des Corvées, des Forêts, St-Marc), centre for dense dark plummy wines (Cailles, Les St-Georges, Vaucrains) and n side for the headiest (Boudots, Cras, Murgers). Many fine growers: Ambroise, ARLOT, CATHIARD, Confuron, *Faiveley*, Gavignet, GOUGES, GRIVOT, J Chauvenet, Lechéneaut, LEROY, *Liger-Belair*, Machard de Gramont, Michelot, *Mugnier*, R CHEVILLON, *Rion*.

Ollier-Taillefer, Dom L'doc ★★★ Dynamic FAUGÈRES family estate. Delicious Allegro from VERMENTINO/ROUSSANNE (w); Collines (r p); Grand Rés (r) from old vines; oaked Castel Fossibus (r). New CUVÉE (r) Le Rêve de Noé, SYRAH/MOURVÈDRE blend.

Orléans Lo r p w ★ DYA. Small AC (88 ha) for white (chiefly CHARD), VIN GRIS, rosé, reds (PINOT N esp PINOT M) around Orléans (13 communes). Formerly famous for vinegar. Try: Deneufbourg, CLOS St Fiacre. 2016 frost forced co-op to close 2017.

Orléans-Clery Lo r ★ DYA. Separate micro-AOP (28 ha); five communes sw of Orléans at n limit for CAB FR, sandy soil. Try: CLOS St Fiacre, Deneufbourg.

Ostertag, Dom Al Bio DOM run with originality in prime RIES country. Ries Muenchberg exquisite 13, maybe also in 17'. Fine PINOT N Fronholtz 15 17.

Pacherenc du Vic-Bilh SW Fr w d r dw sw ★★ →★★★ AOP for MADIRAN's white cousins, based on GROS, PETIT MANSENG, sometimes Petit Courbu and local Aruffiac. Mostly same growers as Madiran but note too ★★CH Mascaaras. Dry DYA, but sweet, esp if oaked, can be kept.

Paillard, Bruno Champ ★★★→★★★★ Youngest major *grande marque*. Excellent BRUT Première CUVÉE NV, Rosé Première Cuvée; exquisite dry refined style esp in long-aged BLANC DE BLANCS *Rés Privée* 02, NPU 02. Bruno P heads LANSON-BCC and owns CH de Sarrin, Prov.

Palette Prov r p w ★★★ Tiny AC nr Aix-en-Prov. Characterful reds, mainly from MOURVÈDRE, GRENACHE, fragrant rosés, intriguing forest-scented whites. Traditional, serious *Ch Simone*; more innovative CH Henri Bonnaud.

Patrimonio Cors r p w ★★ →★★★ AC. Some of island's finest, from dramatic limestone hills in n CORS. Individual reds from NIELLUCCIO, intriguing whites, even *late-harvest*, from *Vermentino*. Top: Antoine Arena, CLOS de Bernardi, Gentile, Montemagni, Pastricciola, Yves Leccia at E Croce. Worth the journey.

Pauillac H-Méd r ★★★ →★★★★ 95' 96' **98** 00' **01** 02 03' 04' **05' 06** 08' **09'** 10' 11 **12 14 15** 16 17 Communal AC in n MÉD with 18 Classed Growths (90 per cent of AC) incl LAFITE, LATOUR, MOUTON. Famous for long-lived wines, the acme of CAB SAUV. Other top CHX: BATAILLEY, CLERC MILON, D'ARMAILHAC, DUHART-MILON, GRAND-PUY-LACOSTE, LYNCH-BAGES, PICHON-BARON, PICHON-LALANDE, PONTET-CANET.

Pays d'Oc, IGP L'doc r p w ★ →★★★ Largest IGP, covering whole of L'DOC-ROUSS. Focus on varietal wines; 58 different grapes allowed. ALBARIÑO latest addition, plus CARIGNAN as single varietal. Technical advances continue apace. Main producers: Jeanjean, DOMS PAUL MAS, GÉRARD BERTRAND, village co-ops. Extremes of quality; best are innovative, exciting.

Pécharmant SW Fr r ★★ **12' 14** 15' 16' 17 Biggest wines (keepers) from BERGERAC (inner AOP) benefit from iron and manganese in soil. Veteran ★★★*Ch de Tiregand*, DOM du Haut-Pécharmant, Les Chemins d'Orient; ★★CLOS des Côtes La Métairie, CHX Beauportail, Champarel, Corbiac, de Biran; Dom des Bertranoux, Ch du Rooy, Hugon, Terre Vieille.

Pélican, Dom du Jura Retired legend Jacques Puffeney's v'yds now run by VOLNAY's MARQUIS D'ANGERVILLE to make fine fresh styles. More to come...

Pernand-Vergelesses C d'O r w ★★★ (r) 99' 02' 03' 05' 08 09' 10' 11 12 13 14 15' (17) Village next to ALOXE-CORTON incl part of CORTON-CHARLEMAGNE, CORTON. Île des Vergelesses v'yd 1st-rate for red, elsewhere chiselled, precise whites. DOMS Rapet and Rollin lead the way but try also from CHANDON DE BRIAILLES, CHANSON, Dubreuil-Fontaine, JADOT.

Perrier-Jouët Champ BRUT NV; Blason de France NV; Blason de France Rosé NV; Brut 02 **04** 06 08. Fine new BLANC DE BLANCS. 1st (in C19) to make dry CHAMP for English market; strong in GRAND CRU CHARD, best for gd vintage and de luxe Belle Epoque 95 **04** 06 and new underrated 07 08' 12 15, Rosé 04 06, in painted bottle.

Pessac-Léognan B'x r w ★★★→★★★★ 00' **01 02 04** 05' **06 08** 09' **10' 11 12 14** 15 16 AC created in 1987 for best part of n GRAV, incl GRANDS CRUS: HAUT-BAILLY, HAUT-BRION, LA MISSION-HAUT-BRION, PAPE-CLÉMENT, etc. Firm, full-bodied, earthy reds; B'x's finest dry whites. Value from Brown, DE ROCHEMORIN, Haut-Vigneau, Lafont-Menaut, Le Sartre, Lespault-Martillac, Rouillac.

Petit Chablis Chab w ★ DYA. Fresh, easy, would-be CHAB from outlying v'yds not on kimmeridgian clay. LA CHABLISIENNE co-op is gd, but prices too close to real thing.

Pfaffenheim Al ★ →★★ Respectable AL co-op. Ripe, balanced wines from warm sites. Dopff & Irion, a once-famous house, now a brand of Pfaffenheim.

Pfersigberg Al GRAND CRU in two parcels; v. aromatic wines. GEWURZ does v. well. RIES from BRUNO SORG, LÉON BEYER (Comtes d'Eguisheim), Paul Ginglinger.

Philipponnat Champ Small house, intense, stylishly vinous at best, basic wines less gd. Now owned by LANSON-BCC group. NV, Rosé NV, BRUT 99 02, CUVÉE 1522 02, remarkable single-v'yd *Clos des Goisses* 85' 92 95 02 04, CHARD-led 08 12', late-disgorged vintage 90.

Picpoul de Pinet L'doc w ★ →★★ DYA. "MUSCADET of Midi". AC since 2013, Grand Vin du L'DOC, from PICPOUL grown around Pinet. Best producers experimenting in cellar to find greater depth. Best: Félines-Jourdan, La Croix Gratiot, St Martin de la Garrigue; co-ops Pinet, Pomérols. Fresh, salty, so perfect *with oysters*, but sadly can be victim of fashion, losing its typical sappy tang.

FRANCE

Pic St-Loup L'doc r (p) ★★→★★★ 11 12 13 14 15 16 17 Coolest, wettest part of L'DOC. Dramatic scenery. AC demands high proportion of SYRAH, plus GRENACHE, MOURVÈDRE. Reds for ageing; white potential considerable but still AC L'doc or IGP Val de Montferrand. Growers: Bergerie du Capucin, Cazeneuve, CLOS de la Matane, Clos Marie, de Lancyre, *Dom de l'Hortus*, Gourdou, Lascaux, MAS BRUGUIÈRE, Mas Peyrolle, Valflaunès.

Pierre-Bise, Ch Lo r p w ★★→★★★★ 03 05' 06 07' (sw) 08 09 10' 11 14' 15 16 (17) Impeccable DOM in COTEAUX DU LAYON, incl Chaume, QUARTS DE CHAUME, SAVENNIÈRES (*Clos de Grand Beaupréau*, ROCHE-AUX-MOINES). Excellent ANJOU-GAMAY, ANJOU-VILLAGES (both CUVÉE Schist, Spilite), Anjou Blanc Haut de la Garde. Patriarch Claude now semi-retired, son René in charge.

Pignier Jura r w sw sp ★★★ Bio producer in s Jura. Great range of fresher styles, eg. Sauvageon and lively reds, plus classics incl quality VIN JAUNE.

Pinon, François Lo w sw sp ★★★ 89 90 95 96 97 02 03 05 08 09 10' 11 14' 15' 16 (17) Excellent organic wines from Vernou, VOUVRAY. François now joined by son Julien.

Piper-Heidsieck Champ Historic house on surging wave of quality. Improved BRUT NV; new, dynamic Brut Essentiel with more age, less sugar, floral yet vigorous; great with sushi, sashimi. Piper Rare, made mainly in challenging vintages, shows precision, energy (98 99, glorious 02 08); 1st release of Rare Rosé 07.

Plageoles, Dom SW Fr r w sp GAILLAC Bernard Plageoles, rebel and purist, mentors growers in defence of true Gaillac style. Organic specialist in rare grapes ie. Ondenc (base of famous sweet ★★★★Vin d'Autan), ★★Prunelard (r, deep fruity), Verdanel (dr w, oak-aged) and countless sub-varieties of Mauzac. Try big spicy red from DURAS, lighter from FER SERVADOU (aka Braucol). *Brilliant dry sparkler* Mauzac Natur just as original.

Plan de Dieu S Rh r ★→★★ 10' 13 15' 16' 17' Rh village nr CAIRANNE with stony, windswept plain. Heady, robust, GRENACHE-inspired, authentic wines; drink with game, stews. Gd choice. Best: CH la Courançonne, CLOS St Antonin, LE PLAISIR; DOMS Aphillantes (character), Arnesque, Bastide St Vincent, Durieu (full), Espiguette, Longue Toque, Martin, Pasquiers, St-Pierre (gd traditional).

Pol Roger Champ Family-owned Épernay house. BRUT Rés NV excels, dosage lowered since 2012; ★★★Brut 02' 04 06 08, lovely 09 12'; Rosé 06 09; BLANC DE BLANCS 09. Fine *Pure Brut* (no dosage). Sumptuous CUVÉE Sir Winston Churchill 98. Always a blue-chip choice. Particularly gd in dry, challenging 15 (from 2024), Indian-summer 16.

Pomerol B'x r ★★★→★★★★ 98' 00' 01 04 05' 06' 08 09' 10' 11 12 14 15 16 Tiny, pricey AC bordering ST-ÉM; MERLOT-led, rich, voluptuous style, but long life. Top CHX on clay, gravel plateau: CLINET, HOSANNA, L'ÉGLISE-CLINET, L'ÉVANGILE, LA CONSEILLANTE, LAFLEUR, LA FLEUR-PÉTRUS, LE PIN, PETRUS, TROTANOY, VIEUX-CH-CERTAN. Occasional value (Bellegrave, BOURGNEUF, CLOS du Clocher, LA POINTE).

Pommard C d'O r ★★★(★) 90' 96' 98 99' 02' 03 05' 06 07 08 09' 10' 11 12 14 15' 16' (17) Antithesis of neighbour VOLNAY; potent, tannic wines to age 10 yrs+. Best v'yds: Rugiens for power, Epenots for grace. Growers: CH de Pommard, COMTE ARMAND, COURCEL, DE MONTILLE, HOSPICES DE BEAUNE, Huber-Vedereau, J-M BOILLOT, Lejeune, Parent, Pothier-Rieusset, Rebourgeon, Violot-Guillemard.

Pommery Champ Historic house; brand now owned by Vranken. BRUT NV steady bet; Rosé NV; Brut 04 08 09 12'. Once outstanding CUVÉE Louise 02 04 less striking recently. Supple Wintertime BLANC DE NOIRS.

Ponsot C d'O r w ★★→★★★★ Idiosyncratic, top-quality MOREY-ST-DENIS DOM, but all change in 2017. Laurent P left to set up on his own. Sister Rose-Marie now in charge. Key wines: *Clos de la Roche*, unique white PREMIER CRU Monts Luisants (ALIGOTÉ).

Pouilly-Fuissé Burg w ★★→★★★ 09' 10' 11 12 14' 15 16 (17) Top AC of MÂCON; potent, rounded but intense whites from around Fuissé, more mineral style by Vergisson. Enjoy young or with age. PREMIERS CRUS about to happen at long last! Top: Barraud, Bret, CH de Beauregard, CH DE FUISSÉ, Ch des Rontets, Cordier, Cornin, Drouin, Ferret, Forest, Merlin, Paquet, Robert-Denogent, Rollet, Saumaize, Saumaize-Michelin, Verget.

Pouilly-Fumé Lo w ★★→★★★ 05' 09' 10 12 14' 15' 16 (17') East-bank neighbour of SANCERRE. 1347 ha SAUV BL. Parts badly frosted 2016, 17. Best improve at least 8–10 yrs+. Growers: Bain, BOURGEOIS, Cailbourdin, Champeau, CH de Favray, Ch de Tracy, Chatelain, DIDIER DAGUENEAU, Edmond and André Figeat, Jean Pabiot, Jonathan Pabiot, LADOUCETTE, Masson-Blondelet, Redde, Saget, Serge Dagueneau & Filles, Tabordet, Treuillet.

Pouilly-Loché Burg w ★★ 14' 15 16 (17) Least known of Mâconnais's Pouilly family. Try CLOS des Rocs, Tripoz, Bret Bros gd, co-op dominant for volume.

Pouilly-sur-Loire Lo w ★★ DYA. In C19, Pouilly supplied Paris with CHASSELAS table grapes. Now only 27 ha remain; same zone as POUILLY-FUMÉ, more neutral wine. Upholding tradition: Gitton, Jonathan Pabiot, Landrat-Guyollot, Masson-Blondelet, Redde, Serge Dagueneau & Filles.

Wettest AOP in France is Irouléguy: c.1500mm (60in) p.a.

Pouilly-Vinzelles Burg w ★★ 12 14' 15 16 (17) Between POUILLY-LOCHÉ and POUILLY-FUISSÉ geographically and in quality. Outstanding v'yd: Les Quarts. Best: Bret Bros, DROUHIN, Valette. Volume from CAVE des GRANDS CRUS Blancs.

Premier Cru First Growth in B'X; 2nd rank of v'yds (after GRAND CRU) in Burg; 2nd rank in Lo: one so far, COTEAUX DU LAYON Chaume.

Premières Côtes de Bordeaux B'x w sw ★→★★ 10' 11 13 14 15 16 Same zone as CADILLAC-CÔTES DE B'X but for sweet whites only. SÉM-dominated *moelleux*. Generally early drinking. Best CHX: Crabitan-Bellevue, du Juge, Fayau, *Suau*.

Prieur, Dom Jacques C d'O ★★★ Major MEURSAULT estate also with range of GRANDS CRUS from MONTRACHET to MUSIGNY. Style aims at weight from late-picking and oak more than finesse. Owners Famille Labruyère also have CHAMP and MOULIN-À-VENT projects plus CH ROUGET, POM.

Prieuré St Jean de Bébian L'doc ★★★ Pézenas estate, once with all 13 grape varieties of CHÂTEAUNEUF-DU-PAPE, on similar soil. Now owned by Russians with talented Aussie winemaker. Three levels: La Chapelle, La Croix, Prieuré (r w); old-vines red 1152.

Primeur "Early" wine for refreshment and uplift; esp from BEAUJ; VDP too. Wine sold en primeur is still in barrel, for delivery when bottled.

Producteurs Plaimont SW Fr SW France's most successful co-op dominates Gascony, reviving forgotten Gascon grapes. Expanding into MADIRAN (acquiring independent DOMS), ST MONT (opening hotel in old abbey), CÔTES DE GASCOGNE. All colours, styles, mostly ★★, all tastes, purses.

Propriétaire récoltant Champ Owner-operator, literally owner-harvester.

Puisseguin St-Émilion B'x r ★★ 08 09' 10' 12 14 15 16 Most e of four ST-ÉM satellites; wines firm, solid. Co-op important. Top CHX: Beauséjour, Branda, Clarisse, DES LAURETS, de Môle, Durand-Laplagne, Fongaban, Guibot la Fourvieille, Haut-Bernat, La Mauriane, Le Bernat, Soleil.

Puligny-Montrachet C d'O (r) w ★★★→★★★★ 02' 04 05' 07 08 09' 10' 11 12 14' 15 16 (17) Should be most floral, fine-boned white burg. V'yds up hill fresh and mineral, richer and softer lower down. Band in middle best: Caillerets, Champ Canet, Combettes, Folatières, Pucelles alongside the MONTRACHET GRANDS CRUS. Producers: *J-M Boillot, Bouchard Père & Fils*, CARILLON, Chartron, CH de Puligny, *Dom Leflaive*, Drouhin, Ente, JADOT, *O Leflaive*, Pernot, *Sauzet*.

Puyméras S Rh r w ★ 15′ 16′ 17′ Respectable, secluded S Rh village, high, breezy v'yds, supple plum-fruited reds centred on GRENACHE, fair whites, decent co-op. Try CAVE la Comtadine, DOM du Faucon Doré (bio), Puy du Maupas.

Pyrénées-Atlantiques SW Fr Mostly DYA. IGP in Gascony and Béarn for wines not qualifying for local AOPS in far sw. Thus ★★★CH Cabidos (superb SWEET WHITE PETIT MANSENG will age), ★★DOM Moncaut (nr Pau), ★Brumont non-AOP varietals and blends. Otherwise pot luck.

Quarts de Chaume Lo w SW ★★★ ⇢★★★★ 89′ 90′ 95′ 96′ 97′ 03 05′ 07′ 10′ 11′ 14′ 15′ 16 (17) 40 ha, slopes close to Layon, CHENIN BL. Admirably strict rules must be enforced for GRAND CRU and price. Best richly textured. Esp Baudouin, Bellerive, Branchereau, CH PIERRE-BISE, FL, Guegniard, Ogereau, Pithon-Paillé, Suronde (bought by Minière, BOURGUEIL). Ignore 2012.

Quincy Lo w ★⇢★★ 14′ 15′ 16 (17) Revived AOP (296 ha, from 60 ha in 1990) SAUV BL from sand/gravel banks se of Vierzon; 1st Loire AC 1936. Growers: Mardon, Portier, Rouzé, Siret-Courtaud, Tatin-Wilk (DOMS Ballandors, Tremblay), Villalin.

Rancio Rouss Most original, lingering, delicious style of VDN, reminiscent of Tawny Port, or old Oloroso Sherry in BANYULS, MAURY, RASTEAU, RIVESALTES, wood-aged and exposed to oxygen, heat. Not to be missed. Same flavour (pungent, tangy) a fault in table wine.

Rangen Al Most s GRAND CRU of AL at Thann. Extremely steep (average 90%) slopes, volcanic soils. Top: majestic RIES ZIND-HUMBRECHT (CLOS St Urbain 05′ 08′ 10′ 17′), SCHOFFIT (St Theobald 08′ 10 17′). Extra finesse in 15.

La Table de la Bergerie: only Lo estate restaurant (Dom de la B) to win Michelin ★.

Rasteau S Rh r (p) (w) br (dr) sw ★★ 10′ 12′ 13 14′ 15′ 16′ 17′ Full-bore reds from clay soils, mainly GRENACHE. Best in hot yrs (09 10 15, 16, 17). NB: Beaurenard (serious, age well), *Cave Ortas* (gd), CH La Gardine, *Ch du Trignon*, Famille Perrin; DOMS Beau Mistral, Collière, Combe Julière, Coteaux des Travers (bio), Didier Charavin, Elodie Balme, Escaravailles, Girasols, Gourt de Mautens (talented, IGP wines from 2010), Grand Nicolet (character), Grange Blanche, Rabasse-Charavin, M Boutin, Soumade (polished), St Gayan, Trapadis. Grenache dessert VDN quality on the up (Doms Banquettes, Coteaux des Travers, Escaravailles, Trapadis).

Raveneau Chab w ★★★★ Along with DAUVISSAT cousins, greatest CHAB producers, using classic methods for *extraordinary long-lived wines*. Excellent value except in secondary market. Look for Blanchots, Les CLOS, Vaillons.

Rayas, Ch S Rh r w ★★★★ 78′ 79 81′ 85 86 88′ 89 90′ 93 94 95′ 96′ 98′ 99 00 01 03 04′ 05′ 06′ 07′ 08 09′ 10′ 11′ 12′ 13′ 14′ 15′ 16′ 17′ Wonderful, time-warp 13-ha CHÂTEAUNEUF estate, tiny yields. Pale, subtle, aromatic, sensuous reds (100% GRENACHE) inimitable, offer delight, age superbly. White Rayas (GRENACHE BL, CLAIRETTE) v.gd over 18 yrs+. Gd-value, elegant second wine: *Pignan*. Supreme CH Fonsalette CÔTES DU RH, incl marvellous SYRAH. Decant them all; each is an occasion. Also gd CH des Tours VACQUEYRAS (peppery), VDP.

Regnié Beauj r ★★ 14 15′ 16 17 Most recent BEAUJ cru, lighter wines on sandy soil, meatier nr MORGON. Try Burgaud, de la Plaigne, Dupré, Rochette, Sunier.

Reuilly Lo r p w ★ ⇢★★★ 10′ 14′ 15′ 16 (17) Revived AC (252 ha, from 30 ha in 1990) neighbour of QUINCY w of Bourges. SAUV BL (127 ha), rosés and *Vin Gris* from PINOT N (75 ha) and/or PINOT GR (50 ha). Some gd Pinot N (r). Best: Claude Lafond, *Jamain*, Mardon, Renaudat, Rouze, Sorbe. Wind machine: frost protection.

Riceys, Les Champ p ★★★ DYA. Key AC in AUBE for a notable PINOT N rosé. Producers: *A Bonnet*, Jacques Defrance, Morize. Great 09; v. promising 14 after lean period 2011–13; 15′ excels.

Richebourg C d'O r ★★★★ 90′ 93′ 95 96′ 98 99′ 00 02′ 03 05′ 06 07 08 09′ 10′ 11 12′ 13 14 15′ 16 (17) VOSNE-ROMANÉE GRAND CRU. Magical Burg with great depth of flavour; vastly expensive. Growers: DRC, GRIVOT, GROS, HUDELOT-NOËLLAT, LEROY, LIGER-BELAIR, MÉO-CAMUZET.

Rimage Rouss A growing mode: vintage VDN, super-fruity for drinking young. Think gd Ruby Port. Grenat is MAURY version.

Rion C d'O r (w) ★★ →★★★ Related DOMS in NUITS-ST-GEORGES, VOSNE-ROMANÉE. Patrice R for excellent Nuits CLOS St Marc, Clos des Argillières and CHAMBOLLE-MUSIGNY. Daniel R for Nuits and Vosne PREMIERS CRUS; Bernard R more Vosne-based. All fairly priced.

Rivesaltes Rouss r w br dr sw ★★ NV or solera, also vintage, young and old VDN from large area in n ROUSS. Grossly underappreciated; deserves revival. Long-lasting wines, esp RANCIOS. Look for: Boucabeille, des Chênes, des Schistes, DOM CAZES, Rancy, Roc des Anges, Sarda-Malet, Vaquer. You will not be disappointed.

Rives-Blanques, Ch L'doc sp w ★★★ LIMOUX. Irish-Dutch couple make BLANQUETTE and more recently CRÉMANT. Limoux white, incl blend Trilogie and age-worthy CHENIN BL Dédicace. Dessert Lagremas d'Aur.

Roche-aux-Moines, La Lo w sw ★★→★★★ 89' 90' 96' 02 03 05' 07 08' 09 10' 11 12 14' 15' 16 33 ha cru of SAVENNIÈRES, ANJOU. Low yields (30 hl/ha), age-worthy CHENIN BL. Try: aux Moines, *Ch Pierre-Bise*, CLOS de la Bergerie (Joly), FL, Forges, Laureau. Severe frost 2017.

Roederer, Louis Champ Peerless family-owned house/DOM. Enviable v'yds: upwards of 40 per cent bio. Flavour, finesse ★★★BRUT Premier NV; Brut 08 09, BLANC DE BLANCS 08' 09 13, Brut Saignée Rosé 09. Magnificent *Cristal* (probably greatest of prestige CUVÉES, 88' 02 08 09) and Cristal Rosé 02' 06. Superb Cristal Oenothèque 95 (best yr of decade.) Brut Nature Philippe Starck (all Cumières 2009). Also owns DEUTZ, PICHON-LALANDE. *See also* California.

Rolland, Michel Fashionable French consultant winemaker and MERLOT specialist (B'x and worldwide). Owner of FONTENIL in FRON. *See* Argentina (Clos de los Siete).

Rolly Gassmann Al w sw ★★★ Revered DOM esp Moenchreben v'yd. Off-dry, rich, sensuous GEWURZ CUVÉE Yves 08 09 11 12 15. New generation Pierre G into bio with more finesse. Mineral zesty RIES 13. Fine PINOT N 15 intense, gentle tannins.

Romanée, La C d'O r ★★★★ 02' 03 05' 06 07 08 09' 10' 11 12' 13 14 15' 16' (17) Tiniest GRAND CRU in VOSNE-ROMANÉE, MONOPOLE of Comte LIGER-BELAIR. Exceptionally fine, perfumed, intense and understandably expensive.

Romanée-Conti, La C d'O r ★★★★ 78' 85' 88' 89' 90' 93' 95 96' 98 99' 00 01 02' 03 05' 06 07 09' 10' 11 12' 13 14' 15' 16' (17) GRAND CRU in VOSNE-ROMANÉE, MONOPOLE of DRC. Most celebrated GRAND CRU in Burg, most expensive wine in world, and on fabulous form these days. But beware fakes.

Romanée-St-Vivant C d'O r ★★★★ 90' 93 95 96' 99' 02' 03 05' 06 07 08 09' 10' 11 12' 13 14 15' 16' (17) GRAND CRU in VOSNE-ROMANÉE. Downslope from LA ROMANÉE-CONTI, haunting perfume, delicate but intense. Ready a little earlier than famous neighbours. Growers: if you can't afford DRC or LEROY, or CATHIARD now, try ARLOT, Follin-Arbelet, HUDELOT-NOËLLAT, JJ Confuron, LATOUR, Poisot.

Rosacker Al GRAND CRU at Hunawihr. Limestone/clay makes some of longest-lived RIES in AL (CLOS STE-HUNE).

Rosé d'Anjou Lo p ★→★★ DYA. Rosé – off-dry to sweet (mainly Grolleau). Big AOP, 2084 ha, 280 producers. V. popular, usually well made. Look for: Clau de Nell, DOMS de la Bergerie, Grandes Vignes, Mark Angeli, Sablonnettes.

Rosé de Loire Lo p ★→★★ DYA. Driest of ANJOU's rosés: six grapes esp GAMAY, Grolleau. AC (1044 ha, 370 producers). Look for: Bablut, Bois Brinçon, Branchereau, Cady, CAVE de SAUMUR, CH PIERRE-BISE, Ogereau, Passavant, Richou, Soucherie.

Rosette SW Fr w s/sw ★★ AOP DYA. Birthplace of BERGERAC wines rediscovered as source of delicious off-dry apéritif whites. Producers to try: CLOS Romain, CHX Combrillac, de Peyrel, Monplaisir, Puypezat-Rosette, Spingulèbre; DOMS de

Coutancie, de la Cardinolle, du Grand-Jaure. Avoid oaked versions. Gd too with foie gras or mushrooms.

Rossignol-Trapet Burg r ★★★ Equally bio cousins of DOM TRAPET, with healthy holdings of GRAND CRU v'yds esp CHAMBERTIN. Gd value across range from GEVREY VIEILLES VIGNES up. Also some BEAUNE v'yds from Rossignol side.

Rostaing, Dom N Rh r w ★★★ 95′ 98′ 99′ 01′ 05′ 06′ 07′ **09′ 11 12′** 13′ 14 15′ 16′ 17′ High-quality CÔTE-RÔTIE DOM: five tightly bound wines, all v. fine, pure, precise, careful oak, wait 6 yrs, decant. Son Pierre started 2015. Complex, enticing, top-class Côte Blonde (5% VIOGNIER), Côte Brune (iron), also La Landonne (dark fruits, 15–20 yrs). Tangy, firm **Condrieu**, also L'DOC Puech Noble (r w).

Rouget, Emmanuel C d'O r ★★★★ Famous for Henri Jayer connection and CROS PARANTOUX but look out for ÉCHÉZEAUX, NUITS-ST-GEORGES, VOSNE-ROMANÉE, now that next generation is involved.

Roulot, Dom C d'O w ★★★→★★★★ Jean-Marc R leads outstanding MEURSAULT DOM, now cult status so beware secondary market prices. Great PREMIERS CRUS esp CLOS des Bouchères, Perrières; value from top village sites Luchets, Meix Chavaux, and esp Clos du Haut Tesson.

Roumier, Georges C d'O r ★★★★ Reference DOM for BONNES-MARES and other *brilliant Chambolle* wines in capable hands of Christophe R. Long-lived wines but still attractive early. Cult status means hard to find now at sensible prices.

Rousseau, Dom Armand C d'O r ★★★★ It's no secret that this unmatchable GEVREY-CHAMBERTIN DOM thrills with balanced, fragrant, refined, age-worthy wines from village to GRAND CRU, and esp CLOS ST-JACQUES.

Roussette de Savoie Sav w ★★ South of Lake Geneva. 100% ROUSSETTE. Ten per cent of SAVOIE wines. Can age. Try: de la Mar, Grisard, Maillet, Quenard.

Roussillon Highly individual Midi region, but often unfairly linked with L'DOC, and incl in AC L'doc. Original, traditional VDN (eg. BANYULS, MAURY, RIVESALTES). Younger vintage RIMAGE/Grenat now competing with aged RANCIO. Also serious age-worthy table wines (r w). *See* COLLIOURE, CÔTES DU ROUSS-VILLAGES, MAURY SEC and IGP CÔTES CATALANES.

Ruchottes-Chambertin C d'O r ★★★★ 90′ 93′ 95 96′ 99′ 00 02′ 03 05′ **06** 07 08 **09′** 10′ **11** 12′ 13 14 15′ 16 (17) Tiny GRAND CRU neighbour of CHAMBERTIN. Less weighty but ethereal, intricate, lasting wine of great finesse. Top growers: MUGNERET-Gibourg, ROUMIER, ROUSSEAU.

Ruinart Champ Oldest house (1729). High standards going higher still. Rich, elegant wines. "R" de Ruinart BRUT NV; Ruinart Rosé NV; "R" de Ruinart Brut 04 06 08. Prestige CUVÉE **Dom Ruinart** is one of two best vintage BLANC DE BLANCS in CHAMP (viz 90′ esp in magnum, '02 **04 08**). DR Rosé also v. special 98′. NV Blanc de Blancs much improved. High hopes for 13, classic cool lateish vintage. Dom R 06 great structure in delicate yr.

Rully Burg r w ★★ (r) 12 14′ 15′ **16** (17) (w) 14′ 15 16′ (17) CÔTE CHALONNAISE village. *Light, fresh, tasty, gd-value whites.* Reds all about the fruit, not structure. Try C Jobard, Devevey, DROUHIN, DUREUIL-JANTHIAL, FAIVELEY, Jacqueson, Ninot, Olivier LEFLAIVE, Rodet.

Sablet S Rh r (p) w ★★ 15′ 16′ 17′ Easy but also serious wines from improving CÔTES DU RH-VILLAGE. Sandy soils, trim red-berry reds esp CAVE co-op Gravillas, CH Cohola (organic), du Trignon, DOMS de Boisson (organic, full), Les Goubert (r w), Pasquiers (full), Piaugier (r w). *Gd full whites* for apéritifs, food, NB: Boissan, St Gayan.

St-Amour Beauj r ★★ **14** 15′ 16 (17) Most n BEAUJ cru: light, fruity, somewhat anonymous. Tediously recommended on 14 Feb. Try: DOM de Fa (Graillot), Janin, *Patissier*, Revillon.

St-Aubin C d'O r w ★★★ (w) **09′ 10′ 11** 12 14′ 15 16 (17) Fine source for *lively, refreshing* *whites*, challenging PULIGNY and CHASSAGNE esp on price. Also pretty reds mostly for early drinking. Best v'yds: Chatenière, En Remilly, Murgers Dents de Chien. Best growers: COLIN-MOREY, JC BACHELET, Lamy, Marc COLIN, Prudhon.

St-Bris Burg w ★ DYA. Unique w for SAUV BL in n BURG. Fresh, lively, but also worth keeping from J-H GOISOT or de Moor. Try also Bersan, Simonnet-Febvre.

St-Chinian L'doc r p ★ →★★★ 11 12 13 14 15 16 17 Large hilly area nr Béziers. Sound reputation. Incl CRUS of Berlou (mostly CARIGNAN) Roquebrun (mostly SYRAH) on schist. Warm, spicy reds, based on Syrah, GRENACHE, Carignan, MOURVÈDRE. Whites from ROUSSANNE, MARSANNE, VERMENTINO, GRENACHE BL. Gd co-op Roquebrun; CH Viranella Madura; DOMS Borie la Vitarèle, des Jougla, la Dournie, LA MADURA, Navarre, Rimbert; CLOS Bagatelle, Mas Champart. Several new estates.

Ste-Croix-du-Mont B'x w sw ★★ 07 09' 10' 11 13 14 15 16 AC making sweet, white *liquoreux*. Faces SAUTERNES across River Garonne. Best: rich, creamy, can age. Top CHX: Crabitan-Bellevue, du Mont, la Rame, *Loubens*, Pavillon.

St-Émilion B'x r ★ →★★★★ 00' 01 03 04 05' 08 09' 10' 11 12 14 15 16 Large MERLOT-led district on B'X's Right Bank, currently on a roll. CAB FR also strong. UNESCO World Heritage site since 1999. ACS St-Ém and St-Ém GRAND CRU. Top designation St-Ém PREMIER GRAND CRU CLASSÉ. Warm, full, rounded style; best firm, v. long-lived. Also modern and traditional styles. Top CHX: ANGÉLUS, AUSONE, CANON, CHEVAL BLANC, FIGEAC, PAVIE. Many attractive value wines.

St-Estèphe H-Méd r ★★ →★★★★ 98 00' 01 02 03 04 05' 06 08 09' 10' 11 12 14 15 16 17 Most n communal AC in the MÉD. Solid, structured wines for ageing; plenty of value to be found. Five Classed Growths: CALON-SÉGUR, COS D'ESTOURNEL, COS-LABORY, LAFON-ROCHET, MONTROSE. Top unclassified estates: CLAUZET, DE PEZ, HAUT-MARBUZET, LE BOSCQ, LE CROCK, MEYNEY, ORMES-DE-PEZ, PHÉLAN-SÉGUR.

L'doc produces twice as much rosé as Prov: three million hl to Prov's 1.5.

St-Gall Champ Brand of Union-CHAMP, top growers' co-op at AVIZE. BRUT NV; Extra Brut NV; Brut BLANC DE BLANCS NV; Brut Rosé NV; Brut Blanc de Blancs 04 06 08'; CUVÉE Orpale Blanc de Blancs 02' 04 08' 10 15' 17'. Fine-value PINOT-led *Pierre Vaudon NV*. Makes top *vins clairs* for some great houses.

St-Georges d'Orques L'doc r p ★★ →★★★ Most individual and historic part of sprawling Grès de Montpellier, aspiring to individual cru status. Try Belles Pierres, CH l'Engarran, DOMS Henry, La Marfée, La Prose.

St-Georges-St-Émilion B'x r ★★ 08 09' 10' 12 14 15 16 Smallest of ST-ÉM satellites. Sturdy, structured. Best CHX: Calon, CLOS Albertus, Macquin-St-Georges, St-André Corbin, ST-GEORGES, TOUR DU PAS-ST-GEORGES.

St-Gervais S Rh r (p) (w) ★ →★★ 15' 16' 17' W-bank Rh village; gd soils but v. limited choice. Co-op low-key; best is long-lived (10 yrs+) DOM Ste-Anne red (fresh, firm, MOURVÈDRE liquorice flavours); gd VIOGNIER. Also Dom Clavel (Syrius red).

St-Jacques d'Albas, Ch L'doc r p w ★★ Dynamic MINERVOIS estate since 2001. English-owned, Oz winemaker: Le Petit St-Jacques, Le DOM, Le CH and SYRAH-dominant La Chapelle (all r). Coteaux de Peyriac from VIOGNIER/VERMENTINO/ROUSSANNE.

St-Joseph N Rh r w ★★ →★★★ 99' 05' 06' 07' 09' 10' 11' 12' 13' 14 15' 16' 17' 40 miles of mainly granite v'yds along w bank of N Rh. SYRAH reds. Best, oldest v'yds nr Tournon: rounded, stylish, red-fruited wines; further in darker, live, peppery, more oak. More complete, detailed than CROZES-HERMITAGE esp CHAPOUTIER (Les Granits), Gonon (top class), *Gripa*, GUIGAL (VIGNES de l'Hospice), *J-L Chave* (gd style); also A Perret (Grisières), Chèze, Courbis (modern), Coursodon (racy, modern), Cuilleron, *Delas*, E Darnaud, Faury, F Villard, Gaillard, J&E Durand (fruit), Marsanne (traditional), Monier Perréol (organic), Nicolas Perrin, P-J Villa, P Marthouret (traditional), Vallet, Vins de Vienne. Gd food-friendly *white (mainly Marsanne)* esp A Perret, Barge, *Chapoutier*

(Les Granits), Cuilleron, Faury, Gonon (fab), Gouye (traditional), Gripa, J Pilon.

St-Julien H-Méd r ★★★→★★★★ 00′ 01 02 03 04 05′ 06 08 09′ 10′ 11 12 14 15 16 17 Small mid-MÉD communal AC. 11 classified (1855) estates own 95 per cent of v′yds. Incl three LÉOVILLES, BEYCHEVELLE, DUCRU-BEAUCAILLOU, GRUAUD-LAROSE, ST-PIERRE. Epitome of harmonious, fragrant, savoury red.

Saint Mont SW Fr r p w ★★ (r) 15′ 16′ 17 (p w) DYA AOP from Gascon heartlands. Saxophonist J-L Garoussia (★DOM de Turet), CH de Bergalasse and ★★Dom des Maouries fight rearguard action to prevent PRODUCTEURS PLAIMONT taking over appellation as a brand.

St-Nicolas-de-Bourgueil Lo r p ★★→★★★ 09′ 10 14′ 15′ 16 (17′) Similar to BOURGUEIL: CAB FR but more popular and expensive. Largely sand/gravel, light wines; more structured from limestone slopes. Wind machines against frost. Try: CLOS des Quarterons, David, Delanoue, Frédéric Mabileau, Laurent Mabileau, Lorieux, Mabileau-Rezé, Mortier, Taluau-Foltzenlogel, Vallée, *Yannick Amirault*.

St-Péray N Rh w sp ★★ 14′ 15′ 16′ 17′ Progressive white Rh (MARSANNE/ROUSSANNE) from hilly granite and lime v′yds opposite Valence, lots of new planting. Once *famous for fizz*; classic-method bubbles well worth trying. (A Voge, J-L Thiers, R Nodin). Still white should have grip, be smoky, flinty. Best: CHAPOUTIER, *Clape* (pure), *Colombo* (stylish), Cuilleron, *du Tunnel* (v. elegant), Gripa (v.gd), J-L Thiers, R Nodin, Vins de Vienne, Voge (oak), TAIN co-op.

St-Pierre de Soucy Sav From steep schist hillsides, this cru makes assertive fresh-tasting mix of Jacquère, CHARD, Mondeuse Blanche. Top: DOM des Ardoisière.

Is Jean-Marc Roulot an actor or winemaker? See *Ce Qui Nous Lie* ("Back to Burgundy").

St-Pourçain Mass C r p w ★→★★ DYA. AC (557 ha in upper Loire [Allier].) Light red, rosé from GAMAY, PINOT N (AOP idiotically bans pure PINOT N), white from local Tressalier and/or CHARD, SAUV BL. Growers: Berioles, DOM de Bellevue, Grosbot-Barbara, Laurent, Nebout, Pétillat, Ray; gd co-op (VIGNERONS de St-Pourçain).

St-Romain C d′O r w ★★ (w) 14′ 15 16 (17) *Crisp whites* from side valley of CÔTE DE BEAUNE. Excellent value by Burg standards. Try Bellene, Buisson, de Chassorney, Gras, HOSPICES. Some fresh reds too.

St-Véran Burg w ★★ 14′ 15 16 (17) S Burg AC either side of POUILLY-FUISSÉ. Try Chagnoleau, Corsin, Deux Roches, Litaud, Merlin for single-v′yd CUVÉES. Gd-value DUBOEUF, Poncetys, TERRES SECRETES co-op.

Ste-Victoire Prov r p ★★ Subzone of CÔTES DE PROV from s slopes of Montagne Ste-Victoire. Dramatic scenery goes with gd wine. Try Mas de Cadenet, Mauvan.

Salon Champ ★★★★ Original BLANC DE BLANCS, from LE MESNIL in Côte des Blancs. Tiny quantities. Awesome reputation for long-lived luxury-priced wines: in truth, sometimes inconsistent. On song recently, viz 83′ 90 97′, but 99 disappoints, where is 02 going? Opinions differ. But 06 looks v.gd. *See also* DELAMOTTE.

Sancerre Lo r (p) w ★→★★★★ 05′ 08′ 10 12 14′ 15′ 16′ (17) Touchstone SAUV BL (2354 ha), many fine reds (PINOT N 600 ha). Exciting new generation. Luck holding: hardly touched by frost 2016/17. Best: ALPHONSE MELLOT, Boulay, BOURGEOIS, Claude Riffault, Cotat (variable), Dezat, Dionysia, Fouassier, François Crochet, Jean-Max Roger, *Joseph Mellot*, Lucien Crochet, Mollet, Natter, Neveu, Paul Prieur, Pierre Martin, Pinard, *P & N Reverdy*, Raimbault, Roblin, Thomas, Thomas Laballe, Vacheron, Vatan, Vattan, Vincent Delaporte.

Santenay C d′O r (w) ★★→★★★ 03 05′ 09′ 11 12 14 15′ 16′ (17) South end of CÔTE DE BEAUNE, potential for fine reds; don′t overlook. Best v′yds: CLOS de Tavannes, Clos Rousseau, Gravières (r w). Producers: Belland, Camille Giroud, Chevrot, Jessiaume, Lamy, MOREAU, Muzard, Vincent. Some gd whites too, eg. CHARMES.

Saumur Lo r p w sp ★→★★★ 09′ 10′ 12 14′ 15′ 16 17 Large AC. Whites: light to v. serious and age brilliantly; mainly easy reds except SAUMUR-CHAMPIGNY; rosés.

FRANCE

Centre of Lo fizz production: CRÉMANT now most important, Saumur Mousseux. Saumur-Le-Puy-Notre-Dame AOP for CAB FR. Producers: Antoine Foucault, BOUVET-LADUBAY, CHAMPS FLEURIS, CH de Brézé, CLOS Mélaric, CLOS ROUGEARD, Ditterie, Guiberteau, Nerleux, Paleine, Parnay, René-Hugues Gay, ROBERT ET MARCEL, Rocheville, St-Just, Targé, VILLENEUVE and Yvonne. 2017 some frost but quality gd.

Saumur-Champigny Lo r ★★→★★★ 05' 09' 10 12 14' 15' 16 (17) Nine-commune AC, v.gd CAB FR, gd vintages age 15–20 yrs+. Best: Bonnelière, Bruno Dubois, CH DE VILLENEUVE, Ch Yvonne, CLOS Cristal, CLOS ROUGEARD, de la Cune, Ditterie, DOM Antoine Sanzay, Dom des Champs Fleuris, Filliatreau, Hureau, Nerleux, Petit St-Vincent, P Vadé, Robert et Marcel (co-op), Roches Neuves, Rocheville, St Just, St-Vincent, Seigneurie, Targé, Val Brun. 2017 some frost.

Saussignac SW Fr w sw ★★ 14 15' 16 17 BERGERAC sub-aop, wines with a shade more acidity than those from adjoining MONBAZILLAC. Best: ★★★DOMS de Richard, La Maurigne, Les Miaudoux, Lestevénie; ★★CHX Le Chabrier, Le Payral, Le Tap.

Sauternes B'x w sw ★★→★★★★ 90' 95 96 97' 98 99' 01' 02 03' 05' 07' 09' 10' 11' 13 14 15 16 AC making France's best *liquoreux* from "noble rotted" grapes. Strong, luscious, golden and age-worthy. Surprisingly food-friendly. Classified (1855) CHX: CLOS HAUT-PEYRAGUEY, GUIRAUD, LAFAURIE-PEYRAGUEY, LA TOUR BLANCHE, RIEUSSEC, SIGALAS-RABAUD, SUDUIRAUT, D'YQUEM. Top non-classified: DOM de l'Alliance, HAUT-BERGERON, Les Justices, RAYMOND-LAFON.

Sauzet, Etienne C d'O w ★★★ Leading bio DOM in PULIGNY with superb range of PREMIERS CRUS (Combettes, Champ Canet best), MONTRACHET and BÂTARD-M. Concentrated, lively wines, once again capable of ageing.

Savennières Lo w dr (sw) ★★→★★★★ 89' 96' 03 05' 07 08 09 10' 11 12 14' 15' (16) Small ANJOU AC, high reputation, big variations in style, quality; v. long-lived whites (CHENIN BL) with marked acidity. Baudouin, *Baumard*, Bergerie, Boudignon, *Ch d'Epiré*, *Ch Pierre-Bise*, CH Soucherie, Closel, DOM FL, Laureau, Mahé, Mathieu-Tijou, Morgat, Ogereau, Pithon-Paillé. Top sites: CLOS du Papillon, COULÉE DE SERRANT, ROCHE-AUX-MOINES.

Savigny-lès-Beaune C d'O r (w) ★★★ 99' 02' 03 05' 09' 10' 11 12 14 15' (17) Important village next to BEAUNE; similar mid-weight wines, savoury touch (but can be rustic). Top v'yds: Dominode, Guettes, Lavières, Marconnets, Vergelesses. Growers: *Bize*, Camus, *Chandon de Briailles*, Chenu, CLAIR, DROUHIN, Girard, Guyon, LEROY, Pavelot, *Tollot-Beaut*.

Savoie r w sp ★★→★★★ Alps. Vin de Sav AC (1980 ha) 16 crus incl APRÉMONT, CHIGNIN, CRÉPY, Jongieux, Ripaille. Separate ACs: Roussette de Sav (Altesse), SEYSSEL. Reds mainly GAMAY, MONDEUSE; whites: Altesse, Jacquère, Mondeuse Blanc, ROUSSANNE.

Schlossberg Al GRAND CRU at Kientzheim famed since C15. Glorious compelling RIES from FALLER 10 and new TRIMBACH; 15 should be great Ries yr here.

Schlumberger, Doms Al w sw ★→★★★ Vast, top-quality AL DOM at Guebwiller owning approx one per cent of all AL v'yds. Holdings in GRANDS CRUS Kitterlé and racy Saering 10' 12 13 15, Spiegel. Rich wines. Rare RIES, signature CUVÉE Ernest and now Grand Cru Kessler GEWURZ lovely in 14 15; great PINOT GR there too.

Schoenenberg Al V. rich, successful Riquewihr GRAND CRU: PINOT GR, RIES, v. fine VENDANGE TARDIVE, SÉLECTION DES GRAINS NOBLES esp DOPFF AU MOULIN. V.gd MUSCAT. HUGEL Schoelhammer from here. 2017 small crop but could be exquisite quality.

Schoenheitz Al Rising DOM; impeccable quality, notable PINOT BL, RIES; exemplary long lees-aged CRÉMANT d'Al 08.

Schoffit, Dom Al w ★★★ Exceptional Colmar grower Bernard S makes superb late-harvest GEWURZ, PINOT GR VENDANGE TARDIVE GRAND CRU RANGEN CLOS St Theobald 08 10' 12' 14 15 on volcanic soil. Contrast with RIES Grand Cru Sonnenberg 10' 13 15 16 17' on limestone. Delicious CHASSELAS.

Sec Literally means dry, though CHAMP so called is medium-sweet (and better at breakfast, teatime, weddings than BRUT).

Séguret S Rh r p w ★★ 12′ 13 14 15′ 16′ **17′** Pretty Prov hillside village nr GIGONDAS. V'yds on both plain and heights. One of top Rh Villages. Mainly GRENACHE, peppery, quite deep reds, some full-on; crisp-fruited whites. Esp CH la Courançonne (gd w), DOMS Amandine, de Cabasse (elegant), *de l'Amauve* (fine), Fontaine des Fées, Garancière, J David (bold, organic), Maison Plantevin, Malmont (stylish), *Mourchon* (robust), Pourra (intense, time), Soleil Romain.

Sélection des Grains Nobles Al Term coined by HUGEL for AL equivalent to German Beerenauslese, subject to ever-stricter rules. *Grains nobles* are grapes with "noble rot" for v. sweet wines.

Selosse, Anselme Champ ★★★★ Leading grower, an icon for many. Oxidative style, oak-fermented; Version Originale still vibrant after 7 yrs on lees. From named sites, top wine probably Mesnil Les Carelles, saline, complex, akin to MEURSAULT Perrières with bubbles. 02 still a baby.

Sérafin, Dom C d'O r ★★★ Deep colour, intense flavours, new wood: Serafin wines need to age. Try GEVREY-CHAMBERTIN VIEILLES VIGNES, Cazetiers, CHARMES-CHAMBERTIN.

Seyssel Sav w sp ★★ AC since 1942. 80 ha. White (from Altesse, Molette), sparkling from CHASSELAS. Try: Lambert de Seyssel, Mollex, Vens-le-Haut.

Sichel & Co B'x r w Respected B'x merchant est in 1883 (Sirius a top brand). Family-run; interests in CHX ANGLUDET, Argadens, PALMER and in CORBIÈRES (Ch Trillol). State-of-art storage facility.

Signargues S Rh ★→★★ 15′ 16′ **17′** Modest CÔTES DU RH village, dry soils between Avignon and Nîmes (w bank). Spicy, robust reds to drink inside 4–5 yrs. NB: CAVE Estézargues (punchy), CH Terre Forte (bio), CLOS d'Alzan, Haut-Musiel, La Font du Vent; DOMS des Romarins (deep), Valériane.

Simone, Ch Prov r p w ★★ →★★★ Historic estate outside Aix-en-Prov, where Winston Churchill painted Mont STE-VICTOIRE. Rougier family for nearly two centuries. Virtually synonymous with AC PALETTE. Age-worthy whites well worth seeking out; characterful rosé, elegant reds from GRENACHE and MOURVÈDRE, with rare grape varieties Castet, Manosquin (r).

Sipp, Louis Al w sw ★★→★★★ Grower/NÉGOCIANT in Ribeauvillé. V.gd RIES GRAND CRU Kirchberg, superb Grand Cru Osterberg GEWURZ VENDANGE TARDIVE, esp 07 09′. Fine in classic drier yrs 08 **10 12 13** 14.

Sipp-Mack Al w sw ★★→★★★ Excellent DOM at Hunawihr. Great RIES from GRANDS CRUS ROSACKER 10 12 **13′ 14** 15′; v.gd PINOT GR.

Sorg, Bruno Al w ★★→★★★ A 1st-class small grower at Eguisheim for GRANDS CRUS Florimont (RIES 10 12 **13′ 14** 15′) and PFERSIGBERG (MUSCAT). Immaculate eco-friendly v'yds.

Sur lie "On the lees". MUSCADET is often bottled straight from the vat, for max zest, body, character.

Tâche, La C d'O r ★★★★ 90′ 93′ 95 **96′ 98** 99′ 00 01 02′ **03 05′ 06** 07 09′ 10′ 11 12′ 13 14 15′ 16′ (17) GRAND CRU of VOSNE-ROMANÉE, MONOPOLE of DRC. One of best v'yds on earth: full, perfumed, luxurious wine, tight in youth.

Taille-aux-Loups, Dom de la Lo w sw sp ★★★ 05′ 07′ 08′ 09 10′ 11 **12 14′ 15′ 16r** (17) Jacky Blot, impeccable producer, now with son Jean-Philippe. Barrel-fermented MONTLOUIS, VIN DE FRANCE (aka VOUVRAY) majority dry esp single v'yds: CLOS Mosny, Michet (Montlouis), Venise (Vouvray); Triple Zéro Montlouis *pétillant* (p w); v.gd BOURGUEIL, DOM de la Butte. Frost 2016/17 (Montlouis).

Tain, Cave de N Rh ★★→★★★ Top N Rh co-op, many mature v'yds, incl 25 per cent of HERMITAGE. Sound to v.gd red Hermitage esp Epsilon, Gambert de Loche, bountiful white Hermitage Au Coeur des Siècles, offer value. Gd ST-JOSEPH (r w), interesting Bio (organic) range (CROZES, St-Joseph), other wines modern, mainstream. Gd recent CROZES reds from hill and plain v'yds, eg. Nord. 2016 whites improved. Distinguished VIN DE PAILLE.

Taittinger Champ BRUT NV, Rosé NV, Brut 04 **06 08**, Collection Brut **89 90** 95' jewels of this again-family-run Reims house. Epitome of apéritif style, exquisite weightlessness. Ace luxury *Comtes de Champagne* 95' **99** 02' **08'**; Comtes Rosé also shines in 06. Excellent single v'yd La Marquetterie. New English bubbly project in Kent, DOM Evremond. (*See also* Dom Carneros, California.) New cellarmaster fills Loec Dupont's big shoes.

Tavel S Rh p ★★ DYA. GRENACHE rosé, should be robust, for vivid Mediterranean dishes. Now many lighter Prov-styles, often for apéritif; a shame. Top: DOM de l'Anglore (no sulphur), Dom de la Mordorée (full), Corne-Loup, GUIGAL (gd), Lafond Roc-Epine, Maby, Moulin-la-Viguerie (organic, traditional), Prieuré de Montézargues (fine), Rocalière (v. fine), Tardieu-Laurent, VIDAL-FLEURY; CHX Aquéria, de Manissy, Ségriès, *Trinquevedel* (fine).

Tempier, Dom Prov r p w ★★★★ Estate where Lucien Peyraud est MOURVÈDRE in AC BANDOL. Wines combine elegance, concentration, longevity. Maintains excellent quality; now rivalled by several others.

Terrasses du Larzac L'doc r ★★ →★★★ Most n part of AC L'DOC. Wild, hilly region from Lac du Salagou to Aniane, incl MONTPEYROUX, St-Saturnin; cooler temperatures make for fresher wines. AC since 2014; 25 new growers in 6 yrs, plus est names: CAL DEMOURA, CLOS des Serres, Jonquières, Mas de l'Ecriture, *Mas Jullien*, MONTCALMÈS, Pas de l'Escalette, Mas Conscience. Over half are organic/bio. *Definitely to watch*. White, rosé are AC L'doc or IGP.

Terres Secretes ★★ Important co-op in Prissé for Mâconnais wines esp ST-VÉRAN and MÂCON-VILLAGES. Sound, gd value.

Thénard, Dom Burg r w ★★→★★★★ Historic producer with large holding of MONTRACHET, mostly sold to NÉGOCIANTS, some v.gd reds from home base in GIVRY.

Thévenet, Jean Burg r w sw ★★★ Top MÂCONNAIS purveyor of rich, some semi-botrytized CHARD, eg. CUVÉE Levroutée at *Dom de la Bongran*.

Thézac-Perricard SW Fr r p w ★★ 15' 16 17 IGP adjoining CAHORS (reds from MALBEC, MERLOT). Worthy ★co-op outclassed by Sandrine Annibal's ★★DOM de Lancement (exciting off-dry white from both MANSENG grapes); reds indistinguishable from lighter Cahors.

Rising stars in the Southwest

Ch de Peyrel, Rosette delicious apéritif off-dry mostly from SÉM, MUSCADELLE. Ideal with foie gras, mushrooms. **Ch Trotteligotte, Cahors** one of CAHORS' most serious bio growers already heading for top. **Dom de Beyssac, Marmande** Right-Bank bio estate with some Abouriou grapes and growing reputation. **Dom de Bias, IGP Aveyron** Alazards noted for PINOT N-based red and delicious white from CHARD, ROUSSANNE. **Dom des Pradelles, Fronton** now among best of this appellation. **Dom la Fon Longue, Côtes de Duras** characterful red from higher ground in Loubès-Bernac area. **Dom Larroudé, Jurançon** Jeremy Estoigt has 7 ha at w end of appellation. Bio. **Dom Peyres-Roses, Gaillac** young grower Charles Bonnafont-Serre challenges best with his entry-style Antidote (w) and Impeccable (r). Passionately bio. **Dom Sédouprat, Côtes de Gascogne** CUVÉE Sanglier consistently wows ex-pats. **Dom Xubialdea, Irouléguy** (w only) Battit Ibagaray plants GROS MANSENG to density of 10,000/ha of which he has seven in all. Bio. **La Vignereuse, Gaillac** Marine Leys a talented disciple of Bernard Plageoles. **Sandrine Annibal, Thézac-Perricard** (IGP) best is off-dry Manseng; v. more-ish. And don't, whatever you do, forget Armagnac from GERS; France's – no, the world's – best brandy.

Thiénot, Alain Champ New generation Stanislas and Garance now at helm. Ever-improving quality: impressive, fairly priced ★★★BRUT NV; Rosé NV Brut; vintage Stanislas 02 04 06 08' 09 12' 13 15. Voluminous VIGNE aux Gamins (single-v'yd AVIZE 02 04 08). CUVÉE Garance CHARD 07 sings, classic 08 for long haul. Also owns CHAMP CANARD-DUCHÊNE, CH Ricaud in LOUPIAC.

Thomas, André & fils Al w ★★★ V. fine grower at Ammerschwihr, rigorously organic, artist-craftsman in cellar. V.gd RIES Kaefferkopf 08 10' 12, magnificent GEWURZ VIEILLES VIGNES 05 09' 10' 12 14 15' 17'.

Tissot Jura Dominant family around ARBOIS. ★★Jacques T offers volume and value. ★★★Stephane T (also as Andre & Mireille Tissot), cult pioneer of single-v'yd CHARD and VIN JAUNE using bio/natural methods; outstanding CRÉMANT du Jura, Indigène.

Tollot-Beaut C d'O r ★★★ Consistent CÔTE DE BEAUNE grower with 20 ha in BEAUNE (Grèves, CLOS du Roi), CORTON (Bressandes), SAVIGNY and at CHOREY-LÈS-BEAUNE base (NB: Pièce du Chapitre). Accessible fruit, slight oak veneer.

Touraine Lo r p w dr sw sp ★→★★★ 14' 15' 16 17 Huge region with many ACS (eg. VOUVRAY, CHINON, BOURGUEIL) plus umbrella AC of variable quality: fruity reds (CAB FR, CÔT, GAMAY, PINOT N), whites (SAUV BL), rosés, sparkling. Touraine Village ACs, see below: Azay-le-Rideau, Chenonceaux, Mesland, Noble-Joué, Oisly. Stocks of Sauv badly depleted: frost 2016/2017, and vine disease. Producers: Biet, Bois-Vaudons, Corbillières, Joël Delaunay, Garrelière, Gosseaume, Jacky Marteau, La Chapinière, Lacour, Mandard, *Marionnet*, Morantin, *Presle*, Prieuré, Puzelat, Ricard, Roussely, Tue-Boeuf, Villebois.

Tavel rosé has two markets, basically: Tavel itself, and Denmark.

Touraine-Amboise Lo r p (w) ★→★★★ TOURAINE Village-AC 60/30/10 per cent r/p/w. François 1er pop blend (GAMAY/CÔT/CAB FR); Côt/Cab Fr top reds; CHENIN BL top white. Best: Bessons, Closerie de Chanteloup, Dutertre, Frissant, Gabillière, Grange Tiphaine, Mesliard, Truet. Aiming for cru for Chenin, Côt.

Touraine-Azay-le-Rideau Lo p w (sw) ★→★★ TOURAINE sub-AC (60 ha). Rosé (60 per cent of AC; Grolleau 60% min); white, dry and off-dry from CHENIN BL. Best: Aulée, Bourse, de la Roche, Grosbois, Nicolas Paget. Frost 2016/17.

Touraine-Mesland Lo r p w ★→★★ 14 15 16 (17) Small TOURAINE villages AC (105 ha) w of Blois. Rarely better than straight Touraine. Best: Grandes Espérances. Girault (bio) sold to DOM Cocteaux.

Touraine-Noble Joué Lo p ★→★★ DYA. V. attractive rosé from three PINOTS (N, M, GR). AOP mainly Indre Valley s of Tours. Best: Astraly, Cosson, Rousseau, Sard-Pierru. Frost-prone, hit 2016/17.

Trapet C d'O r ★★★ Long-est GEVREY-CHAMBERTIN DOM making sensual bio wines from village up to GRAND CRU CHAMBERTIN plus AL whites by marriage. See also cousins ROSSIGNOL-TRAPET.

Trévallon, Dom de Prov r w ★★★ 00' 01 03 04 05 06 07 08 09 10 11 12 13 14 15 16 17 Eloi Dürrbach created this estate in LES BAUX; joined by daughter Ostiane. No GRENACHE, so must be IGP Alpilles. Huge reputation fully justified. Intense, age-worthy CAB SAUV/SYRAH. *Barrique-aged white* from MARSANNE/ROUSSANNE, drop of CHARD and now GRENACHE BL.

Trimbach, FE Al w ★★★→★★★★★ Matchless grower of AL RIES on limestone soils at Ribeauvillé, esp CLOS STE-HUNE 71 89 still great. 10' 13 15 17 classically cool; almost-as-gd (and much cheaper) *Frédéric Emile* 10 12 13 14 15 17. Dry, elegant wines for great cuisine. Look out for 1ST GRAND CRU label: from v'yds of Couvent de Ribeauville, cultivated by Trimbach.

Tursan SW Fr r p w ★★ Mostly DYA. AOP in Landes. Delicious wines (CH de Bachen) made for superstar chef Michel Guérard's restaurants at Eugénie-les-Bains less authentic than ★★DOM de Perchade. Worthy co-op (recently twinned with CHALOSSE) floundering a bit.

Vacqueyras S Rh r (p) w ★★ 07′ 09′ 10′ 11 12′ 13 14 15′ **16′** 17′ Hearty, punchy, peppery, GRENACHE-centred neighbour of GIGONDAS; for game, big flavours. Lives 10 yrs+. Note: JABOULET; CHX de Montmirail, *des Tours* (v. fine); *Clos des Cazaux* (racy, gd value); DOMS Amouriers, Archimbaud-Vache, Charbonnière, Couroulu (v.gd, traditional), Famille Perrin, Font de Papier (organic), Fourmone (gd form), Garrigue (traditional), Grapillon d'Or, Monardière (v.gd), Montirius (bio), Montvac (elegant), Roucas Toumba (organic), Sang des Cailloux (v.gd esp Lopy), Semelles de Vent (clear fruit), Verde. *Full whites* (CLOS des Cazaux, Sang des Cailloux).

Val de Loire Lo r p w DYA. One of France's four regional IGPS, formerly Jardin de la France.

Valençay Lo r p w ★→★★ AOP (165 ha), TOURAINE; esp SAUV BL, (CHARD); reds CÔT, GAMAY, PINOT N. CLOS Delorme, Lafond, Preys, Sébastien Vaillant, Sinson, VIGNERONS de Valençay. Frost 2017.

Valréas S Rh r (p) (w) ★★ 10′ 15′ 16′ 17′ CÔTES DU RH-VILLAGE in n Vaucluse truffle region, quality rising; large co-op. Grainy, peppery, breezy, sometimes heady, red-fruited mostly GRENACHE red, improving white. Esp CH la Décelle, CLOS Bellane (gd white), Mas de Ste-Croix, DOMS Gramenon (bio, stylish), des Grands Devers, du Séminaire (organic), Prévosse (organic), du Val des Rois (best, organic).

VDN (Vin Doux Naturel) ROUSS Sweet wine fortified with wine alc, so sweetness natural, not strength. Speciality of ROUSS based on GRENACHE, Noir, BLANC or Gris, or MUSCAT. Top wines esp aged RANCIOS can finish a meal on a sublime note.

VDP (Vin de Pays) *See* IGP.

VDQS (Vins Délimité de Qualité Supérieure) Now phased out. **VDT (Vin de Table)** Category of standard everyday table wine now replaced by VIN DE FRANCE.

Vendange Harvest. **Vendange Tardive:** late-harvest; AL equivalent to German Auslese but usually higher alc.

Venoge, de Champ Venerable house, precise and more elegant under LANSON-BCC ownership. Gd niche blends: Cordon Bleu Extra-BRUT, Vintage BLANC DE BLANCS 00 04 06 08 12 13 14 15′. Excellent Vintage Rosé 06 09 CUVÉE 20 Ans, Prestige Cuvée Louis XV 10-yr-old BLANC DE NOIRS.

Ventoux S Rh r p w ★★ 15′ **16′** 17′ Widespread AC all around Mont Ventoux between Rh and Prov. A few front-running DOMS v.gd value. Juicy, tangy red (GRENACHE/ SYRAH, café-style to deeper, peppery, rising quality), rosé, gd white (more oak). Best: CH Unang (gd w), Ch Valcombe, CLOS des Patris, Ferme St-Pierre (p w), Gonnet, *La Vieille Ferme* (r, can be VIN DE FRANCE), St-Marc, Terra Ventoux (value), VIGNERONS Mont Ventoux; DOMS Anges, Berane, Brusset, Cascavel, Champ-Long, Croix de Pins (gd w), *Fondrèche* (v.gd), Grand Jacquet, Martinelle (great fruit), Murmurium, Olivier B, PAUL JABOULET (v.gd), *Pesquié* (excellent), Pigeade (genuine), St-Jean du Barroux (organic), Terres de Solence, du Tix, Verrière, VIDAL-FLEURY, Vieux Lazaret, Vindemio (bio); co-op Bédoin.

Vernay, Dom Georges N Rh r w ★★★ 12′ 13′ 14′ 15′ 16′ 17′ Top CONDRIEU name; three wines, much elegance; Terrasses de l'Empire *apéritif de luxe*; Chaillées d'Enfer, richness; Coteau de Vernon, mysterious, supreme style, lives 20 yrs+. CÔTE-RÔTIE, ST-JOSEPH (r) restrained, emphasize purity of fruit. V.gd VIN DE PAYS (r w).

Veronique & Thomas Muré, Clos St-Landelin Al r w ★★→★★★ One of AL's great names; esp fine, full-bodied GRAND CRU *Vorbourg Ries* and PINOT GR 13 14. Pinot N Cuvée "V" ripe, vinous, is region's best, exceptional in 15′ ★★★.

Veuve Clicquot Champ Historic house of highest standing. Full-bodied, rich, fine: one of CHAMP's sure things. Yellow Label NV, White Label DEMI-SEC NV, new CUVÉE

Extra Brut Extra Age ★★★based on reserve wines only, 2010–1990. Vintage Rés 02 04 **06 08** 12', Rosé Rés 08 12'. Luxury La Grande Dame 04, fine **06**, ★★★★La Grande Dame Rosé 06. Part-oak-fermented vintages from 08. CAVE Privée re-release of older vintages esp 89 95 (magnums). Exemplary red winemaking unit for subtlest CHAMP rosés.

Veuve Devaux Champ Premium brand of powerful Union Auboise co-op. Excellent aged Grande Rés NV, and Œil de Perdrix Rosé, Prestige CUVÉE D 08 **09 10**, BRUT Vintage 09 **10 12** 15' 17.

Vézelay Burg r w ★ →★★ Age 1–2 yrs. Lovely location (with abbey) in nw Burg. Promoted to full AC for tasty whites from CHARD. Also try revived MELON (COTEAUX BOURGUIGNON) and light PINOT (generic BOURGOGNE). Best: DOM de la Cadette, des Faverelles, Elise Villiers, La Croix Montjoie.

Vidal-Fleury, J N Rh r w sw ★★ →★★★ GUIGAL-owned Rh merchant/grower of CÔTE-RÔTIE. Top notch, tight, v. stylish *La Chatillonne* (12% VIOGNIER; much oak, wait min 7 yrs). Range wide, improving. Gd CAIRANNE, CHÂTEAUNEUF (r), CÔTES DU RH (r p), MUSCAT DE BEAUMES-DE-VENISE, ST-JOSEPH (r w), TAVEL, VENTOUX.

Vieille Ferme, La S Rh r w ★→★★ Reliable gd-value brand from Famille Perrin of CH DE BEAUCASTEL; much has become VIN DE FRANCE, with VENTOUX (r), LUBÉRON (w) in some countries (France, Japan). Back on form 15. incl rosé.

Vieilles Vignes Old vines, which should make the best wine. Eg. DE VOGÜÉ, MUSIGNY, Vieilles Vignes. But no rules about age and can be a tourist trap.

Vieux Télégraphe, Dom du S Rh r w ★★★ 78' 81' 85 89' 90 95' 96' 97 98' 99' 00 01' 03' 04' 05' 06' **07' 09'** 10' 12' 13 **14** 15' 16' 17' Big, high-quality estate; classic stony soils, intricate, take-your-time robust red CHÂTEAUNEUF; top two wines La Crau (crunchy, packed) and since 2011 Pied Long et Pignan (pure, elegant). Also rich whites *La Crau* (v.gd 15 16), CLOS La Roquète (great with food, note 15 16). Owns fine, slow-to-evolve, complex *Gigondas Dom Les Pallières* with US importer Kermit Lynch.

Vigne or vignoble Vineyard (v'yd), vineyards (v'yds).

Vigneron Vine-grower.

Villeneuve, Ch de Lo r w ★★★★ 96 05 06 08' **09'** 10' 11 **12 14'** 15' 16 (17) Impeccable estate with impressive winery in old caves. Great SAUMUR Blanc (age-worthy Les Cormiers), SAUMUR-CHAMPIGNY (esp VIEILLES VIGNES, Grand CLOS). Organic. Jean-Pierre's daughters now involved.

Vin de France Replaces VDT. At last allows mention of grape variety and vintage. Often blends of regions with brand name. Can be source of unexpected delights if talented winemaker uses this category to avoid bureaucractic hassle. Eg. Yves Cuilleron VIOGNIER (N Rh).

Vin de paille Wine from grapes dried on straw mats, so v. sweet, like Italian passito. Esp in the Jura. *See also* CHAVE, VIN PAILLÉ DE CORRÈZE.

Vin gris "Grey" wine is v. pale pink, made of red grapes pressed before fermentation begins; unlike rosé, which ferments briefly before pressing. Or from eg. PINOT GR, not-quite-white grapes. "Œil de Perdrix" much the same; as is "blush".

Vin jaune w ★★★ Speciality of Jura; inimitable yellow wine. SAVAGNIN, 6 yrs+ in barrel without topping up, develops flor, like Sherry but no added alc. Expensive to make. Separate AC for top spot, CH-CHALON. Sold in unique 62cl Clavelin bottles.

Vin paillé de Corrèze SW Fr r w 25 small growers and a tiny co-op once more laying out grapes on straw in old way to make pungent wine once recommended to breast-feeding mothers. Wines will keep as long as you. If you're brave try ★Christian Tronche.

Vinsobres S Rh r (p) (w) ★★ 10' 12' 13 14 15' **16'** 17' Low-profile AC notable for SYRAH. Best reds can be heady, show decisive red fruit, punch, to drink with red meats. Leaders: CAVE la Vinsobraise; CH Rouanne; DOMS Chaume-Arnaud (organic), Constant-Duquesnoy, Coriançon, Deurre (traditional), Famille Perrin (Hauts de Julien top class, Cornuds value), Jaume (modern, consistent), Moulin (traditional, gd r w), Péquélette (bio), Peysson (organic).

Viré-Clessé Burg w ★★ 14' 15 16 (17) AC based around two of best white villages of MÂCON. Known for exuberant rich style, sometimes late-harvest. Try Bonhomme, Bret Bros, Chaland, DOM de la Verpaille, Gondard-Perrin, Guillemot, J-P Michel, LAFON, **Thévenet**.

Visan S Rh r (p) (w) ★★ 13 15' 16' 17' Improving RH VILLAGE: reds have sound depth, with clear fruit, pepper, some more soft, plenty organic. Whites okay. Best: DOMS Art Mas (organic), Coste Chaude (gd fruit), Montmartel (organic), Dieulefit (bio), Florane, Fourmente (bio esp Nature), Guintrandy (organic), Philippe Plantevin, Roche-Audran (organic, dashing), VIGNOBLE Art Mas.

Vogüé, Comte Georges de C d'O r w ★★★★ A v. grand CHAMBOLLE estate, lion's share of MUSIGNY. Great from barrel, but take many yrs in bottle to reveal glories. Unique white Musigny.

Volnay C d'O r ★★★ →★★★★ 90' 95 96' 99' 02' 03 05' 07 09' 10' 11 14 15' 16 (17) Top CÔTE DE BEAUNE reds, except when it hails. Can be structured, should be silky, astonishing with age. Best v'yds: Caillerets, Champans, CLOS des Chênes, Clos des Ducs, Santenots, Taillepieds. Best growers: Bouley, D'ANGERVILLE, DE MONTILLE, H BOILLOT, HOSPICES DE BEAUNE, LAFARGE, LAFON, N Rossignol, Pousse d'Or.

Food-matching discovery: pale, supple Poulsard (Jura) with raw scallops.

Vosne-Romanée C d'O r ★★★ →★★★★ 90' 93' **95 96'** 99' 02' 03 05' 06 **07 08 09'** 10' 11 12 13 14 15' 16' (17) Village with Burg's grandest crus (eg. ROMANÉE-CONTI, LA TÂCHE) and outstanding PREMIERS CRUS Malconsorts, Beaumonts, Brûlées, etc. There are (or should be) no common wines in Vosne. Many gd if increasingly pricey growers. Top: Arnoux-Lachaux, CATHIARD, Clavelier, DRC, EUGÉNIE, Forey, GRIVOT, GROS, Guyon, Lamarche, LEROY, LIGER-BELAIR, MÉO-CAMUZET, MUGNERET, NOËLLAT, ROUGET, Tardy.

Vougeot C d'O r w ★★★ 99' 02' **03** 05' 06 08 **09'** 10' 11 12' 13 14 15' 16 (17) Mostly GRAND CRU as CLOS DE VOUGEOT but also village and PREMIER CRU, incl outstanding white MONOPOLE, **Clos Blanc de V.** Clerget, HUDELOT-Noëllat, VOUGERAIE best.

Vougeraie, Dom de la C d'O r w ★★★ →★★★★ Bio DOM uniting all BOISSET's v'yd holdings. Reliable BOURGOGNE but most noted for sensual GRANDS CRUS esp BONNES-MARES, CHARMES-CHAMBERTIN, MUSIGNY. Fine whites too, with unique **Clos Blanc de Vougeot** and four GRANDS CRUS incl CHARLEMAGNE.

Vouvray Lo w dr sw sp ★★ →★★★★ (dr) 02' 03 05' 07 08' 09 10 12 14 **15'** 16 (17) (sw) 89' 90' 95' 96' 97' 03' 05' 08 **09' 10 11 15'** 16 AC e of Tours, on n bank of Loire. Best v'yds on *premier côte* above Loire. Top producers reliably gd. DEMI-SEC is classic style, but in best yrs *moelleux* can be lusciously sweet, almost immortal. Fizz variable (60 per cent of production): *pétillant* – recommended speciality. Try: Aubuisières, Autran (rising star), Bonneau, Brunet, Carême, **Champalou**, CLOS Baudoin, Florent Cosme, Fontainerie, Foreau, F PINON, Gaudrelle, **Huet**, Mathieu Cosme, Meslerie (Hahn), Perrault-Jadaud, **Taille-aux-Loups**, Vigneau-Chevreau. Old vintages: 21 24 37 47 59 70 71 must-try.

Wolfberger Al ★★ Principal label of EGUISHEIM CO-OP. V.gd quality for such a large-scale producer. Leading sparkling CRÉMANT producer; high tech for high quality.

Zind Humbrecht, Dom Al w sw ★★★★ Epic bio DOM sensitively run by Olivier H, great winemaker: rich, balanced wines, drier, elegant, v. low yields. Top single-v'yds **Clos St-Urbain Grand Cru Rangen**: RIES 08 10' 15' 16'; 17' a future great; Jebsal, superb PINOT GR 08 10 12 14 16 17 plus GRANDS CRUS Hengst and Brand (Ries 10' 12 14 15), Goldert (MUSCAT 12). Real success in more subtle GC Ries like Brand, already delicious and zesty in 14. New voluptuous PINOT GR CLOS Windsbuhl 15.

Châteaux of Bordeaux

Abbreviations used in the text:

B'x	Bordeaux
Bar	Barsac
Cas	Castillon-Côtes de Bordeaux
E-2-M	Entre-Deux-Mers
Fron	Fronsac
Grav	Graves
H-Méd	Haut-Médoc
L de P	Lalande de Pomerol
List	Listrac
Mar	Margaux
Méd	Médoc
Mou	Moulis
Pau	Pauillac
Pe-Lé	Pessac-Léognan
Pom	Pomerol
Saut	Sauternes
St-Ém	St-Émilion
St-Est	St-Estèphe
St-Jul	St-Julien

AC	appellation contrôlée
ch(x)	château(x)
dom(s)	domaine(s)

A remarkable number of the Bordeaux properties listed below are designated (in red) as good value. Remarkable because the word on the street is that the world's biggest fine-wine region is overpriced. It often looks that way on restaurant wine lists that don't hesitate to mark up cast-iron reputations. It's true that the top growths, sometimes big, sometimes very small, have cult followings and attract "collectors", who are often in reality investors looking for a return. The fact remains that if you are looking for what Bordeaux offers – appetizing, not exaggerated flavours in a digestible partner to food that is available worldwide and keeps for many years, growing more interesting as it goes – this is the

Châteaux of Bordeaux entries also cross-reference to France.

great source of supply. Being so vast and so long-established, Bordeaux offers something nowhere else does.

Compare the prices of mid-to-lower-ranking Bordeaux to similar wines from California or Italy and you find that Bordeaux is highly competitive – and more predictable. Not much novelty – hence less sommelier excitement. The growing Chinese market is certainly helping Bordeaux. Fine; we all benefit from its continuing success.

Frost is the word that encapsulates the 2017 vintage in Bordeaux. April 27–8 saw the worst since 1991, resulting in a crop that was 40–50 per cent down on 2016 (5.77 million hl). Some will not be making any *grand vin* at all. Otherwise, quality is varied, with only the Pomerol and St-Émilion plateaux, vineyards in Pessac and those close to the estuary in the Médoc coming off unscathed. You'll need to pick and choose carefully from the limited offerings. Luckily, producers have two very good vintages in their cellars, 2015 and 2016, with the less showy 2014 offering good-value drinking if you bide your time.

Meanwhile there is a reserve of good red vintages. The luscious 2009s are tempting at whatever level (but don't open them too soon). The 2008s have come into their own. The 2010s are opening, although the Grands Crus need longer. For early drinking try the often-charming 2012s or often-underrated 2011s; austere at first but improving with bottle age. For all sorts of reasons St-Émilion is on a roll just now as the place to look for substantial, satisfying, modern-tasting wines at fair prices that are drinkable within two or three years. They may not be "classic" claret, with the freshness and "cut" of the Médoc, but they suit our crossover cooking, and those who drink red wine without food. Among the Grands Crus the mature vintages to look for are 2000, 2001 (particularly Right Bank), 2002 (top-end Médoc) and 2004, with the very best 2007s still worthy of consideration. The 2006s are just beginning to open, but hang on a little longer for the splendid 2005s. Dry white Bordeaux remains consistent in quality and value. There's not much in 2017 but what there is is good. Remember that fine white Graves ages as well as white burgundy – sometimes better. And Sauternes continues to offer an array of remarkable years, to which 2017 can be added. The problem here is being spoilt for choice: 2016, 2015, 2011, 2009, 2007, 2005 and 2001 are as good as it gets for these luxurious indulgences. And 2014, 2013 and 2010 are not far behind.

A, Dom de L' Cas r ★★ 05' 06 08 09' 10' 11 12 **14** 15 16 MERLOT-led CAS property owned by STÉPHANE DERENONCOURT and his wife. Bio. Punches above its weight.

Agassac, D' H-Méd r ★★ 06 08 09' 10' 11 12 **14** 15 16 Consistent CH in S H-MÉD. Modern, accessible wine. CAB SAUV-led. Tourist-friendly.

Aiguilhe, D' Cas r ★★ 06 07 08 09 10' 11 12 **14** 15 16 Large estate in CAS on high plateau. Same owner as CANON LA GAFFELIÈRE and LA MONDOTTE. MERLOT-led wine with *power and finesse*. Also dry white Le Blanc d'Aiguilhe.

Andron-Blanquet St-Est r ★★ 04 05' 06 08 09' 10' 11 **14** 15 16 Sister CH to COS-LABORY. Often value.

Angélus St-Ém r ★★★★ 96 98' 99 00' 01 02 03 04 05 06 07 08 09' 10' 11 12 13 14 15' 16' 17 PREMIER GRAND CRU CLASSÉ (A) since 2012 so prices up. Imposing cellars with wrought-iron bell tower. Pioneer of modern ST-ÉM; dark, rich, sumptuous. Lots of CAB FR (min 40%). Second label: Le Carillon d'Angélus (new gravity-fed cellar in 2018). Now a 3rd wine, No 3.

Angludet Marg r (w) ★★ 04 05 06 08 09' **10'** 11 12 **14** 15 16 Owned and run by

NÉGOCIANT SICHEL family since 1961. CAB SAUV, MERLOT, 13% PETIT VERDOT. Fragrant, stylish, consistent wines. Value.

Archambeau Grav r w dr (sw) ★★ (r) **08 09** 10 11 14 15 16 (w) 11 12 **13 14 15** 16 Consistent property; v'yd in single block on hill at Illats. Gd *fruity dry white*; fragrant barrel-aged reds. Also rosé.

Arche, D' Saut w sw ★★ 00 01' 02 03' 05 07 09' 10' **11'** 13 14 15 16 Consistent, gd-value Second Growth on edge of SAUT. And a luxury hotel.

Armailhac, D' Pau r ★★★ 00 01 02 04 05' 06 08 09' **10'** 11 12 14 15 16 17 Substantial Fifth Growth. (MOUTON) ROTHSCHILD owned since 1934. On top form, fair value. Supple and expressive earlier (30% MERLOT plus CAB FR).

Arrosée, L' St-Ém r ★★★ 00 01 02 03 04 **05' 06' 07** 08 09' **10' 11 12** RIP from 2013, bought by Dillons of HAUT-BRION, integrated into QUINTUS. Until then on top form since 2003. Mellow, harmonious wines with plenty of CAB FR, CAB SAUV (40%).

Aurelius St-Ém r ★★ **08 09** 10 11 12 14 15 16 Top CUVÉE from the go-ahead ST-ÉM CO-OP – 50,000 bottles/yr. Modern, MERLOT-led, new oak, concentrated.

Ausone St-Ém r ★★★★ 89' 90 95 96' **97 98'** 99 00' 01' 02 03' 04 **05' 06' 07** 08 09' 10' **11 12 13 14** 15' 16' 17 Tiny, illustrious ST-ÉM First Growth (c.1500 cases) named after Roman poet; best position on CÔTES. Vine density up to 12,600 vines/ha. Lots of CAB FR (55%). Long-lived wines with volume, texture, finesse. At a price. Second label: Chapelle d'Ausone (500 cases). *La Clotte*, FONBEL, MOULIN-ST-GEORGES, Simard sister estates.

Balestard la Tonnelle St-Ém r ★★ 01 03 04 05 06 08 09 10 11 12 14 15 16 17 Historic DOM owned by Capdemourlin family on limestone plateau. Recent vintages more modern.

Barde-Haut St-Ém r ★★→★★★ 01 02 03 05' 06 07 08 09 10 11 12 14 15 16 Environmentally friendly GRAND CRU CLASSÉ. Sister property of CLOS L'ÉGLISE, HAUT-BERGEY, Branon in Léognan. Rich, modern, opulent.

Bastor-Lamontagne Saut w sw ★★ 99 01' 02 03' 05 07 09' 10 11 13 14 15 16 Large unclassified Preignac sister to BEAUREGARD and St-Robert in GRAV. Owned by Galeries Lafayette and SMITH-HAUT-LAFITTE. Gd value; pure, harmonious. Second label: Les Remparts de Bastor.

Batailley Pau r ★★★ 03 04 05' 06 08 09' **10' 11 12 13 14** 15 16 17 Gd-value and representative Fifth Growth PAU estate owned by BORIE-MANOUX connections. Second label: Lions de Batailley.

Beaumont H-Méd r ★★ **05' 06** 08 09 10' 12 **14 15** 16 Large estate (around 42,000 cases) between MAR and ST-JUL. Owned by Castel and Suntory; early-maturing, *easily enjoyable wines*.

Beauregard Pom r ★★★ 01 02 04 05' 08 09' **10' 12** 14 15 16 Consistent mid-weight POM, converting to organics. Now more depth. Owned by SMITH-HAUT-LAFITTE and Galeries Lafayette family. Second label: Benjamin de Beauregard. Also Pavillon Beauregard in L DE P.

Beau-Séjour-Bécot St-Ém r ★★★ 95' 96 98' 00' 01 02 03 04 05' 06 08 **09' 10' 11 12** 14 15 16 Distinguished PREMIER GRAND CRU CLASSÉ (B) on limestone plateau. New generation of Bécot family at helm (2017). Lighter touch. Still gd ageing potential.

Beauséjour-Duffau St-Ém r ★★★ 00 01 02 **03 04** 05' 06 08 **09' 10' 11** 12 14 15 16 17

Tiny PREMIER GRAND CRU CLASSÉ estate on côtes. Managed by Thienpont-DERENONCOURT team. Direct sales from property. Second label: Croix de Beauséjour.

Beau-Site St-Est r ★★ 03 04 05 06 08 09 10 11 12 13 14 15 16 Gd-value CRU BOURGEOIS property owned by BORIE-MANOUX. 70% CAB SAUV. Supple, fresh, accessible.

Average size of estate in B'x is 17.2 ha (2015), double that of 20 yrs ago.

Bélair Monange St-Ém r ★★★ **98** 00' 01 02 03 04 05' 06 08 09' **10'** 11 12 13 14 15 16' 17 PREMIER GRAND CRU CLASSÉ on limestone plateau owned by J-P MOUEIX. Loads of investment in v'yd. Fine, fragrant but riper and more intense these days. Second label (since 2014): Annonce de Bélair Monange.

Belgrave H-Méd r ★★ 02' 03 04' 05' 06 08 09' **10'** 11 12 13 14 15 16 17 Fifth Growth managed by DOURTHE since 1979. CAB SAUV dominant. Modern-classic in style. Now consistent quality. Second label: Diane de Belgrave.

Bellefont-Belcier St-Ém r ★★ 04 05' 06 07 08' 09' **10'** 12 14 15 16 17 ST-ÉM GRAND CRU CLASSÉ now (2017) in the hands of Hong Kong businessman Peter Kwok (already owner in St-Ém, POM). Suave, full, fresh.

Belle-Vue H-Méd r ★★ 05 06 08 09 10 11 12 **14** 15 16 Consistent, gd-value s H-MÉD. Dark, dense but firm, fresh, aromatic. 100% PETIT VERDOT CUVÉE in 2016.

Berliquet St-Ém r ★★ 01 02 04 05' 06 08 09 10 11 **14** 15 16 17 Tiny GRAND CRU CLASSÉ on côtes. Sold to owners of CANON in 2017. Fresh, elegant, ages well. Second label: Les Ailes de Berliquet.

Bernadotte H-Méd r ★★→★★★ 01 02 03 04 05' 06 08 09' **10'** 11 **14** 15 16 N H-MÉD CH in St-Sauveur. Owned by a Hong Kong-based group: ANGÉLUS owner consults. Savoury style. Recent vintages more finesse.

Beychevelle St-Jul r ★★★ 00' 01 02 03 04 05' 06 07 08 09' **10'** 11 12 13 14 15 16 17 Fourth Growth with charismatic label: ship with a griffin-shaped prow. Wines of consistent *elegance* rather than power. New gravity-fed winery inaugurated in 2016. Second label: Amiral de Beychevelle.

Biston-Brillette Mou r ★★ 05' 06 08 09 10' 11 12 14 15 16 CRU BOURGEOIS owned by Barbarin family. 50/50 MERLOT, CAB SAUV. Gd-value, attractive, fruit-bound wines.

Bonalgue Pom r ★★ 05 06 08 09 10 11 12 14 15 16 Dark, rich, meaty. Appealing young but will age. As gd value as it gets. Owned by Libourne NÉGOCIANT JB Audy. Sister estates CLOS du Clocher, CH du Courlat in LUSSAC-ST-ÉMILION.

Bonnet B'x r w ★★ (r) 10 12 14 15 16 (w) DYA. Owned by veteran (now 93 yrs old) André Lurton. Big producer of some of best E-2-M and red (Rés) B'x. LA LOUVIÈRE, **Couhins-Lurton**, ROCHEMORIN and Cruzeau in PE-LÉ same stable.

Bon Pasteur, Le Pom r ★★★ 02 03 04 05' 05' 06 08 09' **10'** 11 12 13 14 15 16 Tiny property on ST-ÉM border with 21 different plots. Former owner, MICHEL ROLLAND, makes the wine. Ripe, opulent, seductive wines guaranteed.

Boscq, Le St-Est r ★★ 04 05' 06 08 09' 10 11 12 14 15 16 Quality-driven ST-EST owned by DOURTHE. Consistently great value.

Bourgneuf Pom r ★★ 03 04 05' 06 08 09 10 11 12 14 15 16 17 V'yd situated to w of POM plateau. Subtle, savoury wines. 2015, 16 best yet (racy, balanced). Gd value Pom.

Bouscaut Pe-Lé r w ★★★ (r) 01 04 05' 06 08 09 10' 11 12 14 15 16 (w) 06 07 08 09 10' 11 12 13 14 15 16 17 GRAV Classed Growth. MERLOT-based reds with 10% MALBEC. Sappy, age-worthy *whites*. Tourist-friendly, incl *gîte*.

Boyd-Cantenac Marg r ★★ 02 03 04 05' 06 08 09' **10'** 11 12 14 15 16 Tiny Cantenac-based Third Growth. Same family ownership since 1932. CAB SAUV-dominated. Gd value. POUGET same stable. Second label: Jacques Boyd.

Branaire-Ducru St-Jul r ★★★ 01 02 03 04 05' 06 08 09' **10'** 11 12 13 14 15 16' 17 Consistent Fourth Growth; regularly gd value; ageing potential. RIP (2017) owner Patrick Maroteaux; son François-Xavier now at helm. Second label: *Duluc*.

Branas Grand Poujeaux Mou r ★★ 06 08 09 10 11 12 14 15 16 Tiny neighbour of

Picking on Castillon

Producers in POM and ST-ÉM have clearly earmarked CAS as gd-value area for investment. The following CHX all have ties to prestige Right Bank properties: Ampélia (GRAND-CORBIN-DESPAGNE), CLOS Les Lunelles (PAVIE), D'AIGUILHE (CANON LA GAFFELIÈRE), L'Hêtre (LE PIN), Joanin Bécot (BEAU-SÉJOUR-BÉCOT), l'Aurage (TERTRE-RÔTEBOEUF), Montlandrie (L'EGLISE-CLINET). Consultant STÉPHANE DERENONCOURT owns DOM DE L'A. Tony Laithwaite (La Clarière) got there in 1965.

CHASSE-SPLEEN, POUJEAUX. 50% MERLOT. Ripe, fine, supple tannins. ANGÉLUS owner consults. Sister to Villemaurine in ST-ÉM. Second label: Les Eclats de Branas.

Brane-Cantenac Marg r ★★★→★★★★ 00' 01 02 04 05' 06 08 09' 10' 11 12 13 14 15 16 CAB SAUV-led Second Growth on Cantenac plateau. Classic, fragrant MARG with structure to age. Second label: Baron de Brane. White B'X in pipeline.

Brillette Mou r ★★ 05 06 08 09 10 11 12 14 15 16 CRU BOURGEOIS with v'yd on gravelly soils. Same owner since 1975. Gd depth, fruit. Second label: Haut Brillette.

Cabanne, La Pom r ★★ 05 06' 09 10 11 12 14 15 16 V'yd w of POM plateau. Cellars rebuilt after a fire (2011). Firm when young; needs bottle age. Second label: DOM de Compostelle.

Caillou Saut w sw ★★ 99 01' 02 03' 05' 07 09' 10 11' 13 14 15 16 Discreet Second Growth BAR for pure, fruity *liquoreux*. Neighbour of CLIMENS. Second label: Les Erables. Third wine: Les Tourelles.

Calon-Ségur St-Est r ★★★★ 96' 98 00' 01 02 03' 04 05' 06 07 08' 09' 10' 11 12 13 14 15' 16' 17 Third Growth with great historic reputation. New *cuvier* (2016), barrel cellars and bottle storage gallery. More CAB SAUV now. Estate really flying these days. Second label: Le Marquis de Calon.

Cambon la Pelouse H-Méd r ★★ 05' 06 08 09 10' 11 12 14 15 16 Big, reliable, fruit-forward S H-MÉD CRU BOURGEOIS. Accessible young.

Camensac, De H-Méd r ★★ 05 06 08 09 10' 11 12 14 15 16 Fifth Growth in N H-MÉD. Owned by Merlaut family (GRUAUD-LAROSE, CHASSE-SPLEEN). Steady improvement in recent yrs. Usually benefits from bottle age. Second label: Second de Camensac.

Canon St-Ém r ★★★→★★★★ 01 02 03 04 05' 06 07 08' 09' 10' 11 12 13 14 15' 16' 17 Esteemed PREMIER GRAND CRU CLASSÉ (B) with walled v'yd on limestone plateau. Wertheimer-owned, like BERLIQUET, RAUZAN-SÉGLA, ST-SUPÉRY. Now flying; elegant, long-lived wines. One of top wines of 2016. Nicolas Audebert succeeded John Kolasa as MD in 2015. Second label: Croix Canon (until 2011 CLOS Canon).

Canon la Gaffelière St-Ém r ★★★ 00' 01 02 03 04 05' 06 08 09' 10' 11 12 13 14 15 16 PREMIER GRAND CRU CLASSÉ (B) on S foot slope. Same ownership as AIGUILHE, CLOS DE L'ORATOIRE, LA MONDOTTE. Lots of CABS FR and SAUV (with MERLOT). Stylish, upfront, impressive wines. Organic certification.

Cantemerle H-Méd r ★★★ 04 05' 06 08 09' 10' 11 12 13 14 15 16 17 Large Fifth Growth in S H-MÉD with beautiful wooded park. Average age of v'yd 30 yrs. On gd form & gd value too. Second label: Les Allées de Cantemerle.

Cantenac-Brown Marg r ★★→★★★ 01 02 03 04 05' 06 08 09' 10' 11 12 14 15 16 Third Growth owned by Simon Halabi family. Manager José Sanfins. Previously robust style; now more voluptous, refined. Dry white Alto (90% SAUV BL). Second label: BriO de Cantenac-Brown.

Capbern St-Est r ★★ 04 05 06 08' 09' 10' 11 12 13 14 15 16 17 Capbern-Gasqueton until 2013. Same ownership, management as sister CALON-SÉGUR. Gd form/value.

Cap de Mourlin St-Ém r ★★→★★★ 01 03 04 05 06 08 09 10 11 12 14 15 16 GRAND CRU CLASSÉ on N slopes. V'yd created in C16. MERLOT-led (65%). MICHEL ROLLAND consults. More power, concentration than in past.

Carbonnieux Pe-Lé r w ★★★ 02 04 05' 06 08 09' 10 11 12 15 16 GRAV Classed Growth making sterling red and white; large volumes of both. **Whites**, 65% SAUV BL, eg. 06 07 08 09 10 11 12 13 14 15 16, have ageing potential. Red can age as well. Tourist-friendly. Second label: Tour Léognan.

Carles, De B'x r ★★ 05' 06' 07 08 09 10 11 12 13 14 15 16 FRON property. Haut-Carles is prestige CUVÉE. 20–40,000 bottles depending on yr. Opulent, modern style.

Carmes Haut-Brion, Les Pe-Lé r ★★★ 04 05' 06 07 08 09' 10' 11 12' 13 14 15 16' Tiny walled-in v'yd in heart of B'x; 42% MERLOT, 40% CAB FR, 18% CAB SAUV, structured but suave. New Philippe Starck-designed winery. Second label: Le C des Carmes Haut-Brion.

Caronne-Ste-Gemme H-Méd r ★★ 05 06 08 09' 10' 11 12 14 15 16 Sizeable n H-MÉD estate in St-Laurent-Méd. CAB SAUV led (60%). Wines fresh, structured; more depth recently.

Carruades de Lafite Pau ★★★ Second label of CH LAFITE. 20,000 cases/yr. Second Growth (1855) prices. Refined, smooth, savoury; a junior Lafite, in fact. Accessible earlier but 09 is still young.

Carteau Côtes-Daugay St-Ém r ★★ 05 08 09 10 11 14 15 16 Gd-value ST-ÉM GRAND CRU; full-flavoured, supple wines. Same family ownership since 1850.

Certan-de-May Pom r ★★★ 00' 01' 04 05' 06 08 09' 10' 11 12' 14 15' 16' 17 Tiny neighbour of VIEUX-CH-CERTAN. Former PETRUS winemaker consults. Long-ageing.

Chantegrive, De Grav r w ★★→★★★ 05' 08 09' 10' 11 12 14 15 16 Leading GRAV estate. ANGÉLUS owner consults. V.gd quality, value. Rich, finely oaked reds. CUVÉE Caroline is top, *fragrant white* 10 11 12 13 14 15 16.

Chasse-Spleen Mou r (w) ★★★ 04 05' 06 08 09' 10' 12 14 15 16 17 Big (100 ha), well-known MOU estate run by Céline Villars. Produces gd, often outstanding, long-maturing wine; classical structure, fragrance. Sells at Fifth Growth prices. Makes a little white.

Chauvin St-Ém r ★★ 05 06 08 09 10' 11 12 14 15 16' GRAND CRU CLASSÉ owned by Sylvie Cazes of LYNCH-BAGES. 2016 best yet. New Cupid label.

Cheval Blanc St-Ém r ★★★★ 89 90' 94 95 96' 97 98' 99 00' 01' 02 03 04 05' 06 07 08 09' 10' 11 12 13 14 15' 16' 17 PREMIER GRAND CRU CLASSÉ (A) superstar of ST-ÉM, easy to love. High percentage of CAB FR (60%). Firm, fragrant wines verging on POM. Delicious young; lasts a generation, or two. Second label: Le Petit Cheval (none made 2015). New Le Petit Cheval Blanc from 2014 (100% SAUV BL, vines from B'X, SANCERRE). Sister-CH of YQUEM.

Chevalier, Dom de Pe-Lé r w ★★★★ 00' 01' 02 03 04 05' 06 07 08 09' 10' 11 12 13 14 15' 16' 17 V. special estate in Léognan pine woods, doubled in size from when Bernard family bought in 1983. Pure, dense, finely textured red. Impressive, complex, long-ageing white has remarkable consistency; wait for rich flavours 00 01 02 03 04 05' 06 07' 08' 09' 10 11 12 13 14 15' 16' 17. Second label: Esprit de Chevalier, CLOS des Lunes, DOM de la Solitude, Lespault-Martillac same stable.

Cissac H-Méd r ★★ 00 05 08 09 10 11 12 14 15 16 N H-MÉD estate. Same family ownership since 1895. Firm, CAB SAUV-led wines; used to need time, recent vintages less austere. Second label: Reflets du CH Cissac.

Merlot accounts for 66% of red grapes planted in B'x.

Citran H-Méd r ★★ 00 04 05' 06 08 09 10' 14 15 16 Sizeable s H-MÉD estate. In Merlaut family (GRUAUD-LAROSE) hands since 1996. Medium-weight, ageing up to 10 yrs. Second label: Moulins de Citran.

Clarence de Haut-Brion, Le Pe-Lé r ★★★ 96' 00 01 02 03 04 05' 06 07 08 09' 10' 11 12 14 15 16' 17 Second label of CH HAUT-BRION, until 2007 known as Bahans Haut-Brion. Blend changes considerably with each vintage (anything from 40–80% MERLOT) but same suave texture and elegance as *grand vin*.

Clarke List r (p) (w) ★★ 05' 06 08 09' 10' 11 12 14 15 16 17 Leading LIST owned by

Benjamin de Rothschild. V.gd MERLOT-based red. Dark fruit, fine tannins. Eric Boissenot now consults (previously MICHEL ROLLAND). Also a dry white: Le Merle Blanc du CH Clarke. Ch Malmaison in MOU same stable.

Clauzet St-Est r ★★ 06 08 09 10 11 12 14 15 16' Gd-value CRU BOURGEOIS owned by Baron Velge since 1997. Steady investment, expansion, improvement. CAB SAUV-led. Now consistent quality. Also sister CH de Côme.

Clerc Milon Pau r ★★★ 00 01 02 04 05' 06 07 08 09' 10' 11 12 13 14 15 16' 17 V'yd tripled in size since (MOUTON) Rothschilds purchased in 1970 (now 40 ha). Broader and weightier than sister D'ARMAILHAC. V.gd 2016 but price up. Second label: Pastourelle de Clerc Milon.

Climens Saut sw ★★★★ 96 97' 98 99' 00 01' 02 03' 04 05' 06 07 08 09' 10' 11' 12' 13' 14 15 16' BAR Classed Growth managed with aplomb by Bérénice Lurton. Concentrated wines with vibrant acidity; ageing potential guaranteed. Certified bio. V'yd badly hit by frost in 2017. Second label: Les Cyprès (gd value).

Clinet Pom r ★★★ 01 02 03 05' 06 07 08' 09' 10 11 12 14 15 16 17 Family-owned and -run (Ronan Laborde) estate on POM plateau. MERLOT-dominant (90%). Average 4000 cases/yr. Sumptuous, modern in style. Second label: Fleur de Clinet.

Clos de l'Oratoire St-Ém r ★★ 04 05' 06 08 09 10' 11 12 14 15 16 Gd value GRAND CRU CLASSÉ on ST-ÉM N slopes. Same stable as AIGUILHE, CANON-LA-GAFFELIÈRE, LA MONDOTTE.

Clos des Jacobins St-Ém r ★★→★★★ 01 02 03 04 05' 06 07 08 09' 10' 11 12 14 15 16 Côtes GRAND CRU CLASSÉ at top of game. Renovated, modernized, now showing great consistency; powerful, modern style. ANGÉLUS owner consults. CH La Commanderie (ST-ÉM) same stable.

Clos du Marquis St-Jul r ★★ 03 04 05' 06 07 08 09' 10' 11 12 13 14 15 16' 17 More typically ST-JUL than stablemate LÉOVILLE-LAS-CASES; CAB SAUV dominates (75%). Second label: La Petite Marquise.

Clos Floridène Grav r w ★★ (r) 09' 10' 11 12 14 15 16 (w) 07 08' 09 10 11' 12 13 14 15 16 17 Creation of late Denis Dubourdieu, now run by his sons, Fabrice and Jean Jacques. SAUV BL/SÉM from limestone provides *fine modern white* GRAV, able to age; much-improved red. CHX DOISY-DAËNE, Haura, REYNON in same stable.

Clos Fourtet St-Ém r ★★★ 00 01 02 03 04 05' 06 07 08 09' 10' 11 12 14 15 16 17 PREMIER GRAND CRU CLASSÉ (B) on limestone plateau. Classic, stylish ST-ÉM. Consistently gd form. STÉPHANE DERENONCOURT consults. St-Ém's Côte de Baleau and Les Grandes Murailles same stable. Second label: La Closerie de Fourtet.

Clos Haut-Peyraguey Saut w sw ★★★ 95' 96 97' 98 99 00 01' 02 03' 04 05' 06 07 09' 10' 11' 12 13 14 15 16 Fourth Classed Growth in the hands of magnate Bernard Magrez (FOMBRAUGE, LA TOUR-CARNET, PAPE-CLÉMENT the others). Elegant, harmonious wines with ageing potential. Second label: Symphonie.

Clos l'Église Pom r ★★★ 00' 01 02 03 04 05' 06 07 08 09' 10 11 12 13 14 15 16 Neighbour of L'ÉGLISE-CLINET. Elegant wine that will age. Owned by VIGNOBLES Garcin (as are BARDE-HAUT, Branon, HAUT-BERGEY). Second label: Esprit de l'Église.

Clos Puy Arnaud Cas r ★★ 04 05' 06 08 09' 10 11 12 14 15 16 17 Certified bio (2010). Leading CAS estate. Wines of depth, bright acidity. Earlier-drinking CUVÉE Pervenche.

Sustainable persuasion

B'x still has far to go but growers are being urged to restrict the use of chemicals in the v'yd. Modifications to the guidelines for ACS B'x and B'x SUPÉRIEUR aim to spur things along. It is now forbidden to use herbicides around parcels and in the totality of the surface area. Dead vines must be removed and destroyed and growers should measure and know their "treatment-frequency index". Finally, the cultivation of up to 5% of other grape varieties is now permitted to encourage experimentation with disease-resistant varieties.

Clos René Pom r ★★ 01 04 05' 06 08 09 10 11 12 14 15 16 Family-owned for over a century. MERLOT-led with a little spicy MALBEC. Less sensuous, celebrated than top POM but gd value, can age.

Clotte, La St-Ém r ★★ 04 05 06 08 09' 10' 11 12 15 16' 17 Tiny côtes GRAND CRU CLASSÉ. Steady improvement under AUSONE ownership. Second label: L de La Clotte.

Conseillante, La Pom r ★★★★ 96' 98' 00' 01 02 03 04 05' 06' 07 08 09' 10' 11 12 13 14 15 16' 17 Owned by Nicolas family since 1871. Renovated barrel cellar (2017). Some of noblest, most fragrant POM; almost Médocain in style. 80% MERLOT on clay, gravel soils. Second label: Duo de Conseillante.

Corbin St-Ém r ★★ 04 05 07 08 09' 10' 11 12 14 15' 16 Consistent, gd-value GRAND CRU CLASSÉ. Power, finesse. Annabelle Cruse-Bardinet owner-winemaker.

Just 7% of the B'x v'yd is cultivated organically.

Cos d'Estournel St-Est r ★★★★ 95 96' 98' 00 01 02 03 04 05' 06 07 08 09' 10' 11 12 13 14 15' 16' 17 Big Second Growth on PAU border with eccentric pagoda chai. Refined, suave, hugh-scoring ST-EST. Cutting-edge cellars. Too-pricey SAUV BL-dominated white; now more refined. Second label: Les Pagodes de Cos. Fresh-styled Goulée (MÉD) same ownership (Goulée Blanc too). CH Pomys in St-Est added to stable (2017).

Cos-Labory St-Est r ★★ 98' 00 02 03 04 05' 06 07 08 09' 10' 11 12 14 15 16' 17 Small family-owned Fifth Growth neighbour of COS D'ESTOURNEL; gd value. More depth, structure recently. Second label: Charme de Cos Labory.

Coufran H-Méd r ★★ 04 05 06 08 09 10' 11 12 14 15 16' 17 Sizeable estate in St-Seurin-de-Cadourne. Owned by Miailhe family since 1924. Mainly MERLOT (85%) for supple wine; but can age. Verdignan sister property.

Couhins-Lurton Pe-Lé r w ★★ ⋅★★★ (r) 05 06 08 09 10' 11 14 15 16 (w) 05 06 07 08' 09 10' 11 12 13 14 15 16 *Fine*, tense, long-lived, Classed Growth *white* from SAUV BL (100%). Much-improved, MERLOT-based red. André Lurton-owned.

Couspaude, La St-Ém r ★★★ 04 05 06 07 08 09' 10' 11 12 14 15 16 17 GRAND CRU CLASSÉ on limestone plateau. Owned by Aubert family. Style is rich, creamy with lashings of spicy oak.

Coutet Saut w sw ★★★ 95 96 97' 98'099 01' 02 03' 04 05 07 09' 10' 11' 12 13 14 15' 16 17 Sizeable BAR property owned by Baly family. Consistently v. fine. CUVÉE Madame is a v. rich, old-vine, berry-by-berry selection 89 90 95 97 01 03. Second label: La Chartreuse de Coutet. V.gd dry white, Opalie.

Couvent des Jacobins St-Ém r ★★ 00' 01 03 04 05 06 08 09' 10' 11 12 14 15 GRAND CRU CLASSÉ vinified within walls of town. Same family ownership for over 100 yrs. MERLOT-led with CAB FR. Lighter style but can age.

Crabitey Grav r w ★★ (r) 08 09 10 11 12 14 15 16 (w) 11 12 13 14 15 16 Former orphanage at Portets. Average age of v'yd 30 yrs. Owner Arnaud de Butler now making harmonious MERLOT/CAB SAUV and small volume of lively SÉM/SAUV BL.

Crock, Le St-Est r ★★ 04 05 06 08 09' 10' 11 12 14 15 16' Gd-value CRU BOURGEOIS. Majority MERLOT/CAB SAUV with CAB FR, PETIT VERDOT. Solid, fruit-packed.

Croix, La Pom r ★★ 04 05 06 08 09 10 11 12 14 15 Owned by NÉGOCIANT Janoueix. Organically run. MERLOT-led (60%). Le Castelot, HAUT-SARPE same stable.

Croix-de-Gay, La Pom r ★★★ 01' 04 05 06 08 09' 10' 11 12 14 15 16 17 Tiny MERLOT-dominant (95%) v'yd owned by Chantal Raynaud-Lebreton. Racy, elegant style. SPECIAL CUVÉE La Fleur-de-Gay.

Croix du Casse, La Pom r ★★ 05 06 08 09 10 11 12 14 15 16 Same stable as DOM DE L'ÉGLISE. On S POM sandy/gravel soils. Steady progress. Medium-body; gd value.

Croizet-Bages Pau r ★★⋅★★★ 03 04 05 06 08 09 10' 11 12 14 15 16 17 Striving Fifth Growth; still work to be done. Lately, more consistency but fails to excite. Same family owner since 1934.

Cru Bourgeois Now a certificate awarded annually. 271 CH'X (2015). Quality variable.

Cruzelles, Les L de P r ★★ 08 09 10 11 12 14 15 16 Consistent, gd-value wine. Ageing potential in top yrs. Same stable as L'ÉGLISE-CLINET and Montlandrie (CAS).

Dalem Fron r ★★ 05' 06 08 09' 10' 11 12 14 15 16 17 Same family ownership since 1955. MERLOT-dominated (90%). Smooth, ripe, fresh.

Dassault St-Ém r ★★ 03 04 05' 06 07 08 09' 10 11 12 14 15 16 Consistent, modern, juicy GRAND CRU CLASSÉ in n of AC. Bought by Marcel Dassault in 1955. Second label: D de Dassault. La Fleur and Faurie-de-Souchard sister CHX.

Dauphine, De la Fron r ★★→★★★ 03 04 05 06' 08 09' 10' 11 12' 14 15 17 Substantial FRON estate. Sweeping change from 2000. Renovation of CH, v'yds plus new winery, additional land acquired, organic certification. Now more substance, finesse. Former Ch Haut-Ballet absorbed in 2016. Best of Wine Tourism Award 2018. Second label: Delphis.

Dauzac Marg r ★★→★★★ 98' 00' 01 02 04 05 08' 09' 10' 11 12 14 15 16 Fifth Growth at Labarde; now dense, rich, dark wines. Bio trials. Owned by MAIF insurance company. Second label: La Bastide Dauzac. Also fruity Aurore de Dauzac and CH Labarde (H-MÉD). D de Dauzac is AC B'X.

Desmirail Marg r ★★→★★★ 03 04 05 06 07 09' 10' 11 12 14 15 16 17 Third Growth at Cantenac. CAB SAUV-led (70%). Fine, delicate style. Second label: Initial de Desmirail. Visitor-friendly.

Destieux St-Ém r ★★ 03' 04 05' 06 07 08 09' 10' 11 12 14 15 16 GRAND CRU CLASSÉ located at St-Hippolyte. Solid, powerful style; consistent. MICHEL ROLLAND consults. La Clémence in POM same stable.

Doisy-Daëne Bar (r) w dr sw ★★★ 95 96 97' 98' 99 01' 02 03 04 05' 06 07 09 10' 11' 12 13 14 15' 16 Second Growth owned by Dubourdieu family (CLOS FLORIDÉNE). Produces *fine, sweet* Barsac. L'Extravagant 02 03 04 05 06 07 09 10 11 12 13 14 15 16 an intensely rich, expensive CUVÉE. Also dry white Doisy-Daëne SEC.

Doisy-Védrines Saut w sw ★★★ 95 96 97' 98 99 01' 03' 04 05 07 09 10' 11' 12 13 14 15' 16 BAR estate owned by Castéja family. Richer style than DOISY-DAËNE. *Long-term fave*; delicious, gd value. Second label: Petit Védrines.

Dôme, Le St-Ém r ★★★ 05 06 08 09 10' 11 12 13 14 15 16 Microwine; rich, modern, more freshness than past. Two-thirds old-vine CAB FR, nr ANGÉLUS. NB string of other gd ST-ÉMS in same stable: CH Teyssier (value), Laforge, Le Carré, Le Pontet, Les Astéries, Vieux-Ch-Mazerat.

Dominique, La St-Ém r ★★★ 98 00' 01 04 05' 06 08 09' 10' 11 12 14 15 16 GRAND CRU CLASSÉ next to CHEVAL BLANC. Rich, powerful, juicy style. MERLOT-led (81%). Jean Nouvel-designed winery with rooftop restaurant (La Terrasse Rouge) and shop. Second label: Relais de la Dominique.

Ducru-Beaucaillou St-Jul r ★★★★ 96' 98 99 00' 01 02 03 04 05' 06 07 08 09' 10' 11 12 13 14 15' 16 Outstanding Second Growth in astute hands of Bruno Borie. Heart of ST-JUL. Excellent form; classic cedar-scented claret, suited to long ageing. Croix de Beaucaillou, Lalande-Borie sister estates. Also Fourcas-Borie in LIST.

Duhart-Milon Rothschild Pau r ★★★ 96' 98 00' 01 02 03 04 05' 06 07 08 09' 10' 11

Don't forget to eat

A growing number of CHX are either acquiring or launching restaurants. Witness L'Atelier de Candale (CLOS DES JACOBINS), Les Belles Perdrix (TROPLONG MONDOT), Hostellerie de Plaisance (PAVIE), Logis de la Cadène (ANGÉLUS), La Terrasse Rouge (LA DOMINIQUE) in ST-ÉM; Le Café Lavinal (LYNCH-BAGES), La Table d'Agassac (D'AGASSAC) in the MÉD; La Grande Maison (PAPE CLÉMENT), Les Sources de Caudalie (SMITH-HAUT-LAFITTE) in PE-LÉ. SAUT too, now has culinary offerings at Chx GUIRAUD and LAFAURIE-PEYRAGUEY.

12 13 14 15 16' 17 Fourth Growth stablemate of LAFITE. Same winemaking team. CAB SAUV-dominated (65–80%). V. fine quality esp last 10 yrs. Second label: Moulin de Duhart.

Durfort-Vivens Marg r ★★★ 00 02 03 04 05' 06 08 09' 10' 11 12 13 14 15 16' 17 Much improved MARG Second Growth. CAB SAUV-dominated (70%). Change to bio (certified 2016) has made a difference. Second labels: Vivens and Relais de Durfort-Vivens.

There are 6568 growers in B'x (2016), half the number of 20 yrs ago.

Eglise, Dom de l' Pom r ★★ 00 01 02 03 04 05' 06 08 09 10' 11 12 14 15 16 17 Oldest v'yd in POM (1589). Clay/gravel soils of plateau. Owned by Castéja family since 1973. Consistent, fleshy wines of late.

Église-Clinet, L' Pom r ★★★ →★★★★ 95 96 98' 99 00' 01' 02 03 04 05' 06 07 08 09' 10' 11' 12 13 14 15 16 17 Tiny but high-flying POM estate. Great consistency; full, concentrated and fleshy but expensive. Second label: La Petite Église. LES CRUZELLES, Montlandrie in CAS same stable.

Evangile, L' Pom r ★★★★ 95 96 98' 99 00' 01 02 03 04 05' 06 07 08 09' 10' 11 12 13 14 15 16' 17 Rothschild (LAFITE)-owned property since 1990. Lots of investment. MERLOT-dominated (80%) with CAB FR. 5000 cases/yr (average) of consistently rich, opulent wine. Second label: Blason de L'Evangile.

Fargues, De Saut sw sw ★★★ 98 99' 01 02 03' 04 05' 06 07 08 09' 10' 11' 13 14 15' 16 17 Unclassified but top-quality SAUT owned by Lur-Saluces. First vintage 1943. Classic SAUT: rich, unctuous wines, but refined.

Faugères St-Ém r ★★→★★★ 00' 03 04 05 06 07 08 09' 10 11 12 14 15 16 Sizeable GRAND CRU CLASSÉ in e of ST-ÉM. Rich, powerful, modern wines. Sister CH Péby Faugères (100% MERLOT) also classified. Rocheyron, Cap de Faugères (CAS), LAFAURIE-PEYRAGUEY in same stable. As is Lalique crystal.

Ferrand, De St-Ém r ★★→★★★ 00 01 04 05 06 08 09' 10' 12 14 15 16 Big St-Hippolyte GRAND CRU CLASSÉ owned by Pauline Bich Chandon-Moët. V'yd in a single block. Fresh, firm, expressive.

Ferrande Grav r (w) ★★ 08 09 10 11 12 14 15 16 Substantial GRAVES property owned by NÉGOCIANT Castel (1992). Much improved; easy, enjoyable red; clean, fresh white.

Ferrière Marg r ★★★ 00' 02 04 05 06 08 09' 10' 12 14 15 16 17 Tiny Third Growth in MARG village. Organically certified since 2015. Conversion to bio from 2016. Dark, firm, perfumed wines.

Feytit-Clinet Pom r ★★ →★★★ 00 01 04 05' 05' 06 08 09' 10' 11 12 13 14 15 16' Tiny 6 ha former MOUEIX property run by Jérémy Chasseuil. 90% MERLOT on clay-gravel soils. Top, consistent form. Rich, seductive. Highly prized at fair price.

Fieuzal Pe-Lé r (w) ★★★ (r) 01 06 07 08 09' 10' 11 12 14 15 16 (w) 07 08 09' 10' 11 12 13 14 15 16 Classified PE-LÉ estate with Irish owner. Stephen Carrier winemaker since 2007. Rich, ageable white; generous red. No 2017 (r w) due to frost. Second label: L'Abeille de Fieuzal (r w).

Figeac St-Ém r ★★★★ 96 98' 00' 01' 02 03 04 05' 06 07 08 09' 10' 11 12 13 14 15' 16' 17 Large PREMIER GRAND CRU CLASSÉ (B) owned by Manoncourt family; gravelly v'yd with unusual 70% CAB FR, CAB SAUV. Now richer but always elegant wines; need long ageing. Frost cut crop 50% in 2017. Plans for new winery 2019. Second label: Petit-Figeac.

Filhot Saut w dr sw ★★★ 98 99 01' 02 03' 04 05 07 09' 10' 11' 13 14 15 16 Extensive (350 ha) Second Growth with 62 ha v'yd. Owned and managed by de Vaucelles family. Richer, purer style from 2009.

Fleur Cardinale St-Ém r ★★★ 04 05' 06 07 08 09' 10' 11 12 14 15 16 GRAND CRU CLASSÉ at St-Étienne-de-Lisse. In overdrive for last 15 yrs. Always last to finish harvest. Ripe, unctuous, modern style.

Fleur de Boüard, La B'x r ★★→★★★ 05 06 **07** 08 09 **10 11 12 13** 14 15 16 Leading estate in L DE P. Owned by de Boüard family (ANGÉLUS) since 1998. Unique winery with inverted cone-shaped vats. Dark, dense, modern. Special CUVÉE, Le Plus: 100% MERLOT aged 3 yrs in new oak barrels. Second label: Le Lion.

Fleur-Pétrus, La Pom r ★★★★ 98' **99** 00' 01 02 **03 04** 05' 06 **08 09' 10'** 11 12 13 14 15 16 17 J-P MOUEIX property; 18.7 ha with three distinct parcels. 91% MERLOT, 6% CAB FR, 3% PETIT VERDOT. Finer style than PETRUS or TROTANOY. Needs time.

White B'x accounts for 12% of B'x production; 70 yrs ago it was 45.

Fombrauge St-Ém r ★★→★★★ 00' **01 02 03 04** 05 06 08 **09' 10' 11 12 14** 15 16' A Bernard Magrez (PAPE-CLÉMENT) estate since 1999. GRAND CRU CLASSÉ from 2012. Rich, dark, creamy, modern. Magrez-Fombrauge is special red CUVÉE; also name for dry white B'x. Second label: Prélude de Fombrauge.

Fonbadet Pau r ★★ **03 04** 05' **06 08** 09' **10' 12 14** 15 16 17 Small non-classified estate in PAU. CAB SAUV-led (70%). Less long-lived but reliable, gd value.

Fonbel, De St-Ém r ★★ **07 08** 09 10 11 12 **14 15** 16 Reliable source of juicy, fresh, gd-value ST-ÉM. Same stable as AUSONE, LA CLOTTE.

Fonplégade St-Ém r ★★ **04** 05 06 08 **09' 10 11 12 14** 15 16 American-owned GRAND CRU CLASSÉ. Previously concentrated, modern; now more fruit, balance. Certified organic; in conversion to bio. Second label: Fleur de Fonplégade.

Fonréaud List r ★★ 00' **03 04** 05 06 08 09' **10'** 11 **12 14 15** 16 17 One of bigger, better LIST for satisfying, savoury wines. Renovated cellars (2017). Terra Vitis certification (2015). Small volume of v.gd dry white: Le Cygne.

Fonroque St-Ém r ★★★ **03 04** 05 06 **08** 09' 10' 11 **12 14** 15 16 Côtes GRAND CRU CLASSÉ. Sold to insurance agent 2017. Bio (2008) paying off; more character, elegance.

Fontenil Fron r ★★ 05 06 08 09' **10' 11 12 14** 15' 16 17 Leading FRON, owned by MICHEL ROLLAND. 90% MERLOT. Ripe, opulent, balanced.

Forts de Latour, Les Pau r ★★★★ 95' 96' **98** 00' 01 02 03 04' **05'** 06 07 08 **09' 10'** 11 12 13 14 15 16' Second label of CH LATOUR; authentic flavour in slightly lighter format; high price. Organic certified (2018). No more en PRIMEUR sales; released only when deemed ready to drink (2011 in 2017) but still warrants more time.

Fourcas-Dupré List r ★★ 01 02 03 04 05 06 08 09 **10' 11 12 14** 15 16 17 Well-run property making fairly consistent wine in tight LIST style. A little SAUV BL (67%), SÉM (33%) white since 2014.

Fourcas-Hosten List r ★★→★★★ 03 05 06 08 09 10' 11 12 14 15 16 17 Large LIST estate. Considerable investment and steady improvement since 2006; more precision, finesse. Also a SAUV BL-led dry white.

France, De Pe-Lé r w ★★ (r) 04 05 06 08 09 10 11 12 14 15 16 (w) 07 08 09 10 11 12 13 14 15 16 Unclassified Léognan estate; consistent wines in a ripe, modern style. White fresh and balanced. Second label: CH Coquillas.

Franc-Mayne St-Ém r ★★ 01 03 04 05 08 09 10' 11 12 14 15 16 Tiny GRAND CRU CLASSÉ on côtes. CH DE LUSSAC and Vieux Maillet in POM used to be in same stable. Luxury hotel too. Fresh, fruity, round but structured.

Gaby, Du Fron r ★★ 04 05 06 08 09 10 12 14 15 16 17 Splendid s-facing slopes in CANON-FRON. Mostly MERLOT, ages well. ANGÉLUS owner consults. Organic tendency.

Gaffelière, La St-Ém r ★★★ 96 **98** 00' 01 02 03 04 05' 06 07 08 09' **10'** 11 12 13 14 15 16 First Growth at foot of côtes. Investment, improvement; part of v'yd replanted; modern *cuvier*. Elegant, long-ageing wines. STÉPHANE DERENONCOURT consults. Second label: CLOS la Gaffelière.

Garde, La Pe-Lé r w ★★ (r) 05 **06** 08 09' **10' 11 12 14** 15 16' (w) **08 09 10' 11 12 13** 14 15 16 Owned by DOURTHE; supple, CAB SAUV/MERLOT reds. Tiny production of SAUV BL/Sauvignon Gris white. Second label: La Terrasse de La Garde.

Gay, Le Pom r ★★★ 03 04 05' **06 07** 08 09' 10' 11 12 14 15 16 Fine v'yd on n edge of POM. Major investment, MICHEL ROLLAND consults. Racy and suave with ageing potential. Barrel fermentation since 2014. CH Montviel, La Violette same stable. Second label: Manoir de Gay.

Gazin Pom r ★★★ 96 98' 00' 01 02 03 04 05' 06 08 09' 10' 11 12 13 14 15 16 17 Large MERLOT-led (90%), family-owned POM estate. On v.gd form since mid-90s; generous, long ageing. Second label: L'Hospitalet de Gazin.

Gilette Saut w sw ★★★ 53 55 59 61 67 70 71 75 76 78 79 81 82 83 85 86 88 89 90 96 97 Extraordinary small Preignac CH. Family-owned since C18. Stores its sumptuous wines in concrete vats for 16–20 yrs. Only around 5000 bottles of each. Ch Les Justices is sister 05 07 09 10' 11 13 14 15 16.

Giscours Marg r ★★★ 98 00' 01 02 03 04 05' 06 08 09' 10' 11 12 14 15 16 17 Substantial Third Growth at Labarde. V'yd composed of three gravelly hillocks. Full-bodied, long-ageing MARG capable of greatness (eg 1970). The 80s were wobbly; steady improvement over last 20 yrs with new owner. Second label: La Sirène de Giscours. Little B'x rosé.

Glana, Du St-Jul r ★★ 04 05 06 08 09 10' 12 14 15 16 Big, unclassified CAB SAUV-led (65%) estate. Undemanding; robust; value. Same family ownership since 1961. Second label: Pavillon du Glana.

Gloria St-Jul r ★★ →★★★ 01 02 03 04 05' 06 07 08 09' 10' 11 12 14 15 16 17 A widely dispersed estate with v'yds among the Classed Growths. CAB SAUV-dominant (65%). Sells at Fourth Growth prices. Superb form recently.

Grand Corbin-Despagne St-Ém r ★★ →★★★ 98 00' 01 03 04 05 06 08 09' 10' 11 12 13 14 15 16 Gd-value GRAND CRU CLASSÉ in n ST-ÉM; clay and sand soils. Aromatic wines now with riper, fuller edge. No *grand vin* in 2017 due to frost. Also CH Le Chemin (POM), Ch Ampélia (CAST). Second label: Petit Corbin-Despagne.

Grand Cru Classé St-Ém 2012: 64 classified; reviewed every 10 yrs.

Grand-Mayne St-Ém r ★★★ 96 98 00' 01' 02 03 04 05' 06 07 08 09' 10' 11 12 14 15 16' 17 Impressive GRAND CRU CLASSÉ managed by Jean-Antoine Nony. Consistent, full-bodied, structured wines. Second label: Les Plantes du Mayne.

Grand-Puy-Ducasse Pau r ★★★ 96' 98' 00 01 02 03 04 05' 06 07 08 09' 10' 11 12 14 15 16 17 Fifth Growth owned by a bank. 60% CAB SAUV, 40% MERLOT. Steady improvement over last 10 yrs. Reasonable value. ANGÉLUS owner consults. Second label: Prélude à Grand-Puy-Ducasse.

Grand-Puy-Lacoste Pau r ★★★ 95' 96' 98 00' 01 02 03 04 05' 06 07 08' 09' 10' 11 12 13 14 15 16 Fifth Growth famous for gd-value CAB SAUV-driven (75%) PAU to lay down. A London favourite. Owned and astutely managed by François-Xavier Borie. Eric Boissenot consults. Second label: Lacoste-Borie.

Grave à Pomerol, La Pom r ★★★ 01 02 04 05 06 08 09' 10 11 12 14 15 16' 17 Small property on w slope of POM plateau. Mainly gravel soils. MERLOT-dominant (85%). Reasonable value. Can age.

Greysac Méd r ★★ 05' 06 08 09 10' 11 12 14 15 16 Same stable as HAUT-CONDISSAS. Clay-gravel soils. MERLOT-led, fine, fresh, consistent quality.

Gruaud-Larose St-Jul r ★★★★ 95' 96' 98 99 00' 01 02 03 04 05' 06 07 08 09' 10' 11 12 14 15 16' 17 One of biggest, best-loved Second Growths. Owned by the Merlaut family (CAMENSAC). Smooth, rich, vigorous claret. Visitor-friendly. Second label: *Sarget de Gruaud-Larose.*

Bordeaux's white past

Production figures for commune of Sauveterre-de-Guyenne in E-2-M show how sectors of B'x were predominantly white in the past. *Féret*, the "Bordeaux bible", reveals that from 1874 to 1969 white wine production was 80–98% of volume. From then on red gained pace, with white falling to 40% in 1982, 29 in 1991 and 18 by 2014.

> **Generational change at Lafite**
> It's been all change at CH LAFITE-ROTHSCHILD. After 35 yrs at the helm of DOMS Barons de Rothschild (Lafite), Baron Eric de Rothschild, 78, has handed over the position of chairman to his daughter Saskia. Also a new CEO, Jean-Guillaume Prats, 49, formerly manager of CH COS D'ESTOURNEL, then LVMH's Estates & Wines, who takes over from Christophe Salin, 63. On technical front Eric Kohler had already succeeded long-time winemaker Charles Chevallier.

Guadet St-Ém ★★ 04 05 06 08 09 10 11 12 15 16 Tiny GRAND CRU CLASSÉ run by Lignac family (1844). Better form in last 10 yrs. DERENONCOURT consults. Bio cultivation.

Guiraud Saut (r) w (dr) sw ★★★ 96' 97' 98 99 01' 02 03 04 05' 06 07 08 09' 10' 11' 13 14 15 16 17 Substantial organically certified neighbour of YQUEM. Owners incl long-time manager Xavier Planty. New on-site restaurant from 2018. Visitor-friendly. Top quality – more SAUV BL than most. Dry white G de Guiraud. Second label: Petit Guiraud.

Gurgue, La Marg r ★★ 04 05' 06 08 09' 10 11 12 14 15 16' Neighbour of CH MARGAUX. Same management as FERRIÈRE, HAUT-BAGES-LIBÉRAL. Bio farmed. Fine, gd value.

Hanteillan H-Méd r ★★ 04 05' 06 09' 10 12 14 15 16 Large CRU BOURGEOIS. Almost 50/50 CAB SAUV/MERLOT. Round, balanced, early-drinking. Recent improvement. Second label: CH Laborde.

Haut-Bages-Libéral Pau r ★★★ 00 01 02 03 04 05' 06 08 09' 10' 11 12 14 15 16 Fifth Growth (next to LATOUR) run by Claire Villars Lurton. CAB SAUV-led (70%). Bio farmed. Usually gd value. Second label: La Fleur de Haut-Bages-Libéral.

Haut-Bailly Pe-Lé r ★★★★ 90' 95 96' 98' 99 00' 01 02 03 04 05' 06 07 08' 09' 10' 11' 12 14 15' 16' 17 Top-quality PE-LÉ Classed Growth owned by American family, run by Véronique Sanders. Refined, elegant red (parcel of v. old, 100-yr+ vines); also a little rosé. CH Le Pape (Pe-Lé) same ownership. 50th anniversary of second label, La Parde de Haut-Bailly, in 2017.

Haut-Batailley Pau r ★★★ 00 02 03 04 05' 06 07 08 09' 10' 11 12 13 14 15 Fifth Growth bought by Cazes family of CH LYNCH-BAGES in 2017. Cellars renovated; steady progression in last 10 yrs. Second label: La Tour-l'Aspic.

Haut-Beauséjour St-Est r ★★ 04 05 08 09 10 11 14 15 16 Property created and improved by owner CHAMPAGNE ROEDERER. Juicy but structured. Sister of DE PEZ.

Haut-Bergeron Saut w sw ★★ 02 03 04 05 06 07 09 10 11 13 14 15 16 Preignac estate owned by Lamothe family. Consistent non-classified SAUT. V. old vines (average 50 yrs). Mainly SÉM (90%). Rich, opulent, gd value.

Haut-Bergey Pe-Lé r (w) ★★→★★★ (r) 04 05 06 07 09 10 11 12 14 15 16 (w) 10 11 12 13 14 15 16 Non-classified property with Classed Growth pretentions. Completely renovated in 90s. Rich, bold red. Fresh, concentrated dry white. Tiny production in 2017 (frost).

Haut-Brion Pe-Lé r ★★★★ (r) 88' 89' 90' 93 94 95' 96' 97 98' 99 00' 00' 01 02 03 04 05' 06 08 09' 10' 11' 12 13 14 15' 16 17 Only non-MÉD First Growth in list of 1855, owned by American Dillon family since 1935. Deeply harmonious, wonderful texture, for many no.1 or 2 choice of all clarets. Constant renovation: next stage the *cuvier*. Can be tasted at luxurious new restaurant Le Clarence (two-star Michelin) in Paris. A little *sumptuous dry white* (SAUV BL/SÉM) for tycoons: 02 03 04' 05' 06 07 08' 09 10' 11' 12 13 14 15' 16' 17. *See* LA MISSION HAUT-BRION, LE CLARENCE DE HAUT-BRION, QUINTUS.

Haut Condissas Méd r ★★★ 06 07 08 09' 10' 11 12 14 15 16 17 Garage-style MÉD created in 1995. Annual production 5000 cases. Sister to CH Rollan-de-By. Rich, concentrated, consistent. MERLOT-LED plus 20% PETIT VERDOT.

Haut-Marbuzet St-Est r ★★→★★★ 01 02 03 04 05' 06 08 09' 10' 11 12 14 15 16 Started in 1952 with 7 ha; now 70; owned by Duboscq family. Opulent, easy to love, but unclassified. Two-thirds are sold directly by CH. Rich, unctuous, CAB SAUV/MERLOT wines matured in new oak BARRIQUES in cellars between MONTROSE and COS D'ESTOURNEL. Second label: MacCarthy.

Haut-Sarpe St-Ém r ★★ 04 05 06 08 09 10 11 12 14 15 16 GRAND CRU CLASSÉ owned by Janoueix family; 70% MERLOT, 30% CAB FR. Rich, dark, modern, lashings of oak.

Hosanna Pom r ★★★★ 00 01 03 04 05' 06 07 08 09' 10' 11 12 14 15 16' 17 Tiny 4.5 ha v'yd in heart of POM plateau. 70% MERLOT, 30% CAB FR. Created by J-P MOUEIX since 1999. Wines have power, purity, balance and need time. Stablemate of FLEUR-PÉTRUS, TROTANOY.

Issan, D' Marg r ★★★ 01 02 03 04' 05' 06 07 08 09' 10' 11 12 13 14 15 16' Third Growth with fine moated CH. Fragrant wines; at top of game. Emmanuel Cruse and Jacky Lorenzetti owners (*see* PÉDESCLAUX). Second label: Blason d'Issan.

Jean Faure St-Ém r ★★ 06 08 09 10 11 12 14 15 16 GRAND CRU CLASSÉ on clay, sand, gravel soils. Organic cultivation. 50% CAB FR gives fresh, elegant style. ANGÉLUS owner consults (used to be STÉPHANE DERENONCOURT).

Kirwan Marg r ★★★ 98 00' 01 02 03 04 05' 06 07 08 09 10' 11 12 14 15' 16' 17 Third Growth on Cantenac plateau. New winery for 2017 (37 tulip-shaped concrete vats). CAB SAUV-dominant (60%). Dense, fleshy in 90s; now more finesse. Second label: Charmes de Kirwan.

Labégorce Marg r ★★ →★★★ 03 04 05' 07 08 09 10' 11 12 14 15 16 17 Substantial unclassified MARG owned by the Perrodo family and managed by Marjolaine de Coninck. Considerable investment and progression. Fine, modern style. CH MARQUIS-D'ALESME same stable.

Lafaurie-Peyraguey Saut w sw ★★★ 86' 88' 89' 90' 95 96' 97 98 99 01' 02 03' 04 05' 06 07 09' 10' 11' 13 14 15 16 17 Leading Classed Growth owned by Lalique crystal owner Silvio Denz. 2015 labelled "Hommage à Denis Dubourdieu". Rich, harmonious, sweet 90% SÉM. Upmarket hotel-restaurant in 2018. Second label: La Chapelle de Lafaurie-Peyraguey. Also Sém-led dry white B'X.

Lafite-Rothschild Pau r ★★★★ 89' 90' 93 94 95 96' 97 98' 99 00' 01' 02 03' 04' 05' 06 07 08' 09' 10' 11' 12 13 14 15' 16' 17 Big (112 ha) First Growth of famously elusive perfume and style, never great weight, although more dense and sleek these days. Great vintages keep maturing for decades. Has its own cooperage (La Tonnellerie des Domaines). Joint ventures in Argentina, California, Chile, China, Italy, Portugal and the MIDI. Second label: CARRUADES DE LAFITE. Also owns CHX DUHART-MILON, L'EVANGILE, RIEUSSEC.

Lafleur Pom r ★★★★ 89' 90' 93 94 95 96 98' 99 00' 01' 02 03 04' 05' 06' 07 08 09' 10' 11' 12 13 14 15' 16' 17 Superb but tiny family-owned and -managed property cultivated like a garden. Elegant, intense wine for maturing. Expensive. Renovated, enlarged *cuvier* for 2018 vintage. Second label: *Pensées de Lafleur*.

Lafleur-Gazin Pom r ★★ 04 05 06 08 09 10 11 12 14 15 16' Small J-P MOUEIX estate located between CHX LAFLEUR and GAZIN. Fine, fragrant.

B'x co-ops account for 21% of surface area and 23% of harvest (2016).

Lafon-Rochet St-Est r ★★★ 96' 98 99 00' 01 02 03' 04 05' 06 07 08 09' 10' 11 12 13 14 15 16' 17 Fourth Growth neighbour of COS D'ESTOURNEL run by Michel and Basile Tesseron. On gd form. Former PETRUS winemaker consults. Eye-catching canary-yellow buildings and label. Fermentation in concrete and stainless-steel tanks. Second label: Les Pèlerins de Lafon-Rochet.

Lagrange St-Jul r ★★★ 95 96 98 99 00' 01 02 03 04 05' 06 08 09' 10' 11 12 13 14 15 16 17 Substantial (118 ha) Third Growth owned since 1983 by Suntory. Classic MÉD style. Much investment in v'yd and cellars. CAB SAUV-dominant (67%). Dry white Les Arums de Lagrange. Second label: Les Fiefs de Lagrange (gd value).

Lagrange Pom r ★★ 00 01 04 05 06 09 10 15 16 Tiny POM v'yd located on n border
of plateau. Owned by J-P MOUEIX since 1953. 95% MERLOT. Supple, accessible early.

Lagune, La H-Méd r ★★★ 98 00' 02 03 04 05' 07 08 09' 10' 11 12 14 15 16 17
Third Growth in v. s of MÉD. Dipped in 90s; now on form. Fine-edged with
more structure, depth. Organic certification from 2016, now on conversion to
bio. Second label: Moulin de La Lagune. Also CUVÉE Mademoiselle L from v'yd
in Cussac-Fort-Méd.

Lamarque, De H-Méd r ★★ 00' 04 05' 06 08 09' 10' 11 12 14 15 16 H-MÉD estate
with splendid medieval fortress. V'yd borders MOU. Eric Boissenot consults.
Competent, mid-term wines, charm, value. Second label: D de Lamarque.

Lanessan H-Méd r ★★ 04 05 08 09 10' 11 12 14 15' 16 Distinguished property just
s of ST-JUL, 8th generation of Bouteiller family ownership. Improvement under
manager Paz Espejo. Visitor-friendly.

Langoa-Barton St-Jul r ★★★ 98 00' 01 02 03 04' 05' 06 07 08 09' 10' 11 12 13 14 15
16' 17 Small Third-Growth sister CH to LÉOVILLE-BARTON; charm, elegance. C17 CH
in Barton hands (1821). Consistent value. Second label: Rés de Léoville-Barton.

Larcis Ducasse St-Ém r ★★★ 95 96 98 00 02 03 04 05' 06 07 08 09' 10' 11 12 13 14 15
16 17 Family-owned PREMIER GRAND CRU CLASSÉ. S-facing terraced v'yd. MERLOT-led
(78%). On top form today. Second label: Murmure de Larcis Ducasse.

Larmande St-Ém r ★★ 04 05 06 07 08 09' 10 12 14 15 16 GRAND CRU CLASSÉ owned by
La Mondiale insurance (as is SOUTARD). MERLOT-led but generous amount of CAB FR
(30%). Sound but lighter weight.

Laroque St-Ém r ★★→★★★ 04 05 06 08 09' 10' 11 12 14 15 16 Large GRAND CRU CLASSÉ.
New winemaker from 2015. MERLOT-led (87%). Fresh, terroir-driven wines.

Larose-Trintaudon H-Méd r ★★ 05 06 07 08 09' 10 11 12 14 15 16 Largest v'yd in
MÉD (165 ha). 75,000 cases/yr. Sustainable viticulture. 90 per cent barrel-aged.
Smooth, balanced and generally for early drinking. Second label: Les Hauts de
Trintaudon. Also CHX Arnauld, Larose Perganson.

Laroze St-Ém r ★★ 00 01 05 06 07 08 09' 10' 12 14 15 16' GRAND CRU CLASSÉ run
by Guy Meslin since 1990. Lighter-framed wines from sandy soils; lately more
depth. No *grand vin* in 2017 due to frost. Second label: La Fleur Laroze.

Larrivet-Haut-Brion Pe-Lé r w ★★★ (r) 03 04 05' 06 08 09 10' 11 12 14 15 16
Unclassified PE-LÉ property. 30 yrs under Gervoson family ownership in 2017;
v'yd expanded from 17 to 72.5 ha. STÉPHANE DERENONCOURT consults from 2015.
Rich, modern red. Voluptuous, aromatic, SAUV BL/SÉM barrel-fermented white 08
09 10' 11 12 13 14 15 16 17.

Lascombes Marg r (p) ★★★ 00 01 02 03 04 05' 06 07 08 09' 10' 11 12 14 15 16
17 Large (112-ha v'yd) Second Growth owned by insurance group. Wines were
wobbly; now rich, dark, concentrated, modern with a touch of MARG perfume.
Lots of MERLOT (50%+). Second label: Chevalier de Lascombes.

Latour Pau r ★★★★ 88' 89 90' 91 94 95' 96' 97 98 99 00' 01 02 03' 04' 05' 06 07
08 09' 10' 11' 12 13 14 15' 16' First Growth considered the grandest statement of
B'X. Profound, intense, almost immortal wines in great yrs; even weaker vintages
have the unique taste and run for many yrs. V'yd certified organic in 2018; part
of historical "Enclos" section bio. Ceased en PRIMEUR sales in 2012; wines now
only released when considered ready to drink (2005 in 2017). New cellars for

greater storage capacity. Second label: LES FORTS DE LATOUR; *third label: Pauillac*; even this can age 20 yrs.

Latour-à-Pomerol Pom r ★★★ 95 96 98' 99 00' 01 02 04 05' 06 07 08 09' 10' 11 12 14 15 16 Managed by J-P MOUEIX since 1962. V'yd abuts POM church. Extremely consistent, well-structured wines that age.

Latour-Martillac Pe-Lé r w ★★ (r) 00 01 02 03 04 05' 06 08 09' 10' 11 12 14 15 16 17 GRAV Cru Classé run by Tristan and Loïc Kressmann since 80s. Regular quality; gd value at this level (w) 06 07 08 09 10' 11 12 13 14 15 16 17. Second label: Lagrave-Martillac (r w).

Laurets, Des St-Ém r ★★ 08 09 10 12 14 15 16 Substantial property, sits astride PUISSEGUIN-ST-ÉM and MONTAGNE-ST-ÉM. Les Laurets is 100% MERLOT special CUVÉE. Also CH de Malengin.

Laville Saut w sw ★★ 06 07 09 10 11 13 14 15 16 Preignac estate run by Jean-Christophe Barbe; also lectures at B'X's Faculty of Oenology. SÉM-dominated (85%) with a little SAUV BL, MUSCADELLE. Rich, lush, botrytized wine. Gd-value, non-classified SAUT.

Léoville-Barton St-Jul r ★★★★ 90' 94 95' 96' 98 99 00' 01 02 03' 04 05' 06 07 08' 09' 10' 11 12 13 14 15 16' 17 Second Growth with longest-standing family ownership; in Anglo-Irish hands of Bartons since 1826. Lilian Barton Sartorius currently runs property, assisted by her children, Mélanie and Damien. François Bréhant winemaker. Harmonious, classic claret; CAB SAUV-dominant (74%). Shares cellars with LANGOA-BARTON.

Léoville Las Cases St-Jul r ★★★★ 90' 94 95' 96' 97 98 99 00' 01 02 03' 04' 05' 06 07 08 09' 10' 11' 12 13 14 15' 16' 17 Largest Léoville and original "Super Second"; *grand vin* from Grand Enclos v'yd. Owned by Jean-Hubert Delon. Elegant, complex, powerful wines built for long ageing. Second label: Le Petit Lion; CLOS DU MARQUIS a separate wine. NÉNIN, POTENSAC same ownership.

Léoville-Poyferré St-Jul r ★★★★ 90' 94 95 96' 98 99 00' 01 02 03 04 05' 06 07 08 09' 10' 11' 12 13 14 15 16' Owned by Cuvelier family (1920). Now at "Super Second" level: dark, rich, spicy, long-ageing. *Ch Moulin-Riche* is a separate 21-ha parcel. Second label: Pavillon de Léoville-Poyferré. CH LE CROCK same ownership.

Lestage List r ★★ 04 05 06 08 09 10 11 12 14 15 16 Same Chanfreau-family ownership as FONRÉAUD. Firm, slightly austere. Dry white La Mouette from 2016.

Lilian Ladouys St-Est r ★★ 04 05 06 07 08 09' 10' 11 12 14 15 16 Created in 80s; now 46 ha and 140 parcels of vines. More finesse in recent vintages. Same stable as PÉDESCLAUX. Second label: La Devise de Lilian.

Liversan H-Méd r ★★ 04 05 07 08 09 10 12 14 15 16 CRU BOURGEOIS in n H-MÉD. Owned by part of Advini group; PATACHE D'AUX sister. Round, savoury, approachable.

Visit B'x's wine museum, *Cité du Vin*, great value at €20 entrance.

Loudenne Méd r ★★ 05 06 09' 10' 11 12 14 15 16 Large CRU BOURGEOIS, once Gilbeys, then Lafragette family, now Chinese-owned. Landmark C17 pink-washed *chartreuse* by river. Visitor-friendly. 50/50 MERLOT/CAB SAUV reds. Oak-scented SAUV BL 10 11 12 13 14 15 16. And, of course, a rosé.

Louvière, La Pe-Lé r w ★★★ (r) 04 05' 06 07 08 09' 10' 11 12 14 15 16 (w) 04' 05' 06 07 08 09' 10' 11' 12 13 14 15 16 An André Lurton property since 1965. Excellent *white* (100% SAUV BL), red of Classed Growth standard. *See also* BONNET, COUHINS-LURTON, DE ROCHEMORIN.

Lussac, De St-Ém r ★★ 05 06 08 09 10 11 12 14 15 16 Top estate in LUSSAC-ST-ÉM. Plenty of investment. Supple red and rosé, dry white.

Lynch-Bages Pau r (w) ★★★★ 90' 94 95' 96' 98 00' 01 02 03 04' 05' 06 07 08 09' 10' 11 12 13 14 15 16 17 Always popular, now a star, far higher than its Fifth-Growth rank. Rich, dense CAB SAUV-led. Second label: Echo de Lynch-Bages. Gd white, *Blanc de Lynch-Bages*, now fresher. New winery due for 2019. LES ORMES-DE-PEZ. Villa Bel Air in GRAV same ownership. As is HAUT-BATAILLEY (2017).

Lynch-Moussas Pau r ★★ 01 02 03 04 05' 07 08 09 10' 11 12 14 15 16' 17 Fifth Growth owned by BORIE-MANOUX connections. Lighter-style PAU (75% CAB SAUV) but much improved in recent yrs.

Lyonnat St-Ém r ★★ 06 08 09 10 12 14 15 16 Leading LUSSAC-ST-ÉM owned by Milhade family. More precision of late. Also special CUVÉE Emotion.

Malartic-Lagravière Pe-Lé r (w) ★★★ (r) 00' 01 02 03 04' 05' 06 07 08 09' 10' 11 12 14 15 16 17 (w) 04' 05' 06 07 08 09' 10' 11 12 13 14 15 16 17 GRAV Classed Growth. Owned by Bonnie family since 1997. Loads of investment. Rich, modern red; a little lush white (majority SAUV BL). CH Gazin Rocquencourt (PE-LÉ) same stable. Interests in Argentina.

Mouton Cadet, B'x's biggest brand, sells 12 million bottles/yr (72% red).

Malescasse H-Méd r ★★ 04 05 06 08 09 10 11 12 14 15 16' 17 CRU BOURGEOIS nr MOULIS. New owner and investment from 2012. Supple, value wines; now more depth. 2016 best yet.

Malescot-St-Exupéry Marg r ★★★ 98 00' 01 02 03 04 05' 06 07 08' 09' 10' 11 12 14 15 16 17 On-form MARG Third Growth. Wines ripe, fragrant, finely structured. Second label: Dame de Malescot.

Malle, De Saut r w dr sw ★★★ (w sw) 97' 98 99 01' 02 03' 05 06 07 09 10' 11' 13 14 15' 16 Classified historic monument making v. fine, medium-bodied SAUT; also M de Malle dry white GRAV. Second Growth (1855).

Margaux, Ch Marg r (w) ★★★★ 89' 90' 93 94 95' 96' 97 98' 99 00' 01' 02 03' 04' 05' 06' 07 08 09' 10' 11' 12 13 14 15' 16' 17 First Growth; most seductive, fabulously perfumed, consistent wines. Owned by Mentzelopoulos family since 1977. Special black and gold, "Hommage à Paul Pontallier" bottling for 2015 vintage. Pavillon Rouge 04' 05' 06 08 09' 10' 11 12 14 15 16 17 is second label. Third wine Margaux du Château Margaux from 2009. *Pavillon Blanc* (100% SAUV BL) is best white of MÉD, recent vintages fresher 08 09' 10 11' 12' 13' 14 15 16 17.

Marojallia Marg r ★★★ 02 03 04 05' 06 07 08 09' 10 11 12 15 16 Micro-CH looking for big prices for big, rich, un-MARG-like wines. Philippe Porcheron owner. Second label: CLOS Margalaine.

Marquis-d'Alesme Marg r ★★ →★★★ 01 04 05 08 09' 10' 11 12 14 15 16 Third Growth in MARG village. Investment and steady progress; now more consistency. New Chinese-inspired, high-tech cellars. Same stable as LABÉGORCE.

Marquis-de-Terme Marg r ★★ →★★★ 98 00' 01 02 03 04 05' 06 08 09' 10' 11 12 14 15' 16 17 Fourth Growth with v'yd dispersed around MARG. Recent investment, renovation; previously solid wine, now more seductive. Second label: La Couronne de Marquis de Terme.

Maucaillou Mou r ★★ 05 06 08 09 10 11 12 14 15 16 Fairly consistent MOU estate. Clean, fresh, value wines. Visitor-friendly. Second label: N°2 de Maucaillou.

Mayne Lalande List r ★★ 08 09 10 11 12 14 15 16 Leading LIST estate. CAB SAUV-led (60%). Full, finely textured. B&B too.

Mazeyres Pom r ★★ 04 05' 06 08 09 10 12 14 15 16 Lighter but consistent POM. Supple, earlier-drinking style. Unusual 2–3% PETIT VERDOT. Organic certification. Alain Moueix manages.

Meyney St-Est r ★★ →★★★ 01 02 03 04 05' 06 08 09' 10' 11' 12 14 15 16 Big river slope v'yd, superb site next to MONTROSE. Always robust, structured, age-worthy; CAB SAUV-led (60%). Recent investment. Same stable as GRAND-PUY-DUCASSE, LA TOUR DE MONS (since 2004). ANGÉLUS owner consults. Second label: Prieur de Meyney.

Mission Haut-Brion, La Pe-Lé r ★★★★ 89' 90' 94 95 96' 98' 99 00' 01 02 03 04 05' 06 07 08 09' 10' 11' 12 13 14 15' 16 17 Owned by Dillon family of neighbouring

HAUT-BRION since 1983. Consistently grand-scale, full-blooded, long-maturing wine. V'yd now 26.6 ha. 6000–7000 cases/yr. Second label: La Chapelle de la Mission. Magnificent SÉM-dominated white: previously Laville-Haut-Brion; renamed La Mission-Haut-Brion Blanc (2009) 10 11' 12' 13 14 15 16 17.

Monbousquet St-Ém r (w) ★★★ 03 04 05' 06 07 08 09' 10' 11 12 14 15 16 GRAND CRU CLASSÉ on drained sand/gravel soils. Transformed by Gerard Pérse (*see* PAVIE). Concentrated, oaky, voluptuous, MERLOT-led (60%) wines. Rare *v.gd Sauv Bl/ Sauvignon Gris* (AC B'X). Second label: Angélique de Monbousquet.

Monbrison Marg r ★★ ·★★★ 01 02 04 05' 06 08 09' 10' 11 12 14 15 16 17 Tiny (13.2 ha), family-owned property at Arsac. V'yd 40 yrs old. Delicate, fragrant.

Mondotte, La St-Ém r ★★★★ 98' 99 00' 01 02 03 04 05' 06 07 08 09' 10' 11 12 13 14 15 16 17 Tiny PREMIER GRAND CRU CLASSÉ on the limestone-clay plateau. Old vines (60 yrs). Intense, firm, virile wines. Organic certification from 2014. Same stable as AIGUILHE, CANON-LA-GAFFELIÈRE, CLOS DE L'ORATOIRE.

Montrose St-Est r ★★★★ 90 90 94 95 96' 98 00' 01 02 03 04 05' 06 07 08 09' 10' 11 12 13 14 15' 16' 17 Second Growth with riverside v'yd. Famed for forceful, long-ageing claret. Vintages 1979–85 were lighter. Bouygues brothers owners; huge investment paying off. Environmentally friendly buildings; organic and bio trials. Second label: *La Dame de Montrose*.

Moulin du Cadet St-Ém r p ★★ 01 03 05 08 09 10' 11 12 14 15 16 17 Tiny GRAND CRU CLASSÉ; 100% MERLOT. Same owner SANSONNET. Was robust, now finesse, fragrance.

Moulinet Pom r ★★ 05 06 08 09 10 11 12 15 Large CH for POM: 25 ha on sand and gravel soils. MERLOT-led. Lighter style.

Moulin-Haut-Laroque Fron r ★★ 06 08 09' 10' 11 12 14 15 16 17 Leading FRON property. Family-owned (first bottling 1890). MERLOT-led (65%) with 5% MALBEC. Consistent quality. Structured wines, can age.

Moulin Pey-Labrie Fron r ★★ 04 05' 08 09' 10' 11 12 14 15 16 17 Same Hubau family for over 20 yrs. Limestone-clay soils. Sturdy, well-structured wines that can age.

Moulin-St-Georges St-Ém r ★★★ 03 04 05' 06 08 09' 10' 11 12 13 14 15 16 17 Same stable as AUSONE, LA CLOTTE. 80% MERLOT, 20% CAB FR. Dense, stylish wines.

Mouton Rothschild Pau r (w) ★★★★ 85' 86' 88' 89' 90' 94 95' 96 97 98' 99 00' 01' 02 03 04' 05' 06' 07 08' 09' 10' 11' 12 13 14 15' 16' 17 Rothschild-owned since 1853; current generation Camille, Philippe, Julien. Most exotic, voluptuous of PAU First Growths, now at top of game. 2015 label by German artist Gerhard Richter. 1st signed by Philippe Sereys de Rothschild. White Aile d'Argent (SAUV BL/SÉM). Second label: Le Petit Mouton. *See also* D'ARMAILHAC, CLERC MILON.

Nairac Saut w sw ★★ 98 99 01' 02 03' 04 05' 06 07 09' 10 11 13 14 15 BAR Second Growth run by brother and sister, Nicolas and Eloïse Heeter Tari. Rich but fresh; decent form. Second label: Esquisse de Nairac.

Nénin Pom r ★★★ 98 00' 01 02 03 04 05 06 07 08 09' 10' 11 12 13 14 15' 16' 17 Same owners as LÉOVILLE-LAS-CASES; 20 yrs of investment, evolution; clearly paid off in 2015, 16. MERLOT-led (75%). Restrained style but generous, precise, built to age. Gd-value second label: Fugue de Nénin.

Olivier Pe-Lé r w ★★★ (r) 02 04 05' 06 08 09' 10' 11 12 13 14 15 16 17 (w) 07'

Bordeaux goes west

Philippe de Rothschild started ball rolling in 80s with Opus One. He was followed by Christian MOUEIX with Dominus in 90s. Since then there has been steady trickle of B'X connections making acquisitions in Napa and Sonoma. Think François Pinault (LATOUR) and Araujo; the Wertheimers (CANON, RAUZAN-SÉGLA) and St-Supéry; Gonzague and Claire Lurton (DURFORT-VIVENS, FERRIÈRE) and Trinité, and more recently Alfred and Melanie Tesseron (PONTET-CANET) and Villa Sorriso.

08 09 10' 11 12 13 14 15 16 17 Beautiful classified property with moated castle. Significant investment and change since 2003. Now structured red (55% CAB SAUV) and juicy SAUV BL-led (75%) white.

Ormes-de-Pez, Les St-Est r ★★ 02 03 04 05 06 07 08 09' 10' 11 12 14 15 16 17 Consistent quality. CAZES family of LYNCH-BAGES owners. Full, fleshy, age-worthy.

Ormes-Sorbet, Les Méd r ★★ 04 05 06 08 09' 10' 11 12 14 15 16' Reliably consistent CRU BOURGEOIS. Same family owners since 1764. CAB SAUV dominant (65%). Elegant, gently oaked wines. Drinking window 10 yrs.

Palmer Marg r ★★★★ 88' 89 90 94 95 96' 98' 99 00 01' 02 03 04 05' 06' 07 08' 09' 10' 11' 12 13 14 15' 16' 17 Third Growth on a par with "Super Seconds" (occasionally Firsts). Voluptuous wine of power, delicacy and much MERLOT (40%). Dutch (MÄHLER-BESSE) and British (SICHEL) owners. Certified bio. 54 vats for each v'yd plot. Second label: *Alter Ego de Palmer*. Also original Vin Blanc de Palmer (Loset/ MUSCADELLE/Sauvignon Gris).

Pape-Clément Pe-Lé r (w) ★★★★ (r) 98' 99 00' 01 02 03 04 05 06 07 08 09' 10' 11 12 13 14 15' 16 17 (w) 05' 07 08 09 10 11 12 13 14 15 16 17 Historic estate in B'x suburbs (wine shop and tastings too). Owned by Bernard Magrez; 2010 considered greatest vintage in this era. Dense, long-ageing reds. Tiny production of rich, oaky white. CLOS HAUT-PEYRAUGUEY same stable.

Patache d'Aux Méd r ★★ 05' 06 09 10 11 12 14 15 16 Popular CRU BOURGEOIS at Bégadan. Reliable largely CAB SAUV (60%) wine. DERENONCOURT consults. New ownership 2016 (*see* LIVERSAN).

Pavie St-Ém r ★★★★ 98 99 00' 01 02 04 05' 06 07 08 09' 10' 11 12 13 14 15' 16 17 PREMIER GRAND CRU CLASSÉ (A) splendidly sited on plateau and s côtes. Perse family owners. Intense, oaky, strong wines. MERLOT (60%) but now more CABS FR/ SAUV. Impressive, state-of-the-art winery. Second label: Arômes de Pavie.

Pavie-Decesse St-Ém r ★★★ 01' 02 03 04 05' 06 07 08 09' 10' 11 12 14 15 16 17 Tiny Classed Growth. 90% MERLOT. As powerful, muscular as sister PAVIE.

Pavie-Macquin St-Ém r ★★★ 98' 99 00' 01 02 03 04 05' 06 07 08 09' 10' 11 12 13 14 15 16 17 PREMIER GRAND CRU CLASSÉ (B) with v'yd on limestone plateau. 80%+ MERLOT with 2% CAB SAUV. Winemakers Nicolas and son Cyrille Thienpont. Sturdy, full-bodied wines need time. Second label: Les Chênes de Macquin.

Pédesclaux Pau r ★★ 03 04 05 06 09 10' 11 12 13 14 15 16 Underachieving Fifth Growth revolutionized since 2014. Extensive investment in cellars, more v'yds, glass front to CH. More fruit/flavour. Second label: Fleur de Pédesclaux.

Petit-Village Pom r ★★★ 00' 01 3 04 05 06 07 08 09' 10' 11 12 13 14 15' 16 17 Much-improved POM opposite VIEUX-CH-CERTAN. Owned by AXA Insurance. STÉPHANE DERENONCOURT consults. Suave, dense, increasingly finer tannins. Second label: Le Jardin de Petit-Village.

Petrus Pom r ★★★★ 85' 86 88' 89' 90 93' 94 95' 96' 97 98' 99 00' 01 02 03 04' 05' 06 07 08 09' 10' 11' 12 13 14 15' 16' 17 (Unofficial) First Growth of POM: MERLOT solo *in excelsis*. 11.5 ha v'yd on blue clay gives 2500 cases of massively rich, concentrated wine for long ageing. One of 50 most expensive wines in world. Father, Jean-Claude Berrouet (45 vintages), to son (Olivier since 2007) winemakers. Jean-François MOUEIX owner. No second label.

Pilfering in the vineyard

The disastrous frost in 2017 and consequent loss of crop had further consequences – theft. Six and a half tonnes of grapes were stolen from a v'yd at Génissac in E-2-M and there were reports of further pilfering in POM and L DE P. Thieves even went as far as uprooting 500 vines in MONTAGNE-ST-ÉM. Suspicion fell on brother vintners. Call Inspecteur Clouseau.

Pey La Tour B'x r ★★ 10 11 12 14 15 16 Large DOURTHE property. Quality-driven B'x SUPÉRIEUR. Three red CUVÉES: Rés du CH top selection. Also rosé, dry white B'x.

Peyrabon H-Méd r ★★ 05 06 09' 10 11 12 15 16 17 Consistent CRU BOURGEOIS owned by NÉGOCIANT Millésima. Also La Fleur-Peyrabon in PAU.

Pez, De St-Est r ★★ 03 04 05' 06 07 08 09' 10' 11 12 13 14 15 16 Consistent ST-EST cru owned by ROEDERER (as is PICHON COMTESSE). Mainly MERLOT/CAB SAUV. Dense, reliable style short of poetry.

Phélan-Ségur St-Est r ★★★ 03 04 05' 06 07 08 09' 10' 11 12 13 14 15 16 17 Reliable, top-notch, unclassified CH; long, supple style. New owner in 2017: Belgian shipper; previously Gardinier family. Second label: Frank Phélan.

How much a barrel (225 litres) of wine? Ch Montrose 2016 auctioned: US$119,500.

Pibran Pau r ★★ 03 04 05' 06 08 09' 10' 11 12 13 14 15 16 17 Small property allied to PICHON-BARON. Classy, MERLOT-led (55%+) wine.

Pichon-Baron Pau r ★★★★ 95 96 98 99 00' 01 02 03' 04 05' 06 07 08 09' 10' 11 12 13 14 15' 16' 17 Owned by AXA; formerly CH Pichon-Longueville (until 2012). Revitalized Second Growth; powerful, consistent PAU at a price. Potential for long ageing. Second labels: Les Tourelles de Longueville (approachable: more MERLOT); Les Griffons de Pichon Baron (CAB SAUV dominant).

Pichon-Longueville Comtesse de Lalande (Pichon Lalande) Pau r ★★★★ 95 96 98 99 00 01 02 03' 04 05' 06 07 08 09' 10' 11 12 13 14 15' 16' 17 ROEDERER-owned Second Growth, overlooking estuary. Always among top performers; long-lived wine of famous breed. MERLOT-marked in 80s, 90s; more CAB SAUV in recent yrs (68% in 2015). New high-tech, gravity-fed winery and buildings. Second label: Rés de la Comtesse. DE PEZ, HAUT-BEAUSÉJOUR in same stable.

Pin, Le Pom r ★★★★ 95 96 97 98' 99 00' 01 02 04 05' 06' 07 08 09' 10' 11 12 14 15 16' The original of B'x cult mini-crus (1st vintage: 1979). Only 2.8 ha. Tiny cellar has now given way to modern winery. 100% MERLOT; almost as rich as its drinkers, but prices are out of sight. Ageing potential. L'If (ST-ÉM), L'Hêtre (CAS) new stablemates.

Plince Pom r ★★ 04 05 06 08 09 10 11 12 15 16 Four generations of family ownership. J-P MOUEIX exclusivity. Lighter, fruity style of POM.

Pointe, La Pom r ★★ 04 05 06 07 08 09' 10' 12 14 15 16 Large (for POM), well-managed estate. Investment, progress in last 10 yrs. Hit by frost in 2017.

Poitevin Méd r ★★ 08 09 10 11 12 14 15 16 Supple, elegant CRU BOURGEOIS. Guillaume Poitevin at helm. Consistent quality. Also dry white B'x.

Pontet-Canet Pau r ★★★★ 95 96' 98 99 00' 01 02' 03 04' 05' 06' 07 08 09' 10' 11 12 13 14 15 16' 17 Fashionable, bio-certified, Tesseron-family-owned Fifth Growth. Radical improvement has seen prices soar. New *cuvier* with 32 amphora-shaped vats (all 40 hl) in 2017. Second label: Les Hauts de Pontet-Canet.

Potensac Méd r ★★ 02 03 04 05' 07 08 09' 10' 11 12 13 14 15 16' 17 Same stable as LÉOVILLE LAS CASES. Firm, vigorous wines; need ageing. MERLOT-led (45%) but lots of old-vine CAB FR. Second label: Chapelle de Potensac.

Pouget Marg r ★★ 02 03 04 05' 06 08 09' 10' 11 12 14 15 Obscure Fourth Growth attached to BOYD-CANTENAC. 66% CAB SAUV. Sturdy; needs time.

Poujeaux Mou r ★★ 01 03 04 05 08 09 10' 11 12 14 15' 16' 17 Bought by Cuvelier in 2008 (as is CLOS FOURTET). CAB SAUV-led (50%). Full, robust wines with ageing potential. Second label: La Salle de Poujeaux.

Premier Grand Cru Classé St-Ém 2012: 18 classified; ranked into A (4) and B (14).

Pressac, De St-Ém r ★★ 06 08 09 10 11 12 14 15 16 17 GRAND CRU CLASSÉ at St-Étienne-de-Lisse. MERLOT, CABS FR/SAUV, MALBEC, CARMENÈRE. Quality assured. Value.

Preuillac Méd r ★★ 06 08 09 10 11 12 14 15 Savoury, structured CRU BOURGEOIS. Chinese-owned. MERLOT-led (58%). Second label: Esprit de Preuillac.

St-Émilion classification – current version
The latest classification (2012) incl a total of 82 CHX: 18 PREMIERS GRANDS CRUS CLASSÉS and 64 GRANDS CRUS CLASSÉS. The new classification, now legally considered an exam rather than a competition, was conducted by a commission of seven, nominated by INAO, none from B'X. CHX ANGÉLUS and PAVIE were upgraded to Premier Grand Cru Classé (A) while added to the rank of Premier Grand Cru Classé (B) were CANON LA GAFFELIÈRE, LA MONDOTTE, LARCIS DUCASSE and VALANDRAUD. New to status of Grand Cru Classé were Chx BARDE-HAUT, CLOS de Sarpe, Clos la Madeleine, Côte de Baleau, DE FERRAND, de Pressac, FAUGÈRES, FOMBRAUGE, JEAN FAURE, La Commanderie, La Fleur Morange, Le Chatelet, Péby Faugères, QUINAULT L'ENCLOS, Rochebelle and SANSONNET. Although a motivating force for producers, the classification (which is reviewed every 10 yrs, since 1955) is still an unwieldy guide for consumers.

Prieuré-Lichine Marg r ★★★ 95 96 98' 99 00' 01 02 03 04 05 06 07 08 09' 10' 11 12 14 15 16 17 Fourth Growth owned by a NÉGOCIANT; put on map by Alexis Lichine. Fragrant MARG currently on gd form. STÉPHANE DERENONCOURT consults. Wine shop, tours. Second label: Confidences du Prieuré-Lichine. Gd SAUV BL/SÉM.

Puygueraud B'x r ★★ 03' 05' 06 08 09 10 11 12 14 15' 16' Leading CH of this tiny FRANCS-CÔTES DE B'X AC. Nicolas Thienpont and son Cyrille winemakers (*see* PAVIE-MACQUIN). MERLOT-led. Oak-aged wines of surprising class. Special CUVÉE George, MALBEC (35%+) in blend. A little white (SAUV BL/Sauvignon Gris).

Quinault L'Enclos St-Ém r ★★→★★★ 09 10 11 12 14 15 16 17 GRAND CRU CLASSÉ located in Libourne. Same team and owners as CHEVAL BLANC. Now 20% CAB SAUV; more freshness, finesse. Aged in 500-litre casks.

Quintus St-Ém r ★★★ 11 12 13 14 15 16' 17 Created by Dillons of HAUT-BRION from former Tertre Daugay, L'ARROSÉE (added 2013) v'yds. Now 28-ha. Gaining in stature, finesse but price soared. Second label: Le Dragon de Quintus (gd value).

Rabaud-Promis Saut w sw ★★ →★★★ 01' 02 03' 04 05' 06 07 09' 10 11 12 13 14 15 16 First Growth at Bommes. Déjean family owners. Quality, gd value.

Rahoul Grav r w ★★ (r) 08 09' 10 11 12 14 15 16 17 Owned by DOURTHE; reliable. Balanced red. SÉM-dominated white 11 12 13 14 15 16 17. Gd value.

Ramage-la-Batisse H-Méd r ★★ 05' 08 09 10 11 12 14 15 Reasonably consistent, widely distributed, CRU BOURGEOIS. CAB SAUV-led (56%), MERLOT, PETIT VERDOT, CAB FR.

Rauzan-Gassies Marg r ★★★ 02 03 04 05' 06 07 08 09' 10' 11 12 15 16 Second Growth owned by Quié family since 1946. Lags behind RAUZAN-SÉGLA but making strides to improve. Second label: Gassies.

Rauzan-Ségla Marg r ★★★★ 95 96 98 99 00' 01 02 03 04' 05 06 07 08 09' 10' 11 12 13 14 15' 16' 17 Leading MARG Second Growth long famous for its fragrance; owned by Wertheimers of Chanel since 1994 (*see* BERLIQUET, CANON). Always seeking to improve. Second label: Ségla (value).

Raymond-Lafon Saut w sw ★★★ 96' 97 98 99' 01' 02 03' 04 05' 06 07' 09' 10' 11' 13 14 15 16 17 Small (18 ha) unclassified SAUT producing First Growth-quality wine. Owned by Meslier family. Rich, complex wines that age.

Rayne Vigneau Saut w sw ★★★ 98 99 01' 03 05' 07 09' 10' 11' 13 14 15 16' Substantial First Growth at Bommes. Owned by Trésor du Patrimoine group. SÉM-led (74%) wines now rich, suave, age-worthy. Second label: Madame de Rayne.

Respide Médeville Grav r w ★★ (r) 06 08 09 10 11 12 14 15 16 (w) 11 12 13 14 15 16 Top GRAV property for elegant, CAB SAUV-led red and tiny volume of complex *white*.

Reynon B'x r w ★★ Leading CADILLAC-CÔTES DE B'x estate. Owned by Dubourdieu family (*see* CLOS FLORIDÈNE). Serious MERLOT-led red 06 09' 10 11 12 14 15 16. Fragrant B'x white from SAUV BL (DYA).

Reysson H-Méd r ★★ 06 08 09' 10' 11 12 14 15 16 MERLOT-led (90%) CRU BOURGEOIS owned by NÉGOCIANT DOURTHE. Clay-limestone soils. Rich, modern style.

Rieussec Saut w sw ★★★★ 89' 90' 95 96' 97' 98 99 01' 02 03' 04 05' 06 07 09' 10' 11' 13 14 15 16 Worthy neighbour of YQUEM with substantial v'yd in Fargues, owned by (LAFITE) Rothschilds. Fabulously powerful, opulent wine; SÉM-dominant (90%) is a bargain. Second label: Carmes de Rieussec. Dry wine "R" de Rieussec.

Rivière, De la Fron r ★★ 03 04 05' 06 08 09' 10 12 14 15 16 Largest (65 ha), most impressive FRON property with Wagnerian castle. Chinese-owned. Formerly big, tannic; now more refined. Claude Gros consults. Second label: Les Sources.

Roc de Cambes B'x r ★★★★ 05 06 07 08 09 10 11 12 13 14 15 16 17 Undisputed leader in CÔTES DE BOURG; MERLOT (80%) and CAB SAUV. Savoury, opulent but pricey. Same stable as TERTRE-ROTÊBOEUF.

Rochemorin, De Pe-Lé r w ★★–★★★ (r) 06 08 09' 10' 11 12 14 15 16 (w) 10 11 12 13 14 15 16 Sizeable property at Martillac owned by André Lurton of LA LOUVIÈRE. Fleshy, MERLOT-led (55%) red; aromatic white (100% SAUV BL). Fairly consistent quality. CH Coucheroy (r w) also produced.

Rol Valentin St-Ém r ★★★ 03 04 05' 06 07 08 09' 10' 11 12 13 14 15 16 Once garage-sized; now bigger v'yd with clay-limestone soils. DERENONCOURT consults. Rich, modern wines but balanced.

Rouget Pom r ★★ 03 04 05' 06 07 08 09' 10' 11 12 13 14 15 16 Go-ahead estate on n edge of POM. Owned by Burgundian Labruyère family (*see* DOM JACQUES PRIEUR). Rich, unctuous wines. Second label: Le Carillon de Rouget.

St-Georges St-Ém r ★★ 03 04 05' 06 08 09 10 11 14 15 V'yd represents 25 per cent of ST-GEORGES AC. Owned by Janoueix and Desbois families. MERLOT-led with CABS FR, SAUV. Gd wine sold direct to public. Second label: Puy St-Georges.

St-Pierre St-Jul r ★★★ 96' 98 00' 01' 02 03 04 05' 06 07 08 09' 10' 11 12 13 14 15 16 17 Tiny Fourth Growth to follow, owned by Triaud family. Stylish, consistent, classic ST-JUL. New cellars. *See* GLORIA.

Sales, De Pom r ★★ 04 05 06 08 09 10 12 15 16 Biggest v'yd of POM (10,000 cases). Owner-manager Bruno de Lambert. Reliable lightish wine; never quite poetry. Second label: CH Chantalouette (5000 cases).

Sansonnet St-Ém r ★★ 03 04 05' 06 08 09' 10' 11 12 13 14 15' 16' 17 Ambitious GRAND CRU CLASSÉ on limestone-clay plateau. Modern but refreshing. Second label: Envol de Sansonnet.

Saransot-Dupré List r (w) ★★ 03 04 05 06 09' 10' 11 12 15 16 Small property owned by Yves Raymond. Firm, fleshy, MERLOT-led (2% CARMENÈRE); dry white (SÉM 60%).

Sénéjac H-Méd r (w) ★★ 04 05' 06 08 09' 10' 11 12 14 15 16' S H-MÉD (Pian). Consistent, well-balanced, CAB SAUV-led wines. Drink young or age. Gd value.

Serre, La St-Ém r ★★ 04 05 06 08 09' 10 11 12 14 15 16' Small GRAND CRU CLASSÉ on the limestone plateau. MOUEIX exclusivity. Fresh, stylish wines with fruit.

Sigalas-Rabaud Saut w sw ★★★ 96' 97' 98 99 01' 02 03 04 05' 07' 09' 10' 11 12 13 14 15' 16' 17 Tiny First Growth. *V. fragrant and lovely*. Second label: Le Lieutenant de Sigalas. Also La Sémillante and N°5 (no sulphur).

Siran Marg r ★★ –★★★ 02 03 04 05 06 07 08 09' 10' 11 12 14 15 16 17 Unclassified MARG estate in Labarde. Recent investment and change. Visitor-friendly. Wines have substance, classic MARG fragrance. Second label: S de Siran.

Smith-Haut-Lafitte Pe-Lé r (p) (w) ★★★★ (r) 98 99 00' 01 02 03 04 05' 06 07 08 09' 10' 11 12 13 14 15' 16' 17 (w) 08' 09 10' 11 12 13' 14 15 16 17 Celebrated Classed Growth with spa hotel (Caudalie), regularly one of PE-LÉ stars. White is full, ripe, sappy; red precise/generous. Second label: Les Hauts de Smith. Also CAB SAUV-based Le Petit Haut Lafitte. Cantelys and Le Thil Comte Clary same ownership.

Sociando-Mallet H-Méd r ★★★ 96' 98' 99 00' 01' 02 03 04 05' 06 07 08 09' 10' 11

12 14 15 16 Substantial H-MÉD estate in St-Seurin-de-Cadourne built from scratch by former NÉGOCIANT; managed by daughter Sylvie. Classed-Growth quality. Conservative, big-boned wines to lay down for yrs. Second label: La Demoiselle de Sociando-Mallet. Also special CUVÉE Jean Gautreau.

Sours, De B'x r p w ★★ Valid reputation for popular B'x rosé (DYA). Gd white; improving B'x red. Now owned by Jack Ma of Alibaba fame; more investment.

Soutard St-Ém r ★★★ 00' 01' 05 06 07 08 09 10 11 12 14 15 16' 17 *Potentially excellent* GRAND CRU CLASSÉ on limestone plateau. MERLOT-LED (65%) with 2% MALBEC. Massive investment, still room for improvement; 2016 best yet. Visitor-friendly. Second label: Les Jardins de Soutard.

Suduiraut Saut w sw ★★★★ 95 96 97 98 99' 01' 02 03' 04 05' 06 07' 09' 10' 11' 13 14 15' 16' 17 One of v. best SAUT. SÉM-dominant (90%+). Greater consistency from owner AXA, luscious quality. Second labels: Castelnau de Suduiraut; Lions de Suduiraut (fresher, fruitier). Dry wines "S" and entry level Le Blanc Sec.

Taillefer Pom r ★★ 03 04 05' 06 08 09' 10 11 12 14 15 16 Family property managed by Claire Moueix. Sandier soils. Lighter weight but polished, refined. Can age.

Talbot St-Jul r (w) ★★★ 95 96' 98' 99 00' 00' 01 02 03 04 05' 08' 09' 10' 11 12 14 15 16 Huge (107 ha) Fourth Growth in heart of AC ST-JUL. Wine rich, *consummately charming, reliable* (though wobbly in 2006–7). 66% CAB SAUV. New manager/ winemaker from 2018 (ex-LA CONSEILLANTE). Second label: Connétable de Talbot. Rather gd SAUV BL-based white: Caillou Blanc.

Tertre, Du Marg r ★★★ 03 04 05' 06 08 09' 10' 11 12 14 15 16 Fifth Growth isolated S of MARG. Fragrant (20% CAB FR) fresh, fruity but structured (CAB-SAUV-led) wines. Same Dutch owner/manager as CH GISCOURS. Second label: Les Hauts du Tertre. Also Tertre Blanc VIN DE FRANCE dry white CHARD/VIOGNIER/GROS MANSENG/SAUV BL.

Tertre-Rôteboeuf St-Ém r ★★★★ 95 96 97 98' 99 00' 01 02 03' 04 05' 06' 07 08 09' 10' 11 12 13 14 15 17 Tiny cult star (1979) concentrated, exotic, MERLOT-led. Hugely consistent; can age. Frightening prices. V.gd ROC DE CAMBES, DOM de Cambes.

Thieuley B'x r p w ★★ E-2-M supplier of consistent quality AC B'x (r w); oak-aged CUVÉE Francis Courselle (r w). Also VIN DE FRANCE Les Truffières (CHARD, SYRAH).

Tour-Blanche, La Saut (r) w sw ★★★ 95 96 97' 98 99 01' 02 03' 04 05' 06 07' 09' 10' 11' 13 14 15 16 17 Excellent First Growth SAUT; consistent quality. Rich, bold, powerful wines on sweeter end of scale. Second label: Les Charmilles de La Tour-Blanche. Also dry white B'x Duo de La Tour Blanche.

Tour-Carnet, La H-Méd r ★★★ 01 02 03 04 05' 06 08 09' 10' 11 12 14 15 16 17 North H-MÉD Classed Growth owned by Bernard Magrez (*see* FOMBRAUGE, PAPE-CLÉMENT). MICHEL ROLLAND consults. Rich, concentrated, opulent wines. Second label: Les Douves de Carnet. Also dry white B'x Blanc de La Tour Carnet.

Tour-de-By, La Méd r ★★ 03 04 05' 06 08 09 10 11 12 14 15 16 17 Substantial family-run estate in n MÉD. Sturdy, reliable, CAB SAUV-led (60%) wines with 5% PETIT VERDOT. Also rosé and special CUVÉE Héritage Marc Pagès.

Tour de Mons, La Marg r ★★ 04 05' 06 08 09' 10 11 12 14 15 16 MARG CRU BOURGEOIS named after C17 owner. Now owned by CA GRANDS CRUS (*see* MEYNEY). MERLOT-led (56%). Steady improvement.

Tour-du-Haut-Moulin H-Méd r ★★ 03 04 05' 06 08 09 10 11 12 14 15 16 Family-owned (since 1870) n H-MÉD CRU BOURGEOIS. Intense, structured wines to age.

Tour-du-Pas-St-Georges St-Ém r ★★ 04 05' 06 08 09' 10 11 12 14 15 16 ST-GEORGES-ST-ÉM estate run by Delbeck family. Classic style. Special CUVÉE Ame de St-Georges.

Tour Figeac, La St-Ém r ★★ 02 04 05' 06 07 08 09' 10' 11 12 14 15 16 GRAND CRU CLASSÉ in "graves" sector of ST-ÉM. DERENONCOURT consults. Gd proportion of CAB FR (40%). Fine, floral, harmonious.

Tour Haut-Caussan Méd r ★★ 06 08 09' 10' 11 12 14 15 16 Consistent, family-run CRU BOURGEOIS at Blaignan. MERLOT-led. Value.

Tournefeuille L de P r ★★ 03 04 05' 06 07 08 09 10' 11 12 14 15 16 Reliable L DE P on clay and gravel soils. Owned by Petit family. MERLOT-led (70%). Round, fleshy.

Tour-St-Bonnet Méd r ★★ 06 08 09' 10' 11 12 14 15 16 CRU BOURGEOIS at St-Christoly. Gravel soils. Reliable. Gd value.

Trois Croix, Les Fron r ★★ 07 08 09 10 11 12 13 14 15 16 17 Fine, balanced wines from consistent producer. Clay-limestone soils. 80% MERLOT. Gd value. Owned, managed by Léon family.

Tronquoy-Lalande St-Est r ★★ 05 06 07 08 09' 10' 11 12 14 15 16 17 Same owners as MONTROSE; plenty of investment. MERLOT-led wines (with 5% Petit Verdot) consistent, dark, satisfying. Second label: Tronquoy de Ste-Anne. A little white.

Troplong-Mondot St-Ém r ★★★ 96' 98' 99 00' 01 02 03 04 05' 06 07 08 09' 10 11 12 13 14 15 16 17 PREMIER GRAND CRU CLASSÉ (B) on the limestone plateau. New owner (insurance company) and manager (ex-COS D'ESTOURNEL) in 2017. *Wines of power, depth* with increasing elegance (and price) these days. Second label: Mondot.

Trotanoy Pom r ★★★★ 95 96 98' 00' 01 02 03 04' 05' 06 07 08 09' 10' 11 12 13 14 15' 16' 17 One of jewels in J-P MOUEIX crown. Average age of v'yd 35 yrs. Power, elegance and long ageing. Second label: Espérance de Trotanoy.

Trottevieille St-Ém r ★★★ 95 96 98 99 00' 01 03 04 05' 06 07 08' 09' 10' 11 12 14 15' 16 17 PREMIER GRAND CRU CLASSÉ (B) on limestone plateau. Much improved in new millennium; wines long, fresh, structured. Lots of CAB FR (40–50%) incl some pre-phylloxera vines. Second label: La Vieille Dame de Trottevieille.

Valandraud St-Ém r ★★★★ 96 98 99 00' 01' 02 03 04 05' 06 07 08 09' 10' 11 12 13 14 15 16' 17 PREMIER GRAND CRU CLASSÉ (B) in e ST-ÉM. Initially a garage wonder launched by Jean-Luc and Murielle Thunevin. Formerly super-concentrated; now rich, costly, dense but balanced. Also Valandraud Blanc (SAUV BL/Sauv Gris).

Vieille Cure, La Fron r ★★ 05' 06 08 09' 10' 11 12 13 14 15 16 17 Leading FRON estate; US-owned. Fruity, appetizing. Jean-Luc Thunevin (VALANDRAUD) consults. Value.

Vieux-Ch-Certan Pom r ★★★★ 89 90' 94 95' 96' 98' 99 00' 01' 02 04 05' 06 07 08 09' 10' 11' 12 13 14 15' 16' 17 Rated close to PETRUS in quality; different in style; *elegance, harmony, fragrance*. Average age of v'yd 50 yrs. Alexandre Thienpont and son Guillaume at helm. Second label: La Gravette de Certan.

Vieux Ch St-André St-Ém r ★★ 06 08 09' 10 11 12 14 15 16 Small MERLOT-based v'yd in MONTAGNE-ST-ÉM. Owned by Berrouet family (*see* PETRUS). *Gd value.*

Villegeorge, De H-Méd r ★★ 05 06 08 09' 10 12 14 15 16 Tiny s H-MÉD. CAB SAUV-led (up to 89%). Elegant wines. Marie-Laure Lurton (CH La Tour de Bessan, MAR) owns.

Vray Croix de Gay Pom r ★★ 04 05' 06 08 09' 10' 11 12 14 15 16' 17 Tiny v'yd in best part of POM. More finesse of late. Bio certification from 2018. Second label: L'Enchanteur. CHX Siaurac (L DE P), Le Prieuré (ST-ÉM) same stable.

Yquem Saut w sw (dr) ★★★★ 89' 90' 93 94 95' 96 97' 98 99' 00 01' 02 03' 04 05' 06' 07' 08 09' 10' 11' 13' 14' 15' 16' King of sweet, *liquoreux*, wines. Strong, intense, luscious; kept 3 yrs in barrel. Most vintages improve for 15 yrs+, some live 100 yrs+ in transcendent splendour. 100 ha in production (75% SÉM/25% SAUV BL). No Yquem made 51, 52, 64, 72, 74, 92, 2012. No second label (rejected wine sold to NÉGOCIANTS). Makes small amount (800 cases/yr) of dry, SAUV BL-based "Y" (pronounced "ygrec").

The Place de Bordeaux diversifies

The Place de Bordeaux, a sort of virtual stock exchange for NÉGOCIANTS, brokers (*courtiers*) and CHX, has long been responsible for the distribution of B'X's wines around the world. Now it has a growing list of wines from other regions: Ch de Beaucastel Hommage à Jacques Perrin (Rhône), Masseto, Solaia (Italy), Opus One, Vérité (California), Almaviva, Seña (Chile). If it works for B'x why not give it a go?

Italy

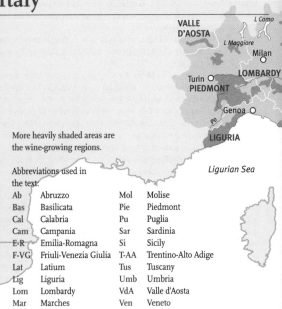

VALLE
D'AOSTA

L Como

L Maggiore

Milan ○

LOMBARDY

Turin ○
PIEDMONT

Genoa ○

Po

LIGURIA

More heavily shaded areas are
the wine-growing regions.

Ligurian Sea

Abbreviations used in
the text:

Ab	Abruzzo	Mol	Molise
Bas	Basilicata	Pie	Piedmont
Cal	Calabria	Pu	Puglia
Cam	Campania	Sar	Sardinia
E-R	Emilia-Romagna	Si	Sicily
F-VG	Friuli-Venezia Giulia	T-AA	Trentino-Alto Adige
Lat	Latium	Tus	Tuscany
Lig	Liguria	Umb	Umbria
Lom	Lombardy	VdA	Valle d'Aosta
Mar	Marches	Ven	Veneto

Wine everywhere is all about people. Italy, too, is all about people:
somehow more memorably, extravagantly and stylishly so than
other countries. You have only to scan this chapter to see the crush of
individuals and their properties thrusting into the limelight. Of course
it is based on geography. Italy has lots of geography; its long mountain
spine sees to that, from the Alps down to its rugged toes, the sea never
very far away. You can also say that "Italy" is only geography; a collection
of passionately individual city-states nominally united 150 years ago,
but loyal to locality in a way foreigners find hard to understand. Tiny
differences in terroir, in history, custom and ownership matter deeply.
"Mine is the *genuino*," says the farmer. "I'm not too sure about next door."

There is plenty of room for self-expression in the current wine boom.
Room, and confidence. A few years ago most of Italy's hundreds of
local grape varieties went unnoticed. Today there's a market for them,
and locals ready to make extravagant claims – and follow them through
with style and relish. Ian D'Agata might be able to tell you how many
he chronicles in his great book, *Native Wine Grapes of Italy*. I can only say
many hundreds – each with its champions.

Don't look in Italy for consensus, or consistency. If the very greatest
wines still come (on the whole) from the hotspots of Piedmont, Tuscany
and the Veneto, a fabulous variety now spreads over the whole country,
matching, in most cases, its irresistible food. I've scattered ideas about
wines for dishes through this chapter. See Italy as a feast. You're invited.

Recent vintages

Amarone, Veneto & Friuli

2017 One of most difficult vintages in memory, non-stop rain.

2016 Very hot summer; big reds, slightly chunky whites.

2015 Very hot summer, early July. Quantity good, quality better.

2014 Cool, wet summer, good September (whites), October (reds). Not memorable for Amarone.

2013 Good whites. Reds, especially passito, suffered late rain/hail.

2012 Prolonged heat, drought hit quantity, quality. Amarone should be good.

2011 "Best year ever" for Amarone. Whites balanced, concentrated. Some reds very tannic, high alcohol.

2010 Cool, good for lighter wines, though Amarone will be fragrant, elegant.

Campania & Basilicata

2017 Tough year for reds especially. Low volume.

2016 Cold spring delayed flowering, hot summer allowed catch-up. Best: Greco.

2015 Wet winter, patchy spring, hot, dry early summer, late autumn. Great.

2014 Production 25 per cent down on 2013. Spotty quality. Choose carefully.

2013 Whites balanced, perfumed; reds less so, especially late-picked Aglianico.

2012 Sept rains saved whites. Indian summer made outstanding Aglianicos.

2011 Wines concentrated; high alcohol, tannin in reds. Whites better balanced.

2010 Whites lightish with good aromas. Late-picked Aglianicos belatedly
judged excellent.

Marches & Abruzzo

2017 Very difficult year, hot and droughty: reds with tough tannins, whites
overripe. Low volume.

2016 Rain, cold and lack of sun made very difficult year. Pecorino probably best.

2015 Hot summer, timely autumn rain, healthy grapes; good whites, better reds.

2014 Marches: good reds and whites. Abruzzo: interesting at higher levels,
mainly late-picked.

2013 Hailstorms and rot. Fine Sept saved whites; reds better than feared.

2012 Warm days and cool nights at vintage. Later-picked varieties best.

2011 Some overconcentrated, alcoholic and tannic reds. Best should age well.

2010 A difficult year but some better-than-expected results. Drinking now.

Piedmont

2017 Among earliest in living memory. Low quantity but good quality.

2016 Potentially top vintage; high quantity, quality, very promising.

2015 Outstanding Barolo/Barbaresco. Should be long-lived. Barbera/Dolcetto
also good. Quantity also up, as no doubt will be price.

2014 Later-picked grapes thrived, early ones (eg. Dolcetto) didn't.

2013 Bright, crisp whites and reds improving with time.

2012 Quality good to very good, volume very low.

2011 Forward, early-drinking, scented reds despite highish alcohol levels.

2010 Patient growers made very good wines. Now seen as potentially top vintage.

Fine vintages: 08 06 04 01 00 99 98 97 96 95 90 89 88. Vintages to keep: 01
99 96. Vintages to drink up: 03 00 97 90 88.

Tuscany

2017 Very difficult vintage. Very hot summer, then rain and cold. Low volume.

2016 Hot summer with a fresher Sept; promising from Chianti to Montalcino
to Maremma. High quality but lower quantity.

2015 Grapes healthy but small: quantity slightly down, quality well up.

2014 Cool, wet summer, fine late season. Quantity up, quality patchy,
buyer beware.

2013 Uneven ripening. Not a great year, but some peaks.

2012 Drought and protracted heat; classic wines saved by early Sept rain.

2011 Some charmingly fruity if alcoholic classic reds. Whites a bit unbalanced.

2010 By no means everywhere wonderful, as has been claimed for Brunello.

Fine vintages: 08 07 06 04 01 99 97 95 90. Vintages to keep: 01 99. Vintages
to drink up: 03 00 97 95 90.

Accorrero Pie ★★★ Italy's best GRIGNOLINO producer. V.gd: Bricco del Bosco (steel
vat) and VIGNE Vecchie (oak-aged). Also gd: BARBERA del Monferrato (Cima and
Bricco Battista) and Brigantino sweet (MALVASIA di Casorzo).

> What do the initials mean?
> **DOC (Denominazione di Origine Controllata)** Controlled Denomination of Origin, cf. AOC in France.
> **DOCG (Denominazione di Origine Controllata e Garantita)** "G" = "Guaranteed". Italy's highest quality designation. Guarantee? It's still *caveat emptor.*
> **IGT (Indicazione Geografica Tipica)** "Geographic Indication of Type". Broader and more vague than DOC, cf. Vin de Pays in France.
> **DOP/IGP (Denominazione di Origine Protetta/IndicazioneGeografica Protetta)** "P" = "Protected". The EU's DOP/IGP trump Italy's DOC/IGT.

Aglianico del Taburno Cam DOCG r dr ★→★★★ Around Benevento, to se. Spicier notes (leather, tobacco) and herbs, higher acidity than other Aglianicos. Gd: CANTINA del Taburno, La Rivolta.

Aglianico del Vulture Bas DOC(G) r dr ★→★★★ 06 07 08 10 11 12 13 15 DOC after 1 yr, SUPERIORE after 3 yrs, RISERVA after 5. From slopes of extinct volcano Monte Vulture. More floral (violet), dark fruits (plum), smoke, spice than other Aglianicos. Gd: Basilisco, CANTINA di Venosa, CANTINE DEL NOTAIO, ELENA FUCCI, Eubea, Grifalco, Madonna delle Grazie, MASTRODOMENICO, PATERNOSTER, Terre degli Svevi.

Alba Pie Major wine city of PIE, se of Turin in LANGHE hills; truffles, hazelnuts and Pie's, if not Italy's, most prestigious wines: BARBARESCO, BARBERA D'ALBA, BAROLO, DOGLIANI (DOLCETTO), Langhe, NEBBIOLO D'ALBA, ROERO.

Albana di Romagna E-R DOCG w dr sw s/sw (sp) ★→★★★ DYA. Italy's 1st white DOCG, justified only by sweet PASSITO; dry and sparkling unremarkable. FATTORIA ZERBINA (esp AR Passito RISERVA), Giovanna Madonia, PODERE Morini (Cuore Matto Riserva Passito), Raffaella Bissoni, Tre Monti.

Allegrini Ven ★★★ Grower world-famous for VALPOLICELLA, though top table wines *La Grola,* Palazzo della Torre, La Poja not DOC, while AMARONE is. Owner of POGGIO al Tesoro in BOLGHERI, Poggio San Polo in MONTALCINO, TUS too.

Alta Langa Pie DOCG (p) w sp ★★→★★★ PIE's major zone for top-quality vintage METODO CLASSICO sparkling, produced only from PINOT N and CHARD. Best: BANFI, Cocchi, FONTANAFREDDA, GANCIA, GERMANO ETTORE, Serafino Enrico.

Altare, Elio Pie ★★★ Past leader of modernist BAROLO. Now run by Sonia, Elio's daughter, who is making her mark. Try Barolos: Arborina, Cannubi, Unoperuno (a selection from Arborina); also Giarborina (LANGHE NEBBIOLO), Langhe Rosso La Villa (BARBERA/NEBBIOLO).

Alto Adige (Sudtirol) T-AA DOC r p w dr sw sp ★★→★★★ Mountainous province of Bolzano (Austrian until 1919); today's best Italian whites? Germanic varieties dominate. Kerner, GEWURZ, SYLVANER, but PINOT GRIGIO too; probably world's best PINOT BIANCO. PINOT N can be excellent, but often overoaked) as can *Lagrein.*

Alto Piemonte Pie Microclimate and soils of ne PIE make it ideal for NEBBIOLO (locally called Spanna), but wines rarely 100%, with additions of other local grapes (Croatina, Uva Rara, Vespolina). Home of the DOC(G): BOCA, BRAMATERRA, Colline Novaresi, Coste della Sesia, Fara, GATTINARA, GHEMME, LESSONA, Sizzano, Valli Ossolane. Many outstanding wines.

Ama, Castello di Tus ★★★ Top CHIANTI CLASSICO estate of Gaiole. Plain *Chianti Classico is one of best,* and most expensive. Worth seeking: TUS/B'x blend Haiku and MERLOT L'Apparita, despite the high price. Outstanding Chianti Classico GRAN SELEZIONE San Lorenzo.

Amarone della Valpolicella Ven DOCG r ★★→★★★★ 06' 07 08 09 10 11' 12 13 15 (16) Intense strong red from winery-raisined VALPOLICELLA grapes; relatively dry version of more ancient RECIOTO DELLA VALPOLICELLA; CLASSICO if from historic zone. (*See also* VALPOLICELLA and box p.153–4.) Older vintages rare, as 1st created in 50s.

Angelini, Paolo Pie ★★→★★★ Small family-run MONFERRATO estate: v.gd GRIGNOLINO del Monferrato Casalese.

Angelini, Tenimenti Tus *See* BERTANI DOMAINS (TOSCANA).

Antinori, Marchesi L&P Tus ★★→★★★★ Historic Florentine house of ancient Antinori family, led by Piero and three daughters. Famous for CHIANTI CLASSICO (Tenute Marchese Antinori and *Badia a Passignano*, latter now elevated to Gran Selezione), also polished but oaky white Cervaro (Umb **Castello della Sala**), PIE (PRUNOTTO) wines. Pioneer TIGNANELLO and SOLAIA among few world-class SUPER TUSCANS. Also estates in BOLGHERI (Guado al Tasso), FRANCIACORTA (*Montenisa*), MONTALCINO (Pian delle vigne), MONTEPULCIANO (La Braccesca), PUG (Tormaresca), TUS MAREMMA (Fattoria Aldobrandesca). RIES-based white from estate of Monteloro n of Florence. Interests in Calfornia, Romania, etc.

Antoniolo Pie ★★★ Age-worthy benchmark GATTINARA. Outstanding Osso San Grato and San Francesco.

Argiano, Castello di Tus ★★★ Beautiful property, next to and distinct from estate called "Argiano", transformed by Sesti family into one of MONTALCINO's finest sources of BRUNELLO. Best is Brunello RISERVA Phenomena.

Argiolas, Antonio Sar ★★→★★★ Top producer using native island grapes. Outstanding crus *Turriga* (★★★), sweet Antonio Argiolas (named for founder, d.2009 age 102), Iselis MONICA, VERMENTINO DI SARDEGNA, and top sweet Angialis (mainly local Nasco grape).

Asti Pie DOCG sw sp ★→★★ NV PIE sparkler from MOSCATO Bianco grapes, inferior to MOSCATO D'ASTI, not really worth its DOCG. Sells like mad in Russia. Try Bera, Cascina Fonda, Caudrina, Vignaioli di Santo Stefano.

Avignonesi Tus ★★★ Large bio estate, Belgian-owned since 2007. 200 ha in MONTEPULCIANO and Cortona. *Italy's best Vin Santo*. VINO NOBILE has returned to 1st division after period in wilderness. Top is VN Grandi Annate but MERLOT Desiderio, CHARD Il Marzocco creditable internationals.

Azienda agricola / agraria Estate (large or small) making wine from its own grapes.

Badia a Coltibuono Tus ★★★ Historic CHIANTI CLASSICO. Star wine is 100% SANGIOVESE barrique-aged Sangioveto, but entry-level Chianti Classico one of best too.

Banfi (Castello or Villa) Tus ★→★★★ Giant of MONTALCINO, 100s of ha, though not in ideal situations, at extreme s of zone; but top, limited-production wine POGGIO all'Oro is a great BRUNELLO.

Barbaresco Pie DOCG r ★★→★★★★ 01 04 06′ 07 08 09 10 11 12 13 14 (15) (16) Wrongly looked down upon as BAROLO's poor cousin: both 100% NEBBIOLO, similar complexity, but plenty of differences. Barbaresco has warmer microclimate, more fertile soils, lower slopes, so less austere, "muscular" than Barolo, but v. elegant. Min 26 mths ageing, 9 mths in wood; at 4 yrs becomes RISERVA. Like Barolo, most these days sold under a cru name or *menzione geografica*. (For top producers *see* box, opposite.)

Barbera d'Alba DOC r ★→★★★ Richest and most velvety of BARBERAS. Gd: GIACOMO CONTERNO (Cascina Francia and Ceretta), GIUSEPPE RINALDI, VIETTI (Scarrone).

Asti Secco: brand-new dry version of Asti DOCG, born 2017. Welcome to our world.

Barbera d'Asti DOCG r ★→★★★ Fruity, high-acid version of BARBERA grape. Higher quality is Barbera d'Asti Superiore Nizza (or simply, Nizza). Gd: BERSANO (Nizza La Generala), BRAIDA (Bricco dell'Uccellone, Bricco della Bigotta, Ai Suma), *Chiarlo Michele* (Nizza La Court), Dacapo (Nizza), Marchesi Gresy (Monte Colombo), Tenuta Olim Bauda (Nizza), *Vietti* (La Crena).

Barbera del Monferrato Superiore Pie DOCG r ★★ Relatively light, fruity BARBERA with sharpish tannins. Gd: Accornero (Cima RISERVA della Casa), Iuli (Barabba).

Barberani ★★→★★★ Brothers Bernardo and Niccolò run organic estate on slopes

> **Barbaresco subzones**
> There are substantial differences between BARBARESCO's four main
> communes – **Barbaresco:** most complete, balanced. Asili (BRUNO GIACOSA,
> CERETTO, Ca' del Baio, PRODUTTORI DEL BARBARESCO), Martinenga (Marchesi
> di Gresy), Montefico (Produttori del Barbaresco, Roagna), Montestefano
> (Produttori del Barbaresco, Rivella Serafino, Giordano Luigi), Ovello
> (CANTINA del Pino, Rocca Albino), Pora (Ca' del Baio, Produttori del
> Barbaresco), Rabaja (CASTELLO DI VERDUNO, Giuseppe Cortese, BRUNO
> GIACOSA, Produttori del Barbaresco, Rocca Bruno), Rio Sordo (Cascina
> Bruciata, Cascina delle Rose, Produttori del Barbaresco), Roncaglie
> (Poderi Colla). **Neive:** most powerful, fleshiest. Albesani (Castello di
> Neive, CANTINA del Pino), Basarin (Marco e Vittorio Adriano, Giacosa
> Fratelli, Negro Angelo), Bordini (La Spinetta), Currá (Rocca Bruno,
> Sottimano), Gallina (Castello di Neive, ODDERO, Lequio Ugo), Serraboella
> (Cigliuti). **San Rocco Seno d'Elvio:** readiest to drink, soft. Sanadaive
> (Marco e Vittorio Adriano). **Treiso:** freshest, most refined. Bernardot
> (CERETTO), Bricco di Treiso (PIO CESARE), Marcarini (Ca' del Baio),
> Montersino (Abrigo Orlando), Nervo (RIZZI), Pajoré (Rizzi, Sottimano).

of Lago di Corbara turning out gd to excellent ORVIETO. Cru Luigi e Giovanna
is star, Orvieto Castagneto and (noble rot) Calcaia also excellent. Reds gd too.

Bardolino Ven DOC(G) r p ★→★★ DYA Light summery red from Lake Garda.
Bardolino SUPERIORE DOCG has much lower yield than Bardolino DOC; its pale-
pink CHIARETTO one of Italy's best rosés. Gd producers: Albino Piona,
Cavalchina, Corte Gardoni, Costadoro, *Guerrieri Rizzardi*, Le Fraghe, Le VIGNE
di San Pietro, ZENATO, Zeni.

Barolo Pie DOCG r ★★★→★★★★ 96' 99' 01' 04' 06' 07 08 09 10' 11 (14) (15) (16)
Italy's greatest red? 100% NEBBIOLO, from any of 11 communes incl Barolo itself.
Traditionally a blend of v'yds or communes, but these days most is single v'yd
(like Burgundian crus), called Menzione Geografica Aggiuntiva. Best are age-
worthy wines of power, elegance, with alluring floral scent and sour red-cherry
flavour. Must age 38 mths before release (5 yrs for RISERVA), of which 18 mths
in wood. (For top producers *see* box, p.131.) Division between traditionalists
(long maceration, large oak barrels) and modernists (shorter maceration, often
barriques) is less helpful these days as producers use techniques of both schools.

Bastianich ★★→★★★ American Joe Bastianich oversees 35 ha from US base, with
star consultant Maurizio Castelli. Knockout Vespa Bianco, typically Friulian
blend of CHARD/SAUV BL with a *pizzico* of native Picolit; outstanding FRIULANO Plus.

Belisario Mar ★★ →★★★ Largest producer of VERDICCHIO DI MATELICA. Many different
bottlings; gd quality/price. Top: RISERVA Cambrugiano e Del Cerro.

Benanti Si ★★★ Benanti family and Salvo Foti (until recently their winemaker)
turned world on to ETNA. Bianco Superiore *Pietramarina* one of Italy's best
whites. V.gd: mono-variety Nerello Cappuccio and NERELLO MASCALESE.

Berlucchi, Guido Lom ★★ Italy's largest producer of METODO CLASSICO fizz; five
million+ bottles from 100 ha v'yd. FRANCIACORTA Brut Cuvée Imperiale is
flagship. New Cuvée J.R.E. N°4 Extra Brut RISERVA.

Bersano Pie ★★★ Large-volume, gd-quality. V.gd: BARBERA, Freisa, GRIGNOLINO.

Bertani Ven ★★ →★★★ Long-est producer of VALPOLICELLA and SOAVE; v'yds in various
parts of Verona province. Basic Veronese/Valpantena lines plus restoration of
abandoned techniques, eg. white using skin maceration, red (Secco Bertani
Original Vintage Edition). *See also* BERTANI DOMAINS (TOSCANA).

Bertani Domains (Toscana) Tus ★★ →★★★ Previously Tenimenti Angelini. Angelini
group has taken over name, using it for all operations incl TUS. Three major

> **Barolo subzones**
> The concept of "cru" is gaining acceptance although it is not allowed on
> the label. It is replaced (in BAROLO and BARBARESCO at least) by "geographic
> mentions" (*Menzioni Geografiche Aggiuntive*), known unofficially as
> subzones. Currently Barolo has 11 village mentions and 170 additional
> geographical mentions. Some of best incl (by commune) – **Barolo:**
> Bricco delle Viole, Brunate, Bussia, Cannubi, Cannubi Boschis,
> Cannubi San Lorenzo, Cannubi Muscatel, Cerequio, Le Coste, Ravera,
> Sarmassa; **Castiglione Falletto:** Bricco Boschis, Bricco Rocche, Fiasco,
> Mariondino, Monprivato, Rocche di Castiglione, Vignolo, Villero;
> **Cherasco:** Mantoetto; **Diano d'Alba:** La VIGNA, Sorano (partly shared with
> Serralunga); **Grinzane Cavour:** Canova, Castello; **La Morra:** Annunziata,
> Arborina, Bricco Manzoni, Bricco San Biagio, Brunate, Cerequio,
> Fossati, La Serra, Rocche dell'Annunziata, Rocchettevino, Roggeri,
> Roncaglie; **Monforte d'Alba:** Bussia, Ginestra, Gramolere, Mosconi,
> Perno; **Novello:** Bergera, Ravera; **Roddi:** Bricco Ambrogio; **Serralunga
> d'Alba:** Baudana, Boscareto, Cerretta, Falletto, Francia, Gabutti,
> Lazzarito, Marenca, Ornato, Parafada, Prapò, Sorano, Vignarionda;
> **Verduno:** Massara, Monvigliero.

wineries: San Leonino, CHIANTI CLASSICO; Trerose, MONTEPULCIANO; Val di Suga, MONTALCINO (esp BRUNELLO Spuntali).

Biondi-Santi Tus ★★★★ Classic wines from traditional MONTALCINO estate that 1st created BRUNELLO, recently sold to Epi group (Piper-Heidsieck): Brunellos and esp RISERVAS high in acid, tannin requiring decades to develop fully. Recently trying more user-friendly style.

Bisol Ven ★★★ Top brand of PROSECCO; outstanding CARTIZZE and owner of beautiful Venissa island retreat in Venice lagoon; also rare, expensive Venissa white from rare Dorona grape.

Boca Pie DOC r ★→★★★★ *See* ALTO PIEMONTE. Potentially among greatest reds. NEBBIOLO (70–90%), incl up to 30% Uva Rara and/or Vespolina. Volcanic soil. Needs long ageing. Best: *Le Piane*. Gd: Carlone Davide, Castello Conti.

Bolgheri Tus DOC r p w (sw) ★★→★★★★ Arty walled village on w coast giving name to stylish, expensive SUPER TUSCANS, mainly French varieties. Big names: ALLEGRINI (POGGIO al Tesoro), ANTINORI (Guado al Tasso), FRESCOBALDI (ORNELLAIA), FOLONARI (Campo al Mare), GAJA (CÀ MARCANDA), outstanding Le Macchiole and MICHELE SATTA, SASSICAIA (the original).

Bolla Ven ★★ Historic Verona firm for AMARONE, RECIOTO DELLA VALPOLICELLA, RECIOTO DI SOAVE, SOAVE, VALPOLICELLA. Today owned by powerful GRUPPO ITALIANO VINI.

Borgo del Tiglio F-VG ★★★→★★★★ Nicola Manferrari is one of Italy's top white winemakers. COLLIO FRIULANO RONCO della Chiesa, Studio di Bianco esp impressive.

Boscarelli, Poderi Tus ★★★ Small estate of Genovese de Ferrari family with reliably high-standard VINO NOBILE DI MONTEPULCIANO, cru Nocio dei Boscarelli and RISERVA.

Botte Big barrel, anything from 6–250 hl, usually between 20–50, traditionally of Slavonian but increasingly French oak. To traditionalists, the ideal vessel for ageing wines in which an excess of oak aromas is undesirable.

Brachetto d'Acqui / Acqui Pie DOCG r sw (sp) ★★ DYA. Pink version of ASTI, similarly undeserving for most part of its DOCG status, equally popular in Russia.

Braida Pie ★★★ Giacomo Bologna's children, Giuseppe and Raffaella, continue in his footsteps; BARBERA D'ASTI Bricco dell'Uccellone remains top, backed by Bricco della Bigotta and Ai Suma.

Bramaterra Pie DOC r *See* ALTO PIEMONTE. Gd: Antoniotti Odilio.

Brezza Pie ★★→★★★ Brezza family run Hotel BAROLO in village while Enzo B makes, from 17 ha+, some of Barolo's most authentic and best-value crus, incl Cannubi, Castellero, Sarmassa. Range incl BARBERA, DOLCETTO, Freisa; surprisingly gd CHARD.

Brigaldara Ven ★★★ Elegant but powerful benchmark AMARONE from estate of Stefano Cesari.Top: Case Vecie. Look for charming Dindarella Rosato.

Brolio, Castello di Tus ★★→★★★ Historic estate, CHIANTI CLASSICO's largest, and supposedly oldest, now thriving again under Francesco RICASOLI after foreign-managed decline. V.gd Chianti Classico and CC Colledilà Gran Selezione (see Chianti Classico box, p.134).

Brunelli, Gianni Tus ★★★ Lovely refined user-friendly BRUNELLOS and ROSSOS from two sites: Le Chiuse di Sotto n of MONTALCINO, and Podernovone to s, with views of Monte Amiata.

Brunello di Montalcino Tus DOCG r ★★★→★★★★ 90' 95 99' 01' 04' 06' 07 09 10' 12 (13) (15') (16) Top wine of TUS, dense but elegant with scent, structure; potentially v. long-lived. Min 4 yrs ageing, 5 for RISERVA. Misguided moves to allow small quantities of eg. MERLOT in this supposedly 100% varietal SANGIOVESE have been fought off, but vigilance needed. (For top producers see box, p.132.)

Bucci Mar ★★★ Quasi-Burgundian VERDICCHIOs, slow to mature but complex with age, esp RISERVA. Red Pongelli is user-friendly, fruity.

Burlotto, Commendatore GB Pie ★★★→★★★★ Commander GB Burlotto was one of 1ST to make/bottle top BAROLO in 1880. Descendant Fabio Alessandria's best: crus Cannubi, Monvigliero and traditional Barolo Acclivi.

Bussola, Tommaso Ven ★★★★ Self-taught maker of some of the great AMARONES, RECIOTOS, RIPASSOS of our time. The great Bepi QUINTARELLI steered him; he steers his two sons.

Ca' dei Frati Lom ★★★ Foremost quality estate of revitalized DOC LUGANA, I Frati a fine example at entry level; Brollettino a superior cru.

Ca' del Baio Pie ★★★ Small family; best-value serious producer in BARBARESCO. Outstanding Asili (RISERVA too) and Pora. V.gd Vallegrande and LANGHE RIES.

Ca' del Bosco Lom ★★★★ No 1 FRANCIACORTA estate owned by giant PINOT GR producer

---

Top Barolos

Here are a few top crus and their best producers: **Bricco Boschis** (Castiglione Falletto) CAVALLOTTO (RISERVA VIGNA San Giuseppe; **Bricco delle Viole** (BAROLO) GD VAJRA; **Bricco Rocche** (Castiglione Falletto) CERETTO; **Brunate** (La Morra, Barolo) Ceretto, GIUSEPPE RINALDI, ODDERO, Vietti; **Bussia** (Monforte) ALDO CONTERNO (Gran Bussia e Romirasco), Poderi Colla (Dardi Le Rose), Oddero (Bussia Vigna Mondoca); **Cannubi** (Barolo): BREZZA, LUCIANO SANDRONE (Cannubi Boschis), E. Pira e Figli – Chiara Boschis; **Cerequio** (La Morra, Barolo): Bordi, Chiarlo Michele, ROBERTO VOERZIO; **Falletto** (Serralunga): BRUNO GIACOSA (Le Rocche del Falletto Riserva); **Francia** (Serralunga): GIACOMO CONTERNO (Barolo Cascina Francia and Monfortino); **Ginestra** (Monforte): CONTERNO FANTINO (Sorì Ginestra and Vigna del Gris), Domenico Clerico (Ciabot Mentin); **Lazzarito** (Serralunga): ETTORE GERMANO (Riserva), VIETTI; **Monprivato** (Castiglione Falletto): GIUSEPPE MASCARELLO (Mauro); **Monvigliero** (VERDUNO): CASTELLO DI VERDUNO, COMM. GB BURLOTTO, PAOLO SCAVINO; **Ornato** (Serralunga): PIO CESARE; **Ravera** (Novello): Elvio Cogno (Bricco Pernice), gd Vajra, Vietti; **Rocche dell'Annunziata** (La Morra): Paolo Scavino (Riserva), Roberto Voerzio, Rocche Costamagna, Trediberri; **Rocche di Castiglione** (Castiglione Falletto): Brovia, Oddero, Vietti; **Vigna Rionda** (Serralunga): Massolino, Oddero; **Villero** (Castiglione Falletto): Boroli, Brovia, Giacomo Fenocchio. And the Barolo of Bartolo MASCARELLO blends together Cannubi San Lorenzo, Ruè and Rocche dell'Annunziata.

> ## The best of Brunello
> Any of the below provide a satisfying BRUNELLO DI MONTALCINO, but we have put a star next to the ones we think are best: Altesino, CASTELLO DI ARGIANO, Baricci★, BIONDI-SANTI★, GIANNI BRUNELLI★, Campogiovanni, Canalicchio di Sopra, Canalicchio di Sotto, Caparzo, CASE BASSE★, Castelgiocondo, CASTIGLION DEL BOSCO, Ciacci Piccolomini, COL D'ORCIA, Collemattoni, Colombini, Costanti, Cupano, Donatella Cinelli, Eredi, FULIGNI, Fossacolle, Franco Pacenti, Il Colle, Il Marroneto★, Il Paradiso di Manfredi, La Gerla, La Magia, La Poderina, Le Potazzine, Le Ragnaie★ LISINI★, Mastrojanni★, PIAN DELL'ORINO★, Pieri Agostina, Pieve di Santa Restituta, POGGIO ANTICO, POGGIO DI SOTTO★, San Filippo, Salvioni★, Siro Pacenti, Stella di Campalto★, TENUTA IL POGGIONE★, TENUTA di Sesta, Uccelliera, Val di Suga.

Santa Margherita, still run by exuberant founder Maurizio Zanella. *Outstanding classico-method fizz* esp Annamaria Clementi (rosé too); both Krug-like. Great Dosage Zero; excellent B'x-style Maurizio Zanella (r); burgundy-style PINOT N Pinero; above-average CHARD, for Italy that is.

Ca' del Prete Pie ★★→★★★ Small estate produces great Freisa d'ASTI, MALVASIA di Castelnuovo Don Bosco.

Caiarossa Tus ★★★ Dutch-owned (Château Giscours' Eric Jelgersma; *see* B'x chapter) estate, n of BOLGHERI. Excellent Caiarossa Rosso plus reds Aria, Pergolaia.

Calcagno Si r w ★★★ Outstanding family estate at top of ETNA's quality hierarchy. Outstanding Feudo di Mezzo and Rosso Arcurìa. V.gd Bianco Ginestra.

Calì, Paolo Si r w ★★→★★★ Paolo Calì's wines express best of Vittoria area. Top: Cerasuolo di Vittoria Forfice and Frappato. V.gd Manene (r) and GRILLO Blues (w).

Caluso / Erbaluce di Caluso Pie DOCG w ★→★★★ Wines can be still, sparkling (dry wines) and sweet (Caluso PASSITO). Gd: Cieck (Misobolo, Brut San Giorgio); Favaro (Le Chiusure and Passito Sole d'Inverno); Ferrando; Orsolani (La Rustia).

Ca' Marcanda Tus ★★★★ BOLGHERI estate of GAJA (founded 1996). Three wines in order of price (high, higher, highest): Promis, Magari, Ca' Marcanda. Grapes mainly international.

Campania We tend to think of Naples and Vesuvius, Capri and Ischia, Amalfi and Ravello when we think of Campania, so called because it was the "country" (*campania*) retreat of the Romans. But best wines come from mts inland. Outstanding red grape AGLIANICO and at least three fascinating whites: FALANGHINA, GRECO, FIANO, all capable of freshness, complexity, character. Prices are not high. Classic DOCs incl FIANO D'AVELLINO, GRECO DI TUFO, TAURASI, with newer areas emerging eg. Sannio, Benevento. Gd producers: Benito Ferrara, Caggiano, CANTINA del Taburno, Caputo, COLLI DI LAPIO, d'AMBRA, De Angelis, *Feudi di San Gregorio*, GALARDI, LA GUARDIENSE, Luigi Tecce, *Mastroberardino*, Molettieri, MONTEVETRANO, Mustilli, Terredora di Paolo, Trabucco, VILLA MATILDE.

Canalicchio di Sopra Tus ★★★ Dynamic Ripaccioli family make beautifully balanced, complex BRUNELLO (and RISERVA), ROSSO DI MONTALCINO. Look for new BRUNELLO cru, Casaccia v'yd, from 2015 vintage.

Cantina A cellar, winery or even a wine bar.

Cantina del Notaio Bas ★★→★★★ Organic and bio estate specializing in AGLIANICO, incl white, rosé, sparkling and PASSITO. Star is La Firma, but super-ripe, AMARONE-like Il Sigillo almost as gd. Repertorio always bitingly tannic and overrated.

Capezzana, Tenuta di Tus ★★★ Noble TUS family estate of late legend Count Ugo Contini Bonacossi, now run by his children. Excellent CARMIGNANO (Villa di Capezzana, Villa di Trefiano) and exceptional VIN SANTO, one of Italy's five best.

Capichera Sar ★★★ Ragnedda family make some of SAR's best whites, noteworthy reds. Outstanding Isola dei Nuraghi Bianco Santigaìni, Vendemmia Tardiva and Vigna'ngena.

Cappellano Pie ★★★ The late Teobaldo Cappellano, a BAROLO hero, devoted part of his cru Gabutti to ungrafted NEBBIOLO (Pie Franco). Son Augusto keeps highly traditional style; also "tonic" Barolo Chinato, invented by an ancestor.

Caprai Umb ★★★ →★★★★ Marco Caprai and consultant Attilio Pagli have turned large estate (nearly 200 ha) into MONTEFALCO leader. Many outstanding wines eg. 25 Anni. Non-cru Collepiano is better for less oak, while ROSSO DI MONTEFALCO is smooth, elegant. GRECHETTO Grecante is reasonably priced.

Carema Pie DOC r ★★→★★★ 06' 07 08 09 10 11 13 (15) (16) Little-known, light, intense, outstanding NEBBIOLO from steep lower Alpine slopes nr Aosta. Best: Luigi Ferrando (esp Etichetta Nera), Produttori Nebbiolo di Carema.

Carignano del Sulcis Sar DOC r p ★★→★★★ 08 09 10 12 13 14 15 (16) Mellow but intense red from SAR's sw. Best: Rocca Rubia from CS di SANTADI, *Terre Brune*.

Carmignano Tus DOCG r ★★★ 02 04 06 07 08 09 10 11 12 13 (15) Fine SANGIOVESE/ B'x-grape blend invented in C20 by late Count Bonacossi of CAPEZZANA. Best: Ambra, CAPEZZANA, Farnete, Piaggia, Le Poggiarelle, Pratesi.

Carpenè-Malvolti Ven ★★ Perhaps 1st to specialize in PROSECCO. Founded 1868 by Antonio Carpene. Range incl Brut, Dry and Extra Dry, though none is all that dry (probably a gd thing).

Carpineti, Marco Lat w sw ★★ Phenomenal bio whites from little-known Bellone and Greco Moro, Greco Giallo varieties. Benchmark Caro and Ludum, one of Italy's best stickies.

Cartizze Ven ★★ DOCG PROSECCO from a hilly, difficult-to-work 106 ha in heart of CONEGLIANO VALDOBBIADENE. Often too sweet even though labelled dry. Best: Col Vetoraz; gd: BISOL.

Case Basse Tus ★★★★ Gianfranco Soldera makes mostly bio, long-oak-aged, definitive-quality BRUNELLO-style (if not DOCG) wines as before. Rare, precious.

Castel del Monte Pug DOC r p w ★→★★ (r) 08 09 10 11 (13) (15) (p w) DYA. Dry, fresh, increasingly serious wines of mid-PUG DOC. Esp *Bocca di Lupo* from Tormaresca (ANTINORI). Il Falcone RISERVA is iconic.

Castel Juval, Unterortl T-AA ★★★ Owned by mountaineer Reinhold Messner. Distinctive, crystalline wines. Difficult to contact, unfortunately. Best: RIES Windbichel, WEISSBURGUNDER. V.gd PINOT N.

Castellare Tus ★★★ Classy Castellina-in-CHIANTI producer of long standing. First-rate SANGIOVESE/MALVASIA Nera I Sodi di San Niccoló and updated CHIANTI CLASSICO esp RISERVA Il Poggiale. Also POGGIO ai Merli (MERLOT), Coniale (CAB SAUV).

Castell' in Villa Tus ★★★ Individual, traditionalist CHIANTI CLASSICO estate in extreme sw of zone. Wines of class, excellence by self-taught Princess Coralia Pignatelli.

Castelluccio E-R ★★→★★★ Quality SANGIOVESE from E-R estate of famous oenologoist Vittorio Fiore, run by son Claudio. IGT RONCO dei Ciliegi and Ronco delle Ginestre are stars. Le More is tasty, relatively inexpensive Romagna DOC.

Castiglion del Bosco Tus ★★★ Ferragamo-owned up-and-coming BRUNELLO producer.

Cataldi Madonna Ab ★★★ Organic certified. Top is PECORINO Frontone, from oldest Pecorino vines in Ab. V.gd: CERASUOLO D'ABRUZZO Piè delle vigne, MONTEPULCIANO d'Ab Toni.

Cavallotto Pie ★★★ Leading BAROLO traditionalist of Castiglione Falletto, v'yds in heart of zone. Outstanding RISERVA Bricco Boschis VIGNA San Giuseppe, Riserva Vignolo, v.gd LANGHE NEBBIOLO. Surprisingly gd GRIGNOLINO, Freisa too.

Cave Mont Blanc VdA Quality co-op at foot of Mont Blanc, with ungrafted indigenous 60–100-yr-old Prie Blanc vines. Outstanding sparkling. Also reviving long-lost Roussin de Morgex red grape. Top Blanc de Morgex et de la Salle Rayon and Brut MC Extreme.

Cerasuolo d'Abruzzo Ab DOC p ★ DYA ROSATO version of MONTEPULCIANO D'ABRUZZO, not to be confused with red CERASUOLO DI VITTORIA from SI. Can be brilliant; best (by far): CATALDI MADONNA (Pie delle Vigne), EMIDIO PEPE, Praesidium, TIBERIO, VALENTINI.

Cerasuolo di Vittoria Si DOCG r ★★ 10 11 13 15 (16) Medium-bodied red from Frappato/NERO D'AVOLA in se of island. To date, absurdly, the only SI DOCG. Try Arianna Occhipinti, COS, Gulfi, Paolo Calì, PLANETA, Valle dell'Acate.

Ceretto Pie ★★★ Leading producer of BARBARESCO (Asili, Bernradot), BAROLO (Bricco Rocche, Brunate, Prapò), plus LANGHE Bianco Blange (ARNEIS). Older generation handing over to Alessandro, Federico, Roberta, Lisa. Organic certified since 2015. Wines recently more classic.

Cerro, Fattoria del Tus ★★★ Estate owned by insurance giant SAI, making v.gd DOCG VINO NOBILE DI MONTEPULCIANO (esp cru Antica Chiusina). SAI also owns Colpetrone (MONTEFALCO SAGRANTINO), La Poderina (BRUNELLO DI MONTALCINO) and 1000-ha in MAREMMA estate of Monterufoli.

Cerruti, Ezio Pie ★★→★★★ Small estate in gd area for MOSCATO: best sweet Sol, naturally dried Moscato. V.gd Fol dry Moscato.

Cesanese del Piglio or Piglio Lat DOCG r ★→★★ Medium-bodied red, gd for moderate ageing. Best: Petrucca e Vela, Terre del Cesanese. Cesanese di Olevano Romano, Cesanese di Affile are similar.

Chianti Tus DOCG r ★→★★ Ancient region between Florence and Siena and its light red. Chianti has come a long way from the raffia-bottle-as-lamp days when it was laced with white grapes and beefed up with imports from the s. Typical TUS wine at a reasonable price.

Chianti Classico Tus DOCG r ★★→★★★ 04 06 07 08 09 10 11 12 13 (15) (16) Historic CHIANTI zone became "CLASSICO" when the Chianti area was extended to most of central TUS in early C20. Covering all or part of nine communes, the land is hilly (altitude 250–500m) and rocky. The "Black Rooster" wine is traditionally blended: the debate continues over whether the support grapes should be French (eg. CAB SAUV) or native. Gran Selezione is new top level, above RISERVA. *See also* box below.

Chiaretto Ven Pale, light-blush-hued rosé (the word means "claret"), produced esp around Lake Garda. *See* BARDOLINO.

Ciabot Berton Pie ★★★ Marco and Paola Oberto, following their father, have turned this La Morra estate into one of best-value serious producers. Blended BAROLO is convincing, crus Roggeri, Rocchettevino have distinctive single-v'yd characters.

Cinque Terre Lig DOC w dr sw ★★ Dry VERMENTINO-based whites from steep LIG coast. Sweet version: Sciacchetrà. Try Arrigoni, Bisson, Buranco, De Battè.

Ciolli, Damiano Lat ★★★ One of most interesting wineries in Italy. Best is Cirsium, 100% Cesanese d'Affile, 80-yr-old vines. V.gd Cesanese d'Affile/Comune, Silene.

Who makes really good Chianti Classico?

CHIANTI CLASSICO is a large zone with hundreds of producers, so picking out the best is tricky. The top get a ★: AMA★, ANTINORI, BADIA A COLTIBUONO★, Bibbiano, BROLIO, Cacchiano, Cafaggio, Capannelle, Casaloste, Casa Sola, CASTELLARE, CASTELL' IN VILLA, FELSINA★, FONTERUTOLI, FONTODI★, I Fabbri★, Il Molino di Grace, ISOLE E OLENA★, Le Boncie, Le Cinciole★, Le Corti, Le Filigare, Lilliano, Mannucci Droandi, MONSANTO★, Monte Bernardi, Monteraponi★, NITTARDI, NOZZOLE, Palazzino, Paneretta, Poggerino, POGGIOPIANO, QUERCIABELLA★, Rampolla, RIECINE, Rocca di Castagnoli, Rocca di Montegrossi★, RUFFINO, San Fabiano Calcinaia, SAN FELICE, SAN GIUSTO A RENTENNANO★, Paolina Savignola, Selvole, Vecchie Terre di Montefili, Verrazzano, Vicchiomaggio, VIGNAMAGGIO, Villa Calcinaia★, Villa La Rosa★, Viticcio, VOLPAIA★.

Cirò Cal DOC r (p) (w) ★★ →★★★ Brisk strong red from Cal's main grape, Gaglioppo, or light, fruity white from GRECO (DYA). Best: Caparra & Siciliani, IPPOLITO, **Librandi** (Duca San Felice ★★★), San Francesco (Donna Madda, RONCO dei Quattroventi), Santa Venere.

Classico Term for wines from a restricted, usually historic and superior-quality area within limits of a commercially expanded DOC. *See* CHIANTI CLASSICO, VALPOLICELLA, VERDICCHIO, SOAVE, numerous others.

Consorzio Chianti Classico turns 90: happy birthday. New director: Carlotta Gori.

Clerico, Domenico Pie ★★★ RIP 2017, one of greatest innovators of Italian wine, modernist BAROLO producer of Monforte d'Alba esp crus Ciabot Mentin Ginestra, Pajana, Percristina. Change of winemaking style towards much less oak.

Coffele Ven ★★★ Sensitive winemaker in up-and-coming SOAVE-land, blessed with grapes on terraces on the higher slopes, v'yds created by father Bepino. Soave CLASSICO, cru Ca' Visco, RECIOTO Le Sponde all just as they should be.

Cogno, Elvio Pie ★★★ Top estate; super-classy, austere, elegant BAROLOS. Best: RISERVA VIGNA Elena (NEBBIOLO Rosè variety), Bricco Pernice, Ravera. V.gd Anas-Cëtta (Nascetta 100%).

Col d'Orcia Tus ★★★ Top-quality MONTALCINO estate (the 3rd-largest) owned by Francesco Marone Cinzano. Best wine: BRUNELLO RISERVA POGGIO al Vento.

Colla, Poderi Pie ★★★ Behind this winery is experience of Beppe Colla (soul and creator of PRUNOTTO 1956–90). Classic, traditional, age-worthy. Top: BARBARESCO Roncaglie, BAROLO Bussia Dardi Le Rose, LANGHE Bricco del Drago.

Colli = hills; singular: Colle. **Colline** (singular Collina) = smaller hills. *See also* COLLIO, POGGIO.

Colli di Catone Lat ★ →★★★ Top producer of FRASCATI and IGT in the Roman hills of Monteporzio Catone. Outstanding aged whites from MALVASIA del Lazio (aka Malvasia Puntinata) and GRECHETTO. Look for Colle Gaio or Casal Pilozzo labels.

Colli di Lapio Cam ★★★ Clelia Romano's estate is Italy's **best Fiano** producer.

Colli di Luni Lig, Tus DOC r w ★★ →★★★ VERMENTINO and Albarola whites; SANGIOVESE-based reds easy to drink, charming. Gd: Ottaviano Lambruschi (Costa Marina); Giacomelli (Boboli), La Baia del Sole (Oro d'Isèe); Bisson (VIGNA Erta).

Collio F-VG DOC r w ★★★ →★★★★ Hilly zone on border with Slovenia. Esp known for complex, sometimes deliberately oxidized whites, some vinified on skins in earthenware vessels/amphorae in ground. Some excellent, some shocking blends from various French, German, Slavic grapes. Numerous gd-to-excellent producers: Aldo Polencic, BORGO DEL TIGLIO, Castello di Spessa, LA CASTELLADA, Fiegl, GRAVNER, MARCO FELLUGA, Livon, Podversic, Primosic, Princic, **Radikon**, Renato Keber, RUSSIZ SUPERIORE, *Schiopetto*, Tercic, Terpin, Venica & Venica, VILLA RUSSIZ.

Colli Piacentini E-R DOC r p w →★★★ DYA Light gulping wines, often fizzy, from eg. BARBERA, BONARDA (r), MALVASIA, Pignoletto (w).

Colterenzio CS / Schreckbichl T-AA ★★ →★★★ Cornaiano-based main player among ALTO ADIGE co-ops. Whites (SAUV Lafoa, CHARD Altkirch, PINOT BIANCO Weisshaus Praedium) tend to be better than reds, despite renown of CAB SAUV Lafoa.

Conegliano Valdobbiadene wh DOCG w sp ★ →★★ DYA. Name for top PROSECCO, tricky to say: may be used separately or together.

Conero DOCG r ★★ →★★★ 09 11 12 13 15 Aka ROSSO CONERO. Small zone; powerful, at times too oaky, MONTEPULCIANO. Try: GAROFOLI (Grosso Agontano), Le Terrazze (Praeludium), Marchetti (RISERVA Villa Bonomi), Moncaro, Monteschiavo (Adeodato), Moroder (Riserva Dorico), UMANI RONCHI (Riserva Campo San Giorgio).

Conterno, Aldo Pie ★★★ →★★★★ Top estate of Monforte d'ALBA, was considered a traditionalist, esp concerning top BAROLOS Granbussia, Cicala, Colonello and esp Romirasco. Sons moving winery in more modernist direction.

Conterno, Giacomo Pie ★★★★ For many, estate's top wine, Monfortino, is best wine of Italy. V'yd (Cascina Francia) is in Serralunga while winery is in Monforte. Roberto C, son of late Giovanni (son of Giacomo), sticks religiously to formula of forebears, incl no temperature control in fermentation. Outstanding BARBERAS.

Conterno Fantino Pie ★★★ Two families joined to produce excellent modern-style BAROLO Sorì Ginestra, Mosconi, and VIGNA del Gris at Monforte d'ALBA. Also NEBBIOLO/BARBERA blend Monprà.

Conterno, Paolo Pie ★★→★★★ A family of NEBBIOLO and BARBERA growers since 1886, current *titolare* Giorgio continues with textbook cru BAROLOS Ginestra and Riva del Bric, plus particularly fine LANGHE *Nebbiolo Bric Ginestra*.

Europe has 1582 Geographical Indication wines (PDO/PGI): 526 of these in Italy.

Contini Sar ★★★ Benchmark VERNACCIA DI ORISTANO, oxidative-styled whites not unlike v.gd Amontillado or Oloroso. Antico Gregori one of Italy's best whites.

Conti Zecca Pug ★★→★★★ SALENTO estate with 320 ha, producing almost two million bottles. Donna Marzia line of Salento IGT wines is gd value, as is SALICE SALENTINO Cantalupi. Many wines; best-known is NEGROAMARO/CAB SAUV blend Nero.

Copertino Pug DOC r (p) ★★★ 08 10 11 12 (13) (15) Smooth, savoury red of NEGROAMARO from heel of Italy. Gd: CS Copertino, MONACI.

Cornelissen, Frank ★★★ From Belgium to ETNA to produce some of Italy's most interesting full-on reds. Outstanding: NERELLO MASCALESE Magma. V.gd VA, CS (r).

Correggia, Matteo Pie r ★★★ Leading producer of ROERO (RISERVA Rochè d'Ampsej, Val dei Preti), Roero ARNEIS, plus BARBERA D'ALBA (Marun).

CS (Cantina Sociale) Cooperative winery.

Cuomo, Marisa Cam ★★★ Fiorduva is one of Italy's greatest whites. V.gd Furore Bianco and Rosso (Costa d'Amalfi).

Cusumano Si ★★→★★★ Recent major player with 500 ha in various parts of SI. Reds from NERO D'AVOLA, CAB SAUV, SYRAH; whites from CHARD, INSOLIA. Gd quality, value. Best from ETNA (Alta Mora).

Dal Forno, Romano Ven ★★★★ V. high-quality VALPOLICELLA, AMARONE, RECIOTO grower; perfectionism more remarkable for fact his v'yds are outside CLASSICO zone.

D'Ambra Cam r w ★★→★★★ On ISCHIA; fosters rare local native grapes. Best: single-v'yd Frassitelli (w, 100% Biancolella). V.gd Per' e Palummo La VIGNA dei Mille Anni TENUTA Migliaccio (r).

De Bartoli, Marco Si ★★★ The late great Marco de Bartoli, scion of two MARSALA houses, fought all his life for "real" Marsala and against cooking or flavoured Marsala. His dry Vecchio Samperi couldn't be called "Marsala" because it wasn't fortified. His masterpiece is 20-yr-old Ventennale, a blend of old and recent wines. His children now in charge. Delicious table wines (eg. GRILLO *Vignaverde*, ZIBIBBO Pietranera), outstanding sweet ZIBIBBO di PANTELLERIA *Bukkuram*.

Dei Pie ★★→★★★ Pianist Caterina Dei runs this aristocratic estate in MONTEPULCIANO, making VINO NOBILES with artistry and passion. Her *chef d'oeuvre* is Bossona.

Derthona Pie w ★→★★★ Timorasso grapes grown in COLLI Tortonesi. One of Italy's unique whites (like v. dry RIES from Rheinhessen). Gd: Boveri Luigi, Claudio Mariotto, La Colombera, VIGNETI MASSA, Mutti.

Di Majo Norante Mol ★★→★★★ Best-known of Mol with decent Biferno Rosso Ramitello, Don Luigi Molise Rosso RISERVA, Mol AGLIANICO Contado. Whites uninteresting; MOSCATO PASSITO Apianae quite gd.

DOC / DOCG Quality wine designation: *see* box, p.127.

Dogliani Pie DOCG r ★→★★★ 10 11 12 13 15 16 DOCG from PIE, Dolcetto *in purezza* though they have forbidden mention of grape on label to confuse you. Some to drink young, some for moderate ageing. Gd: Bricco Rosso, Chionetti, Clavesana, EINAUDI, Francesco Boschis, Marziano Abbona, Osvaldo Barbaris, Pecchenino.

Donnafugata Si r w ★★→★★★ Classy range. Reds Mille e Una Notte, Tancredi; whites Chiaranda, Lighea. Also v. fine MOSCATO PASSITO di PANTELLERIA Ben Ryé.

Duca di Salaparuta ★★ Once on list of every Italian restaurant abroad with Corvo brand, now owned by Ilva di Saronno. More upscale wines incl Kados (w) from GRILLO grapes and INSOLIA (Colomba Platino), (r) NERELLO MASCALESE Làvico and NERO D'AVOLA Suormarchesa, Triskele (+ MERLOT). Plus old favourite Duca Enrico.

Einaudi, Luigi Pie ★★★ 52-ha estate founded late C19 by ex-president of Italy, in DOGLIANI, land in BAROLO. Solid Barolos from Cannubi and Terlo Costa Grimaldi v'yds. Top Dogliani (DOLCETTO) from VIGNA Tecc. Now also in Bussia, Monvigliero.

Elba Tus r w (sp) ★→★★ DYA. Island's white, TREBBIANO/ANSONICA, can be v. drinkable with fish. Dry reds are based on SANGIOVESE. Gd sweet white (MOSCATO) and red (*Aleatico Passito DOCG*). Gd: Acquabona, Sapereta.

Enoteca Wine library; also shop or restaurant with ambitious wine list. There is a national enoteca at the *fortezza* in Siena.

Erbaluce di Caluso (Caluso) DOCG w ★→★★★ Can be still, sparkling (dry wines) also sweet (Caluso PASSITO).

Est! Est!! Est!!! Lat DOC w dr s/sw ★ DYA. Unextraordinary white from Montefiascone, n of Rome.

Etna Si DOC r p w ★★→★★★ (r) 08 09 10 11 12 13 14 15 (16) Wine from high-altitude volcanic slopes, currently right on trend. New money brings flurry of planting and some excellent (and some overrated) wines. Burgundian-styled, but based on NERELLO MASCALESE (r) and CARRICANTE (w). For red try: Benanti (Rovittello, Serra della Contessa, I Monovitigni), Calcagno (Arcuria), Cottanera, Girolamo Russo (FEUDO), Graci (Quota 600), i Vigneri (Vinupetra), Passopisciaro (Porcaria, Rampante, Sciaranuova), TASCA D'ALMERITA (Tascante), TENUTA delle TERRE NERE (Calderara Sottana, La VIGNA di Don Peppino, Guardiola). For white try: Barone di Villagrande (EBS), BENANTI (EBS – Pietramarina), Fessina (EB – Bianco A' Puddara), I Vigneri (EB – Aurora), Girolamo Russo (EB – Nerina), TERRE NERE (Vigne Niche).

Falchini Tus ★★→★★★ Producer of gd DOCG VERNACCIA DI SAN GIMIGNANO.

Falerno del Massico Cam ★★→★★★ DOC r w ★★ (r) 09 10 11 12 13 (15) Falernum was the Yquem of ancient Rome. Today elegant red from AGLIANICO, fruity dry white from FALANGHINA. Best: Amore Perrotta, Felicia, Moio, Trabucco, VILLA MATILDE.

Fara Pie *See* ALTO PIEMONTE.

Faro Si DOC r ★★★ 06' 08 09 10 11 12 13 14 15 Intense, harmonious red from NERELLO MASCALESE and Nerello Cappuccio in hills behind Messina. Salvatore Geraci of Palari most famous, but Bonavita and Cuppari just as gd.

Felluga, Livio F-VG ★★★ Consistently fine FRIULI COLLI ORIENTALI wines, esp blends Terre Alte; *Pinot Gr*, FRIULANO, RIBOLLA GIALLA, PICOLIT (Italy's best?), MERLOT/REFOSCO blend Sossó.

Felluga, Marco F-VG *See* RUSSIZ SUPERIORE.

Felsina Tus ★★★ CHIANTI CLASSICO estate of distinction in se corner of zone: classic RISERVA Rancia and IGT Fontalloro, both 100% SANGIOVESE. Also remarkably gd (for Italy) CHARD, I Sistri. Castello di Farnetella, gd CHIANTI COLLI Senesí in same family.

Most tannic red grape in Italy probably Pignolo. Delicious but handle with care.

Fenocchio Giacomo Pie ★★★ Small but outstanding Monforte d'ALBA-based BAROLO cellar. Traditional style, min intervention, ageing in large Slavonian oak BOTTI. Crus: Bussia, Cannubi, Villero.

Ferrara, Benito Cam ★★★ Maybe Italy's best GRECO DI TUFO producer. Talent shows in excellent TAURASI too.

Ferrari T-AA sp ★★→★★★ Trento maker of best METODO CLASSICO wines outside FRANCIACORTA. Giulio Ferrari is top cru. Also gd: CHARD-based Brut RISERVA Lunelli, new Perlè Bianco, PINOT N-based Extra Brut Perle' Nero.

Ferraris, Luca Pie r ★★★ Top producer of Ruchè di Castagnole MONFERRATO. Top Opera Prima and Vigna del Parroco. V.gd **Clàsic**.

Feudi di San Gregorio Cam ★★→★★★ Much-hyped CAM producer, with DOCGS FIANO DI AVELLINO Pietracalda, GRECO DI TUFO Cutizzi, TAURASI Piano di Montevergine. Also IGT reds Patrimo (MERLOT), Serpico (AGLIANICO); whites **Campanaro** (Fiano/Greco), FALANGHINA. *See also* BASILISCO.

Feudo di San Maurizio VdA ★★★ Outstanding wines from rare native grapes CORNALIN, Mayolet and Vuillermin; last two rank amongst Italy's greatest reds.

Feudo Montoni Si r w ★★★ Fantastic estate. Best: NERO D'AVOLA Lagnusa and Vrucara. V.gd GRILLO della Timpa (w) and Perricone del Core (r).

Fiano di Avellino Cam DOCG w ★★★ 06' 08 10 12 15 (16) Can be either steely (most typical) or lush. Volcanic soils best. Gd: Cirò Picariello, COLLI di Lapio-Romana Clelio, MASTROBERARDINO, Pietracupa, QUINTODECIMO, Vadiaperti, Villa Diamante.

Fino, Gianfranco Pug ★★★ Greatest PRIMITIVO, from old, low-yielding bush vines. Outstanding "Es" among Italy's top 20 reds.

Florio Si Historic quality maker of MARSALA. Specialist in Marsala Vergine Secco. For some reason Terre Arse (= burnt lands), its best wine, doesn't do well in the UK.

Folonari Tus ★★→★★★ Ambrogio Folonari and son Giovanni, ex-RUFFINO, have v'yds in TUS and elsewhere. Estates/wines incl **Cabreo** (CHARD and SANGIOVESE/CAB SAUV), Gracciano Svetoni (VINO NOBILE DI MONTEPULCIANO), La Fuga (BRUNELLO DI MONTALCINO), NOZZOLE (incl top Cab Sauv Pareto). Also wines from BOLGHERI, FRIULI COLLI ORIENTALI, MONTECUCCO.

Fongaro Ven Classic-method fizz Lessini Durello (Durello = grape). High quality, even higher acidity, age-worthy.

Fontana Candida Lat ★★ Biggest producer of once-fashionable FRASCATI. Single-v'yd Santa Teresa much lauded, and that's Frascati's big problem in a nutshell. Part of huge GIV.

Fontanafredda Pie ★★ →★★★ Large producer of PIE wines on former royal estates, incl BAROLOS: Serralunga, VIGNA La Rosa and Fontanafredda. V.gd Alta Langa Brut Nature Vigna Gatinera.

Fonterutoli Tus ★★★ Historic CHIANTI CLASSICO estate of Mazzei family at Castellina with castle and space-age CANTINA in wild heart of TUS hills. Notable: Castellodi Fonterutoli (once v. dark, oaky Chianti Classico, now more drinkable), IGT Siepi (SANGIOVESE/MERLOT). TENUTA di Belguardo in MAREMMA (gd MORELLINO DI SCANSANO) and Zisola in SI under same ownership.

Fontodi Tus ★★★ →★★★★ Outstanding estate at Panzano making one of v. best CHIANTI CLASSICOS, also VIGNA del Sorbo (was RISERVA, now Gran Selezione) and memorable all-SANGIOVESE Flaccianello. IGTS PINOT N, SYRAH Case Via among best of these varieties in TUS. Experimental fermentation in ceramic; resultant wine called Dino (v. limited production).

Foradori T-AA ★★★ Elizabetta F pioneer for 30 yrs, mainly via great red grape of TRENTINO, **Teroldego**. Now ferments in *anfora* with reds like Morei, Sgarzon and whites like Nosiola Fontanabianca. Top wine remains TEROLDEGO-based Granato.

Franciacorta Lom DOCG w (p) sp ★★→★★★★ Italy's major zone for top-quality METODO CLASSICO fizz. Best: Barone Pizzini, Bellavista, **Ca' del Bosco**, Cavalleri, Gatti, Uberti, Villa. Also v.gd: Contadi Castaldi, Monte Rossa, Ricci Curbastri.

Frascati Lat DOC w dr sw s/sw (sp) ★→★★ DYA. Best-known wine of Roman hills, under constant threat from urban expansion and taste-blind tourists. From MALVASIA di Candia and/or TREBBIANO Toscano, most is disappointingly neutral. Gd stuff is Malvasia del Lazio (aka M Puntinata), low crop makes it uncompetitive. Look for Castel de Paolis, Conte Zandotti, Villa Simone, Santa Teresa from FONTANA CANDIDA or Colle Gaio from COLLI DI CATONE, 100% Malvasia del Lazio though IGT.

Frascole Tus ★★→★★★★ Most n winery of most n CHIANTI RÚFINA zone, tucked in foothills of Apennines, small estate run organically by Enrico Lippi, with an eye for typicity. Chianti Rúfina is main driver but VIN SANTO simply to die for.

Frescobaldi Tus ★★→★★★★ Ancient noble family, leading CHIANTI RÚFINA pioneer at NIPOZZANO estate (look for ★★★*Montesodi*), also BRUNELLO from Castelgiocondo estate in MONTALCINO. Sole owners of LUCE estate (MONTALCINO), ORNELLAIA (BOLGHERI). V'yds also in COLLIO, MAREMMA, Montespertoli.

Friuli Colli Orientali F-VG DOC r w dr sw ★★→★★★★ (Was COLLI Orientali del Friuli.) The e hills of F-VG, on Slovenian border. Zone similar to COLLIO but less experimental, making more reds and stickies. Top: Aquila del Torre, Ermacora, Gigante, Iole Grillo, La Busa dla Loft, La Sclusa, LIVIO FELLUGA, Meroi, Miani, Moschioni, Petrussa, Rodaro, Ronchi di Cialla, Ronco del Gnemiz, VIGNA Petrussa. Sweet from VERDUZZO grapes (called Ramandolo if from specific DOCG zone: Anna Berra best) or Picolit grapes (Aquila del Torre, Livio Felluga, Marco Sara, Ronchi di Cialla, Vigna Petrussa) can be amazing.

Friuli Grave F-VG DOC r w ★→★★ (r) 10 11 12 13 (15) (16) Previously Grave del Friuli. Largest DOC of F-VG, mostly on plains. Important volumes of underwhelming wines. Exceptions from Borgo Magredo, Di Lenardo, RONCO Cliona, San Simone, Villa Chiopris.

Friuli Isonzo F-VG DOC r w ★★★ Used to be just Isonzo. Gravelly, well-aired river plain with many varietals and blends. Stars mostly white, scented, structured: JERMANN's Vintage Tunina; LIS NERIS' Gris, Tal Luc and Lis; RONCO del Gelso's MALVASIA, PINOT GRIGIO (Sot lis rivis) and FRIULANO (Toc Bas); VIE DI ROMANS' Flors di Uis and Dessimis. Gd: Borgo Conventi, Pierpaolo Pecorari.

Giro d'Italia 2018 centred on wine and its terroirs. Don't drink and ride...

Friuli-Venezia Giulia F-VG Ne region of Italy. Wine-wise best in the hills on Slovenian border rather than on alluvial plains to the w. DOCS like ISONZO, COLLI ORIENTALI, Latisana, Aquileia all now preceded on label by "Friuli". Only COLLIO, theoretically the best, keeps its old name. Some gd reds, but home to Italy's best whites, along with ALTO ADIGE.

Frizzante Semi-sparkling, up to 2.5 atmospheres, eg. MOSCATO D'ASTI, much PROSECCO, LAMBRUSCO and the like; nw Italy home to large numbers of lightly fizzing wines that never seem to make it out into wider world. It's the world's loss.

Fucci, Elena Bas ★★★ AGLIANICO DEL VULTURE Titolo from 55–70-yr-old vines in Mt Vulture's Grand Cru; one of Italy's 20 best. Seek out 08 11 and outstanding 13 (maybe future RISERVA).

Fuligni Tus ★★★→★★★★ Outstanding producer of BRUNELLO, ROSSO DI MONTALCINO.

Gaja Pie ★★★★ Old family firm at BARBARESCO led by Angelo Gaja, eloquent apostle of top-end Italian wine; daughter Gaia G following. High quality, higher prices. Barbaresco remains DOCG, other previously 100% NEBBIOLO wines Costa Russi, Sorì San Lorenzo, Sorì Tildìn, plus BAROLO Sperss having been declassed to LANGHE DOC, but now going, not surprisingly, back to Barbaresco and Barolo. Splendid CHARD (Gaia e Rey). Also owns Ca' Marcanda in BOLGHERI, Pieve di Santa Restituta in MONTALCINO.

Galardi Cam ★★★ Producer of Terra di Lavoro, much-awarded AGLIANICO/Piedirosso blend, in n CAM. Makes only one wine.

Gancia Pie Famous old brand of MUSCAT fizz; still gd.

Garda Ven DOC r p w ★→★★ (r) 10 11 12 13 15 (p w) DYA. Catch-all DOC for early-drinking wines of various colours from provinces of Verona in Ven, Brescia and Mantua in Lom. Gd: Cavalchina, Zeni.

Garofoli Mar ★★→★★★★ Quality leader in the Mar, specialist in VERDICCHIO (Macrina, Podium, Serra Fiorese), CONERO (Grosso Agontano, Piancarda).

Gattinara Pie DOCG r ★★→★★★ 04' 06 07 08 09 10 11 12 13 (15) Best-known of a cluster of ALTO PIE DOC(G)s based on NEBBIOLO. Volcanic soil. Suitable for long ageing. Best: Antoniolo (Osso San Grato, San Francesco), Bianchi, Iarretti Paride, Nervi, Torraccia del Piantavigna, Travaglini (RISERVA and Tre VIGNE). *See also* ALTO PIEMONTE.

Gavi / Cortese di Gavi Pie DOCG w ★→★★★ DYA. At best, subtle dry white of Cortese grapes, though much is dull, simple or sharp. Most comes from commune of Gavi, hence Gavi di Gavi, now prosaically known as Gavi del Comune di Gavi. Best: Bruno Broglia/La Meirana, Castellari Bergaglio (Rovereto Vignavecchia and Rolona, Fornaci v.gd Gavi di Tassarolo), Castello di Tassarolo, Chiarlo (Rovereto), Franco Martinetti, La Giustiniana, La Raia, La Toledana, Tenuta San Pietro, Villa Sparina.

Alto Piemonte (Boca, Lessona, Gattinara); late C19: 42,000 ha v'yds, now c.700 ha.

Germano, Ettore Pie ★★★ Small family Serralunga estate run by Sergio and wife Elena. Top BAROLOS: RISERVA Lazzarito and Cerretta. Look for 1st cru VIGNA Rionda. V.gd: LANGHE RIES Herzù and ALTA LANGA.

Ghemme Pie DOCG r V.gd PIE red, cf GATTINARA. *See* ALTO PIEMONTE. NEBBIOLO (at least 85%), incl up to 15% Uva Rara and/or Vespolina. Gd: *Antichi Vigneti di Cantalupo* (Collis Braclemae), Ioppa (Balsina), Torraccia del Piantavigna (VIGNA Pelizzane).

Giacosa, Bruno Pie ★★★→★★★★★ Italy's greatest winemaker? He crafts splendid traditional-style BARBARESCOS (Asili, Rabajà), BAROLOS (Falletto, Rocche del Falletto). Top wines (ie. RISERVAS) get famous red label. Range of fine reds (BARBERA, DOLCETTO, NEBBIOLO), whites (ARNEIS), amazing METODO CLASSICO Brut.

GIV (Gruppo Italiano Vini) Complex of co-ops and wineries, biggest v'yd holders in Italy: Bigi, BOLLA, Ca'Bianca, Conti Serristori, FONTANA CANDIDA, Lamberti, Macchiavelli, MELINI, Negri, Santi, Vignaioli di San Floriano. Also in s: SI, Bas.

Grappa Pungent spirit made from grape pomace (skins, etc., after pressing), can be anything from disgusting to inspirational. What the French call "marc".

Grasso, Elio Pie ★★★→★★★★ Tiptop BAROLO producer (crus Gavarini VIGNA Chiniera, Ginestra Casa Maté and RISERVA Rüncot); v.gd BARBERA D'ALBA Vigna Martina, DOLCETTO d'Alba. Son Gianluca now effectively taken over from dad Elio.

Gravner, Josko F-VG ★★★→★★★★ Controversial but talented COLLIO producer (unlike some who copy him), vinifies on skins (r w) in buried amphorae without temperature control; long ageing, bottling without filtration. Wines either loved for complexity or loathed for oxidation and phenolic components. Look out for Breg (white blend) and RIBOLLA GIALLA 2006 for something different.

Greco di Tufo Cam DOCG w (sp) ★★→★★★ DYA. Better versions among Italy's best whites: citrus with hints of orange peel, at best age-worthy. V.gd examples from Benito Ferrara (VIGNA Cicogna), Di Prisco, FEUDI DI SAN GREGORIO (Cutizzi), Macchialupa, *Mastroberardino* (Nova Serra, Vignadangelo), Pietracupa, QUINTODECIMO (Giallo d'Arles), Vadiaperti (Tornante).

Grignolino Pie DOC r ★★→★★★ DYA Two DOCS: Grignolino d'Asti, Grignolino del MONFERRATO Casalese. At best, light, perfumed, crisp, high in acidity, tannin. D'Asti: try BRAIDA, Cascina Tavijin, Crivelli, Incisa della Rocchetta, Spertino. MONFERRATO C: try Accornero (Bricco del Bosco "fresh" version, Bricco del Bosco VIGNE Vecchie "historical" version – vinified like BAROLO), Bricco Mondalino, Canato (Celio), Il Mongetto, PIO CESARE.

Guardiense, La Cam ★★→★★★ Dynamic co-op, 1000+ grower-members, 2000 ha, outstanding-value whites (FALANGHINA Senete, FIANO COLLI di Tilio, GRECO Pietralata) and reds (esp I Mille per l'AGLIANICO); technical direction by Riccardo Cotarella. World's largest producer of Falanghina.

Guerrieri Rizzardi Ven ★★→★★★ Long-est aristocratic producers of Verona wines esp

Veronese GARDA. Gd BARDOLINO CLASSICO Tacchetto, elegant AMARONE Villa Rizzardi and cru Calcarole, and ROSATO Rosa Rosae. V.gd SOAVE Classico Costeggiola.

Gulfi Si ★★★ SI's best producer of NERO D'AVOLA, 1ST to bottle single-*contrada* (cru) wines. Outstanding: Nerobufaleffj and Nerosanlorè. V.gd: Nerojbleo, Nerobaronj and CERASUOLO DI VITTORIA CLASSICO.

Gutturnio dei Colli Piacentini E-R DOC r dr ★→★★ DYA. BARBERA/BONARDA blend from COLLI PIACENTINI; sometimes frothing.

Haas, Franz T-AA ★★★ ALTO ADIGE producer of excellence and occasional inspiration; v.gd PINOT N, LAGREIN (Schweizer), IGT blends esp Manna (w).

Hofstätter T-AA ★★★ Top-quality; gd PINOT N. Look for Barthenau VIGNA Sant'Urbano. Also South Tyrol whites, mainly GEWURZ (esp *Kolbehof*, one of Italy's two best).

IGT (Indicazione Geografica Tipica) Increasingly known as Indicazione Geografica Protetta (IGP). *See* box, p.127.

Ippolito 1845 Cal ★ →★★ This CIRÒ Marina-based winery claims to be oldest in Cal. Run quasi-organically, international and indigenous grapes. Top: Cirò RISERVA COLLI del Mancuso, Pecorello Bianco.

Ischia Cam DOC (r) w ★→★★ DYA. Island off Naples, own grape varieties (w: Biancolella, Forastera; r: Piedirosso, also found in Cam). Frassitelli v'yd best for Biancolella. Best: D'Ambra (Biancolella Frassitelli, Forastera). V.gd: Antonio Mazzella (VIGNA del Lume). Drink on the island.

Isole e Olena Tus ★★★ →★★★★ Top CHIANTI CLASSICO estate run by astute Paolo de Marchi, with superb red IGT Cepparello. Outstanding VIN SANTO; v.gd CAB SAUV, CHARD, SYRAH. Also owns Proprietà Sperino in LESSONA.

Jermann, Silvio F-VG ★★ →★★★ Famous estate with v'yds in COLLIO and ISONZO: top white blend Vintage Tunina and Capo Martino. V.gd Vinnae (mainly RIBOLLA GIALLA) and "Where Dreams ..." (CHARD).

Köfererhof T-AA ★★ →★★★ Great whites: KERNER, SYLVANER; MÜLLER-T excellent too.

Lacrima di Morro d'Alba Mar DYA. Curiously named rose-scented MUSCATTY light red from small commune in the Mar, no connection with ALBA or La Morra (PIE). Gd: Luigi Giusti (Luigino Vecchie VIGNE), Mario Lucchetti (SUPERIORE Guardengo), Marotti Campi (SUPERIORE Orgiolo and Rubico), Stefano Mancinelli (Superiore, Sensazioni di Frutto). For PASSITO: Lucchetti, Stefano Mancinelli (Re Sole).

Lacryma (or Lacrima) Christi del Vesuvio Cam r p w dr (sw) (sp) ★→★★ DOC Vesuvio wines based on Coda di Volpe (w), Piedirosso (r). Despite romantic name Vesuvius comes nowhere nr ETNA in quality stakes. Sorrentino and De Angelis best; Caputo, MASTROBERARDINO, Terredora less inspired.

28% (that's 1368) of the world's wine grapes are Italian.

Lageder, Alois T-AA ★★ →★★★ Top ALTO ADIGE producer. Most exciting wines are single-v'yd varietals: *Sauv Bl Lehenhof*, PINOT GR Benefizium Porer, CHARD Löwengang, GEWURZ Am Sand, PINOT N Krafuss, LAGREIN Lindenberg, CAB SAUV Cor Römigberg. Also owns Cason Hirschprunn for v.gd IGT blends.

Lagrein Alto Adige T-AA DOC r p ★★ →★★★ 06 07 08 09 11 12 13 15 Alpine red with deep colour, rich palate (plus a bitter hit at back); refreshing pink *Kretzer*, *rosé* made with Lagrein. Top Alto Adige: CS Andriano, CANTINA Santa Maddalena, Gojer, Ignaz Niedrist, Josephus Mayr, LAGEDER, MURI GRIES (cru Abtei), Niedermayr, Plattner. From TRENTINO try Francesco Moser's Deamater.

Lambrusco E-R DOC (or not) r p w dr s/sw ★→★★ DYA. Once v. popular fizzy red from nr Modena, mainly in industrial, semi-sweet, non-DOC version. The real thing is dry, acidic, fresh, lively and *combines magically with rich* E-R fare. DOCS: L Grasparossa di Castelvetro, L Salamino di Santa Croce, L di Sorbara. Best: [Sorbara] Cavicchioli (VIGNA del Cristo Secco and Vigna del Cristo Rose), Cleto Chiarli (Antica Modena Premium), Paltrinieri (FRIZZANTE Etichetta Bianca

Fermentazione Naturale and Leclisse). Grasparossa: Cleto Chiarli (Vigneto Enrico Cialdini), Fattoria Moretto (Monovitigno and Vigna Canova), TENUTA Pederzana (Canto Libero Semi Secco), Vittorio Graziano (Fontana dei Boschi). Maestri: CANTINE Ceci (Nero di Lambrusco Otello), Dall'Asta (Mefistofele). Salamino: Cavicchioli (Tre Medaglie Semi Secco), Luciano Saetti (Vigneto Saetti), Medici Ermete (Concerto Granconcerto).

Langhe Pie Hills of central PIE, home of BAROLO, BARBARESCO, etc. DOC name for several Pie varietals plus Bianco, Rosso blends. Those wishing to blend other grapes with NEBBIOLO (ie. GAJA), can at up to 15% as "Langhe Nebbiolo" – a label to follow.

What wine for pizza? Lambrusco di Sorbara or Aglianico.

Le Piane Pie ★★★ BOCA DOC has resurfaced thanks to Christoph Kunzli. Gd: Piane (Croatina) and Mimmo (NEBBIOLO/Croatina).

Les Cretes VdA ★★★ Costantino Charrère is father of modern VALLE D'AOSTA viticulture and saved many forgotten varieties. *Outstanding Petite Arvine*, two of Italy's best CHARDS; v.gd Fumin.

Lessona Pie DOCG r *See* ALTO PIEMONTE. NEBBIOLO (at least 85%). Elegant, age-worthy, fine bouquet, long savoury taste. Best: Proprietà SPERINO (*see also* ISOLE E OLENA). Gd: Colombera & Garella, La Prevostura, TENUTE Sella.

Librandi Cal ★★★ Top producer pioneering research into Cal varieties. V.gd red CIRÒ (*Riserva Duca San Felice* is ★★★), IGT Gravello (CAB SAUV/Gaglioppo blend), Magno Megonio (r) from Magliocco grape, IGT Efeso (w) from Mantonico.

Liguria Lig r w sw ★→★★ Steep, rocky Italian riviera: most wines sell to sun-struck tourists at fat profits, so don't travel much. Main white grapes: VERMENTINO (best are Lambruschi, Giacomelli, La Baia del Sole); Pigato (best are Bio Vio and Lupi). Don't miss CINQUE TERRE'S Sciacchetrà (sw); Ormeasco di Pornassio and ROSSESE DI DOLCEACQUA (r).

Lisini Tus ★★★→★★★★ Historic estate for some of finest, longest-lasting BRUNELLO esp RISERVA Ugolaia.

Lis Neris F-VG ★★★ Top ISONZO estate for whites esp PINOT GR (Gris), SAUV BL (Picol), FRIULANO (Fiore di Campo), plus outstanding blends Confini and Lis. V.gd Lis Neris Rosso (MERLOT/CAB SAUV), sweet white Tal Luc (VERDUZZO/RIES).

Lo Triolet VdA r w ★★★ Top PINOT GR, v.gd Coteau Barrage (SYRAH/Fumin), MUSCAT.

Luce Tus ★★★ FRESCOBALDI now sole owner (bought out original partner Mondavi). SANGIOVESE/MERLOT blend for oligarchs, but lovely Luce BRUNELLO DI MONTALCINO too.

Lugana DOC w (sp) ★★→★★★ DYA. Much-improved white of s Lake Garda, main grape TREBBIANO di Lugana. Best: CA' DEI FRATI (I Frati esp Brolettino), Ottella (Brut, Le Crete), ZENATO (oaked), Fratelli Zeni, Le Morette (owned by Valerio ZENATO). For Trebbiano di SOAVE, try: Suavia (Massi Fitti).

Lungarotti Umb ★★★ Leading producer of TORGIANO, with cellars, hotel, museum, nr Perugia. Star wines DOC Rubesco, DOCG RISERVA *Monticchio*. Gd IGT Sangiorgio (SANGIOVESE/CAB SAUV), Aurente (CHARD), Giubilante. Gd MONTEFALCO SAGRANTINO.

Macchiole, Le Tus ★★★ One of few native-owned wineries of BOLGHERI; one of 1st to emerge after SASSICAIA. Cinzia Merli, with oenologist Luca Rettondini, makes *Italy's best Cab Fr* (Paleo Rosso), one of best MERLOTS (Messorio), SYRAHS (Scrio). V.gd Bolgheri Rosso.

Maculan Ven ★★★ Quality pioneer of Ven, Fausto Maculan continues to make excellent CAB SAUV (Fratta, Palazzotto). Perhaps best-known for sweet TORCOLATO (esp RISERVA Acininobili).

Malvasia delle Lipari Si DOC w sw ★★★ Luscious sweet wine, made with one of the many MALVASIA varieties.

Manduria (Primitivo di) Pug DOC r s/sw ★★→★★★ Manduria is the spiritual home of PRIMITIVO, alias ZIN, so expect wines that are gutsy, alcoholic, sometimes porty to go with full-flavoured fare. Gd producers, located in Manduria or not: Cantele, CS Manduria, de Castris, Gianfranco Fino, Polvanera, Racemi.

Manni Nössing T-AA ★★★ Outstanding KERNER, MÜLLER-T Sass Rigais, SYLVANER. Benchmark wines.

Marcato Ven New owner Gianni Tessari likely to improve already v.gd Lessini Durello sparklers and Durella PASSITO stickie.

Marchesi di Barolo Pie ★★ Large, historic BAROLO producer, making crus Cannubi and Sarmassa, plus other ALBA wines. Favours enlargement of famous Cannubi cru to incl other C areas: C Boschis, C Muscatel, C San Lorenzo, C Valletta.

Maremma Tus Fashionable coastal area of S TUS, largely recovered from grazing and malarial marshland in early C20. DOC(G)S: MONTEREGIO, MORELLINO DI SCANSANO, PARRINA, Pitigliano, SOVANA (Grosseto) Maremma Toscana IGT, more recently Maremma Toscana DOC.

Marrone, Agricola Pie ★★ ·★★★ Small estate, low price but gd-quality BAROLO. Gd: ARNEIS, BARBERA D'ALBA, Pichemej.

Marsala Si DOC w sw SI's once-famous fortified (★·★★★), created by Woodhouse Bros of Liverpool in 1773. Downgraded in C20 to cooking wine (no longer qualifies for DOC). Can be dry to v. sweet; best is bone-dry Marsala Vergine, potentially a useful, if hardly fashionable, apéritif. *See also* DE BARTOLI.

Marzemino Trentino T-AA DOC r ★·★★ 12 13 (15) Pleasant everyday red: sour red berries, violets, fresh herbs, high acid, mid-weight. Isera and Ziresi are subzones. Best: Bruno Grigoletti, Conti Bossi Fredrigotti, Eugenio Rosi (Poiema), Riccardo Battistotti. Gd: De Tarczal, Enrico Spagnolli, Letrari, Longariva, Vallarom, VallisAgri (VIGNA Fornas), Vilar.

Mascarello Pie The name of two top producers of BAROLO: the late Bartolo M, of Barolo, whose daughter Maria Teresa continues her father's highly traditional path; and Giuseppe M, of Monchiero, whose son Mauro makes v. fine, traditional-style Barolo from the great *Monprivato* v'yd in Castiglione Falletto. Both deservedly iconic.

Masi Ven ★★·★★★ Archetypal yet innovative producer of the wines of Verona, led by inspirational Sandro Boscaini. VALPOLICELLA, AMARONE, RECIOTO, SOAVE, etc., incl fine Rosso Veronese *Campo Fiorin*. Also makes Amarone-style wines in F-VG and Argentina. V.gd barrel-aged red IGT Toar, from CORVINA and Oseleta grapes, also Osar (Oseleta). Top Amarones Costasera, Campolongo di Torbe. New F-VG Moxxé fizz from PINOT GRIGIO/partly dried VERDUZZO.

Massa, Vigneti Pie ★★★ Walter Massa brought Timorasso (w) grape back from nr-extinction. Top: Coste del Vento, Montecitorio, Sterpi. Gd: BARBERA Bigolla.

Massolino Vigna Rionda Pie ★★★ One of finest BAROLO estates, in Serralunga. Excellent Parafada, Margheria have firm structure, fruity drinkability; long-ageing VIGNA Rionda best. V.gd Parussi.

Barolo fever rages: over €3 million paid for just 1.5 ha of great Monvigliero cru.

Mastroberardino Cam ★★★ Historic producer of mountainous Avellino province in CAM, quality torch-bearer for Italy's S during dark yrs of mid-C20. Top *Taurasi* (look for Historia Naturalis, Radici), also FIANO DI AVELLINO More Maiorum, GRECO DI TUFO Nova Serra. Antonio M essentially saved Fiano (if not Greco too) from extinction.

Mastrodomenico, Vigne Bas ★★·★★★ Small estate in high-quality Rapolla subzone. Best: AGLIANICO DEL VULTURE Likos.

Melini Tus ★★ Major producer of CHIANTI CLASSICO at Poggibonsi, part of GIV. Gd quality/price esp Chianti Classico Selvanella, RISERVAS La Selvanella, Masovecchio.

Meroi F-VG ★★★ Dynamic estate. Top FRIULANO, MALVASIA Le Zittelle, Ribolla Gialla.

Metodo classico or tradizionale Italian for "Champagne method".

Mezzacorona T-AA ★→★★ Massive TRENTINO co-op in commune of Mezzocorona (sic) with wide range of gd technical wines, esp TEROLDEGO ROTALIANO Nos and METODO CLASSICO Rotari.

Miani ★★★ Enzo Pontoni is Italy's best white winemaker. Top: FRIULANO Buri, Friulano Filip, RIBOLLA GIALLA Pettarin. V.gd: SAUV BL Saurint, MERLOT, REFOSCO Buri.

Mogoro, Cantina di Sar ★★→★★★ 450 ha+ and 900,000 bottles/yr of high-quality wine from co-op. Rare producer of white Semidano variety. Best: Monica San Bernardino and Semidano SUPERIORE Puistéris. V.gd NURAGUS Ajò.

Mollettieri, Salvatore Cam ★★★ Outstanding: TAURASI, RISERVA VIGNA Cinque Querce. V.gd FIANO DI AVELLINO Apianum.

Monaci Pug r p ★★→★★★ Estate owned by family of Severino Garofano, leading oenologist in SALENTO. Characterful NEGROAMARO red (Eloquenzia, I Censi, late-picked Le Braci), ROSATO (Girofle). Uva di Troia (Sine Pari), AGLIANICO (Sine Die).

Monferrato Pie DOC r p w sw ★→★★ Hills between River Po and Apennines. Some of Italy's most delicious and fairly priced wines from typical local grapes BARBERA, Freisa, GRIGNOLINO, MALVASIA di Casorzo and Malvasia di Schierano, Ruché.

Monica di Sardegna Sar DOC r ★→★★★ DYA. Delightfully perfumed, medium-weight wines. Same grape also DOC in Cagliari. Best: Argiolas (Iselis), CANTINA DI MOGORO, CANTINA SANTADI (Antigua), Contini, Dettori (Chimbanta), Ferruccio Deiana (Karel), Josto Puddu (Torremora).

Monsanto Tus ★★★ Esteemed CHIANTI CLASSICO estate, esp for Il POGGIO RISERVA (1st single-v'yd Chianti Classico), Chianti Classico Riserva, IGTS Fabrizio Bianchi (CHARD), Nemo (CAB SAUV).

What wine for *bistecca alla Fiorentina*? Montefalco Sagrantino or Chianti Classico.

Montagnetta, La Pie ★★→★★★ Arguably Italy's best producer of many different Freisas. V.gd: Freisa d'ASTI SUPERIORE Bugianen.

Montalcino Tus Small, exquisite hilltop town in province of Siena, famous for concentrated, expensive BRUNELLO and more approachable, better-value ROSSO DI MONTALCINO, both still 100% SANGIOVESE despite occasional efforts by big boys to squeeze a bit of MERLOT into the Rosso.

Montecarlo Tus DOC r w ★★ (w) DYA. White (increasingly red) wine area nr Lucca.

Monte Carrubo Si r ★★★ Pioneer Peter Vinding-Diers planted SYRAH on a former volcano s of ETNA. Exciting, complex results.

Montecucco Tus SANGIOVESE-based TUS DOC between Monte Amiata and Grosseto, increasingly on-trend as MONTALCINO land prices ineluctably rise. As Montecucco Sangiovese it is DOCG.

Montefalco Sagrantino Umb DOCG r dr (sw) ★★★→★★★★ Super-tannic, powerful, long-lasting wines, potentially great but difficult to tame the phenolics without denaturing the wine. Traditional bittersweet PASSITO version may be better suited to grape, though harder to sell. Gd: Adanti, Antano Milziade, Antonelli, Benincasa, CAPRAI, Colpetrone, LUNGAROTTI, Paolo Bea, Scacciadiavoli, Tabarrini, Terre de' Trinci.

Montepulciano d'Abruzzo Ab DOC r p ★★→★★★ (r) 10 11 12 13 15 1st all-region DOC of Italy. Subdenomination: Colline Teramane (now DOCG), wines often tough, charmless despite hype, and Controguerra (DOC), usually more balanced. Reds can be either light, easy-going or structured, rich. Look for Cataldi Madonna (Toni, lighter Malandrino), EMIDIO PEPE, Marina Cvetic (S Martino Rosso), TIBERIO (COLLE Vota), Torre dei Beati (Cocciapazza, Mazzamurello), *Valentini* (best, age-worthy), Zaccagnini.

Montevertine Tus ★★★★ Organic certified estate in Radda. Outstanding IGT Le Pergole Torte, world-class pure, long-ageing SANGIOVESE. V.gd Montevertine.

Montevetrano Cam ★★★ Iconic CAM *azienda*, owned by Silvia Imparato, consultant

Riccardo Cotarella. Superb IGT Montevetrano (AGLIANICO, CAB SAUV, MERLOT).

Morella Pug ★★★ Gaetano Morella and wife Lisa Gilbee make outstanding PRIMITIVO (Old Vines and La Signora) from c.90-yr-old vines.

Morellino di Scansano Tus DOCG r ★ →★★★ 10 11 13 15 SANGIOVESE red from MAREMMA. Used to be relatively light, simple, now, sometimes regrettably, gaining weight, substance, perhaps to justify its lofty DOCG status. Best: Le Pupille, Mantellasi, **Moris Farms**, PODERE 414, POGGIO Argentiera, Terre di Talamo, *Vignaioli del Morellino di Scansano* (co-op).

Moris Farms Tus ★★★ One of 1st new-age producers of TUS'S MAREMMA; MONTEREGIO and *Morellino di Scansano* DOCS, VERMENTINO IGT. Top cru is own iconic IGT Avvoltore, rich SANGIOVESE/CAB SAUV/SYRAH blend. But *try basic Morellino.*

Moscato d'Asti Pie DOCG w sw sp ★★ →★★★ DYA Similar to DOCG ASTI, but usually better grapes; lower alc, lower pressure, sweeter, fruitier, often from small producers. Best DOCG MOSCATO: L'Armangia, Bera, *Braida*, Ca' d'Gal, Cascina Fonda, Caudrina, Elio Perrone, Forteto della Luja, Il Falchetto, Icardi, Isolabella, La Morandina, Marchesi di Grésy, Marco Negri, Marino, RIVETTI, SARACCO, Scagliola, VIETTI, Vignaioli di Sante Stefano.

Muri Gries T-AA ★★ →★★★ This monastery, in Bolzano suburb of Gries, is a traditional and still top producer of LAGREIN ALTO ADIGE DOC. Esp cru Abtei-Muri.

Nals Margreid T-AA ★★ →★★★ Small quality co-op making mtn-fresh whites (esp PINOT BIANCO Sirmian), from two communes of ALTO ADIGE. Harald Schraffl is an inspired winemaker.

Nebbiolo d'Alba Pie DOC r dr ★★ →★★★ 10 11 12 13 14 15 Sometimes a worthy replacement for BAROLO/BARBARESCO, though it comes from a distinct area between the two and may not be used as a declassification from top DOCGS. Gd: BRUNO GIACOSA (Valmaggiore), Fratelli Giacosa, BREZZA (VIGNA Santa Rosalia), PAITIN, LUCIANO SANDRONE (Valmaggiore).

Nebbiolo Langhe Pie ★★ Like N D'ALBA but from a wider area: LANGHE hills. Unlike N d'Alba may be used as a downgrade from BAROLO or BARBARESCO. Gd: BURLOTTO, GIUSEPPE RINALDI, PIO CESARE, *Vajra. See also* GAJA.

Negrar, Cantina Ven ★★ →★★★ Aka CS VALPOLICELLA. Major producer of high-quality Valpolicella, RIPASSO, AMARONE; grapes from various parts of CLASSICO zone. Look for brand name Domini Veneti.

Niedriest, Ignaz r w ★★★ LAGREIN Berger Gei is reference. So are RIES, WEISSBURGUNDER. V.gd BLAUBURGUNDER and SAUV BL Terlaner.

Nino Franco Ven ★★★ →★★★★ Winery of Primo Franco, named after his grandfather. Among v. finest PROSECCOS: Primo Franco Dry, Rive di San Floriano Brut. Excellent CARTIZZE, *delicious basic Prosecco di Valdobbiadene Brut.*

Nipozzano, Castello di Tus ★★★ FRESCOBALDI estate in RÚFINA, e of Florence, making excellent CHIANTI Rúfina RISERVAS (esp Vecchie Viti) Nipozzano and *Montesodi.*

Nittardi Tus ★★ →★★★ Reliable source of quality modern CHIANTI CLASSICO. German owned; oenologist Carlo Ferrini.

Nozzole Tus ★★ →★★★ Famous estate in heart of CHIANTI CLASSICO, n of Greve, owned by Ambrogio and Giovanni FOLONARI. V.gd Chianti Classico RISERVA, excellent CAB SAUV Pareto.

Nuragus di Cagliari Sar DOC w ★★ DYA. Lively, uncomplicated SAR wine from Nuragus grape, finally gaining visibility. Best: ARGIOLAS (S'Elegas), Pala (I Fiori).

Occhio di Pernice Tus "Partridge's eye". A type of VIN SANTO made predominantly from black grapes, mainly SANGIOVESE. *Avignonesi's is definitive.* Also an obscure black variety found in RÚFINA and elsewhere.

Occhipinti, Arianna Si ★★★ Cult producer, and deservedly so. Organic certified. Happily, wines now less oxidized and more about finesse than power. Top: Il Frappato. V.gd NERO D'AVOLA Siccagno and Nero d'Avola Frappato SP68.

Oddero Pie ★★★ Traditionalist La Morra estate for excellent BAROLO (Brunate, Villero, VIGNA Rionda RISERVA now 10 yrs), BARBARESCO (Gallina) crus, plus other serious PIE wines.

Oltrepò Pavese Lom DOC r w dr sw sp ★→★★★ Multi-DOC, incl numerous varietal and blended wines from Pavia province; best is SPUMANTE. Gd growers: Anteo, Barbacarlo, CS Casteggio, Frecciarossa, Le Fracce, Mazzolino, Monsupello, Ruiz de Cardenas, Travaglino; La Versa co-op.

Ornellaia Tus ★★★★ 04 06' 08 10 11 12 13 15 Fashionable estate nr BOLGHERI founded by Lodovico ANTINORI, now owned by FRESCOBALDI. Top wines of B'x grapes/method: Bolgheri DOC Ornellaia, IGT Masseto (MERLOT). Gd: Bolgheri DOC Le Serre Nuove, IGT Le Volte, POGGIO alle Gazze (w); new Bianco SAUV BL/VIOGNIER.

Orvieto Umb DOC w dr sw s/sw →★★★ DYA Classic Umb white, blend of mainly Procanico (TREBBIANO)/GRECHETTO. *Secco* most popular today. Top: BARBERANI Castagneto, Luigi e Giovanna; *amabile* more traditional. Sweet versions from noble-rot (*muffa nobile*) grapes can be superb, eg. Barberani Calcaia. Other gd: Bigi, Cardeto, *Castello della Sala*, Decugnano dei Barbi, La Carraia, Palazzone.

Pacenti, Siro Tus ★★★ Modern-style BRUNELLO, ROSSO DI MONTALCINO from small, caring producer.

Paitin Pie ★★→★★★ Pasquero-Elia family have been bottling BARBARESCO since C19. Used to be intensely authentic, had a flutter with modernism (new barriques); today back on track making "real" Barbaresco in large barrels. Sorì Paitin is star.

Paltrinieri ★★→★★★ One of top three LAMBRUSCO producers. Among 1st to produce 100% Lambrusco di Sorbara. Best: Secco Radice; v.gd Leclisse.

Pantelleria Si Windswept, black-(volcanic) earth SI island off Tunisian coast, famous for superb MOSCATO d'Alessandria stickies. PASSITO versions particularly dense/intense. Look for DE BARTOLI (Bukkuram), DONNAFUGATA (Ben Ryé), Ferrandes.

Parrina, La Tus ★★ Sizeable estate on TUS coast dominates DOC Parrina; French and indigenous grapes, solid rather than inspired wines.

Passito Tus, Ven One of Italy's most ancient and most characteristic wine styles, from grapes hung up, or spread on trays to dry, briefly under harvest sun (in s) or over a period of weeks or mths in airy attics of winery – a process called *appassimento*. Best-known versions: VIN SANTO (TUS); AMARONE/RECIOTO (Ven), VALPOLICELLA/SOAVE. *See also* MONTEFALCO, ORVIETO, TORCOLATO, VALLONE. Never cheap.

Passopisciaro Si ★★★ ETNA estate run by Franchetti (*see* TENUTA DI TRINORO), contributor to fame of Etna. Outstanding NERELLO MASCALESE single-*contrada* wines. Best: Contrada G (Guardiola) and Contrada C (Chiappemacine). V.gd Contrada R (Rampante).

Paternoster Bas ★★★ Old estate now owned by TOMMASI family. 25 ha organically farmed. Top: Don Anselmo. V.gd AGLIANICO DEL VULTURE Rotondo.

Pepe, Emidio Ab ★★★ Artisanal winery, 15 ha bio and organic certified. Top MONTEPULCIANO D'ABRUZZO. Gd: PECORINO, TREBBIANO D'ABRUZZO.

Pian dell'Orino ★★★ Small MONTALCINO estate, committed to bio. BRUNELLO seductive, technically perfect, Rosso nearly as gd. Many epic wines.

Piave Ven DOC r w ★→★★ (r) 11 12 13 (15) (w) DYA. Volume DOC on plains of e Ven for budget varietals. CAB SAUV, MERLOT, Raboso reds can all age moderately. Above average from Loredan Gasparini, Molon, Villa Sandi.

Picolit F-VG DOCG w sw s/sw ★★→★★★ 08 09 10 12 13 15 Quasi-mythical but inconsistent sweet white from FRIULI COLLI ORIENTALI, might disappoint those who can a) find it and b) afford it. Most from air-dried grapes. Ranges from light/sweet (rare) to super-thick. Gd: Aquila del Torre, Ermacora, Girolamo Dorigo, I Comelli, LIVIO FELLUGA, Marco Sara, Paolo Rodaro, Ronchi di Cialla, VIGNA Petrussa.

Piedmont / Piemonte Alpine foothill region; with TUS, Italy's most important for quality. TURIN is capital, MONFERRATO (ASTI) and LANGHE (ALBA) important centres. No IGTS allowed; Pie DOC is lowest denomination, for basic reds, whites, SPUMANTE, FRIZZANTE. Grapes incl: BARBERA, Brachetto, Cortese, DOLCETTO, Freisa, GRIGNOLINO, MALVASIA di Casorzo, Malvasia di Schierano, MOSCATO, NEBBIOLO, Ruché, Timorasso. *See also* ALTO PIEMONTE, BARBARESCO, BAROLO, ROERO.

Pieropan Ven ★★★ Nino Pieropan is veteran quality leader of SOAVE, the man who brought a noble wine back to credibility. Cru *La Rocca* is still ultimate oaked Soave; Calvarino best of all.

Pio Cesare Pie ★★→★★★ Veteran ALBA producer, offers BAROLO, BARBARESCO in modern (barrique) and traditional (large-cask-aged) versions. Also Alba range, incl whites (eg. GAVI). Particularly gd NEBBIOLO D'ALBA, *a little Barolo at half the price*.

Planeta Si ★★→★★★ Leading SI estate with six v'yd holdings in various parts of island, incl Vittoria (CERASUOLO), Noto (NERO D'AVOLA Santa Cecilia) and most recently on ETNA. Wines from native and imported varieties. La Segreta is brand of gd-value white (CHARD, FIANO, Grecanico, VIOGNIER), red (MERLOT, Nero d'Avola, SYRAH). NB Cometa Fiano.

Podere Tus Small TUS farm, once part of a big estate.

Poggio Tus Means "hill" in TUS dialect. "**Poggione**" means "big hill".

Poggio Antico Tus ★★★ Paola Gloder looks after this 32-ha estate, one of highest in MONTALCINO at c.500m. Style is restrained, consistent, at times too herbal.

Poggio di Sotto ★★★ Small MONTALCINO estate with a big reputation recently. Has purchased adjacent v'yds. Top BRUNELLO, RISERVA and Rosso of traditional character with idiosyncratic twist.

Wild boar eat more grapes in dry yrs, poor thirsty things.

Poggione, Tenuta Il Tus ★★★ MONTALCINO estate making consistently excellent BRUNELLO and Rosso despite huge production (c.500,000 bottles) from 125-ha v'yd in s of zone. Fabrizio Bindocci succeeded legendary Pierluigi Talenti, and is nurturing son Alessandro to take over eventually.

Poggiopiano Tus ★★→★★★ Opulent CHIANTI CLASSICO from Bartoli family. CHIANTIS are pure SANGIOVESE, but SUPER TUSCAN Rosso di Sera incl up to 15% Colorino. V.gd Colorino Taffe Ta'.

Poggio Scalette Tus ★★★ Vittorio Fiore and son Jury run CHIANTI estate at Greve. Top: Il Carbonaione (100% SANGIOVESE); needs several yrs bottle age. Above-average CHIANTI CLASSICO and B'x-blend Capogatto.

Poliziano Tus ★★★ MONTEPULCIANO estate of Federico Carletti. Superior if often v. dark, herbal VINO NOBILE (esp cru Asinone); gd IGT LE Stanze (CAB SAUV/MERLOT).

Pomino Tus DOC r w ★★★ (r) 09 10 11 12 13 (15) Appendage of RÚFINA, with fine red and white blends (esp Il Benefizio). Virtually a FRESCOBALDI exclusivity.

Potazzine, Le Tus ★★★ Giuseppe and Gigliola Gorelli named their wine after their two *potazzine* (little birds, ie. children). V'yd is quite high, just s of MONTALCINO. Outstanding BRUNELLOS and Rossos, serious and v. drinkable. Try them at family's restaurant in town.

Prà Ven ★★★ Leading SOAVE CLASSICO producer, esp crus Monte Grande, Staforte – latter 6 mths in tanks on lees with mechanical *bâtonnage* – v. tasty. Excellent VALPOLICELLAS La Formica, Morandina.

Produttori del Barbaresco Pie ★★★ One of Italy's earliest co-ops, perhaps best in the world. Aldo Vacca and team make excellent traditional straight BARBARESCO plus crus Asili, Montefico, Montestefano, Ovello, Pora, Rio Sordo. Super values.

Prosecco Ven DOC(G) w sp ★→★★ DYA. World has gone mad for Italy's favourite fizz. Why is not clear. For details plus selection of producers *see box, p.148*.

Prunotto, Alfredo Pie ★★★→★★★★ Traditional ALBA firm modernized by ANTINORI in 90s, run by Piero A's daughter Albiera and oenologist Gianluca Torrengo.

V.gd BARBARESCO (Bric Turot), BAROLO (Bussia and VIGNA Colonnello), NEBBIOLO (Occhetti), BARBERA D'ALBA (Pian Romualdo), BARBERA D'ASTI (Costamiole), MONFERRATO Rosso (Mompertone, Barbera/SYRAH blend).

Puglia The 360-km heel of the Italian boot. Generally gd-value, simple wines (mainly red) from various grapes like NEGROAMARO, PRIMITIVO and Uva di Troia, but dubious winemaking talent and old equipment a real problem. Most interesting wines from SALENTO peninsula incl DOCS BRINDISI, COPERTINO, SALICE SALENTINO.

Querciabella Tus ★★★→★★★★ Top CHIANTI CLASSICO estate converted to bio since 2000. Top IGT Camartina (CAB SAUV/SANGIOVESE) and Batàr (CHARD/PINOT BL). V.gd Chianti Classico and Chianti Classico RISERVA. Look for new single-commune wines (Greve in CHIANTI, Radda in Chianti, Gaiole).

Quintarelli, Giuseppe Ven ★★★★ Arch-traditionalist artisan producer of sublime VALPOLICELLA, RECIOTO, AMARONE; plus a fine Bianco Secco, a blend of various grapes. Daughter Fiorenza and sons now in charge, altering nothing, incl the old man's ban on spitting when tasting.

Quintodecimo Cam ★★★ Oenology professor/winemaker Luigi Moio's beautiful estate. Outstanding: TAURASI VIGNA Grande Cerzito; great AGLIANICO (Terra d'Eclano) and GRECO DI TUFO (Giallo d'Arles).

Ratti, Renato ★★→★★★ Iconic BAROLO estate. Son Pietro now in charge. Modern wines; short maceration but plenty of substance esp Barolos Rocche dell'Annunziata and Conca.

Recioto della Valpolicella Ven DOCG r sw (sp) ★★★→★★★★ Historic, made from PASSITO grapes along lines est before C6; unique, potentially stunning, with sumptuous cherry-chocolate-sweet fruitiness.

Recioto di Soave Ven DOCG w sw (sp) ★★★→★★★★ SOAVE from half-dried grapes: sweet, fruity, slightly almondy; sweetness is cut by high acidity. Drink with cheese. Best: Anselmi, COFFELE, Gini, PIEROPAN, Tamellini; often v.gd from Ca' Rugate, Pasqua, PRÀ, Suavia, Trabuchi.

Refosco (dal Peduncolo Rosso) F-VG ★★ 10 11 12 13 15 Must-try gutsy red of rustic style. Best: FRIULI COLLI ORIENTALI DOC, *Volpi Pasini*; gd: Ca' Bolani, Denis Montanara, Dorigo, LIVIO FELLUGA, MIANI, Ronchi di Manzano, Venica in Aquileia DOC.

Ricasoli Tus Historic Tuscan family. First Italian Prime Minister Bettino R devised the classic CHIANTI blend. Main branch occupies medieval Castello di BROLIO. Related Ricasolis own Castello di Cacchiano, Rocca di Montegrossi.

Riecine Tus ★★★→★★★★ Once excellent estate founded by legendary Briton John Dunkley at Gaiole-in-CHIANTI now trying to find its way back. SANGIOVESE specialist; La Gioia potentially outstanding.

Rinaldi, Giuseppe Pie ★★★ Beppe Rinaldi is an arch-traditionalist of BAROLO, v'yds in heart of zone. Outstanding: Brunate and Tre Tine. Don't miss v.gd Freisa and new Namaste (NEBBIOLO/other local varieties).

Ripasso Ven *See* VALPOLICELLA SUPERIORE RIPASSO.

Riserva Wine aged for a statutory period, usually in casks or barrels.

Rivetti, Giorgio (La Spinetta) Pie ★★★ Fine MOSCATO D'ASTI, excellent BARBERA, series of super-concentrated, oaky BARBARESCOS. Also owns v'yds in BAROLO, CHIANTI COLLI Pisane DOCGS, and traditional SPUMANTE house Contratto.

The best of Prosecco

PROSECCO is the wine, GLERA the grape variety with which it is made (meant to ward off copycats). Much is plain ordinary. Quality is higher in the Valdobbiadene. Look for: Adami, Biancavigna, BISOL, Bortolin, Canevel, CARPENÈ-MALVOLTI, Case Bianche, Col Salice, Col Vetoraz, Le Colture, Gregoletto, La Riva dei Frati, Mionetto, NINO FRANCO, Ruggeri, Silvano Follador, Zardetto.

Rizzi Pie ★★→★★★ Sub-area of Treiso, commune of BARBARESCO, where Dellapiana family look after 35 ha v'yd. Top cru is Barbaresco Pajore. V.gd: Nervo and RISERVA VIGNA Boito, also gd METODO CLASSICO Pas Dosè and MOSCATO D'ASTI.

Rocca, Bruno Pie ★★★ Outstanding modern-style BARBARESCO (Rabajà, Coparossa, Maria Adelaide) and other ALBA wines, also v. fine BARBERA D'ASTI.

Rocca Albino ★★★ A foremost producer of elegant, sophisticated BARBARESCO: top crus VIGNETO Loreto, Brich Ronchi.

Rocca delle Macie Tus ★★ Large estate in Castellina-in-CHIANTI run by Sergio Zingarelli, son of spaghetti-western film-maker Italo. Gd quaffing Chianti, plus top wines incl Gran Selezione Sergio Zingarelli and Fizzano. Also Campo Macione estate in Scansano zone.

Roero Pie DOCG r ★★→★★★ 06 07 08 09 10 11 13 (15) (16) Serious, occasionally BAROLO-level NEBBIOLOS from LANGHE hills. Also gd ARNEIS (w ★★→★★★). Best: Agricola Marrone (Langhe Arneis – Tre Fie), Almondo, BRUNO GIACOSA, Ca' Rossa, Cascina Chicco, Correggia, Malvirà, Morra, Negro (Perdaudin), Pioiero, Taliano, Val di Prete, Valfaccenda.

Romagna Sangiovese Mar DOC r ★★→★★★ At times too herbal and oaky, but often well-made, even classy SANGIOVESE red. Gd: Cesari, Drei Donà, Nicolucci, Papiano, Paradiso, Tre Monti, Trere (E-R DOC), Villa Venti (Primo Segno), FATTORIA ZERBINA. Seek also IGT RONCO delle Ginestre, Ronco dei Ciliegi from CASTELLUCCIO.

Ronco Term for a hillside v'yd in ne Italy, esp F-VG.

Ronco del Gelso F-VG ★★★ Tight, pure ISONZO: PINOT GR Sot lis Rivis, FRIULANO Toc Bas and MALVASIA VIGNA della Permuta are regional benchmarks.

Rosato General Italian name for rosé. Other rosé wine names incl CHIARETTO from Lake Garda; CERASUOLO from Ab; Kretzer from ALTO ADIGE.

Rossese di Dolceacqua o Dolceacqua Lig DOC r ★★→★★★ Interesting, fresh, saline reds. Intense, salty, spicy; greater depth of fruit than most. Gd: Ka Mancine, MACCARIO-DRINGBERG, TENUTA Anfosso, Terre Bianche.

Rosso Conero Mar *See* CONERO.

Rosso di Montalcino Tus DOC r ★★→★★★ 10 11 12 13 15 DOC for earlier-maturing wines from BRUNELLO grapes, usually from younger or lesser v'yd sites, but bargains do exist.

Rosso di Montefalco Umb DOC r ★★ 10 11 12 13 15 SANGIOVESE/SAGRANTINO blend, often with a splash of softening MERLOT. *See* MONTEFALCO SAGRANTINO.

Rosso di Montepulciano Tus DOC r ★ 12 13 15 Junior version of VINO NOBILE DI MONTEPULCIANO, growers similar.

Rosso Piceno / Piceno Mar DOC r ★ 10 11 13 15 Generally easy-drinking blend of MONTEPULCIANO/SANGIOVESE now often sold as plain Piceno to help distinguish it from all other Rossos of Italy. SUPERIORE means it come from far s of region. Gd: Boccadigabbia, BUCCI, Fonte della Luna, GAROFOLI, Montecappone, MONTE SCHIAVO, Saladini Pilastri, Terre Cortesi Moncaro, Velenosi Ercole, Villamagna.

Ruffino Tus ★→★★★ Venerable CHIANTI firm, in hands of FOLONARI family for 100 yrs, split apart a few yrs ago. This part, at Pontassieve nr Florence, then bought by US giant Constellation Brands, produces reliable wines such as CHIANTI CLASSICO RISERVA Ducale and Ducale Oro, Greppone Mazzi in MONTALCINO, Lodola Nuova in MONTEPULCIANO, not to mention Borgo Conventi in F-VG.

Rúfina Tus ★★→★★★ Most n sub-zone of CHIANTI, e of Florence in s-facing foothills of Apennines, known for tight, refined wines capable of long ageing. Gd-to-outstanding: CASTELLO DI NIPOZZANO (FRESCOBALDI), Castello del Trebbio, Colognole, Frascole, Grati/Villa di Vetrice, I Veroni, Lavacchio, *Selvapiana*, Tenuta Bossi, Travignoli. Don't confuse with RUFFINO, which happens to have HQ in Pontassieve.

Russiz Superiore F-VG ★★→★★★ LIVIO FELLUGA's brother, Marco, est v'yds in various parts of F-VG. Now run by Marco's son Roberto. Wide range; best is PINOT GRIGIO and COLLIO Bianco blend Col Disòre.

Salento Pug Flat s peninsula at tip of Italy's heel; seems unlikely for quality, but deep soils, old Alberello vines and sea breezes combine to produce remarkable red and rosé from NEGROAMARO, PRIMITIVO, with a bit of help from MALVASIA Nera, MONTEPULCIANO, local Sussumaniello. *See also* PUG, SALICE SALENTINO.

Salice Salentino Pug DOC r ★★→★★★ 08 10 11 13 15 (16) Best-known of Salento's too many NEGROAMARO-based DOCS. RISERVA after 2 yrs. Gd: Agricole VALLONE (Vereto Riserva), Cantele, Due Palme, Leone de Castris (Riserva), Mocavero.

Salvioni Tus ★★★ →★★★★★ Aka La Cerbaiola; small, high-quality MONTALCINO operation of irrepressible Giulio Salvioni and ebullient daughter Alessia. BRUNELLO, ROSSO DI MONTALCINO among v. best available, worth not inconsiderable price.

Sandrone, Luciano Pie ★★★ Modern-style ALBA wines. Deep and concentrated BAROLOS: Aleste (formerly Cannubi Boschis) and Le VIGNE. Look for new Barolo RISERVA. Also gd BARBERA D'ALBA, DOLCETTO, NEBBIOLO D'ALBA.

San Felice Tus ★★ →★★★ Important historic TUS grower, owned by Gruppo Allianz, run by Leonardo Bellaccini. Fine CHIANTI CLASSICO and RISERVA POGGIO Rosso from estate in Castelnuovo Berardenga. Vitiarium is an experimental v'yd for obscure varieties, the excellent Pugnitello (IGT from that grape) a 1st result. Gd too: IGT *Vigorello* (first SUPER TUSCAN, from 1968), BRUNELLO DI MONTALCINO Campogiovanni.

San Gimignano Tus Tourist-overrun TUS town famous for its towers and dry white VERNACCIA DI SAN GIMIGNANO DOCG. Forgettable reds. Producers: Cesani, FALCHINI, Guicciardini Strozza, Il Palagione, Montenidoli, Mormoraia, Panizzi, Pietrafitta, Pietrasereno, Podera del Paradiso.

San Giusto a Rentennano Tus ★★★→★★★★ Top CHIANTI CLASSICO estate owned by cousins of RICASOLI. Outstanding SANGIOVESE IGT Percarlo, sublime VIN SANTO (Vin San Giusto), MERLOT (La Ricolma) and v.gd. Chianti Classico RISERVA Le Baroncole.

San Guido, Tenuta Tus *See* SASSICAIA.

San Leonardo T-AA ★★★ Top TRENTINO estate of Marchesi Guerrieri Gonzaga. Main wine is B'x blend, San Leonardo, Italy's most claret-like wine, with consistent style of a top château.

San Michele Appiano T-AA ★★★ Historic co-op (c.400 ha) run hands-on by Hans Terzer. *Mtn-fresh whites*, brimming with varietal typicity, drinkability, are speciality. PINOT BIANCO Schulthauser, Sanct Valentin SAUV BL impressive, as are CHARD, GEWURZ, PINOT GR, PINOT N.

Santadi Sar ★★★ SAR's, and one of Italy's, best co-ops, esp for CARIGNANO-based reds *Terre Brune*, Grotta Rossa, Rocca Rubia RISERVA (all DOC CARIGNANO DEL SULCIS). V.gd MONICA DI SARDEGNA Antigua.

Santa Maddalena / St-Magdalener T-AA DOC r ★→★★ DYA. Teutonic-style red from SCHIAVA grapes from v. steep slopes behind ALTO ADIGE capital Bolzano. Notable: CS St-Magdalena (Huck am Bach), Gojer, Hans Rottensteiner (Premstallerhof), Heinrich Rottensteiner, Josephus Mayr.

Sant'Antimo Tus DOC r w sw ★★ →★★★ Lovely little Romanesque abbey gives its name to this catch-all DOC for (almost) everything in MONTALCINO zone that isn't BRUNELLO DOCG or Rosso DOC.

Saracco, Paolo Pie ★★★ Top MOSCATO D'ASTI. V.gd: LANGHE RIES, PINOT N.

Sardinia / Sardegna The Med's 2nd-largest island produces much decent and some outstanding wines, incl *Vermentino di Gallura* DOCG, VERMENTINO DI SARDEGNA (little less alc, little less character), Sherry-like VERNACCIA DI ORISTANO, NURAGUS among whites, late-harvest sweet Nasco; CANNONAU (GRENACHE) and CARIGNANO among reds. Outstanding wines: Terre Brune and Rocca Rubia from SANTADI, *Turriga* (r) from ARGIOLAS, VERMENTINO from Capichera. SELLA & MOSCA is great standby.

Sassicaia Tus DOC r ★★★★ 85′ 88′ 90′ 95′ 97 98′ 99 01′ 04′ 05 06 07′ 08 09 10

11 12 **13** (15) Italy's sole single-v'yd DOC (BOLGHERI), a CAB (SAUV/FR) made on First Growth lines by Marchese Incisa della Rocchetta at TENUTA San Guido. More elegant than lush, made for age – and often bought for investment, but hugely influential in giving Italy a top-quality image. The 1985 is/was one of Italy's three greatest wines ever made.

Satta, Michele Tus ★★★ Virtually only BOLGHERI grower to succeed with 100% SANGIOVESE (Cavaliere). Also Bolgheri DOC blends (r) Piastraia, SUPERIORE I Castagni.

Scavino, Paolo Pie ★★★ Modernist BAROLO producer of Castiglione Falletto, esp crus Rocche dell'Annunziata, Bric del Fiasc, Cannubi, Monvigliero. V.gd also Barolo Carobric (traditional blend). Less oaky now.

Schiava Alto Adige T-AA DOC r ★ DYA. Schiava (VERNATSCH in German) gives practically tannin-free, easy-glugging red from most s territory of German-speaking world. Sadly disappearing from Tyrolean v'yds.

Schiopetto, Mario F-VG ★★★→★★★★ Legendary late COLLIO pioneering estate now owned by Volpe Pasini's Rotolo family. V.gd DOC SAUV BL, *Pinot Bl*, RIBOLLA GIALLA, IGT blend Blanc des Rosis, etc.

Sella & Mosca Sar★★ Major SAR grower and merchant with v. pleasant white Torbato (esp Terre Bianche) and light, fruity VERMENTINO Cala Viola (DYA). Gd Alghero DOC Marchese di Villamarina (CAB SAUV) and Tanca Farrà (CANNONAU/Cab Sauv). Also interesting Port-like Anghelu Ruju.

Selvapiana Tus ★★★ CHIANTI RÚFINA estate among Italian greats. Best: RISERVA Bucerchiale, IGT Fornace; but even *basic Chianti Rúfina is a treat*. Also fine red POMINO, Petrognano.

What wine for *fritto misto di mare?* Vermentino, or Fiano.

Settesoli, CS Si★→★★ Co-op with some 6000 ha, giving SI gd name with reliable, gd-value wines.

Sforzato / Sfursat Lom ★★★ AMARONE-like dried-grape NEBBIOLO from VALTELLINA in extreme n of Lom on Swiss border. Ages beautifully.

Sicily The Med's largest island, modern source of exciting original wines and value. Native grapes (r: Frappato, NERO D'AVOLA, NERELLO MASCALESE; w: CATARRATTO, Grecanico, GRILLO, INZOLIA), plus internationals. V'yds on flatlands in w, hills in centre, volcanic altitudes on Mt Etna.

Soave Ven DOC w (sw) ★→★★★ Famous, hitherto underrated, Veronese white. CHARD, GARGANEGA, TREBBIANO di Soave. Wines from volcanic soils of CLASSICO zone can be intense, saline, v. fine, quite long-lived.

Solaia Tus r ★★★★ 85' 90' 95' 97' 99' 01 04 06 07 08 09 10 11 12 13 (15) Occasionally magnificent CAB SAUV/SANGIOVESE blend by ANTINORI, made to highest B'x specs; needs yrs of laying down.

Speri Ven ★★→★★★ VALPOLICELLA family estate, organic certified since 2015, with sites such as outstanding Monte Sant'Urbano. Traditional style. Top: AMARONE VIGNETO Monte Sant'Urbano. V.gd Valpolicella CLASSICO SUPERIORE and RECIOTO.

Spumante Sparkling. What used to be called ASTI Spumante is now just Asti.

Südtirol T-AA The local name of German-speaking South Tyrol ALTO ADIGE.

Superiore Wine with more ageing than normal DOC and 0.5–1% more alc. May indicate a restricted production zone, eg. ROSSO PICENO Superiore.

Super Tuscan Tus Wines of high quality and price developed in 70s/80s to get round silly laws then prevailing. Now, esp with Gran Selezione on up, increasingly irrelevant. Wines still generally considered in Super Tuscan category, strictly unofficially: CA' MARCANDA, Flaccianello, Guado al Tasso, Messorio, ORNELLAIA, Redigaffi, SASSICAIA, Solaia, TIGNANELLO.

Sylla Sebaste Pie ★★★ Illustrates merits of rare NEBBIOLO Rosé variety: lighter, v. perfumed BAROLO. A beauty.

ITALY

Tasca d'Almerita Si ★★★ A new generation of Tasca d'Almeritas runs historic, still prestigious estate, which kept the flag flying for SI in the dark yrs. High-altitude v'yds; balanced IGTs under its old Regaleali label, CHARD and CAB SAUV gd, but star, as ever, is NERO D'AVOLA-based *Rosso del Conte*. V.gd MALVASIA delle Lipari Capofaro.

Taurasi Cam DOCG r ★★★ 04 06 07 08 09 10 11 12 13 15 The s's answer to the n's BAROLO and the centre's BRUNELLO, needs careful handling and long ageing. There are friendlier versions of AGLIANICO but none so potentially *complex, demanding, ultimately rewarding*. Made famous by MASTROBERARDINO, other outstanding: Caggiano, Caputo, FEUDI DI SAN GREGORIO, Luigi Tecce, Molettieri, QUINTODECIMO (VIGNA Grande Cerzito), Terredora di Paulo.

Tedeschi Ven ★★★ Bevy of v. fine AMARONE, VALPOLICELLA. Amarone Capitel Monte Olmi and RECIOTO Capitel Monte Fiontana best.

Tedeschi, Fratelli Ven ★★→★★★ One of original quality growers of VALPOLICELLA when zone was still ruled by mediocrities.

Tenuta An agricultural holding (*see* under name – eg. SAN GUIDO, TENUTA).

Terlano T-AA w ★★→★★★ DYA. ALTO ADIGE Terlano DOC applies to one white blend and eight white varietals esp PINOT BL, SAUV BL. Can be v. fresh, zesty or serious and surprisingly long-lasting. Best: CS Terlano (esp Pinot Bl Vorberg), LAGEDER, Niedermayr, Niedrist.

Teroldego Rotaliano T-AA DOC r p ★★→★★★ TRENTINO's best local variety makes seriously tasty wine on flat Campo Rotaliano. *Foradori* is tops. Gd: Dorigati, Endrizzi, MEZZACORONA'S RISERVA Nos, Zeni.

Terre del Barolo Pie ★→★★ Co-op in Castiglione Falletto, c.700 members; millions of bottles of BAROLO and other LANGHE wines; remarkably consistent quality. Look for new Aldo Rivera, dedicated to the founder.

What wine for white truffles? Old Barolo, Barbera, top Chard.

Terre Nere, Tenuta delle Si ★★★ Italian-American distributor Marc de Grazia shows great wine can be made from NERELLO and CARRICANTE grapes, on coveted n side of Mt Etna. Top: Guardiola, VIGNE Niche and pre-phylloxera La Vigna di Don Peppino.

Terriccio, Castello del Tus ★★★ Large estate s of Livorno: excellent, v. expensive B'x-style IGT Lupicaia, v.gd IGT Tassinaia. Impressive IGT Terriccio, unusual blend of mainly Rhône grapes.

Tiberio ★★★ Outstanding TREBBIANO D'ABRUZZO Fonte Canale (60-yr-old vines) one of Italy's best whites; PECORINO also exceptional. V.gd: CERASUOLO D'ABRUZZO, MONTEPULCIANO D'ABRUZZO.

Tiefenbrunner T-AA ★★→★★★ Grower-merchant in Teutonic castle (Turmhof) in s ALTO ADIGE. Christof T succeeds father Herbert (winemaker since 1943). Wide range of mtn-fresh white and well-defined red varietals: French, Germanic and local, esp 1000m-high MÜLLER-T *Feldmarschall*, one of Italy's best whites.

Tignanello Tus r ★★★★ 04' 06' 07' 08 09 10 11 12 (13) 15 SANGIOVESE/CAB SAUV blend, barrique-aged, wine that put SUPER TUSCANS on map, created by ANTINORI's great oenologist Giacomo Tachis in early 70s. Today one of greatest cash-cows of world wine.

Tommasi Ven ★★★ Fourth generation now in charge. Top: AMARONE, RISERVA Ca' Florian, VALPOLICELLA Rafael. Other estates in Ven (Filodora), PU (Masseria Surani), OLTREPÒ PAVESE (TENUTA Caseo) and Bas (PATERNOSTER).

Torcolato Ven Sweet wine from BREGANZE in Ven; Vespaiolo grapes laid on mats or hung up to dry for mths, as nearby RECIOTO DI SOAVE. Best: CS Beato Bartolomeo da Breganze, MACULAN.

Torgiano Umb DOC r p w (sp) ★★ and **Torgiano, Rosso Riserva** DOCG r ★★★ 01'

04 06 07 08 09 10 11 12 (13) (15) Gd-to-excellent red from Umb, virtually an exclusivity of LUNGAROTTI. **Vigna Monticchio** Rubesco RISERVA is outstanding in vintages: 75 79 85 97; keeps many yrs.

Torrette VdA DOC r ★→★★★ Blend based on Petit Rouge and other local varieties. Gd: Anselmet, L'Atoueyo (T SUPERIEUR), Didier Gerbelle, Elio Ottin (T Superieur), FEUDO DI SAN MAURIZIO (T Superieur), LES CRETES.

Travaglini Pie ★★★ Along with Antoniolo, solid producer of n PIE NEBBIOLO, with v.gd GATTINARA RISERVA, Gattinara Tre VIGNE, and pretty gd Nebbiolo Coste della Sesia.

Trebbiano d'Abruzzo Ab DOC w ★→★★★★ DYA. Generally crisp, simple wine, but VALENTINI's and Tiberio's Fonte Canale are *two of Italy's greatest* whites.

Trediberri Pie ★★★ Dynamic estate, top BAROLO Rocche dell'Annunziata (best value); v.gd BARBERA D'ALBA and LANGHE NEBBIOLO too.

Trentino T-AA DOC r w dr sw ★→★★★ DOC for 20-odd wines, mostly varietally named. Best: CHARD, PINOT BL, MARZEMINO, TEROLDEGO. Provincial capital is Trento, which is DOC name for potentially high-quality METODO CLASSICO wines.

Trinoro, Tenuta di ★★★★ Individualist TUS red wine estate, pioneer in DOC Val d'Orcia between MONTEPULCIANO and MONTALCINO. Heavy accent on B'x grapes in flagship TENUTA di Trinoro, also in Palazzi, Le Cupole and Magnacosta. Andrea Franchetti also has v'yds on Mt Etna.

Tua Rita Tus ★★→★★★★ First producer to est Suvereto, some 20-km down coast, as new BOLGHERI in 90s. Producer of possibly Italy's greatest MERLOT in Redigaffi, also outstanding B'x blend *Giusto di Notri*. *See* VAL DI CORNIA.

Tuscany / Toscana Tus Focal point of Italian wine's late-C20 renaissance, 1st with experimental SUPER TUSCANS, then modernized classics, CHIANTI, VINO NOBILE, BRUNELLO. Development of coastal zones like BOLGHERI, MAREMMA, has been a major feature of Tus wine over last half-century.

Uberti Lom ★★★ Historical estate, excellent interpreter of FRANCIACORTA's terroir. Best Quinque (blend of 5 yrs) and Comarì del Salem. V.gd Dosaggio Zero Sublimis.

Umani Ronchi Mar ★★→★★★ Leading Mar producer, esp for VERDICCHIO (Casal di Serra, Plenio), CONERO Cumaro, IGTS Le Busche (w), Pelago (r).

Vajra, GD Pie ★★★ Leading quality BAROLO producer in Vergne. Outstanding Bricco delle Viole and LANGHE Freisa Kyè. Gd: Langhe RIES Petracine, Barolo Ravera and Serralunga's Luigi Baudana Barolos.

Valdadige T-AA DOC r w dr s/sw ★ Name (in German: *Etschtaler*) for simple wines of valley of Adige, from ALTO ADIGE through TRENTINO to n Ven.

Val di Cornia Tus DOC r p w ★★→★★★ 06 07 08 09 10 11 12 13 (15) Quality zone s of BOLGHERI. CAB SAUV, MERLOT, MONTEPULCIANO, SYRAH. Look for: Ambrosini, Bulichella, Gualdo del Re, Incontri, Jacopo Banti, Montepeloso, Petra, Russo, San Michele, TENUTA Casa Dei, Terricciola, TUA RITA.

Valentini, Edoardo Ab r w ★★★→★★★★ Collectors seek out MONTEPULCIANO D'ABRUZZO and TREBBIANO D'ABRUZZO, among Italy's best wines. Traditional, age-worthy; 70s wines esp memorable.

Valle d'Aosta VdA DOC r p w ★★→★★★ Regional DOC for some 25 Alpine wines, geographically or varietally named, incl Arnad Montjovet, Blanc de Morgex, Chambave, Donnas, Enfer d'Arvier, Fumin, Nus MALVOISIE, Premetta, Torrette. Tiny production, wines rarely seen abroad but potentially worth finding.

Valle Isarco T-AA DOC w ★★ DYA. ALTO ADIGE DOC for seven Germanic varietal whites made along the Isarco (Eisack) River ne of Bolzano. Gd GEWURZ, MÜLLER-T, RIES, SILVANER. Top: Abbazia di Novacella, Eisacktaler, KOFERERHOF, Kuenhof, Manni Nossing.

Valpolicella Ven DOC(G) r ★→★★★★ Complex denomination, running from light quaffers with a certain fruity warmth through stronger SUPERIORES (that may or

> Valpolicella: the best
>
> VALPOLICELLA has never been better than today. AMARONE DELLA VALPOLICELLA and RECIOTO DELLA VALPOLICELLA have now been elevated to DOCG status, while Valpolicella RIPASSO has at last been recognized as a historic wine in its own right. The following producers make gd to great wine: ALLEGRINI★, Begali, BERTANI, BOLLA, Boscaini, Brigaldara★, BRUNELLI, BUSSOLA★, Ca' la Bianca, Ca' Rugate, Campagnola, CANTINA Valpolicella, Castellani, Corteforte, Corte Sant'Alda, CS Valpantena, DAL FORNO★, GUERRIERI-RIZZARDI★, Le Ragose, Le Salette, MASI★, Mazzi★, Nicolis, QUINTARELLI★, Roccolo Grassi★, Serego Alighieri★, SPERI★, Stefano Accordini★, TEDESCHI★, TOMMASI★, Valentina Cubi, Venturini, VIVIANI★, ZENATO, Zeni.

may not be RIPASSO) to AMARONES and RECIOTOS. Today straight Valpol is getting hard to find: a shame, as all best grapes going into trendy, profitable Amarone, which often disappoints (*see* box, above).

Valpolicella Ripasso Ven DOC r ★★→★★★ 09 10 11 12 13 (15) In huge demand, so changes from 2016. Used to be only from VALPOLICELLA SUPERIORE re-fermented (only once) on RECIOTO or AMARONE grape-skins to make a more age-worthy wine. Now can blend ten per cent Amarone with standard Valpolicella and call it Ripasso. Best: BUSSOLA, Castellani, DAL FORNO, QUINTARELLI, ZENATO.

Valtellina Lom DOC/DOCG r ★→★★★ Long e to w valley (most Alpine valleys run n to s) on Swiss border. Steep terraces have for millennia grown NEBBIOLO (here called CHIAVENNASCA) and related grapes. DOCG Valtellina SUPERIORE has five zones: Grumello, Inferno, Sassella, Maroggia, Valgella. Wines and scenery both worth detour. Best today: Fay, Mamete Prevostini, Nera, Nino Negri, Plozza, Rainoldi, Triacca. DOC Valtellina has less stringent requirements. *Sforzato* is its AMARONE.

Vecchio Samperi Si *See* DE BARTOLI.

Verdicchio dei Castelli di Jesi Mar DOC w (sp) ★★→★★★ DYA. Versatile white from nr Ancona on Adriatic; light and quaffable or sparkling or structured, complex, long-lived (esp RISERVA DOCG, min 2 yrs old). Also CLASSICO. Best: Andrea Felici, *Bucci* (Riserva), Borgo delle Oche, Coroncino (Gaiospino e Stracacio), Fazi Battaglia (Riserva San Sisto), GAROFOLI (Podium), La Staffa, Marotti Campi (Salmariano), MONTE SCHIAVO (Le Giuncare), Montecappone (Federico II), Santa Barbara, Sartarelli (Balciana, a rare late-harvest, and Tralivio), UMANI RONCHI (Plenio and Casal di Serra).

Verdicchio di Matelica Mar DOC w (sp) ★★→★★★ DYA. Similar to last, smaller, more inland, higher, so more acidic, so longer lasting though less easy-drinking young. RISERVA is likewise DOCG. Esp Belisario, Bisci, Collestefano, La Monacesca (Mirum), Pagliano Tre, San Biagio.

Verduno Pie DOC r ★★ DYA. Berry and herbal flavours. Gd: Ascheri (Do ut Des), Bel Colle (Le Masche), CASTELLO DI VERDUNO (Basadone), Fratelli Alessandria and GB BURLOTTO.

Verduno, Castello di Pie ★★★ Husband/wife team, v.gd BARBARESCO Rabaja and BAROLO Monvigliero.

Verduzzo F-VG DOC (Friuli Colli Orientali) w dr sw s/sw ★★→★★★ Full-bodied white from local variety. Ramandolo (DOCG) is well-regarded subzone for sweet wine. Top: Anna Berra, Dorigo, Meroi.

Vermentino di Gallura Sar DOCG w ★★→★★★ DYA. VERMENTINO makes gd light wines in TUS, LIG and all over SAR, but best, most intense in ne corner of island, under this its DOCG name. Try Capichera, CS di Gallura, CS del Vermentino/ Monti, CS Giogantino, Depperu.

Vermentino di Sardegna Lig DOC w ★★ DYA. From anywhere on SAR; generally fails to measure up to VERMENTINO DI GALLURA for structure, intensity of flavour. Gd producers: ARGIOLAS, *Santadi, Sella & Mosca*.

Vernaccia di Oristano Sar DOC w dr ★→★★★ SAR flor-affected wine, similar to light Sherry, a touch bitter, full-bodied. SUPERIORE 15.5% alc, 3 yrs of age. Delicious with *bottarga* (dried, salted fish roe). You have to try it. Top: CONTINI. Gd: Serra, Silvio Carta.

Vernaccia di San Gimignano Tus *See* SAN GIMIGNANO.

Vie di Romans F-VG ★★★→★★★★ Gianfranco Gallo has built up his father's ISONZO estate to top FV-G status. Outstanding Isonzo PINOT GR Dessimis, SAUV BL Piere and Vieris (oaked), Flors di Uis blend and MALVASIA. Disappointing CHARD by world standards.

Vietti Pie ★★★ Veteran grower of characterful PIE wines at Castiglione Falletto, incl BARBARESCO Masseria, BARBERA D'ALBA Scarrone, BARBERA D'ASTI la Crena. *Textbook Barolos*: Lazzarito, Brunate, Ravera, Rocche, Villero.

Vignamaggio Tus ★★→★★★ Historic, beautiful CHIANTI CLASSICO estate, nr Greve. Leonardo da Vinci painted the *Mona Lisa* here. RISERVA is called – you guessed it.

Vigna (or vigneto) A single v'yd, generally indicating superior quality.

Vigna Petrussa F-VG ★★★ Small family estate: high-quality Schiopppettino, Picolit.

Villa Matilde Cam ★★★ Top CAM producer of FALERNO Rosso (VIGNA Camarato), Bianco (Caracci), PASSITO Eleusi.

Villa Russiz F-VG ★★★ Historic estate for DOC COLLIO. V.gd SAUV BL and MERLOT (esp "de la Tour" selections), PINOT BL, PINOT GR, CHARD, FRIULANO.

Vino Nobile di Montepulciano Tus DOCG r ★★→★★★ 04 06' 07 08 09 10 11 12 13 (15) Historic Prugnole Gentile aka SANGIOVESE-based wine from the TUS town (as distinct from grape) MONTEPULCIANO. Often tough with drying tannins, but complex and long-lasting from best producers: AVIGNONESI, Bindella, Boscarelli, Canneto, Contucci, La Braccesca, La Calonica, Le Casalte, DEI, Fattoria del Cerro, Gracciano della Seta, Icario, Nottola, POLIZIANO, Romeo, Salcheto, Trerose, Valdipiatta, Villa Sant'Anna. RISERVA after 3 yrs.

Vin Santo / Vinsanto / Vin(o) Santo T-AA, Tus DOC w sw s/sw ★★→★★★★ Sweet PASSITO wine, usually TREBBIANO, MALVASIA and/or SANGIOVESE in TUS (Vin Santo), Nosiola in TRENTINO (Vino Santo). Tus versions extremely variable, anything from off-dry and Sherry-like to sweet and v. rich. May spend 3–10 unracked yrs in small barrels called *caratelli*. *Avignonesi's is legendary*; plus CAPEZZANA, Fattoria del Cerro, FELSINA, FRASCOLE, ISOLE E OLENA, Rocca di Montegrossi, SAN GIUSTO A RENTENNANO, SELVAPIANA, Villa Sant'Anna, Villa di Vetrice. *See also* OCCHIO DI PERNICE.

Voerzio, Roberto Pie ★★★★ BAROLO modernist: conc, tannic Barolos. More impressive/expensive than delicious, usually aged in toasted barriques. Range incl Brunate, Cerequio, Rocche dell'Annunziata-Torriglione, Sarmassa, Serra; excellent BARBERA D'ALBA. Two new Barolos from 2016 vintage.

Volpaia, Castello di Tus ★★→★★★ V.gd CHIANTI CLASSICO estate at Radda. Top Chianti Classico RISERVA and Riserva Coltassala (SANGIOVESE/Mammolo), Balifico (Sangiovese/CAB SAUV).

Zenato Ven ★★ V. reliable, sometimes inspired for GARDA wines, also AMARONE, LUGANA, SOAVE, VALPOLICELLA.

Zerbina, Fattoria E-R ★★★ Leader in Romagna; best sweet ALBANA DOCG (Scacco Matto), v.gd SANGIOVESE (Pietramora); barrique-aged IGT Marzieno.

Zibibbo Si ★★ dr sw Alluring SI table wine from the MUSCAT d'Alessandria grape, most associated with PANTELLERIA and extreme w Si. Dry version exemplified by DE BARTOLI.

Zonin ★→★★★ One of Italy's biggest estate owners, based at Gambellara in Ven, but also big in F-VG, TUS, PUG, SI and elsewhere in world (eg. Virginia, US).

Germany

Abbreviations used in the text:

Bad	Baden
Frank	Franken
M-M	Mittelmosel
M Rh	Mittelrhein
Mos	Mosel
Na	Nahe
Pfz	Pfalz
Rhg	Rheingau
Rhh	Rheinhessen
Sa-Un	Saale-Unstrut
Sachs	Sachsen
Würt	Württemberg

More heavily shaded areas are the wine-growing regions.

The past decade has seen a rise in quality, a refreshment of ideas and a diversification of styles unparalleled in 100 years or more. Germany has developed a style of dry, full-bodied food-enhancing Riesling that Germans love but still confuses some foreigners – especially Brits. What's new is the spectacular rise of the east of the country. It always used to be regarded as too chilly to be really good, and of course, global warming has an effect too. But there is a young generation of growers (see box p.174) who are eager to prove that Sachsen and Saale-Unstrut may rival the best areas of the West. The pioneers of Eastern German viticulture, Prinz zur Lippe, Uwe Lützkendorf and Klaus Zimmerling, must be happy to watch progress. The 20-something generation knows the former GDR only from history books. These growers are well trained, well travelled, and experience will come by itself. Their pragmatism and dynamic spirit is excellent news for German wine.

Recent vintages

Mosel

Mosels (including Saar and Ruwer wines) are so attractive young that their capabilities for developing are not often enough explored. But fine Kabinetts can gain from at least 5 years in bottle and often much more: Spätlese from 5–20, and Auslese and BA anything from 10–30 years. "Racy" is their watchword. Dry Mosels have made significant progress recently; climate change is helping. Saar and Ruwer make leaner wines than Mosel, but surpass the whole world for elegance and thrilling, steely "breeding".

2017 Devastating frost in April (quantity 25 per cent down), but dry summer, low yields gave wines of high extract. Sunny mid-Oct permitted BA, TBA.

2016 Splendid October; quality much better than anticipated, textbook raciness.

2015 Hot, dry summer, damp September, sunny October; Spätlesen, Auslesen to keep.

2014 September saved vintage, but careful selection necessary.

2013 Top wines have freshness, elegance (but rare). Mittelmosel better than Saar, Ruwer.

2012 Classic wines mostly from QbA to Auslese. Low quantity.

2011 Brilliant vintage, particularly in Saar, Ruwer, with sensational TBAs.

2010 High acidity identifying feature, some good Spätlesen, Auslesen.

2009 Magnificent Spätlesen, Auslesen, good balance. Keep.

2008 Kabinetts, Spätlesen can be fine, elegant. Now perfect to drink.

2007 Good quality, quantity. Now approaching maturity.

2005 Very ripe, better acidity than, say, 2003. Exceptional (Saar). Drink or keep.

More fine vintages: 04 03 01 99 97 95 94 93 90 89 88 76 71 69 64 59 53 49 45 37 34 21.

Rheinhessen, Nahe, Pfalz, Rheingau, Ahr

Apart from Mosels, Rheingau wines tend to be longest-lived of all German regions, improving for 15 years or more, but best wines from Rheinhessen, Nahe and Pfalz can last as long. Modern-style dry wines such as Grosses Gewächs (GG) are generally intended for drinking within 2–4 years, but the best undoubtedly have the potential to age interestingly. The same holds for Ahr Valley reds: their fruit makes them attractive young, but best wines can develop for 10 years and longer. Who will give them a chance?

2017 April frost, hail, September rain: a vintage of challenges. Careful selection was necessary. Quantity 20–50 per cent down.

2016 Mildew, plus hot temperatures and sunburn. Quality, quantity very mixed.

2015 Hot, dry summer. Rheingau excellent, both dry and nobly sweet.

2014 Complicated, but Ries, Spätburgunder generally okay, even good with careful selection.

2013 Much variation; best in south Rheinhessen, Franconia, Ahr Valley.

2012 Quantities below average, but very good, classical at every level.

2011 Fruity wines, with harmonious acidity.

2010 Uneven quality, some very good Spätburgunder; dry whites should be drunk now.

2009 Excellent wines, especially dry. Some acidification needed.

2008 Riesling of great raciness, ageing well.

2007 Dry wines now ready to drink.

2005 High ripeness levels, excellent acidity, extract. Superb year. Drink or keep.

More fine vintages: 03 02 01 99 98 97 96 93 90 83 76 71 69 67 64 59 53 49 45 37 34 21.

German vintage notation

The vintage notes after entries in the German section are mostly given in a different form from those elsewhere in the book. If the vintages of a single wine are rated, or are for red wine regions, the vintage notation is identical with the one used elsewhere (*see* front jacket flap). But for regions, villages or producers, two styles of vintage are indicated:

Bold type (eg. **16**) indicates classic, ripe vintages with a high proportion of SPÄTLESEN and AUSLESEN; or, in the case of red wines, gd phenolic ripeness and must weights.

Normal type (eg. 17) indicates a successful but not outstanding vintage. Generally, German white wines, esp RIES, can be drunk young for their intense fruitiness, or kept for a decade or two to develop more aromatic subtlety and finesse.

Adams Rhh ★★→★★★ Family estate led since 2011 by oenologist Simone A, proving why PINOT N from INGELHEIM was considered to be among Germany's best in C19.

Adelmann, Weingut Graf Würt ★★→★★★ Young Count Felix Adelmann now in charge at idyllic Schloss Schaubeck. V.gd 2015 MERLOT and PINOT GR.

Ahr ★★→★★★★ 09 11 12 **13' 14 15'** 16 (17) Small river valley s of Bonn, a sort of PINOT N canyon. Slate brings about fruit and minerality. Best: Adeneuer, Deutzerhof, Heiner-Kreuzberg, Kreuzberg, MEYER-NÄKEL, Nelles, Riske, Schumacher, STODDEN, co-op Mayschoss-Altenahr.

Aldinger, Gerhard Würt ★★★→★★★★ Gerd Aldinger's sons Hansjörg and Matthias go full throttle: TROLLINGER without added sulphur, SEKT with 5 yrs of lees ageing, SAUV BL Ovum fermented and aged in concrete egg. Conventional wines v.gd too.

Alte Reben Old vines. An obvious analogy to the French term vieilles vignes. Analogy is perfect: no min age.

Alter Satz Frank Wines from old co-planted (different varieties all mixed up) v'yds, esp in FRANK, many of them being more than 100 yrs old and ungrafted. Try Otmar Zang (all w), Scheuring, Scholtens or Stritzinger (r).

Amtliche Prüfungsnummer (APNr) Official test number, on every label of a quality wine. Useful for discerning different lots of AUSLESE a producer has made from the same v'yd.

Assmannshausen Rhg ★★→★★★★ 99' 05' 08 09 10 11 12 **13' 14 15** 16 The only RHG village with tradition for *Spätburgunder*. Wines from GROSSE LAGE v'yd Höllenberg (45 ha on slate) age extremely well. Growers: BISCHÖFLICHES WEINGUT RÜDESHEIM, CHAT SAUVAGE, HESSISCHE STAATSWEINGÜTER, KESSELER, König, KRONE, KÜNSTLER, Mumm.

Auslese Wines from selective picking of super-ripe bunches affected by noble rot (*Edelfäule*). Unctuous in flavour, but – traditionally – elegant rather than super-concentrated. When fermented dry elegance is at risk. Equally, GOLD CAPSULE should add finesse and complexity, not only weight.

Ayl Mos ★→★★★ All v'yds known since 1971 by name of historically best site: Kupp. Such are German wine laws. Growers: BISCHÖFLICHE WEINGÜTER TRIER, *Lauer*, Vols.

BA (Beerenauslese) Luscious sweet wine from exceptionally ripe, individually selected berries concentrated by noble rot. Rare, expensive.

Bacharach M Rh ★→★★★ 01 05 08 **09** 11 12 13 14 15 16 17 Small, idyllic town; centre of M RH RIES. Classified GROSSE LAGE: Hahn, Posten, Wolfshöhle. Growers: Bastian, JOST, KAUER, RATZENBERGER.

Baden Bad Huge sw region and former Grand Duchy, 15,000 ha stretched over 230 km, best-known for PINOT N, GRAU- and WEISSBURGUNDER and pockets of RIES, usually dry. Many co-ops.

Bassermann-Jordan Pfz ★★★ 49 ha at DEIDESHEIM, FORST, Ruppertsberg. *Majestic* dry Ries, now also with prolonged cask ageing (Res Probus) and terracotta vinification (Pithium). Breathtaking 2016 GGS from Forst's Kirchenstück and Jesuitengarten v'yds.

Becker, Friedrich Pfz ★★ →★★★★ Outstanding SPÄTBURGUNDER (Kammerberg, Sankt Paul, Res, Heydenreich) 07' 08 09 **10** 11 12 13' 14 15 from most s part of PFZ; some v'yds actually lie across border in Alsace. Gd whites (CHARD, RIES, PINOT GR) too.

Becker, JB Rhg ★★ →★★★ 89 90 92 94 97 01 **05** 07 08 **09** 10 11 12 13 14 15 16 (17) Delightfully old-fashioned, cask-aged (and long-lived) dry RIES, SPÄTBURGUNDER at WALLUF and Martinsthal. Mature vintages are outstanding value.

Bercher Bad ★★★ Cousins Arne and Martin B are experts on PINOT from volcanic soils at Burkheim, Jechtingen and Sasbach.

Bergdolt Pfz ★★★ Organic estate at Duttweiler, known for its WEISSBURGUNDER GG Mandelberg 98' 01' 04' 05 07 08 **09' 10** 11 12' 13 14 15 16. Gd RIES and SPÄTBURGUNDER too.

Bernkastel M-M ★→★★★★ Senior wine town of the M-M, known for timbered houses and flowery, perfectly round RIES. GROSSE LAGE: DOCTOR, Lay. Top growers: Kerpen, JJ PRÜM, LOOSEN, Studert-Prüm, THANISCH (both estates), WEGELER. "Kurfürstlay" GROSSLAGE name is a deception: avoid.

Bischöfliches Weingut Rüdesheim Rhg ★★★ 8 ha of best sites in RÜDESHEIM, ASSMANNSHAUSEN, JOHANNISBERG; vault cellar in Hildegard von Bingen's historic monastery. Peter Perabo (ex-KRONE) is *Pinot N specialist* (brilliant 15s: dense Rüdesheim "S" and fragrant Assmannshausen "S"), RIES also v.gd.

Bischöfliche Weingüter Trier Mos ★★ 120 ha of mostly 1st-class v'yds uniting historical donations. Not v. reliable; do not buy without prior tasting.

Bodensee Bad Idyllic district of s BAD, on Lake Constance, at considerable altitude: 400–580m. Dry MÜLLER-T with elegance, light but delicate SPÄTBURGUNDER. Top villages: Hagnau, Meersburg, Reichenau. Lovely holiday wines.

Boppard M Rh ★→★★★ Wine town of M RH with GROSSE LAGE Hamm, an amphitheatre of vines. Growers: Heilig Grab, Lorenz, M Müller, Perll, WEINGART. Unbeatable *value*.

Brauneberg M-M ★★★ →★★★★★ 59 71 83 90 01 04 05 07 08 09 11 12 13 14 **15** 16 17 Top village nr BERNKASTEL; excellent full-flavoured RIES of great raciness. GROSSE LAGE v'yds Juffer, Juffer-SONNENUHR. Growers: *F Haag, W Haag*, KESSELSTATT, Paulinshof, RICHTER, SCHLOSS LIESER, THANISCH.

Bremer Ratskeller Town hall cellar in n Germany's commercial town of Bremen, founded in 1405, a UNESCO World Heritage Site. Oldest wine is a barrel of 1653 RÜDESHEIMER Apostelwein.

Breuer Rhg ★★★ →★★★★ Exquisite RIES from RÜDESHEIM and RAUENTHAL. Berg Schlossberg has depth at 12% alc, Nonnenberg transforms austerity into age-worthiness, inexpensive Terra Montosa shows what RHG Ries is all about. Gd SEKT, SPÄTBURGUNDER too.

Want a grower to sing opera? Visit Friedrich Bastian at Bacharach. Trained baritone.

Buhl, Reichsrat von Pfz ★★★ Historic PFZ estate at DEIDESHEIM. Since ex-Bollinger cellarmaster Mathieu Kauffmann joined (in 2013), stunning SEKT, and textbook "French-style" GGS, eg. Pechstein 16, Jesuitengarten 15.

Bunn, Lisa Rhh ★★ →★★★ Shooting star in NIERSTEIN, refined Hipping and Oelberg RIES, stylish Res CHARD, remarkable ST-LAURENT (r).

Bürgerspital zum Heiligen Geist Frank ★★★ Ancient charitable estate with great continuity: only six directors in past 180 yrs. Traditionally made whites (*Silvaner*, RIES) from best sites in/around WÜRZBURG. SILVANER GG from sole possession Stein-Harfe 14 15' 16' is a monument.

Bürklin-Wolf, Dr. Pfz ★★→★★★★ Historic estate with 30 ha of best MITTELHAARDT v'yds (estate-own classification since 1994). Bio farming (incl use of horses).

Busch, Clemens Mos ★★★→★★★★ Clemens Busch and son Johannes work steep Pündericher Marienburg all by hand and bio. Breathtaking series of GGs from parcels Fahrlay, Falkenlay, Rothenpfad, Raffes. Now also a Res line: 2 yrs barrel ageing (try Fahrlay Res 14).

Castell'sches Fürstliches Domänenamt Frank ★★→★★★ Superb SILVANER, RIES from monopoly v'yd *Casteller Schlossberg* – mostly dry, but occasionally also TBA (outstanding Ries 06) or BA (Silvaner 67 08).

Chat Sauvage Rhg ★★★→★★★★ 08 09 10 11 12 13' 14 15 16 Founded in 2000, but already among the finest RHG PINOT N producers. V'yds at ASSMANNSHAUSEN, JOHANNISBERG, LORCH, RÜDESHEIM. Some CHARD too, and delicate SEKT (Cuvée S Brut Nature 13).

Christmann Pfz ★★★ VDP President Steffen Christmann is a MITTELHAARDT bio pioneer, best known for his RIES Königsbacher Idig 05' 08' 10' 11 12' 13 14 15' 16. Fine Ölberg Hart "Kapelle" GG 16.

Clüsserath, Ansgar Mos ★★★ Tense RIES from TRITTENHEIMER Apotheke. KABINETTS are delicious, crystalline.

Corvers-Kauter Rhg ★★★ Textbook mineral RÜDESHEIM RIES: crystalline, pure.

Crusius, Dr. Na ★★→★★★ Family estate at TRAISEN, NA. Vivid, age-worthy RIES from sun-baked Bastei and Rotenfels of Traisen and SCHLOSSBÖCKELHEIM.

Deidesheim Pfz ★★→★★★★ Central MITTELHAARDT village and series of GROSSE LAGE v'yds: Grainhübel, Hohenmorgen, Kalkofen, Kieselberg, Langenmorgen, Paradiesgarten. Top growers: BASSERMANN-JORDAN, Biffar, BUHL, BÜRKLIN-WOLF, CHRISTMANN, DEINHARD, Fusser, MOSBACHER, VON WINNING. Gd co-op.

Deinhard, Dr. Pfz ★★→★★★★ Since 2008, a brand of the VON WINNING estate, used for wines with no oak influence.

Diel, Schlossgut Na ★★★→★★★★ Caroline Diel follows her father: exquisite *GG Ries* (best usually Burgberg of Dorsheim). Magnificent SPÄTLESEN, serious *Sekt* (Cuvée Mo 6 yrs on lees).

Doctor M-M Emblematic steep v'yd at BERNKASTEL, the place where TBA was invented (1921, THANISCH). Only 3.2 ha, and five owners: both Thanisch estates, WEGELER (1.1 ha, of which 0.06 ha are leased to KESSELSTATT), Patrick Lauerburg and local Heiliges Geist charity (0.26 ha, leased until 2024 to SCHLOSS LIESER, M MOLITOR). RIES of extraordinary richness, but pricey.

Dönnhoff Na ★★★→★★★★ 90 97 01 05 07 08 09 11 12 13 14 15 16 17 Cornelius D now in charge, in style slightly drier than father Helmut. Gd value are RIES Tonschiefer and Roxheim *Höllenpfad* (fine and elegant). Outstanding GG from NIEDERHAUSEN (Hermannshöhle) and *Norheim (Dellchen)*; SCHLOSSBÖCKELHEIM (Felsenberg). Dazzling EISWEIN.

Germany's priciest v'yd: Doctor of Bernkastel. Rent €8/m²/yr (= €10/vine).

Durbach Bad ★★→★★★ ORTENAU village for full-bodied RIES, locally called Klingelberger, granite soils. Growers: Graf Metternich, LAIBLE (both), Männle (both), MARKGRAF VON BADEN. Reliable co-op.

Egon Müller zu Scharzhof Mos ★★★★ 59 71 76 83 85 88 89 90 93 94 95 96 97 98 99 01 02 03 04 05 06 07 08 09 10 11 12 13 14 15 16 17 Legendary SAAR estate at WILTINGEN with a treasure of old vines. Its racy SCHARZHOFBERGer RIES is among world's greatest wines: sublime, vibrant, immortal. *Kabinetts* feather-light and long-lived (94 showed an aftertaste of white truffle in 2017).

Einzellage Individual v'yd site. Never to be confused with GROSSLAGE.

Eiswein Made from frozen grapes with the ice (ie. water content) discarded, thus concentrated: of BA ripeness or more. Outstanding Eiswein vintages: 98 02 04 08.

New EU terminology
Germany's part in the new EU classification involves, firstly, abolishing the term Tafelwein in favour of plain **Wein**, and secondly changing LANDWEIN to **geschützte geographische Angabe (ggA)** or Protected Geographical Indication. QUALITÄTSWEIN and QUALITÄTSWEIN MIT PRÄDIKAT will be replaced by **geschützte Ursprungsbezeichnung (gU)** or Protected Designation of Origin. The existing terms – SPÄTLESE, AUSLESE and so on (*see* box, p.165) – will be tacked on to gU where appropriate; the rules for these styles won't change.

Less and less produced in past decade: global warming is Eiswein's enemy.

Emrich-Schönleber Na ★★★ Werner S and son Frank make precise RIES from Monzingen's classified Frühlingsplätzchen and Halenberg (usually better).

Erden M-M ★★★ →★★★★ 90 01 03 05 08 09 11 12 13 14 15 16 17 Village on red slate soils; noble AUSLESEN and TROCKEN RIES with rare delicacy. GROSSE LAGE: Prälat, Treppchen. Growers: BREMER RATSKELLER, JJ Christoffel, LOOSEN, MERKELBACH, MARKUS MOLITOR, Mönchhof, Schmitges.

Erste Lage Classified v'yd, 2nd-from-top level, similar to Burgundy's Premier Cru, only in use with VDP members outside AHR, M RH, MOS, NA, RHH.

Erstes Gewächs Rhg "First growth". Only for RHG v'yds, but VDP-members there changed to the GG designation after 2012. Pay attention.

Erzeugerabfüllung Bottled by producer. Incl the guarantee that only own grapes have been processed. May be used by co-ops also. GUTSABFÜLLUNG is stricter, applies only to estates.

Escherndorf Frank ★★★ Village with steep GROSSE LAGE Lump ("scrap" – as in tiny inherited parcels). Marvellous *Silvaner* and RIES, dry and sweet. Growers: Fröhlich, H SAUER, R SAUER, Schäffer, zur Schwane.

Feinherb Imprecisely defined traditional term for wines with around 10–25g sugar/litre, not necessarily tasting sweet. More flexible than HALBTROCKEN. I often choose Feinherbs.

Forst Pfz ★★→★★★★ 01 05 08 09 11 12 13 14 15 16 17 Outstanding MITTELHAARDT village. Full-bodied and fine at the same time. GROSSE LAGE v'yds in descending order of reputation: Kirchenstück, Jesuitengarten, Pechstein, Ungeheuer, Freundstück. Top growers: Acham-Magin, BASSERMANN-JORDAN, BÜRKLIN-WOLF, MOSBACHER, VON BUHL, VON WINNING, WOLF.

Franken / Franconia Region of distinctive dry wines, esp *Silvaner*, mostly bottled in round-bellied flasks (BOCKSBEUTEL). Centre is WÜRZBURG. Top villages: Bürgstadt, ESCHERNDORF, IPHOFEN, Klingenberg, RANDERSACKER.

Franzen Mos ★★ →★★★ From Europe's steepest v'yd, Calmont at Bremm, young Kilian Franzen makes rich and "warm" but also mineral RIES.

Fricke, Eva Rhg ★★ →★★★ Born nr Bremen without viticultural background, now rising star in RHG: expressive, taut RIES (10 ha, organic) from KIEDRICH, LORCH.

Fuder Traditional German cask, sizes 600–1800 litres depending on region, traditionally used for fermentation and (formerly long) ageing.

Fürst, Weingut Frank ★★★ →★★★★ Successful father-son team at Bürgstadt with v'yds there and on steep terraces of Klingenberg. *Spätburgunders* 97' 99 01 05' 08 09 10 11 12 13 14 15 16 of great finesse from red sandstone, dense FRÜHBURGUNDER, excellent whites too. Pur Mineral [sic] is a reliable mid-price label.

Gallais, Le Mos The 2nd estate of EGON MÜLLER ZU SCHARZHOF with 4-ha-monopoly Braune Kupp of WILTINGEN. Soil is schist with more clay than in SCHARZHOFBERG; AUSLESEN can be exceptional.

Geisenheim Rhg Town primarily known for Germany's top university of oenology and viticulture. One GROSSE LAGE too: Rothenberg.

> **Grosse Lage / Grosslage: spot the difference**
> *Bereich* means district within an *Anbaugebiet* (region). *Bereich* on a
> label should be treated as a flashing red light; the wine is a blend from
> arbitrary sites within that district. Do not buy. The same holds for wines
> with a GROSSLAGE name, though these are more difficult to identify. Who
> could guess if "Forster Mariengarten" is an EINZELLAGE or a *Grosslage*?
> (It's Gross.) But now, from the 2012 vintage, it's even more tricky. Don't
> confuse *Grosslage* with GROSSE LAGE: the latter refers to best single v'yds,
> Germany's Grands Crus according to the classification set up by wine-
> grower's association VDP. They weren't thinking about you.

GG (Grosses Gewächs) "Great/top growth". The top dry wine from a VDP-classified
GROSSE LAGE (since 2012). *See also* ERSTES GEWÄCHS.

Goldkapsel / Gold Capsule Mos, Na, Rhg, Rhh Designation (and physical sealing)
mainly for AUSLESE and higher. V. strict selection of grapes. Lange Goldkapsel
(Long Gold Capsule) should be even better.

Graach M-M ★★★ →★★★★ Small village between BERNKASTEL and WEHLEN. GROSSE LAGE
v'yds: Domprobst, Himmelreich, Josephshof. Top growers: Kees-Kieren, LOOSEN,
MARKUS MOLITOR, *JJ* PRÜM, SA PRÜM, SCHAEFER, *Selbach-Oster*, Studert-Prüm, VON
KESSELSTATT, WEGELER. Threatened by planned new Autobahn.

Griesel & Compagnie ★★★ SEKT startup at Bensheim, top Prestige series (Rosé Extra
Brut, Pinot Brut Nature).

Grosse Lage The top level of the VDP's new classification, but only applies to VDP
members. *NB* Not on any account to be confused with GROSSLAGE. The dry wine
from a Grosse Lage site is called GG.

Grosser Ring Mos Group of top (VDP) MOS estates, whose annual Sept auction at
TRIER sets world-record prices.

Grosslage Term destined, maybe even intended, to confuse. Introduced by the
disastrous 1971 wine law. A collection of secondary v'yds with supposedly
similar character – but no indication of quality. Not on any account to be
confused with GROSSE LAGE.

Gunderloch Rhh ★★★ →★★★★ 90 01 05 07 08 09 11 12 13 14 15 16 17 The late
Fritz Hasselbach made ROTER HANG area world-famous (again), son Johannes
builds on this: classics will not change, eg. nobly sweet RIES from GROSSE LAGE
Rothenberg or culinary *Kabinett Jean-Baptiste*. But TROCKEN wines now much
drier than before.

Gut Hermannsberg Na ★★★ Former state domain at NIEDERHAUSEN, privatized 2010.
Powerful, dense RIES GG from Altenbamberg, NIEDERHAUSEN, SCHLOSSBÖCKELHEIM
(extraordinary Kupfergrube 15´), TRAISEN.

Gutsabfüllung Estate-bottled, and made from own grapes.

Gutswein Wine with no v'yd or village designation, but only the producer's name:
entry-level category. Ideally, Gutswein should be an ERZEUGERABFÜLLUNG (from
own grapes), but is not always the case.

Haag, Fritz Mos ★★★★ 90 01 05 07 08 09 10 11 12 13 14 15 16 17 BRAUNEBERG's top
estate; Oliver Haag is following the footsteps of his father, Wilhelm, but wines
are more modern in style. *See also* SCHLOSS LIESER.

Haag, Willi Mos ★★ →★★★ BRAUNEBERG family estate, led by Marcus Haag. Old-style
RIES, mainly sweet, rich but balanced, and inexpensive.

Haart, Julian Mos ★★ →★★★ The talented nephew of Theo Haart, making a name
for dense, spontaneously fermented RIES. Fine 16s: Goldtröpfchen KABINETT and
Schubertslay SPÄTLESE.

Haart, Reinhold M-M ★★★ →★★★★ Best in PIESPORT, aromatic, round RIES. SPÄTLESEN,
AUSLESEN, higher PRÄDIKAT wines *racy, copybook Mosels*: great ageing potential.

Haidle Würt ★★★ Family estate now led by young Moritz Haidle, using the cool climate of Remstal area for RIES, LEMBERGER of distinctive freshness.

Halbtrocken Medium-dry with 9–18g unfermented sugar/litre, inconsistently distinguished from FEINHERB (which sounds better).

Hattenheim Rhg ★★→★★★★ Town famous for GROSSE LAGEN Nussbrunnen, Hassel, Mannberg, Schützenhaus, STEINBERG, Wisselbrunnen. Estates: Barth, HESSISCHE STAATSWEINGÜTER, Kaufmann (ex-Lang), Knyphausen, LANGWERTH, Ress, SPREITZER. Classic RHG RIES. The **Brunnen** ("well") v'yds lie on a rocky basin that collects water, protection against drought.

Heger, Dr. Bad ★★★ KAISERSTUHL estate known for dry parcel selections from volcanic soils in Achkarren and IHRINGEN esp Vorderer Berg for steepest Winklerberg terraces.

Heitlinger / Burg Ravensburg Bad ★★→★★★★ Two leading estates in Kraichgau under same ownership: Heitlinger more modern, elegant in style, Burg Ravensburg full-bodied. Best usually Schellenbrunnen RIES, Königsbecher PINOT N.

Hessische Bergstrasse ★→★★★ Germany's smallest wine region (only 440 ha), n of Heidelberg. Pleasant RIES from Bergsträßer Winzer co-op, HESSISCHE STAATSWEINGÜTER, Simon-Bürkle, Stadt Bensheim.

Hessische Staatsweingüter ★★→★★★★ Rhg State domain of big – and historical – dimensions, holding 220 ha in ASSMANNSHAUSEN, RÜDESHEIM, *Rauenthal*, HATTENHEIM (monopoly STEINBERG), HOCHHEIM and along HESSISCHE BERGSTRASSE. C12 Cistercian abbey KLOSTER EBERBACH has vinotheque, 12 historical presses. Quality is sound, but be selective. SEKT can be exquisite.

Heyl zu Herrnsheim Rhh ★★→★★★ Historic NIERSTEIN estate, bio, part of the ST-ANTONY estate. GG from monopoly site Brudersberg can be excellent.

Heymann-Löwenstein Mos ★★★ Spontaneously fermented RIES from steep terraces at WINNINGEN nr Koblenz, intense and individual in style.

Hochgewächs Designation for a MOS RIES that obeys stricter requirements than plain QbA, today rarely used. A worthy advocate is *Kallfelz* in Zell-Merl.

Hochheim Rhg ★★→★★★★ Town e of main RHG, on River Main. Rich, earthy RIES from GROSSE LAGE v'yds: Domdechaney, Hölle, Kirchenstück, Reichestal. Growers: Domdechant *Werner*, Flick/Königin Victoriaberg, Himmel, *Künstler*, HESSISCHE STAATSWEINGÜTER.

Hock Traditional English term for Rhine wine, derived from HOCHHEIM.

Hövel, Weingut von Mos ★★★ Fine SAAR estate with v'yds at Oberemmel (Hütte – filigree wines – is 4.8 ha monopoly), at KANZEM (Hörecker) and in SCHARZHOFBERG. Now bio.

Huber, Bernhard Bad ★★★→★★★★ Young Julian H is about to gain cult status like his father, esp for supple SPÄTBURGUNDER (*Alte Reben*, Bombacher Sommerhalde) and tight, demanding, burgundy-style CHARD (ALTE REBEN, Hecklinger Schlossberg).

III different vine varieties are on Germany's official register.

Ihringen Bad ★→★★★ Village in KAISERSTUHL known for fine SPÄTBURGUNDER, GRAUBURGUNDER on steep volcanic Winklerberg. Top growers: DR. HEGER, Konstanzer, Michel, Stigler, von Gleichenstein.

Immich-Batterieberg M-M ★★→★★★ Revived historic estate named after slopes that were blasted into the slate rock in C19 ("battery" = bundle of dynamite). TROCKEN and off-dry RIES from Batterieberg, Ellergrub (excellent 16'), Steffensberg v'yds in Enkirch, Gutswein Detonation is light and muscular – purity at its best. But no sweet wines.

Ingelheim Rhh ★★→★★★★ RHH town with limestone beds under v'yds; historic fame for SPÄTBURGUNDER being reinvigorated by estates as ADAMS, Arndt F Werner, Bettenheimer, Dautermann, NEUS, Schloss Westerhaus, Wasem.

Iphofen Frank ★★→★★★ 01' 05' 09 11 12 13 14 15' 16 17 STEIGERWALD village with famous GROSSE LAGE Julius-Echter-Berg. Rich, aromatic, well-ageing SILVANER from gypsum soils. Growers: Arnold, Emmerich, JULIUSSPITAL, RUCK, VETTER, WELTNER, **Wirsching**, Zehntkeller.

Jahrgang Year – as in "vintage".

Johannisberg Rhg ★★→★★★★ RHG village known for berry- and honey-scented RIES. GROSSE LAGE v'yds: Hölle, Klaus, SCHLOSS JOHANNISBERG. GROSSLAGE (avoid!): Erntebringer. Top growers: CHAT SAUVAGE, JOHANNISHOF, PRINZ VON HESSEN, SCHLOSS JOHANNISBERG.

Johannishof (Eser) Rhg ★★→★★★ Family estate with v'yds at JOHANNISBERG, RÜDESHEIM. Johannes Eser makes wine with perfect balance of ripeness and steely acidity.

Josephshöfer Mos ★★→★★★ GROSSE LAGE v'yd at GRAACH, the sole property of KESSELSTATT. Harmonious, berry-flavoured RIES.

Jost, Toni M Rh ★★★ Leading estate in BACHARACH with monopoly Hahn, now led by Cecilia J. Aromatic RIES with nerve, and recently remarkable PINOT N 15'. Family also run estate at WALLUF (RHG).

Juliusspital Frank ★★★ Ancient WÜRZBURG charity with top v'yds all over FRANK known for *dry Silvaners* that age well. Recently less opulence and more structure – GGS now cellared 1 yr more before sale.

Kabinett See box, right. Germany's unique featherweight contribution, but with climate change ever more difficult to produce.

Kaiserstuhl Bad Outstanding district nr Rhine with notably warm climate and volcanic soil. Renowned above all for SPÄTBURGUNDER and GRAUBURGUNDER.

Kanzem Mos ★★★ SAAR village with steep GROSSE LAGE v'yd Altenberg (slate and weathered red rock). BISCHÖFLICHE WEINGÜTER TRIER, **Van Volxem**, VON OTHEGRAVEN.

Karthäuserhof Mos ★★★★ 90 01 05 07 08 09 10 11 12 13 14 15 16 17 Outstanding RUWER estate with monopoly v'yd Karthäuserhofberg. Characteristic neck-only label stands for refreshing dry and sublime sweet wines.

Kauer ★★→★★★ Family estate at BACHARACH. Fine, aromatic organic RIES. Randolf Kauer is professor of organic viticulture at GEISENHEIM.

Keller, Franz Bad See SCHWARZER ADLER.

Keller, Weingut Rhh ★★★→★★★★★ Star of RHH known for powerful GG RIES from Dalsheimer Hubacker and pricey G-Max. Plus Ries from NIERSTEIN (Hipping and Pettenthal) and outstanding PINOT N. From 2018 on, also present in M-M (Piesport Schubertslay).

Kesseler, August Rhg ★★★→★★★★ Outstanding SPÄTBURGUNDER from ASSMANNSHAUSEN and RÜDESHEIM. Also fine RIES, dry and sweet. Passionate August K has now handed over to long-time employees, continues to follow operations.

Kesselstatt, Reichsgraf von Mos ★★→★★★★★ In her 30 yrs+ hard work, Annegret Reh-Gartner (RIP 2016) made this estate splendid: 35 ha top v'yds on MOS and both tributaries, incl remarkable stake in SCHARZHOFBERG.

Kiedrich Rhg ★★→★★★★ Top RHG village, almost a monopoly of the WEIL estate, other growers (eg. FRICKE, Knyphausen, PRINZ VON HESSEN) own only small plots.

Kloster Eberbach Rhg Glorious C12 Cistercian abbey in HATTENHEIM with iconic STEINBERG, domicile of HESSISCHE STAATSWEINGÜTER.

Klumpp, Weingut Bad ★★★ Rising star in Kraichgau. SPÄTBURGUNDER LEMBERGER of depth, elegance. Markus Klumpp is married to Meike Näkel of MEYER-NÄKEL.

Knewitz, Weingut Rhh ★★★ 20-ha family estate puts RHH village of Appenheim on map. Young brothers Tobias and Björn produce focused, skillful whites. Top Hundertgulden RIES and CHARD RES 16, WEISSBURGUNDER ORTSWEIN a best buy.

Knipser, Weingut Pfz ★★★→★★★★ N PFZ family estate, barrique-aged SPÄTBURGUNDER, straightforward RIES (GG Steinbuckel), Cuvée X (B'x blend). Many specialities, incl historical bone-dry Gelber Orleans.

Germany's quality levels

The official range of qualities and styles in ascending order is (take a deep breath):

1 **Wein:** formerly known as Tafelwein. Light wine of no specified character, mostly sweetish.

2 **ggA (geschützte geographische Angabe):** or Protected Geographical Indication, formerly known as Landwein. Dryish *Wein* with some regional style. Mostly a label to avoid, but some thoughtful estates use the *Landwein*, or ggA designation to bypass official constraints.

3 **gU (geschützte Ursprungsbezeichnung):** or protected Designation of Origin. Replacing QUALITÄTSWEIN.

4 **Qualitätswein:** dry or sweetish wine with sugar added before fermentation to increase its strength, but tested for quality and with distinct local and grape character. Don't despair.

5 **Kabinett:** dry/dryish natural (unsugared) wine of distinct personality and distinguishing lightness. Can occasionally be sublime – esp with a few yrs' age.

6 **Spätlese:** stronger, often sweeter than KABINETT. Full-bodied. Today many top SPÄTLESEN are TROCKEN or completely dry.

7 **Auslese:** sweeter and sometimes stronger than Spätlese, often with honey-like flavours, intense and long-lived. Occasionally dry and weighty.

8 **Beerenauslese (BA):** v. sweet, sometimes strong, intense. Can be superb.

9 **Eiswein:** from naturally frozen grapes of BA/TBA quality: concentrated, sharpish and v. sweet. Some examples are extreme, unharmonious.

10 **Trockenbeerenauslese (TBA):** intensely sweet and aromatic; alcohol slight. Extraordinary and everlasting.

GERMANY

Kraichgau Bad Small district se of Heidelberg. Top growers: HEITLINGER/BURG RAVENSBURG, Hoensbroech, Hummel, KLUMPP.

Krone, Weingut Rhg ★★→★★★ 99' 05 06 07 08 09 10 11 12 13' 14 15' 16 Famous SPÄTBURGUNDER estate with old v'yds in ASSMANNSHAUSEN's steep Höllenberg (slate), run by WEGELER. Whites less exciting.

Kühling-Gillot Rhh ★★★★ Top bio estate, run by Caroline Gillot and husband HO Spanier. Best in already outstanding range of ROTER HANG RIES: GG Rothenberg Wurzelecht from ungrafted, 70 yrs+ vines.

Kühn, Peter Jakob Rhg ★★★→★★★★ Excellent estate in OESTRICH led by PJ Kühn and son. Obsessive bio v'yd management and long macerations shape *nonconformist but exciting* RIES. Lenchen TBA 15' is a miracle of freshness.

Kuhn, Philipp Pfz ★★★ Reliable producer in Laumersheim. Dry RIES rich and harmonious (now also SAUMAGEN), barrel-aged SPÄTBURGUNDER succulent, complex and excellent range of specialities (eg. FRÜHBURGUNDER, SAUV BL, SEKT).

Künstler Rhg ★★★ Superb dry RIES in GROSSE LAGE sites at HOCHHEIM, eg. Hölle 03 04 05 07' 08 09' 10 11 12 13 14 15 16, Kostheim, and now on other side of RHG at RÜDESHEIM (15' 16 Berg Schlossberg) and ASSMANNSHAUSEN (15 Höllenberg PINOT N).

Kuntz, Sybille Mos ★★★ Progressive individual organic 12-ha estate at Lieser, esp Niederberg-Helden v'yd. Intense wines, one of each ripeness category, intended for gastronomy, listed in many top restaurants.

Laible, Alexander Bad ★★→★★★ New DURBACH estate of ANDREAS LAIBLE's (see next entry) younger son; aromatic dry RIES and WEISSBURGUNDER.

Laible, Andreas Bad ★★★ Crystalline dry RIES from DURBACH's Plauelrain v'yd and gd SCHEUREBE, GEWÜRZ. In 2014, outstanding PINOT GR *GG Stollenberg*: creamy and tight-knit at same time.

Landwein Now "ggA". *See* box, p.161.

Langwerth von Simmern Rhg ★★→★★★ Famous Eltville estate, traditional winemaking, now back on form. Top v'yds: Baiken (sublime KABINETT), Mannberg (monopoly), Marcobrunn (sensational TBA in yrs like 05 and 15).

Lanius-Knab M Rh ★★★ Often overlooked family estate at Oberwesel, MITTELRHEIN: crystalline but also harmonious RIES at all levels. Superb Oelsberg SPÄTLESE 16 and equally outstanding Engehöll Bernstein Am Lauerbaum GG 15.

Lauer Mos ★★★ Fine, precise RIES: tense, poised. Parcel selections from huge Ayler Kupp v'yd. Best: Kern, Schonfels, Stirn.

Leitz, Josef Rhg ★★★ RÜDESHEIM family estate for rich but elegant dry and sweet RIES esp from classified v'yds.

Liebfrauenstift, Weingut Rhh Owner of best plots of historical LIEBFRAUENSTIFT-KIRCHENSTÜCK v'yd. Formerly linked to a merchant house, but now autonomous. Promising: Katharina Prüm (of JJ PRÜM) consults.

Liebfrauenstift-Kirchenstück Rhh A walled v'yd in city of Worms producing flowery RIES from gravelly soil. Producers: Gutzler, Schembs (01' almost youthful in 2017), WEINGUT LIEBFRAUENSTIFT. Not to be confused with Liebfraumilch, a cheap and tasteless imitation.

Loewen, Carl Mos ★★★ RIES of elegance, tension, complexity. Best v'yd Longuicher Maximin Herrenberg (planted 1896, ungrafted). Entry-level Ries Varidor excellent *value*.

Loosen, Weingut Dr. M-M ★★→★★★ 90 97 01 05 08 09 10 11 12 13 14 15 16 17 Charismatic Ernie Loosen produces traditional RIES from old vines in BERNKASTEL, ERDEN, GRAACH, ÜRZIG, WEHLEN. Erdener Prälat AUSLESE is cultish. Dr. L Ries, from bought-in grapes, is reliable. *See also* WOLF (PFZ), Chateau Ste Michelle (Washington State), J. Christopher (Oregon).

Lorch Rhg ★ →★★★ Village in extreme w of RHG. Sharply crystalline wines, now re-discovered. Best: CHAT SAUVAGE, FRICKE, Johanninger, KESSELER, von Kanitz.

Löwenstein, Fürst Frank, Rhg ★★★ Princely estate with holdings in RHG, FRANK. Classic Rhg RIES from HALLGARTEN, unique *Silvaner, Ries* from ultra-steep v'yd Homburger Kallmuth.

Marcobrunn Rhg Historic 7-ha v'yd in Erbach; in C19 considered one of Germany's v. best, but today much disputed: Has water balance changed? Base of slope nr Bundesstrasse seems to be more humid than before. Potential for outstanding RIES is still there. Growers: HESSISCHE STAATSWEINGÜTER, Knyphausen, LANGWERTH, Schloss Reinhartshausen.

Germany's most party-loving region? Pfz – around 220 wine festivals/yr.

Markgräflerland Bad District s of Freiburg, cool climate due to breezes from Black Forest. Typical GUTEDEL a pleasant companion for local cuisine. Climate change makes PINOT varieties successful.

Markgraf von Baden Bad ★★→★★★ Important noble estate (135 ha) at Salem castle (BODENSEE) and Staufenberg castle (ORTENAU), young Prince Bernhard being more involved than his father was. Rising quality.

Maximin Grünhaus Mos ★★★★ 83 90 97 99 01 05 07 08 09 11 12 13 14 15 16 17 Supreme RUWER estate led by Carl von Schubert, who also presides over GROSSER RING (VDP MOS). V. traditional winemaking shapes herb-scented, *delicate, long-lived Ries*. Astonishing WEISSBURGUNDER, PINOT N.

Merkelbach, Weingut M-M ★★→★★★ Tiny Estate at ÜRZIG, 2 ha. Brothers Alfred and Rolf (both c.80) produce inexpensive MOS made not to sip, but to drink. Superb list of old vintages.

Meyer-Näkel Ahr ★★★→★★★★ Werner Näkel and daughters make fine AHR Valley SPÄTBURGUNDER that exemplifies modern, oak-aged style. Also in S Africa (Zwalu, together with Neil Ellis) and Portugal (Quinta da Carvalhosa).

Mittelhaardt Pfz The n-central and best part of PFZ, incl DEIDESHEIM, FORST, RUPPERTSBERG, WACHENHEIM; largely planted with RIES.

Mittelmosel Central and best part of MOS, a RIES eldorado, incl BERNKASTEL, BRAUNEBERG, GRAACH, PIESPORT, WEHLEN, etc.

Mittelrhein ★★ →★★★ Dramatically scenic Rhine area nr tourist-magnet Loreley. Best villages: BACHARACH, BOPPARD. Delicate yet *steely Ries, underrated* and underpriced.

Until 1925, Mos village Brauneberg was called "Dusemond" (= *mont doux*, "sweet mountain").

GERMANY

Molitor, Markus M-M, Mos ★★★ Growing estate (now 100 ha in 170 parcels throughout M-M and SAAR) led by perfectionist Markus M. Offers styles, v'yds and vintages in amazing depth.

Mosbacher Pfz ★★★ Some of best GG RIES of FORST: rather refined than massive. Traditional ageing in big oak casks. Excellent SAUV BL too ("Fumé").

Mosel (Moselle in French) Wine-growing area formerly known as Mosel-Saar-Ruwer. Conditions on the RUWER and SAAR tributaries are v. different from those along the Mosel. 60% RIES.

Moselland, Winzergenossenschaft Mos Huge MOS co-op, at BERNKASTEL, after mergers with co-ops in NA, PFZ; 3290 members, 2400 ha. Little is above average.

Nackenheim Rhh ★→★★★★ NIERSTEIN neighbour with GROSSE LAGE Rothenberg on red shale, famous for *Rhh's richest Ries*, superb TBA. Top growers: **Gunderloch**, KÜHLING-GILLOT.

Nahe Na Tributary of the Rhine and dynamic region with dozens of lesser-known producers, excellent value. Great variety of soils; best RIES from slate has almost MOS-like raciness.

Naturrein "Naturally pure": designation on old labels (pre-1971), indicating as little technical intervention as possible, esp no chaptalizing (sugar added at fermentation). Should be brought back.

Neipperg, Graf von Würt ★★★ LEMBERGER and SPÄTBURGUNDER of grace and purity, and v. fine sweet TRAMINER. Count Karl-Eugen von Neipperg's younger brother Stephan makes wine at Canon la Gaffelière in St-Émilion and elsewhere.

Neus Rhh ★★★ Revived historic estate at Ingelheim, excellent PINOT N (best: Pares).

Niederhausen Na ★★→★★★★ Village of the middle NA Valley. Complex RIES from famous GROSSE LAGE Hermannshöhle and neighbouring steep slopes. Growers: CRUSIUS, **Dönnhoff**, GUT HERMANNSBERG, J Schneider, Mathern, von Racknitz.

Nierstein Rhh ★→★★★ 90 97 01 05 07 08 09 11 12 13 14 15 16 Important wine town (c.800 ha) with accordingly variable wines. Best are rich, tense, eg. GROSSE LAGE v'yds Bruderberg, Hipping, Oelberg, Orbel, Pettenthal. Growers: BUNN, FE Huff, Gehring, GUNDERLOCH, Guntrum, HEYL ZU HERRNSHEIM, KELLER, KÜHLING-GILLOT, Manz, Schätzel, ST-ANTONY, Strub. But *beware Grosslage Gutes Domtal*: a supermarket deception.

Ockfen Mos ★★→★★★ Village with almost atypical sturdy SAAR RIES from GROSSE LAGE v'yd Bockstein. Growers: OTHEGRAVEN, SANKT URBANS-HOF, WAGNER, **Zilliken**.

Odinstal, Weingut Pfz ★★→★★★ Highest v'yd of PFZ, 150m above WACHENHEIM. Bio farming and low-tech vinification bring pure RIES, SILVANER, GEWURZ. Harvest often extends into Nov.

Oechsle Scale for sugar content of grape juice.

Oestrich Rhg ★★→★★★ Exemplary steely RIES and fine AUSLESEN from GROSSE LAGE v'yds: Doosberg, Lenchen. Top growers: August Eser, KÜHN, Querbach, SPREITZER, WEGELER.

Silvaner goes orange

Fermenting white grapes on their skins – like a red wine – has become fashionable. The tannin of orange wines, however, doesn't suit every grape. SILVANER works well: FRANK's growers are the spearhead of Germany's orange movement, with wines ranging from traditionally Caucasian in style (Manfred Rothe at Nordheim uses terracotta *qvevris* from Georgia) to technically made modern re-interpretations (eg. J STÖRRLEIN & KRENIG Pure Grapes). Many more are experimenting – and the wines are worth a try.

Oppenheim Rhh ★→★★★ Town s of NIERSTEIN, GROSSE LAGE Kreuz, Sackträger. Growers: Guntrum, Kissinger, KÜHLING-GILLOT, Manz. Spectacular C13 church.

Ortenau Bad (r) w ★★ District around and s of city of Baden-Baden. Mainly Klingelberger (RIES) and SPÄTBURGUNDER from granite soils. Top villages: DURBACH, Neuweier, Waldulm.

Ortswein The 2nd rank up in VDP's pyramid of qualities: a village wine, rather than a single v'yd.

Othegraven, von Mos ★★★ Fine SAAR estate with superb GROSSE LAGE Altenberg of KANZEM, as well as parcels in OCKFEN (Bockstein) and Wawern (Herrenberg). Since 2010 owned by TV star Günther Jauch.

Palatinate English for PFALZ.

Pfalz The 2nd-largest German region, balmy climate, Lucullian lifestyle. MITTELHAARDT RIES best; s Pfalz (SÜDLICHE WEINSTRASSE) is better suited to PINOT varieties. ZELLERTAL now fashonable: cool climate.

Piesport M-M ★→★★★★ M-M village for rich, aromatic RIES. GROSSE LAGE v'yds Domherr, Goldtröpfchen. Try: GRANS-FASSIAN, Joh Haart, JULIAN HAART, K Hain, KESSELSTATT, *Reinhold Haart*, SANKT URBANS-HOF. Avoid GROSSLAGE Michelsberg.

Piwi ★→★★ Designation for crossings of European and American vines, for fungal resistance ("Pilz-Widerstandsfähigkeit"). Best known are Johanniter (w), Regent (r).

Prädikat Legally defined special attributes or qualities. *See* QMP.

Prinz von Hessen Rhg ★★★ Glorious wines from historic JOHANNISBERG estate, esp at SPÄTLESE and above, and mature vintages.

Prüm, JJ Mos ★★★★ 71 76 83 88 89 90 94 95 96 97 99 01 02 03 04 05 06 07 08 09 10 11 12 13 14 15 16 17 Legendary WEHLEN estate; also BERNKASTEL, GRAACH. Delicate but extremely long-lived wines with astonishing finesse and distinctive character.

Prüm, SA Mos ★★ Less traditional in style and less consistent than WEHLEN neighbour JJ PRÜM. Be v. selective.

QbA (Qualitätswein bestimmter Anbaugebiete) "Quality Wine", controlled as to area, grape(s), vintage. May add sugar before fermentation (as in French chaptalization). Intended as middle category, but now VDP obliges its members to label their best dry wines (GGS) as QbA. New EU name gU is scarcely found on labels (*see* box, p.161).

QmP (Qualitätswein mit Prädikat) Top category, for all wines ripe enough not to need sugaring (KABINETT to TBA).

Randersacker Frank ★★→★★★ Village s of WÜRZ with GROSSE LAGE: Pfülben. Top growers: BÜRGERSPITAL (remarkable RIES), JULIUSSPITAL, SCHMITT'S KINDER, Staatlicher Hofkeller, STÖRRLEIN & KRENIG.

Ratzenberger M Rh ★★→★★★ Family estate known for racy RIES from BACHARACH and gd SEKT too. Bought 10 ha steep slope Oberdiebacher Fürstenberg in 2017, saving it from becoming fallow.

Rauenthal Rhg ★★→★★★★ Once RHG's most expensive RIES. *Spicy, austere but* *complex* from inland slopes. All the three of Baiken, Gehrn and Rothenberg v'yds contain GROSSE LAGE and ERSTE LAGE parcels, while neighbouring Nonnenberg (sole possession of BREUER) was left unclassified, despite its equally outstanding quality. Top growers: A ESER, Breuer (with monopoly Nonnenberg), HESSISCHE STAATSWEINGÜTER, LANGWERTH VON SIMMERN.

Raumland Rhh ★★★ SEKT expert with deep cellar and a full range of fine, balanced cuvées. Superb CHARD Brut 04, disgorged 2014.

Rebholz, Ökonomierat Pfz ★★★ Top SÜDLICHE WEINSTRASSE estate, bone-dry, zesty and reliable RIES GGS, best usually Kastanienbusch from red schist 05 07' 08' 09 11' 12 14 15 16 (no 2013). Also gd CHARD, SPÄTBURGUNDER.

Restsüsse Unfermented grape sugar remaining in (or in cheap wines added to) wine to give it sweetness. Can range from 1g/l in a TROCKEN wine to 300g in a TBA.

Rheingau Birthplace of RIES. Historic s-facing slopes of Rhine between Wiesbaden and RÜDESHEIM. Classic, substantial Ries, famous for steely backbone, and small amounts of delicate SPÄTBURGUNDER. Also centre of SEKT production.

Rheinhessen Germany's largest region by far (26,600 ha and rising), between Mainz and Worms. Much dross, but also treasure trove of well-priced wines from gifted young growers.

Richter, Weingut Max Ferd M-M ★★→★★★ Reliable estate, at Mülheim. Esp gd RIES KABINETT, SPÄTLESEN: full and aromatic. Round, pretty Brut (EISWEIN dosage). Thoughtful winemaking.

Riffel Rhh ★★★ Organic family estate with holdings in Bingen's once famous Scharlachberg (red soils). RIES Turm has class, ORTSWEIN is a bargain. Now also Pét-Nat (cloudy SEKT) and barrel-fermented SILVANER.

Rings, Weingut Pfz ★★★→★★★★ Brothers Steffen and Andreas have made a name for dry RIES (esp Kallstadt SAUMAGEN), and precise SPÄTBURGUNDER (Saumagen, Felsenberg im Berntal).

Roter Hang Rhh Leading RIES area of RHH (NACKENHEIM, NIERSTEIN, OPPENHEIM). Name ("red slope") refers to red shale soil.

Ruck, Johann Frank ★★★ Spicy and age-worthy SILVANER, RIES, SCHEUREBE, TRAMINER from IPHOFEN.

Rüdesheim Rhg ★★→★★★★★ 90 01 05 08 09 10 11 12 13 14 15 16 17 Most famous RHG RIES on slate, best GROSSE LAGE v'yds (Kaisersteinfels, Roseneck, Rottland, Schlossberg) called Rüdesheimer Berg. Full-bodied but never clumsy wines, floral, gd even in off-yrs. Best growers: *Breuer*, CHAT SAUVAGE, CORVERS-KAUTER, HESSISCHE STAATSWEINGÜTER, *Johannishof*, KESSELER, KÜNSTLER, LEITZ, Ress.

Ruppertsberg Pfz ★★→★★★ MITTELHAARDT village known for elegant RIES. Growers: BASSERMANN-JORDAN, Biffar, BUHL, BÜRKLIN-WOLF, CHRISTMANN, VON WINNING.

Ruwer Mos ★★→★★★★ Tributary of MOS nr TRIER, higher in altitude than M-M. Quaffable light dry and intense sweet RIES. Best growers: Beulwitz, Karlsmühle, KARTHÄUSERHOF, KESSELSTATT, MAXIMIN GRÜNHAUS.

133 of Rheinhessen's 136 villages have v'yds. What do the other three do?

Saale-Unstrut ★→★★★ N-E region around confluence of these two rivers nr Leipzig. Terraced v'yds have Cistercian origins. Quality leaders: Böhme, Born, Gussek, Hey, Kloster Pforta, Lützkendorf (VDP member), Pawis (VDP).

Saar Mos ★★→★★★★ Tributary of Mosel, bordered by steep slopes. Most austere, steely, *brilliant Ries* of all, consistency favoured by climate change. Villages incl: AYL, KANZEM, OCKFEN, SAARBURG, Serrig, WILTINGEN (SCHARZHOFBERG).

Saarburg Mos A small town in SAAR Valley. Growers: WAGNER and ZILLIKEN. GROSSE LAGE: Rausch.

Sachsen ★→★★★ Region in Elbe Valley around Meissen and Dresden. Characterful dry whites. Best growers: Aust, Richter, **Schloss Proschwitz**, Schloss Wackerbarth, Schuh, Schwarz (try co-fermented RIES/TRAMINER), ZIMMERLING.

St-Antony Rhh ★★ →★★★ NIERSTEIN estate with exceptional v'yds. Improvements through new owner (same as HEYL ZU HERRNSHEIM). Not only RIES, also BLAUFRÄNKISCH, PINOT N.

Salm, Prinz zu Na, Rhh Owner of Schloss Wallhausen ★★→★★★ in NA and Villa Sachsen ★→★★ in RHH; ex-president of VDP. RIES at Schloss Wallhausen (organic) has made gd progress recently.

Germany's own wine satisfies only a quarter of domestic consumption: three-quarters imported.

Salwey Bad ★★★ Leading KAISERSTUHL estate. Konrad S picks early for freshness. Best: GGS Henkenberg and Eichberg GRAUBURGUNDER, Kirchberg SPÄTBURGUNDER and WEISSBURGUNDER.

Sankt Urbans-Hof Mos ★★★ Large family estate based in Leiwen, v'yds along M-M and SAAR. Limpid RIES, impeccably pure, racy.

Sauer, Horst Frank ★★★ Finest exponent of ESCHERNDORF's top v'yd Lump. Racy, straightforward *dry Silvaner* and RIES, sensational TBA (prefer 15 over 16).

Sauer, Rainer Frank ★★★ Top family estate producing seven different dry SILVANERS from ESCHERNDORF's steep slope Lump. Best: GG am Lumpen, ALTE REBEN and "L" 99' 03' 04 07' 08 13 14 15 16 17.

Saumagen Popular local dish of PFZ: stuffed pig's stomach. Also one of best v'yds of region: a calcareous site at Kallstadt producing excellent RIES, PINOT N.

Schaefer, Willi Mos ★★★ Willi S and son Christoph finest in GRAACH (but only 4 ha). MOS RIES at its best: pure, crystalline, feather-light, rewarding at all levels.

Schäfer-Fröhlich Na ★★★ Ambitious NA family estate known for spontaneously fermented RIES of great intensity, *GG* incl Bockenau Felseneck and Stromberg.

Scharzhofberg Mos ★★→★★★★ Superlative SAAR v'yd: a rare coincidence of microclimate, soil and human intelligence to bring about the perfection of RIES. Top estates: BISCHÖFLICHE WEINGÜTER TRIER, EGON MÜLLER, KESSELSTATT, VAN VOLXEM, VON HÖVEL.

Schlossböckelheim Na ★★ →★★★★ Village with GROSSE LAGE v'yds Felsenberg, Kupfergrube. Firm RIES that needs ageing. Top growers: C Bamberger, Crusius, DÖNNHOFF, GUT HERMANNSBERG, Kauer, SCHÄFER-FRÖHLICH.

Schloss Johannisberg Rhg ★★→★★★★ Historic RHG estate and Metternich mansion, 100% RIES, owned by Henkell (Oetker group). Usually v.gd SPÄTLESE Grünlack ("green sealing-wax"), AUSLESE Rosalack, reliable GUTSWEIN (Gelblack).

Schloss Lieser M-M ★★★ →★★★★ Since Thomas Haag (elder son of FRITZ HAAG estate) took over in 1997, a big success: textbook RIES both dry and sweet from Lieser (Niederberg Helden), BRAUNEBERG, WEHLEN, PIESPORT. Now also small (leased) plot in BERNKASTEL's DOCTOR. Hotel Lieser Castle has no ties to the wine estate.

Schloss Proschwitz Sachs ★★ Prince Lippe's resurrected estate at Meissen in SACHSEN; the beacon of E Germany, esp with *dry Weissburgunder*, GRAUBURGUNDER. 89 ha, S African winemaker.

Schloss Vaux Rhg ★★→★★★ SEKT house known for single v'yd RIES Sekt (eg MARCOBRUNN, RÜDESHEIMER SCHLOSSBERG). Buys wine from VDP growers, but has now also acquired 7 ha of own v'yds.

Schloss Vollrads Rhg ★★→★★★★ One of greatest historic RHG estates, now owned by a bank. Recently, obvious improvements (eg. silk RIES Edition FEINHERB 15 and ALTE REBEN 16).

Schmitt's Kinder Frank ★★→★★★ Family estate in RANDERSACKER, s of WÜRZBURG, known for classical dry SILVANER, barrel-aged SPÄTBURGUNDER, sweet RIESLANER.

Schnaitmann ★★ →★★★★ Excellent barrel-aged reds from WÜRT: SPÄTBURGUNDER, LEMBERGER from GROSSE LAGE Lämmler v'yd. Wines from lesser grapes (SCHWARZRIESLING, TROLLINGER) tasty too.

Schneider, Cornelia and Reinhold Bad ★★★ Age-worthy SPÄTBURGUNDERS 05 07 08 09 **10 11 12 13 14 15** from Endingen, KAISERSTUHL, denoted by letters – R for volcanic soil, C for loess – and old-fashioned RULÄNDER.

Schneider, Markus Pfz ★★ Shooting star in Ellerstadt, PFZ. A full range of soundly produced, trendily labelled wines.

Schoppenwein Café (or bar) wine, ie. wine by the glass.

Schwarzer Adler Bad ★★★ French restaurant (Michelin star continuously since 1969) at Oberbergen, KAISERSTUHL, and Burgundy-influenced top estate, mainly PINOTS. Top GGS Schlossberg of ACHKARREN and Kirchberg of Oberrotweil.

Schwegler, Albrecht Würt ★★★→★★★★ 7 ha, now led by young Aaron S. Red blends Beryll, Saphir, Granat 90' 94' 99' 03 05' 06' 07 **09** 10' 11 12 13 have ultra-pure fruit. Top selection Solitär only produced once in a decade 03' 11'.

Seeger Bad ★★★ Best producer of Badische Bergstrasse area s of Heidelberg. Makes outstanding PINOT N (Oberklamm GG), BLAUFRÄNKISCH (Spermen GG) and CHARD ("R").

Sekt ★→★★★★ German sparkling wine, v. variable in quality: bottle fermentation is not mandatory, nor is German origin of base wine(s). But serious Sekt producers are making spectacular progress, eg. ALDINGER, Bardong, Barth, BUHL, GRIESEL, Melsheimer, RAUMLAND, RIFFEL, Schembs, Schloss VAUX, Solter, S Steinmetz, WAGECK, WEGELER, Wilhelmshof.

Selbach-Oster M-M ★★★ Scrupulous ZELTINGEN estate with excellent v'yd portfolio, best-known for sweet PRÄDIKAT wines.

Sonnenuhr M-M Sundial. Name of GROSSE LAGE sites at BRAUNEBERG, WEHLEN, ZELTINGEN.

Sorentberg M-M ★★→★★★★ V'yd in a side valley of M-M nr Reil, fallow for 50 yrs (except a tiny plot), now replanted by young Tobias Treis and partner from South Tyrol. Red slate, RIES and promising first results. Sensational **15'** "from 1000 old vines" (but only 650 bottles).

Spätlese Late-harvest. One level riper and potentially sweeter than KABINETT. Gd examples age at least 7 yrs. Spätlese TROCKEN designation is now about to be abandoned by VDP producers: a shame.

Spreitzer Rhg ★★★ Brothers Andreas and Bernd S produce deliciously *racy, harmonious* RIES from v'yds in HATTENHEIM, OESTRICH, Mittelheim. Outstanding 15s, with a breathtaking Rosengarten TBA GOLDKAPSEL on top.

Staatlicher Hofkeller Frank ★★ Bavarian state domain; 120 ha of fine FRANK v'yds, spectacular cellars under great baroque Residenz at WÜRZBURG. Three directors in past 5 yrs: waiting for better times.

Staatsweingut / Staatliche Weinbaudomäne State wine estates or domains exist in BAD (IHRINGEN, Meersburg), WÜRT (Weinsberg), RHG (HESSISCHE STAATSWEINGÜTER), RHH (OPPENHEIM), PFZ (Neustadt), MOS (TRIER). Some have been privatized in recent yrs, eg. at Marienthal (AHR), NIEDERHAUSEN (NA).

The oldest co-ops

Between 1900 and 1930 co-ops spread like mushrooms: mildew, phylloxera and the world economic crisis forced growers to work together. But some co-ops existed long before: as early as 1855, 130 growers formed the Association für Bereitung und Verwertung des Weinmostes (Association for the Preparation and Exploitation of Wine Must) at Neckarsulm-Gundelsheim (WÜRT). In the AHR Valley, the co-op Mayschoss-Altenahr was founded 1868, and at Hagnau, BODENSEE, the village priest initiated a co-op in 1881.

> **Lemberger vs. Blaufränkisch**
> LEMBERGER and BLAUFRÄNKISCH are the same grape. The term "Lemberger"
> was – until now – used in Germany, "Blaufränkisch" in Austria. But
> young German growers (eg. HAIDLE, ST-ANTONY, Seeger) are now favouring
> the name Blaufränkisch for their wines. Easy to see why: more
> international acceptance, less pejorative connotations (Lemberger =
> lean, candy-smelling supermarket wine). But traditionalists are upset,
> and VDP WÜRT restricted the use of "Blaufränkisch" to GUTSWEIN. ORTSWEIN,
> ERSTE LAGE and GG have to be called "Lemberger".

Steigerwald Frank District in e FRANK. V'yds at considerable altitude, but soils allow powerful SILVANER, RIES. Best: CASTELL, Roth, RUCK, VETTER, WELTNER, *Wirsching*.

Steinberg Rhg ★★★ Partly walled v'yd at HATTENHEIM, est by Cistercian monks 700 yrs ago: a German Clos de Vougeot. Monopoly of HESSISCHE STAATSWEINGÜTER. Phyllite schist, berry-scented RIES, fascinating old vintages (eg. NATURREIN 43, TBA 59).

Steinwein Frank Wine from WÜRZBURG's best v'yd, Stein. Goethe's favourite. BURGERSPITAL, JULIUSSPITAL, STAATLICHER HOFKELLER all make it.

Stodden Ahr ★★★→★★★★ AHR SPÄTBURGUNDER with a burgundian touch, delicately extracted and subtle. Best usually ALTE REBEN and Rech Herrenberg. Pricey – but production is tiny.

Störrlein & Krenig Frank ★★→★★★ Family estate at RANDERSACKER known for distinctive dry SILVANER of outstanding ageability. Daughter and son-in-law bring in new ideas but maintain style.

Südliche Weinstrasse Pfz District in s PFZ, famous esp for PINOT varieties. Best growers: BECKER, Leiner, Minges, Münzberg, REBHOLZ, Siegrist, WEHRHEIM.

Taubertal Bad, Frank, Würt ★→★★★ Cool-climate district along Tauber River, divided by Napoleon into BAD, FRANK and WÜRTT sections, SILVANER from limestone soils, local red Tauberschwarz. Frost a problem. Growers: Hofmann, Schlör.

TBA (Trockenbeerenauslese) The sweetest, most expensive category of German wine, extremely rare, viscous and concentrated with dried-fruit flavours. Made from selected dried-out grapes affected by noble rot (botrytis). Half bottles a gd idea.

Thanisch, Weingut Dr. M-M ★★★ BERNKASTEL estate, founded 1636, famous for its share of the DOCTOR v'yd. After family split-up in 1988 two homonymous estates with similar qualities: Erben (heirs) Müller-Burggraef and Erben Thanisch.

Trier Mos The n capital of ancient Rome, on MOS, between RUWER and SAAR. Big charitable estates have cellars here among awesome Roman remains.

Trittenheim M-M ★★→★★★ Racy, textbook M-M RIES if from gd plots within extended GROSSE LAGE v'yd Apotheke. Growers: A CLÜSSERATH, Clüsserath-Weiler, E Clüsserath, FJ Eifel, Grans-Fassian, Milz.

Trocken Dry. Used to be defined as max 9g/l unfermented sugar. Generally the further s in Germany, the more Trocken wines.

Ürzig M-M ★★★→★★★★ 71 83 90 97 01 03 05 07 08 09 11 12 15 16 17 River village on red sandstone and red slate, famous for ungrafted old vines and *unique spicy Ries*. GROSSE LAGE v'yd: Würzgarten. Growers: Berres, Christoffel, Erbes, LOOSEN, MERKELBACH, MOLITOR, Mönchhof, Rebenhof. Threatened by controversial (will it be safe?) Autobahn bridge 160m high.

Van Volxem Mos ★★★ Historical SAAR estate revived by obsessed Roman Niewodniczanski. Low yields from top sites (KANZEM Altenberg, OCKFEN Bockstein, SCHARZHOFBERG, WILTINGEN Gottesfuss). Up to now, mainly dry or off-dry, but in 2016 a brilliant Bockstein SPÄTLESE (and a new cellar).

VDP (Verband Deutscher Prädikatsweingüter) Pace-making association of 200 premium growers. Look for its eagle insignia on wine labels, and for GROSSE LAGE logo on wines from classified v'yds. A VDP wine is usually a gd bet. President: Steffen CHRISTMANN.

Vetter, Stefan Frank ★★→★★★ Natural wine (*see* A Little Learning): SILVANER fermented on skins. To watch.

Vollenweider, Daniel Mos ★★★ A Swiss in M-M: excellent RIES in v. small quantities from Wolfer Goldgrube v'yd nr Traben-Trarbach.

Wachenheim Pfz ★★★ Celebrated village with, according to VDP, no GROSSE LAGE v'yds. See what you think. Top growers: Biffar, BÜRKLIN-WOLF, KARL SCHÄFER, ODINSTAL, WOLF.

Wageck Pfz ★★→★★★ MITTELHAARDT estate for unaffected, brisk CHARD (still and sparkling) and PINOT N of great finesse.

Wagner, Dr. Mos ★★ →★★★ Estate with v'yds in OCKFEN and Saarstein led by young Christiane W. SAAR RIES with purity, freshness.

Wagner-Stempel Rhh ★★★ Seriously crafted RHH wines from Siefersheim nr NA border. Best usually RIES GGS Heerkretz (porphyry soil).

Walluf Rhg ★★★ Underrated village, 1st with important v'yds as one leaves Wiesbaden, going w. GROSSE LAGE v'yd: Walkenberg. Growers: *JB Becker*, Jost.

Wegeler M-M, Rhg ★★ →★★★ Important family estates in OESTRICH and BERNKASTEL (both in top form) plus a stake in the famous KRONE estate of ASSMANNSHAUSEN. Geheimrat J blend maintains high standards, single-v'yd RIES usually outstanding value. Old vintages available.

Wehlen M-M ★★★ →★★★★ 90 97 01 03 05 07 08 09 10 11 12 13 14 15 16 17 Wine village with legendary steep SONNENUHR v'yd expressing RIES from slate at v. best: rich, fine, everlasting. Top growers: JJ PRÜM, Kerpen, KESSELSTATT, LOOSEN, MOLITOR, RICHTER, SA PRÜM, SCHLOSS LIESER, SELBACH-OSTER, Studert-Prüm, THANISCH, WEGELER. Concern that just-built Autobahn above v'yds will affect water balance in subsoil.

Wehrheim, Weingut Dr. Pfz ★★★ Top organic estate of SÜDLICHE WEINSTRASSE. V. dry, culinary style esp white PINOT varieties.

Weil, Robert Rhg ★★★ →★★★★ 17 37 49 59 90 97 01 05 07 08 09 11 12 13 14 15 16 17 Outstanding estate in KIEDRICH with classified v'yds Gräfenberg (steep slope on phyllite schist), Klosterberg, Turmberg. Superb sweet KABINETT to EISWEIN, gd GG; entry-level wines more variable.

Weingart M Rh ★★★ Outstanding estate at Spay, v'yds in BOPPARD (esp Hamm Feuerlay). Refined, taut RIES, low-tech in style, superb value.

Weingut Wine estate.

Weins-Prüm, Dr. M-M 4 ha of prime v'yd holdings in ERDEN, GRAACH, ÜRZIG, WEHLEN. In 2016 bought by Katharina Prüm (of JJ PRÜM) and Wilhelm Steifensand (WEINGUT LIEBFRAUENSTIFT). Label will cease to exist.

On the bulk wine market, Ries is cheaper than Grauburgunder or Sauv Bl.

Weissherbst Pale-pink wine, made from a single variety, often SPÄTBURGUNDER. V. variable quality.

Weltner, Paul Frank ★★★ STEIGERWALD family estate. Densely structured, age-worthy SILVANER from underrated Rödelseer Küchenmeister v'yd and neighbouring plots at IPHOFEN.

Wiltingen Mos ★★→★★★★ Heartland of the SAAR. SCHARZHOFBERG crowns a series of GROSSE LAGE v'yds (Braune Kupp, Braunfels, Gottesfuss, Kupp). Top growers: BISCHÖFLICHE WEINGÜTER TRIER, EGON MÜLLER, KESSELSTATT, LE GALLAIS, SANKT URBANS-HOF, VAN VOLXEM, Vols.

Winning, von Pfz ★★★→★★★★ DEIDESHEIM estate, incl former DR. DEINHARD. *Ries of great purity*, terroir expression, slightly influenced by fermentation in new FUDER casks. Also ambitious PINOT N and SAUV BL.

Winningen Mos ★★ →★★★ Lower MOS town nr Koblenz; powerful dry RIES. GROSSE

LAGE v'yds: Röttgen, Uhlen. Top growers: HEYMANN-LÖWENSTEIN, Knebel, Kröber, Richard Richter.

Wirsching, Hans Frank ★★★ Renowned estate in IPHOFEN known for classically structured dry RIES and *Silvaner*. Andrea W extends range with spontaneously fermented Ries Sister Act and kosher SILVANER. Excellent SCHEUREBE too.

Wittmann Rhh ★★★ Philipp Wittmann has propelled this bio estate to the top ranks. Crystal-pure, zesty dry RIES GG (Morstein 05 06 07' 08 11 12' 13 14 15 16).

Wöhrle Bad ★★★ Organic pioneer at Lahr (25 yrs+), son Markus a PINOT expert, excellent GGS 15' 16 (Kirchgasse GRAUBURGUNDER, Herrentisch WEISSBURGUNDER, Gottsacker CHARD).

Wöhrwag Würt ★★ →★★★ Source of elegant dry RIES – arguably best in all WÜRT. Now children Johanna, Philipp, Moritz involved too. Reds also gd.

Wolf JL Pfz ★★→★★★ WACHENHEIM estate, leased by Ernst LOOSEN of BERNKASTEL. Dry PFZ RIES (esp FORSTER Pechstein), sound and consistent rather than dazzling.

Württemberg Formerly mocked as "TROLLINGER republic", but today dynamic, with many young growers eager to experiment. Best usually LEMBERGER, SPÄTBURGUNDER. Only 30 per cent white varieties. RIES needs altitude v'yds. And, yes, gd Trollinger can be delightful too.

Würzburg Frank ★★→★★★★ Great baroque city on the Main, centre of FRANK wine. Classified v'yds: Innere Leiste, Stein, Stein-Harfe. Growers: BÜRGERSPITAL, JULIUSSPITAL, Reiss, STAATLICHER HOFKELLER, Weingut am Stein.

Zell Mos ★→★★★ Best-known lower MOS village, notorious for GROSSLAGE Schwarze Katz (Black Cat) – avoid! Gd v'yd is Merler Königslay-Terrassen, and top grower is Kallfelz.

Zellertal Pfz ★★→★★★★ Area in n PFZ, high, cool, recent gold-rush: Battenfeld-Spanier, KUHN have bought in Zellertal's best RIES v'yd Schwarzer Herrgott or neighbouring RHH plot Zellerweg am Schwarzen Herrgott. Gd local estates: Bremer, Janson Bernhard, Klosterhof Schwedthelm.

Zeltingen M-M ★★→★★★ Top but sometimes underrated MOS village nr WEHLEN. Rich though crisp RIES. GROSSE LAGE v'yd: SONNENUHR. Top growers: JJ PRÜM, MARKUS MOLITOR, SELBACH-OSTER.

Ziereisen Bad ★★ →★★★★ 05 07 08 09 10 11' 12 13 14 15 16 17 Outstanding estate in MARKGRÄFLERLAND, mainly PINOTS and GUTEDEL. Best are SPÄTBURGUNDERS from small plots: Rhini, Schulen, Talrain. Jaspis = old-vine selections.

Zilliken, Forstmeister Geltz Mos ★★★ →★★★★ 93 94 95 96 97 99 01 04 05 07 08 09 10 11 12 14 15 16 17 SAAR family estate: intense racy/savoury *Ries from Saarburg Rausch* and OCKFEN Bockstein, incl superb long-lasting AUSLESE, EISWEIN. V.gd SEKT too – and Ferdinand's gin.

Zimmerling, Klaus Sachs ★★★ Small, perfectionist estate, one of 1st to be est after the wall came down. Best v'yd is Königlicher Weinberg (King's v'yd) at Pillnitz nr Dresden. RIES, sometimes off-dry, can be exquisite.

Flourishing East

SACHS (around Dresden) has now 499 ha under vines, SA-UN (w of Leipzig) 765 ha. Shooting stars are Matthias Schuh at Sörnewitz, aged 30, producing excellent RIES, GRAUBURGUNDER from Meissen, and Matthias Hey, same age, same grapes plus remarkable red ZWEIGELT at Naumburg. Sa-Un has also a network of young growers: Breitengrad 51 ("Latitude 51"). Surprisingly, state domains have also become motors of the development: Schloss Wackerbarth producing exquisite TRAMINER and astonishing LEMBERGER, Kloster Pforta turning to old varieties, eg. Heunisch. And there is even a 1st East German MW: merchant Janek Schumann from Freiberg/Sachs.

Luxembourg

Luxembourg's wine is Mosel wine, yet really of local interest only, since Luxembourgers drink it all. The Mosel's genius for golden sweetness and fine acidity is in abeyance here; put it this way: no schist – no late harvest. The soil is limestone, and has more in common with Chablis or Champagne than Piesport. Only 11% is Riesling. The big ones are Müller-Thurgau (aka Rivaner), Auxerrois and Pinots Blanc and Gris. Crémant fizz is a strong speciality. Climate change has been kind, even if frost is still a danger (and hit in 2016 and 2017). Most whites have strong acidity and some sweetness – labels don't differentiate between dry and off-dry. A common term (but of little significance) is "Premier Grand Cru". More reliable are groups of winemakers who come together to promote their high standards: Domaine et Tradition (eight producers) has most credibility.

Alice Hartmann ★★★→★★★★ 11 12 13 14 15' 16 Star producer, in Wormeldange, with parcel selections from Luxembourg's best RIES v'yd, Koeppchen (best Les Terrasses from 70-yr-old vines). Sélection du Château has oak influence (full-bodied Ries Au Coeur de la Koeppchen, refined CHARD, remarkable PINOT N). Excellent Crémant too (Grande Cuvée, Rosé Brut). Also owns v'yds in Burgundy (St-Aubin), Mittelmosel (Trittenheim) and leases a plot in Scharzhofberg. Sells out fast.

Aly Duhr ★★→★★★ V.gd PINOT GR from Machtum, gd off-dry RIES from Ahn and elegant Ries Vendange Tardive.

Bernard-Massard ★→★★★ Big producer esp Crémant. Top labels: Château de Schengen and Clos des Rocher. Makes Sekt in Germany too.

Château Pauqué ★★★→★★★★ Passionate Abi Duhr bridges gap between Burgundy (CHARD Clos de la Falaise, Clos du Paradis AUXERROIS oak-aged) and Germany (substantial RIES Paradaïs Vieilles Vignes, Botrytis Ries in exceptional sweet/sour Auslese style).

Gales ★★→★★★ Reliable producer at Remich. Best: Crémant (value Héritage Brut, Prestige Cuvée G Brut) and Domaine et Tradition labels (eg. smoky PINOT GR 15, nuanced PINOT N 15'). Gd De Nos Rochers range. Old cellar labyrinth worth seeing.

Schumacher-Knepper ★★→★★★ Some v.gd wines produced here under Ancien Propriété Constant Knepper label (Wintringer Felsberg RIES 15'). Floral PINOT BL and savoury Elbling.

Sunnen-Hoffmann ★★★ Corinne Sunnen and brother Yves (5th generation), once merchants, turned organic growers in 2001. Now textbook whites from 9 ha around Remerschen: tense, slightly oaked CHARD Schwabsange Kolteschbierg 16, outstanding RIES Wintrange Felsbierg VV Domaine et Tradition 16 from a v'yd planted in 1943.

Other good estates: Mathis Bastian, Cep d'Or, Duhr Frères/Clos Mon Vieux Moulin, Fränk Kayl, Paul Legill, Ruppert, Schmit-Fohl, Stronck-Pinnel. Domaines Vinsmoselle is a union of co-ops.

Spain

Abbreviations used in the text:

PORTUGAL			
Alen	Alentejo	Jum	Jumilla
Alg	Algarve	La M	La Mancha
Bair	Bairrada	Mad	Madeira
Bei Int	Beira Interior	Mall	Mallorca
Lis	Lisboa	Man	Manchuela
Min	Minho	Mén	Méntrida
Set	Setúbal	Mont-M	Montilla-Moriles
Tej	Tejo	Mont	Montsant
Vin	Vinho Verde	Mur	Murcia
		Nav	Navarra
		Pen	Penedès
SPAIN		Pri	Priorat
Alel	Alella	P Vas	País Vasco
Alic	Alicante	Rib del D	Ribera
Ara	Aragón		del Duero
Bier	Bierzo	Rio	Rioja
Bul	Bullas		
Cád	Cádiz		
Can	Canary Islands		
C-La M	Castilla-		
	La Mancha	R Ala	Rioja Alavesa
C y L	Castilla y León	R Alt	Rioja Alta
Cat	Catalonia	R Baj	Rioja Baja
Cos del S	Costers del Segre	Rue	Rueda
Emp	Empordà	Som	Somontano
Ext	Extremadura	U-R	Utiel-Requena
Gal	Galicia	V'cia	Valencia

It's hard to see a direction of travel in Spanish wine today – except upwards. New terroirs, lost grape varieties, new techniques borrowed from the ancients, new rules and definitions... everywhere aspiration. What has seemed for years a pretty simple story – Tempranillo under various names, oak and time, Albariño for refreshment – has gone all fireworks. This chapter now holds as much excitement, or at least as many works in progress, as any in the book. Terroir: how to claim it, name it, legislate for it – the talk is all about the soil (it used to be the cellar, and how long in the barrel). Should we, can we, name the terroir and the particular vineyard parcel on the label? Aren't the terms Reserva and Gran Reserva long overdue for retirement? Much better to use the terroir, they say, to classify quality. You could say it's the wine world's direction of travel. The problem is that plenty of Spanish regions still seem in a daze about their soils. Where they have done research, they have not done anything sensible with the results. It's up to the wine-grower. So, as I say, much unfinished business – and lots of fireworks.

Recent Rioja vintages

2017 Calamitous frosts in many zones (April). Harvest much reduced, but quality very good.

Portugal & Spain

2016 Difficult spring, very hot summer, rain at harvest. Best have fine wines.
2015 Reliably gd Rioja again. Top wines may be as good as 2010.
2014 After two small vintages, a return to form in quality and quantity.
2013 Cool, wet year, small harvest, with some good wines.
2012 Good. One of lowest yields for two decades.
2011 Officially *excelente*; some jammy fruit, developing well.
2010 *Excelente*. A perfect year, proving itself as the wines mature.
2009 Can drink now, but will develop further.
2008 Cool year, wines fresh and aromatic, a little lower in alcohol. Ready.
2007 Difficult vintage, ready for drinking.
2006 Light fragrant vintage. Drink up.

Aalto Rib del D r ★★★→★★★★ Big, polished, structured wines: Aalto; flagship
PS (from 200 small plots). Mariano García, ex-VEGA SICILIA, builds wines for
cellaring. García's family wineries: San Román (TORO), MAURO (C Y L), Garmón (RIB
DEL D). MD Javier Zaccagnini makes own elegant Sei Solo, Preludio in winery.
Abadal, Bodegas Cat Family business in Plà de Bages DO has popular wines and CAT
specialities under series of brands: Abadal, La Fou (in Terra Alta DO), Ramón
Roqueta. Also makes wine in ancient stone tanks in National Park. Result:
fascinating, fresh, PINOT-like reds.

Abadía Retuerta C y L r ★★→★★★ Height of luxury, Michelin-starred restaurant, glam hotel – and winery. Just outside RIB DEL D. V.gd white blend DYA Le Domaine. Single-v'yd international reds steadily improving, eg. Pago Garduña SYRAH. Also PETIT VERDOT.

Abel Mendoza R Ala ★★→★★★ For knowledge of RIO villages and v'yds Abel Mendoza has few equals. Works in small batches with careful barrel selections. Five fine varietal whites. Grano a Grano range for long cellaring – every-berry-hand-selected TEMPRANILLO and GRACIANO.

Alexander Jules Sherry ★★→★★★ US-based négociant bottling selected BUTTS from eg. Juan Piñero in SANLÚCAR.

Algueira Gal r w ★★ V. fine selection, elegant reds from local varieties: Brancellao, MENCÍA. Outstanding Merenzao (aka Jura's Trousseau), almost burgundian in style.

Alicante r w sw ★→★★★ Spiritual home of MONASTRELL; spicy reds, fortified **Fondillón**. Heritage of old bush vines on interior high plateau. Top: ARTADI, Bernabé Navarro (gd natural wines, uses clay *tinajas*), ENRIQUE MENDOZA, Iberica Bruno Prats.

Almacenista Sherry, Man ★★→★★★★ A Sherry stockholding cellar, often v. small; ageing wines to sell to BODEGAS to refresh existing stocks. Important in MANZANILLA production. Can be terrific. Few left; many prefer to sell on open market eg. GUTIÉRREZ COLOSÍA.

Alonso, Bodegas Man ★★★→★★★★ Exciting new entrant to Sherry. Owners Asencio brothers also own Dominio de Urogallo (Asturias). Bought bankrupt stock of Pedro Romero, who had v. fine SOLERAS of Gaspar Florido. Their 1st release is Velo Flor, fresh 9–10 yr MANZANILLA and four-bottle set of exceptional releases of Gaspar Florido Sherries, though priced to match. One to watch.

A chance to dress up as a phylloxera louse: Sant Sadurní d'Anoia phylloxera festival.

Alonso del Yerro Rib del D, Toro r ★★→★★★ Stéphane Derenoncourt (B'x consultant) eliciting elegance from extreme continental climate of RIB DEL D. All estate wines. Top: María, inky but not in least overblown. Paydos is its wine in TORO.

Álvaro Domecq Sherry, Man ★★→★★★ Fine old BODEGA based on SOLERAS of JEREZ's oldest bodega. Polished wines. Gd FINO La Janda. Excellent 1730 VORS series.

Alvear Mont-M, Ext ★★→★★★★ Historic Alvear has superb array of PX wines in MONT-M. Gd, dry FINO CB and Capataz, lovely sweet SOLERA 1927, unctuous DULCE Viejo. V. fine vintage wines. Also owns Palacio Quemado BODEGA in Ext. Promising new wine project with ENVINATE.

Añada Vintage.

Argüeso, Herederos de Man ★★→★★★ One of SANLÚCAR's top producers, now owned by Yuste. V.gd San León, dense and salty **San León Res** and youthful Las Medallas; also impressively lively VORS AMONTILLADO Viejo.

Arrayán, Bodegas Mén ★★ Has restored reputation of MÉN with its fine GARNACHAS. Albillo Real (w) also promising.

Artadi Alic, Nav ★★→★★★★ Formed in 1985 from a growers' co-op. Since then Juan Carlos López de Lacalle has led it to outstanding success. Left RIO DO end 2015, believed it failed to defend quality. Gd-value VIÑAS de Gain, luxuriant La Poza de Ballesteros, dark, stony El Carretil; outstanding single-v'yd El Pisón. Also in ALIC with v.gd El Sequé (r), NAV with Artazuri (r, DYA p).

Arzuaga Rib del D ★★ Generous, approachable, classic GRAN RES. Hotel within v'yds.

Atlantic Wines Gal, P Vas r p w Collective term for bright, unoaked or lightly oaked style of wine, with usually firm acidity. Increasingly used to describe crisp, delicate reds. Specifically relates to wine grown close to the Atlantic – in RÍAS BAIXAS – or the Cantabrian Sea – the TXAKOLÍS. Also used to describe cool climatic influences, eg. inland GAL DOS, and specific vintages in R Ala and R Alt.

Baigorri R Ala r w ★★→★★★ Wines as glamorous as glassy architecture. Bold, modern RIO. Fine white. Polished Garage wins prizes. Top-end Belus, B70. RES v. approachable. Gd restaurant with v'yd views.

Barbadillo Man ★ ·★★★★ Grandly dominates SANLÚCAR's upper town. Range runs from supermarket to superb. Pioneer of MANZANILLA EN RAMA. Reliquía range unbeatable esp AMONTILLADO, PALO CORTADO. Outstanding century-old Versos Amontillado, just 100 bottles released 2016. Sherry guru Armando Guerra advising on adventurous new releases to transform image of traditional business. Also DYA Castillo San Diego (w), local bestseller, from PALOMINO. Also owns Vega Real (RIB DEL D), BODEGA Pirineos (SOM).

Báscula, La Alic, Rio, Jum r w sw ★★ Reliable, gd-value wines from upcoming regions, plus classics. Run by S African Bruce Jack, British MW Ed Adams.

Belondrade C y L, Rue r w ★★·★★★ Didier Belondrade was one of 1st to show potential of VERDEJO when he launched his lees-aged-in-oak RUE in 1994. Quinta Apollonia (w) and light, summery, Quinta Clarisa TEMPRANILLO (r), both C y L.

Beronia Rio r p w ★·★★★ Much improved RIO BODEGA. Classic styles are bestsellers. RES v. reliable. Top: glossy but unpronounceable III a. C. GONZÁLEZ BYASS owns.

Bierzo r w ★·★★★ There's more to Spain than TEMPRANILLO. Bierzo proves it with crunchy *Pinot-like red – Mencía* – grown on slate soils. Best sites are high altitude, and made without (too much) oak. Look for DESCENDIENTES DE J PALACIOS, RAÚL PÉREZ, plus Dominio de Tares, Losada, Luna Berberide, MENGOBA, Vino Valtuille. Bierzo also has fine GODELLO (w).

Bodega A cellar; a wine shop; a business making, blending and/or shipping wine.

Butt Sherry 600-litre barrel of long-matured American oak used for Sherry. Filled ⅚ full, allows space for FLOR to grow. Popular in Scotland, post-Sherry use: adds final polish to whisky. Trend for whites aged in ex-FINO butts – CVNE's Monopole Clasico, revival of old style.

Calatayud Ara r p w ★·★★★ Old-vine GARNACHA grown at 700–900m finally putting Calatayud on map, though still best known for cheap co-op wines. Best: Ateca, EL ESCOCÉS VOLANTE, San Alejandro.

Callejuela Sherry, Man ★★·★★★ Blanco brothers plus SANLÚCAR winemaker Ramiro Ibañez and Jerezano Willy Pérez have v'yds in some of Sherry's most famous PAGOS. Vintage releases of MANZANILLA.

Campo de Borja Ara r p w ★·★★★ Self-proclaimed "Empire of GARNACHA". Heritage of old vines, plus young v'yds makes 1st choice for gd-value Garnacha, now showing serious quality, eg. BODEGAS Alto Moncayo, Aragonesas, Borsao.

Campo Viejo r p w sp ★·★★★ RIO's biggest brand. In addition to value RES, GRAN RES, has varietal GARNACHA, and adds TEMPRANILLO Blanco to white RIO. V.gd top Res Dominio. Part of Pernod Ricard (also Calatrava-designed Ysios winery in Rio).

Canary Islands r p w ★·★★★ Ancient v'yds (*see* Falstaff) reviving; seven main islands, nine DOS. Tenerife alone has five DOs. Unusual varieties, old vines, distinct microclimates, volcanic soils. Fresh, tasty wines. Dry white LISTÁN (aka PALOMINO) and Marmajuelo, black Listán Negro, Negramoll (TINTA NEGRA), Vijariego offers *enjoyable original flavours*. Gd dessert MOSCATELS, MALVASÍAS esp fortified El Grifo from Lanzarote. ENVINATE, SUERTES DEL MARQUÉS top producers.

Cañas, Luis R Ala r w ★·★★★ One of RIO's safest buys. Classics eg. Selección de la Familia RES, youthful, enjoy-now GRAN RES, as well as moderns eg. ultra-concentrated Hiru 3 Racimos, Amaren, styles that need cellaring.

Cangas ★·★★ Isolated DO in wild Asturias beginning to export. Fresh (w) Albarín Blanco, firm red from Albarín Negro, Verdejo Negro, and most promising, Carrasquín. Producers: Dominio de Urogallo (owned by owners of BODEGAS ALONSO), Monasterio de Corias.

Capçanes, Celler de Mont r p w sw ★·★★ One of Spain's top co-ops. Great-value, expressive wines from MONT. Kosher specialist esp Peraj Ha'abib.

Cariñena Ara r p w ★→★★ The one DO that is also name of a grape variety. Solid, not exciting, but gd value; promising 3 de Tres Mil from VINOS DE PAGO FINCA Aylés. Consultant Jorge Navascués is also winemaker at CONTINO, makes own wines at Navascués Enologia: Cutio and Mas de Mancuso.

Casa Castillo Jum r ★★→★★★ Proves JUM can be tiptop. Family business high up in Jum *altiplano*. Excellent El Molar GARNACHA, Valtosca SYRAH, v. fine Las Gravas single-v'yd blend, MONASTRELL esp PIE FRANCO (plot escaped recent phylloxera).

Castell d'Encús Cos del S r w ★★→★★★ CAT wineries are searching for climates. Raül Bobet (also of PRI FERRER-BOBET) there 1st. At 1000m, he has all the cool climate he wants for *superbly fresh, original wines*. Ancient meets modern: grapes fermented in stone *lagares*, winery is up to date. In less than a decade Ekam RIES, Thalarn SYRAH, Acusp PINOT have become classics.

Castilla y León r p w ★→★★★ Spain's largest wine region. Best are v.gd; plenty to enjoy. DOS: Arlanza, Arribes, BIERZO, CIGALES, RUE, Tierra de León, Tierra del Vino de Zamora, TORO, Sierra de Salamanca, Valles de Benavente, Valtiendas, Vinos de Calidad. Red grapes: Juan García, MENCÍA and clones of TEMPRANILLO. White: Doña Blanca. Gd, deeply coloured ROSADO from Prieto Picudo. Plus independent stars: ABADÍA RETUERTA, Dehesa La Granja, MAURO, Prieto Pariente.

Castillo de Cuzcurrita R Alt Walled v'yd, C14 castle, excellent consultant Ana Martín. Great basis for v. fine RIO.

Castillo Perelada Emp, Nav, Pri r p w sp ★→★★★ Glamorous estate. Vivacious CAVAS, esp Gran Claustro; modern reds. Rare 12-yr-old, SOLERA-aged GARNATXA de l'EMPORDÀ. V. fine Casa Gran del Siurana from PRI. Recently bought CHIVITE group, an old fave of mine.

Catalonia r p w sp Vast DO, covers whole of Cat: seashore, mtn, in-between. Top chefs and top BODEGAS (eg. TORRES), many v. creative. Yet actual DO is just umbrella, too large to have identity.

Cava Spain's traditional-method sparkling. Zero dosage Brut Nature popular given ripeness of Mediterranean fruit. Majority made in PEN – in or around San Sadurní d'Anoia – also RIO (esp MUGA Conde de Haro), V'CIA. Local grapes back in favour: MACABEO (VIURA of RIO), PARELLADA, XAREL.LO (best for ageing). Best can age 10 yrs, though 9 mths is legal min. New highest category for single-v'yd wines with lower yields is CAVA DE PARAJE CALIFICADO. Still too much low-quality fizz, so producers have left DO. TORRES chose not to release new sparkler as Cava. *See* CAVA DE PARAJE CALIFICADO, CLÀSSIC PENEDÈS, CONCA DEL RÍU ANOIA.

Cava de Paraje Calificado Launched 2017 as top category of single-v'yd CAVA with stringent rules, tasting panel. Min 36 mths age, most exceed that. 14 wines passed the test: Alta Alella, Mirgin; Castellroig, Sabaté i Coca; CODORNÍU, La Pieta, El Tros Nou, La Fideura; FREIXENET, Casa Sala; GRAMONA, Enoteca, Celler Batlle, III Lustros; JUVÉ Y CAMPS, La Capella; RECAREDO, Turó d'en Mota, Serrall del Vell; Torelló, Gran Torelló; Vins el Cep, Claror.

César Florido Sherry ★→★★★ Master of MOSCATEL, since 1887. Explore gloriously scented, succulent trio: Dorado, Especial, Pasas.

Chacolí *See* TXAKOLI.

Chipiona Sherry's MOSCATEL grapes come from this sandy coastal zone. Mainly co-ops. CÉSAR FLORIDO leads the way.

Chivite Nav r p w sw ★★→★★★ Popular DYA range Gran Feudo esp ROSADO Sobre Lías (*sur lie*). Pale Las Fincas Rosado. Colección 125, incl outstanding CHARD, *one of Spain's top Chards* (the late Denis Doubordieu consulted). Gd late-harvest MOSCATEL. Sold to CASTILLO PERELADA 2017.

Clàssic Penedès Pen Category of DO PEN for traditional-method fizz, higher quality than CAVA. Min 15 mths ageing. Since 2017, organically grown grapes. Members incl Albet i Noya, Colet, LOXAREL, Mas Bertran.

Clos Mogador Pri r w ★★★ René Barbier was one of PRI's founding quintet, mentor to many. Still commands respect. One of 1st to gain a VI DE FINCA designation.

Codorníu Raventós Cos del S, Pen, Pri, Rio r p w sp ★·★★★★ Spain's oldest family BODEGA; art nouveau winery worth a visit. CAVA winemaker Bruno Colomer has innovated, raised quality across range. Outstanding Ars Collecta Cavas: Jaume Codorníu; three single-v'yd, single-variety CAVAS DE PARAJE CALIFICADO; and 456, a blend of three v'yds and most expensive Cava ever produced. Elsewhere, Legaris in RIB DEL D and Raimat in COS DEL S continue to improve. BODEGA Bilbaínas in RIO has bestseller VIÑA Pomal, top Altos de la Caseta, Vinos Singulares varietals incl Maturana Blanca, original Cava Blanc de Noirs (GARNACHA). *See also* SCALA DEI.

Conca de Barberà Cat r p w Small CAT DO once purely a feeder of quality fruit to large enterprises, now some excellent wineries, incl bio Escoda-Sanahuja. Top TORRES wines Grans Muralles, Milmanda both made in this DO.

Conca del Ríu Anoia Cat Small traditional-method sparkling DO created in 2013 by RAVENTÓS I BLANC to provide tighter quality controls than CAVA. Organic production, lower yields, min ageing 18 mths, only local grape varieties.

Consejo Regulador Organization that controls a DO – each DO has its own. Quality as inconsistent as wines they represent: some bureaucratic, others enterprising.

Contador Cat, R Alt r w ★★★ Benjamin Romeo (ex-ARTADI) is scrupulously focused on his terroir and his 20 small v'yds. Rich, *top white Que Bonito Cacareaba.* Flagship red Contador, "super-second" La Cueva del Contador. Dense but elegant single-v'yd La Viña de Andrés. Wines to lay down. Macizo is his powerful, silky GARNACHA BLANCA/XAREL·LO blend (w) in CAT.

Contino R Ala r p w ★★·★★★★ Estate incl one of RIO's great single v'yds. New winemaker Jorge Navascués took over from Jesús Madrazo 2017. A big task: Madrazo's dedication produced outstanding RES, tiptop GRACIANO, lovely white Rio and pale ROSADO. Now fully integrated into CVNE.

Costers del Segre r p w sp ★·★★★ Geographically divided DO somehow manages to draw mountainous CASTELL D'ENCÙS and lower-lying Castell del Remei, Raimat, within same boundary.

Cota 45, Bodegas Cád ★·★★ From SANLÚCAR Sherry star Ramiro Ibáñez. Ube brand is PALOMINO from different famous PAGOS, eg. Carrascal, Miraflores. Unfortified but aged in Sherry BUTTS to give FINO character. Reveals strong terroir differences.

Crianza Guarantees ageing of wine, not quality. New or unaged wine is Sin Crianza (without oak) or JOVEN. In general Crianzas must be at least 2 yrs old (with 6 mths to 1 yr in oak) and must not be released before 3rd yr. *See* RES.

Amphoras (aka *tinajas*)

The revival of amphoras is part of turning back from industrial winemaking to artisanship. Some make a specific 100-per-cent amphora wine; others keep a few lurking in corners, beside the concrete eggs, for blending and experiments esp in CAT: Josep Mitjans of LOXAREL has been a pioneer. He buys his 700–1000-litre amphoras in Ext and coats them with beeswax or pitch to keep oxygen out. Try his BIO A Pèl wines (r w). In ALIC, Rafa Bernabé of Bernabé Navarro makes his peachy Benimaquia MOSCATEL (sweet, finishing dry) in amphoras, with 4 mths on skins. Sara Pérez of MAS MARTINET (PRI) uses smaller amphoras, saying a barrel hides the wine like make-up; in pottery you see the real wine. In the name of terroir, Heretat Mont Rubi in PEN has locally made amphoras for its Sumoll (r) grapes; amphoras soften tannin. You can even find amphora wines in supermarkets, eg. U-R's Toro Loco Edición Memoria, which contains amphora wine. In MONT-M, ALVEAR still uses large old amphoras for storage, an impressive sight that has hardly changed in centuries.

Cuevas de Arom Ara r ★★ Young project from Fernando Mora MW and team, also make v.gd VDT Valdejalón at BODEGAS Frontonio, also in CAMPO DE BORJA. Elegant GARNACHAS, with focus on fruit rather than new oak.

Cusiné, Tomás Cos del S r w ★★→★★★ Innovative winemaker, now returned to CASTELL DEL REMEI; group incl Cara Nord, Cérvoles, FINCA Racons, Vilosell. Individual, modern; incl ten-variety white blend Auzells.

CVNE R Ala, R Alt r p w ★★→★★★★ One of RIO's great names. Pronounced *"coonee"*, Compañia Vinícola del Norte de España, founded 1879. Four wineries: CONTINO, CVNE, Imperial, VIÑA Real. Most impressive at top end, ethereal, less oak than most in Rio. At Imperial winery gd RES; outstanding, elegant GRAN RES; modern Real de Asúa. Viña Real is in R Ala. Recent white is Monopole Classico aged in American oak then blended in Sherry BUTTS, following traditional recipe. The great wines are long-lived; seek out 64 70.

Delgado Zuleta Man ★→★★ Oldest (1744) SANLÚCAR firm. Flagship is 6/7-yr-old *La Goya* MANZANILLA PASADA, served at wedding of King Felipe VI of Spain; also 10-yr-old Goya XL EN RAMA. Impressively aged 40-yr-old Quo Vadis? AMONTILLADO.

Díez-Mérito Sherry ★→★★★★ Cellars now owned by Salvador Espinosa. Reliable Bertola range; plus fine aged VORS Sherries: AMONTILLADO *Fino Imperial*, Victoria Regina OLOROSO, Vieja SOLERA PX.

DO / DOP (Denominación de Origen / Protegida) Former Denominación de Origen (DO)/DO Calificada (DOC) now grouped as DOP along with singleestate PAGO denomination.

Domaines Lupier Nav r ★★★ Young couple rescuing scattered v'yds of old GARNACHA focus on making two v. fine wines: floral La Dama; dense, bold El Terroir. Bio.

Dominio do Bibei Gal r w ★★★ Launched international fame of DO. Major project with start-up advice from MAS MARTINET and CLOS MOGADOR. Lapena is GODELLO grown on schist; Lalama is spicy MENCÍA blend.

Dulce Sweet.

Emilio Hidalgo Sherry ★★★→★★★★ Outstanding small family BODEGA. All wines (except PX) start by spending time under FLOR. Excellent unfiltered 15-yr-old La Panesa FINO, thrilling 50-yr-old AMONTILLADO Tresillo 1874, rare Santa Ana PX 1861.

Emilio Rojo Gal w ★★★ One man, one winery, one wine. His eponymous wine is Treixadura/LOUREIRO/ALBARIÑO/Lado/TORRONTÉS/GODELLO. Superb, with thrilling freshness. Star of RIBEIRO.

Empordà Cat r p w sw ★→★★ One of number of centres of creativity in CAT. Best: CASTILLO PERELADA, Celler Martí Fabra, Pere Guardiola, Vinyes dels Aspres. Quirky, young Espelt grows 17 varieties: try GARNACHA/CARIGNAN Saúló. Sumptuous natural sweet wine from Celler Espolla: SOLERA GRAN RES.

Enrique Mendoza Alic r w sw ★★★ Pepe, son of Enrique, serious winemaker and lively host, spokesman for ALIC and its MONASTRELLS. Top wines from dry inland *altiplano*: vibrant Tremenda, single-v'yd Las Quebradas. Honeyed MOSCATEL. Interested in FONDILLÓN.

Envínate Team of four young winemakers consulting in different regions; exemplary fresh, modern wines. Working for ALVEAR at Palacio Quemado, and at MONT-M making amphora wines. Also Almansa, Extremadura, RIBEIRA SACRA, Tenerife.

Epicure Wines Cat, Pri r w sp ★★ Sommelier Franck Massard building portfolio of characterful wines from DOS across Spain, incl CAVA, MONT, RIBEIRA SACRA, Terra Alta, VALDEORRAS. Lively ROSADO Mas Amor.

Equipo Navazos Sherry ★★★→★★★★ Jesús Barquín and Eduardo Ojeda transforming perception of Sherry with négociant approach, selecting outstanding BUTTS. Collaborations incl Dirk Niepoort, Colet-Navazos (sparkling; uses Sherry in *liqueur d'expedition*), Navazos-Palazzi (brandy), Perez Barquero (MONT-M), RAFAEL PALACIOS. FLOR Power is unfortified, flor-aged wine: homage to a JEREZ tradition.

Escocés Volante, El Gal, Ara r w ★→★★★ Norrel Robertson, Scot, MW, was flying winemaker across Spain. Settled in CALATAYUD in 2003 focusing on old-vine GARNACHA grown at altitude. Chooses to release some wines outside DO. El Mondongo blends four Garnacha v'yds fermented in egg-shaped vats. El Cismático old-vine Garnacha is 1st of series of single v'yds. Also makes ALBARIÑO in RÍAS BAIXAS, GODELLO in MONTERREI.

Espumoso Sparkling, but not made according to traditional method, unlike CAVA, so usually cheaper.

Ferrer-Bobet Pri r ★★★ Complex wines by Sergi Ferrer-Salat (who owns Barcelona's Monvinic wine bar/shop) and Raül Bobet (CASTELL D'ENCÚS). Slate soils, old vines culminate in Selecció Especial Vinyes Velles, 100% CARIÑENA (variety becoming ever more popular in PRI; Ferrer-Salat, Bobet among 1st to embrace it). Spectacular winery.

Finca Farm or estate (eg. FINCA VALPIEDRA).

Finca Allende R Alt r w ★★→★★★★ Top (in all senses) RIO BODEGA at BRIONES in ancient merchant's house with tower looking over town to v'yds, run by irrepressible Miguel Ángel de Gregorio. Single-v'yd, mineral Calvario; pure, fine Aurus. Leader in white: powerful Allende Blanco, v. fine, aromatic Martíres. FINCA Nueva is pret-à-porter range. Also Finca Coronado in LA MANCHA.

Finca Sandoval Man r ★★→★★★ Victor de la Serna, leading wine writer/critic, has own winery in DO MANCHUELA, campaigns for Manchuela and its native varieties BOBAL, MONASTRELL. FINCA Sandoval is top wine, Salia 2nd.

Flor Sherry Spanish for "flower": refers to the layer of *Saccharomyces* yeasts that grow and live on top of FINO/MANZANILLA Sherry in a BUTT ⅙ full. Flor consumes oxygen and other compounds ("biological ageing") and protects wine from oxidation. Traditional AMONTILLADOS begin as Finos or Manzanillas before the flor dies naturally or with addition of fortifying spirit. Flor grows a thicker layer nearer the sea at EL PUERTO DE SANTA MARÍA and SANLÚCAR, hence finer character of Sherry there. Most abundant in spring, autumn. Increasing trend to age unfortified wines for a short time with flor.

Fondillón Alic sw ★→★★★ Fabled unfortified *rancio* semi-sweet wine from overripe MONASTRELL grapes, made to survive sea voyages. Now matured in oak for min 10 yrs; some SOLERAS of great age. Sadly shrinking production: Brotons, GUTIÉRREZ DE LA VEGA, PRIMITIVO Quiles.

Freixenet Pen, Cava r p w sp ★→★★★ Biggest CAVA producer. Best-known for black-bottled Cordón Negro. Elyssia is step up with CHARD, PINOT N. Casa Sala is prestige top label, single-v'yd CAVA DE PARAJE CALIFICADO. La Freixeneda (r) newly launched from family's C13 estate. Other Cava brands in Ferrer family: Castellblanch, Conde de Caralt, Segura Viudas. Plus: Morlanda (PRI), Solar Viejo (RIO), Valdubón (RIB DEL D), Vionta (RÍAS BAIXAS). Also B'x négociant Yvon Mau, Henri Abelé (Champagne), Gloria Ferrer (US), Katnook (Australia), Finca Ferrer (Argentina).

Fundador Pedro Domecq Sherry Former Domecq BODEGAS sliced up through multiple mergers. VORS wines now owned by OSBORNE; *La Ina, Botaina, Rio Viejo*, VIÑA 25 by LUSTAU. Andrew Tan of Emperador, world's largest brandy company, bought remainder, focus on Fundador brandy. Group also incl Harvey's, famed for Bristol Cream and v. fine VORS, and Garvey, known for *San Patricio* FINO.

Galicia r w (sp) Isolated nw corner of Spain, destination of pilgrims walking Camino de Santiago; some of Spain's best whites (*see* MONTERREI, RÍAS BAIXAS, RIBEIRA SACRA, RIBEIRO, VALDEORRAS), bright crunchy reds (MENCÍA). Plenty of interest esp in re-emerging smaller DOS of Monterrei, Ribeira Sacra, Ribeiro.

Genéricos Rio Unappealing word in RIO to describe important, often appealing category: wines (usually prestige) that only declare vintage, avoid regulations on ageing (eg. RES or GRAN RES). GENÉRICOS need not follow DO winemaking, ageing rules. Gives flexibility to express terroir better, but some overextracted.

González Byass Sherry, Cád ★★→★★★★ Founded 1845, remains a family business. Cellarmaster Antonio Flores is a debonair, poetic presence. From the most famous of FINOS, *Tío Pepe*, Flores has developed *a fascinating portfolio: en rama and the Palmas Finos*. Alongside remain consistently polished VIÑA AB AMONTILLADO, Matúsalem OLOROSO, Noë PX. Also gd brandies; table wines, incl BERONIA (RIO), Pazos de Lusco (RÍAS BAIXAS), Vilarnau (CAVA), Viñas del Vero (SOMONTANO); plus (not so gd, but popular) Croft Original Pale Cream. FINCA Moncloa, close by to JEREZ, produces still reds; also Tintilla de Rota (sweet red fortified).

Gramona Pen, Cava r w sw sp ★★→★★★★ A taste of what CAVA can achieve. Cousins make impressively long-aged Cavas esp Enoteca, *III Lustros*, *Celler Batlle* (all three CAVA DE PARAJE CALIFICADO). Hive of investigation too, incl bio; sweet incl Icewines, experimental wines.

Gran Reserva In RIO Gran Res spends min 2 yrs in 225-litre barrique, 3 yrs in bottle. Seek out superb old Rio Gran Res, often great value. Many recent less exciting.

Guímaro Gal r w ★★ Leading name in revival of DO's reputation. Local family returning to traditional techniques: wild yeast, foot-treading, used oak barrels, single v'yds. Cepas Viejas GODELLO from oldest vines is intense, structured. FINCA Pombeiras is old-vine MENCÍA. Makes Ladredo with Dirk Niepoort.

Guita, La Man ★→★★★ Reliable *Manzanilla*. Grupo Estévez-owned (also VALDESPINO).

Gutiérrez Colosía Sherry ★→★★★ Rare remaining riverside BODEGA in EL PUERTO DE SANTA MARÍA. Former ALMACENISTA. Excellent old PALO CORTADO.

Gutiérrez de la Vega Alic r w sw ★★→★★★ Remarkable BODEGA dedicated to sweet wine. In ALIC, but no longer in DO, after disagreement over regulations. Lovely expression of MOSCATEL esp Casta Diva. Expert in FONDILLÓN. Cellar full of SOLERAS.

Hacienda Monasterio Rib del D r ★★★ PETER SISSECK still consults on 160-ha property. More accessible in price, palate than PINGUS, wines becoming more approachable.

Visiting Rio? Seven v.gd bodegas close to Haro station. Easiest oenotourism ever.

Haro R Alt Picturesque city at heart of R Alt, reputation made when railway built enabling exports to n coast and B'x. Visit great names of RIO clustered in station district: BODEGAS BILBAÍNAS, CVNE, Gomez Cruzado, LA RIOJA ALTA, LÓPEZ DE HEREDÍA, MUGA, RODA.

Harvey's Sherry ★→★★★ Once-great Sherry name, famed for Bristol Cream. Now owned by Emperador, along with Fundador Pedro Domecq and Garvey. Small range of mature VORS Sherries.

Hidalgo-La Gitana Man ★★→★★★★ Historic (1792) SANLÚCAR firm. V. refined MANZANILLA La Gitana a classic. Finest Manzanilla is single-v'yd *Pastrana Pasada*, verging on AMONTILLADO maturity. Outstanding VORS, incl Napoleon Amontillado, Triana PX, Wellington *Palo Cortado*.

Jerez de la Frontera Capital of Sherry region, between Cádiz and Seville. "Sherry" is corruption of C8 "Sherish", Moorish name of city. Pronounced "*hereth*". In French, Xérès. Hence DO is Jerez-Xérès-Sherry. MANZANILLA has own DO: Manzanilla-SANLÚCAR DE BARRAMEDA.

Joven Young, unoaked wine. *See also* CRIANZA.

Juan Carlos Sancha Rio r w ★★ Winemaker turned university professor of oenology turned winemaker, Sancha is a man who understands the soils, rare varieties and traditions of RIO. Works with lesser-known varieties – TEMPRANILLO Blanco, Maturana Tinta, Maturana Blanca, Monastel – as well as with GARNACHA.

Juan Gil Family Estates Jum r w ★→★★★ Family BODEGA; has helped transform reputation of JUM. Gd young MONASTRELLS (eg. 4 Meses); powerful, long-lived top Clio, El Nido. Group also owns impressive modern wineries, incl Ateca (CALATAYUD), Can Blau (MONT), Shaya (RUE).

Jumilla Mur r (p) (w) ★→★★★ Arid v'yds in mts n of Mur; old MONASTRELL vines revived by committed growers. TEMPRANILLO, MERLOT, CAB, SYRAH, PETIT VERDOT too. Top: CASA CASTILLO, JUAN GIL. Also: Agapito Rico, Carchelo, Castaño.

Juvé & Camps Pen, Cava w sp ★★→★★★ Consistently gd family firm for quality CAVA. RES de la Familia is stalwart, CAVA DE PARAJE CALIFICADO La Capella.

La Mancha r p w ★→★★ Quixote country, but Spain's least impressive (except for its size) wine region, s of Madrid. Key sources of grapes for distillation to brandy. Too much bulk wine, yet excellence still possible: JUAN GIL Volver, MARTÍNEZ BUJANDA's FINCA Antigua, PESQUERA's El Vínculo.

León, Jean Pen r w ★★→★★★ TORRES-owned since 1995, Mireia Torres runs this as an independent label. Earliest pioneer of CAB, CHARD in Spain, now gd, oaky Chards, expressive 3055 *Merlot*. Getting better all the time; showing a more playful side with packaging of eg. XAREL·LO.

López de Heredia R Alt r p w ★★→★★★ One of R Alt's old guard (1877), with remarkable aged wines that have magically become fashionable again. Worth a visit for Swiss "château" BODEGA, cobwebbed cellars and Zaha Hadid-designed shop. Place to see how RIO was made (as it still is). Cubillo is younger range with GARNACHA; darker Bosconia; delicate, ripe *Tondonia*. Whites have seriously long barrel and bottle age, the GRAN RES ROSADO is like no other.

Loxarel Pen r p w sp ★★ Josep Mitjans is passionately committed to his terroir and to XAREL·LO variety. (Loxarel is anagram). Range incl skin contact and amphora wines. Cora is fun, fresh (w). Cent Nou 109 Brut Nature RES is quirky treat: traditional-method fizz, but lees never disgorged. Complex, cloudy, unsulphured, v. youthful after 109 mths. Bio.

Lustau ★★★→★★★★ Launched original ALMACENISTA collection. Sherries from JEREZ, SANLÚCAR, EL PUERTO. Only BODEGA to produce EN RAMA from three Sherry towns – fascinating contrasts. Emilín is superb MOSCATEL, VORS PX is outstanding, carrying age and sweetness lightly. One of few bodegas to release vintage Sherries.

Maestro Sierra, El Sherry ★★★ Discover how a small, family BODEGA used to be. Run by Mari-Carmen Borrego, following on from her mother Pilar Plá. Fine AMONTILLADO 1830 VORS, FINO, OLOROSO 1/14 VORS. Brilliant quality wines.

Málaga r w sw ★→★★★ MOSCATEL-lovers should explore hills of Málaga. TELMO RODRÍGUEZ revived ancient glories with subtle, sweet *Molino Real*. Barrel-aged No 3 Old Vines Moscatel from Jorge Ordóñez is gloriously succulent. Bentomiz has impressive portfolio of Moscatels. Sierras de Málaga DO for dry Moscatel table wines; Ordóñez' Botani is delicately aromatic.

Mallorca r w ★→★★★ Constantly improving, if high-priced and hard to find off island. Incl 4 Kilos, Án Negra, Biniagual, Binigrau, Hereus de Ribas, Son Bordils. Reds blend traditional varieties (Callet, Fogoneu, Mantonegro) with CAB, SYRAH, MERLOT. Whites (esp CHARD) improving fast. DOS: BINISSALEM, PLÁ I LLEVANT.

Manchuela C-La M r w sw ★→★★ Traditional region for bulk wine, now showing some promise eg. Bobal, MALBEC, PETIT VERDOT. Pioneer FINCA SANDOVAL followed by Alto Landón and Ponce, producer of PIE FRANCO (rare, ungrafted vines) wine.

Marqués de Cáceres R Alt r p w ★→★★ Significant contribution to RIO in 70s, introducing French winemaking techniques. Fresh white, rosé. Gaudium is modern top wine; GRAN RES traditional classic. Owns Deusa Nai in RÍAS BAIXAS.

Marqués de Murrieta R Alt r p w ★★★→★★★★ Murrieta was in at start of RIO and kept on growing. Major investment in winery, step change in quality. Classic and modern: makes one of Rio's traditional greats, long-aged Castillo de Ygay GRAN RES. Latest release Gran Res Blanco is 86 (!), Gran Res Tinto 75. Best-value is ripe, classic RES. Dalmau is impressive contrast, modern approach to Rio, v. well made. *Capellania* is taut, complex white, one of Rio's v. best; 1st ROSADO, v. pale Primer Rosé (CARIÑENA), launched 16; v.gd Pazo de Barrantes ALBARIÑO (RÍAS BAIXAS).

Marqués de Riscal R Ala, C y L, Rue r (p) w ★★→★★★★ Riscal is living history of RIO, able to put on a tasting of every vintage going back to its 1st in 1862. Take your pick of styles today: reliable RES, modern, youthful FINCA Torrea, balanced GRAN RES. Powerful, modern style *Barón de Chirel Res.* The *marqués* discovered and launched RUE (1972). Makes vibrant DYA SAUV BL, VERDEJO, though chose to put v.gd new Barón de Chirel Verdejo in C Y L not Rue. Eye-popping Frank Gehry hotel attached.

Martínez Bujanda, Familia C-La M, Rio r p w ★→★★ Commercially astute business with a number of wineries; also makes private-label wines. Most attractive are *Finca Valpiedra*, charming single estate in RIO; FINCA Antigua in LA M.

Mas Doix Pri ★★→★★★★ Fine family business in Poboleda, blessed with 70–100-yr-old GARNACHA and CARIÑENA grown on slate. Treasure is rare, superb Cariñena, all blueberry and velvet, astonishingly pure, named after yr v'yd was planted, *1902*.

Mas Martinet Pri r ★★→★★★★ Wines of Sara Pérez have fine pedigree. Daughter of Josep Lluís Pérez, one of original PRI quintet, most passionate of Pri's 2nd generation, ever innovating, fermenting freshly picked grapes in vats in v'yds, and in *amphoras*. Venus La Universal is other project.

Mauro C y L r w ★★→★★★ Founded by Mariano García of AALTO and formerly VEGA SICILIA. Full-bodied, oak-aged style of García with Tereus and VS. Latest release is GODELLO. Now joined by sons Eduardo and Alberto, also working at San Román (TORO), Garmón (RIB DEL D).

Mengoba Bier r p w ★→★★★ Grégory Pérez makes range of wines, not all accepted within DO. In Le Vigne de Sanchomartín he co-ferments a field blend of MENCIA, GARNACHA Tintorera and GODELLO. Las Tinajas is amphora-aged Godello with 4 mths skin contact; orange wine, complex and textured. Las Botas is Godello aged in MANZANILLA butts for 10 mths.

At last count there were 1,325,629 barrels of wine gently ageing in Rio's cellars.

Méntrida C-La M r p ★→★★ Former co-op country s of Madrid, now being put on map by ARRAYÁN, Canopy and Jiménez-Landi with GARNACHA, Albillo grapes.

Monterrei Gal r w ★→★★★ Small DO on Portuguese border, where once Romans made wine. Discovering its potential, with impressive array of local varieties, blends. Best: Quinta da Muradella: fascinating parcels of unusual vines.

Montilla-Moriles ★→★★★ Andalucian DO nr Córdoba. Hidden treasure, too often regarded as JEREZ's poor relation. Makes dry to sweetest wines all with PX. Best to shop nr top end for superbly rich PX, some with long ageing in SOLERA. Top: ALVEAR, PÉREZ BARQUERO, TORO ALBALÁ. Important source of PX for use in Jerez DO.

Montsant Cat r (p) w ★→★★★ Tucked in around PRI, in the shadow of its famous neighbour. Result: better value. Varied soils, incl slate. Fine GARNACHA BLANCA esp Acústic. Dense, balsamic reds: Alfredo Arribas, Can Blau, CAPÇANES, Domènech, Espectacle, Joan d'Anguera, Mas Perinet, Masroig, Venus la Universal.

Muga R Alt r p w (sp) ★★→★★★★ The tall Muga brothers and cousin are the friendly giants of HARO, producing some of RIO's finest reds. Gd DYA VIURA; new wave pale ROSADO; lively CAVA; classic reds delicately crafted. Best: Selección Especial, wonderfully fragrant GRAN RES *Prado Enea*. Also modern Rios: powerful *Torre Muga*; expressive, complex Aro.

Mustiguillo V'cia r w ★★→★★★ Dynamic BODEGA led renaissance of unloved local Bobal grape. Created a PAGO, El Terrerazo. Mestizaje is juicy; FINCA Terrerazo more refined. Top wine is Quincha Corral. Reviving local Merseguera grape with Finca Calvestre white. Member of GRANDES PAGOS.

Navarra r p (w) sw ★→★★★ Next door to RIO and always in its shadow. Early focus on international varieties confused its identity. Best: old-vine GARNACHA from eg. DOMAINES LUPIER. Also CHIVITE, Nekeas, OCHOA, Otazu, Tandem, VIÑA Zorzal.

Ochoa Nav r p w sw sp ★→★★ Ochoa *padre* led modern growth of NAV, daughters now carry the torch. Winemaker Adriana O calls her range "8a", incl Mil Gracias Graciano and fun, sweet, Asti-like sparkling MdO.

Osborne Sherry ★★→★★★★ Osborne (1772) is all about fine old age. Outstanding v. old SOLERAS incl AOS AMONTILLADO, PDP PALO CORTADO, OLOROSO Seco BC 200, PX Solera Vieja. Owns former DOMECQ VORS incl 51–1a Amontillado. Based in EL PUERTO; its FINO Quinta and mature Coquinero FINO typical of zone. Also makes table wines in RIO, RUE, RIB DEL D.

Pago, Vinos de Pago denotes (single) v'yd. Implies top wine; not always so. Lack of objective assessment makes them much criticized. Obvious absentees incl ALVARO PALACIOS' L'Ermita, PINGUS, Calvario (FINCA ALLENDE), CONTINO's VIÑA del Olivo, TORRES properties. Pri Vi de Finca, CAVA DE PARAJE CALIFICADO go some way to find a different quality category.

Pago de los Capellanes Rib del D ★★→★★★ V. fine estate, once belonging to chaplains as name suggests, BODEGA founded 1996. All TEMPRANILLO, modern, expressive, matured in French oak. El Nogal has plenty of yrs ahead; top El Picon reveals best of RIB DEL D.

Pagos, Grandes Network of mainly family-owned BODEGAS across Spain with commitment to quality. Work together for collective marketing. Confusion of term with VINO DE PAGO. Some are Vinos de Pago but not all.

Palacio de Fefiñanes Gal w ★★★→★★★★ Standard DYA *Rías Baixas* one of finest ALBARIÑOS. Two superior styles: barrel-fermented 1583 (yr winery was founded, oldest winery of DO); super-fragrant, pricey, lees-aged, mandarin-scented "III". Visit historic palace/winery in main square at Cambados.

Palacios, Álvaro Bier, Pri, Rio r ★★★→★★★★ Álvaro P helped build global reputation for Spanish wine by his obsession with quality. One of quintet who revived PRI; his wines live up to hype. Old-vines Les Terrasses; Gratallops, polished, structured village wine; FINCA Dofí mainly GARNACHA, superbly aromatic. Les Aubaguetes, from Bellmunt, boosted by 20% CARIÑENA. Super-pricey L'Ermita, powerful, from low-yielding Garnacha. At PALACIOS REMONDO restoring reputation of RIO Baja and its Garnachas. Also with nephew at DESCIENDIENTES DE J. PALACIOS.

Palacios, Descendientes de J Bier r ★★★→★★★★ Superb wines, showing MENCÍA at its best. Ricardo Pérez Palacios, Álvaro's nephew, grows old vines on steep slate. Sadly not all BIER lives up to this promise. Gd-value, floral *Pétalos*. Villa de Corullón both superb; Las Lamas and Moncerbal are two fine, v. different soil expressions, one more clay, the other rocky. Exceptional single-v'yd La Faraona (but only one barrel), grows on complex tectonic fault. New winery. Bio.

Palacios, Rafael Gal w ★★★→★★★★ Rafael Palacios, ÁLVARO's younger brother, can't put a foot wrong in VALDEORRAS. Singular focus on GODELLO across many tiny v'yds over more than a decade. Results in textured Louro do Bolo; As Sortes, a step up; most recently *O Soro*, surely Spain's best white.

Palacios Remondo R Baj r w ★★→★★★ ALVARO PALACIOS' return to family winery has helped turn R Baj round, spotlights forgotten potential of region. Promotes concept of villages or crus, as in Burgundy. Complex, oaked Plácet (w) originally created by brother Rafael. Reds: organic, GARNACHA-led, red-fruited La Montesa; big, mulberry-flavoured, old-vine Propriedad. Top wine is Quiñon de Valmira from slopes of Monte Yerga.

Pariente, José Rue w ★★→★★★ Victoria P makes VERDEJOS of shining clarity under her father's name. Cuvée Especial fermented in concrete eggs gains fascinating complexity. Silky late-harvest Apasionado. Daughter Martina runs Prieto Pariente with brother Ignacio (also in C Y L and with GARNACHA in Sierra de Gredos).

Pazo Señorans Gal w ★★★ Consistently excellent ALBARIÑOS from beautiful RÍAS BAIXAS estate. V. fine Selección de AÑADA, proof v. best Albariños age beautifully.

Penedès Cat r w sp ★→★★★★ Demarcated region w of Barcelona, best-known for CAVA. Identity confused since arrival of all-embracing CAT DO. Best producers: Agustí Torelló Mata, Alemany i Corrio, Can Rafols dels Caus, GRAMONA, JEAN LEÓN, Parés Baltà, TORRES.

Pérez, Raúl Bier Creative winemaker. Family winery is Castro Ventosa, BIER. Works mainly in nw. Experimental, terroir-driven; many interesting wines. Provides house-room for new winemakers in his cellar. Magnet for visiting (eg. Argentine) winemakers keen to share ideas.

Pérez Barquero Mont-M ★→★★★ Part of revival of MONT-M PX. GD Gran Barquero FINO, AMONTILLADO, OLOROSO; La Cañada PX. Supplier to EQUIPO NAVAZOS.

Pérez Pascuas Rib del D r ★★→★★★★ Family business making classic RIB DEL D wines from TINTO FINO. Gd-value RES.

Pesquera, Grupo Rib del D r ★★ Veteran farmer/tractor-dealer Alejandro Fernández helped launch RIB DEL D with his excellent, simply named, Tinto Pesquera; less exciting now. Daughters now joined business. Also at Condado de Haza, Dehesa La Granja (C Y L), El Vínculo (LA MANCHA), plus hotel, restaurant and farm.

Pie franco Ungrafted vine, on own roots. Typically on sandy soils where phylloxera could not penetrate. Some are well over a century old.

Pingus, Dominio de Rib del D r ★★★★ One of RIB DEL D's modern treasures. Tiny bio winery of Pingus (PETER SISSECK's childhood name), made with old vine TINTO FINO, shows refinement of variety. *Flor de Pingus* from younger vines; Amelia is single barrel named after his wife. PSI uses grapes from growers, long-term social project to encourage them to preserve vines and stay on land.

Priorat r w ★★→★★★★ Some of Spain's finest wines. Magical isolated mtn, named after old monastery tucked under craggy cliffs. Rescued in 80s by quintet of René Barbier of CLOS MOGADOR, ÁLVARO PALACIOS, others. Experience, expense stopped early overoaking. In its place is remarkable purity, sense of place. Pri has pioneered introduction of "village" crus within Pri and Vi de FINCA.

Puerto de Santa María, El One of three towns forming "Sherry Triangle". Production now in decline; remaining BODEGAS: GUTIÉRREZ COLOSÍA, OSBORNE, TERRY. Puerto FINOS prized as less weighty than JEREZ, not as "salty" as SANLÚCAR. Taste Lustau's three EN RAMAS to taste different characters of Sherries aged in the three towns.

Raventós i Blanc Pen p w ★★→★★★ One of stars of traditional-method sparkling. Pepe R left CAVA and created higher specification CONCA DEL RÍU ANOIA DO. V. fine ROSADO De Nit. Zero SO2 Extrem (no added sulphur) v. lively, textured. Textures de Pedra is ringingly pure Blanc de Noirs. Bio.

Recaredo Pen, Cava w sp ★★→★★★ Outstanding CAVA producer, small family concern. Few wines, all outstanding. Hand-disgorges all bottles. Tops is characterful, mineral *Turó d'en Mota*, CAVA DE PARAJE CALIFICADO, from vines planted 1940, ages brilliantly. Bio.

Remelluri, La Granja Nuestra Señora R Ala r w ★★→★★★ TELMO RODRIGUEZ returned to his family property. Makes his original multi-varietal white here. Developing single v'yds nearby. Campaigns for quality, terroir, traditional methods, varieties.

Reserva (Res) Unusually in the wine world, Res has actual meaning in RIO, where Res means aged for min 3 yrs of which 1 yr is in oak. Increasingly producers prefer to ignore regulations, in order to choose barrels larger than regulation 225 litres, and to age for different periods.

Rey Fernando de Castilla Sherry ★★→★★★★ Gloriously consistent quality. Seek out Antique Sherries; all qualify as VOS or VORS, but label doesn't say so. Youngest of these, Antique FINO, is fascinating, complex, fortified to historically correct 17% alc. Also v. fine brandy, vinegar. Favoured supsplier to EQUIPO NAVAZOS.

Rías Baixas Gal (r) w ★★→★★★ Atlantic DO growing ALBARIÑO in five subzones, mostly DYA. Best: Forjas del Salnés, Gerardo Méndez, Martín Códax, PALACIO DE

FEFIÑANES, Pazo de Barrantes, *Pazo Señorans*, Terras Gauda, ZÁRATE. Until recently Spain's premier DO for whites, now at risk of overproduction. Influential new generation of consultant winemakers: Dominique Roujou de Boubée (As Bateas for ADEGA Pombal), RAÚL PÉREZ (Sketch).

Ribeira Sacra Gal r w ★★→★★★ Magical DO with v'yds running dizzyingly down to River Sil. Increasingly fashionable esp for fresh reds. Top: ADEGAS Moure, ALGUEIRA, DOMINIO DO BIBEI, GUÍMARO.

Ribeiro Gal (r) w ★→★★★ Historic region, famed in Middle Ages for Tostado sweet wine. Undergoing revival, with fresh, light whites made from GODELLO, LOUREIRO, Treixadura. Top: Casal de Armán, Coto de Gomariz, EMILIO ROJO, FINCA Viñoa.

Ribera del Duero r p (w) ★→★★★★ Ambitious DO with great appeal in Spain, created 1982. Anything that incl AALTO, HACIENDA MONASTERIO, PESQUERA, PINGUS, VEGA SICILIA has to be serious, but with 280 BODEGAS consistency hard to find. Too many v'yds planted in wrong places. With time elegance breaking through. Other top names: ALIÓN, ALONSO DEL YERRO, Cillar de Silos, *Pago de los Capellanes*. Also of interest: ARZUAGA, Bohórquez, Dominio de Atauta, Emilio Moro, FINCA Villacreces, Garmón, La Horra, O Fournier, PÉREZ PASCUAS, Sastre, Tomás Postigo. *See also* C Y L neighbours ABADÍA RETUERTA, MAURO.

Rioja r p w sp ★→★★★★ Spain's most famous wine region. Three sub-regions: R Alt, R Baj and R Ala. Range of soils and altitudes. Many classic wines, but also undergoing a transformation, with more varieties, fresher styles.

Rioja Alta, La R Ala, R Alt r ★★→★★★★ For lovers of classic RIO, an easy choice. Vanilla-edged *Gran Res 904* and GRAN RES 890, aged 6 yrs in oak are stars. But rest of range from *Ardanza*, down to Arana, Alberdi each carry classic house style. Also owns R Ala modern-style Torre de Oña with new Martelo, RÍAS BAIXAS Lagar de Cervera, RIB DEL D Àster.

Sherry is on the move at last: six new bodegas registered in 2017 alone.

Rioja 'n' Roll Something new for RIO. New generation of winemakers formed a network for fun and for marketing. All small production, with serious focus on v'yds. Seek them out: Alegre & Valgañón, Artuke, Barbarot, Exopto, Laventura, Olivier Rivière, Sierra de Toloño.

Roda Rib del D, R Alt r ★★→★★★ Modern HARO BODEGA, though at 30+ yrs more of a modern classic. Serious RES reds from low-yield TEMPRANILLO, backed by continued research: Roda, Roda I, Cirsión and approachable Sela. Doing it again with RIB DEL D Bodegas La Horra, making Corimbo and Corimbo I.

Rosado Rosé. NAV GARNACHA rosados finally gave in to Provençal paleness. Recently Spain been fighting back esp with: SCALA DEI's Pla dels Àngels (PRI), Ramón Bilbao's Lalomba (RIO), MARQUÉS DE MURRIETA's Primer Rosé (Rio), Flor de MUGA (Rio).

Rueda C y L w ★→★★★ Spain's response to SAUV BL: zesty VERDEJO. Mostly DYA whites. "Rueda Verdejo" is 85%+ indigenous Verdejo. "Rueda" is blended with eg. Sauv Bl, VIURA. Too much poor quality. Best: *Belondrade*, JOSÉ PARIENTE, MARQUÉS DE RISCAL, Naia, Ossian, Viñedos de Nieva.

Saca A withdrawal of Sherry from the SOLERA (oldest stage of ageing) for bottling. For EN RAMA wines most common *sacas* are in *primavera* (spring) and *otoño* (autumn), when FLOR is richest, most protective.

Sacramento, El Rio ★→★★★ Impressive new estate: new winery, with old-vine v'yds outside Laguardia. Project of Etienne Cordonnier-Lezaola, with Jesús Madrazo, formerly of CONTINO. Still early days, but great pedigree. v. promising.

Sánchez Romate Sherry ★★→★★★ Old (1781) BODEGA with extensive range, also sourcing and bottling rare BUTTS for négociants and retailers. 8-yr-old *Fino Perdido*, nutty AMONTILLADO NPU, PALO CORTADO Regente, excellent VORS AMONTILLADO and OLOROSO La Sacristía de Romate, unctuous Sacristía PX.

SPAIN

Sandeman Sherry ★→★★ More famous for its Port than its Sherry. Interesting VOS wines: Royal Esmeralda AMONTILLADO, Royal Corregidor Rich Old OLOROSO.

Sanlúcar de Barrameda Sherry-triangle town (with JEREZ, EL PUERTO DE STA MARÍA) at mouth of River Guadalquivír. The port where Magellan, Columbus and the CO of the Armada set off. Humidity in low-lying cellars encourages FLOR. Sea air said to give wines perfect microclimate. Wines aged under flor in Sanlúcar BODEGAS qualify for DO MANZANILLA-Sanlúcar de Barrameda.

Scala Dei Pri r w ★★★ Tiny v'yds of "stairway to heaven" cling to craggy slopes above old monastery. Managed by part-owner CODORNÍU. Winemaker Ricard Rofes restoring old methods, fermenting in stone *lagares*. Focus on local varieties esp GARNACHA. Single-v'yds Sant'Antoni and Mas Deu show character. Pla dels Àngels is refreshing ROSADO. At Monasterio de Poblet in COS DEL S, UNESCO World Hertitage Site, Rofes is reviving use of Garnacha, Garrut, Trepat grapes.

Sierra Cantabria R Ala, Toro r w ★★★ Persistent quiet excellence. Eguren family specialize in single-v'yd, min-intervention wines. Organza (w). Reds, all TEMPRANILLO. At Viñedos de Paganos, superb El Puntido; powerful, structured La Nieta. Other properties: Señorío de San Vicente in RIO and Teso la Monja in TORO.

Sisseck, Peter Rib del D *See* PINGUS.

Solera Sherry System for blending Sherry and, less commonly, Madeira (*see* Portugal). Consists of topping up progressively more mature BUTTS with younger wines of same sort from previous stage, or *criadera*. Maintains vigour of FLOR, gives consistency, refreshes mature wines.

Somontano r p w ★→★★ DO in Pyrénéan foothills still searching for an identity, growing many international varieties. Opt for GEWURZ – rare for Spain. Try Enate, Viñas del Vero (owned by GONZÁLEZ BYASS) – its high-altitude Secastilla has gd old-vine GARNACHA, GARNACHA BLANCA.

Suertes del Marqués Can r w ★→★★ Rising star in Tenerife. Founded 2006, works with 21 plots of LISTÁN Blanco and Listán Negro. Exceptional v'yds, with unique *trenzado* – plaited vines.

Telmo Rodríguez, Compañía de Vinos Rio, Mál, Toro r w sw ★★→★★★ Telmo Rodríguez has returned to REMELLURI. His pioneering business, rediscovering old vines across Spain, still continues. MÁLAGA (*Molino Real* MOSCATEL), ALIC (Al-Murvedre), RIO (Lanzaga), RUEDA (Basa), TORO (Dehesa Gago), Cigales (Pegaso), *Valdeorras* (DYA Gaba do Xil GODELLO). Return to Rio has led to launch of exceptionally pure Las Beatas, tiny single v'yd of old-vine GARNACHA.

Toro r ★→★★★ Small DO w of Valladolid famed for rustic wines from Tinta del Toro (TEMPRANILLO). Today best more restrained, but still firm tannic grip. Dense old-vine San Román. Glamour from VEGA SICILIA-owned Pintia, and LVMH property Numanthia. Also: PAGO la Jara from TELMO RODRÍGUEZ, Paydos, Teso la Monja.

Toro Albalá Mont-M ★→★★★★ From young dry FINOS to glorious sweet wines, a triumph for MONT-M. Among them lively AMONTILLADO Viejísimo. Seek out remarkable, sumptuous Don PX Convento Selección 1931.

Torres Cat, Pri, Rio r p w sw ★★→★★★★ Spain's leading BODEGA for many yrs continues to make the news. Miguel Jr and sister Mireia are full-time, Miguel Sr is busy on many fronts. Latest release is long-awaited Vardon Kennett, oddly named but beautifully packaged traditional-method sparkling (not CAVA). Best reds: outstanding, elegant B'x-blend *Res Real*, top PEN CAB *Mas la Plana*; CONCA DE BARBERÀ duo (burgundy-like *Milmanda*, one of Spain's finest CHARDS, *Grans Muralles* blend of local varieties) is stunning. In RIB DEL D Celeste continues to improve as does RIO Ibéricos, and PRI Salmos. Owns JEAN LEÓN. Ahead-of-time pioneer in Chile; noble wines there too.

Tradición Sherry ★★→★★★★ BODEGA assembled by the great José Ignacio Domecq from an exceptional selection of SOLERAS. Based on the oldest-known Sherry

Sherry styles

Manzanilla: fashionable pale, dry, low-strength (15% alc): supposedly green-appley. The world's best-value dry white wine; sip it with almost any food, esp crustaceans. Matured by the sea at SANLÚCAR where the FLOR grows thickly and the wine grows salty. Drink cold and drink up; it fades when open like any top white. Eg. HEREDEROS DE ARGÜESO, San León RES.

Manzanilla Pasada: mature MANZANILLA, where flor is fading; v. dry, complex. Eg. HIDALGO-LA GITANA's single-v'yd Manzanilla Pasada Pastrana.

Fino: pale, dry, biologically aged in JEREZ or EL PUERTO DE SANTA MARÍA; weightier than Manzanilla; 2 yrs age min (as Manzanilla). Eg. GONZÁLEZ BYASS 4-yr-old Tío Pepe. Serve as Manzanilla, don't keep more than one week once opened. Trend for mature Finos aged more than 8 yrs, eg. FERNANDO DE CASTILLA Antique, González Byass Palmas range.

Amontillado: FINO in which layer of protective yeast flor has died. Oxygen gives more complexity. Naturally dry. Eg. LUSTAU Los Arcos. Commercial styles sweetened.

Oloroso: not aged under flor. Heavier, less brilliant when young, matures to nutty intensity. Naturally ultra-dry, even fierce. May be sweetened with PX and sold as Cream. Eg. EMILIO HIDALGO Gobernador (dr), Old East India (sw). Keeps well.

Palo Cortado: v. fashionable. Traditionally wine that had lost flor – between AMONTILLADO and v. delicate OLOROSO. Difficult to identify with certainty, though some suggest it has a keynote "lactic" or "bitter butter" note. Rich, complex: worth looking for. Eg. BARBADILLO Reliquía, Fernando de Castilla Antique. Drink with meat or cheese.

Cream: blend sweetened with grape must, PX and/or MOSCATEL for a commercial medium-sweet style. Few great Creams as old VORS: EQUIPO NAVAZOS La Bota No. 21 is outstanding exception.

En Rama: Manzanilla or Fino bottled from BUTT with little or no filtration or cold stabilization to reveal full character of Sherry. More flavoursome, said to be less stable. Seasonal bottlings, in small batches, sell out fast. *Saca* or withdrawal is typically when flor is most abundant. Keep in fridge, drink up quickly.

Pedro Ximénez (PX): raisined sweet, dark, from partly sun-dried PX grapes (grapes mainly from MONT-M; wine matured in Jerez DO). Unctuous, decadent, bargain. Sip with ice-cream. Tokaji Essencia apart, world's sweetest wine. Eg. Emilio Hidalgo Santa Ana 1861, LUSTAU VORS.

Moscatel: aromatic appeal, around half sugar of PX. Eg. Lustau Emilín, VALDESPINO Toneles. Now permitted to be called "Jerez".

VOS / VORS: age-dated Sherries: some of treasures of Jerez BODEGAS. A v. necessary move to raise the perceived value of Sherry. Wines assessed by carbon dating to be more than 20 yrs old are called VOS (Very Old Sherry/Vinum Optimum Signatum); those over 30 yrs old are VORS (Very Old Rare Sherry/Vinum Optimum Rare Signatum). Also 12-yr-old, 15-yr-old examples. Applies only to Amontillado, Oloroso, PALO CORTADO, PX. Eg. VOS Hidalgo Jerez Cortado Wellington. Some VORS wines are softened with PX: sadly producers can be overgenerous with PX. VORS with more than 5 g/l residual sugar are labelled Medium.

Añada "Vintage": Sherry with declared vintage. Runs counter to tradition of vintage blended SOLERA. Formerly private bottlings now winning public accolades. Eg. Lustau Sweet Oloroso Añada 1997.

house (1650). Glorious VOS, VORS Sherries, also a 12-yr-old FINO. Outstanding art collection and archives of Sherry history.

Txakolí / Chacolí P Vas (r) (p) w (sw) ★→★★ Wines from Basque country DOS in Getaria, Bizkaya and Alava. Many v'yds face Atlantic winds and soaking rain, hence sharp crunchiness of *pétillant* whites esp in Getaria where DYA Txakolí is poured into tumblers from a height to add to spritz. Bizkaya wines, with less exposed v'yds, can have depth and need not be DYA. Top: Ameztoi, Astobiza, Doniene Gorrondona, Txomín Etxaníz. Also Gorka Izagirre, with Michelin three-star restaurant Azurmendi, nr Bilbao airport.

Utiel-Requena U-R r p (w) ★→★★ Marriage of two towns, slowly forging its own identity with Bobal grape. Try: Bruno Murciano, Caprasia, Cerrogallina.

Valdeorras Gal r w ★→★★★ Warmest, most inland of GAL's DOS, named after gold Romans found in valleys. Exceptional GODELLO, potentially more interesting than ALBARIÑO, driving change. Best: Godeval, RAFAEL PALACIOS, TELMO RODRÍGUEZ, Valdesil.

Valdepeñas C-La M r (w) ★→★★ Large DO s of LA MANCHA. Known for cheap reds (eg. Albali), but losing importance to eg. CAMPO DE BORJA.

Valdespino Sherry ★★→★★★★ Home to Inocente FINO from top Macharnudo single-v'yd, rare oak-fermented Sherry (EN RAMA version bottled by EQUIPO NAVAZOS). Terrific dry AMONTILLADO Tío Diego; vibrant SOLERA 1842 OLOROSO VOS; outstanding 80-yr-old *Toneles* MOSCATEL, JEREZ's v. best. Winemaker is Eduardo Ojeda. Owned by Grupo Estévez (also owns LA GUITA).

Valencia r p w sw ★→★★ Known for anonymous bulk wine and cheap, sweet MOSCATEL, and still guilty. One producer to note: Murviedro. Higher-altitude old vines and min-intervention winemaking: eg. Aranleon, Celler del Roure, El Angosto, Los Frailes could change things.

VDT (Vino de la Tierra) Table wine usually of superior quality made in a demarcated region without DO. Covers immense geographical possibilities; category incl many prestigious producers, non-DO by choice to be freer of inflexible regulation and use varieties they want. (*See* Super Tuscan, Italy).

Vega Sicilia Rib del D r ★★★★ Spain's First Growth has a new winemaker. But these wines take yrs, so any change of style will be slow. Único, aged 6 yrs in oak; second wine *Valbuena* outstanding despite lesser status. Flagship: RES Especial, NV blend of three vintages, with up to 10 yrs in barrel; v. fine. Neighbouring Alión shows modern take on RIB DEL D. Owns TORO property Pintia, Oremus in Tokaji (Hungary), joint-venture project Macan in RIO with Rothschild.

Vendimia Harvest.

Vi de Finca Pri Single-v'yd category: in PRI, wine made for 10 yrs from same single v'yd and commercially recognized as such. Pioneered by ÁLVARO PALACIOS and colleagues, following Burgundian model.

Viña Literally, a v'yd.

Viña Zorzal Nav, Rio Entrepreneurial new generation making young gd-value wines, eg. GRACIANO. Restoring old-vine NAV GARNACHA eg. Malayeto.

Vivanco, Bodegas R Alt r p w sw ★→★★ Big Briones BODEGA, *outstanding wine museum*.

Williams & Humbert Sherry ★→★★★★ Historic BODEGA on the up, specialities, eg. vintage EN RAMA FINO 2006. Bestsellers: Dry Sack, Winter's Tale AMONTILLADOS. V.gd mature wines: *Dos Cortados* PALO CORTADO, *As You Like It* sweet OLOROSO, VOS Don Guido PX.

Ximénez-Spínola Sherry V. fine small producer of PX. Grows PX in JEREZ: v. rare; most source from MONT-M. Intriguing rarity, Exceptional Harvest, from overripe PX, unfortified.

Zárate Gal (r) w ★★→★★★★ BODEGA in Val do Salnés. Elegant ALBARIÑOS with long lees ageing. El Palomar is from centenarian v'yd, one of RÍAS BAIXAS' oldest, on own rootstock, aged in *foudre* for texture, complexity. Ethereal.

Portugal

Plenty of countries are advancing in unexpected ways, and faster than we ever imagined possible, but Portugal has sprung more surprises than most. It is home to over 250 native varieties – some of which do not exist elsewhere in the world – and Portuguese wine-growers have shown a heroic determination to preserve this heritage – vines like Alvarinho, Arinto, Encruzado, Fernão Pires for whites or Baga, Castelão, Tinta Roriz, Touriga Nacional, Trincadeira for reds. Added to this diversity are vastly different microclimates, soils and the effects of Atlantic or Continental influences. Blends are what Portugal does best. While Port is the best-known example, throughout the country it is blends that go beyond the merely fruity to make wines of compelling moreishness. Bairrada's Baga blends; the Alicante Bouschet blends of the Alentejo; the increasingly elegant whites as well as reds of the Douro; all show different facets. If there is a Portuguese character, it is perhaps rich fruit, balance and a certain herbal complexity.

Recent Port vintages

A vintage is "declared" when the wine is outstanding and meets the shippers' highest standards; something of a parallel to Champagne. In good but not quite classic years most shippers use the names of their quintas (estates) for single-quinta wines of real character but needing less ageing in bottle. The vintages to drink now are 63 66 70 77 80 83 85 87 92 94, though very young Vintage Port is an unconventional delight, specially with chocolate cake or even with peppered steak.

2017 Exceptionally early harvest after a very dry, warm year in Douro. Expected to be widely declared.
2016 Patchy, challenging harvest. Probably single-quinta year.
2015 Single-quinta year with notable exceptions: Niepoort, Noval; very dry, hot.
2014 Excellent from vineyards that ducked September's rain; production low.
2013 Single-quinta year; mid-harvest rain. Stars: Vesuvio, Fonseca Guimaraens.
2012 Single-quinta year. Very low-yielding, drought-afflicted. Stars: Noval, Malvedos.
2011 Classic year, widely declared. Inky, outstanding concentration, structure. Stars: Noval Nacional, Vargellas Vinha Velha, Fonseca.
2010 Single-quinta year. Hot, dry but higher yields than 2009. Stars: Vesuvio, Senhora da Ribeira.
2009 Controversial year. Declared by Fladgate, but not Symingtons or Sogrape. Stars: Taylor, Niepoort, Fonseca, Warre.
2008 Single-quinta year. Low-yielding, powerful wines. Stars: Noval, Vesuvio, Terra Feita, Passadouro. Sandeman's LBV is v.gd.
2007 Classic year, widely declared. Deep-coloured, rich but well-balanced wines. Stars: Taylor, Vesuvio.
2006 Difficult; a few single quintas. Stars: Vesuvio, Roriz, Barros Q. Galeira.
2005 Single-quinta year. Stars: Niepoort, Vargellas, Senhora da Ribeira – iron fist in velvet glove.

Recent table wine vintages

2017 Exceptionally early harvest. Very dry, warm year. Great quality all around.
2016 Patchy, complicated year. Very good quality (red and white) for those who waited.

See Portugal map p.176.

2015 Great quality with quantity: aromatic, intense, balanced wines.

2014 Excellent fresh whites and bright, intense reds (if picked before rain).

2013 Great for (most) whites, and reds picked before rain; mixed results after.

2012 Concentrated wines, good balance, especially whites.

2011 Well-balanced year; outstanding Douro, Alentejo reds.

2010 Good quality and quantity all round. Bairrada had another excellent year.

Açores / Azores w sw (r) ★→★★★ 15' Mid-Atlantic archipelago of nine volcanic islands with DOCS Pico, Biscoitos and Graciosa for whites and traditional *licoroso* (late-harvest/fortified). Pico landscape, incl vine-protecting *currais* (pebble walls), is UNESCO World Heritage Site. New dynamic winemakers, and arrival of budget flights, producing exciting volcanic-soil wines. Best: Arinto dos Açores, Terrantez do Pico, VERDELHO from Azores Wine Company, Cancela do Porco, Curral Atlantis, Insula.

Adega A cellar or winery.

Alenquer Lis r w ★★→★★★ 11' 12 13 14 15' Microclimatic DOC, home to LIS's best reds. Age-worthy SYRAH pioneer MONTE D'OIRO, great-value CHOCAPALHA and Pinto.

Alentejo r (w) ★→★★★★ 08' 09 10 11' 12 13 14 15' Reliably warm popular s region, divided into subregional DOCS Borba, Redondo, Reguengos, PORTALEGRE, Évora, Granja-Amareleja, Vidigueira (known for quality white), Moura. Ancient clay amphora technique Vinho de Talha seeing a comeback. More liberal VR Alentejano preferred by many top estates. Rich, ripe reds esp from Alicante Bouschet, SYRAH, TRINCADEIRA, TOURIGA N. Whites fast improving. CARTUXA, ESPORÃO, JOÃO PORTUGAL RAMOS, Malhadinha Nova, MOUCHÃO, MOURO, Sonho Lusitano have potency, style. Watch: Dona Maria, FITA PRETA, MONTE DE RAVASQUEIRA, QUINTA do Peso, Quinta do Rocim, SUSANA ESTEBAN, Terrenus.

Algarve r p w sp ★→★★ S coast producing mostly Vinho Regional, national and international varieties. Recent advances means wines are progressing but still fall short of famous beaches and Michelin-starred gastronomy. Barranco Longo and QUINTA dos Vales honourable mentions.

Aliança Bair r p w sp ★→★★★ Large firm with gd reds and *sparkling*. Wines shown with art at Aliança Underground Museum. Interests in ALEN (QUINTA da Terrugem, Alabastro), DÃO (Quinta da Garrida), DOU (Quinta dos Quatro Ventos). Owner of popular Casal Mendes brand.

Ameal, Quinta do Vin w sw sp ★★★ 00 03 04 05 07' 09 11 14 15 Superior, age-worthy, organic LOUREIRO incl oaked Escolha and, in top yrs (11 14) low-yield low-intervention Solo. Gd wine tourism project, incl accommodation.

Andresen Port ★★→★★★★ Family-owned house. Excellent wood-aged Ports, esp 20-yr-old TAWNY. Outstanding *Colheitas* 1900' 1910' (still bottled on demand) 68' 80' 91' 03'. Pioneered age-dated WHITE PORTS 10-, 20-, v.gd 40-yr-old.

Aphros Vin r p w sp ★★★ Bio pioneer, "natural" wine player, nr Ponte de Lima. V.gd LOUREIRO and Vinhão (both sp and oak-aged Silenus) will age beautifully. New cellar frees up old "medieval" one for traditional winemaking (no electricity/ amphoras/*lagares*). Secluded retreat for wine-lovers.

Aveleda, Quinta da Vin r p w ★→★★ DYA Home of Casal García, VIN's biggest seller since 1939. Nr Penafiel. Regular range of estate-grown wines. Now owns DOU's QUINTA DO VALE DONA MARIA. Newly opened visitor centre.

Bacalhôa Vinhos Alen, Lis, Set r p w sw sp ★★→★★★ Principal brand and headquarters of billionaire and art-lover José Berardo's group. Also owns National Monument QUINTA da Bacalhôa (v.gd CAB SAUV 1st planted 1974 also used in top red Palácio da Bacalhôa), sparkling estate Quinta dos Loridos. Top MOSCATEL DE SETÚBAL barrels, incl rare Roxo. Owner of historic Quinta do Carmo brand making v.gd ALEN reds. Modern, well-made brands: Serras de

Azeitão, Catarina, Cova da Ursa (SET), TINTO da Ânfora (ALEN). Also amazing garden in Funchal.

Baga Friends Bair Group of BAIR producers mad about BAGA grape. They'll convert you too. BUÇACO, Dirk NIEPOORT, FILIPA PATO, LUIS PATO, Quinta da Vacariça, QUINTA DAS BAGEIRAS, Sidonio de Sousa.

Bágeiras, Quinta das Bair r w sp ★★★ →★★★★ 04′ 05′ 08′ 09 10 11 Iconic BAIR producer. Remarkable, v. age-worthy range: whites (esp Avô Fausto barrique-aged 100% MARIA GOMES), BAGA reds (esp GARRAFEIRA – RES, Pai Abel and Avô Fausto blended with TOURIGA N), fizz and fortified Baga Abafado. Most made traditionally – fermented in open cement vats (reds 100 per cent whole-bunch fermentation) then matured in old *toneis* (wooden vats).

Bairrada r p w sw sp ★→★★★★ 03′ 04 05′ 06 07 08′ 09′ 10′ 11′ 12 13 14′ Atlantic-influenced DOC and Vinho Regional Beira Atlântico. Age-worthy, structured BAGA reds, sparklings (new Baga Bair designation for best). Top Baga specialists: FILIPA PATO, LUÍS PATO, Casa de Saima, CAVES SÃO JOÃO, QUINTA DAS BÁGEIRAS, Sidónio de Sousa. Watch: ALIANÇA, Campolargo, Colinas de S. Lourenço, Quinta de Baixo (NIEPOORT-owned), Vadio, V Puro. *See* BAGA FRIENDS.

Barbeito Mad ★★→★★★★ Innovative MAD producer with striking labels. Unique, single-v'yd single-cask COLHEITAS. Outstanding 20-, 30-, 40-yr-old MALVASIAS. New 50-yr-old Bastardo. Excellent Ribeiro Real range with 20-yr-old BOAL, Malvasia, SERCIAL, VERDELHO, with dash of 50S TINTA NEGRA. Sublime use of hard-to-reach Fajã dos Padres v'yds. 96 Colheita 1st to mention Tinta Negra on front label. Historic Series: MAD most coveted wine in US in C18 and C19.

Barca Velha Dou r ★★★★ 65 66 78 81 82′ 83 85 91′ 95′ **99 00** 04 08′ Portugal's iconic red, created in 1952 by FERREIRA, forging DOU's reputation for world class. Released in exceptional yrs, only 18 times. Aged several yrs pre-release. Second label, also released in exceptional yrs from CASA FERREIRINHA's best barrels (when Barca Velha not made), *Res Especial*, v.gd, esp 62 80′ **84** 86′ 89′ 94′ 97′ 01′ **07** 09. Arguably 80′ 86′ 89′ 94′ 97′ 01′ 09 could have been Barca Velha.

Barros Port ★★→★★★★ Founded 1913, Sogevinus-owned since 2006, maintains substantial stocks of aged TAWNY and COLHEITA. V.gd Colheitas 35′ 38′ 41′ 44′ 50′ 57′ 60′ 66′ 63 66′ 74′ 78 80′ 97′. V.gd 20-, 30-, 40-yr-old Tawny. VINTAGE PORT: 95 87 05 07 11. Very Old Dry White and Colheita (35) WHITE PORTS.

Barros e Sousa Mad ★★→★★★★ Acquired by neighbour PEREIRA D'OLIVEIRA (2013) who will bottle remaining stock under its name. Old lodge to be new visitor centre. Look for rare Bastardo Old RES.

Beira Interior r p w ★→★★★ Unique DOC with some of highest mtns in Portugal, between DÃO and Spanish border. Huge potential from old, high (up to 750m) v'yds, esp for white Siria, Fonte Cal. V.gd-value Beyra, QUINTAS do Cardo. ANSELMO MENDES (VIN) also in area. Watch: Quintas dos Currais, dos Termos.

Blandy Mad ★★→★★★★ Historic MAD family firm with young, dynamic CEO Chris Blandy. *Funchal lodges* showcase history, incl vast library of FRASQUEIRA (BUAL 1920′ 1957′ 1966′, MALMSEY **1988**′, SERCIAL 1975′ 1988′, VERDELHO 1979′). V.gd 20-yr-old Terrantez and COLHEITAS (Bual 1996 **2008**, Malmsey 1999, Verdelho 2000, Sercial 2002). New: superb 50-yr-old Malmsey, outstanding Terrantez 1980′, TINTA NEGRA 95; Atlantis table wine: white Verdelho, rosé Tinta Negra.

Borges, HM Mad ★→★★★ Sisters Helena and Isabel Borges hold tiny amounts of

---

Azores UNESCO Heritage Site
On volcanic, barren Pico Island, you will find hills sloping down to the sea, marked by a grid of black stone walls separating the v'yds. Generations of small farmers tamed a hostile environment to create their own way of life and a wine of great quality.

fine Terrantez 1877 demi-john from founding yr. V.gd 30-yr-old MALVASIA incl wine from 1932. V.gd SERCIAL 1990.

Branco White.

Bual (or Boal) Mad Classic MAD grape: medium-rich (sweet), tangy, smoky wines; less rich than MALVASIA. Perfect with harder cheeses and lighter desserts. Tends to be darkest in colour.

Buçaco Bei At r w ★★★ Manueline-Gothic monument *Bussaco Palace hotel* lists its classic austere wines back to 40s. Blends of two regions. Reds: BAGA (BAIR), TOURIGA N (DÃO). Whites: Encruzado (Dão), MARIA GOMES, Bical (Bair). Barriques and new oak since 2000 have slightly modernized style esp whites and single-v'yd red Vinha da Mata (VM). Member of BAGA FRIENDS.

Bucelas Lis w sp ★★ Tiny DOC making crisp, dry, racy, min 75% ARINTO. Gd-value sparkling. Widely popular in C19 England as "Lisbon Hock". Best: QUINTAS DA ROMEIRA, da Murta.

Burmester Port ★→★★★ Est 1730, Sogevinus-owned since 2005. Elegant, wood-aged, gd-value Ports esp 20-, 40-yr-old TAWNY. 1890 1900' 37' 52' 55' 57' COLHEITAS. Age-dated WHITE PORTS, incl fine 30-, 40-yr-old. Gd VINTAGE PORT and single-QUINTA do Arnozelo.

Cálem Port ★→★★★ Est 1859, Sogevinus-owned since 1998. Popular entry-level fruity Velhotes. Best are COLHEITAS 61', 10-, 40-yr-old TAWNY. Lodge in Gaia gets over 100,000 visitors/yr.

Campolargo Bair r w sp ★→★★★ Large estate, idiosyncratic pioneer with B'x varieties. V.gd native ARINTO, Bical, CERCEAL (w), Alvarelhão, PINOT N, Rol de Coisas Antigas blend, B'x blend Calda Bordaleza (r).

Canteiro Mad Method of naturally cask-ageing finest MAD in warm, humid lodges for greater subtlety/complexity than ESTUFAGEM.

Carcavelos Lis br sw ★★★ Unique, mouthwatering, gripping, off-dry fortified. New Villa Oeiras breathed life into v. old, tiny, ailing DOC, with v'yd area of 12.5 ha.

Cartuxa, Adega da Alen r w sp ★★→★★★★ C17 cellars, wine restaurant, modern art centre a tourist magnet, while flagship Pêra Manca red 98 01 03 05' 07 08' 10' 11' 13' and white draw connoisseurs. Gd-value volume Vinea and EA (organic version available) reds. Consistent best-buy Cartuxa RES 10 11' 12' 13'. Scala Coeli, reputed single variety (different each yr).

Carvalhais, Quinta dos Dão r p w sp ★→★★★ SOGRAPE-owned. V.gd, consistent, estate-grown, age-worthy range, esp oak-aged Encruzado, RES (r w), TOURIGA N, Alfrocheiro, TINTA RORIZ, Único. Unusual oxidative BRANCO Especial (w) a delight. Home of Duque de Viseu and Grão Vasco.

Castro, Álvaro de Dão ★★→★★★★ Emblematic producer, characterful wines mostly under QUINTA names, gd-value Saes and superior Pellada. Superb Primus (w) and *Pape* (r). Carrocel 06 07 08' 10 11' (TOURIGA N) released in great yrs. Limited-release single-barrel/-v'yd Muleta and Dente d'Ouro preserve old field-blend heritage.

Cello, Casa de Dão, Vin ★★ Family-run project in VIN and DÃO. Unique QUINTA de San Joanne (Vin) age-worthy range (w), incl outstanding Superior (only in v.gd years). V.gd Escolha, gd-value Terroir Mineral. Distinctive classic Quinta da Vegia (DÃO) range (r) esp RES and Superior.

Chaves, Tapada do Alen ★★★ Historic property now owned by CARTUXA. Unique old, high-altitude v'yds making gd white and v.gd age-worthy red esp Vinhas Velhas, Frangoneiro.

Chocapalha, Quinta de Lis r p w ★★★ Family-run, Atlantic-influenced estate blending old and new, native and international varieties. Winemaker Sandra Tavares da Silva (WINE & SOUL). *Among Lisboa's best reds* esp CASTELÃO, CAB SAUV and flagship TOURIGA N CH. Vibrant, fresh whites esp new RES.

> **Almost extinct treasure**
> COLARES is continental Europe's most westerly wine region, right on the beach nr Sintra, and one of its most intriguing. Reds, made mainly from the highly tannic Ramiro, need patient ageing. Whites, from saline, tangy MALVASIA de Colares, not so much. Being planted in sandy soil, vines survived phylloxera, ungrafted. But there are hardly any left.

Chryseia Dou r ★★ ·★★★ 07 08' 09 11' 12' 13 14 15' Bruno Prats (B'x) and SYMINGTON FAMILY ESTATES partnership. Polished TOURIGA-driven (Nacional and Franca) red. Fresher, finer since sourced from QUINTA de Roriz. Second label: *Post Scriptum*. Prazo de Roriz gd value.

Churchill Dou, Port r p w sw ★★ Port house est 1981 by John Graham, whose family founded GRAHAM. V.gd DRY WHITE PORT (10 yrs old), 20-, 30-yr-old (new), unfiltered LBV, VINTAGE PORT 82 85 91 94 97 00 03 07' 11'. QUINTA da Gricha is source of old-vine, grippy Single QUINTA Vintage Port and v.gd single-v'yd DOU red. Gd Churchill's Estates label (esp TOURIGA N).

Cockburn Port ★★ ·★★★ Part of SYMINGTON FAMILY ESTATES and back on form esp drier, fresher style of VINTAGE PORT in 11' 15' (esp lush, tense Bicentenary Vintage Port). Extraordinary 08' 27' 34 63 67. Consistently gd Special RES aged longer in wood than others. Vibrant LBV aged 1 yr less. V.gd single-QUINTA dos Canais. New Gaia visitor centre incl Symington's cooperage tour.

Colares Lis r w ★★★ Unique, historic coastal DOC (1908). Windswept ungrafted vines on sand produce Ramisco **tannic reds**, MALVASIA fresh, salty whites. Fundação Oriente and Casal Santa Maria bring modern flair to traditional style of ADEGA Regional de Colares and Viúva Gomes.

Colheita Port, Mad Vintage-dated Port or MAD of a single yr. Cask-aged: min of 7 yrs for TAWNY Port (often 50 yrs+, some 100 yrs+); min 5 yrs for MAD. Bottling date shown on label. Serve chilled.

Conceito Dou, Port r w sp ★★★ Winemaker Rita Ferreira Marques does style and substance. Strikingly labelled DOU Superior wines (esp Conceito red and white) bring finesse to local grapes, incl traditional now-rare PINOT N-like Bastardo and new single-v'yd (90-yr-old vines) Conceito Único.

Cortes de Cima Alen r w ★★★ Built from scratch by Danish/Californian couple in 1988. ALEN SYRAH pioneer with (v.gd, now more elegant, top red) Incógnito 11' 12'. Consistent range, esp RES and varietals (ARAGONEZ, Syrah, TRINCADEIRA). V.gd whites from new Alen coastal v'yds incl ALVARINHO, SAUV BL.

Cossart Gordon Mad ★★★ MADEIRA WINE COMPANY-owned brand. Drier style than BLANDY esp fortifying BUAL 1962' is bottled electricity.

Covela, Quinta de Vin w ★★ Uplifting revival of impressive C16 property on VIN/DOU border. V.gd age-worthy Avesso-based range. Single-variety Edição Nacional, Avesso/CHARD Escolha, Avesso/ARINTO/Chard/VIOGNIER oak-aged RES. Solid cellar-aged TOURIGA N/CAB SAUV red. Gd rosé.

Crasto, Quinta do Dou, Port r w ★★★ ·★★★★ (r) 07' 08 09' 10 11' 12 13 14 One of DOU's most reputed estates. Striking hilltop location. Jewels in crown are two v. old field-blend single-v'yd reds Vinha da Ponte 03 04 07' 10' 12 13 14, Maria Teresa 05' 06 07 09' 11' 13. Great-value old-v'yd RES. Superb single-variety TINTA RORIZ. Great TOURIGA N. Dou Superior v'yds brought gd-value wines to market, incl attractive red, innovative acacia-aged white and SYRAH with VIOGNIER dash. Gd VINTAGE PORT and unfiltered LBV.

Croft Port ★★ ·★★★ Fladgate-owned historic shipper with visitor centre in glorious v'yds nr Pinhão. Sweet, fleshy VINTAGE PORT 66 70 75 77 82 85 91 94 00 03' 07 09' 11'. Single-QUINTA da Roêda Vintage Port 03 04 07 08' 09 12' 15' v.gd value. Popular: Indulgence, Triple Crown, Distinction and Pink ROSÉ PORT.

Crusted (Port) Gd-value, rare, traditional NV Port style. I keep a bottle handy all winter. Blend of two or more vintage-quality yrs, aged up to 4 yrs in casks, released 3 yrs after bottling. Unfiltered, forms deposit ("crust") so decant. Look for DOW, FONSECA, GRAHAM, NIEPOORT, NOVAL.

Dão r p w sp ★★ →★★★ 05 06 07' 08' 09 10 11' 12 13 Historic mtn-fenced DOC recently on a roll. Modern pioneers ÁLVARO DE CASTRO, CARVALHAIS, Dão Sul, Falorca, Maias, Roques make fine age-worthy reds, textured, tasty whites (Encruzado is reputed king). Second wave incl Caminhos Cruzados, CASA DA PASSARELLA, CASA DE MOURAZ, Julia Kemper. To watch: António Madeira, Conciso (NIEPOORT-owned), outstanding Druida, Lemos, MOB, Ribeiro Santo, Vegia. Top Dão Nobre ("noble") designation now used. Superb, gd-value GARRAFEIRAS.

DOC / DOP (Denominacão de Origem Controlada / Protegida) Quality-oriented protected designation of origin controlled by a regional commission. Similar to France's AC. *See also* VINHO REGIONAL.

Doce (vinho) Sweet (wine).

Douro r p w sw World's 1st demarcated and regulated wine region (1756), named after its river. Dramatic UNESCO World Heritage Site. Formerly inaccessible, now wine-tourism ready. Famous for Port, now produces just as much quality table wine (Dou DOC). Three subregions (Baixo Corgo, Cima Corgo and fast-expanding Dou Superior); great diversity of terroir. Over 100 native varieties (often planted together, 80 yrs+) in terraces of unforgiving schist. Powerful, increasingly elegant, age-worthy reds; fine, characterful whites. Best: ALVES DE SOUSA, BARCA VELHA, CASA FERREIRINHA, CHRYSEIA, CRASTO, *Niepoort*, POEIRA, QUINTA DAS CARVALHAS, QUINTA Nova, RAMOS PINTO, *Vale Dona Maria*, *Vale Meão*, VALLADO, WINE & SOUL. To watch: Boavista, Foz Torto, Maria Izabel, Murças, NOVAL, POÇAS, Pôpa, Quanta Terra, REAL COMPANHIA VELHA, S. José, Síbio, Vesuvio. VR is Duriense.

Dow Port ★★★ →★★★★ Historic SYMINGTON-owned shipper. Drier VINTAGE PORT 66' 70' 72 75 77' 80' 83 85' 91 94' 97 00' 03 07' 11'. Single-QUINTAS do Bomfim and Senhora da Ribeira (v.gd 15) in non-declared vintage yrs. Beautiful riverside Bomfim winery visitor centre in Pinhão.

Duorum Dou, Port r w ★★ →★★★ Consistent DOU Superior project of JOÃO PORTUGAL RAMOS and ex-FERREIRA/BARCA VELHA José Maria Soares Franco. Gd-value, fruity, entry-level *Tons*, COLHEITA. Fine RES and O. Leucura from v. old vines. V.gd dense, pure-fruited VINTAGE PORT 07 11' 12 15' from 100-yr-old vines. Fine second label Vinha de Castelo Melhor and gd-value LBV.

Esporão, Herdade do Alen r w sw ★★ →★★★ Landmark estate, increasingly certified organic. High-quality, fruit-focused, modern. Gd-value entry-level Monte Velho, reputed RES (r w). V.gd single-v'yd/variety range. Sophisticated GARRAFEIRA-like Private Selection and rare Torre do Esporão 07' 11. New *talha* (old clay amphora) red back to ALEN tradition. Auspicious DOU project (QUINTA das Murças) making gd organic, single-v'yd reds.

Iconic Barca Velha is Dou's oldest red table wine, 1st released 1952; little left, though.

Espumante Sparkling. Generally gd value. Best from BAIR (esp BÁGEIRAS, Colinas São Lourenço, Kompassus, lookout for BAGA Bairrada designation), DOU (esp Vértice), Távora-Varosa (esp MURGANHEIRA) and VIN (esp SOALHEIRO).

Esteban, Susana Alen r w ★★ →★★★ Her own boutique label. Stunning flagship Procura (r w), from PORTALEGRE's v.old low-yield v'yds (red adds Alicante Bouschet from Évora). Gd-value second label Aventura. Innovative Sidecar invites other winemakers (most recently Spaniard Eulogio Tavares).

Estufagem Tightly controlled "stove" process of heating MAD for min 3 mths for faster ageing and characteristic scorched-earth tang. Used mostly on entry-level wines. Finer results with external heating jackets and lower max temperature (45°C/113°F).

Falua Tej r p w ★→★★ JOÃO PORTUGAL RAMOS' TEJO outpost. Well-made export-focused Tagus Creek blends native and international grapes. Gd-value entry-level Conde de Vimioso (RES a step up).

Favaios, Adega de Dou (r) (w) sw 600-member co-op making 70 per cent of DOU fortified MOSCATEL do Dou. Top aged vintage examples retain delicacy, freshness (80' 89').

Dão is Portugal's Burgundy, available at Languedoc prices.

Ferreira Port ★★→★★★ SOGRAPE-owned historic Port house. Winemaker Luis Sottomayor (BARCA VELHA) reckons LBV now as gd as last decade's VINTAGE PORT, both categories on the up here. Vintages 11' 15' stand out. V.gd-value spicy TAWNY incl Dona Antonia RES, 10-, 20-yr-old Tawny (QUINTA do Porto, *Duque de Bragança*).

Ferreirinha, Casa Dou r w ★★→★★★★ SOGRAPE-owned. Remarkable range of age-worthy DOU wines. Gd-value entry-level Callabriga, Esteva, Papa Figos, Vinha Grande. Superb Dou QUINTA da Leda and Antónia Adelaide Ferreira (r w). Rarely-released RES Especial and (iconic) BARCA VELHA.

Fita Preta Alen r w ★★ António Maçanita scored with populist Sexy sister-brand. Fita Preta label more serious, esp Palpite (v.gd white and Grande RES red). Signature Series flirts with unusual techniques (skin contact, *talha*, unoaked TOURIGA N) and varieties eg. BAGA.

Fladgate Port Independent family-owned partnership. Owns leading Port houses (TAYLOR, FONSECA, CROFT, KROHN) and luxury wine hotels: The Yeatman (VILA NOVA DE GAIA), Vintage House (Pinhão).

Fonseca Port ★★★→★★★★ FLADGATE-owned Port house, founded 1815. Voluptuous Bin 27, organic Terra Prima RES. V.gd 20-,40-yr-old TAWNY. Excellence in VINTAGE PORT 27' 63' 66' 70 75 77' 80 83 85' 92 94' 97 00' 03' 07 09 11'. Superb second label Fonseca Guimaraens. Single-QUINTA Panascal.

Fonseca, José Maria da Lis r p w sw sp ★→★★★★ 200-yr-old, 7th-generation producer; extensive v'yds (650 ha) and portfolio. LANCERS, PERIQUITA are bread-and-butter brands. Cherry on cake is fortified MOSCATEL DE SETÚBAL, which mines aged stock to great effect (great-value 20-yr-old Alambre, Roxo, remarkable SUPERIOR 11' 18 34' 35 42 55' 66 71). Innovative wine bar in Lisbon. Pioneer of modern *talha* wines under historic, characterful ALEN José de Sousa label.

Frasqueira Mad Top MAD category. Also called Vintage. Single-yr, single-noble-variety aged min 20 yrs in wood, usually much longer. Date of bottling required. Expensive these days.

Garrafeira Label term for superior quality. Traditionally a merchant's "private RES". Must be aged for min 2 yrs in cask and 1 yr in bottle (often much longer). Whites need 6 mths in cask, 6 mths in bottle. Special use in Port by NIEPOORT.

Global Wines Bair, Dão r w sp ★★→★★★ Also known as Dão Sul. One of Portugal's biggest producers, DÃO-based, with estates in many other regions. Great-value popular brands Cabriz (esp RES) and Casa de Santar (esp Res, superb Nobre). Classy Paço dos Cunhas single-v'yd Vinha do Contador. Modern wines, striking architecture, visitor centre at BAIR's QUINTA do Encontro. Other brands: Grilos, Encostas do Douro (DOU), Monte da Cal (ALEN), Quinta de Lourosa (VIN).

Graham Port ★★★→★★★★ SYMINGTON-owned Port house. 1st division Ports from RES RUBY Six Grapes to VINTAGE PORT 45' 63' 66 70' 75 77' 80 83' 85' 91' 94' 97 00' 03' 07' 11', incl limited release Stone Terraces 11' 15' and single-QUINTA dos Malvedos. V.gd-value, attractive 20-, 30-, 40-yrs-old TAWNY, LBV. Fine Single-Harvest (COLHEITAS) esp 52' 69' 72'. Trumping them all, sublime Ne Oublie Very Old Tawny, one of three 1882 casks laid down by AJ Symington.

Gran Cruz Port ★→★★★ French group La Martiniquaise runs Port's largest brand (Porto Cruz), focused on volume and cocktails. VILA NOVA DE GAIA museum, rooftop terrace bar tourist attraction. Dalva brand has gd VINTAGE PORT, outstanding TAWNY stocks (esp COLHEITAS, white 52' 63' 73). New Pinhão-based QUINTA de Ventozelo has gd range of wines.

Henriques & Henriques Mad ★★ →★★★★ Only MAD shipper to own v'yds (incl rare Terrantez plot). Owned by rum giant La Martiniquaise. Unique extra-dry apéritif Monte Seco. Best are 20-yr-old MALVASIA and Terrantez, 15-yr-old (NB *Sercial*), Single Harvest (aged in old bourbon barrels, **1997**', **1998**', BUAL **2000**'), Vintage (VERDELHO **1957**, Terrantez **1954**', SERCIAL **1971**'). V.gd new TINTA NEGRA 50-yr-old.

Horácio Simões Set r w sw ★★ Innovative boutique producer. Dynamic range incl late-harvest and fortified MOSCATEL (esp single-cask Roxo and Excellent). Thrilling, rare fortified Bastardo. Table wines to watch: light, fruity Bastardo, BOAL (esp 100-yr-old vines Grande RES), CASTELÃO.

Justino Mad ★→★★★ Largest MAD shipper, owned by rum giant La Martiniquaise, makes Broadbent label. Fairly large entry-level range. Some jewels: Terrantez Old Res (NV, probably around 50-yrs-old), Terrantez **1978**' (oldest in cask), MALVASIA **1964**' **1968**' **1988**'.

Kopke Port ★ →★★★★ Oldest Port house, est 1638, now Sogevinus owned. Well-known for v.gd spicy, structured COLHEITAS 35' 41' 57' 64' 65' 66 78 80' 84 87 from middle/upper slopes of QUINTA S. Luiz. Unique WHITE PORT range esp now-rare 1935' and 30-, 40-yr-olds.

Krohn Port ★→★★★ Now FLADGATE-owned. Exceptional stocks of aged TAWNY (rich 10-, 20-yr-old), COLHEITA 61' 66' 67' **76**' **82**' **83**' **87**' 91 97 dating back to 1863 (source of TAYLOR 1863 Single Harvest). VINTAGE PORTS improving.

Lancers p w sp ★ JOSÉ MARIA DA FONSECA's semi-sweet, semi-sparkling, ROSADO, now white, fizzy (p w) and alc-free versions.

Lavradores de Feitoria Dou r w ★★ →★★★ Well-run collaboration of 15 producers (19 v'yds). Gd whites, esp SAUV BL, Meruge (100-per-cent oak-aged old-vines Viosinho). Value reds, incl Três Bagos RES. V.gd Grande Escolha (esp long-aged Estágio Prolongado), QUINTA da Costa das Aguaneiras, elegant Meruge (mostly TINTA RORIZ from a n-facing 400m v'yd).

LBV (Late Bottled Vintage) Port Affordable and ready-to-drink alternative to VINTAGE PORT. A single-yr wine, aged 4–6 yrs in cask, twice as long as VINTAGE PORT. V.gd, age-worthy, unfiltered versions eg. DE LA ROSA, FERREIRA, NIEPOORT, NOVAL, RAMOS PINTO, Romaneira, SANDEMAN, WARRE.

Lisboa r p w sp sw ★ →★★ Large, hilly region around capital; varied terroir, muddle of local and international grapes. Best-known DOCS: ALENQUER (pioneering boutique wineries CHOCAPALHA, MONTE D'OIRO for best reds) and traditional BUCELAS, COLARES. Fresh dry whites growing in strength, esp from limestone, coastal/elevated v'yds eg. ADEGA Mãe (Viosinho), Casal Figueira (Vital), Casal Sta Maria (COLARES), QUINTA de Sant'Ana (PINOT N, RIES), Quinta do Pinto (blends), Quinta da Serradinha, Vale da Capucha (organic).

Madeira r w ★ →★★★★ Island and DOC, famous for fortifieds. Modest table wines (Terras Madeirenses VR, Madeirense DOC). VERDELHO best. Look for Atlantis, Barbusano, Moledo, Palmeira, Primeira Paixão, Terras do Avô.

Madeira Wine Company Mad Association of all 26 British MAD companies, est 1913. Owns BLANDY, COSSART GORDON, Leacock, Miles and accounts for over 50 per cent of bottled Mad exports. Since BLANDY family gained control, almost exclusively focused on promoting Blandy brand.

Malvasia (Malmsey) Mad Sweetest and richest of traditional MAD noble grape varieties, yet with Mad's unique sharp tang. Delightful with rich fruit, chocolate puddings or just dreams.

Mateus Rosé p (w) sp ★ World's bestselling, medium-dry, lightly carbonated rosé now in transparent bottles and available in white (drier, no spritz) or fully fizzy (p w). Expressions range: (MARIA GOMES/CHARD) and three rosé blends (BAGA/SHIRAZ, Baga/MUSCAT; ARAGONEZ/ZIN).

Mendes, Anselmo Vin r w sw sp ★★★ Acclaimed winemaker and consultant. Several benchmark, age-worthy ALVARINHOS, incl gd-value (aged on lees) Contacto, excellent oaked voluptous Curtimenta, superb single-v'yd Parcela Única, classy Muros de Melgaço and vibrant new Expressões. Gd LOUREIRO, silky, modern red VIN (Parducso), surprising orange Vin Tempo. Watch out for new BEI INT, DÃO, DOU wines.

Minho Vin River between n Portugal and Spain, also VR covering same region as VIN. Some leading Vin producers prefer VR Minho label.

Monte de Ravasqueira Alen ★★→★★★ Great terroir (high amphitheatre, clay-limestone, granite), precision viticulture and experienced winemaker make gd range esp single-v'yd Vinha das Romãs, MR Premium (r p w).

Monte d'Oiro, Quinta do Lis r p w ★★→★★★ Family estate started with Hermitage vines from Chapoutier. Now makes savoury, creamy SYRAH, peculiar VIOGNIER (Madrigal), fine TINTA RORIZ (Têmpera) esp Ex-Aequo, Bento & Chapoutier Syrah/TOURIGA N blend.

Moscatel de Setúbal Set sw ★★★ DOC s of Lisbon. Fortified sweet MOSCATEL with exotic scents; incl rare Roxo. "Superior" label. JOSÉ MARIA DA FONSECA (oldest) owns old stocks incl famous 100-yr-old Round Trip. Best: BACALHÔA VINHOS and HORÁCIO DOS SIMÕES, QUINTA do Piloto. Value: ADEGA DE PEGÕES, Casa Ermelinda Freitas, SIVIPA.

Moscatel do Douro Dou The high Favaios region produces surprisingly fresh, fortified MOSCATEL Galego Branco (MUSCAT Blanc à Petit Grains) that rival those of SET. Look for: ADEGA FAVAIOS, Niepoort, POÇAS, Portal.

Alicante Bouschet, French crossing in Alen since 1901, far outpaces any French version.

Mouchão, Herdade de Alen r w sw ★★★ 05′ 06 07 08′ 09 10 11′ Historic family-run estate focuses on ALICANTE BOUSCHET. V.gd museum release (COLHEITAS Antigas) 02 03, *Tonel 3–4* 03 05′ 08 11′, fortified *licoroso*. Gd-value Ponte das Canas blend (incl SYRAH), Dom Rafael.

Mouraz, Casa de Dão r w ★★ Boutique organic pioneer. Modern but charcterful (esp Elfa) wines from family-owned v'yds at 140–400m. Lost cellar, some v'yds in forest fires. Actively rebuilding via crowdfunding campaign. AIR label from bought-in ALEN, DOU, VIN organic grapes.

Mouro, Quinta do Alen r w ★★→★★★ Reliable ALEN producer. Imposing reds; native grapes plus CAB SAUV (also single-variety). V.gd Mouro, excellent Gold label in top yrs 05 06′ 07′ 08 09 10 11. Vinha do Malhó is savoury Centurion/PETITE SIRAH blend. Charcterful Erros (Mistakes) range. Value Vinha do Mouro, Zagalos.

Murganheira, Caves sp ★★★ Largest ESPUMANTE producer; owns RAPOSEIRA. Blends and single varietal (native, French grapes) fizz: Vintage, Grande RES, Czar rosé.

Niepoort Bair, Dão, Dou r p w ★★★→★★★★ Family-owned Port shipper and DOU pioneer with many interests. Port highlights: VINTAGE PORT, unique demijohn-aged GARRAFEIRA and single v'yd Bioma. V.gd TAWNY esp elegant bottle-aged COLHEITAS. Fine DOU range, esp *Redoma* (r p w Res w), Coche (superb w), Batuta, iconic Charme and unique 130-yr-old single-v'yd Turris. Exciting Projectos portfolio incl cross-region/winemaker wines esp António Madeira (DÃO), DODA (Dão), Ladredo (Ribeira Sacra, Spain), Navazos (Spain). Dirk Niepoort's vision now in BAIR (esp GARRAFEIRA, Poeirinho, VV), Dão (esp Conciso) and VIN.

Noval, Quinta do Dou, Port r w ★★★→★★★★ Historic estate bought by AXA in 1993. Consistent, fine (esp since 1994) VINTAGE PORT 63′ 66 67 70 75 78 82 85 87 91 94′ 95 97′ 00′ 03′ 04 07′ 08′ 11′ 12′ 13′ 14 15′. Extraordinary *Nacional* 62 63′ 66′ 70 94′ 96′ 97′ 00′ 01′ 03′ 04′ 11′ from 2.5 ha ungrafted vines is pricey jewel in crown. Second vintage label: Silval. Superb COLHEITAS, 20-, 40-yrs-old, unfiltered LBV. Since 2004 making DOU wines incl gd-value Cedro (native/SYRAH blend), v.gd Noval, varietal TOURIGA N.

Offley Port ★→★★ Old house now owned by SOGRAPE. Gd recent fruit-driven VINTAGE PORT, unfiltered LBV, TAWNY. Apéritif/cocktail styles: Cachuca RES WHITE PORT, ROSÉ PORT.

Palmela Set r w ★→★★★ Castelão-focused DOC. Best: Herdade Pegos Claros, HORÁCIO SIMÕES, QUINTA do Piloto. To watch.

Passarella, Casa da Dão r p w ★★→★★★ Revival of C19 DÃO estate. V.gd range esp flagship Villa Oliveira: Encruzado, TOURIGA N (from old field-blend v'yd), single v'yd Pedras Altas (r), Vinha do Províncio (w), 1ª Edição (five vintage ENCRUZADO blend), oustanding 125 Anos (r). V.gd boutique Fugitivo range esp Enólogo, Enxertia (Jaen), Vinhas Centenárias (red blend of 100-yr-old vines); new Curtimenta. Excellent (value) GARRAFEIRA (w).

Pato, Filipa Bair r w sp sw ★★→★★★ Daughter of LUIS PATO (below) stresses terroir in "Wines with no make-up"; 90-yr-old-vine Nossa Calcario is flagship label: silky, perfumed BAGA (r) and complex Bical (w). V.gd old-vine, oak-*lagares* fermented Territorio Vivo. Tests boundaries (like her father), esp with thrilling amphora-aged Post Quercus (r w).

Pato, Luís Bair r w sw sp ★★→★★★★ Justifiably self-assured BAIR grower. Made his "Mr BAGA" name with *seriously age-worthy, single-v'yd Baga* (Vinhas Barrio, Barrosa, Pan) and two Pé Franco wines from ungrafted vines (sandy-soil QUINTA do Ribeirinho, chalky-clay Valadas). Ready-to-drink, gd-value: Vinhas Velhas (r w), Baga Rebel, wacky red FERNÃO PIRES (fermented on Baga skins). V.gd whites incl Vinhas Velhas (single-v'yd Vinha Formal), fizzy MARIA GOMES Método Antigo, early-picked (Informal).

Pegões, Adega de Set r p w sw sp ★→★★★ Dynamic co-op. Stella label and low-alc Nico white offer gd clean fruit. COLHEITA Seleccionada (r w) gd value.

Península de Setúbal Set ★→★★ Formerly Terras do Sado. Atlantic-facing region s of Lisbon. VR wines mostly from chalky or sandy banks of Sado and Tagus Rivers. Est: ADEGA DE PEGÕES, Bacalhôa Vinhos, Casa Ermelinda Freitas, JOSÉ MARIA FONSECA, SIVIPA. Watch: António Saramago, Herdade do Portocarro, Soberanas.

Pereira d'Oliveira Vinhos Mad ★★→★★★★ Family-run producer with vast stocks (1.6 million litres) of bottled-on-demand FRASQUEIRA, many available to taste at characterful 1619 cellar door. Best incl stunning C19 vintages (MOSCATEL 1875, SERCIAL 1875, Terrantez 1880) and rare Bastardo 1927.

Periquita Grape also known as CASTELÃO. Also trademark of JOSÉ MARÍA DA FONSECA'S successful brand.

Atlantic-influenced wines are best pairing for Portugal's many seafood dishes.

Poças Dou, Port ★★→★★★ Family-owned firm est 1918. V.gd COLHEITAS 64 67' 92 94 95 97 00 01. Old stocks allow for 20-, 30-, 40-yr-old TAWNY. Gd VINTAGE PORT. Table wines improving. V.gd Símbolo in partnership with B'x-owner (Angélus) Hubert de Bouard.

Poeira, Quinta do Dou r w ★★★ Consultant Jorge Moreira's own project. Cool n-facing slopes make intense yet softly spoken wines, esp red. Now more bottle age. V.gd CAB SAUV blend, single-v'yd Ímpar. Taut, keen, oaked ALVARINHO. Classy second label Pó de Poeira (r w).

Portalegre Alen r p w ★→★★★ Ongoing revival of most n subregion of ALEN. Acquisition of high-altitude v'yds (SYMINGTON), historic estates (TAPADA DO CHAVES) signal comeback. Started by wine writers Richard Mayson (QUINTA do Centro) and João Afonso (Solstício/Equinócio), chef Vitor Claro, consultant RUI REGUINGA (Terrenus), winemaker SUSANA ESTEBAN, ESPORÃO. Elevation, granite and schist, old vines, gd rainfall account for fresh, structured wines with depth. To watch.

Quinta Portuguese for "estate". "Single-quinta" denotes single-estate VINTAGE PORTS made in non-declared yrs (increasingly in top yrs too by single-estate producers).

Ramos, João Portugal Alen r w ★ ★★★ One of Portugal's most respected winemakers, now works under own name (VIN) and other brands (DUORUM, FALUA, Foz de Arouce, QUINTA da Viçosa, Vila Santa). Recipe: gd-value, true-to-region wines, commercial appeal. Classy top wines: Estremus, Marquês de Borba RES.

Ramos Pinto Dou, Port ★★★ 1880 pioneering Port and DOU producer owned by Champagne Roederer. Consistent esp Duas Quintas RES (r), Res Especial (mainly TOURIGA N from Bom Retiro). V.gd age-worthy VINTAGE PORT incl single-QUINTA Vintage (de Ervamoira). Complex single-quinta TAWNY 10-yr-old (de Ervamoira) and best-in-class 20-yr-old (Bom Retiro). Gd 30-yr-old incl a dash of centenarian Tawny. Winemaker Ana Rosas replaces retired João Nicolau de Almeida.

Montado: traditional landscape of cork oaks, Holm oaks, cattle, black pigs for gd ham.

Raposeira Dou sp ★★ MURGANHEIRA-owned. Classic-method fizz. Flagship Velha RES, CHARD/PINOT N lees-aged 4 yrs.

Real Companhia Velha Dou, Port r p w sw ★ ★★★ Silva Reis family have renewed their Port (incl Royal Oporto and Delaforce) and DOU portfolio thanks to precision viticulture (540 ha) and winemaking (led by POEIRA's Jorge Moreira). V.gd old-vine flagship QUINTA das Carvalhas (r w), VINTAGE PORT, 20-yr-old TAWNY. Value brands Aciprestes, Evel. Quinta de Cidrô (v.gd CAB SAUV/TOURIGA N). Gd experimental project Séries. New, thrilling whites from Quinta do Síbio (esp rare Samarrinho). Grandjó is best late-harvest in Portugal. Unique 149-yr-old Carvalhas Memories Very Old Tawny.

Reserve / Reserva (Res) Port Higher quality than basic or ages before being sold (or both). In Port, bottled without age indication (used in RUBY, TAWNY). In table wines, ageing rules vary between regions.

Romeira, Quinta da r p w sp ★ ★★ Historic BUCELAS estate. Consolidating position under new owner Wine Ventures. Extended v'yd (75 ha, mostly ARINTO) now offers s and n aspects for slightly different styles. V.gd Arinto (Prova Régia RES, oaked Morgado Sta Catherina Res). Gd-value Prova Regia Arinto, Principium French/native grape blends (VR LISBOA).

Rosa, Quinta de la Dou, Port r p w ★★★ Lovely riverside estate at Pinhão. Port and DOU's range rapidly increasing in quality under winemaker Jorge Moreira (POEIRA). V.gd VINTAGE PORT, LBV. Rich but elegant wines esp RES (r w). DouROSA is entry level. Generous gd-value Passagem label.

Rosado Rosé. Growing category. Best: Colinas São Lourenço Tête de Cuvée, Cortes de Cima, Covela, Monte da Ravasqueira, QUINTA Nova, SOALHEIRO (sp), Vértice (sp).

Rosé Port Pioneered by Croft's Pink (2005) now made by other shippers (eg. KROHN, Poças). Quality variable. Serve chilled, on ice, or, if you must, in a cocktail.

Rozès Port ★★★ Port shipper owned by Vranken-Pommery. VINTAGE PORT, incl LBV, sourced from DOU Superior QUINTAS (Grifo, Anibal, Canameira). Terras do Grifo Vintage is blend of all three; v.gd LBV from Grifo only.

Ruby Port Most simple, young, cheap sweet Port style. Can still be gd drink. RES better.

Rui Reguinga Alen, Tej ★★★ Consultant winemaker with own projects. ALEN: v.gd old-vines Terrenus range, incl single-v'yd, 100-yr-old vines Vinha da Serra (w). TEJO: v.gd Rhône-inspired Tributo (SYRAH/GRENACHE/VIOGNIER). Also in Argentina.

Sandeman Port Port ★★ ★★★ Historic house owned by SOGRAPE. V.gd age-dated TAWNY esp 20-, 30-, 40-yr-old, unfiltered LBV. Great old VINTAGE PORT 07' 11' bring back quality. Second label: forward Vau Vintage. Superb Very Old Tawny Cask 33.

São João, Caves Bair r w sp ★★ ★★★ Traditional, family-owned firm known for gd old-fashioned red/white, esp *Frei João*, Poço do Lobo (BAIR), Porta dos Cavaleiros

> **Talha wines**
> The technique of making wine in clay amphoras, called *talhas*, was probably introduced by the Romans 2000 yrs ago. Now they're a trend. Top producers: Cortes de Cima, ESPORÃO, Herdade dos Outeiros Altos, Herdade do Peso, Herdade do Rocim, José de Sousa, Piteira. BAIR, VIN also trying amphoras. Better wine?

(DÃO). Regular gd-value museum releases from vast stock (back to 1963). Gd ARINTO/CHARD white, sparkling blends.

Sercial Mad White grape. Makes driest MAD. *Supreme apéritif*, gd with gravlax or sushi. *See* Grapes chapter.

Smith Woodhouse Port ★★★ SYMINGTON-owned small Port firm est 1784. Gd unfiltered LBV; some v.gd drier VINTAGE PORT 66 70 75 77' 80 83 85 91 94 97 00' 03 07 11'. Single-quinta da Madelena.

Soalheiro, Quinta de Vin r p w sp ★★ →★★★ Leading ALVARINHO specialist with partly organic range worth aging. V.gd subtly barrel-fermented old-vine Primeiras Vinhas, oak-aged RES (w), chestnut barrel/partial malolactic fermentation Terramatter, unfiltered Pur Nature. First red, Oppaco, is unique Vinhão/Alvarinho blend. V.gd fizz (p w).

Sogrape Vin ★→★★★★ Portugal's most successful firm. MATEUS ROSÉ, BARCA VELHA jewels in crown for contrasting reasons. Portfolio encompasses ALEN (Herdade do Peso), DÃO (CARVALHAIS), DOU (Casa Ferreirinha, Legado), Port (FERREIRA, SANDEMAN, OFFLEY), VIN (incl gd-value Azevedo).

Sousa, Alves de Dou, Port r w ★★→★★★ Family-owned DOU pioneer. Characterful range from various QUINTAS, incl late releases. polished Vinha de Lordelo. Expanding Port range incl elegant VINTAGE PORT, v.gd 20-yr-old TAWNY.

Symington Family Estates Dou, Port r w ★★→★★★★ DOU's biggest landowner with 27 QUINTAS, a clutch of top Port houses (incl COCKBURN, DOW, GRAHAM, VESUVIO, WARRE); classy Dou range (CHRYSEIA, Vesuvio and well-made organic Altano). Now also in n ALEN.

Tawny Wood-aged Port (hence tawny colour), ready to please on release. RES, age-dated (10-, 20-, 30-, 40-yr-old) wines go up in complexity, price. Single-year COLHEITAS can cost gd deal more than VINTAGE. Luscious Very Old Tawny Ports (min 40 yrs old, most much older) rare, may cost more than Vintage, rarely worth it.

Taylor Port ★★ →★★★★ Historic Port shipper, FLADGATE's jewel in the crown. Imposing VINTAGE PORTS 66 70 75 77' 80 83 85 92' 94 97 00' 03' 07' 09' 11', incl single-QUINTAS (Terra Feita, Vargellas), rare Vargellas Vinha Velha from 70-yr-old+ vines. Market leader for TAWNY incl v.gd age-dated, 50-yr-old COLHEITAS and luscious Very Old Tawny (Scion, 1863).

Tejo r w DOC and VR around River Tagus (Tejo). Quantity-to-quality shift but still little sets pulse racing. Solid: FALUA, QUINTAS da Alorna, da Lagoalva, da Lapa. More ambitious: Encosta do Sobral, RUI REGUINGA/Tributo show potential of top terroir. Old vines produce gd results with stalwart CASTELÃO (Casal Branco), FERNÃO PIRES.

Tinto Red.

Trás-os-Montes Mountainous inland DOC, just n of DOU. Valle Pradinhos is well-known reference. Promising: Encostas de Sonim, Valle de Passos, Sobreiró de Cima. (VR Transmontano.)

Vale Dona Maria, Quinta do Dou, Port r p w ★★ →★★★ Now owned by AVELEDA. V.gd plush yet elegant reds incl two single-parcel wines: Vinha do Rio, Vinha da Francisca. Smoky, oaky but brisk whites feature in labels made with bought-in fruit, incl flagship CV, mid-range Van Zellers, new VVV and entry level Rufo. Port also gd.

Vale Meão, Quinta do Dou r w ★★★ Leading DOU Superior estate; once source of BARCA VELHA. Fine, age-worthy, elegant top red. Gd-value second label Meandro (also w). Gd single-QUINTA VINTAGE PORT. Single-varietal Monte Meão range.

Vallado, Quinta da Dou r p w ★★→★★★ Family-owned Baixo Corgo estate with modern hotel/winery. DOU Superior QUINTA do Orgal (boutique Casa do Rio) with new, fresh organic red. Range of Dou (r w), incl RES field blend, worth following. Gd 10-, 20-, 30-, 40-yr-old TAWNY. Adelaide designates top Dou red, VINTAGE PORT, thrilling Tributa Very Old (pre-phylloxera) Tawny.

Vasques de Carvalho Dou, Port ★★★ New producer (2012) est by António Vasques de Carvalho (inherited family cellars, stock, v'yd) and business partner Luís Vale (injected capital). V.gd, stylish 10-, 20-, 30- and 40-yr-old TAWNY.

Verdelho Mad Style and grape of medium-dry MAD; pungent but without spine of SERCIAL. Gd apéritif or pair with pâté. Increasingly popular for table wines.

Vértice Dou sp ★★★ Reputed DOU fizz producer. V.gd-value Gouveio. Superb, high-altitude, 8-mth-aged PINOT N.

Vesuvio, Quinta do Dou, Port ★★★★ Magnificent QUINTA and Port on par with best VINTAGE PORT 00' 01 03' 04 05' 06 07' 08' 09 10 11' 12 13' 15. Only SYMINGTON FAMILY ESTATES Port still foot-trodden by people (not robotically). V.gd age-worthy old-vine Vesuvio (r), gd-value second label Pombal do Vesuvio (r).

Vila Nova de Gaia Dou, Port Historic home of major Port shippers' lodges, across River Douro from Oporto. Hotels, restaurants have sprung up. Many lodges have moved out.

Vinho Verde r p w sp ★ →★★★ Portugal's biggest DOC in cool, rainy, verdant nw. Adequate for decades; now signs of renaissance: fresh, better blends. Best: high-end, subregional, varietal QUINTA wines, incl ALVARINHO from Monção & Melgaço (eg. ADEGA DE MONÇÃO, ANSELMO MENDES, da Pedra, do Regueiro, Luis Seabra, Reguengo de Melgaço, SOALHEIRO), LOUREIRO from Lima (eg. APHROS, Paço de Palmeira, QUINTA DO AMEAL). Avesso from Baião (COVELA). Red Vinhão grape now targeted for makeover by leading players (eg. Anselmo Mendes, Aphros, SOALHEIRO). Large brands are spritzy; DYA. Watch: Quinta de Santiago, da Lixa, de San Joanne.

Vintage Port Classic vintages are best wines declared in exceptional yrs by shippers between 1 Jan and 30 Sept in 2nd yr after vintage. Bottled without filtration after 2 yrs in wood, mature v. slowly in bottle, throwing a deposit: always decant. Modern vintages broachable earlier (and hedonistic young), best will last more than 50 yrs. Single-QUINTA Vintage Ports also drinking earlier; best can last 30 yrs+.

VR / IGP (Vinho Regional / Indicação Geográfica Protegida) Same status as French Vin de Pays. More leeway for experimentation than DOC/DOP.

Warre Port ★★★→★★★★ Oldest of British Port shippers (1670), now owned by SYMINGTON FAMILY ESTATES. Rich, long-aging VINTAGE 63 66 70' 75 77' 80' 83 85 91 94 **97** 00' 03 07' 09' 11' and unfiltered LBV. Elegant Single-QUINTA and 10-, 20-yr-old TAWNY Otima reflect Quinta da Cavadinha's cool elevation.

Old-vine field blends can have more than 40 different varieties planted together.

White Port Port from white grapes. Ranges from dry to sweet (*lágrima*); mostly off-dry and blend of yrs. Apéritif straight or drink iced with tonic and fresh mint. Growing, high-quality, varietal: age-dated (10-, 20-, 30-, or 40-yr-old), eg. ANDRESEN, KOPKE, QUINTA de Santa Eufemia; rare COLHEITAS eg. C DA SILVA's Dalva.

Wine & Soul Dou, Port r w ★★★★ Boutique DOU project of Sandra Tavares and Jorge Serôdio Borges, making terroir-expressive wines, incl v.gd, oak-aged Guru (w), superb old-vine QUINTA da Manoella Vinhas Velhas and complex, dense (80-yr-old vine) Pintas. V.gd Pintas Character and second-label Manoella esp white. V.gd Pintas VINTAGE PORT. Oustanding 5G (120-yr-old barrel kept from five generations) Very Old TAWNY Port.

Switzerland

Abbreviations used in the text:

Aar	Aargau
Ber	Bern
Gris	Grisons
Luc	Lucerne
Neu	Neuchâtel
Schaff	Schaffhausen
Thur	Thurgau
Tic	Ticino
Val	Valais
Vd	Vaud
Zür	Zürich

High prices haven't put drinkers off burgundy yet; sadly they do when it comes to Swiss wines. Few foreigners drink them, though skiers soon become aware of Fendant and its deceptive kick. The rare grapes of the Alps have unique qualities, and surprising variety. The most impressive are dense, often sweet, golden-amber and live for years. The most useful are sharp and full-bodied whites, great food wines such as Petite Arvine and Completer, or the ubiquitous red Dôle, though the Swiss have better and more interesting reds: Cornalin and Humagne Rouge, Merlot with an Italian-Swiss accent in Ticino and some impressive Syrah in the Valais. The most prestigious are Chardonnay and Pinot Noir from Bündner Herrschaft. The best advice to off-piste skiers, wine-lovers too, is to employ a guide.

Recent vintages

2017 Frost, drought, hail; some cantons have only 20 per cent of a normal year. Quality is promising.

2016 Frost in April, rainy summer then sun: late, healthy harvest; mostly mid-weight wines.

2015 Great vintage, maybe best in 50 years: ripe fruit, perfectly balanced acidity.

2014 Dry, sunny September saved crop; a year of classically structured wines.

2013 Very small crop; eastern Switzerland outstanding, great freshness, purity.

2012 A winemaker's vintage. Difficult year with hail and rain.

Fine vintages: 2009, 2005 (all), 2000 (esp Pinot N, Valais reds), 1999 (Dézaley), 1997 (Dézaley), 1990 (all).

Aargau Wine-growing canton se of Basel, mainly PINOT N, MÜLLER-T. Gd growers incl Döttingen co-op, Haefliger (bio), Hartmann, LITWAN, Meier (zum Sternen).

Aigle Vd ★★ Commune for CHASSELAS known for BADOUX v. light Les Murailles. Try Terroir du Crosex Grillé.

AOC The equivalent of French Appellation Contrôlée, but unlike in France, not nationally defined and every canton has its own rules. 85 AOCs countrywide.

Bachtobel, Schlossgut Thur ★★★ Since 1784 owned by descendants of Kesselring family, known for refined PINOT N from slopes nr Weinfelden.

Bad Osterfingen Schaff ★★★ Restaurant and wine estate in historical baths (est 1472). Michael Meyer is a PINOT specialist. Co-producer of ZWAA.

Badoux, Henri Vd ★★ Big producer; his CHASSELAS AIGLE les Murailles (classic lizard label) is most popular Swiss brand, though seldom convincing.

Baumann, Ruedi Schaff ★★★ Leading estate at Oberhallau; berry-scented, ageable PINOT N esp -R., Ann Mee. ZWAA collaboration with nearby BAD OSTERFINGEN estate.

Bern Capital and canton. Villages Ligerz, Schafis, Twann (Lake Biel), Spiez (Lake Thun): mainly CHASSELAS, PINOT N. Top: Andrey, Johanniterkeller, Schlössli, Steiner.

Besse, Gérald et Patricia Val ★★★ Leading VAL family estate, mostly on steep-sloping terraces up to 600m; superb old-vines *Ermitage Les Serpentines* 08 09 10' **12 13'** 14 15 bears its name: MARSANNE from granite soils, planted 1945.

Blattner, Valentin Vine-breeder in the Jura canton, known for crossings like Cabertin and Pinotin, bringing together fungal resistance and high quality.

Bonvin Val ★★→★★★ An old name of VAL, recently much improved, esp local grapes: *Nobles Cépages* series (eg. HEIDA, PETITE ARVINE, SYRAH).

Bovard, Louis Vd ★★→★★★★ Family estate (ten generations) famous for its textbook DÉZALEY La Médinette 99' 03 05' 08 09 10 11 12' **13** 14 15 16, old vintages back to 2000 available from the domaine.

Bündner Herrschaft Gris ★★→★★★★ 05' 09' 10 11 12 13' 14 15' 16 17 Switzerland's Burgundy: PINOT N (BLAUBURGUNDER) with structure, fruit and age-worthiness, individualistic growers. But only four villages: FLÄSCH, Jenins, Maienfeld, MALANS. Climate balanced between mild s winds and cool climate from nearby mts.

Calamin Vd ★★★ GRAND CRU of LAVAUX, tarter CHASSELAS than neighbour DÉZALEY. Only 16 ha, growers incl BOVARD, Dizerens, DUBOUX.

Castello di Morcote Tic ★★★ One of most scenic v'yds of TIC, tended by art historian Gaby Gianini, well-balanced, warm, supple MERLOT with small amounts of CAB FR.

Chablais Vd ★★→★★★ Wine region at upper end of Lake Geneva, top villages: AIGLE, YVORNE. Name is derived from Latin *caput lacis*, head of the lake.

Changins Secondary wine town of LA CÔTE, home of Switzerland's centre for viticultural and oenological teaching and research.

Chanton, Josef-Marie and Mario Val ★★★ *Terrific Valais spécialités*; v'yds up to 800m: Eyholzer Roter, Gwäss, HEIDA, Himbertscha, Lafnetscha, Resi.

Chappaz, Marie-Thérèse Val ★★★→★★★★★ Small bio estate at Fully, famous for magnificent sweet wines of local grape Petite ARVINE 00 02 03 **04' 06'** (430g/l residual sugar!) **09 10** and Ermitage (MARSANNE). Hard to find.

Côte, La Vd ★→★★★ 2000 ha w of Lausanne on Lake Geneva, mainly CHASSELAS of v. light, commercial style. Best-known villages: FÉCHY, Mont-sur-Rolle, Morges.

Cruchon, Henri Vd ★★ →★★★ Bio producer of LA CÔTE, lots of SPECIALITÉS (VIOGNIER, Altesse, Servagnin, BLATTNER-breedings). Top growth: PINOT N Raissennaz.

Dézaley Vd ★★★→★★★★★ 90' 97 99 03 05' 09' 10 11 12 **13 14** 15' 16 17 Celebrated LAVAUX GRAND CRU on steep slopes of Lake Geneva, 50 ha; planted in C12 by Cistercian monks. Potent CHASSELAS develops with age. Best: DUBOUX, *Fonjallaz*, *Louis Bovard*, Monachon, Ville de Lausanne. Tiny red production too, mostly blends.

Dôle Val ★★ VAL's answer to Burgundy's Passetoutgrains: PINOT N plus GAMAY. Buy only reliable producers. Lightly pink Dôle Blanche pressed straight after harvest.

Swiss wine and global warming
Switzerland's Bundesamt für Umwelt (Federal Insitute for the
Environment) has published a comprehensive study about the impact
of global warming on the country and its agriculture. Conclusion:
the negatives surpass the positives by far. Longer growing seasons
are positive, but will not compensate for higher chances of drought,
heatwaves, floodings and landslides. And shorter winters mean less
tourism – which might affect wine consumption. Will 2017 snowfall
change their minds?

Donatsch, Thomas Gris ★★★ Barrique pioneer (1974) at MALANS, joined by son Martin; rich, supple PINOT N, crisp CHARD. Family restaurant, zum Ochsen, gd place to have a bottle opened.

Duboux, Blaise Vd ★★★ 5-ha family estate in LAVAUX. Outstanding DÉZALEY *vieilles vignes* Haut de Pierre (v. rich, mineral), CALAMIN Cuvée Vincent.

Epesses Vd ★→★★★ Well-known LAVAUX AOC, 130 ha surrounding GRAND CRU CALAMIN: sturdy, full-bodied whites. Growers incl BOVARD, DUBOUX, Fonjallaz, Luc Massy.

Féchy Vd ★→★★★ Famous though unreliable AOC of LA CÔTE, mainly CHASSELAS.

Federweisser / Weissherbst German-Swiss pale rosé or even Blanc de Noirs made from BLAUBURGUNDER.

Fendant Val ★→★★★ Full-bodied VAL CHASSELAS, ideal for fondue or raclette. Try BESSE, Domaine Cornulus, GERMANIER, Provins, SIMON MAYE. Name derived from French *se fendre* (to burst) because ripe berries of local Chasselas clone crack open if pressed between fingertips.

Fläsch Gris ★★★→★★★★ Village of BÜNDNER HERRSCHAFT on schist and limestone, producing mineral, austere PINOT N. Lots of gd estates, esp members of Adank, Hermann, Marugg families. *Gantenbein* is outstanding.

Flétri / Mi-flétri Late-harvested grapes for sweet/slightly sweet wine.

Fribourg 115 ha on shores of Lake Murten (Mont Vully): powerful CHASSELAS, elegant TRAMINER, round PINOT N. Try Château de Praz, Chervet, Cru de l'Hôpital, Derron.

Fromm, Georg Gris ★★★ 04 05' 09' 10 11 **12 13'** 14 15' 16 17 Top grower in MALANS, 5 ha in conversion to bio, known for subtle single-v'yd PINOT N (Fidler, Schöpfi, Selfi, Selvenen). Constructing new cellar with architect Peter Zumthor.

Gantenbein, Daniel & Martha Gris ★★★★ 05 09' 10' 11 12 13' 14 15' 16 17 Star growers, based in FLÄSCH. Top PINOT N from DRC clones (*see* France), RIES clones from Loosen (*see* Germany), exceptional CHARD in v. limited quantity.

Geneva City surrounded by 1400 ha of vines remote from homonymous lake (v'yds there belong mainly to neighbouring canton VD). A wide range of varieties, growers incl Balisiers, Grand'Cour, Les Hutins, Novelle.

Germanier, Jean-René Val ★★→★★★ Important VAL estate, reliable FENDANT Les Terrasses, elegant SYRAH Cayas, AMIGNE from schist at Vétroz (dr sw – "Mitis").

Glacier, Vin du (Gletscherwein) Val ★★★ Fabled oxidized, (larch)-wooded white from rare Rèze grape of Val d'Anniviers. Find it at the Rathaus of Grimentz. A sort of Alpine Sherry.

Grain Noble ConfidenCiel Val Quality label for authentic sweet wines, eg. CHAPPAZ, DOMAINE DU MONT D'OR, Dorsaz (both estates), GERMANIER, Philippe Darioli, PROVINS.

Grand Cru Val, Vd Inconsistent term, in use in VAL (commune Salgesch for PINOT N) and in VD (as "Premier Grand Cru" for a wide range of single-estate wines). Switzerland has only two Grands Crus in the sense of a classification of v'yd sites: CALAMIN, DÉZALEY.

Grisons (Graubünden) Mtn canton, German-speaking. PINOT N king. *See* BÜNDNER HERRSCHAFT. Best growers in other areas: Manfred Meier, VON TSCHARNER.

Huber, Daniel ★★→★★★ Pioneer who reclaimed possibly historical sites from fallow in 1981. Bio since 2003. Now joined by son Jonas. Reliable MERLOT Fusto 4, premium label Montagna Magica 03 05' 07 08 09 10 11 12.

Johannisberg Val VAL name for SILVANER, often off-dry or sweet; great with fondue. Excellent: *Domaine du Mont d'Or*.

Joris, Didier Val ★★★→★★★★ Only 3 ha, but a dozen varieties bringing wines of depth and complexity, incl outstanding (and rare) MARSANNE. Now also to revive nearly extinct local white grape Diolle.

La Colombe, Domaine Vd ★★→★★★ Family estate of FÉCHY, LA CÔTE, 15 ha, bio. Best known for range of ageable CHASSELAS, eg. La Brez.

La Rodeline, Domaine Val ★★★ VAL family estate known for local varieties from prime terraced single v'yds at Fully and Leytron: La Chaille CORNALIN, Les Claives MARSANNE and Petite ARVINE, Plamont HEIDA, Raffort HUMAGNE Blanc.

Lavaux Vd ★★→★★★★ 30 km of steep s-facing terraces e of Lausanne; UNESCO World Heritage site. Uniquely rich, mineral CHASSELAS. GRANDS CRUS DÉZALEY, CALAMIN, several village AOCS.

Litwan, Tom Aar ★★★ Newcomer who studied in Burgundy. Delicate, fine-grained PINOT N Auf der Mauer ("On Top of the Wall") and Chalofe ("Lime Kiln").

Malans Gris Village in BÜNDNER HERRSCHAFT. Top PINOT N producers incl DONATSCH, FROMM, Liesch, Studach, Wegelin. Late-ripening local grape Completer gives a long-lasting phenolic white. Monks used to drink it with day's last prayer (Compline). Adolf Boner (01' 05') is keeper of the Grail.

Maye, Simon et Fils Val ★★★ Perfectionist estate at St-Pierre-de-Clages. Dense SYRAH *vieilles vignes* 00 07 09 10 11' 12; spicy, powerful Païen (HEIDA), FENDANT v.gd too.

Mémoire des Vins Suisses Union of 56 leading growers in effort to create stock of Swiss icon wines, to prove their ageing capacities. Oldest wines from 1999.

Mercier Val ★★★→★★★★ SIERRE family estate, Anne-Catherine and Denis M now joined by daughter Madeleine. Meticulous v'yd management: dense, aromatic reds, eg. archetypal CORNALIN 99 02 03 05' 07 09' 10' 11 12 13 14 15 and SYRAH.

Mont d'Or, Domaine du Val ★★→★★★★ Emblematic VAL estate for semi- and nobly sweet wines, esp JOHANNISBERG Saint-Martin 07 08' 09 10 11 12.

Neuchâtel ★→★★★ 600 ha around city and lake on calcareous soil. Slightly sparkling CHASSELAS, exquisite PINOT N from local clone (Cortaillod). Best: Château d'Auvernier (also PINOT GR), La Maison Carrée, Porret, TATASCIORE.

Oeil de Perdrix Neu "Partridge's eye": PINOT N Rosé, originally from NEU, now found elsewhere.

Pircher, Urs Zür ★★★→★★★★ Top estate at Eglisau, steep s-facing slope overlooking Rhine. Outstanding PINOT N Stadtberger Barrique 05' 09' 10 11 12 13' 14 15' 16 from old Swiss clones. Whites of great purity.

Provins Val ★→★★★ Co-op with 4000+ members, Switzerland's biggest producer, 1500 ha, 34 varieties. Sound entry-level, v.gd oak-aged Maître de Chais range.

Rouvinez Vins Val ★→★★★ Famous producer at SIERRE, best known for cuvées La Trémaille (w) and Le Tourmentin (r). Controls also BONVIN, Caves Orsat, Imesch.

Ruch Schaff ★★★ Excellent PINOT N from HALLAU, eg. Chölle from 60-yr-old vines, Haalde from steep slope. Amphora-fermented MÜLLER-T. Only 2.5 ha.

St. Jodern Kellerei Val ★★→★★★★ VISPERTERMINEN co-op famous for **Heida Veritas** from ungrafted old vines: superb reflection of Alpine terroir.

St-Saphorin Vd ★→★★★★ Neighbour AOC of DÉZALEY, lighter, but equally delicate. Try Monachon's Les Manchettes.

Schaffhausen ★→★★★ Canton/town on Rhine with famous falls, BLAUBURGUNDER stronghold. Best-known village is Hallau, but be v. careful. Top growers: BAD OSTERFINGEN, BAUMANN, RUCH, Strasser.

Schenk SA Vd ★→★★★ Wine giant with worldwide activities, based in Rolle, founded 1893. Classic wines (esp VD, VAL); substantial exports.

SWITZERLAND

> Wine regions
> Switzerland has six major wine regions: VAL, VD, GENEVA, TIC, Trois Lacs (NEU, Bienne/BER, Vully/FRIBOURG), German Switzerland, which comprises ZÜR, SCHAFF, GRIS, AAR, St Gallen, Thur, some smaller wine cantons.

Schwarzenbach, Hermann Zür ★★★ Leading family estate on Lake ZÜRICH, crisp whites (local Räuschling, MÜLLER-T) match freshwater fish.

Sierre Val ★★→★★★ VAL town on six hills, home of rich, luscious wines. Best-known: des Muses, Imesch, MERCIER, ROUVINEZ, Zufferey.

Sion Val ★★→★★★ Capital/wine centre of VAL, domicile of big producers: *Charles Bonvin* Fils, Gilliard, PROVINS, Varone.

Specialités / Spezialitäten Quantitatively minor grapes producing some of best Swiss wines, eg. Räuschling, GEWURZ or PINOT GR in German Switzerland, or local varieties (and grapes like JOHANNISBERG, MARSANNE, SYRAH) in VAL.

Sprecher von Bernegg Gris ★★★ Historic estate at Jenins, BÜNDNER HERRSCHAFT, revived by young Jan Luzi esp PINOT N: Lindenwingert, vom Pfaffen/Calander.

Stucky, Werner Tic ★★★→★★★★ Pioneer of MERLOT del TIC now joined by son Simon. Three wines: Temenos (Completer/SAUV BL), Tracce di Sassi (Merlot), Conte di Luna (Merlot/CAB SAUV). Stucky's best v'yd is only accessible via a funicular.

Tatasciore, Jacques Neu ★★★★ Shooting star in NEU, refined PINOT N to show that Burgundy isn't far away.

Ticino ★→★★★ Italian-speaking; mainly MERLOT. Best wines avoid international style, eg. Agriloro, CASTELLO DI MORCOTE, Gialdi, HUBER, Klausener, Kopp von der Crone Visini, STUCKY, Tamborini, Valsangiacomo, Vinattieri, ZÜNDEL.

Tscharner, Gian-Battista von ★★→★★★ Family estate at Reichenau Castle, GRAUBÜNDEN; tannin-laden PINOT N (Churer Gian-Battista 99 00 05' 07 09 10 11) to age.

Valais (Wallis) Largest wine canton, in dry, sunny upper Rhône Valley. Mostly too warm for PINOT N, but local varieties are outstanding, and best MARSANNE, SYRAH rival French legends downstream. Top: BESSE, CHANTON, CHAPPAZ, Cornulus, darioli, des Muses, Dorsaz, GERMANIER, JORIS, MAYE, MERCIER, MONT D'OR, PROVINS, ROUVINEZ, ST. JODERN, Zufferey (both).

Vaud (Waadt) Wine canton known for conservative spirit. Important big producers: Bolle, Hammel, Obrist, SCHENK. CHASSELAS is main grape – but only gd terroirs justify growers' loyalty.

Visperterminen Val w ★→★★★ Upper VAL v'yds, esp for HEIDA. One of highest v'yds in Europe (at 1000m+; called Riben). Try CHANTON, ST. JODERN KELLEREI.

Yvorne Vd ★★→★★★ CHABLAIS village with v'yds on detritus of 1584 avalanche, eg. Château Maison Blanche, Commune d'Yvorne, Domaine de l'Ovaille.

Until the 60s, B'x was aged, bottled in cellars under Zürich's main railway station.

Zündel, Christian Tic ★★★→★★★★ 02 05' 09 10 11 12 13 14 15 German Swiss geologist in TIC. Wines of great purity and finesse, esp MERLOT/CAB SAUV Orizzonte. CHARD Dosso was about to become cultish when disease *flavescence dorée* killed the v'yd. Last vintage: 2015.

Zürich Largest wine-growing canton in German Switzerland, 610 ha. Mainly BLAUBURGUNDER, Räuschling a local SPECIALITY. Best growers: Gehring, Lüthi, PIRCHER, SCHWARZENBACH, Zahner.

Zur Metzg, Winzerei Zür ★★→★★★ Banker turned winemaker, refined PINOT N, barrel-fermented MÜLLER-T (mainly bought-in grapes), vinified in old grocery.

Zwaa Schaff ★★★ Collaboration of two leading, complementary SCHAFF estates (BAUMANN – calcareous, deep soil; BAD OSTERFINGEN – light, gravelly). PINOT N 94' 97 98 99 99 01 02 03 04 05 06 07 09' 10 11 12 13' 14 15', white counterpart a blend PINOT BL/CHARD 00' 04 05' 06 07' 08 09 10 11' 12 13 14.

Austria

Abbreviations used in the text:

Burgen	Burgenland
Carn	Carnuntum
Kamp	Kamptal
Krems	Kremstal
Nied	Niederösterreich
S Stei	Südsteiermark
Therm	Thermenregion
Trais	Traisental
V Stei	Vulkanland Steiermark
Wach	Wachau
Wag	Wagram
Wein	Weinviertel
W Stei	Weststeiermark

This Alpine republic makes wine to probably the highest average quality in Europe – perhaps the reason why in some markets it is more fashionable than its two obvious siblings, Germany and Alsace. The style is pristine, crystalline, balanced, with ample alcohol and with an emphasis on showing off the vineyard; producers are mostly small-scale and family-owned – and ambitious. The Austrian quality system is gradually moving from the old Germanic system based on sugar levels to one based on provenance, which also enshrines local styles and grape varieties: Grüner Veltliner has established an international reputation, while Blaufränkisch and Zweigelt suit a very modern idiom of lighter, fresher reds. The creation of Austria's first DAC for Weinviertel in 2002 was the opening shot. The 10th DAC, Schilcherland, was ratified in 2017, and further Styrian DACs as well as Rosalia and Ausbruch in Burgenland are on the cards.

Recent vintages

2017 Hail, frost, heat, drought, but in the end normal yields, decent quality.

2016 Spring frost, mildew, hail reduced yield. What's left is good.

2015 Very good quality. Summer heat spikes did little harm.

2014 Tricky weather necessitated scrupulous selection. Quality meant sacrificing quantity.

2013 Hot, dry summer, rain in September; very good for sweet wines.

2012 Quantities down from 2011. Quality satisfactory or better.

2011 One of finest vintages in living memory. Try it while you can.

Don't hesitate to try more mature vintages from good producers.

Achs, Paul Burgen r (w) ★★★ 10 12 13 14 15 16 Exacting producer of vivid reds. Esp BLAUFRÄNKISCH Edelgrund, Heideboden.

Allram Kamp w ★★★ 10 11 12 13 14 15 16 Consistently gd GRÜNER V (esp Renner, Gaisberg), RIES, RES Heiligenstein.

Alphart Therm w ★★ Regional focus on ROTGIPFLER, ZIERFANDLER; HEURIGER destination.

Alzinger Wach w ★★★★ 06 08 09 10 12 13 14 15 Underrated but 1st rate. Look out for RIES, GRÜNER V, Steinertal and Loibenberg.

Arndorfer Kamp r w ★★★ Enterprising, experimenting couple, gd across board. Esp ZWEIGELT, oaked RIES.

Ausbruch Quality/style designation for Prädikat wine; restricted to RUST and botrytized, dried grapes. Min must weight 27°KMW or 138.6°Oechsle. Ratification of DAC expected.

Ausg'steckt ("Hung out") Traditional signal of open HEURIGEN or *Buschenschank*: entrance decorated with fresh greenery.

Bauer, Anton Wag r w ★★★→★★★★ Est WAG producer of uncompromising quality. Famed GRÜNER V: single-v'yds Rosenberg, Spiegel. Astonishing, elegant PINOT N.

Beck, Judith Burgen r w ★★→★★★ Experimental bio youngster to watch for blends from indigenous reds.

Braunstein, Birgit Burgen r w ★★★ 10 12 13 15 16 Bio winemaker of rare intuition, experimental spirit, amazing reds BLAUFRÄNKISCH LEITHABERG, PINOT N, ST-LAURENT. Experimental amphora-aged Magna Mater CHARD. To try.

Bründlmayer, Willi Kamp r w sw sp ★★★★ 06 08 10 11' 12 13 14 15 Deservedly celebrated top producer, at Langenlois. GRÜNER V, RIES esp Heiligenstein and Steinmassl. Beautiful *méthode traditionelle*, impressive PINOT N.

Burgenland Burgen r (w) Federal state and wine region bordering Hungary. Warmer than NIED, hence reds like BLAUFRÄNKISCH, ST-LAURENT, ZWEIGELT prevalent. Shallow NEUSIEDLERSEE, eg. at RUST, creates ideal botrytis conditions.

Carnuntum Nied r w Undeservedly overlooked region se of VIENNA specialized in reds, esp ZWEIGELT marketed as Rubin Carnuntum. Best: G Markowitsch, MUHR-VAN DER NIEPOORT, Netzl, TRAPL.

Christ Vienna r w ★★★ Dynamic VIENNA producer and HEURIGEN pushing boundaries. Textbook GEMISCHTER SATZ and experimental red blends.

DAC (Districtus Austriae Controllatus) Provenance- and quality-based appellation system denoting regionally typical wines and styles. Creation of 1st, WEIN DAC 2001, prompted regional quality turnaround. Currently ten DACs: EISENBERG, KAMP, KREMS, LEITHABERG, MITTELBURGENLAND, NEUSIEDLERSEE, TRAIS, Wein, Wiener GEMISCHTER SATZ. Latest SCHILCHERLAND. More in pipeline. Often stratified into Klassik and RES with varietal and ageing stipulations.

Domäne Wachau Wach w ★★★→★★★★ Top Austrian co-op specialized in single v'yds like Achleiten, Bruck, Kellerberg. Impressive across board. Great-value SMARAGD and Terrassen series.

Ebner-Ebenauer Wein w sp ★★★ Dynamic young couple with uncompromising quality focus. Esp single-v'yd GRÜNER V Hermanschachern, Bürsting, Sauberg. Gorgeous Blanc de Blancs *méthode traditionelle* 08 10.

Green heroes

Organic or bio-dynamic methods are big in Austria: some ten per cent of growers are certified, and many more farm with these methods. Pioneers like NIKOLAIHOF (WACH), JOSEF UMATHUM (BURGEN) and FRED LOIMER (KAMP) have super quality and resounding success. Also look for BECK, BRAUNSTEIN, GEYERHOF, GUT OGGAU, JURSCHITSCH, Meinklang. And don't be shy of asking for experimental natural and orange wines; there are more and more of them.

Eichinger, Birgit Kamp w ★★★→★★★★ Top-class KAMP stalwart for RIES, esp Heiligenstein and exceptionally expressive GRÜNER V, esp Hasel.

Eisenberg Burgen Small DAC (since 2009) restricted to BLAUFRÄNKISCH from local slate soil. Powerful but elegant.

Erste Lage Premier Cru designation according to ÖTW v'yd classification; currently 59 v'yds in KAMP, KREMS, TRAIS, WAGRAM.

Esterhazy Burgen r (w) ★★★ Historic Schloss (Haydn worked here) in Eisenstadt (BURGEN), renewed quality focus and dynamic management.

Partially fermented grape must, *Sturm*: seasonal but dangerous autumn speciality.

Federspiel Wach VINEA WACHAU middle category of ripeness, min 11.5%, max 12.5% alc. Understated, gastronomic wines as age-worthy as SMARAGD. Name refers to falconry.

Feiler-Artinger Burgen r w sw ★★★→★★★★ 06 07 08 10 13 14 15 16 First-class RUST estate famed for AUSBRUCH dessert wines. Subtle BLAUFRÄNKISCH Umriss. Picturesque historic buildings.

Gemischter Satz Vienna Revived historic concept of co-planted and co-fermented field-blend of white varieties. Prevalent in WEIN and VIENNA: determined producers achieved DAC status in 2013 for Vienna. No variety to exceed 50%. Look for CHRIST, GROISS, LENIKUS, WIENINGER.

Gesellmann, Albert & Silvia Burgen r w (sw) ★★★ Renowned for powerful blends of indigenous reds.

Geyerhof Krems r w ★★→★★★ Consistent top-class bio producer of RIES, esp Sprinzenberg. Notable entry-level Stockwerk.

Gols Burgen r (w) Wine village on n shore of NEUSIEDLERSEE. Top: BECK, G HEINRICH, NITTNAUS, PITTNAUER, PREISINGER.

Gritsch Mauritiushof Wach w ★★→★★★ Expressive SMARAGD, esp RIES from 1000-Eimberberg; new high-altitude GRÜNER V plantings.

Groiss, Ingrid Wein w ★★ Experimental, talented young grower specializing in old v'yds. Peppery GRÜNER V, GEMISCHTER SATZ from unusual varieties.

Grosse Lage Stei Highest v'yd classification in STEI, work still in progress along Danube (*see* ERSTE LAGE).

Gumpoldskirchen Therm Once famed, still popular HEURIGEN village s of VIENNA, centre of THERM. Home to rarities ZIERFANDLER, *Rotgipfler.*

Gut Oggau Burgen r w ★★→★★★ Creative, experimental, thoughtful bio producer.

Harkamp S Stei w sp ★★★ Top S STEI producer of SAUV BL but particularly admired for exquisite *méthode traditionelle* Sekts.

Heinrich, Gernot Burgen r w dr sw ★★★ 08 10 12 13 15 PANNOBILE member. Beautiful BLAUFRÄNKISCH, esp Alter Berg and CHARD under LEITHABERG appellation.

Heinrich, J Burgen r w ★★★ 08 09 12 13 14 15 Known for full-bodied but expressive BLAUFRÄNKISCH, esp Goldberg.

Heuriger Wine of most recent harvest. **Heurigen** homely taverns where growers serve own wines with rustic, local food – integral to VIENNA life. *See* AUSG'STECKT.

Hiedler Kamp w sw ★★★ Focused, age-worthy and precise RIES Steinhaus, vivid GRÜNER V Thal and Kittmannsberg.

Hirsch Kamp w ★★★ 10 12 13 14 15 16 Stylish, classy RIES and GRÜNER V from Heiligenstein, Lamm. Fun entry-level GRÜNER V Hirschvergnügen.

Hirtzberger, Franz Wach w ★★★★ 06 07 08 10 13 14 15 16 WACH beacon of powerful, concentrated RIES, GRÜNER V, esp Honivogl, Singerriedel v'yds.

Huber, Markus Trais w ★★★ Energetic, enterprising producer focusing on filigree TRAIS style.

Illmitz Burgen sw SEEWINKEL town on NEUSIEDLERSEE, famous for BA, TBA (*see* Germany). Best from KRACHER, Opitz.

Jäger Wach w ★★★ Incisive GRÜNER V and RIES esp Achleiten, Klaus.

Jalits Burgen ★★★ Top range EISENBERG producer of elegant if powerful BLAUFRÄNKISCH esp Res Szapary and Diabas.

Jamek, Josef Wach w ★★→★★★ Danube-facing WACH stalwart with famed *restaurant*, back with renewed vigour. RIES, GRÜNER V esp Achleiten, Klaus.

Johanneshof Reinisch Therm r w ★★★→★★★★ Top THERM estate with absolute focus. Stellar PINOT N, ROTGIPFLER, ST-LAURENT, ZIERFANDLER. Esp single-v'yds Frauenfeld, Holzspur, Satzing, Spiegel.

Roast chestnuts are the traditional accompaniment for racy new Schilcher.

Jurtschitsch Kamp w sp ★★★→★★★★ Re-invigorated bio estate; impressive across board. Gd sparkling.

Kamptal Nied (r) w Wine region along Danube tributary Kamp n of WACH; rounder style, less altitude. Top v'yds: Heiligenstein, Käferberg, Lamm. Best: BRÜNDLMAYER, EICHINGER, HIEDLER, HIRSCH, JURTSCHITSCH, LOIMER, SCHLOSS GOBELSBURG. Kamp is DAC for GRÜNER V, RIES.

Kerschbaum, Paul Burgen ★★★ 09 12 13 14 15 16 BLAUFRÄNKISCH specialist, notable single v'yd Hochäcker.

Klosterneuburg Wag r w Wine town in WAG, seat of 1860-founded viticultural college and research institute. *See also* KMW.

KMW Abbreviation for KLOSTERNEUBURGER Mostwaage ("must level"), Austrian unit denoting must weight, ie. sugar content of grape juice. 1°KMW = 4.86°Oe (*see* Germany). 20°Bx = 83°Oe.

Knoll, Emmerich Wach w ★★★★ 05 06 07 08 10 11 13 14 15 16 Leading, iconic WACH producer of incisive, layered, *long-lived Ries*, GRÜNER V at any level. Notable Auslese. Best when mature.

Kollwentz Burgen r w ★★★ 10 11 13 15 16 Great reds and red blends.

Kracher Burgen sw ★★★★ 03 04 05 06 07 08 10 11 13 14 Botrytis specialist in ILLMITZ famed for TBA (*see* Germany). Nouvelle Vague series is oak-matured.

Kremstal (r) w Wine region and DAC for GRÜNER V, RIES. Top: MALAT, MOSER, NIGL, SALOMON-UNDHOF, STIFT GÖTTWEIG, WEINGUT STADT KREMS.

Krutzler Burgen r ★★★ 08 09 11 13 14 15 Famous for exacting, powerful, long-lived BLAUFRÄNKISCH. Top wine: Perwolff.

Lagler Wach w ★★★ Precise RIES, GRÜNER V; one of few to make NEUBURGER SMARAGD.

Laurenz V Kamp ★★★ Tiered range of GRÜNER VS aimed at international markets.

Leithaberg Burgen DAC on n shore of NEUSIEDLERSEE, limestone and schist soils. Red restricted to BLAUFRÄNKISCH, whites can be GRÜNER V, PINOT BL, CHARD or NEUBURGER.

Lenikus Vienna w ★★ VIENNA start-up, clean-cut GEMISCHTER SATZ from Bisamberg.

Lesehof Stagård Krems w ★★★ Long-est KREMS estate, vibrant flair for thrilling RIES.

Loimer, Fred Kamp (r) w sp ★★★→★★★★ 10 11 13 14 15 16 Ambitious bio pioneer. Known for expressive whites from single-v'yds Heiligenstein, Steinmassl. Branching out into impressive PINOT N and *lovely sparkling*.

Malat Krems w ★★★→★★★★ Pure RIES and GRÜNER V: real drive esp single-v'yds Gottschelle, Silberbichl.

Mantlerhof Krems w ★★★ Bio producer with rounded, but precise GRÜNER V from loess soils.

Mayer am Pfarrplatz Vienna (r) w ★★ VIENNA stalwart and HEURIGER destination.

Mittelburgenland Burgen r DAC (since 2005) on Hungarian border: structured, age-worthy BLAUFRÄNKISCH. Producers: GESELLMANN, J HEINRICH, KERSCHBAUM, WENINGER.

Moric Burgen ★★★→★★★★ 06 08 10 11 12 13 15 World-class, elegant, long-lived BLAUFRÄNKISCH, note single-v'yds Neckenmarkt, Lutzmannsburg.

Moser, Lenz Krems ★→★★ Austria's largest producer (17 million bottles p.a.).

Muhr-van der Niepoort Carn r w ★★★ Quality-focused BLAUFRÄNKISCH producer instrumental in Spitzerberg revival. Look for approachable Liebeskind, Samt & Seide and Sydhang SYRAH.

Netzl, Franz & Christine Carn ★★★ Leading estate for expressive, age-worthy ZWEIGELT esp Haidacker. Also notable red blends, gd-value Rubin CARN Zweigelt.

Neumayer Trais w ★★★ Quality pioneer in TRAIS, great GRÜNER V, RIES.

Neumeister V Stei ★★★ 09 11 12 13 14 15 16 Top W STEI SAUV BL specialist esp single-v'yds Klausen, Moarfeitl. Look for Stradener Alte Reben.

Neusiedlersee (Lake Neusiedl) Burgen Shallow lake on Hungarian border, largest steppe-lake in Europe, important nature reserve. Lake humidity key to botrytis development. Eponymous DAC limited to ZWEIGELT.

Niederösterreich (Lower Austria) Ne region comprising three parts: Danube (KAMP, KREM, TRAIS, WACH, WAGRAM), WIEN (ne) and CARN, THERM (s) representing 59 per cent of Austria's v'yds.

Nigl Krems w ★★★★ Quality producer of stylish RIES, GRÜNER V esp Privat bottlings.

Nikolaihof Wach w ★★★→★★★★ 08 09 10 13 14 15 16 Outstanding bio producer and pioneer. Thrilling, world-class RIES and GRÜNER V esp late Vinothek releases.

Nittnaus, Anita & Hans Burgen r w sw ★★★→★★★★ Bio producer of elegant, nuanced reds. Top BLAUFRÄNKISCH Tannenberg, LEITHABERG. Note PANNOBILE blend and Comondor.

Nittnaus, Hans & Christine Burgen ★★★ Quality GOLS producer of fine reds esp ZWEIGELT Heideboden, BLAUFRÄNKISCH Edelgrund; red blend Nit'ana. Also notable for TBA and Eiswein.

Ott, Bernhard Wag w ★★★ GRÜNER V specialist in WAG. Cult following for rich, rounded style, esp Fass 4, Rosenberg, Spiegel.

ÖTW (Österreichische Traditionsweingüter) Kamp, Krems, Trais, Wag Private association working on v'yd classification. See ERSTE LAGE, GROSSE LAGE. Currently 33 members; excludes WACH.

Pannobile Burgen Union of nine NEUSIEDLERSEE growers centred on GOLS. Pannobile bottlings may only use indigenous reds (ZWEIGELT, BLAUFRÄNKISCH, ST-LAURENT), whites only PINOTS BL, GR, CHARD. Members: ACHS, BECK, G HEINRICH, NITTNAUS, PITTNAUER, PREISINGER. NB for interesting wines.

Pfaffl Wein r w ★★→★★★ 13 14 15 16 Large, leading WEIN player. Notable RES wines. Creator of ultra-successful brand The Dot Austrian Pepper, Austrian Cherry, etc.

Pichler, Franz X Wach w ★★★★ 06 07 08 09 11 13 14 15 16 Incisive, concentrated, intense, *iconic Ries*, GRÜNER V, from top WACH sites.

Pichler, Rudi Wach w ★★★★ 09 10 11 13 14 15 16 Exacting producer of precise, stellar RIES, GRÜNER V from single-v'yds Achleiten, Steinriegl.

Pichler-Krutzler Wach w ★★★ Marriage of Austrian wine royalty. Outstanding whites from top WACH single v'yds, *thrilling Ries*.

Pittnauer, Gerhard Burgen r ★★★ Gifted, intuitive producer of Austria's finest ST-LAURENT esp Rosenberg; great-value entry-level Pitti.

Polz, Erich & Walter S Stei ★★★ 12 13 15 16 Ambitious s STEI estate. Top v'yd Hochgrassnitzberg: SAUV BL, CHARD.

For particularly rich, nutty white taste indigenous Austrian Neuburger.

Prager, Franz Wach w ★★★★ 07 08 09 10 12 13 14 15 16 Stellar, incisive RIES, GRÜNER V; impressive holding of top sites. Winemaker of engaging intellect and curiosity.

Preisinger, Claus Burgen r ★★★ Creative and irreverent PANNOBILE member. Try fun, crown-capped red Puszta Libre.

Prieler Burgen r w ★★★→★★★★ Super-focused, longstanding producer of age-worthy BLAUFRÄNKISCH and PINOT BL, notably Haidsatz and Seeberg.

Proidl, A & F Krems w ★★★ Consistently reliable RIES, GRÜNER V, both from Ehrenfels. Ask for library RIES releases.

Reserve (Res) Attribute for min 13% alc and prolonged (cask) ageing.

Ried V'yd. As of 2016 compulsory term for single-v'yd bottlings.

Rust Burgen r w d sw Picturesque fortified C17th town on NEUSIEDLERSEE. Home to numerous nesting storks. Famous for Ruster AUSBRUCH. Top: E TRIEBAUMER, FEILER-ARTINGER, SCHRÖCK.

Sabathi, Hannes S Stei w ★★★ Top-range SAUV BL. Notable single-v'yd Pössnitzberg.

Salomon-Undhof Krems w ★★★ →★★★★ Stylish, thrilling GRÜNER V, RIES, always whistle-clean style, esp single-v'yds Kögl, Pfaffenberg.

Kitzeck in S Stei is Austria's highest wine village: 564m (1850ft). Don't look down.

Sattlerhof S Stei w ★★★ 10 12 13 15 16 Iconic STEI producer: clean, oak-aged SAUV BL, MORILLON, esp single-v'yds Kranachberg, Sernauberg.

Schiefer, Uwe Burgen r ★★★ Characterful, edgy; elegant BLAUFRÄNKISCH in EISENBERG.

Schilcher W Stei Racy, peppery rosé from indigenous Blauer Wildbacher grape, speciality of W STEI. Own DAC in 2017 for SCHILCHERLAND.

Schilcherland W Stei Latest Austrian and 1st STEI DAC for SCHILCHER, created 2017.

Schilfwein (Strohwein) Sweet wine made from grapes dried on reeds from NEUSIEDLERSEE. *Schilf* = reed, *Stroh* = straw.

Schloss Gobelsburg Kamp r w d sp sw ★★★★ 09 10 12 13 14 15 16 Former Cistercian estate with top-quality track record. RIES, GRÜNER V of exceptional purity, esp single-v'yds Gaisberg, Heiligenstein, Lamm, Renner. Gd sparkling.

Schlumberger sp High-volume, value producer of *méthode traditionelle* fizz.

Schmelz Wach w ★★★ Underrated producer of quietly outstanding whites.

Schröck, Heidi Burgen (r) w sw ★★★ Top-range RUST producer determined to broaden gastronomic use of AUSBRUCH.

Schuster, Rosi Burgen r ★★★ 13 15 Young BURGEN red specialist.

Seewinkel Burgen ("Lake corner") nature reserve and region e of NEUSIEDLERSEE; ideal conditions for botrytis.

Smaragd Wach Ripest category of VINEA WACHAU, min 12.5% alc but often exceeding 14%, dry, potent, age-worthy, expressive. Depending on producer often botrytis-influenced but dry. Named after local lizard.

Spätrot-Rotgipfler Therm Blend of ROTGIPFLER/Spätrot = synonym for ZIERFANDLER. Aromatic, weighty, textured. Typical for GUMPOLDSKIRCHEN. *See* Grapes chapter.

Spitz an der Donau Wach w Dramatic Danube-facing town at narrowest and coolest part of WACH. Famous v'yds Singerriedel and 1000-Eimerberg. GRITSCH MAURITIUSHOF, HIRTZBERGER, LAGLER.

Stadlmann Therm r w sw ★★ →★★★ Exacting producer of textbook ZIERFANDLER/ROTGIPFLER, delicate Gelber MUSKATELLER, real talent for PINOT N.

Steiermark (Styria) Most s region of Austria, known for aromatic fresh dry whites, esp SAUV BL. *See* S STEI, V STEI, W STEI, SCHILCHERLAND.

Steinfeder Wach Lightest VINEA WACHAU category for delicate, dry wines should be to modern taste. Max 11.5% alc. Named after fragrant Steinfeder grass.

Stift Göttweig w ★★ →★★★ Baroque Benedictine monastery (= Stift) nr Krems; uncompromising quality. Precise single-v'yd Gottschelle, Silberbichl (RIES, GRÜNER V).

Südsteiermark (South Styria) STEI region close to Slovenian border, famed for light but highly aromatic MORILLON, MUSKATELLER, SAUV BL from steep slopes. Best growers: GROSS, POLZ, SABATHI, SATTLERHOF, TEMENT, WOHLMUTH.

Tegernseerhof Wach w ★★ →★★★ V. clean, zesty RIES, GRÜNER V. Lovely FEDERSPIEL.

Tement, Manfred S Stei w ★★★ 09 10 12 13 15 16 World-class oaked SAUV BL, MORILLON. Top sites Grassnitzberg, Zieregg.

Thermenregion Nied r w Spa region e of VIENNA. Famous for indigenous ZIERFANDLER and ROTGIPFLER, historic hotspot for PINOT N. Producers: ALPHART, JOHANNESHOF REINISCH, STADLMANN.

Tinhof, Erwin Burgen r w ★★★ Talented producer of elegant BLAUFRÄNKISCH, esp Gloriette; ST-LAURENT esp Feuersteig. Age-worthy PINOT BL Golden Erd; NEUBURGER.

Traisental Nied Small district s of Krems. Limestone soils are prevalent and explain filigree style. Top: HUBER, NEUMAYER.

Trapl, Johannes Carn r ★★ ⁺★★★ Talented, ambitious newcomer; poised, floral BLAUFRÄNKISCH, esp Sitzerberg and Pinot-esque ZWEIGELT.

Triebaumer, Ernst Burgen r (w) (sw) ★★★★ 08 09 10 12 13 14 15 Iconic RUST estate. Pioneered indigenous red esp BLAUFRÄNKISCH revival, notably Mariental. Plus v.gd AUSBRUCH.

Umathum, Josef Burgen r w dr sw ★★★ ⁺★★★★ Top-range bio grower of intuitive, elegant reds. Unusually serious rosé Rosa.

Velich w sw ★★★ CHARD winemaker with cult following. Outstanding sweet wines in SEEWINKEL.

Veyder-Malberg Wach ★★★ Exacting WACH boutique producer, super-pure style of RIES and GRÜNER V.

Vienna (Wien) (r) w Capital boasting 612 ha v'yds within city limits. Ancient tradition, reignited quality focus. Local field-blend tradition enshrined as DAC GEMISCHTER SATZ in 2013. *Heurigen visit a must.* Best: CHRIST, LENIKUS, WIENINGER and Zahel.

Vinea Wachau Prestigious WACH growers' association founded 1983. Strict quality charter with three-tier ripeness scale for dry wine: FEDERSPIEL, SMARAGD, STEINFEDER.

Vulkanland Steiermark (Southeast Styria) (r) Formerly known as Süd-Oststeiermark, famous for aromatic varieties. Best: NEUMEISTER, Winkler-Hermaden.

Wachau Nied World-famous Danube region, home to some of Austria's most expressive, long-lived RIES, GRÜNER V. Top: ALZINGER, DOMÄNE WACHAU, F PICHLER, HIRTZBERGER, JAMEK, KNOLL, NIKOLAIHOF, PICHLER-KRUTZLER, PRAGER, R PICHLER, TEGERNSEERHOF, VEYDER-MALBERG.

Wachter-Wiesler, Weingut Burgen r ★★★ Notable BLAUFRÄNKISCH illustrative of EISENBERG DAC.

Wagentristl Burgen (w) ★★ Watch out for this young grower with talent for PINOT N and BLAUFRÄNKISCH.

Wagram Nied (r) w Region w of VIENNA, incl KLOSTERNEUBURG. Vast bank of loess soil ideal for GRÜNER V and increasingly also PINOT N. Best: BAUER, Ehmoser, Leth, OTT.

Weingut Stadt Krems Krems r w ★★ ⁺★★★ Co-op making quality strides. Same winemaker as STIFT GÖTTWEIG.

Weinviertel (r) w ("Wine Quarter") Largest Austrian wine region, 13,356 ha between Danube and Czech border, eponymous DAC. Region formerly slaked VIENNA's thirst, still grows base for sparkling but quality ethos now surging with GRÜNER V fame. Try: EBNER-EBENAUER, GROISS, PFAFFL.

Weninger, Franz Burgen r (w) ★★★★ 08 10 12 13 15 16 Promising, ambitious and elegant BLAUFRÄNKISCH.

Weststeiermark (West Styria) Small wine region specializing in SCHILCHER. New DAC SCHILCHERLAND from 2017.

Bi-annual VieVinum wine fair, held in even yrs in Vienna, open to consumers.

Wieninger, Fritz Vienna r w sp ★★★ ⁺★★★★ 13 14 15 16 Vienna stalwart, bio pioneer, key to GEMISCHTER SATZ revival. Viennese HEURIGEN an institution. Best v'yds: Nussberg and Rosengartl.

Winzer Krems Krems w Quality-oriented co-op of 962 growers covering 990 ha. Gd RIES, GRÜNER V, easy ZWEIGELT.

Wohlmuth S Stei w ★★★ ⁺★★★★ World-class STEI producer of SAUV BL esp from single-v'yds Edelschuh and Steinriegl. *Do not miss* weightless, aromatic Gelber MUSKATELLER.

England

If the release of a raft of super-priced deluxe cuvées is a sign of confidence, then English sparkling wine has confidence in truckloads. Nyetimber and Gusbourne are joining Sugrue Pierre and Kit's Coty at the super-expensive end of the market, and there'll be more. Which brings us to another matter. All English sparkling is not equal. From the ratings here you can see the ones to buy. Sadly, the best companies are not always the biggest, and the wines you're most likely to come across may not give the best impression of English sparkling. As the best producers draw further ahead of the rest of the field, it's more important than ever to be discriminating. Abbreviations: Berkshire (Berks), Buckinghamshire (Bucks), Cornwall (Corn), East/West Sussex (E/W S'x), Hampshire (Hants), Herefordshire (Heref).

Bluebell Vineyard Estates E S'x Blanc de Blancs is best bet here: subtle, balanced. Classic Cuvée is richer. Fizz from classic varieties much better than SEYVAL BLANC. Barrel Aged B de B a bit heavy.

Breaky Bottom E S'x Best: SEYVAL BL-based Cuvée Koizumi Yakumo, Champagne-blend Cuvée Gerard Hoffnung.

Bride Valley Dorset ★★ Spurrier v'yd. Juicy, fresh, fruity; appley Brut, quite dark Rosé.

Camel Valley Corn Bob Lindo reckons his warm, ancient slate soils are better suited to the English climate than chalk. Try CHARD Brut, White Pinot (that's PINOT N).

Kent's Greensand Ridge used to be nicknamed "England's Banana Belt": gd for growing fruit.

Chapel Down Kent Big producer making accessible style. Kit's Coty, single-v'yd Blanc de Blancs and Coeur de Cuvée more interesting but super-pricey.

Coates & Seely Hants ★★★ Lovely ripe Brut Res NV and savoury, spicy Rosé NV. Rich Blanc de Blancs. Lots of expertise, v. assured. Uses name "Britagne" for fizz.

Court Garden E S'x ★★ Gd rich style with bit of power. Subtle, taut Blanc de Blancs; elegant Classic Cuvée; rich, pretty Blanc de Noirs. Rosé is red-fruited, crunchy.

Denbies Surrey UK's largest single v'yd. Well-organised tourism.

Digby Hants, Kent, W S'x ★★★ Négociant buying grapes from several counties. Well-aged, assured wines made by Dermot SUGRUE under contract at WISTON. PINOT-led NV, stylish Res Brut 10 and v.gd Leander Pink NV, hard to resist.

Exton Park Hants ★★★ Mouthwatering, characterful wines, balanced at quite low dosage. Blanc de Noirs is supple, fresh; Brut Res has classic English elderflower note. Blanc de Blancs 11, with age, is aromatic, crisp.

Greyfriars Surrey Best are balanced Classic Cuvée 13 and Blanc de Blancs 13. NV from CHARD/PINOT N/PINOT M also worth a look.

Gusbourne Kent, W S'x ★★★ V'yds on clay in Kent and chalk in Sussex. v.gd Blanc de Blancs, improves with age. Also Brut Res, still wines CHARD, crunchy PINOT N. New deluxe cuvée awaiting release.

Hambledon Vineyard Hants ★★★ Accomplished, beautifully made wines. Everything under Hambledon label is v.gd, top level. PINOT M Rosé is planned; zero dosage cuvée a possibility. Meonhill label cheaper, also gd.

Harrow & Hope Bucks ★★ Sounds like a pub; vines planted 2010, 1st release 2016. Elegant Blanc de Blancs, balanced Brut Res NV, pale, spice, raspberry Brut Rosé.

Hart of Gold New négociant-style label owned by MW Justin Howard-Sneyd; impressive Champagne blend Hart of Gold 10, made with Heref grapes.

Hattingley Valley Hants ★★★ Doing things seriously, and it shows. Classic Res has a touch of barrel fermentation for weight, subtlety; Rosé 14 has lovely poise. Tops is Blanc de Blancs 11 with four yrs on lees: savoury, creamy.

Henners E S'x ★★ Classic ripeness, balanced Brut 11, Brut Res 10; cherry-spice Rosé.

Herbert Hall Kent Promising wines, often a bit young, Rosé 14 is pretty.

Hoffmann & Rathbone ★ Sussex-based, using bought-in fruit for gd toasty, creamy Blanc de Blancs; Classic Cuvée also worth tasting.

Hush Heath Estate Kent ★★★ Immaculate Wealden v'yds growing Champagne varieties. Best: Balfour Brut Rosé, Leslie's Res, 1503 NV range. New Skye Blanc de Blancs is ripe, elegant. Cider too, and owns local pubs.

Jenkyn Place Hants ★★★ Fresh, floral, hedgerow style, confident and harmonious. V.gd Brut 10, characterful, rich Blanc de Noirs 10.

Leckford Estate Hants From Waitrose's own estate, vinified by RIDGEVIEW. Fair balance, a bit short on oomph.

Nyetimber W S'x ★★★★ On a roll, with Classic Cuvée NV (3 yrs on lees), v. pure; taut Blanc de Blancs 10 (5 yrs on lees); elegant Rosé; balanced Demi-Sec. Single-v'yd Tillington has character, linear elegance. New deluxe cuvée for release 2018.

Plumpton College E S'x Promising UK's only wine college; growing influence and now own wines. Gd still, sparkling. Best sparklers Dean Brut NV, Rosé NV.

Rathfinny E S'x Much-hyped new producer on windswept E S'x downs; 1st release is impressive still PINOTS BL/GR, intense flavour, purity; 1st sparkling release 2018.

Ridgeview E S'x ★★ Invariably well made, enjoyable, reliable, gd value. Now run by 2nd generation. Various cuvées: tops are Blanc de Blancs, Blanc de Noirs, Rosé de Noirs. Makes South Ridge (1st, 1996) for Laithwaite's.

Simpsons Kent Promising newcomer. Ruth and Charles S make wine in Languedoc. Gd s-facing chalk slopes nr Canterbury. Gd still CHARD; 1st fizz released 2018.

Sugrue Pierre E S'x ★★★ Dermot Sugrue is winemaker at WISTON, where he also makes JENKYN PLACE, DIGBY, Black Dog Hill under contract. He makes one (CHARD-dominant) wine/yr from his own vy'ds, and it's glorious. The 13, The Trouble with Dreams, is all lemon shortbread, exuberant fruit, complex, tense and crystalline.

The Bolney Estate W S'x Long-est estate, slightly mixed quality. Cuvée Rosé (100% PINOT N) best bet.

Windsor Great Park Berks Tony Laithwaite, of Laithwaite's and *The Sunday Times* Wine Club, grew up in Windsor and now grows CHARD, PINOTS N/M on 4 ha of s-facing slope in, yes, the royal park itself. Second vintage still slightly raw 14.

Wiston W S'x ★★★★ In the top rank of English wine. Superb Blanc de Blancs 10; 09 for release later, possibly as prestige cuvée. Proper lees ageing shows in depth with tension across the range. Brut NV now has up to 40% Res wines: big plus. Cuvée Brut gets 100% old oak barriques, for creaminess, not oakiness.

Wyfold Oxon Tiny (1-ha) Champagne-variety v'yd at 120m above sea level in Chilterns, part-owned by hands-on Laithwaite family. Best: Brut 11, Rosé 14.

A question of balance

English sparkling has high acidity – there's no getting away from that. The typical style is super-fresh, elegant, with notes of apple and sometimes white flowers. Dosage is no higher than in Champagne, however: a surprise to drinkers who assume producers might balance higher acidity with more dosage. But residual sugar doesn't cancel out acidity; instead, it delays the moment when you perceive acidity on the palate. So upping dosage would unbalance the wine, when what you actually want is a wine that unfolds on the palate. Acidity in English sparkling has to be balanced with fruit, and plenty of time on lees. At least 3 yrs seems to be essential for depth and ageability. Some examples with 7 yrs bottle age are in fine shape.

Central & Southeast Europe

More heavily shaded areas are the wine-growing regions.

Abbeviations used in the text:

Bal	Balaton
Cri & Mar	Crişana & Maramures
Cro Up	Croatian Uplands
Dalm	Dalmatia
Dan P	Danubian Plain
Dob	Dobrogea
Is & Kv	Istria & Kvarner
Mold	Moldova / Moldavia
Mun	Muntenia & Oltenia Hills
N Hun	North Hungary
N/S Pann	North/South Pannonia
Pod	Podravje
Pos	Posavje
Prim	Primorje
Sl & CD	Slavonia & Croatian Danube
Thr L	Thracian Lowlands
Tok	Tokaj
Trnsyl	Transylvania

HUNGARY

At last Hungary is gaining global recognition for its historic wine industry, ranging from superb Cabernet Franc to dry Furmints with class and complexity to match white burgundies, all in addition to the wonderful sweet wines of Tokaj. There's still room for discoveries with 137 varieties being grown and more being rescued from extinction. Many of these are fascinating, but in Furmint Hungary has a genuinely world-class white grape. Volcanic soils help too. They're a feature of most of Hungary's 22 wine regions, and they add an extra dimension and depth, particularly to whites.

Aszú Tok Botrytis-shrivelled grapes and the resulting sweet wine from TOK. From 2014, legal minimum sweetness is 120g/l residual sugar, equivalent to 5 PUTTONYOS. Option to label as 5 or 6 Puttonyos but not obligatory. 3 and 4 Puttonyos still allowed on labels provided wines meet new higher standards. Gd Aszú in 99' 05 06 07 08 09 13' 16. V. wet in 10 14 so limited Aszú with careful selection; not much botrytis in 11 12 15. Reports for 17 optimistic.

Aszú Essencia / Eszencia Tok Term for 2nd-sweetest TOK level (7 PUTTONYOS+), only permitted up to 2010. Do not confuse with ESSENCIA/ESZENCIA.

Badacsony Bal ★★ →★★★ Volcanic slopes n of Lake Balaton; full, rich whites. Look for Gilvesy, Laposa (Bazalt Cuvée, KÉKNYELŰ, 4-Hegy OLASZRIZLING), *Szeremley* (age-worthy KÉKNYELŰ, SZÜRKEBARÁT), Villa Sandahl (excellent RIES esp 15 Citrus x Lime, Dry Honey Bishop, Bear Glue), Villa Tolnay (esp GRÜNER V, RIES).

Balassa Tok w dr sw ★★ →★★★ 13 15 16 Excellent Mézes-Mály FURMINT, Villő ASZÚ from personal winery of GRAND TOKAJ's viticulturalist.

Balaton Region, and Central Europe's largest freshwater lake. Incl BADACSONY, Balatonmelléke, CSOPAK, Zala, SOMLÓ to n, BALATONBOGLÁR to s.

Balatonboglár Bal r w dr ★★ →★★★ Wine district, also major winery of TÖRLEY, s of Lake Balaton. Gd: Budjosó, GARAMVÁRI, IKON, KONYÁRI, Kristinus, Légli Géza, Légli Otto, Pócz, Varga.

Barta Tok w dr sw ★★ →★★★ 13 15 16' (17) Highest v'yd in TOK with gd female winemaker producing impressive dry whites, esp Öreg Király FURMINT, HÁRSLEVELŰ, v.gd sweet Szamorodni, ASZÚ.

Béres Tok w dr sw ★★ →★★★ 08 11 13 15 Handsome winery at Erdőbénye producing v.gd ASZÚ and dry wines esp Lőcse FURMINT, Diókút HÁRSLEVELŰ.

Bikavér r ★ →★★★ 12' 13' 15 16 Means "Bull's Blood". PDO only for EGER and SZEKSZÁRD. Always a blend, min three varieties. In Szekszárd, KADARKA is compulsory, max 7%, with min 45% KÉKFRANKOS with no new oak. Look for: Eszterbauer Tüke, HEIMANN, Meszáros, Sebestyén Iván-Völgyi, TAKLER, VIDA. Egri Bikavér is majority Kékfrankos and no grape more than 50%, oak-aged for min 6 mths. Superior is min five varieties, 12 mths in barrel, from restricted sites. Best for Egri Bikavér: BOLYKI, DEMETER, GÁL TIBOR, Grof Buttler, ST ANDREA, Thummerer.

Bock, József S Pann r ★★ →★★★ 12 13 15 16 Leading family winemaker in VILLÁNY, making rich, full-bodied, oaked reds. Try: Bock CAB FR Fekete-Hegy, Bock & Roll, SYRAH, Capella Cuvée.

Bolyki N Hun r p w ★★ 12 13 15 16 Notable winery in a quarry in EGER, great labels. V.gd EGRI CSILLAG, Meta Tema, rosé, Indián Nyár (lit, Indian Summer) and excellent BIKAVÉR esp Bolyki & Bolyki.

Csányi S Pann r p ★ →★★ 12 13 15 16 Largest winery in VILLÁNY with ambitious plans. Csányi is a prominent banker. Look for: Chateau Teleki CAB FR, Kővilla Cab Fr, unoaked KÉKFRANKOS.

Csopak Bal N of Lake Balaton. Protected status for top v'yd OLASZRIZLING. Look for: Figula (v.gd Sóskút), Homola (Sáfránykert), Jasdi (esp single-v'yd selections), St Donát (Slikker, Meszes).

Degenfeld, Gróf Tok w dr sw ★★ →★★★ 13' 15 16 Improved estate with luxury hotel and new manager from ROYAL TOKAJI. Sweet wines best: 6 PUTTONYOS, Szamorodni. Decent HÁRSLEVELŰ 15. And fizz.

Demeter, Zoltán Tok w dr sw sp ★★★★ 13' 15 16 Benchmark cellar in TOKAJ for elegant, intense dry wines esp Boda, Veres FURMINTS; excellent Szerelmi HÁRSLEVELŰ, lovely Oszhegy MUSCAT. V.gd 100% Furmint PEZSGŐ (sp). Eszter late-harvest cuvée and superb ASZÚ 08.

Dereszla, Chateau Tok w dr sw ★★ →★★★ 08' 09' 13' for excellent ASZÚ. Gd DYA dry FURMINT and Kabar from new Henye cellar in Bodrogkerezstur. Also gd PEZSGŐ. Rare flor-aged dry Szamorodni Experience.

DHC (Districtus Hungaricus Controllatus) Term for Protected Designation of Origin (PDO). Symbol is a local crocus and DHC on label.

Disznókő Tok w dr sw ★★ →★★★★ 07' 08' 09 11' 13' 15 (16) Prominent Fiirst Growth estate with focus on long-lived sweet. Fine expressive ASZÚ, superb *Kapi* cru in top yrs incl 11. Also gd-value late-harvest and Édes (sw) Szamorodni. Useful restaurant. Belongs to AXA.

Dobogó Tok (r) w dr sw ★★★ 07 **08**' 09 11 12 13' 15 Impeccable small estate in TOK (name means "Clip Clop"). Benchmark ASZÚ and late-harvest Mylitta, thrilling dry FURMINT, esp Betsek DŰLŐ and *pioneering Pinot N* Izabella Utca.

Dűlő Named single v'yd. Top names in TOK: Betsek, Király, Mézes-Mály, Nyúlászó, Szent Tamás, Úrágya etc.

Duna Duna Great Plain. Districts: Hajós-Baja (try Sümegi, Koch – also VinArt in VILLÁNY), Csongrád (Somodi), Kunság (Frittmann, Font).

Eger N Hun ★→★★★ Top red region of n producing more burgundian-style reds and noted for Egri BIKAVÉR. Try: BOLYKI, Gróf Buttler, Demeter, *Gál Tibor*, Kaló Imre (noted for natural wines), KOVÁCS NIMRÓD, Pók Tamás, ST ANDREA, Thummerer.

Egri Csillag N Hun "Star of Eger". Dry white blend modelled on BIKAVÉR. Min 4 grapes.

Essencia / Eszencia Tok ★★★★ Legendary, luscious free-run juice from ASZÚ grapes, occasionally bottled, alc usually well below 5%, sugar off the charts. Reputed to have medicinal/aphrodisiac properties.

Etyek-Buda N Pann Dynamic region noted for expressive, crisp whites, fine sparklers and promising for PINOT N. Leading producers: Etyeki Kúria (esp Pinot N, SAUV BL), György-Villa (premium estate of TÖRLEY), Haraszthy (Sauv Bl, Sir Irsai, Oreghegy), Nyakas (v.gd CHARD), Kertész, Rókusfalvy.

Gál Tibor N Hun r w ★★ 13 15' 16 New cellar and natural winemaking have brought huge improvements.Try appealing EGRI CSILLAG DYA, fine KADARKA and vibrant, modern TiTi BIKAVÉR.

Garamvári Bal r p w dr sp ★→★★★ Leading producer of bottle-fermented fizz (previously Chateau Vincent). Try Optimum Brut, FURMINT Brut Natur, PINOT N Evolution Rosé. Also DYA Lellei label for IRSAI OLIVÉR, SAUV BL, PINOT N, SYRAH Rosé.

Gere, Attila S Pann r p ★★★→★★★★ 09' 11 12' 13 15 16 Leading light in VILLÁNY making some of country's best reds, esp rich Solus MERLOT, intense Kopar Cuvée, top Attila barrel selection. New Fekete-Járdovány is rare historic grape.

Gizella w ★★ 15 16 Small family winery in TOK, making delicious dry whites from FURMINT, HÁRSLEVELŰ and blends.

Grand Tokaj Tok w dr sw ★→★★ 13' 15' 16 Previously Crown Estates, fresh start from 2013. New winery, new winemaker (Karoly Áts, ex-ROYAL TOKAJI). Appealing Arany Késői Late-Harvest; Dry FURMINT Kővágó DŰLŐ; v.gd Szarvas ASZÚ 6 PUTTONYOS.

Heimann S Pann r ★★→★★★ 13' 14 15 16 Impressive family winery in SZEKSZÁRD, esp intense Barbár and BIKAVÉR. Key focus is local grapes, esp fine KADARKA, Alte Reben KÉKFRANKOS.

Hétszőlő Tok w dr sw ★★ Historic cellar and stunning v'yd, owned by Michel Reybier of Cos d'Estournel (B'x). 6 PUTTONYOS ASZÚ 13 is impressive.

Heumann S Pann r p w ★★→★★★ 13' 14 15 16 Small German/Swiss-owned estate in Siklós making great KÉKFRANKOS Res, CAB FR, appealing SYRAH and Lagona (r).

Hilltop Winery N Pann r p w dr ★★ In Neszmély. Meticulous, gd-value DYA varietals, Hilltop, Moonriver labels. V.gd Premium range (esp CHARD, Cserszegi Fűszeres).

Holdvölgy Tok w dr sw ★★→★★★ 13 15 16 Super-modern winery in MÁD, noted for complex dry wines, fun Hold and Hollo range, plus gd sweet wines.

Ikon Bal r w ★★ Well-made wines from KONYÁRI and former Tihany abbey v'yds. Try Evanglista CAB FR.

Szamorodni

Literally "as it was born". Produced from whole bunches with no separate ASZÚ harvest. Mini-renaissance for sweet (*édes*) version as a more authentic TOK name than late-harvest, helped by new rules from 2016: 1 yr ageing, min 6 mths in barrel, 9% alc. Try BARTA, Bott, HOLDVÖLGY, KIKELET, OREMUS, SZENT TAMÁS, SZEPSY. Best dry versions are flor-aged lke Sherry; try CHATEAU DERESZLA, Karádi-Berger, *Tinon*.

Kikelet Tok w dr sw ★★★ 09 11 13 15 16 One of TOK's inspirational women wine-makers. In Tarcal. Wonderful Váti FURMINT, Lónyai HÁRSLEVELŰ, fine Szamorodni.

Királyudvar Tok w dr sw sp ★★★→★★★★ 08 09 12′ 13 Bio producer In old royal cellars at Tarcal. Highly regarded for FURMINT Sec, Henye PEZSGŐ, Cuvée Ilona (late-harvest), flagship 6 PUTTONYOS Lapis ASZÚ.

Konyári Bal r p w ★★→★★★ 12 13 15 16 Gd family estate nr BALATON. Try DYA rosé; Loliense (r w), lovely Szarhegy 15. Top reds: Jánoshegy KÉKFRANKOS, Páva.

Kovács Nimród Winery N Hun r p w ★★→★★★ 13′ 14 15 16 EGER producer, jazz-inspired labels. Try Battonage CHARD, Blues KÉKFRANKOS, 777 PINOT N, top: NJK 09.

Kreinbacher Bal w dr sp ★★ ★★★ 13 15 Hungary's best fizz? Excellent Classic Brut PEZSGŐ based on FURMINT. V.gd dry Juhfark, HÁRSLEVELŰ, Öreg Tőkék (old vines).

Mád Tok Historic town in TOK with Mád Circle of leading producers: Árvay, Áts, BARTA, Budaházy, Demetervin (gd dry FURMINT, sweet Elvezet), HOLDVÖLGY, Lenkey, Orosz Gabor, ROYAL TOKAJI, SZENT TAMÁS WINERY, SZEPSY, Tok Classic, Úri Borok.

Malatinszky S Pann r p w ★★★ 08′ 09 11′ 12 13′ 15′ Certified organic VILLÁNY cellar. Top, long-lived Kúria **Cab Fr**, Kövesföld (r). Gd: Noblesse Rosé, CHARD, Serena (w).

Mátra N Hun ★→★★ N hill region for decent-value, fresh whites, rosé and lighter reds. Better producers: Balint, Benedek, Gábor Karner, NAG, NAGYRÉDE, Szöke Mátyás, Naygombos (rosé).

Mór N Pann w ★→★★ Small region, famous for fiery local *Ezerjó*. Also promising for CHARD, RIES, TRAMINI. Try Czetvei Winery.

Nagyréde N Hun (r) p w ★ Gd-value, commercial DYA varietal wines under Nagyréde and MÁTRA Hill labels.

Oremus Tok w dr sw ★★★★ 07 08 09 11 12 13 15 16 Perfectionist Tolcsva winery owned by Spain's Vega Sicilia: top ASZÚ; v.gd late-harvest, dry FURMINT *Mandolás*.

Pajzos-Megyer Tok w dr sw ★★→★★★ 06′ 07 08 09 11 12 13′ 15 French-founded (1991) winery in Sarospatak. Megyer label for modern dry and late-harvest (sw) varietals. Pajzos for premium, esp age-worthy ASZÚ, lovely late-harvest HÁRSLEVELŰ 11, plus complex dry wines.

Pannonhalma N Pann r p w ★★→★★★ 13 15 16 800-yr-old Pannonhalma Abbey, focused, aromatic whites: RIES, SAUV BL, TRAMINI. Lovely *Hemina* (w), decent PINOT N.

Patricius Tok w dr sw ★★→★★★ 13 15 16 Family winery in Bodrogkisfalud. Consistent dry FURMINT esp Selection, gd late-harvest Katinka, ASZÚ 06 08.

Pendits Winery Tok w dr sw ★★ 06 08 09 11 13 Demeter-certified bio estate in Abaujszanto. Luscious long-ageing ASZÚ, pretty, dry DYA MUSCAT.

Pezsgő Hungarian for sparkling wine. Growing trend. In TOK must be bottle-fermented from 2017.

Puttonyos (putts) Traditional indication of sweetness in TOKAJI ASZÚ. Optional since 2013 (*see* ASZÚ). Historically a *puttony* was a 25-kg bucket or hod of Aszú grapes, sweetness determined by number of Puttonyos added to a 136-litre barrel of base wine.

Royal Tokaji Wine Co Tok dr sw ★★→★★★★ 09′ 11′ 13′ 15 16 MÁD winery that led renaissance of TOK in 1990 (I am a co-founder). Mainly First Growth v'yds. 6-PUTTONYOS single-v'yd bottlings: esp Betsek, *Mézes-Mály*, Nyulászó plus 5 PUTTONYOS, SZENT TAMÁS. V.gd dry FURMINT, The Oddity. New By Appointment for winemaker projects: try No2 HÁRSLEVELŰ, Dry SZAMORODNI. **Dry Muscat**.

St Andrea N Hun r p w ★★★ 12 13′ 15 16 Leading name in EGER for modern, high-quality BIKAVÉR (Áldás, Hangács, Merengő). Gd white blends: Napbor, Örökké and delicious Szeretettel rosé. Flagships: Mária (w) and Nagy-Eged-Hegy (r).

Sauska S Pann, Tok r p w ★★→★★★★ 11′ 12 13′ 15′ Immaculate winery in VILLÁNY. V.gd KADARKA, KÉKFRANKOS, CAB FR and impressive red blends, esp Cuvée 7 and Cuvée 5. Also Sauska-TOK with focus on excellent dry whites, esp Medve and Birsalmás FURMINTS. V.gd PEZSGŐ **Extra Brut fizz**.

Somló Bal Dramatic extinct volcano famous for long-lived, austere white *Juhfark* ("sheep's tail"), FURMINT, HÁRSLEVELŰ, OLASZRIZLING. Region of small producers esp Fekete, Györgykovács, Kolonics, Royal Somló, Somlói Apátsági, Somlói Vándor, Spiegelberg. Bigger TORNAI (esp Grofi HÁRSLEVELŰ, Juhfark), KREINBACHER also v.gd.

Sopron N Pann r ★★→★★★ Dynamic district on Austrian border overlooking Lake Fertő. KÉKFRANKOS most important, plus CAB SAUV, PINOT N, SYRAH. Bio *Weninger* is excellent, maverick Ráspi for natural wines. Try: Luka, Pfneiszl, Taschner, Wetzer.

Szekszárd S Pann r p ★★→★★★ Ripe, rich reds. Increasing focus on BIKAVÉR, KÉKFRANKOS and reviving KADARKA. Look for: Dúzsi (rosé), Eszterbauer (esp Tüke Bikavér, Nagyapám Kadarka), HEIMANN, Mészáros, Remete-Bor (Kadarka), newcomer Schieber (CAB FR, Kékfrankos), Sebestyén (Ivan-Volgyi Bikavér), TAKLER, Vesztergombi (Csaba's Cuvée, Turul), VIDA (Hidaspetre Kékfrankos, La Vida).

Szent Tamás Winery Tok w sw ★★★ 09 11 12' 13' 15 Important winery (with handy café) in MÁD with ISTVÁN SZEPSY Jr. Gd dry FURMINTS: Dongó, Percze. Sweet focus now on Szamorodni; Nyulászó, Dongó superb. Reliable village-level Mád label.

Bor is "wine": *vörös* is red; *fehér* is white; *édes* is sweet, *száraz* is dry, *válogatás* is selected.

Szepsy, István Tok w dr sw ★★★★ 07' 08 09' 11' 12 13' 15' Brilliant, soil-obsessed, no-compromise 17th-generation TOK producer in MÁD. Now focusing on dry FURMINT (esp Urágya, Betsek and Nyúlászó DŰLŐ) and reviving sweet Szamorodni. Superb ASZÚ (esp Dűlő Urágya) and now bottling amazing ESZENCIA 07.

Szeremley Bal w dr sw ★★ 09 11' 12 13 15 Pioneer in BADACSONY. Intense, fine RIES, *Szürkebarát*, (aka PINOT GR), KÉKNYELŰ, appealing sweet Zeus.

Takler S Pann r p ★★ 13 15 16 Super-ripe, supple SZEKSZÁRD reds. Decent, gd value, entry-point red, rosé. Best: Res selections of CAB FR, KÉKFRANKOS.

Tinon, Samuel Tok w dr sw ★★★ 07 08 09 15 16 Sauternais in TOK since 1991. Fine v'yd selection dry FURMINTS. Distinctive complex ASZÚ with v. long maceration and barrel-ageing. Excellent sweet and iconic dry flor-aged *Szamorodni*.

Tokaj Nobilis Tok w dr sw ★★★ 12 13 15 16 Fine small producer in Bodrogkisfalud run by Sarolta Bárdos, one of TOK's inspirational women. Excellent dry Barakonyi HÁRSLEVELŰ, FURMINT, v.gd Szamorodni, rare Kövérszőlő Edes (sw).

Tokaj / Tokaji ★★→★★★★ Tokaj is the town and wine region; Tokaji the wine. Recommended producers without individual entries here: Árvay, Bardon (Alpha), Bodrog Borműhely (Lapis FURMINT, HÁRSLEVELŰ, Szamo), Bott Pince (esp late-harvest Bott-rytis), Carpinus, Demetervin, Erzsébet, Füleky, Hommona Attila (esp Határi, Rány), Karádi-Berger, Lenkey, Orosz Gábor.

Törley r p w dr sp ★→★★ Innovative large company. Chapel Hill is major brand name. Well-made, gd-value DYA international and local varieties IRSAI OLIVÉR, Zenit, Zefir. Major fizz producer (esp *Törley*, Gala, Hungaria labels), v.gd classic method, esp François President Rosé Brut, CHARD Brut. György-Villa for top selections (try Juhfark, SYRAH).

Tornai Bal w ★★ 13 15 2nd-largest SOMLÓ estate. Gd-value entry-level varietals, excellent top Grofi HÁRSLEVELŰ, Juhfark.

Tűzkő S Pann r w ★★ 13 15 16 Antinori-owned estate in Tolna. Gd TRAMINI, KÉKFRANKOS, MERLOT.

Vida S Pann r ★★ 13 14 15 Family estate in SZEKSZÁRD. V.gd BIKAVÉR, old-vine KADARKA, Hidaspetre KÉKFRANKOS.

Villány S Pann Most s wine region. Noted for serious ripe B'x varieties (esp CAB FR) and blends; juicy examples of *Kékfrankos*, PORTUGIESER. High quality: ATTILA GERE, *Bock*, CSÁNYI, Gere Tamás & Zsolt, HEUMANN, Hummel, Jackfall, Janus, Kiss Gabor, *Malatinszky*, Polgar, Riczu-Stier, Ruppert, *Sauska*, Tiffán, *Vylyan*, WENINGER-GERE.

Villányi Franc S Pann New classification for CAB FR from VILLÁNY. Premium version has restricted yield, 1 yr in oak. Super-premium from 2015 is max 35 hl/ha.

Vylyan S Pann r p ★★→★★★ 12' 13 14 15 16 Red specialist making v.gd v'yd selections, esp Gombás PINOT N, Mandolás CAB FR, Montenuovo, Pillangó MERLOT. *Duennium Cuvée* is flagship red. Also delicious rare Csoka.

Weninger N Hun r p w ★★★ 13' 14 15 16 Benchmark bio winery in SOPRON run by Austrian Franz Weninger Jr. Single-v'yd *Steiner Kékfrankos* is superb. SYRAH, CAB FR and red Frettner blend also impressive. Intriguing Orange Zenit.

Weninger-Gere S Pann r p ★★→★★★ 13' 15 16 Joint-venture between Austrian Franz WENINGER Sr and ATTILA GERE. Excellent CAB FR, tasty Tinta (TEMPRANILLO), Cuvée Phoenix and DYA fresh rosé.

BULGARIA

New wineries continue to appear in Bulgaria; the total has now reached over 200. The first wave of private wineries started in the mid-2000s and they are now seeing the benefits of maturing vines with deeper roots. Their wines are often better balanced as a result. There's a new focus on regionality led by producers in three areas: Melnik, South Sakar and Plovdiv. Local grape varieties are also gaining more attention as drinkers look for authenticity and more interesting flavours than just another Cabernet or Chardonnay.

Angel's Estate Thr L r p w ★★ 13 15 16 17 Ripe, oaky, polished reds and smooth whites under Stallion label, guided by Alex Velianov (RIP in 2017). Deneb CAB FR 13', CAB SAUV 13' particularly impress.

Bessa Valley Thr L r p ★★★ 11 12 13' Stephan von Neipperg (Canon la Gaffelière, B'x) and K-H Hauptmann's pioneering estate winery nr Pazardjik. Smooth, rich reds; firm, fresh rosé. Try Enira, v.gd SYRAH and Enira Res, excellent Grande Cuvée 13'.

Black Sea Gold Thr L r p w ★ 15 16 Black Sea coastal winery; 700 ha. Better labels: Golden Rhythm, Pentagram, Salty Hills (all blends), Villa Marvella micro-winery.

Borovitsa Dan P r w ★★★ 10 13 15 16 Adriana Srebinova makes hand-crafted parcels of terroir wines – among Bulgaria's best. Dux is long-lived flagship. Also v.gd The Guardians MRV (Rhône white grapes), Cuvée Bella Rada (RKATSITELI), Granny's and Black Pack (both GAMZA), Orange Garden CHARD, Vox Dei PINOT N, Sensum (r) and Maxxima range.

Boyar, Domaine Thr L r p w ★→★★★ 13 15 16 Produces everything from DYA entry-level labels via mid-range Ars Longa, Deer Point, Dom Boyar, Platinum, Elements, Quantum, to boutique Korten label incl v.gd MERLOT, SYRAH, CAB FR and Natura for local grapes.

Bratanov Thr L r w ★★ 13 15 16 New-wave family estate using wild fermentations. V.gd Tamianka, CHARD *sur lie*, SYRAH and red blends.

Burgozone, Chateau Dan P r w ★★ 13 14 15 16 Gd whites from family estate close to Danube esp VIOGNIER, SAUV BL and Iris Creation. Decent PINOT N.

Castra Rubra Thr L r p w ★★→★★★ 11' 12 13 15 16 Michel Rolland from B'x consults. B'x blend Castra Rubra and impressive Butterfly's Rock are best. Also decent: Dominant blends, Via Diagonalis and Motley Cock.

Damianitza Thr L r p w ★★ 13 15 16 Holistic producer with some certified organic wines in Struma Valley. Try Ormano (w), Tipsy Virgin Rosé, Volcano SYRAH and flagship Kometa.

Dragomir Thr L r p w ★★→★★★ 11' 12 13' 15 16 Garage winery, highly regarded for intense full-bodied reds, esp Pitos, flagship RUBIN Res, plus fresh Sarva, Dragomir barrel-fermented rosé.

Katarzyna Thr L r p w ★→★★ 15 16 Large modern winery in border zone nr Greece. Noted for ripe soft reds. Try La Vérité CAB FR, Harvest MERLOT 10, Encore MALBEC.

Independent estates
Many dynamic new estates in Bulgaria. Recommended: Alexandra Estate (VERMENTINO, rosé), Bendida (RUBIN), Better Half (Zmeevo red, SYRAH blend), Bononia (Ooh La La, Res), Chateau Copsa (Zeyla MISKET), Eolis (CAB FR, Inspiration), Gulbanis (Cab Fr), Ivo Varbanov (CHARD), Karabunar (Orange DIMIAT, Misket), Rouse Wine House (RIES, Vrachanski Misket), Maryan (Orange Dimiat, Res), Salla (Ries, Vrachanski Misket), Stratsin (Sauv Rosé, MERLOT), Tohun (whites, Cab/Merlot), Tsarev Brod (Gergana, Chard Amber Harvest), Varna Winery, Villa Yustina (4 Seasons range, Monogram Rubin/MAVRUD), Yalovo (Misket blend, Rubin, sparkling) Yamantiev (Marble Land, Syrah), Zelanos (PINOT GR, PINOT N).

Logodaj Thr L r p w sp ★★★ 13 14 15 16 (17) In Struma Valley with protégé of Riccardo Cotarella in charge. V.gd bottle-fermented Satin esp rosé. Rich CHARD and excellent Nobile MELNIK 15', serious Incantesimo SYRAH.

Lovico Suhindol Dan P r w ★ Historic producer, est 1909, noted for CAB SAUV, GAMZA.

Medi Valley Thr L r p w ★★ 15 16 17 Highest commercial v'yd in Bulgaria, plus plot nr Vidin. Try eXentric MELNIK 55, MAVRUD, premium Incanto SYRAH, Incanto Black.

Melnik Thr L Dynamic region in sw with several wineries co-operating on new PDO. Promising local grapes; esp Shiroka MELNIK, Melnik 55, Sandanski MISKET. Names to watch: Orbelia, Orbelus (organic), Rupel, Villa Melnik, Zlaten Rozhen.

Menada Thr L r p w ★ Third-biggest producer, noted for cheerful Tcherga blends.

Midalidare Estate Thr L r p w ★★ 13 15 16 Boutique winery with 60 ha. Try SAUV BL Premium, rosé, Nota Bene and Mogilovo Village selections and Grand Vintages: MALBEC, CAB FR.

Minkov Brothers Thr L r p w ★→★★ 13' 15 16 More boutique arm of one of Bulgaria's largest producers. Ethno is basic blends with local grapes. Jamais Vu, Le Photografie, Oak Tree are better.

Miroglio, Edoardo Thr L r p w sp ★★→★★★ 13' 14 15 16 (17) Italian-owned v'yds at Elenovo. Consistently gd bottle-fermented sparkling esp Blanc de Blancs, Brut Rosé 11'. Gd PINOT N in all styles from Blanc de Noirs to RES, v.gd flagship Soli Invicto. Try Elenovo CAB FR, MAVRUD. EM varietals are reliable; interesting bio blends incl Bouquet, Mavrud/RUBIN.

Neragora Thr L r w ★★ 15' 16 Organic estate producing v.gd MAVRUD and blends Ares (with MERLOT), Cherno (with CAB SAUV).

Preslav, Vinex Thr L r w ★→★★ 13 15 16 Whites best here esp long-lived Rubaiyat CHARD, though long-standing winemaker recently departed. Also try Novi Pazar PINOT GR, RIES. Entry-level label: Khan Krum.

Rossidi Thr L r p w ★★ 15 16' Boutique winery nr Sliven. Fine, part concrete-egg fermented CHARD. V.gd Rubin, elegant PINOT N. Intriguing orange wine now GEWURZ.

Rumelia Thr L r w ★★ 13 14 V.gd MAVRUD specialist, alone and in Erelia blends.

Santa Sarah Thr L r w ★★★ 11 13 15 16 17 Pioneering *garagiste*. Bin reds are v.gd, long-lived Privat is flagship. New: Petite Sarah smooth red, We Are No Saints rosé, v.gd Santa Sarah SAUV BL.

Slavyantsi, Vinex Thr L r p w ★→★★ "Fair for Life" certified for work with local Roma community. Great job with budget varietals and blends esp under Leva brand.

Terra Tangra r p w ★★ 12 15 16 Large estate in Sakar, certified organic red v'yds. Now more fruit-focused. Gd MAVRUD rosé, MALBEC and serious Roto.

VP Brands r p w ★ Formerly Vinprom Peshtera. Owns Villa Yambol (entry-level wines, better Kabile range) and New Bloom in Saedinenie for easy-drinking Pixels, Verano Azur labels, plus characterful F2F reds.

Zagreus Thr L r p w ★★ 13 14 15 MAVRUD in all styles from acacia-fermented rosé to complex Amarone-style Vinica from semi-dried grapes.

SLOVENIA

Slovenia is consolidating its reputation as one of the stars of Central Europe. Its winemakers are gaining confidence across a range of styles, including fine sparkling, crisp and appetizing whites in the east and rich, complex ones in the west. Reds are becoming more balanced, while being in the heartland of the orange wine scene has done the country's image no harm. A beautiful country to visit, with amazing scenery and a serious food culture too.

Batič Prim r p w sw ★★ 09 11 13 15 Bio/natural wines in VIPAVA. Rosé is top seller. Also Angel Blends, Valentino (sw).

Bjana Prim sp ★★→★★★ V.gd traditional-method PENINA from BRDA esp fine Brut Rosé, NV, Brut Zero.

Blažič Prim w ★★→★★★ 11 13 14 15 16 From BRDA. Long-ageing, complex REBULA, SAUVIGNONASSE and Blaž Belo (w) in top yrs.

Brda (Goriška) Prim Top-quality district in PRIM. Many leading wineries: BJANA, BLAŽIČ, Dolfo (esp sparkling Spirito, SIVI PINOT, Škoaj), EDI SIMČIČ, Erzetič, JAKONČIČ, KLET BRDA, KRISTANČIČ, MOVIA, Prinčič, Reya, ŠČUREK, Zanut (SAUV BL, SAUVIGNONASSE, top Brjač MERLOT in gd yrs), orange wines from KABAJ and Klinec.

Burja Prim r w ★★★ 13 14 15 16 Bio VIPAVA estate. Excellent Burja Bela, Burja Noir (PINOT N) and Burja Reddo based on SCHIOPPETTINO. New Stranice field blend and Žorž single-v'yd Pinot N.

Čotar Prim r w ★★ 09 11 12 13 15 Intriguing, long-lived organic/natural wines from KRAS esp Vitovska (w), MALVAZIJA, SAUV BL, TERAN, Terra Rossa red blend.

Cviček Pos Traditional low-alc, sharp, light red blend of POS, based on Žametovka. Try Bajnof, Frelih.

Dveri-Pax Pod r w sw ★★→★★★ 13 15 16 Benedictine-owned estate nr Maribor. Crisp, taut, gd-value whites esp FURMINT, PINOT GR, SAUV BL. V.gd old-vine selections: RIES, GEWURZ. Superb sweet wines and new PENINA Brut and Rosé.

Gašper Prim r w sp ★★ 13 14 15 16 Brand of Slovenia's top sommelier. V.gd MALVAZIJA, PENINA, REBULA.

Guerila Prim r w ★★ 13 15 16 Bio producer in VIPAVA. V.gd local DYA PINELA, Zelen.

Istenič Pos sp ★→★★ Fizz specialist. Try N°1, Barbara Sec, Gourmet Rosé 13, Prestige Extra Brut 11.

Istria Coastal zone extending into Croatia; main grapes: REFOŠK, MALVAZIJA. Best: Bordon (E Vin rosé, Malvazija), Korenika & Moškon (PINOT GR, REFOŠK, Kortinca red), Rodica, Rojac (Renero, Stari d'Or), Pucer z Vrha (Malvazija), SANTOMAS, Steras (Refošk Kocinski), VINAKOPER.

Jakončič Prim r w sp ★★★' 15 16 V.gd BRDA producer esp Carolina REBULA, Bela (w), Red. Also gd PENINA.

Joannes Pod r w ★★ 10 11 13 14 15' RIES specialist nr Maribor; wines age well. Also fresh light PINOT N.

Slovenian wine consumption 4th highest in world: 44.07 l/head. More than France.

Kabaj Prim r w ★★★ 08 11 12 13 15 French-directed. Noted for Orange REBULA, Amfora, Ravan (FRIULANO), Luisa Prestige (w) and long-aged reds.

Klet Brda Prim r w sp ★★ →★★★ 13 14 15 16 Slovenia's largest co-op, surprisingly gd, forward-thinking. Bright modern DYA Quercus varietal whites, Krasno unoaked blends, v.gd Colliano (US). Bagueri premium v'yd selections. Excellent A+ (r w).

Kobal Pod w ★★ Former PULLUS winemaker gone solo. V.gd FURMINT, SAUV BL.

Kogl Pod r p w ★★ 15 16 Hilltop estate nr Ormož, dating from 1542. Vibrant precise whites esp Mea Culpa AUXERROIS, Ranina (aka BOUVIER), Primus Inter Pares (w). Flavoursome PINOT N rosé.

> **Europe's orange centre**
> Slovenia is right in the centre of Europe's orange wine country, which crosses the border into the Italian hills of Collio, where it has been revived by such producers as Gravner, Radikon and Prinčič. Making whites with extended skin contact has long been a tradition in Slovenia and Croatia, with time on the skins varying from just a few days to wks or even mths for a full orange style, often with min sulphites. Long-lived, complex, food wines are (or can be) the result. Look for BATIČ, ČOTAR, JNK, KABAJ, Klinec, Mlecnik, MOVIA, plus Clai, KABOLA, KOZLOVIČ, Roxanich, TOMAC over the Croatian border.

Kras Prim Renowned district on Terra Rossa soil in PRIM. Best-known for TERAN, MALVAZIJA. Try Vinakras (esp Prestige Teran, Vitovska).

Kristančič r w ★★→★★★ 13 15 16 Family producer in BRDA (don't confuse with same winemaking surname at MOVIA). Pavó wines recommended.

Kupljen Pod r p w ★★ 15 16 Dry wine pioneer nr Jeruzalem. Reliable white varietals.

Marof Pod r w ★★→★★★ 13 15 Pioneering winery in Prekmurje. All wines now oak-aged. Try Breg CHARD, SAUV BL and Mačkovci Cru BLAUFRÄNKISCH.

Movia Prim r w sp ★★★→★★★★ 08' 10 13 14 15 High-profile bio winery led by charismatic Aleš Kristančič. Excellent v. long-lived Veliko Belo (w), Veliko Rdeče (r); v.gd MODRI PINOT, showstopping Puro Rosé (sp). Orange Lunar (esp CHARD) is notable.

Penina Name for quality sparkling wine (Charmat or traditional method). V. trendy.

Podravje Largest wine region covering Štajerska and Prekmurje in e. Best for crisp dry whites, gd sweet wines, reds typically lighter styles from MODRA FRANKINJA (aka BLAUFRÄNKISCH), PINOT N.

Posavje Region in se. Best: sweet esp Mavretič (superb ★★★★SAUV BL Icewine, gd Yellow MUSCAT), Prus (★★★★sweet esp Icewines, botrytis wines), Šturm (★★★★ Icewine, botrytized Muscat). Improving reds eg. Klet Krško MODRA FRANKINJA.

PRA-VinO Pod w sw 12 13 14 15 70s pioneer of private wine production. Best for ★★★★sw incl Icewine (*ledeno vino*), botrytis wines from LAŠKI RIZLING, RIES, ŠIPON.

Primorje Region in w covering Slovenian ISTRIA, BRDA, VIPAVA, KRAS. Aka Primorska.

Puklavec Family Wines Pod r w sp ★★→★★★ 15 16 Large family winery offering v.gd-value, *consistent crisp aromatic whites* in Puklavec & Friends and Jeruzalem Ormož ranges. Top selections under Seven Numbers label are superb esp FURMINT, PINOT GR.

Pullus Pod r p w ★★ 15 16 Crisp, modern whites from Ptuj winery: Pullus SAUV BL, RIES. Excellent "G" wines (notable 777); superb sweet LAŠKI RIZLING, Rumeni MUSCAT.

Oldest known wheel came from Ljubljana Marshes, carbon-dated at 5000 yrs+ old.

Radgonske Gorice Pod sp ★→★★ Producer of bestselling Slovenian sparkler Srebrna (silver) PENINA, classic-method Zlata (golden) Penina and popular demi-sec black label TRAMINEC.

Santomas Prim r p w ★★→★★★ 12 13 14 15 Leading ISTRIAN estate. Some of country's best *Refošk* and REFOŠK/CAB SAUV blends esp Antonius from 60-yr-old vines and Grande Cuvée blend.

Ščurek Prim r p w sw ★★→★★★ 12 13 15 16 Family estate in BRDA, five sons. Gd DYA varieties CAB FR, Jakot, PINOT BL, REBULA, plus Strune blends. Best wines from local grapes esp Kontra, Pikolit, Stara Brajda (r w).

Simčič, Edi Prim r w ★★★→★★★★ 11' 12 13 14 15 Perfectionist in BRDA; red wine superstar with Duet Lex and barrel-selection Kolos. Excellent whites: MALVAZIJA, REBULA, SAUV BL, Triton Lex. Superb Kozana single-v'yd CHARD.

Simčič, Marjan Prim r w sw ★★★→★★★★ 12' 13' 14 15 Whites: CHARD, REBULA, SAUV BL,

Selekcija, SIVI PINOT and Teodor blends always v.gd. MODRI PINOT is elegant. V. fine Opoka single-v'yd range esp CHARD, Sauv Bl, RIBOLLA. Great Leonardo (sw).

Štajerska Pod Large e wine region incl important districts of Ljutomer-Ormož, Maribor, Haloze. Crisp, refined whites and top sw. Best (without individual entries): Doppler, Gaube (Kaspar CHARD), Gross (SJI FURMINT, Gorca Furmint), Heaps Good Wine, Krainz (ŠIPON), Miro, M-vina (esp ExtremM SAUV BL), Valdhuber, Zlati Grič (Rosé PENINA, Sauv Bl).

Steyer Pod w sw sp ★★ 15 16 TRAMINER specialist in ŠTAJERSKA: dry, sparkling, oak-aged, Vaneja sweet.

Sutor Prim r w ★★★ 12 13 14 Excellent small producer from VIPAVA. Try Sutor White from REBULA/MALVAZIJA, also v.gd SAUV BL, fine CHARD, elegant red.

Tilia Prim r w ★★ →★★★ 12 13 14 15 16 "House of Pinots" in VIPAVA since co-owner gained PhD studying PINOT N. Sunshine range for appetizing gd-value whites. Black label for more serious reds incl gd Pinot N, White label in top yrs.

Verus Pod r w ★★★ 15' 16 Fine, focused, brisk whites esp v.gd FURMINT, crisp SAUV BL, flavoursome PINOT GR, refined RIES. Promising PINOT N.

Vinakoper Prim r p w sp ★→★★ 13 15 16 Large producer in ISTRIA. Look for DYA MALVAZIJA, REFOŠK Rex Fuscus, Capris Malvazija (part-acacia-aged).

Vipava Prim Valley noted for cool breezes in PRIM, source of some fine wines. Recommended: BATIČ, Benčina (PINOT N), BURJA, Frlanova (BARBERA), Guerila, Jangus (SAUV BL, MALVAZIJA), JNK (orange wines), Lepa Vida (Malvazija, oOo orange wine), Miška (PINELA), Mlečnik (orange/natural wines), Pasji Rep (Jebačin), Štokelj (Pinela), SUTOR, TILIA, Vina Krapež (excellent Lapor Belo).

CROATIA

Croatia still both excites and frustrates. The largest wine producer is in administration at the time of writing after high-profile arrests, and at the other end of the scale several hundred small commercial wineries produce individual wines from the country's huge range of unique local varieties, with more and more emerging from obscurity. Strong tourism supports high prices, so exports are relatively limited; but expect more as all-inclusive cruises mean the tourists don't come ashore to spend.

Agrokor r p w ★→★★ In extraordinary administration after management arrests. Watch this space for future of generally gd brands: Agrolaguna in ISTRIA with Vina Laguna Festigia (v.gd MALVAZIJA in all forms esp Vižinada); Vina Belje nr Danube (esp Goldberg GRAŠEVINA, premium CHARD).

Ahearne r p w ★★ British Master of Wine Jo Ahearne making a name with Rosina Darnekuša rosé, Pošip, Wild Skins (w), PLAVAC MALI.

Arman, Franc Is & Kv r w ★★ 13' 15' 16 A 6th-generation family winery. V.gd TERAN and DYA MALVAZIJA and skin-contact Malvazija Classic. Also gd MERLOT, CAB FR.

Badel 1862 r w ★★ 12 13 14 15 Group of wineries. Best: Korlat SYRAH, MERLOT. Gd-value Duravar range esp SAUV BL, GRAŠEVINA. Gd PLAVAC and DINGAČ 50° from Peljesac.

Babić is grape to look out for in n Croatia esp at Šibenik. Fine aromatic reds.

Benvenuti Is & Kv r w ★★★ 13' 15 16 Impressive family winery. V.gd reds esp Caldierosso, TERAN. Benchmark fresh MALVAZIJA, complex Anno Domini (w).

BIBICh Dalm r p w ★★→★★★ 13 15 16 Highly regarded producer; focus on local grapes esp Debit (w), plus SYRAH. Try Lučica single-v'yd and sweet Ambra. Also R6 Riserva, Bas de Bas Crno.

Bolfan Cro Up r p w ★→★★ 13 15 Bio/natural wine. Gd Primus RIES, SAUV BL, PINOT N.

Bura-Mrgudić Dalm r ★★ 11 14 15 Brother/sister; renowned DINGAČ and Mare POSTUP. Also work with Benmosche of Villa Splendid.

Cattunar Is & Kv r w ★★ 15 16 Hilltop estate with gd range of MALVAZIJA from four soils. V.gd late-harvest Collina, TERAN Kappi 06.

Coronica Is & Kv r w ★★ 13 15 16 Notable ISTRIAN winery esp barrel-aged Gran MALVAZIJA and benchmark Gran TERAN.

Dalmatia Rocky coastal region and its lovely islands to s of Zadar. Tourism hotspot.

Vrhunsko vino: premium-quality wine; *Kvalitetno Vino:* quality wine; *Stolno Vino:* table wine. *Suho:* dry; *Polsuho:* semi-dry.

Dingač Dalm 10 11' 12 13 (15) First quality designation (1961), now PDO, on s DALM's Pelješac peninsula. Full reds from PLAVAC MALI. Try: BURA-MRGUDIČ, Kiridžija, Lučič, Madirazza, Matuško, Miličič, SAINTS HILLS, Skaramuča, Vinarija Dingač.

Enjingi, Ivan Sl & CD w sw ★★ Cult natural winemaker in SLAVONIJA. Noted for GRAŠEVINA and long-lived Venje.

Fakin Is & Kv r w ★★→★★★ 15 16 Young *garagiste* winemaker impressing with MALVAZIJA esp La Prima, Il Primo TERAN.

Feravino Sl & CD r p w ★ One of largest small producers with 160 ha. Entry-level wines modern, decent value.

Galić Sl & CD r w ★★ 13 14 15 16 Promising new producer in SLAVONIJA esp GRAŠEVINA, red blend Crno 9.

Gerzinić Is & Kv r p w ★★ 13 14 15 16 Brothers make v.gd TERAN (r p), MALVAZIJA, SYRAH.

Gracin Dalm r p ★★→★★★ 12 13 (15) Small exciting winery; rocky coastal v'yds nr Primošten. Prof Leo Gracin owns; country's *best Babič*, Opol (p), Prošek (sw).

Grgić Dalm r w ★★→★★★ 11 13 15 Napa Valley legend for Montelena CHARD that won Judgement of Paris in 76. Returned to Croatian roots to make PLAVAC MALI, rich POŠIP on Pelješac peninsula with daughter and nephew.

Hvar Beautiful island with world's oldest continuously cultivated v'yd and UNESCO protection. Noted for PLAVAC MALI, incl Ivan Dolac designation. Gd: Carič, PZ Svirče, TOMIČ, ZLATAN OTOK and new AHEARNE.

Ilocki Podrumi Sl & CD r p w ★★→★★★ 15 16 Claims 2nd-oldest wine cellar in Europe: built in 1450. Superb Premium GRAŠEVINA, TRAMINAC, Principovac range.

Istria North Adriatic peninsula. MALVAZIJA is main grape. Gd also for CAB SAUV, MERLOT, TERAN. Look for: F ARMAN, Banko Mario (benchmark Malvazija 16), BENVENUTI, Capo (Malvazija, Stellae range), CATTUNAR, Clai (orange wines esp Sveti Jakov), CORONICA, Cossetto, Damjanič (Borgonja, Clemente), Degrassi (VIOGNIER, CAB FR), Deklič, Domaine Koquelicot (Belaigra Grand Cru), FAKIN, Frankovič, GERZINIČ, KABOLA, KOZLOVIČ, MATOŠEVIČ, Medea, MENEGHETTI, Novacco, Peršurič, PILATO, Piquentum, Radovan (REFOŠK, Merlot), ROXANICH, SAINTS HILLS, Sirotic, Tomaz (Avantgarde, Sesto Senso), TRAPAN, Zigante.

Kabola Is & Kv r p w ★★→★★★ 13' 14 15' 16 Immaculate ISTRIAN estate. V.gd MALVAZIJA as fizz, young wine, cask-aged Unica, Amfora. Tasty DYA Rosé; v.gd TERAN.

Katunar Is & Kv r w ★★ 16 Leading producer of Žlahtina only found on island of Krk. Try Sv. Lucija.

Korta Katarina Dalm r p w ★★→★★★ 09' 11' 12 13 15 Modern winemaking from Korcula. Excellent POŠIP, PLAVAC MALI esp Reuben's Res.

Kozlović Is & Kv r w ★★★ 13' 15 16 *Benchmark Malvazija* in all its forms esp exciting, complex Santa Lucia, Pomojem. Also v.gd Santa Lucia Crna; MUŠKAT Momjanski.

Croatia's Hvar island enjoys around 2800 hrs of sunshine/yr, highest in Europe.

Krajančič w ★★ 15 Leader in showing the potential of POŠIP: try Sur Lie, Intrada.

Krauthaker, Vlado Sl & CD r w sw ★★★ 13 15 16 Top producer from KUTJEVO esp GRAŠEVINA Mitrovac, Izborna Berba. Also v.gd PINOT N, Zelenac, CHARD.

Kutjevo Cellars Sl & CD w dr sw ★★ 13 15' 16 800-yr-old cellar in Kutjevo town – noted for gd GRAŠEVINA esp De Gotho, Turkovič and lovely Icewine.

Maraština Alias of the common MALVAZIJA of the coast; often fair refreshment.

Matošević Is & Kv r w ★★ 14 15 16 Benchmark MALVAZIJA esp Alba, Alba Robinia (aged in acacia), Antiqua. V.gd Grimalda (r w).

Meneghetti Is & Kv r w ★★ 13 15 Sleek blends (r w), fine precise MALVAZIJA.

Miloš, Frano Dalm r p ★★ 07 12 13 Much admired for legendary Stagnum, also easier PLAVAC and rosé.

Pilato Is & Kv r w ★★ 13 15 16 Family winery; v.gd MALVAZIJA, PINOT BL, TERAN, MERLOT.

Postup Dalm Famous v'yd designation nw of DINGAČ. Full-bodied, rich red from PLAVAC MALI. Try: Donja Banda, Miličič, Mrgudič Marija, Vinarija Dingač.

Prošek Dalm Historic sw made from sun-dried local grapes in DALM; 1st mention 1556. Gd versions: GRACIN, STINA, TOMIČ Hectorovich.

Roxanich Is & Kv r w ★★→★★★ 08 09 11 13 15 Natural producer making powerful, intriguing orange wines (MALVAZIJA Antica, Ines U Bijelom); impressive complex reds esp TERAN Ré, Superistrian Cuvée, MERLOT.

Saints Hills Dalm, Is & Kv r p w ★★→★★★ 13 14 15 Two wineries and three locations with consultant Michel Rolland. V.gd Nevina white from ISTRIA; richly fruity PLAVAC MALI St Roko, serious DINGAČ.

Croatian Slavoljub Penkala invented the mechanical pencil. Not named after him.

Slavonija Region in ne, famous for oak, and for whites esp from GRAŠEVINA. Also gd reds appearing now. Look for Adzič, Antunovič (Premium Graševina 13), Bartolovič, Belje, ENJINGI, FERAVINO, GALIČ, KRAUTHAKER, KUTJEVO, Orahovica (Silvanac Zeleni 15).

Stina Dalm r p w ★★→★★★ 13 15 16 Dramatic steep v'yds on Brač island; v.gd POŠIP, PLAVAC MALI esp Majstor label. Gd Tribidrag (AKA ZIN), Opol rosé, PROŠEK.

Tomac Cro Up r w sp ★★ Estate nr Zagreb with 200-yr history, famous for sparkling and pioneering amphora wines.

Tomič Dalm r p w ★★ 13 15 16 Outspoken personality on island of HVAR, with organic PLAVAC MALI v'yd. Gd reds esp Plavac Barrique, Hectorovich PROŠEK.

Trapan, Bruno Is & Kv r w ★★ 14 15 16 Dynamic young producer. Try MALVAZIJA, incl natural Uroboros, orange Istraditional and DYA Ponente. Also sleek reds: Terra Mare TERAN, The One! (r).

Veralda Is & Kv r p w ★★ 13 15 Award-winning winery impressing with rich polished reds, bright whites and orange amphora wine.

Zlatan Otok Dalm r p w ★★ 10 11 12 13 15 Family winery from HVAR with v'yds also at Makarska. Famous for ripe reds esp BABIČ, Crljenak, PLAVAC MALI. Gd DYA POŠIP.

BOSNIA & HERZEGOVINA, KOSOVO, MACEDONIA (FYROM), SERBIA, MONTENEGRO

The wine scene across the Balkans is evolving fast as more and more quality-focused producers appear and former state dinosaurs die out or reinvent themselves.

Bosnia & Herzegovina's 3500 ha have seen a real step-up in quality. Local grapes dominate, esp aromatic white Žilavka and vibrant red Blatina. Names to look for: Andrija, Carski, Crnjac & Zadro (esp Selekcija Žilavka, CZ Selekcija), Hepok, Hercegovina Produkt (Zlatna Dolina, Charisma Blatina), Nuič, Tvrdos, Vukoje, Podrum Vilinka (X-line, Žilavka). Also some gd Vranac.

Kosovo has 3200 ha and 12 commercial wineries but still lags behind rest of region. Stonecastle is the biggest.

Macedonia (Republic of, or even Former Yugoslav Republic of Macedonia because of ongoing disagreements with Greece) still remains dependent on cheap bulk though efforts continue to raise quality and switch towards bottled wines. Many smaller investments have disappeared/fail to find a market. Here the bigger wineries drive quality and invest in research. Giant Tikveš has a French-trained winemaker and continues to impress with Bela Voda and Barovo single v'yd wines; gd Special Selection range (esp GRENACHE BLANC, Temjanika, Vranec) and rich oaky Domaine Lepovo CHARD, Grand Cuvée. Stobi sources only from its own 600 ha of v'yds; try Vranec Veritas, Vranec classic, Aminta (r), Žilavka and refined PETIT VERDOT. Château Kamnik is leading boutique winery, with gd CARMENÈRE, SYRAH 10 Barrels, Temjanika Premium, Vranec Terroir. Other wineries to look out for: Ezimit (Stardust range, Vranec Barrique), Popov, Popova Kula (Stanušina in three styles), Skovin (Markov Manastir Vranec, Temjanika).

Montenegro has 2651 ha of v'yds and more than 500 growers but 13 Jul Plantaže dominates with 2310 ha, one of Europe's largest v'yds, but wines are pretty gd (try Medun Vranac, Vladika, Stari Podrumi, Vranac RES). Also Lipovac, Sjekloča, Vinarija Krgovic. Vranac dominates, present in 97 per cent of v'yds but recent research indicates that Kratošija/ZIN may originate here and not in Croatia.

Serbia has 22,300 ha of registered v'yds and around 400 wineries, many new and tiny. There's a focus on reinventing former workhorse grapes like Prokupac as a Serbian red flagship variety. Producers to try: Aleksandrovič (Trijumf range, Regent, Rodoslav), Aleksič (Arno, Kardaş), Botunjac (Sveti Grai), Budimir (Triada, Svb Rosa, Boje Lila), Cilič, Čokot (Experiment), Despotika (Morava, Dokaz), Deurič, Doja (Prokupac), Ivanovič (Prokupac, No.1/2), Janko (Vrtlog, Misija), Kovačevič (CHARD, Aurelius), Matalj (Kremen Chard, Kremen Kamen), Pusula (CAB FR), Radovanovič (Cab Res), Saga, Temet (Ergo, Tri Morave), Virtus (Credo), Zivković, Zvonko Bogdan (rosé, Chard, Cuvée No.1).

CZECH REPUBLIC

The Czech Republic has two wine regions, the tiny Bohemia (Boh) and 25-times larger Moravia (Mor) with a total vineyard area of 17,200 ha. Although scarcely known to the outside world, Czech and Moravian wine have a long history. Semi-sweet wines make up much of the production. Huge grants as well as a patriotic drinking culture have encouraged investment on a scale unimaginable 20 years ago, transforming many small producers into swanky operations with super-modern facilites, as well as on-site tasting rooms and accommodation for busloads of thirsty visitors, where wine flows to the sound of folk music. But the wines of the Czech Republic are still trying to find their niche beyond its borders. The market is dominated by several giants producing large quantities of supermarket-quality stuff, much of it blended from imported bulk wine.

Baloun, Radomil Mor ★→★★★ Medium-sized producer, wide range of highly quaffable wines, all dry. PINOT N Blanc, BLAUFRÄNKISCH Blanc curiosities.

Dobrá Vinice Mor ★★★ One of the so-called "authentists" specializing in wines matured in amphora-like *qvevri* imported from Georgia. Also Brut Nature.

Dufek, Josef Mor ★★ Dynamic family winery, over 30 organically grown varieties.

Dva Duby Mor ★★★ Dedicated terroirist, bio principles. Flagship is Rosa Inferni (BLAUFRÄNKISCH/ST LAURENT). Other red blends Vox In Excelso and Ex Opere Operato also v.gd.

Lobkowicz, Bettina Boh ★→★★★ Outstanding PINOT N and classic-method sparkling RIES, Pinot N Blanc de Noirs, Cuvée Pinot N/PINOT GR.

Plešingr & Sons Mor ★★→★★★ Brothers Michal and Patrik follow in footsteps of their father. Emphasis on PINOTS N/GR.

Spielberg Mor ★★→★★★ Winemaker of the Year in 2017 with modern operation nr the site of Battle of the Three Emperors at Austerlitz. BLAUER PORTUGIESER is particularly gd.

Stapleton & Springer Mor ★★★ Joint-venture between Jaroslav Springer and ex-US ambassador Craig Stapleton with brother Benjamin, both burgundy fans. Single-v'yd PINOT N a speciality.

Stávek, Richard Mor ★→★★★ Natural wine specialist. Orange wines a hit in some top restaurants/wine bars, esp in NYC.

Vinselekt Michlovský Mor ★→★★★ Innovator and technologist, wide range of grapes, incl some bred by himself. WELSCHRIESLING is a must.

SLOVAK REPUBLIC

Classic Central European vines dominate here, alongside international favourites. Slovakia's vineyard area of 12,000 ha starts around Bratislava on the Danube, then continues along the foothills of the Lesser Carpathians (L Car) to Nitra (Nit), Central Slovakia (C Slo) while in Southern Slovakia (S Slo) it follows the Hungarian border for 450 km east to the small Slovak Tokaj (Tok) region, adjacent to its more illustrious Hungarian namesake, and further northeast to Eastern Slovakia (E Slo). Vinárske závody Topoľčianky and Sekt JE Hubert Sered' (both Nit) are the country's largest wine and sekt producers, respectively.

Château Belá S Slo ★★★ Fine RIES with Egon Müller zu Scharzhof (*see* Germany).
Elesko L Car ★★★ Huge winery unrivalled in Central Europe; modern art gallery.
J&J Ostrožovič Tok ★★★ V.gd Slovak Tok.
Karpatská Perla L Car ★★ V.gd wines from immaculately maintained v'yds.
Malík & Sons L Car ★★ University professor and international wine judge planted 14 ha in Modra with LEANYKA, SAUV BL, PINOT BL. Also Modragne classic sparkler.
Movino C Slo ★★ Most important Central Slovakia producer, est in Veľký Krtíš 1973.
Víno Matyšák L Car ★→★★★ Large modern winery in Pezinok.

ROMANIA

Romania is taking too long to re-emerge as the leading wine country of Eastern Europe – its historic role. But it had a good harvest in 2017, which is good news for drinkers abroad. New quality-focused boutique wineries continue to pop up, but in reality few are anywhere near making money and are fighting for customers. Fallout is still settling after the failure of the country's biggest producer, bringing changes on the domestic scene too. Romania's significant vineyard area of 182,363 ha and 85 grape varieties make the country an important producer in Europe (the 6th biggest). Keep watching.

Avincis Mun r w p ★★ 13' 15 16 Dramatic historic family estate and state-of-art winery in DRĂGĂŞANI. V.gd Cuvée Grandiflora, Cuvée Andréi, Negru de Drăgăşani, Crâmpoşie Selecţionată, PINOT N and new sweet TĂMÂIOASĂ.

Balla Géza Cri & Mar r p w ★★ 12 13 15 16 Much-improved leading producer in Miniş. Best is Stone Wine range from v'yd at 500m esp CAB FR, FETEASCĂ NEAGRĂ, FURMINT. V.gd Cadarca.

Banat Wine region in w; incl DOC Recaş.

Bauer Winery Mun r w ★★ 13 15 16 Family winery of winemaker at PRINCE ŞTIRBEY. V.gd Crâmpoşie, FETEASCĂ NEAGRĂ. One of Romania's 1st orange wines (SAUVIGNONASSE).

Budureasca Mun r w ★→★★ 15 16 Large DEALU MARE estate with British winemaker. Consistent Budureasca (esp Fumé, Tămâioasă (MUSCAT), premium FETEASCĂ NEAGRĂ) and top Origini range.

Corcova Mun r p w ★★ 13 15' 16 Hillside v'yds and renovated C19 royal cellar. Try FETEASCĂ NEAGRĂ, SYRAH, appealing SAUV BL, rosé.

Cotnari Mold DOC region in MOLD, only grows local varieties esp FETEASCĂ ALBĂ, Frâncușă, GRASĂ, TĂMÂIOASĂ. Historic renown for sweet wines.

Cotnari Wine House Mold p w ★→★★ 15 16 Next-generation producer in COTNARI, 350 ha, dry wine focus. Best is Colloquium label esp GRAȘA de Cotnari, Busuioaca de Bohotin.

Cotnari Winery Mold w sw ★ Former collectivized winery with 1360 ha, replanted 2006/7. Mostly dry and semi-dry whites from local grapes. Aged sweet Collection wines *can be impressive*.

Crișana & Maramures Region in nw incl DOC Minis. Carastelec (focus on bottle-fermented sparkling incl Vinca and Carassia labels) and renovated natural producer Nachbil.

Davino Winery Mun r w ★★★ 12' 13' 15 16 Top producer in DEALU MARE. Focus on blends for v.gd Dom Ceptura, Flamboyant, Revelatio and Rezerva. Local varieties feature in Alba and Purpura Valahica.

Dealu Mare / Dealul Mare Mun Means "The Big Hill". DOC on s-facing slopes. Location of several leading producers (*see* individual entries). Also Crama Basilescu (MERLOT, FETEASCĂ NEAGRĂ), Merlot specialist Rotenberg, organic Domeniile Franco Romane. Domenille Tohani is biggest.

Dobrogea Nr Black Sea. Incl DOC regions of Murfatlar, Badabag and Sarica Niculițel (also winery of same name). Regarded for ripe reds today; sweet whites were historically famous.

DOC Romanian term for PDO. Sub-categories incl DOC-CMD: harvest at full maturity, DOC-CT: late-harvest, DOC-CIB: noble-harvest. PGI is Vin cu indicatie geografică or simply IG.

Domeniul Coroanei Segarcea Mun r p w ★→★★ 11 13' 15 Historic royal estate. Famous for TĂMÂIOASĂ Roze. Also try Minima Moralia CAB SAUV, Principesa Margareta Marselan, Simfonia red blend.

Drăgășani Mun Dynamic region on River Olt for aromatic whites and intriguing reds. Leading producers: AVINCIS, BAUER, PRINCE ȘTIRBEY.

Girboiu, Crama Mold r w ★→★★ 200 ha in earthquake-prone Vrancea, hence Tectonic label (try Șarba, FETEASCĂ NEAGRĂ) and Epicentrum blends. Only grower of rare Plavaie grape under DYA Livia brand and in Cuartz sparkling.

Halewood Romania Mun r p w sp ★→★★ 13 15 16 consistent gd-value commercial range esp La Umbra and v'yd selections. Hyperion is top label: try Chairman's Res, CAB SAUV. Also Rhein sparklings.

Romania in current form was a century old in 2018.

Jidvei Trnsyl w ★→★★ 15 16 Romania's largest v'yd with 2460 ha in TRNSYL. Consultancy from Marc Dworkin (also Bulgaria's Bessa Valley). Stick to premium dry wines esp Owner's Choice Ana CHARD, Maria FETEASCĂ ALBĂ, Mysterium white blend.

LacertA Mun r w ★★ 13 15 16 Quality estate in DEALU MARE, named after local lizards. Try Cuvée IX (r) and Cuvée X (w), SHIRAZ.

Liliac Trnsyl r p w ★★→★★★ 15 16 V.gd Austrian-owned estate; name means "bat". Crisp fine whites esp FETEASCĂ REGALĂ, FETEASCĂ ALBĂ, delicious sweet Nectar and new Icewine with Kracher (Austria). Pioneers of orange wine and gd PINOT N (r p).

Metamorfosis, Viile Mun r w ★★ 13 15 16 Antinori-owned (*see* Italy) estate in DEALU MARE. Top: Cantvs Primvs in best yrs. V.gd v'yd selections esp Negru de DRĂGĂȘANI, FETEASCĂ NEAGRĂ, fresh fruit-driven Metamorfosis range.

Moldova Largest wine region ne of Carpathians. Borders Republic of Moldova.

Muntenia & Oltenia Hills Major wine region in s, covers DOC areas of DEALU MARE, Dealurile Olteniei, DRĂGĂŞANI, Pietroasa, Sâmbureşti, Stefaneşti, Vanju Mare.

Murfatlar Winery Dob r w Previously major producer in Murfatlar region, lost licence to produce wine after fraud.

Oprişor, Crama Mun r p w ★★ 13' 15 16 La Cetate range consistently gd. Try Caloian Rosé, vibrant Rusalca Alba, Crama Oprişor CAB SAUV, Smerenie red blend and top cuvée Ispita.

Petro Vaselo Ban r p w ★★ 13 14 15 16 Italian investment in BANAT with organic vineyards. Gd Bendis (sp), Melgris FETEASCĂ NEAGRĂ, Ovas (r). V.gd entry-level Alb, Roşu and rosé.

Prince Ştirbey Mun r p w sp ★★ ··★★★ 13 15 16 Pioneering estate in DRĂGĂŞANI. V.gd dry whites, esp local Crâmposie Selectionată (still and sparkling), SAUV BL, FETEASCĂ REGALĂ, TĂMÂIOASĂ Sec. V.gd local reds (Novac, Negru de Drăgăşani).

Recaş Winery Ban r p w ★★ ··★★★ 13 15' 16 Romania's most successful exporter, crushing over 20,000 tonnes. Progressive, consistent wines with longstanding Australian and Spanish winemakers. V.gd-value, bright varietal wines sold as Calusari, Dreambird, Frunza, I am, I heart, Paparuda, Werewolf. Mid-range: La Putere, Sole. Excellent premium wines esp Cuvée Uberland, Selene reds, Solo Quinta.

Senator Mold r w ★ 850 ha across four regions. Monser and Glia (try Sarba, BABEASCĂ NEAGRĂ) ranges feature Romanian varieties, Omnia is organic, Varius for international grapes.

S.E.R.V.E. Mun r p w ★★··★★★★ 14 15 16 First private winery in Romania, founded by late Corsican Count Guy de Poix. Reliable entry-point Vinul Cavalerului, Res Contelui. V.gd Terra Romana esp PINOT N, rosé, Cuvée Amaury (w). *Cuvée Charlotte 11* quality red benchmark.

Transylvania Cool mtn plateau, central Romania. Mostly whites with gd acidity.

Villa Vinèa Trnsyl r w ★★ 13 15 16 Young Italian-owned estate. Gd whites esp GEWURZ, SAUV BL, FETEASCĂ REGALĂ and red blend Rubin (not made from Bulgaria's grape).

Vinarte Winery Mun r w ★★ 13 14 15 16 Italian-led investment with three estates, 20 yrs old in 2018: Castel Bolovanu in DRĂGĂŞANI, Terase Danubiane in Vanju Mare, Villa Zorilor in DEALU MARE. Best: Prince Mircea MERLOT, Nedeea red blend, fruity Castel Starmina FETEASCĂ NEAGRĂ.

Vincon Winery Mold r p w sw ★ Major domestic-focused producer with 1500 ha in Vrancea.

Visineşcu, Aurelia Mun r w ★★ 14 15 16 DEALU MARE estate. Try Artizan (r w) based on local grapes. Anima is top label esp Fete Negre 3.

MALTA

A couple of years of drought here have reduced quantities, and Malta and Gozo's roughly 300 ha of vineyards don't seem able to meet demand for the local product. Most growers sell their crop to the large wineries, including Delicata, Marsovin and Antinori-owned Meridiana. In addition wines are produced from imported Italian grapes. If you want something typically Maltese, look for local grapes Gellewza (light red, also makes acceptable fizz) and white Girgentina, which is often blended with Chardonnay to produce a succulent full-fruited wine. Malta's most celebrated wine is Marsovin's Grand Maître, an equal blend of Cabernets Sauvignon and Franc, aged in new oak, costly but hardly good value. There are a handful of boutique wineries, some rustic, but others, such as San Niklaw, making high quality but in very limited quantities. San Niklaw's Vermentino, Sangiovese and Syrah are noteworthy.

Greece

The resilience of good Greek wine through the country's years of economic crisis owes a lot to tourists. In every corner of Greece, one can find wine bars, restaurants, resorts or hotels that not only respect wine but also understand that original, delicious wines can be the greatest ambassadors of this nation. Greece has far more of these than most people realize. And far more adventurous and ambitious producers to discover. Is there a national style of wine? Clean, gutsy, with flavours just beyond the usual. *See* Grape Varieties for new names to start conjuring with. Abbreviations: Aegean Islands (Aeg), Central Greece (C Gr), Ionian Islands (Ion), Macedonia (Mac), Peloponnese (Pelop), Thessaloniki (Thess).

Alpha Estate Mac ★★★ Acclaimed estate in AMYNTEO with outstanding v'yds. Excellent MERLOT/SYRAH/XINOMAVRO blend, pioneering Ecosyste range, Xinomavro Res from old, ungrafted vines is stunning.

Amynteo Mac (POP) XINOMAVRO-dominated. Fresh reds, excellent rosés (still and sparkling). Greek cool climate at its best.

Argyros Aeg ★★★★ Top SANTORINI producer; several magnificent VINSANTOS (20-yrs-old version is ★★★★). KTIMA (w) and Vareli (w) age for a decade. Spicy, rare MAVROTRAGANO (r) is a top example.

Avantis C Gr ★★★ Boutique winery in Evia. Exquisite Aghios Chronos SYRAH/VIOGNIER, Rhône-like Collection Syrah and rich MALAGOUSIA. Plagies Gerakion range is oaky but balanced. New winery in SANTORINI looks v. promising.

Biblia Chora Mac ★★★ Popular benchmark SAUV BL/ASSYRTIKO. Ovilos range (r w), could rival B'x at triple the price. Slow takeover by Greek varieties; try Vidiano and AGIORGITIKO. Sister estate of GEROVASSILIOU.

Boutari, J & Son ★→★★★★ Historic producer across regions but with heart in NAOUSSA. Excellent value, esp *Grande Res Naoussa* to age for 40 yrs+. Top wines: Oropedio MOSCHOFILERO and 1879 Legacy Naoussa, from a v. old v'yd.

Carras, Domaine Mac ★★ Historic estate at Halkidiki, with own red and white POP (Côtes de Meliton). Chateau Carras is a classic; ambitious Grand Blanc (magnums only) and SYRAH, floral MALAGOUSIA; LIMNIO (r) might be *best value* of all.

Cephalonia Ion Important Ionian sland with three POPs: mineral ROBOLA (w), rare MUSCAT (w sw) and excellent MAVRODAPHNE (r sw). Dry Mavrodaphne is a trend here (as elsewhere in Greece) but cannot be POP.

Dalamaras ★★★→★★★★ Stellar producer in NAOUSSA. XINOMAVROS of great purity. Palaiokalias single v'yd is one of best Xinomavros around.

Dougos C Gr ★★★ Rich reds with local and international grapes, but focus is now on RAPSANI, esp Old Vines. Try Acacia (w).

Driopi Pelop ★★★ Venture of TSELEPOS in NEMEA. Top wine: single-v'yd Res. New winery underway, should push quality even higher.

Economou Crete ★★★ One of Greece's great artisans; brilliant, burgundian Sitia (r).

Gaia Aeg, Pelop ★★★ Top NEMEA and SANTORINI producer. Great Thalassitis Santorini (Submerged is aged underwater), modern VINSANTO and elegantly oaked *wild-ferment* Assyrtiko. Top wine: ever evolving *Gaia Estate* from Nemea. Dazzling "S" red (AGIORGITIKO with touch of SYRAH).

Greek appellations

Terms are changing in line with other EU countries. Quality appellations of OPAP and OPE now fused together into POP (or PDO) category. Regional wines, known as TO, will now be PGE (or PGI).

Gentilini Ion ★★ →★★★ Leading CEPHALONIA name, incl **steely Robola**. Wild Paths shows what ROBOLA can be. Marvellous dry MAVRODAPHNE Eclipse (r).

Gerovassiliou Mac ★★★ Quality (and trend) leader. Original ASSYRTIKO/MALAGOUSIA and top Malagousia, a grape of which he is the leading light. Top reds Avaton from indigenous varieties and BIBLIA CHORA. All are must try.

Goumenissa Mac (POP) ★ →★★★ Earthy, expressive XINOMAVRO/Negoska (r). Try Chatzyvaritis (★★★), natural-style Tatsis (★★★), Aidarinis (single-v'yd ★★★), BOUTARI (Filiria).

Hatzidakis Aeg ★★★★ Top-class producer who tragically took his own life in August 2017. All remaining bottles should be treated like national treasures. Future seems unclear but there are hopes.

Helios C Gr, Pelop Umbrella name for Semeli, Nassiakos and Orinos Helios, gd value across rapidly expanding range. Top Nassiakos MANTINIA.

Karydas Mac ★★★ Tiny family estate and amazing v'yd in NAOUSSA, crafting classic, compact but always refined XINOMAVRO. A gem of this POP.

Katogi Averof Pelop, Epir ★★→★★★ Initially from mountainous Epirus. Katogi was the original cult Greek wine. Top: KTIMA Averoff and Rossiu di Munte range from plots at 1000m+.

Limnio and Limniona: two different red varieties. Very elegant so try them both.

Katsaros Thess ★★★ Small winery on Mt Olympus. KTIMA (CAB SAUV/MERLOT) is Greek classic. Tight XINOMAVRO Valos is full of varietal definition.

Kechris ★★→★★★ Maker of The Tear of the Pine, possibly **world's best Retsina**: fantastic wine.

Kir-Yanni Mac ★★→★★★ V'yds in NAOUSSA, AMYNTEO. Trendsetting, age-worthy reds incl Ramnista Naoussa, Diaporos, Blue Fox. Akakies sparklings (p w) are notable, Tarsanas ASSYRTIKO is fab. Consistently excellent.

Ktima Estate. Some insist on using the term "Ktima" on export labels instead of "Estate". They are correct.

Lazaridi, Nico Mac ★ →★★★ Wineries in Drama, Kavala. Gd Château Nico Lazaridi (r w), Black Sheep value range. Top: Magiko Vouno red (CAB SAUV), white (SAUV BL).

Lazaridis, Kostas Att, Mac ★★★ Wineries in Drama and Attica (under Oenotria Land label). Popular Amethystos label. Top wine: amazing Cava Amethystos CAB FR, followed by Oenotria Land CAB SAUV/AGIORGITIKO. Trendy, Provence-like Julia pink.

Ligas Mac ★★★ Full-blown natural producer in Pella. Fans of this style should try Kydonitsa orange wine.

Lyrarakis Crete ★★ →★★★ Producer from Heraklio, reviving old Cretan varieties like Plyto, Dafni and Melissaki, practically saving these from extinction. Hard-to-find **single-v'yd versions** extraordinary, mainly from old-vine blocks. Some of most elegant whites on island.

Malvasia Group of appellations created in the early 2010s, to recreate wine of Middle Ages. Not from MALVASIA grapes but a reflection of the local varieties. Four POPs: Monemvassia-Malvasia in Laconia (from Monemvassia/ASSYRTIKO/ Kydonitsa), Malvasia of Paros (from Monemvassia/Assyrtiko), Malvasia Chandakas-Candia (from Assyrtiko/Vidiano/MUSCAT) and Malvasia of Sitia (ditto plus Thrapsathiri), both from Crete.

Manoussakis Crete ★★★ Great estate with Rhône-inspired blends but Greek varieties on way. ASSYRTIKO is lovely, MUSCAT of Spinas a revelation.

Mantinia Pelop (POP) w High-altitude, cool region. Fresh, crisp, low-alc, almost Germanic styles from charming, MUSCAT-like **Moschofilero**. Excellent sparklers from TSELEPOS too.

Mercouri Pelop ★★★ One of Greece's most beautiful estates, on w coast. V.gd KTIMA (r), delicious RODITIS (w), complex dry MAVRODAPHNE (r), REFOSCO (r).

> Assyrtiko – beyond the volcano
> An increasing number of varietal ASSYRTIKOS from around Greece prove
> this is a top-quality grape, even away from its birthplace, the lunar-like
> terroir of SANTORINI. Outside Greece, it's in Australia's Clare Valley (Jim
> Barry), Italy's Alto Adige (Alois Lageder), S Africa's Swartland (E Sadie).

Naoussa Mac ★★→★★★ (POP) Top-quality region for sophisticated, fragrant
XINOMAVRO. Best examples on par in quality and style (but not price) with Barolo.
Top: DALAMARAS, KARYDAS, KIR-YIANNI, THIMIOPOULOS.

Nemea Pelop ★★→★★★ (POP) AGIORGITIKO reds. Huge potential for quality; styles
from fresh to classic to exotic. (Try DRIOPI, GAIA, HELIOS, Nemeion, PAPAÏOANNOU,
SKOURAS.) Single-v'yd bottlings on rise.

Palyvos Pelop ★★→★★★ Excellent producer in NEMEA making modern, big-framed
reds. Excellent single-v'yd selections. Try ultra-premium NV Nohma.

Papaïoannou Pelop ★★★ If NEMEA were Burgundy, Papaïoannou would be Jayer.
Benchmark range: excellent value KTIMA, Palea Klimata (old vines), Microklima
(micro-single-v'yd), top-end Terroir. Most vintages need at least a decade.

Pavlidis Mac ★★★ Outstanding estate at Drama. Trendy Thema (w) ASSYRTIKO/
SAUV BL. Emphasis range: varietals incl classy AGIORGITIKO and TEMPRANILLO.

Rapsani Thess POP on Mt Olympus. Made famous in 90s by TSANTALIS (try Grande
Res); but DOUGOS has different interpretations esp Old Vines label. XINOMAVRO,
Stavroto, Krasato.

Retsina New Retsinas (eg. GAIA, KECHRIS), packed with freshness, a great alternative to
Fino Sherry. Yes, great, even age-worthy Retsinas exist.

Samos Aeg ★★→★★★★ (POP) Island famed for sweet MUSCAT Blanc. Esp (fortified)
Anthemis, sun-dried Nectar. Rare old bottlings are steals at their price, eg. hard-
to-find Nectar 75 or 80.

New oak is on the way out for most Greek reds. Finally...

Santo Aeg ★★→★★★ Most successful SANTORINI co-op. Dazzling Grande Res, rich yet
crisp VINSANTOS. Great-value ASSYRTIKO, Nyhteri. Exciting sparklers.

Santorini Aeg ★★★→★★★★ Dramatic volcanic island and POP for white (dr sw).
Luscious VINSANTOS, salty, **bone-dry Assyrtiko**. Top: GAIA, HATZIDAKIS, SANTO, SIGALAS.
Possibly cheapest ★★★★ dry whites around, able to age for 20 yrs. World class.
MAVROTRAGANO reds (not incl in POP) can be sublime. Apex of Greek wine.

Sigalas Aeg ★★★★ Leading light of SANTORINI. Stylish VINSANTO, excellent
MAVROTRAGANO. Nyhteri and Cavalieros (dr w) out of this world; Seven Villages
micro-cuvées must-try.

Skouras Pelop ★★★ V. consistent range. Lean, wild-yeast Salto MOSCHOFILERO
rewards keeping. Top reds: high-altitude Grande Cuvée NEMEA, Megas Oenos.
Solera-aged, multi-vintage Labyrinth is weird but beautiful.

Tatsis Mac ★★★ Natural producer in GOUMENISSA. Top wine is Old Roots XINOMAVRO.

Thimiopoulos Mac ★★★★ New-age NAOUSSA with spectacular export success, sold
as Earth and Sky or Uranos. New projects in RAPSANI, SANTORINI. Popular, value
Atma range.

Tsantalis Mac ★→★★★★ Long-est producer. Huge range. Gd Metoxi (r), RAPSANI Res,
Grande Res, gd-value wines from Thrace. Made monastery wines from **Mount
Athos** famous, eg. excellent Avaton.

Tselepos Pelop ★★★ Leader in MANTINIA and NEMEA (*see* DRIOPI), intriguing range all
around. Greece's best MERLOT (★★★★ Kokkinomylos) and single-v'yd Avlotopi CAB
SAUV not far behind. Venture in SANTORINI with Canava Chrysou.

Vinsanto Aeg ★★★★ Sun-dried, cask-aged luscious ASSYRTIKO and Aidani from
SANTORINI can age forever. Insanely low yields.

Eastern Mediterranean & North Africa

EASTERN MEDITERRANEAN

The eastern Med has an older wine tradition than the western, by far. Then came Islam. Buried tradition includes new possibilities: of ancient local grapes, for example. So the region is increasingly looking to its own native vines for inspiration. In Lebanon that means Merweh and Obaideh; in Israel Bittuni, Dabouki, Marawi. Cyprus and Turkey have a rich choice of indigenous varieties already. Traditional workhorse varieties (Cinsault in Lebanon, Carignan in Israel), also producing better results.

Cyprus

The new generation of Cyprus winemakers is led by producers who make their living from wine, so they're really committed to better quality. Most are focusing on their local varieties. Hobby wineries belonging to rich investors are now appearing and may stir up the wine scene, while at the same time the demands for cheap wines for tourism and all-inclusive holidays are forcing prices down at the bottom end.

Aes Ambelis r p w br ★→★★ 15 16 Consistent, appealing XYNISTERI and rosé. V.gd modern version of COMMANDARIA 10.

Argyrides Vasa Winery r w ★★ 13 14 15 16 Immaculate pioneering estate winery. Top MARATHEFTIKO, MOURVÈDRE. V.gd VIOGNIER, MERLOT/CAB SAUV. VLASSIDES consults.

Ayia Mavri w br sw ★→★★ Recommended for sweet wines only esp v.gd sweet MUSCAT 15, COMMANDARIA 11.

Commandaria Rich, sweet PDO wine from sun-dried XYNISTERI and MAVRO grapes. Probably most ancient named wine still in production. New-generation producers: AES AMBELIS, Anama, GEROLEMO, KYPEROUNDA, TSIAKKAS. Traditional styles: St Barnabas (KAMANTERENA), St John (KEO), Centurion (ETKO).

Constantinou r w ★→★★ In Lemesos region; Ayioklima XYNISTERI DYA and gd SHIRAZ.

ETKO & Olympus r w br ★→★★ Former big producer, improving since move to Olympus winery. Best for St Nicholas COMMANDARIA 13 and superior Centurion.

Gerolemo w ★→★★ Up-and-coming; noted for local grapes. Try Morokanella, MUSCAT.

K&K Vasilikon Winery r p w ★★ 13 14 15 16 Family winery owned by three brothers. Gd DYA XYNISTERI, Einalia rosé and consistent reds: Ayios Onoufrios, Methy.

Kamanterena (SODAP) r p w ★→★★ 14 15 16 Winery name of large SODAP co-op in Pafos hills. Gd-value competent DYA whites and rosé, young unoaked MARATHEFTIKO. V.gd COMMANDARIA St Barnabas 02.

Cyprus is phylloxera-free with ungrafted vines; 15 indigenous varieties identified.

KEO r p w br ★ 14 15 16 Winemaking now at Mallia Estate in hills. Ktima Keo range is best esp Altesse (w), Heritage (r). Classic St John ★★COMMANDARIA.

Kyperounda r p w br ★★→★★★ 13' 15' 16 Some of Europe's highest v'yds at 1450m. Petritis is standard-setting XYNISTERI. Flagship Epos CHARD and red from own-v'yd. V.gd: SHIRAZ, Andessitis blend. Excellent modern COMMANDARIA.

Makkas r p w ★→★★ 15 16 Former economist with garage winery in Pafos region. Gd XYNISTERI, MARATHEFTIKO, SYRAH, Rodostafylo rosé.

Tsiakkas r p w br ★★→★★★ 15 16 Banker turned winemaker. Expressive whites esp SAUV BL, XYNISTERI. Also v.gd COMMANDARIA, Vamvakada (aka MARATHEFTIKO), Yiannoudi. Promising experiments with orange wine and local Promara.

Vlassides r p w ★★→★★★ 13' 15 16 UC Davis-trained Vlassides makes benchmark SHIRAZ, gd DYA Grifos range in all colours, CAB SAUV, excellent long-ageing Private Collection.

Vouni Panayia r p w ★★ 14 15 16 Dynamic family winery with local grape focus. Try Alina XYNISTERI, MARATHEFTIKO, Promara, Yiannoudi.

Zambartas r p w ★★→★★★ 13 15 16 Young Australia-trained winemaker making intense CAB FR/LEFKADA rosé, v.gd SHIRAZ/Lefkada red, excellent MARATHEFTIKO, zesty XYNISTERI esp exciting single v'yd version. Promising local Yiannoudi with MOURVÈDRE in Epicurean.

Oldest known pet cat (not Pét-Nat) found on Cyprus, buried 9500 yrs ago.

Israel

Israeli wines are showing more elegance, better varietal character and a greater sense of place. The trend is to Mediterranean-style blends, red and white, rather than overripe varietals; there is also a great deal of interest in researching local varieties. Best regions remain the high-altitude Upper Gailiee (Up Gal), Golan Heights (Gol) and Judean Hills (Jud). Abbreviations: Gailiee (Gal), Negev (Neg), Samson (Sam), Shomron (Shom).

Abaya Gal r ★★ Terroirist. Moving towards natural wines. Intense, rustic SYRAH.

Agur Jud r w ★→★★ Elegant reds. 100% Oseleta (N Italian grape) of interest.

Ashkar Gal ★→★★ Connects a people, land and their heritage. Unique SAUV BL.

Barkan-Segal Gal, Sam r w ★→★★ Israel's largest winery. Great hopes from new winemaker. New Segal Petit UF, fruity and oaky CAB.

Bar-Maor Shom r ★★ Min-intervention winemaking. Archetype rare prestige blend.

Carmel Up Gal r w sp ★★ Complex Kayoumi v'yd RIES, fruity 4 Vats (r). Gd value Private Collection. Vacated historic Rishon Le Zion Cellars.

Château Golan Gol r (w) ★★★ Geshem (r w) v.gd Mediterranean blends. Great, rare ROUSSANNE. Bold Eliad. Innovative winemaker.

Clos de Gat Jud r w ★★★→★★★★ Classy estate exuding quality, style, individuality. Powerful Sycra SYRAH 07' 09 11, rare MERLOT rich and concentrated. Traditional, quality CHARD. Fresh entry-level Chanson (w) gd value.

Cremisan Jud r w ★→★★ Palestinian wines made in a monastery from indigenous grapes: Baladi, Dabouki, Hamdani, Jandali.

Dalton Up Gal r w ★★ Family winery, creative winemaker. Vibrant FUMÉ BLANC.

Domaine du Castel Jud r w ★★★→★★★★ Pioneer of JUD. Set standards in Israel for style, quality. Beautiful winery. Characterful, supple, consistent Grand Vin 09' 10 11 12 13' 14' 15. Plush Petit Castel. La Vie gd commercial white and red. Benchmark CHARD. Characterful rosé.

Feldstein Gal r w ★★ Artisan. Excellent GRENACHE and interesting indigenous Dabuki (aka Dabouki).

Flam Jud, Gal r (w) ★★★ Founded by brothers. Superb, elegant B'x blend Noble 08' 09 10' 11' 12 13'. Fruit-forward SYRAH, deep MERLOT. Classico great value. Excellent, fresh, fragrant white (SAUV BL/CHARD), crisp rosé.

Galilee Quality region in n esp higher altitude Up Gal.

Galil Mountain Up Gal r w ★→★★ Prestige blend Yiron always gd value.

Golan Heights High-altitude plateau, with volcanic tufa and basalt soil.

Gush Etzion Jud r w ★→★★ Central mtn v'yds; PINOT N, GRENACHE/SYRAH/MOURVÈDRE.

Jezreel Valley Shom ★→★★ Gd old-vine Argaman, Israeli variety. Pét-Nat Dabouki.

Judean Hills Quality region rising towards Jerusalem. Terra rossa on limestone.

Kosher Necessary for religious Jews. Irrelevant to quality. Wines can be v.gd.

Lahat Gol, Jud ★★→★★★ Rhône specialist. Well-integrated red (N Rhône style), complex white (S Rhône style).

Lewinsohn Gal r w ★★★ Quality *garagiste* in a garage. Exquisite, lean CHARD. Red: chunky, spicy, yet elegant blend of PETITE SIRAH/Marselan.

Maia Shom r w ★★ Med-style. Greek consultants. Mare Nostrum chewy, refreshing.

Margalit Gal, Shom r ★★★→★★★★ Israel's 1st cult wine. Father and son. Rare Special Res. B'x blend Enigma 12 13' 14 15. Complex CAB FR. Fine CAB SAUV. Excellent ageing potential. Perfumed Paradigma GRENACHE/SYRAH/MOURVÈDRE. New Optima White and RIES.

Mia Luce Gal ★★→★★★ *Garagiste*. SYRAH with stems: N Rhône feel. Superb Marselan.

Negev Desert region in s of country. V'yds at high elevations.

Pelter-Matar Gol r w (sp) ★★ Fresh whites. Matar gd CHARD, SAUV BL/SEM.

Psagot Jud ★★ Central mtn v'yds. Peak is a succulent Mediterranean blend.

Recanati Gal r w ★★★ Quality at every price point. Special Res 11' 12' 13. Complex, wild CARIGNAN. Flowery Marawi and 1st-ever Bittuni (local r variety), fruity, young.

Samson Central region incl the JUD plain and foothills, se of Tel Aviv.

Sea Horse Jud r (w) ★★ Artistic winemaker. New chewy Counoise.

Seror Gol r w ★→★★ Deep complex SYRAH. Fresh rosé. One to watch.

Shomron Region with v'yds mainly around Mt Carmel and Zichron Ya'acov.

Shvo Up Gal r w ★★★ Non-interventionist grower-winemaker. Super-rustic Mediterranean red. Rare Gershon SAUV BL, racy CHENIN BL. Characterful rosé.

Sphera Jud w ★★★→★★★★ White only. Racy, minerally White Concepts varietals (RIES, CHARD, SAUV BL) and crisp blend First Page. Outstanding, rare White Signature (SEM/Chard).

Tabor Gal r w sp ★★→★★★ V.gd whites esp SAUV BL. Adama label v.gd value. Complex Malkiya. Bright single-v'yd TANNAT, fruity Marselan.

Teperberg Jud, Sam r w sp ★→★★ Israel's largest family winery. Fifth generation. Excellent CAB FR; crisp PINOT GR.

Tulip Gal r (w) ★★ Innovative, progressive. Opulent Black Tulip. Deep SHIRAZ. Refreshing Net SAUV BL. Noble contribution to adults with special needs.

"If there is wine, send quantity": request for supplies on pottery fragment, 600BC.

Tzora Jud r w ★★★★ Terroir-led; talented winemaker (Israel's only MW). Crisp Shoresh (SAUV BL). JUD Red excellent value. Complex, elegant prestige Misty Hills (CAB SAUV/SYRAH) 10' 11 12' 13' 14'. Rare luscious Or dessert.

Tzuba Jud r w ★→★★ Well-balanced CHARD. Gd Metzuda blend.

Vitkin Jud r w ★★→★★★ Quality CARIGNAN. Complex GRENACHE BL. Gt-value entry level.

Vortman Shom ★→★★ One to watch: COLOMBARD, FUMÉ, GRENACHE/CARIGNAN blend.

Yaacov Oryah Sam ★★→★★★ Creative artisan. V.gd orange wines and red blends.

Yarden Gol r w sp ★★★ Brought New World technology to Israel. Rare, prestige Katzrin 08' 11' 12 13. Bold Bar'on CAB/SYRAH. Big-selling brand Hermon Red. Regular Cab Sauv shows quality, consistency and value. Gd Blanc de Blancs and Brut Rosé. Delicious sweet Heights Wine.

Yatir Jud r (w) ★★★ Desert winery with high-altitude v'yds. Velvety, concentrated Yatir Forest 10 11 12' 13'. Lively VIOGNIER.

Lebanon

Problems never seem to leave poor Lebanon. We write this every year but the country is shown at its best through its wines. Reds have warmth and spice and whites showing better freshness than previously.

Atibaia r ★★★ *Garagiste*. Elegant red B'x style blend with soft tannins.

Chateau Belle-Vue r (w) ★★ Le Château a plush blend of B'x grapes and SYRAH.

Château Ka r w ★→★★ Great-value, fruity cherry-berry Cadet de Ka.

Château Kefraya r w ★★→★★★★ Fine, ripe, concentrated, complex *Comte de M* 09' 10 11' 12'. Full, fragrant, oaky Comtesse de M (CHARD/VIOGNIER). Fresh crisp rosé.

Chateau Ksara r w ★★ Founded 1857. Res du Couvent is fruity, easy-drinking and full of flavour.

Château Marsyas r (w) ★★ Deep, powerful, fruity (mainly CAB/SYRAH). Owner of complex ★★★Bargylus (Syria), a miracle wine made in impossible conditions.

Chateau Musar r w ★★★→★★★★ Icon wine of the e Med, CAB SAUV/CINSAULT/ CARIGNAN 02 03 04 05' 07' 08 09. *Unique recognizable style.* Best after 15–20 yrs in bottle. Indigenous Obaideh and Merweh (w) age indefinitely; second label Hochar (r) now higher profile. Musar Jeune is softer, easy-drinking.

Clos St. Thomas r w ★→★★ Pioneer in revival of local varieties. Try aromatic Obaidy (sic).

Domaine de Baal r (w) ★★ Crisp CHARD/SAUV BL, heady estate red from organic v'yd.

Domaine des Tourelles r w ★★→★★★ Blockbuster SYRAH, gd Marquis des Beys. Outstanding new CINSAULT from 70-yr-old vines. Fast improving winery.

Domaine Wardy r w ★→★★ Gd value. Soft and elegant Obeideh (sic).

IXSIR r w ★★→★★★ Stony SYRAH-based blends, floral whites and prestige El.

Massaya r w ★★ Terraces de Baalbeck a refined, elegant GSM. Entry-level v.gd value.

Turkey

It does not get easier to make wine in Turkey. The enemies are within: the government and a traditional conservative agricultural sector that would prefer to sell raisins. Those making the effort deserve support. Boğazkere, Narince and Oküzgözü in particular, of interest.

Büyülübağ r (w) ★★ One of new small, quality wineries. Gd CAB SAUV.

Corvus r w ★★★ Bozcaada island. Intense, concentrated Corpus, luscious Passito.

Doluca r w ★→★★ DLC label showcases local varieties. Gd rounded OKÜZGÖZÜ.

Bronze Age grape seeds found in Turkey believed to be Muscat Blanc à Petits Grains.

Kavaklidere r w sp ★→★★★ Pendore estate is best, esp ÖKÜZGÖZÜ, SYRAH. Gd value at every price. Stéphane Derenoncourt consults.

Kayra r w ★→★★ Spicy SHIRAZ, fresh NARINCE. Ripe OKÜZGÖZÜ from E Anatolia.

Sevilen r w ★→★★ International variety specialist. Deep SYRAH, aromatic SAUV BL.

Suvla r w ★→★★ Full-bodied B'x blend Sur, and fruity SYRAH backed by oak.

Urla r w ★★ Tempus is red blend with complexity, depth and length.

Vinkara r w ★ Charming NARINCE and cherry-berry KALECIK KARASI.

NORTH AFRICA

It's hard to imagine how important North Africa was to wine trade only 50 years ago. Now Algeria is out of picture, Tunisian (Tun) wine is mainly for tourists; only Morocco (Mor), with French investment, keeps flag flying.

Bernard Magrez Mor r ★★ Investment by B'x tycoon.Tannic, spicy SYRAH/GRENACHE, S Rhône style. Meaty.

Castel Frères Mor r p ★ Gd-value brands like Bonassia, Halana, Larroque, Sahari.

Celliers de Meknès, Les Mor r p w ★→★★ Virtual monopoly in Mor. Château Roslane is best.

Domaine Neferis Tun r p w ★→★★ Calastrasi joint venture. Selian CARIGNAN best.

Ouled Thaleb Mor r p w ★★ Medaillon generous blend of CAB SAUV/MERLOT/SYRAH. Lively Syrah Tandem (Syrocco in US): Thalvin and Graillot (Rhône) joint venture.

Val d'Argan Mor r p w ★→★★ At Essaouira. Gd value: Mogador. Best: Orients.

Vignerons de Carthage Tun r p w ★ Best from UCCV co-op: Magon Magnus (r).

Vin Gris ★ Pale pink resort of the thirsty. Castel Boulaouane brand best known.

Volubilia Mor r p w ★→★★ Best delicate pink *vin gris* in Morocco.

Asia & Old Russian Empire

ASIA

China The news about Chinese wine is that if it wins another gold medal or trophy in an international wine tasting, it's not news any more. This is quite an achievement when you consider than it was only in 2011 that Jia Bei Lan CAB 2009 did just that. V'yd plantings have soared nearly 20 per cent from 680,000–800,000 ha. Only 15 per cent of the grapes go to make wine, but it's a fast-growing percentage. Far-flung nw Xinjiang and n-central Ningxia have half the total. Hebei and coastal Shandong, combined, share another quarter, with the remaining quarter in other provinces incl Yunnan, where Moët-Hennessy Shangri-La Winery's Ao Yun (Cab/MERLOT, China's most expensive wine) is grown in the Himalayan foothills. China's love affair and obsession with B'x is reflected in its plantings. CAB SAUV leads with 60%, followed by Merlot, CHARD, Cab Gernischt (aka CARMENÈRE), Marselan (Cab Sauv x GRENACHE), SYRAH, CAB FR and WELSCHRIESLING. Other varieties incl RIES, UGNI BL, SEM, PETIT MANSENG, PINOT N, GAMAY, PETIT VERDOT. China's most impressive dessert wines to date, inspired by Canada's Icewine, are made from VIDAL. Ningxia wears the crown of being the "B'x of China". Gd reds are made by Jia Bei Lan, Silver Heights, Legacy Peak, Domaine Helan Mountain (owned by Pernod Ricard), Leirenshou and Domaine Fontaine Sable. Sha Po Tou at the foot of the Xiangshan Mtn, also in Ningxia, has a 100% Cab Gernischt from 22-year-old vines. Meanwhile, Li's Family Treasures SHIRAZ is getting gd reviews. So is Taila Winery in Shandong for its VIOGNIER. Grace V'yd in Shanxi produces a cracking Marselan. Tiansai, aka Skyline of Gobi, in Xinjiang on the historic Silk Road is said to make the best rosé (and probably Chard) from the Middle Kingdom.

India's viticultural challenges incl monsoons, scorching heat, humidity and the resultant fungal threats. There are about 115,000 ha of vines but only about 2000 ha make wine; these are mainly in Maharashtra, Karnataka and Andhra Pradesh. Sula's consistent SAUV BL is the go-to white. Gd Sauv Bl is also made by Indus, Charosa and Grover (esp Zampa Art Collection). For fizz, tops are Moët Hennessy's Domaine Chandon and York Sparkling Cuvée (CHENIN BL). Its late-harvest Chenin is gd with Indian food, esp seafood and vegetarian. Also Fratelli Vitae Barrel Fermented CHARD, Chard/Sauv Bl, SANGIOVESE and Sangiovese Bianco. Reds tend to be overoaked, but KRSMA Estates CAB SAUV stands out. So does the more est Grover Zampa La Res Cab Sauv/SHIRAZ.

Japan now makes more Koshu than all its reds put together.

Japan Leading the field is KOSHU, acidic, floral, citrus, zesty, from grape of the same name, which has become the darling of writers, sommeliers. Top names: Aruga Branca, Chateau Mercian, Domaine Hide, Grace Wine (also gd Blanc de Blancs fizz), Haramo, Lumiere, Soryu. Hybrid Muscat Bailey A is most planted red, with a candy-floss aroma. Chitose Winery on Hokkaido makes a v.gd PINOT N. Red B'x blends tend to be overoaked. The biggest challenge is lack of sun: typhoon season is May to October, and esp July to September, mths critical for ripening. Total vine plantings are 19,000 ha, but wine represents only about six per cent, with around 280 wineries. Most are in Yamanashi, w of Tokyo (Koshu is ancient name of this prefecture), followed by Nagano, Hokkaido, Yamagata, Niigata. The wine landscape is dominated by large corporations that also happen to be the country's biggest brewers, namely Sapporo, Kirin and Suntory. Their distribution is guaranteed and the envy of smaller producers.

THE OLD RUSSIAN EMPIRE

The Black Sea and the Caucasus are the centres of wine-growing in western Asia, and attention is turning their way again. Crimea, famous for its sweet and sparkling wines under the last tsars, is reinventing itself with dry styles. Georgia's ancient techniques and grape varieties have found relevance in the fashion for alternatives. Its buried clay *qvevris* (amphorae), long considered archaic, are now seen as valid vessels for long fermentations. Georgian Saperavi is acknowledged a first-class red wine grape. Armenia, another country with a real wine heritage, is worth watching too. Off the beaten track is new wine production, above 1000m (3281ft), in Kazakhstan.

Armenia Vies with Georgia as a birthplace of winemaking (the most ancient winery dates back 6100 yrs). Its remote mountainous v'yds are phylloxera-free. Indigenous white Voskeat, Garandamak; red Areni, Hindogny, Kakhet can give high quality. Private investment and internationally renowned consultants drive the standards at ArmAs, Tierras de Armenia, Zorah Karasi.

Georgians were making wine 2500 yrs before wheel was invented; 1st things 1st.

Georgia Private households own 90 per cent of Georgia's 48,000 ha of v'yds. Wine is a lifestyle choice, and with over 7000 yrs of unbroken viticultural history, Georgia has preserved its unique grapes (around 500), viticulture, wine styles. Principal varieties are red SAPERAVI (from easy and semi-sweet to robust, tannic, age-worthy) and white RKATSITELI (lively, refreshing). Handmade *qvevris*, protected by UNESCO, are a symbol of Georgian winemaking and inspire winemakers worldwide. Historic production of skin-macerated whites is known as Kakheti method, and more fashionably as orange wine. Leading producers incl Badagoni, Château Mukhrani, GWS, Jakeli Khashmi, Kindzmarauli Marani, Marani (TWC), Pheasant's Tears, Schuchmann, Tbilvino.

Moldova This tiny country's agriculture is based on winemaking: 110,000 ha of v'yds need the hands of ten per cent of the population. European grapes are historically grown along with typically Romanian (w) FETEASCĂ ALBĂ, FETEASCĂ REGALĂ, (r) Rară Neagră, FETEASCĂ NEAGRĂ and others. Wines offer gd value. Historic red blends Roşu de Purcari (CAB SAUV, MERLOT, MALBEC) and Negru de Purcari (Cab Sauv, SAPERAVI, Rara Neagră) can be seriously interesting. Vinăria Purcari is most acclaimed. Producers of note: Asconi, Château Vartely, Cricova (sp), Et Cetera, Fautur, Gitana, Lion Gri, Vinăria Bostavan, Vinăria din Vale.

Russia has introduced, prematurely you may well think, geographic indications and protected names of origin. There are 60,000 ha, yet over half of "Russian" wine is made with cheap bulk. The Krasnodar region leads with favourable conditions by the Black Sea and the River Kuban. International grapes (incl RIES) lead. Harsh climate in the Don Valley, known for indigenous grapes (red Krasnostop, Tsimliansky), means they have to bury vines in winter. Château le Grand Vostock and Lefkadia have consistent high quality. Est large producers are Château Tamagne, Fanagoria, Myskhako, Yubileinaya, Abrau Durso (sparkling); small are Burnier, Gai-Kodzor, Rayevskoye.

Ukraine Wine production is concentrated around the Black Sea, particularly in the Crimea where quality is also highest. International grapes are common, also some local hybrids. Producers with own v'yds are raising stakes for quality dry wines: Inkerman (Special Res), Guliev Wines, Prince Trubetskoy Winery, Satera (Esse, Kacha Valley), Oleg Repin, Uppa Winery, Veles are of note. Massandra, Solnechnaya Dolina, Koktebel, Magarach continue strong tradition of fortified styles. Wines modelled on Champagne are another heritage: try Artyomovsk Winery, Novy Svet, Zolotaya Balka.

United States

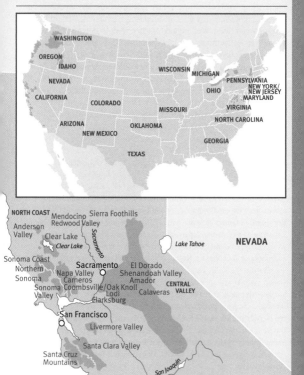

WASHINGTON
OREGON
IDAHO
NEVADA
CALIFORNIA
COLORADO
ARIZONA
NEW MEXICO
TEXAS
OKLAHOMA
MISSOURI
WISCONSIN MICHIGAN
OHIO
PENNSYLVANIA
NEW YORK/
NEW JERSEY
MARYLAND
VIRGINIA
NORTH CAROLINA
GEORGIA

NORTH COAST Mendocino Sierra Foothills
Anderson Redwood Valley
Valley
Clear Lake *Clear Lake*
Sonoma Coast
Northern
Sonoma Napa Valley El Dorado
Sonoma Carneros Shenandoah Valley
Valley Coombsville/Oak Knoll Amador
Lodi Calaveras CENTRAL
Clarksburg VALLEY
San Francisco
Livermore Valley
Santa Clara Valley
Santa Cruz
Mountains
Monterey Salinas
Carmel Valley/ Arroyo Seco CENTRAL COAST
Santa Lucia
Highlands San Lucas
Pacific Ocean Paso Robles
CALIFORNIA

NEVADA
Lake Tahoe
Sacramento
CENTRAL
VALLEY
Fresno
San Joaquin

UNITED STATES

Abbreviations used in the text
(*see also* Principal Vineyard/
Viticultural Areas p.247, p.263, p.268):

CA	California
Clark	Clarksburg, CA
Coomb	Coombsville, CA
Mad	Madera, CA
Mend	Mendocino, CA
Mont	Monterey, CA
Oak Knoll	Oak K, CA
San LO	San Luis Obispo, CA
Santa B	Santa Barbera, CA
Santa Cz Mts	Santa Cruz Mountains, CA
Son	Sonoma, CA
ID	Idaho
NJ	New Jersey

San Luis Obispo
Edna Valley/Arroyo GV
Santa Maria Valley
Santa Barbara
Sta Rita Hills
Santa Ynez Valley
Santa Barbara

Los Angeles

OH	Ohio
OR	Oregon
PA	Pennsylvania
PNW	Pacific Northwest
TX	Texas
VA	Virginia
WA	Washington

There's no denying the predominance of California in US wine – 90 per cent of it comes from here. But while other states can't match up in terms of volume, we are seeing definite stylistic differences, with different states establishing different personalities. Oregon for elegant, fresh Pinot; Washington for riper, rounder Merlot and Cab Sauv; Virginia for concentrated but fresh blends with Viognier, Petit Manseng, Tannat and Petit Verdot (not all at once); New York State for cool-climate Riesling. And that's before we look at the differences within California, which is not just one place. Napa is beginning to see the virtues of balance (at last); coastal Sonoma is taut and tight; and there are many, many individual producers of talent and imagination taking risks and defying the luxury-goods image of the state. The US is becoming once again a country of mavericks.

Arizona

Research has revealed soils and climate zones "similar to" Burgundian conditions. High-desert terroir of volcanic rock and limestone soils, gd ripening weather. Wineries incl **Arizona Stronghold**: ★ flagship red Rhône blend Nachise and excellent white blend Tazi. **Alcantara Vineyards**: elegant and earthy reds, esp Confluence IV and Grand Rouge, a six-wines blend. **Burning Tree Cellars**: artisanal, small batch, intense red blends. **Caduceus Cellars**: ★★→★★★ ownership by Alt-rocker Maynard James Keenan gave winery early buzz and wines stepped up too; excellent white blend Dos Ladrones, top reds Sancha, Nagual del Marzo. **Callaghan Vineyards**: ★★ served at the White House, TANNAT and red blends stand out; top-rated Caitlin made by vintner's daughter. **Chateau Tumbleweed**: up-and-coming small-batch producer esp Dr. Ron Bot SYRAH blend. **Four Eight Wineworks**: incubator co-op for emerging winemakers, features Kindred, proprietary red blend. **Page Springs Cellars**: GSM, other white Rhône single-varietal esp Dragoon MARSANNE, and blends. **Pillsbury Wine Company**: ★ filmmaker Sam Pillsbury producing excellent dessert wine Symphony Sweet Lies, PETITE SIRAH Special Res, v.gd CHENIN BL, Double-Gold winning GRENACHE and Guns & Kisses SHIRAZ.

California

No longer is it possible to stereotype CA wines as sunny fruit-bombs smothered in new oak. They are there, of course, some of them with eye-stretching prices. But more wineries are exploring cooler climates along the coasts of Santa B, Son and Mend as well as rockier, high-elevation sites in Mend Co, Lake County and the Sierra Nevada mtns, looking for better balance, finesse and "minerality". Critics and younger consumers (as well as I) demanded less ripe, less oaky wines – and a new generation of winemakers is delivering the goods. Not all at once, but you can find racy, refreshing SAUV BL, CHARD and PINOT N, focused, peppery SYRAHS and CABS with more balance and less bombast. Millennial wine-drinkers are famously open to new things. Amphoras of course, but also esoteric varieties like Trousseau Gris, Italian novelties and some of the Iberian varieties like TEMPRANILLO, VERDEJO and TOURIGA N. Even a revival of CHENIN BL. Anderson V has booked its place as a world-class source of harmonious Pinot N and Chard, while star producers inland in El Dor Co, Lake County and Lodi, and up the Son coast towards Alaska, are no longer considered eccentric. On the negative side some low-end red wines are adding sugar and oak flavourings. This last bit is depressing, but from the bow of the ship, the future looks bright.

Recent vintages

California is too diverse for simple summaries. There can certainly be differences between the North, Central and Southern thirds of the state, but there have been no "bad" vintages in over a decade, and some that have been difficult for winemakers have made drinkers happy. Here are some brief overviews of recent vintages in cellars, in stores and a couple on the way.

2017 Ample winter rains at last. Catastrophic wildfires in Napa, Sonoma, but after most grapes picked; may be talk of "smoke taint", but quality mostly very good.

2016 Good quality, quantity, early harvest. Wines look balanced.

2015 Dry year, low yields, but quality surprisingly good.

2014 Despite a 3rd year of drought, quality high.

2013 Another large harvest with excellent quality prospects.

2012 Cab Sauv oustanding. Very promising for most varieties.

2011 Difficult. Later pickers reported gd Cab Sauv/Pinot N. Zin suffered.

2010 Cool, wet. But some outstanding bottlings esp Rhône varieties, Zin.

2009 Reds/whites good balance, ageing potential. Napa Cab Sauv excellent.

Principal vineyard areas

There are well over 100 AVAs in CA. Below are the key players.

Alexander Valley (Alex V) Son. Warm region in upper Son. Best-known for gd Zin, Cab Sauv on hillsides.

Amador County (Am Co) Warm Sierra County with wealth of old-vine Zin; Rhône grapes also flourish.

Anderson Valley (And V) Mend. Pacific fog and winds follow Navarro River inland; superb Pinot N, Chard, sparkling, v.gd Ries, Gewurz, some stellar Syrah. Wild, stellar potential.

Arroyo Seco Mont. Warm AVA; gd Ries, Merlot, Chard.

Atlas Peak Napa. Exceptional Cab Sauv, Merlot.

Calistoga (Cal) Warmer n end of Napa V. Red wine territory esp Cab Sauv.

Carneros (Car) Napa, Son. Cool AVA at n tip of SF Bay. Gd Pinot N, Chard; Merlot, Syrah, Cab Sauv on warmer sites. V.gd sparkling.

Coombsville (Coomb) Napa. Cool region nr SF Bay; top Cab Sauv in B'x pattern.

Diamond Mtn Napa. High-elevation vines, outstanding Cab Sauv.

Dry Creek Valley (Dry CV) Son. Outstanding Zin, gd Sauv Bl; gd hillside Cab Sauv and Zin.

Edna Valley (Edna V) San LO. Cool Pacific winds; v.gd Chard.

El Dorado County (El Dor Co) High-altitude inland area surrounding Placerville. Some real talent emerging with Rhône grapes, Zin, Cab and more.

Howell Mtn Napa. Classic Napa Cab Sauv from steep hillside v'yds.

Livermore Valley (Liv V) Alameda. Historic gravelly white-wine district mostly swallowed by suburbs; regaining some standing with new-wave Cab Sauv, Chard.

Mendocino Ridge (Mend Rdg). Emerging region in Mendocino County, dictated by elevation over 365m. Cool, above fog, lean soils.

Mt Veeder Napa. High mtn v'yds for gd Chard, Cab Sauv.

Napa Valley (Napa V) Cab Sauv, Merlot, Cab Fr. Look to sub-AVAs for meaningful terroir-based wines, and mtn areas for most complex, age-worthy.

Oakville (Oak) Napa. Prime Cab Sauv territory on gravelly bench.

Paso Robles (P Rob) San LO. Popular with visitors; Rhône, B'x varieties, reds prominent.

Pritchard Hill (P Hill). Elevated, rugged, prime terrritory for Cab Sauv.

Red Hills of Lake County (R Hills). N extension of Mayacama range, huge Cab Sauv potential.

Redwood Valley (Red V) Mend. Warmer inland region; gd Zin, Cab Sauv, Sauv Bl.
Russian River Valley (RRV) Son. Pacific fog lingers; Pinot N, Chard, gd Zin on benchland.
Rutherford (Ruth) Napa. Outstanding Cab Sauv esp hillside v'yds.
Saint Helena (St H) Napa. Lovely balanced Cab Sauv.
Santa Lucia Highlands (Santa LH) Mont. Higher elevation, s-facing hillsides, great Pinot N, Syrah, Rhônes.
Santa Maria Valley (Santa MV) Santa B. Coastal cool; gd Pinot N, Chard, Viognier.
Sta Rita Hills (Sta RH) Santa B. Excellent Pinot N.
Santa Ynez (Santa Ynz) Santa B. Rhônes (r w), Chard, Sauv Bl best bet.
Sierra Foothills El Dor Co, Am Co, Calaveras County. All improving.
Sonoma Coast (Son Coast) V. cool climate; edgy Pinot N, Chard.
Sonoma Valley (Son V) Gd Chard, v.gd Zin; excellent Cab Sauv from Sonoma Mountain (Son Mtn) sub-AVA. Note Son V is area within Sonoma County.
Spring Mtn Napa. Elevated Cab Sauv, complex soil mixes and exposures.
Stags Leap (Stags L) Napa. Classic red, black fruited Cab Sauv; v.gd Merlot.

American Viticultural Areas

I'm not sure AVAs will ever catch on with the public as USPs. They're not exactly (or even approximately) like Appellations Contrôlées. One thing they do is stimulate local feelings and claims for specialness, which is, overall, a gd thing. Federal regulations on appellation of origin in the US were approved in 1977. There are two categories: 1st is a straightforward political AVA, which can incl an entire state, ie. CA, WA, OR and so on. Individual counties can also be used, ie. Santa B or Son. When the county designation is used, all grapes must come from that county. The 2nd category is a geographical designation, such as Napa V or Will V, within the state. These AVAs are supposed to be based on similarity of soils, weather, etc. In practice, they tend to be inclusive rather than exclusive. Within these AVAs there can be further sub-appellations, eg. the Napa V AVA contains Ruth, Stags L and others. When these geographical designations are used, all grapes must come from that region. A producer who has met the regulatory standards can choose a purely political listing, such as Napa, or a geographical listing, such as Napa V. It will probably be many yrs before the public recognizes the differences, but there is no doubt that some AVAs already fetch hefty premiums.

Abreu Vineyards Napa V ★★★→★★★★ 07 09 10 11 12 13 14 Supple CAB SAUV-based wines from selected v'yds. Madrona v'yd leads the way with powerful, balanced opening, long, layered finish. V.gd cellar choice for 10–15 yrs.
Acaibo ★★★ B'x-like estate of Gonzague and Claire Lurton in Chalk Hill is called Trinité (CAB SAUV, MERLOT, CAB FR). Acaibo is top wine; a winner. Also seductive *G&C Lurton* blend.
Alban Vineyards Edna V ★★★→★★★★ 10 11 12 13 14 (15) John Alban, a SYRAH frontiersman and original Rhône Ranger, still making great wine. Top VIOGNIER, GRENACHE, splendid Syrah capable of extended ageing.
Albatross Ridge Mont ★★★ Bowlus family rules a special high-elevation roost seven miles from Pacific nr Carmel. Early CHARD, PINOT N fresh, lively, warrant watching.
Alma Rosa Santa RH ★★★→★★★★ Dick Sanford's 2nd act after selling namesake winery. Continuing tradition of refined PINOT N, CHARD, also v.gd rosé.
Andrew Murray Santa B ★★★ Rhônes around the clock and hits keep coming. SYRAH leads pack, but VIOGNIER, ROUSSANNE, fresh GRENACHE BL hits too.
Antica Napa V ★★★ Piero Antinori's mtn SANGIOVESE venture initially flopped, but

subsequent lessees improved v'yds, proving potential for fine CAB SAUV, CHARD. Antinori wisely re-claimed property.

Araujo Napa V *See* EISELE VINEYARD.

A Tribute to Grace N Coast ★★★ Kiwi Angela Osborne's homage to GRENACHE. Fruit from exceptional v'yds, diverse terroirs all over state, none more exciting than 975m (3199ft), mtn-ringed Santa Barbara Highlands.

Au Bon Climat Santa B ★★★ Jim Clendenen made PINOT N before it was hip, and advocated the balanced wine style now trending. Fomented rise of Central Coast with Burg-style CHARD, Pinot N. Other small lots under Clendenen Family label.

Banshee Wines Son Coast ★★★ Three wine-industry vets used insider connections to buy unsold barrels of juice from other wineries and reblend into PINOT N gold. Growing national presence. New line of well-made single-v'yd wines.

Beaulieu Vineyard ("BV") Napa V ★→★★★ Iconic Georges de Latour Private Res CAB SAUV back on track, with other reds. Cheap Coastal Estate brand fine in a pinch.

Beckmen Vineyards Santa B ★★★ Steve Beckmen's bio Purisma Mtn estate produces formidable SYRAH, GRENACHE and GRENACHE BL. Rhône blend Cuvée le Bec is rightly popular nationwide.

Bedrock Wine Co. Son V ★★★ Morgan Peterson's (son of RAVENSWOOD founder Joel P) label is a paean to CA heritage ZIN v'yds and old-school co-fermentation techniques. Great to see wisdom of ages through clear young eyes.

Benziger Family Winery Son V ★★★ Heart's in right place with this family-run pioneer of bio/organic farming; some wines better than others. Tribute, CAB SAUV-based blend, complex, structured for ageing. Gorgeous estate worth visiting.

Beringer Napa ★★→★★★ (Private Res) 07 08 09 10 12 Big producer of average grocery-level wines, but Private Res CAB SAUV and single-v'yd Cabs are serious and age-worthy. Howell Mtn Cab Sauv strong, CHARDS now fresher, better. Winemaker Mark Beringer is direct descendant of founder.

Bokisch Lodi ★★→★★★ Markus B is CA leader when it comes to Spanish varieties. V.gd TEMPRANILLO leads list backed by superb GRACIANO, ALBARIÑO, flirty rosado.

Bonny Doon Mont ★★★ 10 12 13 14 15 (Le Cigar Volant) Randall Grahm's marketing is whimsical, but his wines are serious, more terroir-driven than ever. *Vin gris* is superb, Le Cigare Volant Rhône blend impressive; many tricks up his sleeve.

Bonterra *See* FETZER.

Brewer Clifton Santa B ★★★ Following recent sale, one of CA's original cult PINOT N brands back on game: bold, ripe Pinot; impressive CHARD with balance, verve.

Broc Cellars N Coast ★★→★★★ Adventurous Berkeley-based urban winery, not striving for critics' points, but making delicious, quaffable wine like Vine Star red, fruity Beaujolais-like CARIGNAN. Takes risks wkds.

Bronco Wine Company Provocateur, populist Fred Franzia's company, famous for Two-Buck Chuck and scores of other commercial labels.

Cakebread Napa V ★★★ CAB SAUV still has massive cachet with baby boomers. SAUV BL popular, CHARD v.gd; management has diversified direct-to-consumer offerings.

Calera ★★★→★★★★ Josh Jensen, Cent Coast PINOT N pioneer, sought property with limestone and altitude, struck gold. Jensen sold to DUCKHORN in 2017, brand in gd hands. Selleck and Jensen v'yds always stylish.

Caymus Napa V ★★★ 09 11 12 13 One of Napa's foremost international status brands. CAB SAUVS, esp iconic Special Selection, seem riper, sappier. High-quality, dense for sure, but don't hold forever.

Cedarville Sierra F'hills ★★★ Bootstrappers Jonathan Lachs and Susan Marks have built a powerhouse in the granite-rich Fairplay District of El Dor Co. Superb wines across board, mostly red. GRENACHE and SYRAH, fine CAB SAUV, ZIN, VIOGNIER.

Chalone Mont ★★★ A *sui generis* v'yd in Gavilan mts, e of Mont, with limestone (rare in CA), giving PINOT N, CHARD stony lift.

Chappellet Napa V ★★★★ P Hill original, great since 60s. Rugged terrain gives v. durable reds. Signature series CAB SAUV superb, affordable. CHARD v.gd; dry CHENIN BL a treat. Still family-owned, also owns SONOMA-LOEB.

Charles Krug Napa V ★★→★★★ Historically important winery made recent comeback, demanding recognition for role in modern Napa V. Late owner Peter Mondavi was Robert's estranged brother. Supple CAB SAUV, crisp, pure SAUV BL.

Chateau Montelena Napa V ★★★ →★★★★ Tons of history, occasional troubles, but great continuity of ownership and style. Serious, age-worthy CAB SAUV; CHARD holds up well too. Grand stone winery warrants a visit.

Chateau St Jean Son V ★★★ Rock of Son V, solid wines on all fronts, but consensus flagship wine for decades has been Cinq Cépages blend of five B'x varieties, reliable and age-worthy.

Chimney Rock Stags L ★★★ 07 08 10 12 14 Underrated Stags L making best wines ever under graceful stewardship of WM Elizabeth Vianna. Tomahawk V'yd CAB SAUV top-notch.

Cliff Lede Stags L ★★★ 10 11 12 13 14 Brilliant Stags L CAB SAUV is big but balanced with tannin, gd acid. Small production Cabs from Howell Mtn, Diamond Mtn, Oak; leesy SAUV BL also notable.

Clos du Val Napa V ★★★ Stags L classic. New owners slashed production, moved to upscale, estate-based model. Can estate v'yds make cut? CAB SAUV can improve, Car PINOT N solid, jury still out.

Clos Pegase Napa V ★★★ Look-at-me winery, v.gd MERLOT from Car v'yd, gd CAB SAUV.

Cobb Wines Son Coast ★★★ Ross Cobb is captain of family ship, making wonderful Son Coast PINOT N, CHARD from select v'yds. Restrained, balanced, natural. Pinots improve with few yrs. Emaline Ann, Coastlands top sites.

Time to explore Dry CV, Son Coast and And V: better value than Napa.

Constellation ★→★★★ Massive wine/beer/spirits company, publicly traded; 90+ million cases/yr. Owns famed CA brands like Estancia, Franciscan, MT VEEDER, Ravenswood, ROBERT MONDAVI, Simi, creates many of its own.

Continuum St H, Napa V ★★★★ 09 10 11 12 13 14 Tim Mondavi broke with family tradition by leaving benchland for heights of P Hill, spared no expense or effort developing extraordinary estate wine from B'x varieties. Among best of Napa V.

Copain Cellars And V ★★★ Successful endeavour aimed at developing Old World-influenced, classically proportioned wines; recently sold to JACKSON FAMILY. PINOT N is strong suit esp bright, spicy Kiser v'yd versions. Tous Ensemble line easy-going, balanced wines.

Corison Napa V ★★★★ 06 07 09 10 12 13 14 While many in Napa V follow ★iren call of powerhouse wines for big scores, diminishing pleasure, Kathy Corison continues to make elegant, fresh wines esp fresh, focused Kronos V'yd CAB SAUV.

Cuvaison Car ★★★ Quiet top estate, making great wine yr after yr. Top marks to PINOT N, CHARD from Car estate; gd SYRAH, superb CAB SAUV from Mt Veeder. Single Block bottlings incl lovely rosé, v.gd SAUV BL.

Daou P Rob ★★★ Elevated estate in Adelaida Dist is driving CABS SAUV and FR in Paso to new heights literally, figuratively. Wines in high demand.

Dashe Cellars Dry CV, N Coast ★★★ RIDGE veteran Mike Dashe makes tasteful, balanced Dry CV and Alex V ZIN from urban winery in Oakland. Also terrific old-vine CARIGNANE, zesty GRENACHE rosé.

Davis Bynum RRV ★★→★★★ Early RRV PINOT N pioneer still makes big, juicy single-v'yd RRV Pinot and rounded CHARD. Style evolving, more elegant than past.

Dehlinger RRV ★★★→★★★★ PINOT N master still at top of game after more than four decades. Also v.gd CHARD, SYRAH and balanced, elegant CAB SAUV.

Diamond Creek Napa V ★★★★ 06 07 09 10 12 13 14 Napa Mtn jewel. Prices v. high for age-worthy, minerally CAB SAUV from famous hillside v'yds on Diamond Mtn. Patience rewarded.

Domaine Carneros Car ★★★ Taittinger outpost in Car offering consistently gd fizzes esp vintage Blanc de Blancs Le Rêve. V.gd NV Rosé. Vintage Brut may even be on par with French product. The Famous Gate PINOT N formidable.

Domaine Chandon Napa V ★★→★★★ Moët outpost in Yountville's top bubbly is v.gd. NV Res Étoile Blanc and Rosé. Pairings and great nibbles on outdoor patio.

Domaine de la Côte Santa RH ★★★ Exacting, Burgundian-style estate PINOT N from coolest w reaches of Sta RH by brilliant wine mind, former sommelier Rajat Parr and winemaker Sashi Moorman. *See also* SANDHI.

Dominus Estate Napa V ★★★★ 07 08 10 12 13 Moueix-owned (*see* France) Herzog de Meuron-designed winery, dazzling but sadly not open to public. Wines from gravelly, bench soils consistently elegant, impressive. Second wine Napanook v.gd.

Donum Estate N Coast ★★★→★★★★ Anne Moller-Racke has passionately worked Car soils since 1981, her aim is true. PINOT N from four sites is focused, generous, complex. Among leaders of region.

Drew Family And V ★★★ Mend Rdg pioneer making minimalist, savage PINOT N from And V and higher up hills. Look for estate Field Selections Pinot N from Mend Rdg, SYRAH from coastal Valenti V'yd.

Dry Creek Vineyard Dry CV ★★★ Dry C standard-bearer back on A game. Tried-and-true Loire-inspired, grassy FUMÉ BLANC and other SAUV BL always delicious, reds like CAB SAUV, MERLOT, ZIN all improved.

Duckhorn Vineyards ★★★→★★★★ Crowd-pleasing, super-consistent CAB SAUV, MERLOT esp Three Palms v'yd, gd SAUV BL. Second label Decoy wines better than ever. Also owns Migration brand, Goldeneye in And V, and CALERA.

Dunn Vineyards Howell Mtn ★★★→★★★★ Mtn man Randy Dunn stubbornly resisted stampede to jammy, lush CAB SAUV styles, favouring restraint, ageability. Wines aren't always spotless, but when great, they can last decades.

Dutton-Goldfield RRV ★★★ Steady-handed, classical cool-climate CA PINOT N, CHARD from RRV-based powerhouse grower, not super edgy or risky: maybe a gd thing.

Edna Valley Vineyard Edna V ★★★ Easy-drinking varietals from gentle Central Coast. Lovely, lilting SAUV BL, crisp but tropical CHARD. Impressive SYRAH, gd CAB SAUV from top v'yd.

Eisele Vineyard Napa V ★★★★ In 2016 this canonical CAB SAUV name changed from Araujo to Eisele V'yd (effective 2013 vintage), after historic planting from which it comes. Also, refreshing SAUV BL, v.gd VIOGNIER, SYRAH. Now a Pinault (*see* Château Latour, B'x) property.

Ernest Vineyards Son ★★★ Who would've thought we need more PINOT N, CHARD in the state, but this newcomer brings verve, acidity and style to a roster of excellent regional and single v'yd wines. Complex, racy, addictively drinkable.

Etude Car ★★★→★★★★ Winery started by Tony Soter now belongs to Treasury group, but team remains true to his vision, issuing artful PINOT NS from several terroirs. Heirloom Grace v'yd bottling is special. Napa CAB SAUV also better than most Cab specialists. Pinot Rosé to die for.

Failla Son Coast ★★★ One of savviest, most talented winemakers in CA, Ehren Jordan effortlessly tempers CA fruit to make savoury, compelling, complex PINOT N, SYRAH, CHARD from cool coastal sites.

Far Niente Napa V ★★★→★★★★ Pioneer of single-v'yd CAB SAUV, CHARD in generous, Napa style. Hedonism with soul. Dolce: celebrated botrytized sweet wine.

Fetzer Vineyards N Coast ★★→★★★ Pioneer in organic/sustainable viticulture in Mend Co, still decent wines. After selling to Brown Forman, Fetzer family members spun off to other sites in Mend Co.

Field Recordings P Rob ★★★ Impressively subtle, perceptive wines from P Rob's Andrew Jones. Best are blends Neverland and Barter & Trade, but don't miss Alloy and Fiction, delicious in 500 ml cans.

Firestone Santa Y ★★→★★★ Solid Santa Y brand founded by tyre heirs sold to Foley Estates (2007), still relevant with array of Rhône, B'x wines. Founders retained brewery of same name.

Flowers Vineyard & Winery Son Coast ★★★→★★★★ Extreme Son Coast pioneer (1st Chard planted 1991) sold in 2009 to Huneeus Co, but wines remain great. Now organic, making pure PINOT N, CHARD.

Foppiano Son ★★→★★★ Honest RRV wines loaded with sunny fruit and little pretence. PETITE SIRAH, SAUV BL notable.

Forlorn Hope N Coast ★★★ Name says it all: Matthew Rorick's devotion to overlooked v'yds, forgotten grapes, from VERDELHO, Alvarelão to unique Portuguese-variety field blends, all compelling and v.gd.

Forman Vineyard Napa V ★★★ Ric Forman is a dedicated, even fanatic terroirist making elegant, age-worthy CAB SAUV-based wines from hillside v'yds. Also v.gd CHARD with nod to Chablis.

Fort Ross ★★★→★★★★ Son Coast Ultra-cool estate a stone's-throw from Pacific metes out terrific, savoury PINOT N, zesty CHARD and surprisingly gd PINOTAGE (!).

Freeman RRV, Son Coast ★★★→★★★★ Restrained terroir-driven PINOT N, CHARD from cool-climate Son Coast and RRV, with nod to Burgundy. The Ryo-fu Chard ("cool breeze" in Japanese) is amazing, as is Akiko's Cuvée Pinot N.

Freemark Abbey Napa V ★★★ Claimed by JACKSON FAMILY FARMS in 2006, improved. Great values, incl classic single-v'yd Sycamore, Bosché CAB SAUV bottlings.

Freestone Son Coast ★★★ Fine expression of Son Coast. Intense, racy CHARD, PINOT N from vines only few miles from Pacific show gd structure, long finish esp Chard. Investment by Napa's JOSEPH PHELPS.

Frog's Leap Ruth ★★★ John Williams, true champion of organic and bio viticulture, coaxes best out of valley-floor estate. Supple CAB SAUV and MERLOT, elegant CHARD, popular SAUV BL and great ZIN. Value.

Gallo of Sonoma Son ★★★ Formidable wines drawn from great Son v'yd sources and broader lands, un-fussy as founders would have wanted. Fruit quality speaks loudly.

Gallo Winery, E&J ★→★★ Gigantic, privately held company, key to development of post-prohibition wine culture in US and beyond. Populist at core, also secretive. Barefoot, Ecco Domani, LOUIS MARTINI, Turning Leaf, more. *See* GALLO OF SONOMA.

Gary Farrell RRV, Son Coast ★★★ Namesake vintner sold it yrs ago, but high performance continues. Excellent PINOT N, CHARD from cool-climate v'yds. Rocholi v'yd Chard superb.

Gloria Ferrer Car ★★★ Exceptional bubbly. A toast to decades-long collaboration between owners, growers and winemakers that made this Freixenet-owned venture extraordinary. All wines v.gd, Royal Cuvée best.

Grace Family Vineyard Napa V ★★★★ 05 06 07 09 10 11 12 Stunning CAB SAUV shaped for long ageing. One of few cult wines that might actually be worth price.

Graziano Family Mend ★★★ Best-known for Italian varietals made under Enotria and Monte Volpe labels, namely BARBERA, MONTEPULCIANO, PINOT GRIGIO, SANGIOVESE. Savvy veteran, Champion of Mend Co.

Here come the machines

A perfect storm of anti-immigration politics, an improving Mexican economy and increasing min wages is making seasonal migrant labour scarcer. CA wineries are turning to machines like mechanical harvesters and sophisticated optical laser sorters. The robots are coming.

Green and Red Napa V ★★★ Named for colours of its v'yd soils (iron red and green serpentine), Napa classic specializes in old-school, savoury, balanced ZIN. Exotic SAUV BL from new winemaker is a real head-turner.

Grgich Hills Cellars Napa V ★★★ Beret-wearing hall-of-famer Mike Grgich built one of Napa V's great early achievers esp with CHARD, but CAB, delicious ZIN also blossomed. In latter days he adopted bio growing.

Gundlach Bundschu Son V ★★★ CA's oldest family-operated winery. Welcoming vibe makes it popular tasting destination with adventurous concerts for younger set. Best bets MERLOT, CAB SAUV, *Gewurz*.

Hahn Santa LH ★★★ Always overdelivers for $. B'x varieties combine Monterey/Paso fruit to great effect, MERITAGE often killer. Lucienne PINOT N releases fantastic.

Hall Napa V ★★★→★★★★ No expense spared on winery or wines, St H winery makes great Napa CAB SAUV, but bewildering variety of selections. Signature offering outstanding, velvety SAUV BL v.gd, MERLOT among best in CA. Also owns WALT coastal PINOT N, CHARD brand.

Hanna Winery Son ★★★ Son classic with outstanding SAUV BL, PINOT N; Res CAB SAUV, MERLOT superb. Merlot-based rosé a treat.

Hanzell Son V ★★★ Pinot pioneer of 50s still making CHARD, PINOT N from estate vines. Both reward cellar time. Arguably among best of CA. Sebella Chard, from young vines, all bright, crisp fruit.

Harlan Estate Napa V ★★★★ Concentrated, robust CAB SAUV – one of original cult wines only available via mailing list at luxury prices. Still all those things today.

HdV Wines Car ★★★ Underrated Son gem makes fine complex *Chard* with a honed edge and v.gd PINOT N, from grower Larry Hyde in conjunction with Aubert de Villaine of DRC (*see* France). V.gd CAB SAUV, SYRAH.

Heitz Cellar Napa V ★★★→★★★★★ Everyone focuses on iconic, age-worthy Martha's V'yd CAB SAUV. Basic Napa V Cab is always delicious. Gd *Sauv Bl*, even GRIGNOLINO.

Heller Estate Mont ★★★ Founded Carmel V AVA and still prevails there with signature CHENIN BL, supple CAB SAUV, v.gd MERLOT and rosé.

Hendry Oak K ★★★ Classic, est 1939, with tremendous, distinctive CAB SAUV and ZIN (try Block 28) from a cool pocket of the valley nr Napa town.

Hess Collection, The Napa V ★★★ Great Napa V visit with world-class art gallery, also makes gd wine. CAB SAUV from MOUNT VEEDER WINERY hits new quality level esp exceptional 19 Block Cuvée, blockbuster with gd manners.

Hirsch Son Coast ★★★ Pioneer of Son Coast, David Hirsch's v'yd won acclaim growing premium grapes; now family label gets cream of crop from towering Pacific ridge. Lithe PINOT N, breathtaking CHARD.

Honig Napa V ★★★→★★★★ Sustainably grown Napa CAB SAUV and SAUV BL are nationwide benchmarks thanks to consistent quality, hard-working family and team. Top Cab from Bartolucci v'yd in St H.

Inglenook Oak ★★★★ FF Coppola's Rubicon, now under Inglenook label, marks return to classic Napa CAB SAUV – balanced, elegant, true to great tradition. Also CHARD, MERLOT.

Iron Horse Vineyards Son ★★★ Amazing selection of 12 vintage bubblies, all wonderfully made. Ocean Res Blanc de Blancs is v.gd, Wedding Cuvée a winner. V.gd CHARD, PINOT N.

Jackson Family Farms ★★★→★★★★ Visionary, massive v'yd owner in CA with prime elevated sites, owns hugely-popular Kendall-Jackson brand, and high achievers like Lokoya, MATANZAS CREEK, Verité. Jackson Estate series great for mtn CABS.

Jordan Alex V ★★★ Adjustments in grape sourcing led to brilliant revival of balanced, elegant wines from showcase Alex V estate. CAB SAUV homage to B'x: and it lasts. Zesty, delicious CHARD.

Joseph Phelps Napa V ★★★★ (Insignia) 07 08 09 10 **11 12 13** Expensive Napa First

Growth Insignia CAB SAUV not to be underestimated for moderate ageing. Most offerings excellent quality esp SYRAH. *See also* Son outpost FREESTONE.

Joseph Swan Son ★★★ Long-time RRV producer of intense old-vine ZIN and single-v'yd PINOT N. Often overlooked Rhône varieties also v.gd, esp ROUSSANNE/MARSANNE blend and orange GRENACHE BL.

Kenwood Vineyards Son V ★★→★★★ Landmark Son V producer reinvented itself with focus on finer quality. CAB SAUV leads way; epic Jack London v'yd bottling.

Kistler Vineyards RRV ★★★★ Change in style: buttery CHARD, potent PINOT N become better, more lean and racy. Still from a dozen designated v'yds in any given yr. Still highly sought.

Kongsgaard Napa ★★★→★★★★ There are few more delightful personalities than 5th-generation Napa-ite John Kongsgaard. He also makes incredible wine, notably *Chard* from Judge v'yd and excellent CAB SAUV, SYRAH.

Korbel ★★ Cheap fizz sold in grocery stores, but all traditional method and remarkably decent for price. Also, fun visit by Russian River.

Kunin Santa B ★★★ Popular founder, sommelier, retailer and winemaker Seth Kunin died in late 2017 at age 50. Hoping his wife and partner will carry the torch for Rhône and Loire-inspired wines in Santa B County.

Ladera Napa V ★★★→★★★★ Stotesbery clan sold their Howell Mtn winery and set up shop in St H. Hillside CAB SAUVS and MALBEC are great; don't miss superb SAUV BL from NZ winemaker.

Lagier-Meredith Mt Veeder ★★★ Wine from renowned UC Davis vine researcher Carole Meredith and oenologist husband Steve Lagier. Handmade, tiny production of beautiful, pure SYRAH, MONDEUSE, MALBEC and ZIN (whose ancestry in Croatia Meredith famously decoded).

Lamborn Family Vineyards Howell Mtn ★★★★ Superstar winemaker Heidi Barrett makes intense, age-worthy CAB SAUV and big full-flavoured ZIN from estate v'yd.

Lang & Reed Mend, Napa ★★★ No one in CA has flown CAB FR banner more passionately than L&R's John Skupny. Wines capture perfume, litheness with Napa generosity. Also delicious Mend CHENIN BL.

Larkmead Napa V ★★★★ 10 11 13 14 Historic Cal estate revived; *outstanding Cab Sauv*, supple, balanced; bright, delicious SAUV BL. New release Tocai FRIULANO is a delight.

Laurel Glen Son ★★★ Always seems to exceed expectations, arguably in better hands than ever with Bettina Sichel, Phil Coturri et al. Hillside CAB fruit from Son Mtn always core of brand.

Lewis Cellars Napa V ★★★★ CAB SAUV, CHARD, SYRAH from former racing driver Randy Lewis can only be described as full-throttle. Unapologetic Napa hedonism at best.

Lioco N Coast ★★★ Intended to prove that CA can make lean, mineral CHARD. Mission accomplished. Now also excellent PINOT N, scrumptious red and rosé Indica CARIGNAN from Mend. Winemaker is John Raytek of Ceritas.

Littorai Son Coast ★★★★ Burgundy-trained Ted Lemon's P NOIRS and CHARDS are pure, articulate, focused, inspiring. Modern CA wines worth seeking out.

Lohr, J ★★→★★★ Prolific producer of Central Coast makes CAB SAUV, PINOT N, CHARD for balance and gd value. Cuvée Pau and Cuvée St E pay homage to B'x. Don't miss floral red Wildflower VALDIGUIÉ.

Long Meadow Ranch Napa V ★★★→★★★★ Smart, holistic vision incl destination winery with restaurant, cattle on organic farm. Supple, age-worthy CAB SAUV has reached ★★★★ status; lively Graves-style SAUV BL.

Louis M Martini Napa ★★→★★★ Since buying the Martini brand and epic Monte Rosso v'yd, GALLO has restored latter to greatness. Martini brand is solid for workaday CABS, ZINS.

MacPhail Son Coast ★★★ Strong 2015 vintage was James MacPhail's last here. Bold

PINOT N, CHARD from prime sources is the strategy. MacPhail moves on to Tongue Dancer and other gigs. Still merits endorsement.

MacRostie Son Coast ★★★ New tasting room is a modern beauty; screwcapped wines steadily improved. Lovely PINOT N, SYRAH; Son Coast CHARD absolute delight.

Marimar Torres Estate RRV ★★★ Great Catalan family's CA outpost issues several bottlings of CHARD, PINOT N. V'yds now all bio. Chards are excellent, long-lived, esp Acero (unoaked, *fresh, expressive*). Pinot N from Doña Margarita v'yd nr ocean is intense, rich.

Masút Mend ★★★ Newish, elevated Eagle Peak property run by Ben and Jake Fetzer shines brightly. Estate PINOT NS ethereal. Will inspire others to explore area.

Matanzas Creek Son ★★★ Exceptional JACKSON FAMILY property in cool Bennett Valley makes top MERLOT and SAUV BL, just as it should in this precious climate.

Matthiasson ★★★ Experimental wines have become cult hits. Racy CHARD, elegant CAB SAUV, epic white blend, plus esoterica like RIBOLLA GIALLA, SCHIOPPETINO.

Mayacamas Vineyards Mt Veeder ★★★★ Under new ownership (Charles Banks, former partner in SCREAMING EAGLE), CA classic has not changed classic style, only improved. Age-worthy CAB SAUV, CHARD recall great bottles of 70s, 80s.

Melville Santa RH ★★★ Family-run anchor of Sta RH, with bold, v.gd CHARD, PINOT N, but estate SYRAH steals show. Worth tasting too is SamSara, Chad and Mary Melville's personal label.

What do well-heeled LA wine tourists want? High-end Cab Sauv from Paso Robles.

Meritage Basically a B'x blend (r or w). Term invented for CA but has spread. It's a trademark, and users have to belong to The Meritage Alliance. Insider tip: not a French term – it rhymes with "heritage".

Merry Edwards RRV ★★★ One of great CA winemakers, and PINOT N pioneer. Single v'yds from Son always wildly popular. Ripe, rounded, layered, tad sweet by today's standards. Slightly sweet musqué SAUV BL also popular.

Meteor Coomb ★★★ Another rising name from suddenly fashionable Coomb. Coolish site produces wonderfully dense CAB SAUV from estate v'yd. Second wine, Perseid, v.gd for earlier drinking.

Mount Eden Vineyards Santa Cz Mts ★★★ V'yd high up in Santa Cz Mts, one of CA's 1st boutique wineries, tight, structured CAB SAUV, PINOT N, CHARD since 1945. Current ownership since 1981.

Mount Veeder Winery Mt Veeder ★★★ Classic CA mtn CAB SAUV, CAB FR grown at 500m on rugged, steep hillsides. Big, dense wines with ripe, integrated tannins.

Mumm Napa Valley Napa V ★★★ Stylish bubbly esp *delicious Blanc de Noirs* and rich, complex DVX single-v'yd fizz to age a few yrs in bottle; v.gd Brut Rosé.

Nalle Dry CV ★★★ Family winery crafts elegant, lower alc, claret-style ZIN. Once quite fashionable, still excellent. Great stop in Dry CV.

Newton Vineyards Spring Mtn ★★→★★★★ Impressive estate at base of Spring Mtn, now LMVH-owned; wines have improved recently. Look for CAB SAUV and opulent unfiltered CHARD.

Neyers Napa V ★★★ Complex CHARD, floral GRENACHE, silky CAB SAUV. French in sensibility, looking for substance beyond grape variety. Prices more than fair.

Niebaum-Coppola Estate *See* INGLENOOK.

Niner Edna V, P Rob Young, ambitious family estate with excellent CAB SAUV from P Rob, great CHARD and ALBARIÑO from Edna V. CA cuisine restaurant gd for lunch in P Rob countryside.

Obsidian Ridge Lake ★★★ Star of Lake County stretch of Mayacamas range. True mtn wine, from hillside v'yds at 780m, volcanic soils sprinkled with black glass. Res Cab Half Mile is excellent, as is estate CAB SAUV and SYRAH. Also owns Poseidon brand from Car.

Ojai Santa B ★★★ In a change of style from big, super-ripe to leaner, finer, former AU BON CLIMAT partner Adam Tolmach making best wines of his career. V.gd PINOT N, CHARD, Rhône styles. Syrah-based rosé is delicious.

Opus One Oak ★★★★ Still standard-bearer for fine Napa CAB SAUV, CONSTELLATION-Rothschild collaboration in gd form; popular CA export. Wines designed to cellar 10 yrs+.

Ovid St H ★★★ Cult-styled, ultra-luxurious organic estate on Pritchard Hill. Supple B'x blends star turn but SYRAH also fine.

Natural wines loved by sommeliers. Need distinction between interesting and gd.

Pahlmeyer Napa V ★★★★ Fashionable estate from decades of CA's 1st ascent. Wines massive, jammy, but supple. B'x blend most famous, gd for short ageing.

Palmina Santa B ★★★ Accurate Italian styles, unusual vines. CA flair: sumptuous, meant for food. FRIULANO, VERMENTINO, LAGREIN, NEBBIOLO.

Patz & Hall N Coast ★★★★ James Hall one of CA's most thoughtful winemakers culling fruit from top v'yds from Central Coast to Mend. Style is generous, tasteful, super-reliable. Zio Tony CHARD v. special, lemony, electric, opulent.

Paul Hobbs N Coast ★★★→★★★★ Globe-trotting winemaker Paul Hobbs' bread still buttered in CA. Bottlings of single-v'yd CAB SAUV, CHARD, PINOT N, SYRAH are top. Second label Crossbarn v.gd value.

Peay Vineyards Son Coast ★★★→★★★★ Standout brand from one of coast's coldest zones. Finesse-driven CHARD, PINOT N, SYRAH superb. Second label, Cep, also v.gd esp rosé. Weightless, impeccably made wines.

Pedroncelli Son ★★ Old-school Dry CV winery updated v'yds, winery; still makes bright, elbow-bending CAB SAUV, ZIN, solid CHARD. Refreshingly unpretentious.

Peju Napa V ★★★ Immensely popular showcase winery on tasting-room circuit; quality underrated esp balanced, supple CAB SAUV.

Peter Michael Winery Mont, Son ★★★★ *Sir* Peter Michael to you. Brit in Knight's Valley sells mostly to restaurants, mailing list. Quality outstanding: rich, dense CHARD, B'x blend Les Pavots (r), hedonist's PINOT N.

Philip Togni Vineyards Spring Mtn ★★★★ 05 07 09 10 11 12 13 14 Living link to classic, early Napa, Togni, a student in B'x of Émile Peynaud, arrived in Napa in 1959. Outstanding estate mtn CAB SAUV-based red, powerful, age-worthy.

Pine Ridge Napa V ★★★ Outstanding CAB SAUV made from several Napa v'yds. Estate Stags L bottling is silky, graceful. Gd CHARD, lively CHENIN BL/VIOGNIER blend.

Pisoni Vineyards Santa LH ★★★ Family winery in Santa LH became synonymous with PINOT N explosion and big, jammy wines. Still, Pinot N is and always was v. well made and remains popular.

Presqu'ile Santa MV ★★★ New Central Coast winery, elegant PINOT N, SYRAH. To watch.

Quintessa Ruth ★★★★ Magnificent estate at heart of Napa V owned by international player Augustin Huneeus makes a single-estate wine; superb, refined B'x blend justifies triple-digit price.

Qupé Santa B ★★★→★★★★ One of original SYRAH champions, brilliant range of Rhônes esp X Block, from one of CA's oldest v'yds. Epic Hillside Estate; don't miss unshakeable MARSANNE, ROUSSANNE. Central Coast Syrah unbeatable for $.

Ravenswood *See* CONSTELLATION.

Red Car Son Coast ★★★ Move from Central Coast to Son Coast highly successful for small, artsy producer: now crisp, finely drawn. Precise CHARD, lacy, fruit-forward PINOT N, killer rosé.

Ridge N Coast, Santa Cz Mts ★★★★ Saintly founder Paul Draper has retired, but his spirit lives on. Supple, harmonious estate *Montebello Cab Sauv* is superb. Outstanding single-v'yd ZIN from Son, Napa V, Sierra F'hills, P Rob. Don't overlook *outstanding Chard*.

Robert Mondavi ★★→★★★ Owned by CONSTELLATION since 2004, many wines could be better; changing of winemaking guard appears at hand. Home To Kalon v'yd still a great site, potential there.

Robert Sinskey Vineyards Car ★★★ Great, idiosyncratic Napa estate favouring balance, restraint. Great CAB SAUV and Car PINOT N. Racy Abraxas white blend and Pinot rosé excellent.

Rodney Strong Son ★★★ Strong indeed, across the board, from 14 significant v'yds. Strong coastal PINOT N, CHARD, super Alex V CAB SAUV from Alexander's Crown, Rockaway V'yds. Also owns DAVIS BYNUM.

Roederer Estate And V ★★★★ Champagne Roederer-owned. Finesse, class esp luxury cuvée L'Ermitage. Also SCHARFFENBERGER. Domaine Anderson PINOT NS excellent.

Saintsbury Car ★★★ Region pioneer still making v.gd, relevant PINOT N, CHARD, yummy Vincent Van Gris rosé.

St-Supéry Napa ★★★ Bought by owners of Chanel (and Château Rausan-Ségla), but some continuity of talent. Tasteful, balanced Virtú (w) and Élu (r) B'x blends and SAUV BL, highlights.

Sandhi Santa RH ★★★ *See* DOMAINE DE LA CÔTE. Same winemaking team, grapes bought from top local v'yds. Must for lovers of white Burg: racy, intense CHARD, gd PINOT N.

Sandlands N Coast ★★★ Turley winemaker Tegan Passalaqua seeks out venerable, forgotten v'yds for his own brand. Exciting CHENIN BL, Trousseau N, CARIGNANE.

Scharffenberger Mend ★★★ Bubbly brand revived and refreshed by Champagne Roederer. V.gd value, quality. Nod to Brut Rosé.

Schramsberg Napa V ★★★★ Best bubbles in CA? Exacting quality in every cuvée esp luxurious J Schram and Blanc de Noirs. Great tours of historic caves.

Screaming Eagle Napa V Excessive CAB SAUV to the Nth degree; thousands of dollars a bottle. Whatever.

Scribe Son ★★★ Appealing to millennial set, gentleman-farmer-chic tasting room pours well-made esoterica like SYLVANER, ST-LAURENT and PINOT N rosé all day.

Sea Smoke Santa RH ★★★ Bold PINOT N style earned cult following; still rare, but better balanced.

Seghesio Son ★★★ Classic Sonoma ZINS. Rich, strong, but graceful. Old Vine bottling is benchmark, Rockpile Zin also dynamite.

Selene Napa V ★★★ Lovely B'x reds, whites from prominent consulting winemaker Mia Klein, incl great CAB FR, Hyde V'yd SAUV BL *Musqué*.

Sequoia Grove Napa V ★★★ Rutherford staple for more than 30 yrs, still v.gd. Flagship Cambium is stunning CAB blend, balanced, age-worthy. CHARD v.gd.

Shafer Vineyards Napa V ★★★→★★★★ Hillside Select CAB SAUV a lavish CA classic, One Point Five also a beaut. Fine MERLOT and CHARD sourced from nearby Car.

Shannon Ridge Lake ★★★ Ambitious, large, v. successful development in elevated High Valley of Lake County. Honest, well-made wines that overdeliver for the $. Fast-growing brand, incl second label Vigilance.

Silverado Vineyards Stags L ★★★ V'yds owned by Disney descendants since 1976, has kept up with times. Single-v'yd Solo CAB SAUV is powerful, smooth; new release of Geo B'x blend from Coomb AVA is dark, dense. CAB FR v.gd.

Silver Oak Alex V, Napa V ★★★ So popular in 90s that sommeliers in 2000s turned backs on it. Napa and Alex V CABS still made in juicy, supple style: favourites.

> **Pink turns to orange**
> America's two-decade rosé craze has in many ways democratized wine, and the quality of American rosé has surely improved. Are trendy orange wines (*see* p.262) the next trend? Plenty of CA wineries are flirting with international fad, incl BROC CELLARS, FORLORN HOPE, WIND GAP.

CALIFORNIA

> **Evolving Sauvignon Blanc**
> New Zealand SAUV BL's popularity has pointed CA winemakers toward fresher, less oaky styles. Some greats are DRY CREEK VINEYARD, Geyser Peak River Ranches, GREEN AND RED, Grey Stack Rosemary's Block, LADERA, SPRING MOUNTAIN, ST-SUPÉRY.

Smith-Madrone Spring Mtn ★★★ Serious, purist producer, daring to dry farm in hot climate. Superb RIES with brilliant floral briskness. Also v.gd powerful CAB SAUV from high-elevation v'yd.

Sonoma-Cutrer Vineyards Son ★★★ Flagship CHARD a classic, still by glass at restaurants all over country. Owsley PINOT N from RRV lush with black fruit.

Sonoma-Loeb Car, RRV ★★★ Precise, cool-climate PINOT N, CHARD, by CHAPPELLET'S winemaker at its winery for 20 yrs, so 2011 sale to Napa brand made sense.

Spottswoode St H ★★★★ Crown jewel of St H, sublime estate. CAB SAUV pricey, worth it. Value Lyndenhurst Cab Sauv, SAUV BL delightful.

Spring Mountain Vineyard Spring Mtn ★★★★ Top-notch estate delivers site-driven, age-worthy mtn wines. Signature Elivette B'x blend layered and sturdy, Estate CAB SAUV v.gd, estate SAUV BL is Rubenesque treat.

Staglin Family Vineyard Ruth ★★★★ Perennial 1st-class, nuanced CAB SAUV from family-owned estate; powerful, complex Salus CHARD.

Stag's Leap Wine Cellars Stags L ★★★→★★★★ Gd to see quality maintained since founder Winiarski sold to large corp. Flagships still silky, seductive CABS (top-of-line Cask 23, Fay, SLV), but don't miss excellent CHARD.

Sterling Napa V ★★ Fun; take aerial tram to tasting room (view of valley).

Stony Hill Vineyard Spring Mtn ★★★★ Famous (since 60s) antidote to oaky, buttery CA CHARD complaint; always been crisp. Restrained, balanced CAB SAUV, gd RIES, GEWURZ, sweet SEM.

Sutter Home *See* TRINCHERO FAMILY ESTATES.

Tablas Creek P Rob ★★★→★★★★ Joint venture between Beaucastel (*see* France) and importer Robert Haas with vine cuttings from Châteauneuf-du-Pape. Red and white blends are the way to go: Patelin, Côtes de Tablas and Esprit lines all 1st rate.

Tatomer Santa B ★★★ Graham T learned to make exceptional dry RIES, GRUNER V in Austria. Now he's state leader in these grapes and on every list in LA and SF.

Thomas Fogarty Santa Cz Mts ★★★ There's a spark and energy here, from focused PINOT N to zesty GEWURZ and CHARD. Do not overlook.

Trefethen Family Vineyards Oak K ★★★ Historic family winery in cool zone makes elegant CAB SAUV, MERLOT, crisp long-living CHARD and v. nice Napa *Ries*.

Trinchero Family Estates ★→★★★ Foundational Napa producer with bewildering number of labels; ahead of pack is affordable, v. pleasing CAB SAUV under Napa Wine Company label.

Truchard Car ★★★ Look for zesty CHARD, focused MERLOT, and slightly rustic, earthy PINOT N from this storied Car producer.

Turley Wine Cellars N Coast ★★★★ Selling mostly to mailing list, so rare in market. Known for big, brambly old-vine ZIN from century-old v'yds. True CA treasures.

Unti Dry CV ★★★ Wines start in Dry CV v'yds; grower always refining range of luscious, tasty SYRAH, GRENACHE, ZIN, BARBERA.

Viader Estate Howell Mtn ★★★★ Ripe, powerful expression of Howell Mtn still turns heads. "V" is marvellous B'x blend based on PETIT VERDOT, CAB FR.

Vineyard 29 Napa V ★★★ Top winemaker Philippe Melka's fingerprints all over gorgeous CABS at maturing estate venture. Gd but oaky SAUV BL.

Vino Noceto Sierra F'hills ★★★ Among best SANGIOVESE in state, star of Cal-Ital movement in Sierras.

Volker Eisele Family Estate Napa V ★★★ Special site tucked way back in Napa's Chiles Valley continues to overdeliver with CAB s and more. Looking for an adventure? Chiles V road trip!

Wente Vineyards ★★ → ★★★★ Oldest continuing family winery in CA makes better whites than reds. Outstanding gravel-grown SAUV BL leads way.

Wind Gap Son Coast ★★★ Pax Mahle one of CA's most talented winemakers esp in cool climates. PINOT N, CHARD v.gd but in gd vintages Son Coast SYRAH genius.

Wine Group, The Central V ★ By volume, world's 2nd-largest wine producer; budget brands like Almaden, Big House, Concannon, Cupcake, Glen Ellen.

Colorado

Worth exploring for experiments with lesser-known grapes. Some of highest-altitude v'yds in nation and a climate similar to Rhône and Central Coast. AVAs incl Grand Valley and West Elks. Wineries on radar: **Bookcliff**: ★★ excellent MALBEC, SYRAH, Res CAB FR, CAB SAUV, VIOGNIER. **Boulder Creek**: ★ Governor's Cup-winning wines: Ensemble B'x blend; Cab Sauv, Syrah, MERLOT, v.gd RIES. **Canyon Wind**: excellent Anemoi Lips Syrah, gd PETIT VERDOT/Syrah Notus and B'x blend IV. **Carlson**: unpretentious winery with whimsical names but well-made, value-priced wines esp award-winning Ries. **Creekside**: v.gd Cab Fr aged in Appalachian oak, gd Petit Verdot. **Grande River**: focus on traditional B'x, Rhône styles, but intense, floral Viognier shines here too. **Guy Drew**: ★★★ ambitious whites incl Viognier, dry Ries, unoaked CHARD, Metate; successful Syrah. New tasting room open to public. **Infinite Monkey Theorem**: hip, urban winery with v.gd red blend, 100th Monkey, and Viognier/ROUSSANNE, Blind Watchmaker White; wines on tap and by the can. **Jack Rabbit Hill**: bio/organic, M&N v.gd PINOT M/PINOT N. **Plum Creek**: ★ superb, restrained Chard, v.gd Merlot. **Snowy Peaks (Grande Valley)**: v. high-altitude vines, v.gd Petit Verdot. Oso blends use hybrid grapes. **Sutcliffe**: v.gd Cab Fr, Syrah, Merlot. **Turquoise Mesa**: ★ award-winning Syrah. **Two Rivers**: ★ excellent Cab Sauv, v.gd Chard, Ries and Port-style. **Whitewater Hill V'yds**: excellent Cab Sauv Res; exceptional red blend Ethereal. **Winery at Holy Cross**: ★ red-driven historic winery; award-winning Res Merlot, blend Sangre de Cristo Nouveau.

Georgia

Expanding region with increasingly sophisticated wines, incl CHARD, CAB, MERLOT, TANNAT, TOURIGA N, also native muscadine. Top estates: **Château Élan**, **Crane Creek**, **Engelheim**, **Frogtown**, **Habersham**, **Sharp Mountain**, **Stonewall Creek**, **Three Sisters**, **Tiger Mountain**, **Wolf Mountain**, **Yonah Mountain**.

Once wiped out by Prohibition, Georgian wine is thriving. Muscadine, mostly.

Idaho

ID has a young, small but growing wine industry, with only 1200 acres of v'yds and about 50 wineries. There are three approved growing regions: Snake River Valley (approved in 2007), Eagle Foothills, and Lewis-Clark Valley, both recently approved. Growers and winemakers still determining what grows best where but early returns impressive, particularly for SYRAH.

Cinder Wines Snake RV ★★ Winemaker Melanie Krause has shown a knack for producing high-quality SYRAH and RIES. VIOGNIER also v.gd.

Coiled Snake RV ★★ One of state's top producers, making tasty dry RIES, SYRAH.

Ste Chapelle Snake RV ★ ID's 1st and largest winery, owned by WA-based Precept Wines. Dry and off-dry style reds and whites, incl quaffable RIES.

Maryland

Roughly the size of Belgium, with 88 wineries. Leaders: original pioneer **Boordy**, plus **Big Cork**, **Black Ankle**, **Bordeleau**, **Knob Hall**, **Old Westminster** and **Sugarloaf**. Rising stars: **Dodon** (for SAUV BL and red B'x blends), **Port of Leonardtown** (notable ALBARIÑO, BARBERA, PETIT VERDOT). Chesapeake Bay, which plays a critical role in moderating the climate, cuts through state (top to bottom).

Michigan

136 wineries. PINOT N now most widely planted red, with RIES, GEWURZ, PINOT GR, CAB FR also strong. Current leaders: **Bel Lago**, **Black Star**, **Boathouse**, **Bowers Harbor**, **Brys**, **Chateau Chantal**, **Chateau Fontaine**, **Chateau Grand Traverse**, **12 Corners**, **Fenn Valley**, **Hawthorne**, **2 Lads**, **Laurentide**, **Lawton Ridge**, **Left Foot Charley**, **L Mawby**, **Mari**, **45 North**, **Rove Estate**, **St Ambrose Cellars**, **St Julian**, **Tabor Hill**, **WaterFire**.

Michigan's wine industry creates 28,000 jobs and $773 million in direct wages.

Missouri

The University of Missouri has a new experimental winery to test techniques and grape varieties in local conditions, which are warm and humid. Best so far: Chambourcin, SEYVAL BL, VIDAL, Vignoles (sweet and dry). **Stone Hill** in Hermann produces v.gd Chardonel (frost-hardy hybrid, Seyval Bl x CHARD), Norton and gd Seyval Bl, Vidal. **Hermannhof** is notable for Vignoles, Chardonel, Norton. Also: **St James** for Vignoles, Seyval, Norton; **Mount Pleasant** in Augusta for rich fortified and Norton; **Adam Puchta** for fortifieds and Norton, Vignoles, Vidal; **Augusta Winery** for Chambourcin, Chardonel, Icewine; **Les Bourgeois** for SYRAH, Norton, Chardonel, Montelle, v.gd Cynthiana, Chambourcin. How's that for a start?

Nevada

Limited commercial wineries. **Churchill Vineyards**: in high desert region producing gd SÉM/CHARD. **Pahrump Valley**: oldest winery here, v.gd PRIMITIVO, ZIN. Sanders Family, former owners of Pahrump Winery.

New Jersey

Cool in n, warmer in s. 50 wineries. Leaders: Alba, Beneduce, Cape May, Unionville Vineyards. CHARD, RIES, PINOT N esp successful in recent vintages.

Alba ★★★ 14 15 16 Exceptional CHARD, gd RIES, GEWURZ; one of largest PINOT N plantings on East Coast.

Unionville Vineyards ★★ 14 15 16 17 Large estate with five separate v'yds. UC-Davis-trained winemaker produces gd CHARD, rosé, SYRAH, B'x-style blends.

New Mexico

High-altitude v'yds and diurnal variations give wines crisp character and lower alc. French-hybrid grape varieties; sparkling wines excel. **Black Mesa**: ★★ excellent SYRAH, v.gd PETITE SIRAH, CHARD. **Casa Abril**: Family-owned, Spanish and Argentine varieties. **Gruet**: ★★★ still the regional standard for sparkling, blending Wash State and Lodi, CA fruit. Esp Blanc de Noirs and Gilbert Gruet Grand Res; v.gd Chard, PINOT N. **La Chiripada**: ★ oldest continuously owned winery in state. Top-notch Res CAB SAUV and v.gd Petite Sirah, VIOGNIER. **Noisy Water**: ★ excellent Cab Sauv, v.gd SHIRAZ. **Vivác**: ★★ excellent red blends Divino (Italian grapes) and Diavolo (French) and v.gd Port-style Amante.

New York (NY)

Largest and fastest-growing East Coast wine state with more than 420 wineries and ten AVAs. Abbreviations: Finger Lakes (Finger L), Long Island (Long I), North Fork (North F).

21 Brix ★★ 15 16 17 Exceptional estate on Lake Erie with 1st-rate RIES, CHARD, GEWURZ, GRÜNER V, Noiret; aromatic BLAUFRÄNKISCH, CAB SAUV.

Anthony Road Finger L ★★★ **13** 14 15 16 17 Gold Standard dry and semi-dry RIES (some of best in US), also outstanding GEWURZ, GRÜNER V, PINOT GR, MERLOT, PINOT N.

Brotherhood is the oldest continuously operating winery in the US: founded 1839.

Bedell Long I ★★ →★★★ 13 14 15 16 17 Leading LONG I estate since 1980. Prestigious winemaker turns out classy white blend, fragrant VIOGNIER, focused SAUV BL and CHARD; noteworthy SYRAH, MALBEC, MERLOT and exceptional red blends. Artist labels, eg. April Gornik, Chuck Close.

Boundary Breaks Finger L ★★★ 15 16 17 Peerless bone-dry to dessert RIES, serious GEWURZ and red B'x-style CAB-based blends.

Casa Larga Finger L ★★ 14 16 17 Fine family-run estate with commendable CHARD, RIES, CAB-based red, PINOT N, VIDAL Icewine.

Channing Daughters Long I ★★★ 14 15 16 17 Deliciously experimental wines from South Fork producer, incl BLAUFRÄNKISCH, DORNFELDER, LAGREIN, MALVASIA, RIBOLLA GIALLA and a range of *pétillants*, plus CAB FR, MERLOT, SYRAH.

Finger Lakes One of most exciting wine regions in US, with 140 wineries today. While RIES undoubtedly est its reputation, other varieties incl GEWÜRZ, GRÜNER V, CAB FR, SYRAH gaining stature. Up-and-coming wineries: Atwater, Billsboro, Domaine Leseurre, Hector, Kemmeter, Ventosa.

Fox Run Finger L ★★★ 14 15 16 17 Excellent RIES, plus gd CHARD, rosé, CAB FR, PINOT N. Café overlooking Lake Seneca.

Frank, Dr. Konstantin (Vinifera Wine Cellars) Finger L ★★★★ **13** 14 15 16 17 The pioneer, still one of country's leading RIES producers. Also outstanding GEWURZ, GRÜNER V, PINOT GR, RKATSITELI, old-vine PINOT N, plus impeccable Château Frank sparkling. Est 1961, with 4th generation now involved.

Hamptons, The (aka South Fork) Long I Beach community whose population nearly doubles in summer with invasion of chic Manhattanites; three wineries: CHANNING DAUGHTERS, Duckwalk, WÖLFFER.

Heart & Hands Finger L ★★★ 13 15 16 17 On shores of Cayuga Lake; classic cool-climate RIES, rosé, delicate PINOT N.

Hermann J Wiemer Finger L ★★★★ 14 15 16 17 Est 1979 by German winemaker. One of best RIES producers in US; fine CHARD, GEWURZ, CAB FR, PINOT N, sparkling.

Hudson River Region Scenic region 90 minutes from Manhattan, with 42 wineries. Leaders: Benmarl, Hudson-Chatham, Whitecliff. Also excellent Fjord, Milea, MILLBROOK, Nostrano, Robibero, Tousey, Whitecliff. Grapes are CHARD, Baco Noir, CAB FR, PINOT N.

Lake Erie Tri-state AVA. Standout producers: 21 BRIX and Mazza Chautauqua Cellars. Look for CHARD, PINOT GR, RIES, Icewine, high-quality eau de vie.

Long Island

Jutting e into the Atlantic some 80 km (50 miles) from Manhattan, Long I's relatively mild climate lets vintners concentrate on classic vinifera grapes, esp CAB FR, MERLOT, CHARD, SAUV BL. With 30 wineries and three AVAs – Long I, North Fork of Long I, and THE HAMPTONS (aka South Fork). Leaders: BEDELL, CHANNING DAUGHTERS, MACARI, MARTHA CLARA, PAUMANOK, SPARKLING POINTE, WÖLFFER. Up and coming: Matabella.

> No oranges were harmed in the making of this wine
> Growing phenomenon in e esp NY state: emergence of orange wines.
> On Long I, CHANNING DAUGHTERS offers Ramato (PINOT GRIGIO). In FINGER L,
> RED TAIL RIDGE makes CHARD/RIES blend Miscreant, "a white that drinks like
> a red" according to the winemaker. Atwater Estate offers GEWURZ, while
> ANTHONY ROAD makes Skin Ferment Chard and Skin Ferment Ries. Like
> many other wineries they prefer not to use the word "orange" on the
> label as they worry consumers will think citrus is involved.

Lakewood Finger L ★★★ 14 16 17 High-quality GEWURZ, RIES, CAB FR, PINOT N.

Lamoreaux Landing Finger L ★★★ 14 16 17 Greek Revival building overlooking Lake Seneca; superb RIES, excellent *Chard*, GEWURZ, Icewine, plus CAB FR, MERLOT, PINOT N.

Macari Long I, North F ★★★ 14 16 17 Set on Macari family's 500-acre waterfront estate. Top-notch SAUV BL; premium reds incl CAB FR, MERLOT and B'x-style blends.

McCall Long I, North F ★★★ 13 14 16 17 Praiseworthy red blends, incl CAB FR, MERLOT, other B'x varieties. gd PINOT N, CHARD. Also home to Charolais cattle.

McGregor Finger L ★★ 13 14 16 17 On scenic Keuka Lake, with gd RIES, PINOT N and exciting SAPERAVI/Sereksiya Charni blend.

Martha Clara Long I, North F ★★★ 13 14 15 16 17 V'yds thriving on former potato farm produce superb MERLOT, MALBEC; v.gd CHARD, PINOT GR, SAUV BL.

Millbrook Hudson ★★★ 15 16 17 Gd CHARD, RIES, Tocai (FRIULANO), CAB FR.

North Fork Long I One of longest growing seasons in ne. Top estates: BEDELL, MACARI, MARTHA CLARA, MCCALL, PAUMANOK, SPARKLING POINTE. Up and coming: Hound's Tree.

Paumanok Long I ★★★ 10 13 14 15 16 17 First-rate establishment, with succulent CHENIN BL, excellent red B'x-style blends; fine CHARD, RIES, MERLOT.

Paumanok, native name for Long I, was home to 13 different Indian tribes in 1643.

Ravines Finger L ★★★ 12 14 15 16 17 *Inspired Ries*, GEWURZ, CAB FR, PINOT N, plus sparkling CHARD/Pinot N blend. Sophisticated bistro.

Red Newt Finger L ★★★ 13 14 15 17 Elegant GEWURZ, PINOT GR, RIES; gd CAB FR, MERLOT, PINOT N. Cosy bistro.

Red Tail Ridge Finger L ★★★ 14 15 16 17 Superb CHARD, RIES, PINOT N, TEROLDEGO, fizz.

Rhode Island Although smallest state in US, Rhode I has a dozen wineries, and is growing rapidly. Leading: Greenvale, Newport, Nickle Creek, Sakonnet.

Shinn Estate Long I ★★★ 14 15 16 17 Lively SAUV BL, earthy CAB FR, fine MERLOT, crisp Blanc de Blancs fizz. Attractive farmhouse inn.

Silver Thread Finger L ★★★ 14 15 16 17 Laudable RIES and GEWURZ, also worthy rosé, PINOT N and B'x-style red blend.

Sparkling Pointe Long I ★★★ *Superior sparkling* produced exclusively from traditional Champagne grape varieties.

Swedish Hill Finger L ★★★ 15 16 17 Est 1968; notable GEWURZ, PINOT GRIGIO, Ries, CAB FR and Blanc de Blancs.

Wölffer Estate Long I ★★★★ 13 14 15 16 17 Premier South Fork estate where German-born winemaker's classical approach results in superlative CHARD, MERLOT, CAB SAUV and gd rosé.

North Carolina

200 wineries, incl **Biltmore, Childress, Cypress Bend** (for muscadine), **Duplin** (likewise for muscadine), **Grandfather, Hanover Park, Jones von Drehle, Laurel Gray, McRitchie, Old North State, Ragapple Lassie, Raffaldini, RayLen, Saint Paul Mountain Vineyards, Shelton.** Top varieties: CHARD, VIOGNIER, CAB FR and native muscadine.

C17 colonists grew native scuppernong: sounds/tastes more like insult than vine.

Ohio

Extreme cold in winter is moderated by Lake Erie. 278 wineries, five AVAs. PINOT GR, RIES, PINOT N, Icewine can be excellent, and CAB FR in s OH. Top: **Breitenbach**, **Debonné**, **Ferrante**, **Firelands**, **Harpersfield**, **Laurentia**, **Markko**, **M Cellars**, **Paper Moon**, **St Joseph**, **Valley Vineyards**.

Oklahoma

Nearly 50 wineries, one AVA, Ozark Mtn. Mostly reds esp CAB SAUV. **Chapel Creek**: Norton, TEMPRANILLO; **Clauren Ridge**: Meritage, PETITE SIRAH, VIOGNIER; **Durso Hills**: Norton; **Redbud Ridge**: SYRAH; **Sand Hill**: wide range esp Cab Sauv; **Stable Ridge**: v.gd Bedlam CHARD; **The Range Vineyard**: white blend Jackwagon.

Oregon

Oregon's climate is perhaps the most n-European in the US. It rains. PINOT N remains the state's standout variety. Pushed by climate change and runaway v'yd costs at home, producers from CA and Burgundy are buying land, planting vines and building wineries; notably Foley Family Wines, Henriot, Jackson Family Wines, Louis Jadot. But outside Will V AVA, Mediterranean varieties are now growing too.

Principal viticultural areas

Southern Oregon (S OR) encompasses much of w OR, s of Will V, incl sub-AVAs Applegate (App V), Rogue, Umpqua (Um V) Valleys. Amidst expansive experimentation, Albariño, Gewurz, Grüner V, Viognier, Cab Fr, Syrah and Tempranillo are standouts.

Willamette Valley (Will V) has well-defined sub-AVAs incl Chehalem Mts, Dundee Hills (Dun H), Eola-Amity Hills, McMinnville (McM), Ribbon Ridge (Rib R), Yamhill-Carlton (Y-Car). Apart from Pinot N, Chard, Pinot Bl, Pinot Gr, Ries also excel here.

Rocks District of Milton-Freewater (Walla Walla Valley [Walla]) entirely in OR, produces cult wines from Cayuse and ★★★★Syrahs from others.

Abacela Um V ★★★ 12' 13 14' 15 16 Planted first TEMPRANILLO in US; Barrel Select v.gd, Fiesta and NV Vintner's Blend for value. Deep, potent Res MALBEC, SYRAH.

Adelsheim Will V ★★★ 12' 13' 14' 15 16 New owners for founding winery; outstanding single-v'yd PINOT N (brown label) and Caitlin's Res CHARD.

Alloro Chehalem Mts ★★★ 12' 13 14' 15 16 Beautiful site with elegant PINOT NS and CHARDS. Riservata and Justina age v. well.

Anam Cara Will V ★★ →★★★ 12' 13 14' 15 16 Mark V top PINOT N; Nicholas Estate Res also v.gd dry RIES.

Archery Summit Will V ★★★ 12' 13 14' 15 16 Top-tier Dun H producer. Try Archery Summit Estate, Arcus, Renegade Ridge for PINOT NS; exotic Ab Ovo PINOT GR fermented in concrete egg.

Argyle Will V ★★ →★★★ 12' 13 14 15' 16 V.gd vintage **bubbly** and Brut Rosé; Master Series CHARD, RIES better than spotty PINOT NS.

A to Z Wineworks S OR ★★ 13 14' 15' 16' Value-priced, soundly made and widely available CHARD, RIES, PINOT GR, PINOT N principally sourced from S OR.

Beaux Frères Rib R ★★★ →★★★★ Robert Parker co-founded this winery, recently sold to Maisons & Domaines Henriot. No expansion plans; winemaker Mike Etzel still on board. Sequitur is v.gd companion label.

Bergström Will V ★★★ 12 13' 14' 15' 16 Rib R winery; elegant, powerful PINOT N, CHARD. Sigrid Chard ethereal, Old Stones Chard v.gd value. Bergström, Shea, Silice best Pinot N designates.

Bethel Heights Will V ★★★ →★★★★ 12 13 14' 15' 16 Single block and Casteel PINOT N are dense, dark and muscular. Old-vine CHARD and occasional PINOT BL v.gd.

Big Table Farm Will V ★★★ 13 14' 15' 16 Distinctive hand-drawn labels; quirky, complex wines. Wirtz v'yd PINOT N. Unique Edelzwicker is aromatic white blend.

Brick House Rib R ★★★★ 11' 12' 13' 14' 15 16 Bio leader owned by ex-newsman Doug Tunnell. Evelyn's, Les Dijonnais and Cuvée du Tonnelier PINOT NS show gamey, earthy, textural strengths. Rare GAMAY Noir gd.

Brooks Will V ★★★ 12 13 14' 15' 16 Bio producer and RIES champion with zesty dry, balanced sweet Ries. V.gd PINOT NS; also Amycas white blend.

Chehalem Will V ★★ →★★★ 12 13 14 15' 16' Sturdy, single-v'yd dry RIES and v.gd INOX CHARD; PINOT NS variable in recent vintages.

Cowhorn App V ★★★ 12' 13 14 15' 16' App V AVA bio family-owned makes dense, detailed VIOGNIER, GRENACHE, SYRAH and v.gd Rhône blends (r w).

How to be trendy: drink OR Pinot N Blanc. Taste is between Pinot Bl and Chard.

Cristom Will V ★★★ 12' 13' 14' 15 16 Lifted, lively PINOT N from Louise, Marjorie, Jessie estate v'yds. VIOGNIER is bright, aromatic.

DanCin S OR ★★★ 12' 13' 14 15' 16 Fine range of v.gd-value CHARD (esp Chassé) and PINOT N from throughout w OR. Winery to watch.

Domaine Drouhin Oregon Will V ★★★ →★★★★ 12' 13' 14 15 16 The 1st Burgundy producer to invest in OR (1987). Édition Limitée, Lauren, Arthur designates are world class. New Roserock Res are compelling.

Domaine Serene Dun H ★★★★ 12' 13' 14' 15' 16 Superb single-v'yd CHARD and PINOT N esp Grace and Evanstad Res. Coeur Blanc is white Pinot N. New sparkling wine facility and vast visitor centre recently opened. Industry leader.

Elk Cove Will V ★★★ 12' 13 14' 15 16 2nd-generation winemaker; reliable single-v'yd PINOT NS esp La Bohème and Res. New Pike Road label v.gd value.

Erath Will V ★★ 12 13 14 15 16 Widely available line of reliable but ordinary PINOTS BL/GR/N. Founding OR winery now owned by WA's Ste Michelle Wine Estates.

Evening Land Will V ★★★ 12' 13 14' 15 Prestige producer; Seven Springs Summum PINOT N, CHARD rare, but among best on either side of Atlantic.

Gran Moraine Y-Car ★★★ 12' 13 14 15 16 OR estate of CA giant Jackson Family Wines; expansive v'yds in development with dedicated winery. Winery to watch.

Hyland Estates McM ★★★ 12' 13' 14 15 16 OR veteran Laurent Montalieu's PINOT NS show expressive minerality esp single-clone wines. Old Vine RIES v.gd.

Ken Wright Will V ★★★★ 12' 13 14 15 16 Consistent, deeply fruited, sometimes high-alc, single-v'yd PINOT NS demonstrate range of sub-AVA terroirs. Not expensive for such quality.

King Estate OR ★★ →★★★ 12' 13 14 15' 16 Now 100 per cent bio and incl in newly expanded single V AVA. PINOT GR specialist with improving PINOT N. Domaine and Backbone are tops. NxNW label for WA wines incl Red Blend, RIES.

Lange Estate Will V ★★★ 12' 13 14 15 16 CHARD rules here; Estate lively, rich, Three Hills tropical toasty. Muscular, age-worthy PINOT N Res, Freedom Hill v'yd excel.

Ovum OR ★★★ 15' 16' Artisanal, impressive RIES, GEWURZ from both n and S OR.

Patricia Green Will V ★★★ 12 13 14 15' 16 Cult-calibre, impeccable single-v'yd PINOT N. Founder now deceased; still essential winery to watch.

Ponzi Will V ★★★ →★★★★ 12' 13' 14' 15' 16 2nd-generation Luisa Ponzi making outstanding wines across all price points. Aurora, Abetina PINOT NS knockout; Res CHARD standout. Don't miss brilliant ARNEIS. Entry Tavola Pinot N v.gd value.

Quady North App V ★★ →★★★ 12 13' 14 15' 16 Winemaker Herb Quady deftly mixes Rhône and Loire influences esp VIOGNIER, CAB FR, SYRAH. Winery to watch.

Résonance Will V ★★★ 13' 14' 15 16 New OR project from Maison Louis Jadot; Jacques Lardière makes PINOT N, CHARD. Eponymous v'yd one of OR's finest.

Bio, LIVE, Salmon Safe — free the grapes!
OR's artisan winemakers are an independent bunch, many with strong feelings about keeping wines as natural and hands-off as possible. Hence recent rise in bio wines and v'yds, which seem to be multiplying like rabbits throughout state. Certifications such as LIVE and Salmon Safe are also proliferating, but Demeter-approved bio producers from Cayuse in far ne to COWHORN in deep s are proving that all that extra time and effort does indeed result in better, more complex and interesting wines. Trend is now spreading to big estates farming hundreds of acres, notably KING ESTATE, Momtazi, Montinore, REX HILL.

Rex Hill Will V ★★★ →★★★★ 12' 13 14' 15 16 Well-chosen v'yd selects, incl Antiquum Farm, Jacob-Hart, La Colina, Shea, Sunny Mt among outstanding line of PINOT N.

Shea Wine Cellars Will V ★★★ 12' 13 14' 15' 16 Top-tier clients purchase Shea grapes; but in-house wines every bit as gd. Among numerous block and clone selections, Homer Res is bomb. Some excellent CHARD too.

Sineann Will V ★★★ 12' 13' 14' 15 16 Brightly fruity PINOT N from Will V and Col Gorge sites; v.gd old-vine ZIN.

Sokol Blosser Will V ★★→★★★ 12' 13 14 15 16 Son Alex took over winemaking in 15, does best with value Evolution wines. Among multiple estate PINOT N: Big Tree, Goosepen, Orchard esp gd.

Soter Will V ★★★★ CA legend Tony Soter moved to OR to make PINOT N. Estate *Mineral Springs Ranch Pinot N* is sublime.

Stoller Family Estate Will V ★★★ 12' 13 14' 15' 16 Beautifully balanced PINOT N exemplify Dun H. V.gd Elsie's and Nancy's cuvées tops, along with Res.

Teutonic Wine Company ★★★ Iconoclastic, Mosel-inspired RIES, crisp white blends, Germanic-styled PINOT N. Up-and-comer generating buzz.

The Eyrie Vineyards Dun H ★★★★ 11' 12 13' 14' 15 16 Founder David Lett planted 1st Will V PINOT N in 1965, 1st US PINOT GR shortly after. Today son Jason continues traditional, elegant, age-worthy style. Original Vines and Res wines highlight top-notch, long-aging lineup.

Trisaetum Will V ★★★ 12' 13' 14' 14' 15' 16 Owner, artist, winemaker James Frey makes superior RIES, bone-dry to late-harvest and Res. V.gd PINOT N, CHARD, sparkling and B'x blend from Walla grapes. Ribbon Ridge Estate is top drop. The 1st vintages of Jadot's RÉSONANCE were produced here.

Oregon's smallest AVA, Red Hill Douglas County: no wineries, just one small v'yd.

Willamette Valley Vineyards Will V ★★→★★★ 12 13 14 15 16 Hundreds of shareholder/owners; extensive v'yd holdings and diverse line-up, principally PINOT N and CHARD. Elton now its own label; new v'yd project just planted in Walla.

Winderlea Will V ★★★ 12 13 14' 15' 16 Top bio producer; vibrant single-v'yd PINOT N, notably Shea, Weber, Winderlea. V.gd, age-worthy CHARD. Philippe Armenier (Domaine de Marcoux) consults; Napa legend Robert Brittan makes wines.

Wine by Joe OR ★★ 12 13 14 15 16 Budget label from Joe Dobbes; gd PINOTS GR/BL and CHARD. PINOT N less successful.

Pennsylvania

220+ wineries. Some exploration now with GRÜNER V and other Austrian varieties. Top estates: **Allegro** (red B'x blend), **Blair** (PINOT N, CHARD), **Briar Valley** (RIES, CAB FR), **Galen Glen** (excellent aromatic whites eg. Grüner V, Ries), **Galer Estate** (fine Chard, Cab Fr), **Karamoor** (Meritage, PETIT VERDOT, Chard, MERLOT), **Manatawny Creek** (consistently delicious red blends), **Mazza** (VIDAL Icewine, Ries), **Nimble Hill** (Ries, Grüner V), **Penns Woods** (some of best reds in PA),

Pinnacle Ridge (aromatic whites, sparkling, gd reds), **Seven Mountains** (Ries), **The Vineyard at Grandview** (some of state's best red B'x blends, ALBARIÑO), **Waltz** (v. fine Chard, CAB S, Merlot), **Va La** (Italian varieties), **Vox Vineti** (top red blends).

Texas

First vines were planted by missionaries in the 1650s. TX now the nation's 3rd-largest wine tourism destination, with steady innovations in dozens of wineries, led by Texas Fine Wine, a five-member association promoting Texas-appellation wines (for which 75 per cent or more of the content must be grown in state). Despite weather disasters elsewhere in state, last yr's harvest was exceptional, with ripe fruit and lower alc esp in Hill County and High Plains AVAs. Mediterranean varieties thrive here: look for MARSANNE, ROUSSANNE, VERMENTINO, VIOGNIER, AGLIANICO, GARNACHA/GRENACHE, MONTEPULCIANO, MOURVEDRE, TEMPRANILLO, TOURIGA. TANNAT and Portuguese Souzão show particular promise.

Becker Vineyards ★★★ Wide range B'x, Burgundian, Rhône-styled wines. Top picks: TEMPRANILLO Res, Prairie Rotie and MALBEC/PETIT VERDOT blend Raven. CAB SAUV Res Canada Family, Res Newsom V'yd Cab Sauv, Res Malbec, rosé Provencal.

Bending Branch ★★ Pioneering sustainable winery in picturesque setting. Specializing in robust Mediterranean varieties; TANNAT a signature grape. V.gd Souzão, ROUSSANNE, Newsom V'yds TEMPRANILLO. Single Barrel PICPOUL Blanc is aged in used Bourbon barrels.

Brennan Vineyards ★★→★★★ Known for dry VIOGNIER, white Rhône blend Lily; Res TEMPRANILLO; v.gd NERO D'AVOLA called Super Nero.

Cap Rock ★★→★★★ Much-medalled High Plains winery esp MERLOT, **Roussanne**.

Duchman Family Winery ★★★★ All TX grapes, specializes in Italian varieties, blends. Award-winning DOLCETTO, VERMENTINO. Gd TEMPRANILLO, refreshing Grape Growers (w) Blend, AGLIANICO rosé; v.gd Salt Lick Cellars GSM and BBQ White.

Fall Creek Vineyards ★★★ Pioneering winery in Hill Country. Gorgeous Salt Lick TEMPRANILLO and GSM, consistently excellent B'x blend Meritus, old-vine whites, v.gd Res CHARD, delicious off-dry CHENIN BL.

Haak Winery ★★ Gd dry Blanc du Bois from coastal area; exceptional "Madeira" copies from a Spanish winemaker.

Inwood Estates ★★★ Exceptional TEMPRANILLO and Mericana CAB SAUV, v.gd PALOMINO/ CHARD blend and Dallas County Chard. Small but special producer worth checking out. 100 per cent TX grapes.

Kuhlman Cellars Three-yr-old winery with proprietary red blends driven by PETITE SIRAH. Gd 100% VIOGNIER. Offers two price levels of wine and small plate pairings.

Lewis Wines ★★→★★★ Quality grape grower, rosé specialist (three labels). Impressive reds: TEMPRANILLO (varietal and CAB SAUV blends), Portuguese TINTA CÃO.

TX sunny and dry climate attracts comparisons with s Portugal.

Llano Estacado ★→★★★ Historic winery, mix of outstanding and plain but drinkable wines. Excellent MALBEC, 1836 (r w). V.gd Viviana (w) and Viviano (r) that mimics a Super Tuscan.

Lost Draw Vineyards ★★★ Small-batch wines, Mediterranean varieties: CARIGNAN, PICPOUL Blanc, VIOGNIER. Signature is Gemütlich white blend GRENACHE BLANC/ VIOGNIER/ROUSSANNE. V.gd TEMPRANILLO.

McPherson Cellars ★★★ Delicious Les Copains, excellent Res ROUSSANNE. One of TX best winemakers.

Messina Hof Wine Cellars ★→★★★ Big range. Excellent RIES esp late-harvest. V.gd Papa Paolo Port-style, Res CAB FR, unoaked CHARD.

Pedernales Cellars ★★★ →★★★★ Top VIOGNIER Res, excellent TEMPRANILLO, GSM. Old World-style; all TX grapes.

Perissos Vineyard and Winery ★★ Reds shine here esp excellent AGLIANICO, PETITE SIRAH, TEMPRANILLO.

Ron Yates Up-and-coming winery, same owner as SPICEWOOD, opened in 2016. Nine wines, focus on Rhône, Spanish, Italian styles. Too soon for stars.

Southold Farm and Cellar Ambitious new winery in Fredericksburg by artisanal winemaker Regan Meador, back to TX after successful run on Long Island. Whimsically named wines belie serious intent. Plantings of Counoise, MOURVÈDRE and Terret Noir.

Spicewood Vineyards ★★→★★★ Estate-grown; exceptional Sancerre-like SAUV BL, v.gd SEM. Gd TEMPRANILLO, dry MOURVÈDRE rosé, Portuguese varieties.

William Chris Vineyards On pricey side, but best buys are MALBEC rosé, PETIT VERDOT and red blend Enchante.

Virginia

Vines defy the hot, humid summers here to produce wines of remarkable elegance and balance. VIOGNIER is a star, and PETIT VERDOT and TANNAT make some terrific reds. CAB FR does well, CAB SAUV less well. With 280 wineries, growth is being driven by small estates and increasingly sophisticated winemaking. New v'yds continue to crop up across the state.

Ankida Ridge ★★★ 14 15 16 17 Founded 2008; already what many consider best PINOT N in VA. Gd CHARD too. Vines high on steep slopes of Blue Ridge Mts.

Barboursville **★★★★** 13 14 15 16 17 One of top estates in e (founded 1976 by Italy's Zonin family); elegant B'x-style reds eg. Octagon, plus superb CAB SAUV, NEBBIOLO, PETIT VERDOT. Paxxito is luscious VIDAL/MUSCAT Ottonel blend. Outstanding restaurant and inn on historic site frequented by Thomas Jefferson.

"No nation is drunken where wine is cheap; and none sober, where the dearness of wine substitutes ardent spirits as the common beverage," said Thomas Jefferson.

Boxwood ★★★ 14 15 16 17 Reds from five B'x grapes, also SAUV BL (1st vintage 2016). Short drive from Washington DC.

Breaux ★ 15 16 17 Hilltop v'yd, hr from Washington DC. Gd MERITAGE, CAB FR, CHARD.

Chrysalis ★★★ 13 14 15 16 17 Pioneering VIOGNIER producer, plus ALBARIÑO, PETITE VERDOT, TEMPRANILLO, VA native Norton.

Delaplane ★★★ 14 15 16 17 In scenic, mtn country overlooking historic Crooked Run Valley nr Paris, VA, with CHARD, PETIT MANSENG, B'x style reds, CAB FR, TANNAT.

Gabriele Rausse ★★ 15 16 17 Small estate nr Jefferson's Monticello; owned by VA's 1st commercial grape-grower. CHARD, CABS SAUV, FR, MERLOT, NEBBIOLO.

Glen Manor Vineyards ★★★ 13 14 15 16 17 V'yds on historic farm in Blue Ridge Mts; crisp SAUV BL, excellent red B'x-style blend, gd rosé, CAB FR, PETIT VERDOT.

Keswick ★★★ 14 15 16 17 Stellar estate with exceptional CHARD and VIOGNIER, age-worthy B'x-style red blends, excellent CAB FR, MERLOT, PETIT VERDOT, TOURIGA.

King Family Vineyards ★★★ 14 15 16 17 Serious, age-worthy MERITAGE, gd CHARD, VIOGNIER, CAB FR, PETIT VERDOT, luscious *vin de paille*-style PETIT MANSENG dessert wine. Polo matches on estate.

Linden ★★★★ 14 15 16 17 Just 100 km w of Washington DC. Leading VA estate with notable high-altitude wines incl rich CHARD, vivacious SAUV BL, savoury PETIT VERDOT, elegant, complex B'x-style red blends, delicious demi-sec PETIT MANSENG.

Michael Shaps Wineworks ★★★ 14 15 16 17 Innovative producer with luscious VIOGNIER and CHARD, layered PETIT MANSENG blend, tasty TANNAT, savoury PETIT VERDOT, also stylish MERITAGE and unique, concentrated late-harvest Raisin d'Etre.

Pollak ★★★ 15 16 17 superior VIOGNIER, PINOT GR, MERITAGE, MERLOT, PETIT VERDOT.

RdV Vineyards ★★★★ 13' 14 15 16 17 Top e estate, focus on B'x-inspired red blends characterized by elegance, complexity, power. Reservations for visits required.

Sunset Hills ★★ 15 16 17 Scenic winery in renovated barn; gd CHARD, VIOGNIER, CAB SAUV, outstanding B'x-style red blend.

Upper Shirley Vineyards ★★★ 15 16 17 Perched above the picturesque James River, with nice VIOGNIER, high-quality Blanc de Blanc (sp), CHARD, MERLOT, PETIT VERDOT, TANNAT, savory red blend.

Veritas ★★ 14 15 16 17 Gd bubbly, opulent VIOGNIER, gd CHARD, CAB FR, MERLOT, PETIT VERDOT and B'x-inspired red blend.

Washington

Wine-growing is a v. different proposition in WA from the almost-French conditions of OR. Behind the Cascade Mts it doesn't rain. Given irrigation, though, from the Columbia and other rivers, the continental climate suits many grapes, and many farmers. While there are over 70 varieties planted in state, CHARD, RIES, CAB SAUV, MERLOT and SYRAH make up over 75 per cent of production. In recent yrs, it's Cab Sauv that has increasingly become the dominant player, with production increasing a whopping 50 per cent in 2016. The market calls the shots. While Cab will no doubt raise its profile even higher, don't look for experiments to stop any time soon. WA has diverse talents.

Principal viticultural areas

Columbia Valley (Col V) Huge AVA in central and e WA with a touch in OR. High-quality Cab Sauv, Merlot, Ries, Chard, Syrah. Key sub-divisions incl Yakima Valley (Yak V), Red Mtn, Walla AVAs.

Red Mountain (Red Mtn) Sub-AVA of Col V and Yak V. Hot region known for Cabs and B'x blends.

Walla Walla Valley (Walla) Sub-AVA of Col V with own identity and vines in WA and OR. Home of important boutique brands and prestige labels focusing on quality. Cab Sauv, Merlot, Syrah.

Yakima Valley (Yak V) Sub-AVA of Col V. Focus on Merlot, Syrah, Ries.

Abeja Walla ★★★ Producer of top Col V CAB SAUV, CHARD. VIOGNIER v.gd.

Andrew Will Col V, Red Mtn ★★★→★★★★ 10' 11 12' 13' 14' (15) Long-time producer of some of state's best, most age-worthy single-v'yd red blends. Winery on Vashon Island, grapes from top v'yds. Sorella is flagship but no misses in line-up.

Avennia Col V, Yak V ★★★ 12' 13' 14' 15 Focuses on old vines, top v'yds. Turning heads with cellar-worthy B'x, Rhône styles. Sestina B'x blend and Arnaut SYRAH tops. Les Trouves gd value.

Betz Family Winery Col V ★★★→★★★★ 10 11 12' 13 14' 15 (16) Maker of high-quality Rhône, B'x styles. Pére de Famille CAB SAUV consistently stands out as a keeper.

B Leighton Yak V Side project for Brennon Leighton, formerly at CHATEAU STE MICHELLE and current winemaker for K VINTNERS. Rhône blend Gratitude, SYRAH, PETIT VERDOT v.gd.

In 2000, WA had fewer than 200 wineries. It now has more than 900.

Brian Carter Cellars Col V ★★★ 10 11' 12' 13 14 Blend specialist, with wines aged additional time before release. Try unconventional PETIT VERDOT-driven Trentenaire, Solesce B'x blend.

Cadence Red Mtn ★★★ 10' 11 12' 13' 14 (15) Dedicated to B'x-style blends from Red Mtn fruit. Some of state's most age-worthy wines. Cara Mia is own v'yd.

Cayuse Walla ★★★★ 10 11 12' 13' 14 15 (16) Mailing list only, yrs-long wait. All estate v'yd wines from Rocks District of Walla receive stratospheric scores. Earthy, savoury SYRAH (esp Cailloux and Bionic Frog) and God Only Knows GRENACHE tops. Sister wineries No Girls, Horsepower, Hors Categorie also top-notch.

Charles Smith Wines Col V ★★ Sold to Constellation in 2016 for $120 million. Focus on value wines. Look for Kung Fu Girl RIES.

Chateau Ste Michelle Col V ★★→★★★ Largest single producer of RIES in world; all prices/styles: v.gd quaffers (excellent Col V Ries) to TBA-style rarities (Eroica Single Berry Select). Gd-value reds and whites from Col V as well as estate offerings from Cold Creek, Canoe Ridge.

Chinook Wines Col V ★★★ Husband (vines) and wife (wines) have a history of fine, value CAB FR, MERLOT, CHARD, SAUV BL.

Col Solare Red Mtn ★★★→★★★★ 09' 10 11 12' 13 14 (15) Partnership between Ste Michelle Wine Estates and Tuscany's Antinori. Focus on single CAB SAUV from Red Mtn. Complex, long-lasting.

Columbia Crest Col V ★★→★★★ WA's top value producer and by far largest winery makes oodles of v.gd, affordable wines under Grand Estates, H3, Res labels. Res wines offer v.gd value esp CAB SAUV and Walter Clore (r).

Corliss Estates Col V ★★★ 08' 09' 10 11 12' 13 (14) Producer of high-end B'x blend. All wines see substantial time in barrel and bottle before release. Sister winery Tranche offers v.gd value.

Côte Bonneville Yak V ★★★ 09' 10 11 12' 13 14 (15) Estate winery for highly regarded DuBrul v'yd making age-worthy wines in sophisticated style. *Carriage House* v.gd value. Don't overlook CHARD, RIES.

Col V gets just 6–10 in of rain/yr. Don't bother with your brolly.

DeLille Cellars Red Mtn, Col V ★★★ 10' 11 12' 13 14' 15 (16) Long-time maker of B'x and Rhône styles. Chaleur Estate Blanc one of state's best whites. D2 (r) v.gd value.

Doubleback Walla ★★★ 10' 11 12' 13' 14' 15 (16) Former footballer Drew Bledsoe makes one wine, CAB SAUV, a feminine expression of Walla fruit with cellaring potential. Bledsoe Family sister winery making v.gd SYRAH.

Dusted Valley Vintners Walla ★★★ 11 12' 13 14 15 (16) B'x and Rhône styles. Stoney Vine SYRAH from estate plantings worth seeking out. Boomtown label gd value.

Efesté Yak V, Col V, Red Mtn ★★★ 10 11 12' 13 14 15 (16) Woodinville producer of zesty RIES, racy CHARD from cool Evergreen V'yd, also v.gd SYRAHS and old-vine CAB SAUV. Final Final gd value.

Fidélitas Red Mtn ★★★ 10 11 12' 13 14 15 (16) Producer of B'x style blends and CAB SAUV from Red Mtn. Quintessence V'yd Cab Sauv top-notch.

Fielding Hills Col V ★★★ Small producer focusing on estate v'yd on Wahluke Slope. CAB SAUV, MERLOT outstanding as well as v.gd value.

Figgins Walla ★★★ 10 11 12' 13' 14 15 Second-generation winemaker Chris Figgins also winemaker at famed LEONETTI. Makes single-estate B'x blend, RIES. Toil new OR PINOT N project.

Force Majeure Red Mtn ★★★ Producer of estate B'x and Rhône styles. VIOGNIER a standout. Cult winery in making.

Gramercy Cellars Walla ★★★ 12' 13 14' 15 (16) Founder master sommelier Greg Harrington produces lower alc, higher acid wines. Speciality earthy SYRAHS (esp Lagniappe), herby CAB SAUV. Lower East value label.

Hedges Family Estate Red Mtn ★★★ Venerable family winery; polished, reliable wines esp estate red blend and DLD SYRAH.

Hogue Cellars, The Col V ★★ Owned by Constellation Brands; value single-variety wines. Genesis, Res labels more focused, smaller production.

Januik Col V ★★★ 10 11 12' 13 14' 15 (16) V.gd-value B'x styles. Single v'yds a step above. Champoux V'yd CAB SAUV stands out. Novelty Hill sister winery.

K Vintners Col V, Walla ★★★ Rock-star winemaker Charles Smith focuses on single-v'yd SYRAH, plus Syrah/CAB SAUV blends. Sixto CHARD-focused sister winery.

L'Ecole No 41 Walla, Col V ★★★ 10 11 12' 13 14 15 (16) One of Walla's founding wineries; wide range. Ferguson top B'x blend. CHENIN BL, SEM v.gd value.

Leonetti Cellar Walla ★★★★ 10' 11 12' 13 14 15 (16) Founding Walla winery has cult status and steep prices for collectable CAB SAUV, MERLOT and SANGIOVESE. Res B'x blend flagship.

Long Shadows Walla ★★★→★★★★ Former Ste Michelle Wine Estates CEO Allen Shoup brings group of globally famous winemakers to WA to make a wine each.

Maison Bleue Walla ★★★ 12' 13 14 15 (16) Rhône-focused winery using Walla fruit, turning heads with GRENACHE, SYRAH.

Mark Ryan Yak V, Red Mtn ★★★ Producer of big, bold B'x and Rhône styles. MERLOT-based Long Haul and Dead Horse CAB SAUV stand out. Crazy Mary MOURVÈDRE swoonworthy. Board Track Racer second label.

Milbrandt Vineyards Col V ★★ Focus on value. The Estates is higher-tier, single-v'yd wines from Wahluke Slope and Ancient Lakes. Look for PINOT GR, RIES.

Northstar Walla ★★★ 10' 11 12' 13 14' (15) MERLOT-focused winery. Premier Merlot (made to age) is gorgeous.

Pacific Rim Col V ★★ RIES specialist making oceans of tasty, inexpensive yet eloquent Dry to Sweet and Organic. For more depth *single v'yd releases*.

Pepper Bridge Walla ★★★ 10' 11 12 13 14 (15) B'x styles from estate fruit. Pepper Bridge and Seven Hills v'yd blends among WA's best.

Quilceda Creek Col V ★★★★ 04' 05' 06 07 09 10 11' 12' 13 14' (15) Flagship producer of cult status CAB SAUV known for ageing potential. One of most lauded producers in US. Sold by allocation. Find it if you can.

Unlike almost all the world's vines, WA's grow on their own roots.

Reynvaan Family Vineyards Walla ★★★→★★★★ 10' 11 12' 13 14 15 (16) Family winery with estate v'yds in Rocks District and foothills of Blue Mtn. Dedicated to SYRAH, CAB SAUV, Rhône-style whites. Wait-list winery but worth it.

Rôtie Cellars Walla Top-flight Rhône styles. Northern Blend a consistent standout.

Saviah Cellars Walla Exquisite SYRAH, TEMPRANILLO, B'x blends. Stones Speak Syrah is knee-buckler.

Seven Hills Winery Walla ★★★ 10 11 12' 13 14 15 (16) One of Walla's oldest, most respected wineries, known for age-worthy reds. Res CAB SAUV and Ciel du Cheval V'yd tops. Recently bought by Crimson Wine Group.

Sleight of Hand Walla Winemaker and audiophile Trey Busch makes dazzling B'x blends, Rhône styles. Psychedlic SYRAH from Rocks District worth seeking out.

Sparkman Cellars Yak V, Red Mtn ★★★ 10 11 12' 13 14 15 Woodinville producer makes a staggering 27 wines, focus on power. Stella Mae and Ruby Leigh B'x blends: excellent quality, value. Evermore Old Vines CAB SAUV cellar-worthy.

Spring Valley Vineyard Walla ★★★ 10' 11' 12' 13 14' (15) All estate wines. Uriah MERLOT blend consistent standout. Katherine Corkrum CAB FR also superb.

Syncline Cellars Col V ★★★ Rhône-dedicated producer; wines in distinct, fresh style. Subduction Red is v.gd value. NB MOURVÈDRE. Sparkling GRÜNER delicious.

Woodward Canyon Walla ★★★★ 09 10 11 12' 13 14 15 (16) One of oldest Walla producers, focusing on B'x styles. *Old Vines Cab Sauv* is complex, age-worthy. CHARD one of best in state. Nelms Road value label.

Wisconsin

Wollersheim Winery (est 1840s) is one of best estates in midwest, with hybrid and Wisconsin-native American hybrid grapes. Look for Prairie Fumé (SEYVAL BL) and Prairie Blush (Marechal Foch).

Mexico

Mexico's Napa is Guadalupe in Baja California, 80 miles south of San Diego, 20 from Ensenada and the Pacific. Its Robert Mondavi, inspirer and leader of a young quality industry, is Hugo d'Acosta. He owns three wineries, a wine school and custom-crush plant. Baja California boasts 90 per cent of Mexico's production, with a growing number of small producers clustered in the Valle de Guadalupe. Though you can book a day-long tour with UberValle, it's still a more low-key experience than Napa and Sonoma. The hip vibe has caught on with the culinary and hospitality sets. There's increasing visibility and press coverage of Mexico as a burgeoning farm-to-table food destination, and wineries stay authentic, producing from high-altitude, cool-climate vineyards, and wines that often have a saline character. The better wines are produced on hillsides where the water comes from mountain springs.

Adobe Guadalupe ★★→★★★ Hugo d'Acosta consults at this hacienda-style winery, founded by Dutch expat Tru Miller. Wines incl B'x blends, named after angels. Noteworthy: Rafael 2013, a blend of NEBBIOLO/CAB SAUV. V.gd quality, balanced, flavourful. Gd restaurant, B&B.

Bibayoff Vinos ★★→★★★ Outstanding ZIN and v.gd Zin/CAB SAUV blend. Zesty CHENIN BL all from dry-farmed hillside vines.

Casa de Piedra ★★→★★★ Hugo d'Acosta at work here too, making Vino de Piedra, v.gd blend of CAB SAUV/TEMPRANILLO; Piedra del Sol, CHARD, traditional-method fizz.

Château Camou ★★→★★★ French-inspired winery with serious B'x credentials. CAB SAUV-based blend Gran Vino Tinto is velvety with a supple, elegant finish. Aged El Gran Vino Tinto is noteworthy.

Finca La Carrodilla First certified organic winery in Valle de Guadalupe, UC Davis-trained winemaker specializes in single varietals – CAB SAUV and SHIRAZ among the best. Small, careful production.

Las Nubes Young winery, est 2008, wines named for clouds in English and native Kiliwa language. Gd Res red blends.

Monte Xanic ★★→★★★ First premium winery here, now a speakeasy-like setting with excellent CAB SAUV, v.gd MERLOT. Award-winning whites; look for SAUV BL, unoaked CHARD, fresh CHENIN BL.

Paralelo ★★ Cutting-edge project by Hugo d'Acosta, designed by his star architect brother. Small production. Emblema SAUV BL, two versions of B'x style Ensamble.

Rincón de Guadalupe ★★→★★★ Oldest TEMPRANILLO vines in Mexico; v.gd SAUV BL and excellent red blend, Viejo Tinto.

Roganto ★★→★★★ Small winery using estate fruit, making excellent CAB SAUV and super red blend, Tramonte: layers of flavour, lasting finish, potential for ageing.

Tres Mujeres ★★→★★★ Rustic co-op owned by women reflects new wave of artisan producers in Baja. Top TEMPRANILLO; v.gd GRENACHE/CAB SAUV, La Mezcla del Rancho.

Once a rugged outpost, now increasingly visible/hip destination for wine and food.

Tres Valles Powerful Guadalupe, Santo Tomas, San Vincente Valley reds. V.gd Kuwal blend driven by TEMPRANILLO. Kojaa, from Durif (PETITE SIRAH) is cult quality.

Vena Cava ★★ Hip winery owned by UK-born former music exec, constructed from reclaimed fishing boats. Well-priced, modern, organic wines. V.gd complex oak-aged CAB SAUV and TEMPRANILLO. Signature is Res, Cab Sauv/SYRAH blend. Farm-to-table restaurant next door.

Viñas Pijoan Honest wines, *garagista* in spirit and style. Family run, mostly French varieties. B'x blend Leonora is flagship wine, named for winemaker's wife.

Canada

Canada entered the wine world with Ontario's super-sweet Icewine. Now the focus is shifting west to British Columbia. New-generation vineyards continue to spread across diverse regions that stretch from 42–52°N and beyond, in a climate that defines cool. Canada's sporting 700+ wineries and 12,000 ha+ under vine. Authentic, pristine wine with generous acidity and moderate alcohol is the Canadian USP, a refreshing alternative among New World styles. Chardonnay, Riesling and sparkling are foremost among whites; the most talked-about reds are Pinot Noir and Syrah, with Cabernet Franc and Meritage blends coming on nicely.

Ontario

Three prime appellations of origin: Niagara Peninsula, Lake Erie North Shore and Prince Edward County (P Ed). Within the Niagara Peninsula: two regional appellations – Niagara Escarpment (Niag E) and Niagara-on-the-Lake (Niag L) – and ten sub-appellations.

Bachelder Niag r w ★★★★ 12' 13 14 15 16' Pure, precise, elegant, age-worthy CHARD, PINOT N in Burgundy, Oregon and on the Dolomitic limestone and clay of Niag.

Cave Spring Niag r w sw sp ★★★ 14' 15' 16' (17) Respected pioneer; CSV (old vines) esp RIES, CHARD. Estate labels age gracefully. Elegant CAB FR, Chard, top late-harvest, Icewine.

Château des Charmes Niag r w sw sp ★★ 14 15 16' (17) The 114-ha Bosc family farm is a charter member of Sustainable Winegrowing Ontario. RIES from bone-dry to Icewine, sparkling and Equuleus: flagship red blend.

Creekside Niag r w sp ★★ 14 15 16' (17) Eclectic group defying convention; focus on SYRAH, SAUV BL incl sparkler; experimental, edgy wines. A visitor experience.

Flat Rock Niag r w (sp) ★★★ 14 15 16' (17) 32 ha on Twenty Mile Bench; a rich selection of juicy, crisp RIES, PINOT N, CHARD. Top picks: single-block Nadja's Ries, Rusty Shed Chard. All screwcapped.

Henry of Pelham Niag r w sw sp ★★★ 13' 14' 15 16' (17) Speck brothers make CHARD, RIES, exceptional Cuvée Catherine Brut fizz, Speck Family Res (SFR), unique Baco Noir, Ries Icewine.

Hidden Bench Niag r w ★★★★ 13 14 15 16' (17) Classic artisanal Beamsville Bench producer. RIES, PINOT N, CHARD; top Terroir Series Roman's Block Ries plus Nuit Blanche and La Brunate blends.

Huff Estates P Ed r w sp ★★ 15 16' (17) 9-ha South Bay v'yd on clay/shale loam over limestone. Traditional-method sparkler, still CHARD, PINOT N, PINOT GR.

Inniskillin Niag r w sw 14 15 16' (17) Icewine pioneer making juicy Res RIES, PINOT GR, PINOT N and super CAB FR; single-v'yd series CHARD, Pinot N only in best yrs.

Malivoire Niag r p w (sp) ★★★ 15' 16' (17) Shiraz Mottiar makes eco-friendly GAMAY,

---

Home-grown oranges

Canadians are in the orange wine business too, with VQA Ontario approving a new category for skin-fermented white wines as of summer 2017. Look for **Southbrook Vineyards 2016 Vidal Skin-Fermented White**, Ontario: VIDAL, in steel, 25 days on skins. **Pearl Morissette 2016 Cuvée Bleu**, Niag: CHARD, PINOT GR, SAUV BL, in amphora, 3.5 mths on skins. **Little Farm Winery 2016 Pied de Cuve Orange**, BC: RIES, in steel, 6 mths on skins. **Haywire 2016 Free Form Natural and Unfiltered White**, Ok V: Sauv Bl, in steel, 9 mths on skins. **The Hatch 2016 Rhymes with Door Hinge**, Ok V: KERNER, Schönburger/Chard, co-fermented in old puncheons, 6 wks on skins.

plus CAB FR, CHARD; tasty PINOT N, GEWURZ; trio of rosés from four Niag E v'yds.

Norman Hardie r w ★★★★ 14' 15 16' (17) Iconic P Ed pioneer hand-crafting CHARD, PINOT N, RIES, CAB FR on limestone-clay soils. Cuvée L Chard, Pinot N in best yrs.

Ontario produces 90 per cent of Canada's Icewine: about 850,000 litres annually.

Pearl Morissette Niag r w ★★★ 14 15 16' (17) No-dogma RIES aged in *foudre*, CHARD, CAB FR, PINOT N with concrete eggs and *foudres*.

Ravine Vineyard Niag r w ★★★ 14 15 16' (17) Organic 14-ha St David's Bench v'yd spans former riverbed. Top Res CHARD, CAB FR; drink-now label: Sand and Gravel.

Stratus Niag r w ★★★★ 13 14 15 16' (17) Iconoclast JL Groux works 25 ha of Niagara Lakeshore fruit at eco-certified winery. Blends (r w) reflect a quest for somewhereness; v.gd RIES, SYRAH.

Tawse Niag r w (sp) ★★★★ 13 14 15 16' (17) Winemaker Paul Pender makes outstanding CHARD, RIES, gd PINOT N, CAB FR, MERLOT; v'yds certified organic and bio.

British Columbia

The prescribed Geographical Indications for BC wines of distinction are BC, Fraser Valley, Okanagan Valley (Ok V), Golden Mile Bench (subdivision of Ok V), Similkameen Valley, Vancouver Island, Gulf Islands.

Blue Mountain Ok V r w sp ★★★ 14' 15 16' (17) Next generation continue traditional-method fizz incl smart RD versions; reliable age-worthy PINOT N, CHARD, PINOT GR, GAMAY. Outstanding Res Pinot N.

Burrowing Owl Ok V r w ★★ 15' 16' (17) Pioneer estate; excellent CAB FR, v.gd PINOT GR, SYRAH on Black Sage Bench; successful boutique hotel/restaurant.

Every bottle of 100% BC wine sold there generates $95.34 in economic activity.

CedarCreek Ok V r w ★★★ 14' 15 16' (17) Expect a starry line-up of aromatic RIES, GEWURZ, Ehrenfelser and Platinum single-v'yd blocks PINOT N, CHARD.

Church & State Wines Ok V r w (sp) 14' 15 16' (17) Lost Inhibitions blends are west-coast casual. Serious picks Trebella (Rhône white), Quintessential (B'x red).

Haywire Ok V r w sp ★★★ 15 16' (17) Hipster Summerland uses natural, Pét-Nat, organics, concrete ferments, amphora. CHARD, PINOT GR, PINOT N, GAMAY, sparkling.

Mission Hill Ok V r w ★★★ 13' 14 15 16' Australian Darryl Brooker is tweaking the texture of his elite Legacy Series: Oculus, Perpetua, Quatrain, Compendium. Benchmark visitor centre/outdoor restaurant.

Nk'Mip Ok V r w ★★★ 14' 15 16' (17) Steady, fresh RIES, PINOT N; top-end Qwam Qwmt Pinot N, SYRAH. Part of $25 million aboriginal resort/Desert Cultural Centre.

Osoyoos Larose Ok V r ★★★ 14' 15 (16') B'x-based Groupe Taillan owns this 33-ha single v'yd. Track record of age-worthy Le Grand Vin echoes B'x, sings Ok.

Painted Rock Ok V r w ★★★ 14 15 16' (17) Skaha Bench, steep, 24-ha maturing v'yd. B'x consultant Alain Sutre; v.gd SYRAH, CAB FR, CHARD, signature red blend Icon.

Quails' Gate Ok V r w ★★★ 14 15 16' (17) Inspired style: fresh, aromatic RIES, CHENIN BL; continued refinement of core PINOT N, CHARD and limited Collector Series.

Road 13 Ok V r w (sp) ★★★ 14 15 16' (17) Treasured old-vine CHENIN BL (w sp), plus premium Jackpot series VIOGNIER, SYRAH, PINOT N, CAB FR on Golden Mile Bench.

Stag's Hollow Ok V ★★★ 15 16' (17) Winemaker Dwight Sick is creating ALBARIÑO, VIOGNIER, GRENACHE, PINOT N, SYRAH; one-off, top-lot Renaissance labels in great yrs.

Tantalus Ok V r w sp ★★★ 15 16 (17) Natural, terroir-driven RIES, PINOT N, CHARD from oldest (1927) continuously producing Ok V v'yds.

Nova Scotia

Benjamin Bridge ★★★ 07 08' 09 11' 12 Gaspereau Valley; traditional-method fizz. Excellent age-worthy vintage and NV Brut from CHARD/PINOTS N/M blends.

South America

CHILE
Antofagasta
JUJUY
SALTA Salta Salta
Calayate Valley
TUCUMAN
FORMOSA
CATAMARCA
CHACO
SANTIAGO
DEL ESTERO
SANTA FE
COQUIMBO La Rioja La Rioja
Elqui LA RIOJA
La Serena SAN JUAN
Limarí San Juan San Juan
Choapa
Valparaíso Aconcagua Mendoza
Casablanca Santiago Mendoza
San Antonio Maipo ARGENTINA
Leyda Rapel (incl Cachapoal/Colchagua)
Curicó San Rafael
Maule
Itata
Bío Bío
Malleco
NEUQUÉN
RÍO NEGRO Viedma
PATAGONIA
Rawson
Chubut
CHUBUT
CÓRDOBA
Córdoba
ENTRE
RÍOS
Santa Fe
BUENOS AIRES
Buenos Aires
LA PAMPA
Colorado
Negro
South Atlantic Ocean

Abbreviations used in the text:

CHILE

Aco	Aconcagua
Bío	Bío-Bío
Cach	Cachapoal
Casa	Casablanca
Cho	Choapa
Col	Colchagua
Coq	Coquimbo
Cur	Curicó
Elq	Elqui
Ita	Itata
Ley	Leyda
Lim	Limarí
Mai	Maipo
Mal	Malleco
Mau	Maule
Rap	Rapel
San A	San Antonio

ARGENTINA

Cata	Catamarca
La R	La Rioja
Luján	Luján de Cuyo
Men	Mendoza
Neu	Neuquén
Pat	Patagonia
Río N	Río Negro
Sal	Salta
San J	San Juan
Uco V	Uco Valley

CHILE

Keeping up with Chile is a full-time job. The wine valleys are evolving faster than ever, in a continual expansion to extremes of south, north, east and west. Coastal vineyards start barely a mile from the icy Pacific, and mountain vineyards continue to creep higher into the Andes with plantings now far above the 2000m line. In the north, the Atacama Desert is home to more and more vineyards, and looking south, Chile has now the most austral wine region in the world, stealing the thunder from New Zealand. Chile embraces both its traditional varieties – País, Cinsault, Muscat, Malbec and Carignan – as well as its modern mainstays of Sauvignon Blanc, Cabernet Sauvignon, Syrah, Chardonnay and Pinot Noir. Look away and you'll miss the next big thing.

Recent vintages

While Chile's climate is more consistent than many other wine countries, vintage variation is increasing as climate change has its effects. A vintage in Chile is rarely bad everywhere – the diverse range of varieties and regions ensures that there will always be some successes. 2017 was an early and hot vintage in which picking at the right time was paramount, most especially due to the forest fires that hit the south.

Aconcagua Andes region above Santiago making top blends. Coastal sites are increasingly recognized for gd CHARD, SYRAH, PINOT N.

Almaviva Mai ★★★★ One of Chile's 1st luxury brands making just one wine: a rich, complex, age-worthy B'x-style blend. CONCHA Y TORO/Baron Philippe de Rothschild joint venture in Puente Alto, MAI.

Altaïr Wines Rap ★★★ Luxury house of SAN PEDRO making a top, eponymous CAB SAUV blend and younger second label blend, Sideral.

Antiyal Mai ★★★ Chile's bio guru Alvaro Espinoza consults for many but this is his family project, making understated, elegant reds.

Apaltagua ★★ Diverse portfolio from Central Valley and always gd value. Gd CARMENÈRE, CARIGNAN.

Aquitania, Viña Mai ★★★ Well-respected MAI producer and pioneer in Mal. Excellent Lazuli CAB SAUV; elegant CHARD, PINOT N, SAUV BL.

Arboleda, Viña Aco ★★ →★★★ Cool, ACO coastal range from ERRÁZURIZ; v.gd SAUV BL, CHARD, PINOT N.

Aristos Cach ★★★ →★★★★ Top wines from this small Franco-Chilean venture: stylish CAB SAUV, stellar CHARD.

Bío-Bío Large s region, deeply rooted in Chile's history and now growing again. Crisp RIES, SAUV BL, PINOT N, CHARD.

Bodegas RE Casa ★★★ Exciting portfolio of experimental, often excellent, wines by Pablo Morandé Jr. and Sr. Orange wines, clay amphoras, cloudy bubbles and off-beat blends.

Bouchon Mau ★★ →★★★ Full-fruit reds, fresh whites. V.gd Canto blends; PAÍS Salvaje is natural wine. Traditional MAU, reinvented.

Caliboro Mau ★★ →★★★ Italian Count Francesco Cinzano's Chile investment; lively red blends, rare Torontel (MUSCAT family) Late Harvest.

Caliterra Casa, Col, Cur, Ley ★★ →★★★ Col winery from the ERRÁZURIZ group. MALBEC is flagship, Cenit is top blend.

Chile's 1st indigenous vine found in Atacama: Tamarugal, 2 ha, parents unknown.

Calyptra Cach ★★★ High-altitude, juicy CAB SAUV, rich CHARD and superb barrel-aged SAUV BL. François Massoc is winemaker.

Carmen, Viña Casa, Col, Mai ★★ →★★★ V'yd where CARMENÈRE variety was first identified. New additions to the DO range incl v.gd SEM, MALBEC. SANTA RITA own.

Casablanca The 1st cool, coastal wine region, but now superceded (temperature-wise) by regions closer to the coast. Still leading in quantity and quality. CHARD, SAUV BL, PINOT N, SYRAH.

Casa Marín San A ★★★ Mother-and-son duo, Maria Luz and Felipe Marin, make excellent RIES, SAUV BL, SYRAH, and one of Chile's only Sauvignon Gris. Just 2.5 miles from coast.

Casas del Bosque Casa, Mai ★★ →★★★ Cool, sloping site. Consistently gd-quality SAUV BL, SYRAH, CHARD through the ranges esp Pequeñas Producciones.

Casa Silva Col, S Regions ★★ →★★★ The Silva family is a local wine dynasty with v'yds since 1892. Today's portfolio is diverse: robust CARMENÈRE, fresher Col coastal whites and v.gd SAUV BL, PINOT N from Pat.

Clos des Fous Cach, Casa, S Regions ★★ →★★★ The "Clos of Madmen" is actually v. smart. Pedro Parra and François Massoc spearhead this terroir-focused collection of juicy red blends, PINOT N.

Clos Ouvert Mau ★★ French expat Louis Antoine Luyt pioneered modern "natural" wine movement in Chile with this portfolio of PAÍS, CARIGNAN, CINSAULT from MAU.

Concha y Toro Cent V ★ →★★★★ Producing 14 million cases/yr, Concha y Toro isn't small. The portfolio is eye-watering and covers all the major valleys in Chile. Highlights incl Terrunyo SAUV BL, CAB SAUV; Maycas de Limarí CHARD, PINOT N,

Sauv Bl, SYRAH from LIM; Gravas Syrah from MAI, and top Cab Sauv in Marques and **Don Melchor**. Lion's share of production goes into classic and consistent Casillero del Diablo brand. See also ALMAVIVA, Trivento (Argentina).

Cono Sur Casa, Col, Bio ★★ →★★★ Focused on PINOT N; the Bicicleta is most sold Pinot N in UK. Great quality at all prices (esp Res Especial) and all grape varieties. Top CAB SAUV Silencio is excellent.

Cousiño Macul Mai ★★→★★★ Historic family winery in outskirts of Santiago. Reliable wines in Antiguas line leads up to top blend, **Lota**.

De Martino Cach, Casa, Elq, Mai, Mau, Ita ★★ →★★★★ One of Chile's star wineries, and star winemakers, pioneering new valleys and styles. Reds are fresh with fruit and little oak, whites are balanced. Single-v'yd delights incl 2000m ELQ SYRAH, old-vine MALBEC, CARIGNAN. Viejas Tinajas from ITA is amphora-aged.

Elqui Steep n valley in Andes mainly known for Pisco but also v.gd mtn SYRAH, SAUV BL, PX. World-class star-gazing.

Emiliana Casa, Rap, Bio ★ →★★★ Chile's leading organic/bio specialist involving Alvaro Espinoza (see ANTIYAL). Complex, SYRAH-heavy G and Coyam show almost Mediterranean-style wildness; Adobe and Novas v.gd everyday ranges.

Errázuriz Aco, Casa ★★ →★★★★ Exciting ACO producer: quality, innovation. Coastal and mtn v'yds diversify portfolio. V.gd wild-ferment SAUV BL, CHARD, PINOT N, SYRAH. Rich CAB SAUV blend Don Maximiliano, perfumed CARMENÈRE KAI. Superb Pizarras Chard, Pinot N. See also CALITERRA, SEÑA, VIÑA ARBOLEDA, VIÑEDO CHADWICK.

Falernia, Viña Elq ★★→★★★ First commercial producer in ELQ, still leads. Excellent Rhône SYRAH, herbaceous SAUV BL, uncommon PX. Labels incl Alta Tierra, Mayu.

Fournier, Bodegas O Ley, Mau ★★ MAU and Ley portfolio with old-vine CARIGNAN and fresh coastal SAUV BL. Spanish-owned (see Spain, Argentina).

Garcés Silva, Viña San A ★★→★★★ SAN A producer with opulent, oaked SAUV BL, CHARD, PINOT N, SYRAH. Boya is fresher, fruitier line.

Haras de Pirque Mai ★★→★★★ Based in heart of MAI, reds are strength (CAB SAUV, SYRAH), but a v.gd flinty SAUV BL too.

Itata Coming back into fashion, this s valley is a heartland of old vines and natural wines. Top CINSAULT, PAÍS, MUSCAT.

Lapostolle Cach, Casa, Col ★★→★★★ Bio and undoubtedly chic. Prized Apalta (Col) estate producing lush CARMENÈRE-based Clos Apalta and bold whites. Collection range boasts fresher style of single-site SYRAHS and Carmenères.

Leyda, Viña Col, Mai, San A ★★→★★★ Gd-value SAN A producer with zesty, coastal whites (CHARD, SAUV BL, Sauvignon Gris), spicy SYRAH, juicy PINOT N.

Limarí The limestone soils are ideal but rainfall is minimal. Drought is scaring off some investment, but those who do get v.gd CHARD, SAUV BL, SYRAH, PINOT N.

Loma Larga Casa ★★ Unique in CASA for its steep hillsides and focus on reds. Top MALBEC and CAB FR.

Maipo Chile's Grand Cru and cradle of top CAB SAUV. Nr Santiago with alluvial soils and mtn influence. Look for Pirque, Puente Alto, Alto Jahuel.

Matetic Casa, San A ★★★ Consistent and quality-oriented. Large bio estate stradling CASA and SAN A. Try SYRAH, **Sauv Bl**, PINOT N.

Maule Workhorse region with large volume and sometimes exciting old-vine wines. Try CARIGNAN (see VIGNO) and PAÍS.

Ring of fire

Sitting on the Ring of Fire, Chile has long been on the risk radar for earthquakes, but there's another life-threatening phenomenon putting Chile on the edge: forest fires. In 2017, over 2000 fires spread through Chile's s affecting over 500,000 ha, claiming 11 lives. Irresponsible forestry management, arson, climate change being held equally culpable.

> **Mountains to coast**
> When you think Chile, forget North to South – think East to West. Chile's wine regions and appellation system are divided into Andes (East), Entre Valles (Central Valleys) and Costa (West, Coastal). Division marks impact of mtns and coast – more important than latitude in Chile's case. Just as in California.

Maycas del Limarí Lim ★★ ⟶★★★ LIM brand in CONCHA Y TORO stable. V.gd *Sauv Bl*, CHARD, PINOT N, SYRAH reflecting cool coast and limestone soils.

Montes Casa, Col, Cur, Ley ★★⟶★★★★ Innovative COL winery with Aurelio Montes Jr. now in charge. Intense, complex reds (Alpha CAB SAUV, *Folly Syrah*, Purple Angel CARMENÈRE) are complemented by fresher coastal wines incl v.gd Outer Limits range (SAUV BL, PINOT N) from Zapallar and CINSAULT from ITA.

MontGras Col, Ley, Mai ★★ Wide portfolio incl gd-value reds from Col, Intriga CAB SAUV from MAI and excellent Amaral SAUV BL from Ley.

Montsecano Casa ★★★ Boutique production of bio PINOT N from cool, granite hillsides of CASA. *Top stuff.*

Morandé Casa, Mai, Mau ★★⟶★★★ Large and consistent producer making wines all over Chile. Try the Limited Edition lines for intrigue; Brut Nature NV (CHARD, PINOT N) is a top Chilean *bubbly*.

Neyen Col ★★★ Rich, complex CARMENÈRE/CAB SAUV blend from old vines in Apalta. Tranforming into bio; owned by VERAMONTE.

Odfjell Mai, Mau ★⟶★★★ Strong portfolio with rich MAI CAB SAUV, aromatic CARIGNAN from MAU, v.gd MALBEC/CARIGNAN/SYRAH Winemaker's Travesy blend.

Pérez Cruz, Viña Mai ★★⟶★★★ Family producer with MAI estate, specializing in B'x varieties, blends. Top CAB SAUV, interesting PETIT VERDOT.

Polkura Col ★★⟶★★★ Sven Bruchfeld makes v.gd SYRAH from Marchigue. Also SAUV BL and MALBEC.

Quebrada de Macul, Viña Mai ★★⟶★★★ Cult-status CAB SAUV Domus Aurea is a top wine from Macul MAI.

Rapel Large Central Valley denomination; stretches mtn to coast; covers Cach, Col.

Ribera del Lago Mau ★★⟶★★★ Winemaker Rafael Tirado makes excellent SAUV BL and Laberinto PINOT N from maze-shaped v'yds in MAU.

San Antonio West of Santiago, next to CASA, but cooler. Known for SAUV BL, CHARD, SYRAH, PINOT N and Ley subregion.

San Pedro Cur ★⟶★★★ The 2nd-largest winery in Chile, Cur-based San Pedro makes wines from all major valleys. 35 South (35 Sur) and Castillo de Molina are entry level; 1865 Limited Edition starts to get exciting with single-v'yd wines. Top of range is Cabo de Hornos. Group also owns ALTAÏR, Missiones de Rengo, Santa Helena, TARAPACÁ, Viña Mar.

Santa Carolina, Viña ★★⟶★★★ One of Chile's oldest but still innovative. V.gd CAB SAUV, CARMENÈRE across ranges, and fresh whites from coast and s. Luis Pereira Cab Sauv is superb; Herencia (Carmenère) one of Chile's best.

Santa Rita Mai ★★⟶★★★★ Historic MAI winery with impressive, diverse portfolio. 120 and Medalla Real are solid everyday wines, Floresta range has exciting SEM and CARMENÈRE, *Casa Real Cab Sauv* is a Chilean icon. Sebastian Labbé now head winemaker in charge of 380-ha replant.

Seña Aco ★★★★ One of Chile's best: CAB SAUV-based B'x blend from ACO valley. A single wine made by Chadwick/ERRÁZURIZ.

Tabalí Lim ★★ ⟶★★★ Leader in LIM making cool, coastal wines from limestone soils. V.gd CHARD, SAUV BL, PINOT N, SYRAH and mtn MALBEC.

Tarapacá, Viña Casa, Ley, Mai ★★ Part of VSPT group, classic range from main Chile valleys: Tara-Pakay (CAB SAUV/SYRAH), Etiqueta Negra Gran Res (Cab Sauv).

> **Orange fever**
> Chile has become a hotbed for orange and amphora-aged wines. You'll find excellent and profusely aromatic old-vine field blends of MUSCAT and SEM on the orange side; and a return to ageing in clay amphoras is also popular with old-vine CARIGNAN, CINSAULT and PAÍS reds. Try: DE MARTINO, Huaso de Sauzal, Louis-Antoine Luyt, RE, Rogue Vine.

Torres, Miguel Cur ★★→★★★★ One of Chile's most important foreign investments. Spanish family revolutionized Chile's industry with stainless-steel tanks in 1979. Still innovative today. V.gd CAB SAUV (esp **Manso de Velasco**), delightful sparkling PAÍS, complex Escaleras de Empedrado PINOT N. All worth trying.

Undurraga Casa, Ley, Lim, Mai ★→★★★ Large producer of sparkling and still. TH (Terroir Hunter) series is a highlight with single-v'yd wines from around Chile.

Valdivieso Cur, San A ★→★★★ Diverse portfolio from main valleys. Gd Res and Single V'yd range (esp CAB FR, MALBEC, **Ley Chard**). Excellent Caballo Loco and CARIGNAN-based Éclat. Big name in Chile for bubbles too.

Vascos, Los Rap ★→★★★ Col-based estate is joint venture by Lafite-Rothschild making B'x-style reds, now improving. Top: Le Dix, Grande Res.

Ventisquero, Viña Casa, Col, Mai ★→★★★ Sizeable winery with v'yds all over Chile. Most interesting is Atacama v'yd, Tara (PINOT N, CHARD) V.gd Enclave CAB SAUV, Pangea SYRAH. Kalfu gd for weekdays.

Veramonte Casa, Col ★★→★★★ Rodrigo Soto converted traditional CASA estate to bio, now making v.gd PINOT N, SYRAH, SAUV BL (esp Ritual). Owned by González Byass (*see* Spain).

Vigno Mau Appellation-style association of several producers making old-vine CARIGNAN from MAU. Wines must be 70% Carignan, 30-yr-old+ v'yds, dry-farmed.

Local legend says conquistador Francisco de Aguirre was 1st to plant vines, 1554.

Villard Casa, Mai ★★ French-born Thierry Villard makes sophisticated MAI reds, v.gd PINOT N, MERLOT, Equis CAB SAUV, fresh CASA whites.

Viñedo Chadwick Mai ★★★→★★★★ Excellent, single-label CAB SAUV from Puente Alto. Elegant and stylish. Owned by Chadwick/ERRÁZURIZ.

Viu Manent Casa, Col ★★ Col-based producer, MALBEC specialist, even making one in Argentina. Other highlights: CARMENÈRE-based El Incidente, zesty CASA SAUV BL.

Von Siebenthal Aco ★★→★★★ Concentrated and rich reds from ACO incl juicy Parcela 7 blend, luscious CARMENÈRE, full-bodied PETIT VERDOT. Also VIOGNIER.

ARGENTINA

A steak bigger than the plate and a bottle of red: that's Argentina. Or perhaps a half-bottle of red. Argentines are drinking less. It's down to 20 litres a head a year – where once it was 90. But notably better. It's gone far beyond a simple hearty Malbec, good as that could be. Today Argentina is a titan of the wine world, making world-class reds (Malbec, Cabernets Franc and Sauvignon) and some very fine Chardonnays too. Light Bonarda red and peppery Torrontés white are mainstays. Mendoza is still the heart of the Argentine wine scene, but you'll find good *vino* coming from way up north towards Salta. Down south, too: Río Negro is in Patagonia. 99 per cent of Argentina's wine production is along the spine of the Andes mountains. Their rain shadow protects the vineyards below while their snowmelt provides water for irrigation. Nothing grows without it. Between the dry bright atmosphere of high altitude and total water control you have ideal growing conditions.

Achaval Ferrer Men ★★→★★★ Luján winery focusing mainly on single-v'yd MALBECS. Owned by Stolichnaya spirits group.

Aleanna Men ★★→★★★ Better known by its label, El Enemigo. CATENA winemaker Alejandro Vigil and youngest Catena daughter, Adrianna, make top CHARD, CAB FR, MALBEC from excellent sites in Uco V.

Alta Vista Men ★ →★★★ Handsome old winery in Luján, where French investors have spent more than a pretty penny. First to work on single-v'yd concept in Argentina. Top MALBECS.

Altocedro Men ★★→★★★ La Consulta is at the heart of this small winery owned by winemaker Karim Mussi. Distinctive style, v.gd TEMPRANILLO, MALBEC.

Altos las Hormigas Men ★★★ Forward-thinking wines by Italians Alberto Antonini and Attilio Pagli with Chilean terroir specialist Pedro Parra, winemaker Leo Erazo. Excellent single-v'yd MALBEC. Try BONARDA (sparkling and still) in sister winery Colonia Las Liebres.

Antucura Men ★★ B'x varieties made in Vista Flores under guidance of Michel Rolland (*see* France).

Atamisque Men ★ →★★★ Large Uco V estate making wide range of great-value wines. V.gd Catalpa CHARD, PINOT N. Top value Serbal CAB FR, SAUV BL.

Benegas Men ★★ →★★★ Benegas family founded TRAPICHE in 1883, sold it 1971 to start this premium winery. Top-notch CAB FR and B'x blend.

Bressia Men ★★ →★★★ Walter Bressia is famous here. His family winery makes v.gd complex, age-worthy red blends (Profundo, Conjuro), top Monteagrelo SYRAH, CAB FR and Lagrima Canela CHARD.

Caelum Men ★★ Luján winery owned and run by young Buenos Aires family. Italian winemaker has fondness for FIANO and makes gd CHARD, MALBEC.

Callia San J ★→★★ SAN J powerhouse, making gd-value, fruity SYRAH and off-dry whites for local market.

Canale, Bodegas Humberto Rio N ★ →★★★ Historic RÍO N specialist with top old-vine RIES and distinctly s style of MALBEC.

Caro Men ★★★ →★★★★ Luxury B'x-style blend made in joint venture by CATENA and Rothschilds of Lafite (France). Top blend is Caro followed by Amancaya.

Casa Bianchi Men ★ →★★ Leading producer in San Rafael making lots of bubbles and wide range of still.

Casarena Men ★★→★★★ Growing portfolio of premium wines under Casarena label; Ramanegra for everyday, 505 for value. V.gd Casarena single-v'yd MALBEC, CAB FR, CAB SAUV.

Catena Zapata, Bodega Men ★★ →★★★★ One of biggest names in Argentina, Nicolas Catena pioneered high-altitude in MEN and led way for quality in 90s. Today Catena owns a wide range of brands, wineries. Top: Adriana Gualtallary MALBEC, CHARD, CAB FR. Alamos (distributed by Gallo) is worthy workhorse.

Chacra Rio N ★★★ *Superb Pinot N* from old vines in bio estate in RÍO N, Pat. Brainchild of Piero Incisa della Rocchetta of Sassicaia (*see* Italy) making elegant, collectable wines. Chacra 32 from 1932 plantation is superb. Barda is v.gd second label.

Clos de los Siete Men ★★ Collection of four bodegas in Uco V owned by Bordelais incl Michel Rolland, blended by Rolland into one wine. What's not used for that wine is bottled separately by owner (*see* DIAMANDES, MONTEVIEJO).

Cobos, Viña Men ★★★ →★★★★ One of Argentina's 1st consultants, Paul Hobbs, making his own premium wines in Luján and Uco V. Top CAB SAUV (Volturno, Bramare), v.gd MALBEC, CHARD.

Colomé, Bodega Sal ★★→★★★ Some of world's highest vines, at 3100m (10,171ft); n winery in Calchaquí. Intense MALBEC-based reds, lively TORRONTÉS.

Decero, Finca Men ★★ →★★★ Luján winery, Swiss owners. Precise reds and v.gd PETIT VERDOT.

> **Cab Franc fanatics**
> CAB FR is one of most exciting reds in Argentina today. Plantings may have tripled in a decade to over 900 ha, but there's still relatively little (compared to 40,000 ha of MALBEC), so it goes into premium wines only. Spicy, floral, concentrated, it performs best in Uco V at altitude. Try ALEANNA, CASARENA, CATENA ZAPATA, PULENTA ESTATE, Zaha, ZORZAL.

DiamAndes Men ★★★ Ultra-modern winery in Uco V owned by Bonnie family of Château Malartic-Lagravière (B'x). Rich reds, lively whites. In CLOS DE LOS SIETE neighbourhood.

Dominio del Plata Men ★★ → ★★★★ Best known as Susana Balbo's winery. Queen of Torrontés still makes top whites (incl v.gd blend) but also complex, rich MALBEC and **blends**, CAB SAUV (try Ben Marco, Nosotros).

Doña Paula Men ★★ → ★★★★ Diverse portfolio, consistent in all labels. Excellent single-v'yd MALBECS (try Parcel range), also some of best SAUV BL, RIES in MEN. Owned by Santa Rita (*see* Chile) group.

Etchart Sal ★ → ★★ Leader in Cafayate making emblematic TORRONTÉS and solid high-altitude reds.

Fabre Montmayou Men, Rio N ★★ → ★★★ MEN and RIO N producer, old vines in both. French-owned. Diverse portfolio from both. Gd second label Phebus.

Fin del Mundo, Bodega Del Neu ★ → ★★ Biggest Neu producer covering all bases. Postales is entry level, also gd-value Ventus, Newen. Top is Special Blend; try single-v'yd Fin range (esp CAB FR).

Flichman, Finca Men ★★ → ★★★ In hills overlooking Lunlunta (MAI), but v'yds all over MEN. Dedicado is top terroir red blend, v.gd Paisaje reds and CHARD. Caballero de la Cepa is solid everyday brand.

Fournier, O Men ★★ → ★★★ Spanish investment in Uco V making top TEMPRANILLO in blends and varietals, solid SAUV BL, MALBEC. V.gd Urban Uco entry-level range. *See* Chile.

Kaikén Men ★★ → ★★★ Tucked into Luján making v.gd reds mainly from Vistalba but sometimes further afield. Top MALBEC, CAB SAUV. Owned by Montes (*see* Chile).

La Anita, Finca Men ★★ → ★★★ Traditional Luján with a focus on deep reds. Try Varúa CAB SAUV, gd SYRAH and MALBEC, unusual FRIULANO white.

La Riojana La R ★ → ★★ Argentina's largest co-op with over 500 growers in Famatina Valley. All the classics and gd-value TORRONTÉS. Fairtrade and organic.

Las Moras, Finca San J ★ → ★★ Owned by TRAPICHE. Gd SYRAH, BONARDA across ranges.

Luca / Tikal / Tahuan / Alma Negra / Animal Men ★★ → ★★★ Family of premium labels owned by CATENA children, now adults, Laura (Luca) and Ernesto (T/T/A/A) with a focus on complex red blends, sophisticated PINOT N and top sparkling.

Luigi Bosca Men ★★ → ★★★ Lots to discover in this large Luján winery. Highlights incl Finca Las Nobles complex old-vine reds, Las Compuertas RIES, and La Linda for everyday. Icono is top of range (MALBEC/CAB SAUV).

Manos Negras / Tinto Negro / TeHo / ZaHa Men ★★ → ★★★ Innovative project of many labels focused on Uco V and beyond. V.gd single-vineyard MALBEC, CAB FR.

Marcelo Pelleriti Men ★★ → ★★★ Personal label from MONTEVIEJO winemaker. Uco V MALBEC is stronghold but elegant Abremundos Malbec/CAB FR is worth seeking out. Pelleriti also makes several labels with Argentine rockstars.

Masi Tupungato Men ★★ → ★★★ Italian investment in Uco V combining MALBEC and Veneto heritage with *ripasso*-style Passo Doble Malbec/CORVINA/MERLOT; and Amarone-style *Corbec* (Corvina/Malbec).

Matias Riccitelli Men ★★ → ★★★ Son of one of Argentina's best-known winemakers, Matias Riccitelli makes his own mark with portfolio from MEN and RÍO N. V.gd old-vine SEM, rich MALBEC and fun, young label Hey Malbec.

Mendel Men ★★★ Maipú winery with some v. old vines. Bright SEM, top MALBECS and red blends. Lunta gd value. Roberto de la Motta in charge.

Mendoza Producing the lion's share of Argentine wine, Men province can be split in three: closest to city is historic, and warmer, Maipú; further s is larger Luján, cradle of MALBEC; furthest s, highest and coolest is Uco V (incl Gualtallary, Altamira, La Consulta).

Michel Torino Sal ★★ →★★★ One of largest producers in Cafayate. Gd-value table wine (esp TORRONTÉS) and premium El Esteco brand (v.gd CAB SAUV).

Moët-Hennessy Argentina Men ★→★★ First foreign investment in Argentina brought bubbles to MEN in 50s. Its big business today is Charmat-method party fizz (Chandon), and smaller, traditional-method label Baron B. *See* TERRAZAS DE LOS ANDES.

Monteviejo Men ★★→★★★ Owned by B'x family behind Château Le Gay with winemaker Marcelo Pelleriti. First winery of CLOS DE LOS SIETE. Superb, tiny La Violeta; v.gd Lindaflor ranges.

Neuquén Pat Main region in s Pat concentrated in San Patricio del Chañar. Hearty reds (esp MALBEC, CAB FR) and fruity PINOT N.

Nieto Senetiner, Bodegas Men ★→★★★ Originally founded 1888 in Vistalba, but has outgrown its Luján base with v'yds across MEN today. Diverse portfolio incl range of v.gd single-v'yd reds, fresh SEM. Big in bubbles.

Noemia Pat ★★★→★★★★ Best MALBEC of Pat. Old vines in RÍO N produce elegant, age-worthy wines. Winemaker Hans Vinding-Diers also master of blends.

Norton, Bodega Men ★→★★★ Founded 1895 by British engineer, today owned by Swarovski of crystal fame. Large portfolio of gd-value wines, superb single-v'yd Lot MALBEC, top Gernot Lange blend. Plethora of gd fizz.

Passionate Wine Men ★★→★★★ Matias Michelini is one of S America's most exciting, and experimental, winemakers, championing Uco V. Try Demente (MALBEC/CAB FR), Agua de Roca SAUV BL. Orange wines too.

Peñaflor Men ★→★★★ Ginormous wine group. Owns Finca Las Moras, Andean V'yds (SAN J), MICHEL TORINO (SAL), Santa Ana, TRAPICHE (MEN).

Piatelli Sal ★★ Two wineries and v'yds in Cafayate and Luján. Smart reds and bright TORRONTÉS.

Piedra Negra Men ★→★★★ François Lurton from B'x making v.gd MALBEC in Uco V. Also great white blends (PINOT GR base).

Poesia Men ★★→★★★ French winemakers in Luján making rich reds from old vines of MALBEC, CAB SAUV and SYRAH from Uco V.

Porvenir de Cafayate, El Sal ★★→★★★ Modern wines from Cafayate. Laborum is varietal range, Amauta blends. Best for TORRONTÉS, TANNAT, MALBEC, CAB SAUV.

Pulenta Estate Men ★★ →★★★ Wine dynasty that previously owned Trapiche. Family winery in Luján with v.gd value La Flor range, excellent single-v'yd range of CAB FR and MALBEC.

Renacer Men ★★→★★★ Energetic young team in Luján; winery owned by Chilean family. Solid MALBEC, fresh SAUV BL from Casa in Chile, Amarone-style Enamore.

Riglos Men ★★→★★★ Gd CAB FRANC and CAB SAUV from Uco V producer; solid MALBEC.

How do you date old vines? With difficulty. Vines don't have growth rings like trees.

Río Negro Milder Pat region known for PINOT N. Gd old-vine SEM, RIES, MALBEC, MERLOT.

Ruca Malén Men ★★ Founded at turn of this century, Ruca Malén makes consistently rich reds. V.gd blends and PETIT VERDOT.

Salentein, Bodegas Men ★★ →★★★ One of Uco V's most eyecatching investments. Dutch-owned winery and art gallery. V.gd single-v'yd and Primus range. El Portillo is gd value.

Salta Original high-altitude region of S America, over 2300m (7546ft), only topped by Bolivia. Known for best TORRONTÉS (esp Calchaquí) and rich, concentrated TANNAT and MALBEC.

San Juan Workhorse region next to MEN renowned for rich, ripe SYRAH, BONARDA from the flats. Exciting cooler wines closer to mts.

Malbec: red forever, pink for 50 yrs, sparkling in last decade. Now made as white too.

San Pedro de Yacochuya Sal ★★★ Pioneer of high quality in Cafayate, joint venture with Michel Rolland (*see* France) and ETCHART family. Fragrant TORRONTÉS, dense MALBEC SPY, powerful Yacochuya blend.

Schroeder, Familia Neu ★★ NEU producer with dinosaur fossils in cellar. Gd PINOT N and bubbly.

Sophenia, Finca Men ★★→★★★ Top Uco V producer in Gualtallary. Solid SAUV BL, v.gd MALBEC, BONARDA. Synthesis is top range.

Tapiz Men ★★→★★★ Classic Luján winery working in collaboration with B'x winemaker (ex-Petrus) Jean-Claude Berrouet. Attractive reds (top MERLOT, Black Tears MALBEC).

Terrazas de los Andes Men ★★→★★★★ Fine-wine sister of CHANDON and best-known for single-v'yd MALBEC series and superb *Cheval des Andes* blend made with Cheval Blanc (B'x).

Toso, Pascual Men ★★→★★★ Italian family est winery in MEN in 1880s. Mainly MALBEC focus; top wine Magdalena Toso is superb.

Trapiche Men ★→★★★★ Long history; has passed through many hands. Today part of PEÑAFLOR and one of biggest brands in Argentina with endless portfolio. Try *Medalla* CAB SAUV; Iscay MALBEC/CAB FR blend; single-v'yd Finca range Malbec; Costa & Pampa range from coast.

Trivento Men ★→★★ Argentine outpost of Chile's Concha y Toro. Consistent wines in entry-level range. Eolo MALBEC is pricey flagship.

Val de Flores Men ★★★ Also known as Bodega Rolland. Michel Rolland's Vistaflores venture in CLOS DE LOS SIETE. Concentrated, age-worthy MALBEC. Mariflor (single varieties) ready to drink now. Superb Camille blend.

Viña Alicia Men ★★★ Private venture part-owned by LUIGI BOSCA family. Old-vine wines and interesting blends. Try Tiara (RIES/ALBARIÑO/SAVAGNIN), NEBBIOLO.

Vines of Mendoza / Winemaker's Village Men ★★ Lifestyle hotel and winery in Uco V making hundreds of micro-vinifications for private labels. Also small village of winemakers. Look for: Abremundos (*see* MARCELO PELLERITI), Corazon del Sol, Recuerdo, Super Uco.

Zorzal Men ★★★ Wide portfolio from Gualtallary. V.gd CAB FR, SAUV BL, PINOT N. Eggo range made in cement eggs, no oak.

Zuccardi Men ★★→★★★★ Wine dynasty now run by 3rd-generation Sebastian Zuccardi. Maipú is home to everyday Santa Julia brand, Uco V is home to premium Zuccardi wines. Excellent single-v'yd Alluvional wines, v.gd Emma BONARDA. Cemento is top unoaked MALBEC.

BRAZIL

Forget Copacabana. Brazil's wine country is in the far south, where the hills look more like those of Italy's Piedmont than the Sugar Loaf Mountain. Rio Grande do Sul is home to Brazil's main wine region, Vale dos Vinhedos, which makes good bubbles, Merlot and Chardonnay. There's also a host of Italian and Portuguese varieties, reflecting the mixed European heritage of the region. Other places to look out for in the south include Campanha, Serra do Sudeste, Planalto Catarinense and Campos de Cima de Serra. In the north, tropical Vale do São Francisco is an anomoly with its two harvests a year.

Aurora ★→★★ Brazil's largest co-op with over 1000 growers in Serra Gaucha. Mostly fair-value table wines.

Casa Valduga ★→★★★ Predominantly bubbles (v.gd traditional method) but also a top MERLOT (Storia) from well-known Serra Gaucha producer.

Cave Geisse ★★★ The 1st serious traditional-method producer of sparkling, pioneered by ex-Chandon winemaker Chilean Mario Geisse. Try the Nature.

Lidio Carraro ★→★★ Min-intervention winery making juicy, vibrant reds in Vale dos Vinhedos and Serra do Sudeste. V.gd Quorum blend.

Miolo ★→★★★ Leading premium category, large producer with wineries and v'yds in all major regions. V.gd MERLOT, CHARD, TOURIGA N; top sparkling Millésime.

Pizzato ★→★★★ Passionate producer in Vale dos Vinhedos making one of Brazil's top MERLOTS (DNA 99) and v.gd CHARD, sparkling. Fausto is young range.

Salton ★→★★ Large winery with long history. Youngest gen Gregorio Salton winemaker today. Gd party fizz, v.gd Salton Gerações blend.

URUGUAY

The smallest wine country in South America, but the highest per capita wine consumption (and beef!). Most of what locals drink is simple jug wine and producers export most of the good stuff. Atlantic maritime influence makes it closer to Bordeaux than Chile in style with aromatic whites (especially Albariño) and energetic reds with spine of tannin and acidity. Tannat rules the reds esp in main region Canelones – just outside capital Montevideo.

Alto de la Ballena ★→★★ Pioneer in Punta del Este region; boutique production of v.gd SYRAH, CAB FR and juicy TANNAT/VIOGNIER blend.

Bouza ★★→★★★ Galician family brought ALBARIÑO to Uruguay, now make super whites in Montevideo, Pan de Azucar further up coast. V.gd single-v'yd TANNAT.

Garzón, Bodega ★→★★★ $85 million investment by Argentine billionaire, with Alberto Antonini as consultant. Fresh, energetic wines in Maldonado.

Juanico Establecimiento ★→★★★ Largest producer in Uruguay with a wide portfolio. Gd-value everyday wines (esp SAUV BL, TANNAT) to complex Familia Deicas range with Paul Hobbs as consultant. Excellent Preludio CHARD blend and single-v'yd terroir Tannat collection.

Marichal ★→★★ Family winery in Canelones focused on PINOT N (incl world's 1st blend with TANNAT).

Pisano ★→★★★ Fantastic family producer in Canelones with new generation now taking reins. V.gd TANNAT, TORRONTÉS, VIOGNIER.

Viñedo de los Vientos ★★→★★★ Off-beat winemaker Pablo Fallabrino is wild child of Uruguay. Unique white blends, interesting TANNAT (try *ripasso* method), indulgent dessert wines.

OTHER SOUTH AMERICAN WINES

Bolivia If high altitude is in fashion, Bolivia is haute couture. All v'yds above 1800m (5906ft), some top 3000m (7843ft). Result is racy acidity and most impressive colour esp gd for SYRAH, CAB SAUV, dry MUSCAT. Try Sausini, La Concepción, Campos de Solana, Kohlberg and Kuhlmann (fizz). Unfortunately few of these unique wines make it out of Bolivia, but you might find Singani (local brandy).

Peru The original S American wine country, today more focused on Pisco (local brandy) than wine. Coastal Ica is main wine region, couple of hrs south of Lima. For wine, try Tacama (founded 1540, esp sparkling) Vista Alegre, Intipalka, Quebrada de Ihuanco and Mimo. Rich TANNAT, Ancellota and wines from Pisco grapes best.

Australia

Abbreviations used in the text:

Ad H	Adelaide Hills, SA
Bar V	Barossa Valley, SA
Beech	Beechworth, Vic
Can	Canberra, NSW
Coon	Coonawarra, SA
Fra R	Frankland River, WA
Gra	Grampians, Vic
Hea	Heathcote, Vic
Hunt V	Hunter Valley, NSW
Kang I	Kangaroo Island, SA
Lang C	Langhorne Creek, SA
Mac	Macedon, Vic
N/S Tas	North/South Tasmania
Qld	Queensland
Ruth	Rutherglen, Vic
Marg R	Margaret River, WA
McL V	McLaren Vale, SA
Mor P	Mornington Penninsula, Vic

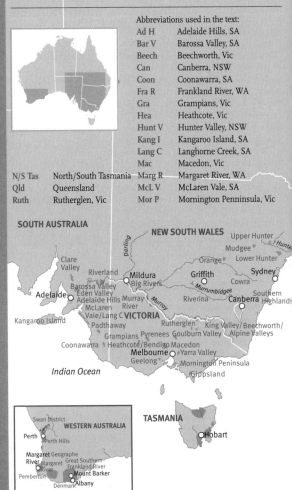

It's hard to find an Australian winemaker nowadays without a pet project. It might be Tempranillo, or Fiano, or Pét-Nat, or cool-climate Shiraz, or natural wine, or Grenache made with an eye to Pinot Noir, or long, complex Chardonnay, or rich, unabashed Shiraz, or a fresher face of Cabernet, or the rabbit hole of Pinot Noir; and so on. The point is that Australian wine is full of niche wines now. Even Riesling – so loved by enthusiasts, so unloved commercially – is slowly being "discovered", with grape prices at the farm-gate on the mouthwatering march. Buoyant is the word. The marketplace has fragmented and so too has the offering. Australian wine is enjoying the sun again. It doesn't hurt of course that Australian wine exports to China are soaring. Enthusiasm runs high when the wine is flying out the door. In 2017 Australian wine exports to its key markets, the UK and the US, both slipped (marginally) but its exports to China climbed a remarkable 63 per cent by value, 15 per cent by volume. Shiraz and traditional red varieties are the drivers but when Chinese buyers discover and embrace Australian white wine, which its food culture would suggest it eventually will, then it will be on for young and old, and the Australian wine landscape will never be the same again.

Recent vintages

New South Wales (NSW)

2017 Hot summer followed a wet spring; whites lapped it up; reds too, in general.
2016 Challengingly wet in the Hunter but good/excellent everywhere else.
2015 Difficult in most parts, but Orange, Canberra excellent; Hilltops very good.
2014 Hunter Shiraz will be exceptional. Canberra Ries, Shiraz right up there.
2013 Rich reds, whites. Hunter Sem and Canberra Ries especially good.
2012 Wet, cold. Sem may be okay, perhaps Cab Sauv, generally disappointing.

Victoria (Vic)

2017 One for the ages. A great year all around.
2016 Dry but otherwise average year. No disasters but no raves either.
2015 Strong year across the board.
2014 Frost damage galore but very good red vintage for most.
2013 Wet winter followed by a hot, dry summer. Quality surprisingly high.
2012 Turning out better than first expected. Red/white very good to exceptional.

South Australia (SA)

2017 Biggest issue was yield, which was high; quality should be above average.
2016 Hopes are high that this is a special vintage for both reds and whites.
2015 Warm regions coped well with a summer of wild temp swings.
2014 Hot, low-yield year has produced generous whites, reds.
2013 Water a problem so yields generally well down. Streaky vintage.
2012 Yields down but a brilliant year. Great for Ries; excellent Cab Sauv.

Western Australia (WA)

2017 Anxious vintage, cool and at times wet, but looks promising, especially aromatic varieties.
2016 Humid, sultry vintage but ultimately a good one.
2015 Challenging, mixed results; pays to be selective, but gems will be found.
2014 The luck continues; almost getting monotonous. Another tiptop year.
2013 Cab Sauv, Chard very strong. Some rain but, again, gods were kind.
2012 Drought continued, so too the run of beautiful, warm/hot vintages.

Accolade Wines r w Name for wines/wineries previously under the once-mighty CONSTELLATION, HARDYS groups. The master of the false dawn, though wine quality is generally v.gd.

Adelaide Hills SA Cool 450m (1476ft) sites in Mt Lofty ranges. CHARD, SAUV BL, SHIRAZ outgun PINOT N. ASHTON HILLS, HENSCHKE, HAHNDORF HILL, MIKE PRESS, JERICHO, MURDOCH HILL, SHAW & SMITH, TAPANAPPA all in excellent form.

Adelina Clare V, SA r w Reds (SHIRAZ, GRENACHE, MATARO, NEBBIOLO) are the stars. Imposing and intense, but polished. Whites (RIES) are no slouches but when you make reds like this...

Alkoomi Mt Barker, WA r w (RIES) 05' 10' 13' 17 (CAB SAUV) 04' 10' 12' 13' 14 Veteran maker of fine Ries; rustic reds; more accessible young than previously.

All Saints Estate Ruth, Vic br ★ Great fortifieds, past and present. Hearty table wines.

Alpine Valleys Vic In valleys of Victorian Alps. Best: BILLY BUTTON, MAYFORD, Ringer Reef. TEMPRANILLO the star, though aromatic whites have come out swinging.

Andevine Hun V, NSW r w ★ Shot from blocks with initial SHIRAZ, SEM, CHARD releases from mature HUNTER v'yds; 2nd-album blues since; now back on form.

Andrew Thomas Hun V, NSW r w ★★ Alpha producer. Old-vine SEM; silken SHIRAZ. Reds particularly gutsy in HUNTER context.

Angove's SA r w (br) ★★ MURRAY V family business. Cheapies (r w) often the stand-outs of a broad range, Mainstream face of organic grape-growing.

Annie's Lane Clare V, SA r w Part of TWE. Boldly flavoured wines. Flagship Copper Trail (can be) excellent, esp RIES, SHIRAZ. Has fallen off a cliff in terms of prominence.

Arenberg, d' McL V, SA r w (br) (sw) (sp) ★★ Sumptuous SHIRAZ, GRENACHE. Many varieties, wacky labels (incl The Cenosilicaphobic Cat SAGRANTINO). The Elton John of Oz wineries, fancy shirts and all. Often at best at value end.

A.Rodda Beech, Vic r w ★★ Bright CHARD from est v'yds; whole-bunch-fermented TEMPRANILLO grown at high altitude is routinely a beauty.

Ashton Hills Ad H, SA r w (sp) ★★★ (PINOT N) 05' 10' 1'2 13' 15 Totemic AD H producer. Compelling Pinot N from 30-yr-old+ v'yds. Bought in 2015 by WIRRA WIRRA.

Bailey's NE Vic r w br ★★ Rich SHIRAZ, magnificent dessert MUSCAT (★★★★) and TOPAQUE. V'yds all organic. Sold by TWE to CASELLA in 2017.

Balgownie Estate Bendigo, Vic, Yarra V, Vic r ★ Capable of medium-bodied, well-balanced, minty CAB of elegance, finesse and character from its BENDIGO heartland. Separate YARRA V arm.

Balnaves of Coonawarra SA r w ★★★ Family-owned COON champion. Lusty CHARD; v.gd spicy, medium-bodied SHIRAZ, full-bodied Tally CAB SAUV flagship. New "joven-style" Cab gd.

Bannockburn Vic r w ★★★ (CHARD) 10' 12' 14' 15 (PINOT N) 08' 10' 12' 14 Intense, complex Chard, spice-shot Pinot N. Put GEELONG region on map.

Barossa Valley SA Ground zero of Aussie red wine. V.-old-vine SHIRAZ, MOURVÈDRE, CAB SAUV, GRENACHE. Can produce bold, black, beautiful reds with its eyes closed,

---

Natural runs wild

If there's a new trend, Australian wine is on it. The combination of a relative lack of rules and regulations in the great southern land and the wide range of climates, soils and varieties mean that there's barely a windmill that can't be tilted at. Pét-Nat, natural wine and orange wine (much to distaste of Orange wine region of NSW) have all taken such robust foothold in the Australian wine scene that they've invigorated it as a whole. Producers Blind Corner, Brave New Wines, Cobaw Ridge, Frederick Stevenson, Gentle Folk, Jauma, KALLESKE, Latta, Lucy M, Patrick Sullivan, RAVENSWORTH, Shobbrook, Si Vintners, The Wine Farm, TORBRECK, TRIPE.ISCARIOT are just a fraction of the wide band of producers either wholly or partly involved in what is an incredibly dynamic natural wine scene. Concrete and/or clay eggs and/or amphora are commonplace in Australian wineries now, and can pop up in the most unlikely places. Inner-city bar scene of nation's capital cities is main driver and target market but ripple effect is significant.

and has done for just about ever. The best bits are known, but often blended (eg. GRANGE). New guard chasing fresher, (slightly) lighter styles.

Bass Phillip Gippsland, Vic r ★★★★ (PINOT N) 10' 12' 14' 15 Ultimate soloist. Tiny amounts of variable but mostly exceptional Pinot N. Gives idiosyncrasy a gd name. In top form.

Bay of Fires N Tas r w sp ★★★ ACCOLADE empire's TAS outpost. Stylish table wines and Arras *super-cuvée sparkling(s)*. PINOT N shouldn't be passed over. Oz's top sparkling house.

Beechworth Vic The rock-strewn highlands of ne Vic. Tough country. CHARD, SHIRAZ best-performing varieties. NEBBIOLO rising from the (winter) fog. CASTAGNA, DOMENICA, FIGHTING GULLY ROAD, GIACONDA, SAVATERRE, Schmölzer & Brown, SORRENBERG essential producers.

Bendigo Vic Hot central Vic region. BALGOWNIE ESTATE the stalwart. Home of rich SHIRAZ, CAB SAUV.

Best's Great Western Gra, Vic r w ★★★ (SHIRAZ) 05' 10' 11' 12' 13' 14' 15 Shiraz master; *v.gd mid-weight reds*. Thomson Family Shiraz from 120-yr-old vines superb. Sparkling Shiraz worth tracking down.

Billy Button Alpine V, Vic r w So many wines, such small quantities. Everything from SHIRAZ and CHARD to VERDUZZO, VERMENTINO, SCHIOPPETTINO, SAPERAVI. Every wine balanced on a pinhead.

Bindi Mac, Vic r w ★★★★ (PINOT N) 04' 06' 10' 12' 13' 15 Ultra-fastidious maker of outstanding, long-lived Pinot N (esp), CHARD. Tiny production.

Bortoli, De Griffith, NSW, Yarra V, Vic r w (br) dr sw ★★→★★★ (Noble SEM) Both irrigation-area winery and leading YARRA V producer. Excellent cool-climate PINOT N, SHIRAZ, CHARD, SAUV BL and gd sweet, botrytized, Sauternes-style Noble Sem. YARRA V arm is where interest lies.

Brash Higgins McL V, SA ★★★ Brad Hickey is a smart cookie. He has degrees in English and botany but has also worked as a brewer, baker, sommelier and now maker of radical expressions of MCL V (r w). You'd reckon he knows a thing or two about yeast. Has fast become a star of region.

Bremerton Lang C, SA r w ★★ Silken CAB, SHIRAZ with mounds of flavour.

Brokenwood Hun V, NSW r w ★★ (ILR Res SEM) 03' 05' 06' 09' 11 (Graveyard SHIRAZ) 00' 06' 09' 13'. Outside of the *Cricket Pitch* Sem/SAUV BL can be hard to find value, but quality generally gd.

Brown Brothers King V, Vic r w br dr sw sp ★ Wide range of crowd-pleasing styles, varieties. General emphasis on sweetness.

By Farr / Farr Rising Vic r w ★★★★ 10' 12' 13' 14 15' 16 (PINOT N) Superb producer, at Bannockburn. CHARD, Pinot N can be minor masterpieces.

Campbells Ruth, Vic (w) br ★★ Smooth ripe reds (esp Bobbie Burns SHIRAZ); extraordinary Merchant Prince Rare MUSCAT, Isabella Rare TOPAQUE (★★★★).

Canberra District NSW Both quality, quantity rising; site selection important; cool climate. CLONAKILLA best known. New guns: COLLECTOR WINES, EDEN ROAD and RAVENSWORTH.

Cape Mentelle Marg R, WA r w ★★★ (CAB SAUV) 01' 10' 11' 12' 13' 14' 15 Pioneer in excellent form. Robust Cab has become more elegant (with lower alc), CHARD v.gd; also ZIN, v. popular SAUV BL/SEM. Owned by LVMH Veuve Clicquot.

Casella Riverina, NSW r w ★ Casella's Yellow Tail range of budget reds/whites have helped build an Australian wine empire. Now owner of BAILEY'S, Brand's of Coonawarra, MORRIS , PETER LEHMANN.

Castagna Beech, Vic r w ★★★ (SYRAH) 05' 06' 08' 10' 12' 14 Julian C leads Oz bio brigade. Estate-grown SHIRAZ/VIOGNIER, SANGIOVESE/Shiraz excellent.

Chambers Rosewood NE Vic (r) (w) br ★★★ Viewed with MORRIS as greatest maker of sticky TOPAQUE, *Muscat*.

Chapel Hill McL V, SA r (w) ★★ Leading MCL V producer. SHIRAZ, CAB the bread and butter but TEMPRANILLO and esp GRENACHE on rise.

Charles Melton Bar V, SA r w (sp) ★ Tiny winery with bold, ripe, traditional reds, esp Nine Popes, an old-vine GRENACHE/SHIRAZ blend.

Chatto Tas r ★★★★ Jim C's (MOUNT PLEASANT winemaker) secret TAS assignment. Tiny producer makes PINOT N of fruit, spice and all things nice. Ultra savoury. Ultra gd.

Clarendon Hills McL V, SA r ★★ Full-Monty reds (high alc, intense fruit) from grapes grown on hills above MCL V. Cigar wines.

Clare Valley SA Small, pretty, high-quality area 161 km (100 miles) n of Adelaide. Best toured by bike, some say. Australia's most prominent RIES region. Gumleaf-scented SHIRAZ; earthen, tannic CAB SAUV. GROSSET, KILIKANOON, KIRRIHILL, MOUNT HORROCKS, TIM ADAMS, WENDOUREE lead way.

Clonakilla Can, NSW r w ★★★★ (SHIRAZ) 05' 06' **07' 09'** 10' 13' 14' 15' 16 *Deserved leader of the Shiraz/Viognier brigade.* RIES, VIOGNIER excellent. CANBERRA region superstar. Varietal SYRAH may well be best of lot.

Clos du Tertre Fra R w Stunning RIES. Textural, intense, layered, long. Ries fanatics.

Clyde Park Vic r w ★★ Broody single-v'yd CHARD, PINOT N in stellar form. SHIRAZ turning heads.

Coldstream Hills Yarra, Vic r w (sp) ★★★★ (CHARD) 10' 11' 12' **13' 14'** 15' (PINOT N) 06' 10' 12' 13' 14' 15' Est 1985 by critic James Halliday. Delicious PINOT N to drink young, *Res to age.* Excellent Chard (esp Res). Head-turning *single-v'yd releases.* Part of TWE.

Collector Wines Can, NSW r ★ 07' 09' 12' 13' Res SHIRAZ is the one. Layered, spicy, perfumed, complex.

D'Arenberg's new visitor centre is shaped like a cube, of the Rubik variety, unsolved.

Coonawarra SA Most s v'yds of state: home to some of Australia's best (value, quality) CAB SAUV; land of richest red soil (on limestone). WYNNS is senior, and champion, resident. BALNAVES, KATNOOK, LINDEMANS, MAJELLA, RYMILL, YALUMBA all key.

Coriole McL V, SA r w ★★★ (Lloyd Res SHIRAZ) 98' 02' **04'** 10' 12' 13' 14 To watch, esp for SANGIOVESE and old-vine Shiraz Lloyd Res. Interesting Italians: FIANO, SAGRANTINO, NERO D'AVOLA. Heart and soul producer.

Craiglee Mac, Vic r w ★★★ (SHIRAZ) 00' 08' 10' 12' 13' 14 Salt-of-the-earth producer. Northern Rhône inspired. Fragrant, peppery Shiraz, age-worthy CHARD.

Crawford River Hea, Vic w ★★★ Outstanding RIES producer. Cool, cold, scintillating (dry) style, great for seafood, highly age-worthy.

Cullen Wines Marg R, WA r w ★★★★ (CHARD) 09' 10' 11' 12' **13'** 14' 15' 16 (CAB SAUV/ MERLOT) 04' 05' **09'** 11 12' 13' 14' 15 Second-generation star Vanya Cullen makes substantial but subtle SEM/SAUV BL, outstanding Chard, elegant, sinewy Cab/ Merlot. Bio in all she does. Extreme quality, forever inching higher.

Curly Flat Mac, Vic r w ★★★ (PINOT N) 10' 11' 12' 13' 14' 15 Robust but perfumed Pinot N on two price/quality levels. Full-flavoured CHARD. Both age-worthy. Departure of founding winemaker Phil Moraghan a blow.

David Franz Bar V, SA r w SEM from 100+-yr-old vines, a rose made with 108 different varieties (yes 108), old-vine CAB SAUV, experimental VERMENTINO, pristine CHARD. You name it, they're playing with it here. Hit and miss, but when it hits...

Deakin Estate Vic r w ★ V.-low-alc MOSCATO. Spicy SHIRAZ, CAB SAUV. Keeps delivering value hits.

Devil's Lair Marg R, WA r w ★ Opulent CHARD, CAB SAUV/MERLOT. Fifth Leg gd second label. Owned by TWE.

Domaine A S Tas r w ★★ Swiss owners/winemakers Peter and Ruth Althaus are perfectionists; v.gd oak-matured SAUV BL. Polarizing cool-climate CAB SAUV. Let's say charismatic.

Domaine Chandon Yarra V, Vic r (w) sp ★★ Cool-climate sparkling and table wine. Owned by Moët & Chandon (*see* France). Known in UK as Green Point. NV cuvées in best ever shape.

Domenica Beech, Vic ★★★ Flashy new BEECH producer with est v'yds. Exuberant, spicy SHIRAZ. Textural MARSANNE.

Eden Road r w ★★ Elegant SHIRAZ, CHARD, CAB SAUV from Hilltops, TUMBARUMBA, CANBERRA DISTRICT regions.

Eden Valley SA Hilly region home to Chris Ringland, HENSCHKE, PEWSEY VALE, Radford, TORZI MATTHEWS and others; racy RIES, (perfumed, bright) SHIRAZ, CAB SAUV of top quality.

Elderton Bar V, SA r w (br) (sp) ★★ Old vines; rich, oaked CAB SAUV, SHIRAZ. All bases covered. Some organics/bio. Rich reds in excellent form.

Eldorado Road Ruth, Vic r Paul Dahlenburg has a day job (Bailey's winemaker) but his home pet project is a beauty. DURIF, SHIRAZ and NERO D'AVOLA show that elegance and power are not mutually exclusive.

Eldridge Estate Mor P, Vic r w ★★★ Winemaker David Lloyd is a fastidious experimenter. PINOT N, CHARD worth the fuss. Varietal GAMAY really quite special.

Epis Mac, Vic r w ★ (PINOT N) Long-lived Pinot N; elegant CHARD. Cold climate. Powerful at release; complexity takes time.

Evans & Tate Marg R, WA r w ★★ Owned by MCWILLIAM'S since 2007. Quality better since. SHIRAZ, CAB SAUV, CHARD. Value mostly but more aspirational wines gd.

Faber Vineyards Swan V, WA r ★★★ (Res SHIRAZ) 07' 09' 11' 12' 13' 14 John Griffiths is a guru of WA winemaking. Home estate redefines what's possible for SWAN V Shiraz.

Fighting Gully Road Beech, Vic r w ★ Touchstone producer of the BEECH region. CHARD, AGLIANICO, TEMPRANILLO kicking goals.

Flametree Marg R, WA r w ★★ Exceptional CAB SAUV; spicy, seductive SHIRAZ; occasionally compelling CHARD.

Fraser Gallop Estate Marg R, WA r w ★★ Concentrated CAB SAUV, CHARD, (wooded) SEM/SAUV BL. On cusp of top tier.

Freycinet Tas r w (sp) ★★★ (PINOT N) 10' 11' 12' 13' 15 Pioneer family winery on TAS's e coast producing dense Pinot N, gd CHARD, excellent Radenti sparkling.

Garagiste Mor P, Vic r w ★★★ CHARD and PINOT N of both intensity and finesse. Quality is super-reliable across board but really pulls out some pearlers.

Geelong Vic Region w of Melbourne. Cool, dry climate. Best names: BANNOCKBURN, Bellarine Estate, BY FARR, LETHBRIDGE, Provenance.

Gemtree Vineyards McL V, SA r (w) ★★ Warm-hearted SHIRAZ alongside TEMPRANILLO and other exotica, linked by black bio. Largely bio.

Giaconda Beech, Vic r w ★★★★ (CHARD) 08' 10' 11' 12' 13' 14' 15 (SHIRAZ) 08' 10' 13' 14 In the mid-80s Rick Kinzbrunner walked up a steep, dry, rock-strewn hill and came down a winemaking legend. In the process he kickstarted BEECH region. Australian Chard royalty. Tiny production of powerhouse wines.

Giant Steps Yarra V, Vic r w ★★★ Top single-v'yd CHARD, PINOT N. Vintages 12' 13' 14' 15' (and 17) all exciting for both main varieties. Innocent Bystander brand sold to BROWN BROTHERS.

Glaetzer-Dixon Tas r w ★★★ Nick Glaetzer turned his family history on its head by setting up camp in cool TAS. Euro-style RIES, Rhôney SHIRAZ, meaty PINOT N. Different in gd way. Reaches for stars.

Glaetzer Wines Bar V, SA r ★★ Big, polished reds with eye-catching packaging to match. V.-ripe old-vine SHIRAZ led by iconic Amon-Ra.

Goulburn Valley Vic Temperate region in mid-Vic. Full-bodied, earthy table wines. MARSANNE, CAB SAUV, SHIRAZ the pick, MITCHELTON, TAHBILK perpetual flagbearers. Aka Nagambie Lakes.

Grampians Vic Temperate region in nw Vic previously known as Great Western. High-quality spicy SHIRAZ, sparkling Shiraz. Home to SEPPELT (for now), BEST'S, MOUNT LANGI, The Story.

Granite Belt Qld High-altitude, (relatively) cool, improbable region just n of Qld/NSW border. Spicy SHIRAZ, rich SEM, eg. Boireann, Golden Grove.

Grant Burge Bar V, SA r w (br) (sw) (sp) ★ Smooth reds, whites from best grapes of Burge's large v'yd holdings. Acquired by ACCOLADE in 2015.

Great Southern WA Remote cool area in s of WA; Albany, Denmark, Frankland River, Mount Barker, Porongurup are official subregions. First-class RIES, SHIRAZ, CAB SAUV. Style, value here.

Grosset Clare V, SA r w ★★★★ (RIES) 05' 10' 12' 13' 15' 16' 17 (Gaia) 04' 05' 12' 13' 14 Fastidious winemaker. Foremost Oz Ries, lovely CHARD, v.gd *Gaia* CAB SAUV/MERLOT. Beetrooty PINOT N.

Hahndorf Hill Ad H, SA r w ★★ Much experimentation, wonder across wide range of varieties, but makes fascinating fist of GRÜNER V, and has made variety its own in Oz.

Hardys r w (sw) sp ★★★ (Eileen CHARD) 06' 10' 12' 13' 15 (Eileen SHIRAZ) 04' 06' 10' 12' 13' Historic company now part of ACCOLADE. Chard excellent. Shiraz not far off.

Heathcote Vic The region's 500-million-yr-old Cambrian soil has great potential for high-quality reds esp SHIRAZ. It's slowly being realized.

Henschke Eden V, SA r w ★★★★ (SHIRAZ) 96' 04' 06' 09' 12 (CAB SAUV) 90' 96' 02' 04' 06' 09' 10' Pre-eminent 150-yr-old family business known for delectable Hill of Grace (Shiraz), v.gd Cab Sauv, red blends, gd whites and truly scary prices.

Hentley Farm Bar V, SA r w ★★ Consistently produces SHIRAZ of immense power and concentration – wall-of-flavour territory – though importantly in a (generally) fresh, almost frisky, context.

Hewitson SE Aus r (w) ★★ (*Old Garden Mourvèdre*) 06' 09' 10' 12' 13' 14 Dean Hewitson sources parcels off the "oldest MOURVÈDRE vines on the planet". V.gd SHIRAZ at various price levels.

Houghton Swan V, WA r w ★★★ (Jack Mann) 08' 11' 12' 13' 14' 15 Once-legendary winery of Swan Valley nr Perth. Part of ACCOLADE. Inexpensive white blend once considered *a national classic*. V.gd CAB SAUV, SHIRAZ, etc. sourced from GREAT SOUTHERN, MARG R. Jack Mann Cab blend is seriously gd.

Howard Park WA r w ★★★ (RIES) 11' 12' 13' 14' 15' 16' (CAB SAUV) 01' 05' 09' 10' 11' 12' 13' Scented Ries, CHARD; earthy Cab. Second label *MadFish* v.gd value. PINOT N improving.

Hunter Valley NSW It makes no sense but it works. Sub-tropical coal-mining area 160-km (100-miles) n of Sydney. Mid-weight, earthy SHIRAZ, gentle SEM can live for 30 yrs. Arguably most terroir-driven styles of Oz. MOUNT PLEASANT, *Tyrrell's* (esp) the pillars.

Inkwell McL V, SA r (w) ★★ High polish, high opinion, high character. Full house of intriguing wines, mostly SHIRAZ-based.

Jacob's Creek Bar V, SA r w (br) (sw) sp ★ Owned by Pernod Ricard. Almost

---

Nouveau Gamay

Varietal GAMAY may rank low on the identity charts, though of course Beaujolais does not. A small band of Australian producers have tinkered with Gamay over the past decade or two, ELDRIDGE ESTATE and SORRENBERG most notably, though a broader movement may be about to erupt. BASS PHILLIP, De Bortoli, Farr Rising, Marq, OCHOTA BARRELS, Pfeiffer, Punt Road, TYRRELL'S all make interesting Gamay – when they can get hold of enough grapes. You heard it here first. The canary is moving in the mine of Oz Gamay.

totally focused on various tiers of uninspiring-but-reliable Jacob's Creek wines, covering all varieties, prices. New red range aged in whisky barrels; say no more.

Jasper Hill Hea, Vic r w ★★ (SHIRAZ) 04' 06' 10' 13' Emily's Paddock Shiraz/CAB FR blend, Georgia's Paddock Shiraz from dry-land estate are intense, burly, long-lived and bio.

Jericho Ad H, SA, McL V, SA r w ★★ Excellent fruit selection and skilled/considered winemaking combine to produce a suite of thoroughly modern, tasty wines esp SHIRAZ and TEMPRANILLO.

Jim Barry Clare V, SA r w ★★ Great v'yds provide v.gd RIES, McCrae Wood SHIRAZ and richly robed, pricey, oaked-to-the-devil The Armagh Shiraz.

John Duval Wines Bar V, SA r ★★★ John Duval – former maker of PENFOLDS Grange – makes *delicious Rhôney reds* of great intensity, character.

Kalleske r ★★ Old family farm at Greenock, nw corner of BAROSSA, makes rather special single-v'yd SHIRAZ among many other (intensely flavoured) things.

Kate Hill Tas r w Complex PINOT N from tiny plots but rise, complete with a whisper of sweetness, is stunningly intense and arresting in quality.

Katnook Estate Coon, SA r w (sw) (sp) ★★★ (Odyssey CAB SAUV) 00' 04' 05' 10' Pricey icons Odyssey, Prodigy SHIRAZ. Concentrated fruit, and too much oak.

Kilikanoon Clare V, SA r w ★★★ RIES, SHIRAZ excellent performers. Luscious, generous, beautifully made. Sold to Chinese investment group in 2017.

King Valley Vic Altitude between 155–860m (509–2821ft) has massive impact on varieties, styles. Over 20 brands headed quality-wise by BROWN BROTHERS, Chrismont, Dal Zotto and esp PIZZINI.

Kirrihill Clare V, SA r w ★★ V.gd CAB SAUV, SHIRAZ, RIES at, often, excellent prices. Affordable way to stock mid-term cellar.

Knappstein Wines Clare V, SA r w ★★ Reliable RIES, SHIRAZ, CAB SAUV. Sold by LION NATHAN to ACCOLADE in 2016. Addition of medium-bodied, perfumed Shiraz/MALBEC and skin-contact Ries adds much-needed charm/energy to range.

Kooyong Mor P, Vic r w ★★★ PINOT N, *superb Chard* of harmony, structure. PINOT GR of charm. High-quality single-v'yd wines.

Lake Breeze Lang C, SA r (w) ★★ Succulently smooth, gutsy, value SHIRAZ, CAB SAUV; has mid-level wines thoroughly licked.

Lake's Folly Hun V, NSW r w ★★ (CHARD) 09' 13' 14' (CAB SAUV) 05' 13' 14' Founded by surgeon Max Lake, pioneer of HUNTER V Cab Sauv. Chard often better than Cab Sauv blend. Variable but can be excellent.

Langmeil Bar V, SA r w ★★ Owns some of the world's oldest SHIRAZ vines (planted mid-1800s), plus other old v'yds, employed to produce full-throttle Shiraz, GRENACHE and CAB SAUV.

Larry Cherubino Wines Fra R, WA r w ★★★ Intense SAUV BL, RIES, *spicy Shiraz*, polished CAB SAUV. Ambitious label now franking its early promise in full.

Leasingham Clare V, SA r w ★ Once-important brand now a husk of its former self. Owned by ACCOLADE.

Leeuwin Estate Marg R, WA r w ★★★★ (CHARD) 06' 08' 10' 12' 13' 14' Iconic producer. All about Chard. Full-bodied, age-worthy Art Series rendition. SAUV BL, RIES less brilliant. *Cab Sauv* can be v.gd.

Leo Buring Bar V, SA w ★★ 02' 05' 13' 14' Part of TWE. Exclusively RIES; Leonay top label, *ages superbly*. Maybe a step behind where it once was.

Lethbridge Vic r w ★★★ Small, stylish producer of CHARD, SHIRAZ, PINOT N, RIES. Forever experimenting. Cool climate but wines have ample meat on their bones.

Limestone Coast Zone SA Important zone, incl Bordertown, COON, Mt Benson, Mt Gambier, PADTHAWAY, Robe, WRATTONBULLY.

Lindemans r w ★ Owned by TWE. Low-price Bin range now main focus, far cry from former glory. Lindemans' COON Trio reds still okay.

Lion Nathan Brewery. Sold its Oz wine holdings (KNAPPSTEIN, PETALUMA, ST HALLETT, STONIER, Tatachilla) to ACCOLADE in 2016.

Luke Lambert Yarra V, Vic ★★ Hip young producer of stylish (cool climate, mostly) SHIRAZ, PINOT N and NEBBIOLO.

Macedon and Sunbury Vic Adjacent regions: Macedon higher elevation, Sunbury nr Melbourne airport. Quality from BINDI, CRAIGLEE, CURLY FLAT, EPIS, Granite Hills, Hanging Rock.

Mac Forbes Yarra V, Vic ★★★ Myriad (in both number and styles) single-v'yd releases, mainly PINOT N, CHARD, RIES. Fast becoming one of the real movers and shakers of the YARRA V.

McHenry Hohnen Marg R, WA ★★ Among the best producers of MARG R CHARD, and on the rise too.

McLaren Vale SA Beloved maritime region on s outskirts of Adelaide. Big-flavoured reds in general but BRASH HIGGINS, CHAPEL HILL, CORIOLE, GEMTREE, INKWELL, SC PANNELL, WIRRA WIRRA and growing number of others show elegance as well as flavour. SHIRAZ the hero but varietal GRENACHE the big quality mover.

McWilliam's SE Aus r w (br) (sw) ★★ Family-owned. EVANS & TATE, Hanwood, MOUNT PLEASANT key pillars.

Main Ridge Estate Mor P, Vic r w ★★ Rich, age-worthy CHARD, PINOT N. Founder Nat White is legend of MOR P wine; hard to imagine place without him. Changed hands in 2015.

Majella Coon, SA r (w) ★★ As reliable as the day is long. Opulent SHIRAZ, CAB SAUV. Essence of modern COON.

Penfolds new NV red, G3, blends three vintages of Grange. Costs more than buying the three separately.

Margaret River WA Temperate coastal area s of Perth. Powerful CHARD, structured CAB SAUV, spicy SHIRAZ. Try CULLEN, DEVIL'S LAIR, FRASER GALLOP, LEEUWIN ESTATE, MOSS WOOD, VOYAGER ESTATE and many others. Great touring (and surfing) region.

Marius McL V, SA r ★★★ Varietal SHIRAZ and blends of dramatic concentration. Quality in inverse proportion to fuss; latter kept to a min.

Mayford Vic r w ★★ Tiny v'yd in private, hidden valley. Put ALPINE VALLEYS region on map. SHIRAZ, CHARD, exciting spice-shot TEMPRANILLO.

Meerea Park Hun V, NSW r w ★ Brothers Garth and Rhys Eather create age-worthy SEM, SHIRAZ often as single-v'yd expressions.

Mike Press Wines Ad H, SA r (w) ★★ Tiny production, tiny pricing. CAB SAUV, SHIRAZ, CHARD, SAUV BL. Crowd favourite of bargain hunters.

Mitchelton Goulburn V, Vic r w (sw) ★★ Stalwart producer of CAB SAUV, SHIRAZ, RIES, plus speciality of *Marsanne*, ROUSSANNE. Top spot to vist; fancy new hotel set among those fab river red gums.

Mitolo r ★ Quality SHIRAZ, CAB SAUV. Heroic style.

Montalto Mor P, Vic r w ★★★ For some yrs was a nice restaurant, gallery. Recently, wine quality skyrocketed. Firmly "must try" of MOR P region.

Moorilla Estate Tas r w (sp) ★★ Pioneer nr Hobart on Derwent River. Gd CHARD, RIES; PINOT N. V.gd restaurant, extraordinary art gallery.

Moorooduc Estate Mor P, Vic r w ★★★ Long-term producer of stylish, sophisticated CHARD, PINOT N. Just a bit special.

Moppity Vineyards Hilltops, NSW r w ★★ Stern, tannic SHIRAZ/VIOGNIER, CAB SAUV (Hilltops). Elegant CHARD (TUMBARUMBA). Quality ambitions but best known as a value producer.

Mornington Peninsula Vic Coastal area 25 miles se of Melbourne. Quality boutique wineries abound. Cool, windy climate. PINOT N, CHARD, PINOT GR. Wine/surf/beach/food playground.

Morris NE Vic (r) (w) br ★★★ RUTH producer of Oz's greatest dessert *Muscats*, TOPAQUES. Owned by CASELLA.

Moss Wood Marg R, WA r w ★★★ (CAB SAUV) 01' 04' 05' 12' 13' 14 MARG R's most opulent (red) wines. SEM, CHARD, super-smooth *Cab Sauv*. Oak-and-fruit-rich.

Mount Horrocks Clare V, SA r w ★★ Fine dry RIES, sweet Cordon Cut Ries. SHIRAZ, CAB SAUV in fine form.

Mount Langi Ghiran Gra, Vic r w ★★★★ (SHIRAZ) 04' 08' 09' 10' 12' 13' 14' 15 Rich, peppery, *Rhône-like Shiraz*. Excellent Cliff Edge Shiraz. Special patch of dirt. Special run of form.

Mount Mary Yarra V, Vic r w ★★★★ (PINOT N) 05' 10' 12' 13' 14' 15 (Quintet) 00' 04' 10' 12' 13' 14' 15 Late Dr. Middleton made tiny amounts of suave CHARD, vivid Pinot N, elegant CAB SAUV blend. All age impeccably. Remarkably, post-Dr. era is improvement, if anything.

Mount Pleasant Hun V, NSW ★★★★ Old HUNTER producer owned by MCWILLIAM'S, now re-invigorated. NB single-v'yd SEMS (esp Lovedale), SHIRAZ.

Mudgee NSW Region nw of Sydney. Earthy reds, fine SEM, full CHARD. Gd quality but needs a hero.

Murdoch Hill Ad H, SA r w ★ Stunningly peppery PINOT N; SYRAH. Just keeps on producing hits.

Murray Valley SA Vast irrigated v'yds. Key figure in climate-change discussions.

Ngeringa Ad H, SA r w ★★ Perfumed PINOT N and NEBBIOLO. Rhône style SHIRAZ. Savoury rosé. Bio.

Ochota Barrels Bar V, SA r w ★★ Quixotic producer making hay with (mostly) old-vine GRENACHE, SHIRAZ from MCL V, BAROSSA.

O'Leary Walker Clare V, SA r w ★★ Low profile but excellent quality. CLARE V RIES, CAB SAUV standout. MCL V SHIRAZ oak-heavy but gd.

Orange NSW Cool-climate, high-elevation region. Lively SHIRAZ (when ripe) but best suited to (intense) aromatic whites and CHARD.

Out of Step Yarra V, Vic r w ★★★ Took on YARRA V SAUV BL and won. Now doing likewise with CHARD, PINOT N and NEBBIOLO from various v'yds. Only the brave.

Padthaway SA V.gd SHIRAZ, CAB SAUV. Soil salinity ongoing issue.

Paringa Estate Mor P, Vic r (w) ★★★ Maker of irresistible PINOT N and SHIRAZ. Fleshy, fruity and flashy styles.

Passing Clouds Bendigo, Vic ★★ Pioneer of modern era of Vic wine though off radar for many yrs. Burst back in 2016 with a gloriously elegant, textured release of its signature CAB blend and has continued gd form since.

Paxton McL V, SA r ★★ One of Australia's most prominent organic/bio grower/producers. Ripe but elegant SHIRAZ, GRENACHE.

Pemberton WA Region between MARG R and GREAT SOUTHERN; initial enthusiasm for PINOT N replaced by RIES, CHARD, SHIRAZ.

Penfolds r w (br) ★★★★ (Grange) 55' 60' 62' 63' 66' 71' 76' 86' 90' 96' 98' 99' 02' 04' 05' 06' 08' 10' 12' 13 (CAB SAUV Bin 707) 91' 96' 98' 02' 04' 06' 10' 12' 14' 15 and of course *St Henri*, "simple" SHIRAZ. Originally Adelaide, now SA. Oz's best warm-climate red wine company. *Yattarna* CHARD, Bin Chard now right up there with reds.

Petaluma Ad H, SA r w sp ★★ (RIES) 02' 11' 12'' 13' 16 (CHARD) 12' (CAB SAUV COON) 04' 05' 08' 12' Seems to miss ex-owner/creator Brian Croser. Gd, but low-key now.

Peter Lehmann Wines Bar V, SA r w (br) (sw) (sp) ★★ Well-priced wines incl easy RIES. Luxurious/sexy Stonewell SHIRAZ among many others (r w). Peter died 2013; company sold 2014 to CASELLA (Yellow Tail).

Pewsey Vale Ad H, SA w ★★ V.gd RIES, standard and (aged-release) The Contours, grown on lovely tiered v'yd.

Pierro Marg R, WA r w ★★ (CHARD) 12′ 13′ **14′** 15′ 16 Producer of expensive, tangy SEM/SAUV BL and full-throttle Chard.

Pipers Brook Tas r w sp ★★ (RIES) 09′ 13′ (CHARD) 13′ Cool area pioneer; gd Ries, *restrained Chard and sparkling* from Tamar Valley. Second label: Ninth Island. Owned by Belgian Kreglinger family.

Pizzini King V, Vic r ★★ (SANGIOVESE) 13′ 14′ 15 A leader of Italian varieties in Oz, esp NEBBIOLO, SANGIOVESE (recently stepped up a gear). Dominant KING VALLEY producer.

Primo Estate SA r w dr (sw) ★★ Joe Grilli's many successes incl rich MCL V SHIRAZ, tangy COLOMBARD, potent Joseph CAB SAUV/MERLOT.

Punch Yarra V, Vic r w ★★★ Lance family ran Diamond Valley for decades. When they sold, they retained the close-planted PINOT N v'yd. It can grow detailed, decisive, age-worthy wines.

Pyrenees Central Vic region making rich, often minty reds. Blue Pyrenees, Dalwhinnie, Dog Rock, Mount Avoca, TALTARNI leading players.

Ravensworth Can, NSW r w ★★ Suddenly in hot demand for various wine experiments. SANGIOVESE is best-known but there's a buzz over skin-contact whites and GAMAY Noir.

Riverina NSW Large-volume irrigated zone centred on Griffith.

Robert Oatley Wines Mudgee, NSW r w ★★ Ambitious venture of ROSEMOUNT ESTATE creator Robert Oatley. Quality/price ratio usually well-aligned.

Rockford Bar V, SA r (w) sp ★★ Sourced from various old, low-yielding v'yds; reds best; also iconic sparkling Black SHIRAZ.

Rosemount Estate r w ★ Periodically loses its way but reds can be gd.

Ruggabellus Bar V, SA r ★★ Causing a stir. Funkier, more savoury version of BAROSSA. Old oak, min sulphur, wild yeast, whole bunches/stems. Blends of CINSAULT, GRENACHE, MATARO, SHIRAZ.

Rutherglen & Glenrowan Vic Two of four regions in warm ne Vic zone, justly famous for sturdy reds, magnificent fortified dessert wines.

Rymill Coon, SA r ★★ Well-est. Ever-reliable but has shifted CAB SAUV quality up a gear of late.

St Hallett Bar V, SA r w ★★★ (Old Block) 02′ **04′ 06′ 08′** 12′ 13′ Old Block SHIRAZ the star; rest of range is smooth, sound, stylish. ACCOLADE-owned.

Saltram Bar V, SA r w ★ Value Mamre Brook (SHIRAZ, CAB SAUV) and (rarely sighted) No 1 Shiraz are leaders. One of TWE's many "where are they now?" brands.

Samuel's Gorge McL V, SA r ★★ Justin McNamee makes (at times) stunning GRENACHE, SHIRAZ, TEMPRANILLO of character and place.

Savaterre Beech, Vic r w ★★★ (PINOT N) **04′ 06′ 10′** 12′ 13′ Excellent producer of full-bodied CHARD, meaty Pinot N, close-planted SHIRAZ.

Scarborough Hun V, NSW ★ Just to prove the baby hasn't been thrown out with the bathwater. Yellow Label CHARD is old-school rich in fruit and oak, done well.

SC Pannell McL V, SA r ★★★ Excellent (spicy, whole-bunch-fermented) SHIRAZ (often labelled SYRAH) and (esp) GRENACHE-based wines. NEBBIOLO to watch. Meticulous.

Seppelt Gra, Vic r w br sp ★★★ (St Peter's SHIRAZ) 02′ **04′ 08′ 10′** 12′ 13′ 14′ Historic name owned by TWE. Impressive CHARD, RIES, (esp) peppery Shiraz. Brand remains as a husk; winery shut down.

Oldest extant v'yd in NSW is 1.1 ha planted 1867, owned by Tyrrell's.

Seppeltsfield Bar V, SA r br ★★ National Trust Heritage Winery bought by KILIKANOON in 2007. Fortified wine stocks back to 1878.

Serrat Yarra V, Vic r w ★★★ Micro-v'yd of noted winemaker Tom Carson (YABBY LAKE) and wife Nadege. Complex, powerful, precise SHIRAZ/VIOGNIER, PINOT N, CHARD.

Seville Estate Yarra V, Vic r w ★★★ (SHIRAZ) **05′ 06′ 10′** 13′ 14′ 15 Excellent CHARD, spicy Shiraz, delicate PINOT N. YARRA V pioneer still showing 'em how it's done.

> **The thrill of Tasmania**
> If fine wine and the thrill of the chase go hand-in-hand for you, then train your glasses on Tassie. There's been a buzz about Tassie wine for roughly 30 yrs but it has only been in the past handful that a swag of tiny producers has achieved high-class PINOT N. We're into exciting territory. Est names like BAY OF FIRES, FREYCINET, Meadowbank, MOORILLA, PIPERS BROOK, STEFANO LUBIANA have been joined and/or surpassed by CHATTO, Dr Edge, GLAETZER-DIXON, Holyman, Hughes & Hughes, Lisdillon, Pooley, Sailor Seeks Horse, Small Island, Stargazer, TOLPUDDLE, Two Tonne Tasmania and others. Many of these wines are only a barrel or two, but hooley dooley, are they gd!

Shadowfax Vic r w ★★ More than just a tourist adjunct to the historic Werribee Park. V.gd CHARD, PINOT N, SHIRAZ. Never a bad wine.

Shaw & Smith Ad H, SA r w ★★★ Savvy outfit, black turtlenecks and all. Crisp and *harmonious* SAUV BL, complex M3 CHARD and – surpassing them both – *Shiraz*. PINOT N slowly improving.

Simao & Co Ruth, Vic r w ★★ Young Simon Killeen, of STANTON & KILLEEN family, released an undeniably scrumptious TEMPRANILLO in 2015. New range but rich in story, personality, interest.

Sorrenberg Beech, Vic r w ★★★ No fuss but highest of quality. SAUV BL/SEM, CHARD, (Australia's best) GAMAY, B'x blend. Every egg a bird. One of great "in the know" wineries of Oz.

Southern NSW Zone NSW Incl CANBERRA, Gundagai, Hilltops, TUMBARUMBA. Savoury SHIRAZ; lengthy CHARD.

Spinifex Bar V, SA r w ★★★ Bespoke BAROSSA producer. Complex SHIRAZ, GRENACHE blends. Routinely turns out rich-but-polished reds.

Stanton & Killeen Ruth, Vic (r) ★ Fortified vintage the main attraction.

Stefano Lubiana S Tas r w sp ★★★ Beautiful v'yds on the banks of Derwent River, 20 mins from Hobart. Excellent PINOT N, sparkling, MERLOT, CHARD. Homely but driven and ambitious.

Stella Bella Marg R, WA r w ★★★ Humdinger wines. CAB SAUV, SEM/SAUV BL, CHARD, SHIRAZ, SANGIOVESE/Cab Sauv. Sturdy, characterful.

Stoney Rise Tas r w ★★★ Joe Holyman was wicketkeeper for TAS; holds 1st-class record for highest number of catches on debut; now looks after all winemaking tasks for his outstanding PINOT N, CHARD.

Stonier Wines Mor P, Vic r w ★★ (CHARD) 12' 13' 15 (PINOT N) 06' 12' 13' 15' Consistently gd. Res notable for elegance. PINOT N in fine form. Myriad single-v'yd releases now.

Sunbury Vic *See* MACEDON and SUNBURY.

Swan Valley WA Located 20 mins n of Perth. Birthplace of wine in the w. Hot climate makes strong, low-acid wines. FABER VINEYARDS leads way.

Tahbilk Goulburn V, Vic r w ★★★ (MARSANNE) 06' 08' 13' 14' 16 (SHIRAZ) 04' 06' 10' 12' Historic Purbrick family estate: long-ageing reds, also some of Oz's best old-vine *Marsanne*. Res CAB SAUV can be outstanding. Rare 1860 Vines Shiraz. For lovers of rustic.

Taltarni Pyrenees, Vic r w sp ★★ SHIRAZ, CAB SAUV in best shape in yrs. Long-haul wines but jackhammer no longer required to remove tannin from your gums. Crowbar still helps.

Tamar Ridge N Tas r w (sp) Big fish in the small TAS pond. Owned by BROWN BROTHERS. Value and volume come before quality on the agenda.

Tapanappa SA r ★★★ WRATTONBULLY collaboration between Brian Croser, Bollinger, J-M Cazes of Pauillac. Splendid CAB SAUV blend, SHIRAZ, MERLOT, CHARD. Surprising *Pinot N* from Fleurieu Peninsula.

AUSTRALIA

Tar & Roses Hea, Vic r w ★★ SHIRAZ, TEMPRANILLO, SANGIOVESE of impeccable polish, presentation. Modern success story. Passing of co-founder Don Lewis in 2017 a great loss.

Tarrawarra Estate Yarra V, Vic r w ★★ (Res CHARD) 10' 12' 13' 15 (Res PINOT N) 04' 06' 10' **12**' 13' 15 Moved from hefty, idiosyncratic to elegant, long. Res generally a big step up on standard.

Tasmania Cold island region with hot reputation. Outstanding sparkling, PINOT N, RIES. V.gd CHARD, SAUV BL, PINOT GR. Future looks bright.

Taylors Wines Clare V, SA r w ★ Large-scale production led by RIES, SHIRAZ, CAB SAUV. Exports under Wakefield Wines brand.

Ten Minutes by Tractor Mor P, Vic r w ★★★ Wacky name, smart packaging, even better wines. *Chard, Pinot N both excellent* and will age. Style meets substance.

Teusner Bar V, SA r ★★ Old vines, clever winemaking, pure fruit flavours. Leads a BAROSSA V trend towards "more wood, no good".

Thousand Candles Yarra V, Vic r w ★★ A couple of missteps but this grand v'yd estate has PINOT N and SHIRAZ humming. One to watch.

Tim Adams Clare V, SA r w ★★ Ever-reliable (in a gd way) RIES, CAB SAUV/MALBEC blend, SHIRAZ and (full-bodied) TEMPRANILLO.

Tolpuddle Tas ★★★ SHAW & SMITH bought this outstanding 1988-planted v'yd in TAS's Coal River Valley in 2011. Scintillating PINOT N, CHARD in lean, lengthy style.

Topaque Vic Replacement name for iconic RUTH sticky "Tokay", thanks to EU. Still provokes a double-take.

Torbreck Bar V, SA r (w) ★★★ Dedicated to (often old-vine) Rhône varieties led by SHIRAZ, GRENACHE. Ultimate expression of rich, sweet, high-alc style. Quality has cruised through internal ructions unaffected.

Torzi Matthews Eden V, SA r ★★ Aromatic, stylish, big-hearted SHIRAZ. Value RIES. Incredible consistency yr-on-yr.

Tripe.Iscariot Marg R, WA r w ★★ Hard to spell, easy to drink. Complex whites/reds by its own design. Impossible to pigeonhole.

Tumbarumba Cool-climate NSW region tucked into the Australian Alps. Sites 500–800m. CHARD the star. PINOT N a long way behind, and unlikely ever to catch up.

Turkey Flat Bar V, SA r p ★★★ Top producer of bright-coloured rosé, GRENACHE, SHIRAZ from core of 150-yr-old v'yd. Controlled alc and oak. New single-v'yd wines. Old but modern. Winner of coveted Jimmy Watson Trophy in 2016 with, remarkably, its Grenache.

TWE (Treasury Wine Estates) Aussie wine behemoth. Dozens of well-known brands: COLDSTREAM HILLS, DEVIL'S LAIR, LINDEMANS, PENFOLDS, ROSEMOUNT, SALTRAM, WOLF BLASS, WYNNS among them.

Two Hands Bar V, SA r ★★★ Big reds and many of them, though here's the thing; they've finally turned the volume down a fraction and the glory of the fruit seems all the clearer/louder.

Rise and rise of Grenache: one took Jimmy Watson Trophy 2016 for 1st time, most coveted Oz prize.

Tyrrell's Hun V, NSW r w ★★★★ (SEM) 10' 11' 13' 14' 15' 16' 17 (Vat 47 CHARD) 10' 12' 13' 14' 15' 16 Oz's greatest maker of Sem, Vat 1 now joined with series of individual v'yd or subregional wines. *Vat 47*, Oz's 1st Chard, continues to defy climatic odds. Outstanding old-vine 4 Acres SHIRAZ, Vat 9 Shiraz. One of true greats.

Vasse Felix Marg R, WA r w ★★★ (CHARD) 10' 13' 15' 16 (CAB SAUV) 08' 09' 10' 11' 12' 13' With CULLEN, pioneer of MARG R. Elegant Cab Sauv for mid-weight balance. Complex/funkified Chard. Returning to estate-grown roots.

Voyager Estate Marg R, WA r w ★★ Big volume of (mostly) estate-grown, rich, powerful SEM, SAUV BL, (esp) CHARD and CAB SAUV/MERLOT.

> Do you really want to drink this?
> The Rootstock Festival in Sydney – dedicated to all things "natural" and
> organic – took previous yr's spit buckets (you read correctly) and had
> them distilled. The resultant limited, er, release spirit was bottled under
> Kissing A Stranger label. For real.

Wantirna Estate Yarra V, Vic r w ★★★ Regional pioneer showing no sign of slowing down. CHARD, PINOT N, B'x blend all in excellent form. Small on quantity, big on quality.

Wendouree Clare V, SA r ★★★★ Treasured maker (tiny quantities) of powerful, tannic, concentrated reds, based on CAB SAUV, MALBEC, MATARO, SHIRAZ. Recently moved to screwcap; the word "longevity" best defined with a picture of a Wendouree red. Beg, borrow or steal.

West Cape Howe Denmark, WA r w ★ Affordable, flavoursome reds the speciality.

Westend Estate Riverina, NSW r w ★★ Thriving family producer of **tasty bargains** esp Private Bin SHIRAZ/Durif. Recent cool-climate additions gd value.

Willow Creek Mor P, Vic r w ★★ Gd gear. Impressive producer of CHARD, PINOT N in particular. Power and poise.

Wirra Wirra McL V, SA r w (sw) (sp) ★★ (RSW SHIRAZ) 04' 05' 10' 12' (Angelus CAB SAUV) 05' 10' 12' 13' High-quality, concentrated wines in flashy livery. The Angelus Cab Sauv named Dead Ringer outside Australia.

Wolf Blass Bar V, SA r w (br) (sw) (sp) ★★ (Black Label CAB SAUV blend) 04' 05' 10' 12' 13 Owned by TWE. Not the shouty player it once was but still churns through an enormous volume of clean, inoffensive wines.

Woodlands Marg R, WA r ★★★ 7 ha of 40-yr-old+ CAB SAUV among top v'yds in region; younger but v.gd plantings of other B'x reds. Reds of brooding impact.

Wrattonbully SA Important grape-growing region in LIMESTONE COAST ZONE; profile lifted by activity of TAPANAPPA, Terre à Terre, Peppertree.

Wynns Coon, SA r w ★★★★ (SHIRAZ) 06' 10' 12' 13' 14' 15 (CAB SAUV) 91' 98' 00' 04' 05' 06' 10' 12' 13' 14' 15 TWE-owned COON classic. RIES, CHARD, Shiraz, *Cab Sauv* all v.gd esp Black Label Cab Sauv (15' release is one for the ages), *John Riddoch Cab Sauv*. Recent single-v'yd releases the icing.

Yabby Lake Mor P, Vic r w ★★★ CHARD, PINOT N, SHIRAZ all generally/routinely tiptop.

Yalumba Bar V, SA, SA r w sp ★★★ 168 yrs young, family-owned. *Full spectrum of high-quality wines*, from budget to elite single v'yd. Entry level Y Series v.gd value.

Yangarra Estate McL V, SA r w ★★★★ Conventional in some ways, inventive in others. Whatever it takes to make great wine. You get the full box and dice here, across most price points.

Yarraloch Yarra V, Vic r w ★★★ CHARD can be "to die for". Capable of exceptional PINOT N too.

Yarra Valley Vic Historic area just ne of Melbourne. Growing emphasis on v. successful CHARD, PINOT N, SHIRAZ, sparkling. Understated, elegant CAB SAUV.

Yarra Yering Yarra V, Vic r w ★★★ (Dry Reds) 00' 04' 05' 06' 10' 12' 15' YARRA V pioneer. Powerful PINOT N; deep, herby CAB SAUV (Dry Red No 1); SHIRAZ (Dry Red No 2). Luscious, daring flavours (r w).

Yellow Tail NSW *See* CASELLA.

Yeringberg Yarra V, Vic r w ★★★★ (MARSANNE/ROUSSANNE) 06' 09' 12' 13' 14 (CAB SAUV) 00' 04' 05' 06' 10' 12' 13' 14 Historic estate still in hands of founding (1862) Swiss family, the de Purys. Extremely small quantities of v.-high-quality CHARD, Marsanne, Roussanne, Cab Sauv, PINOT N.

Yering Station / Yarrabank Yarra V, Vic r w sp ★★★ On site of Vic's 1st v'yd; replanted after 80-yr gap. Snazzy table wines (Res CHARD, PINOT N, SHIRAZ, VIOGNIER); Yarrabank (sparkling wines in joint venture with Champagne Devaux).

AUSTRALIA

New Zealand

Abbreviations used
in the text:

Auck	Auckland
B of P	Bay of Plenty
Cant	Canterbury
N/C Ot	North/Central Otago
Gis	Gisborne
Hawk	Hawke's Bay
Hend	Henderson
Marl	Marlborough
Mart	Martinborough
Nel	Nelson
Waih	Waiheke Island
Waip	Waipara Valley
Wair	Wairarapa

We're buying more than ever of New Zealand's pungent Sauvignon Blanc; far more than we do of its fragrant, supple, often distinguished Pinot Noir. Albariño is carving out a niche, while rosé production is soaring, in both volume and quality. But there is a whiff of consolidation in the air. Kiwis are drinking fractionally less wine than five years ago, and the ranks of the country's wineries have started to thin, with small, family-owned vineyards established in the 90s being snapped up by giant, often overseas-based, companies. With increasingly mature vines and winemakers – many have now been in place for 20 years – new quality heights are being scaled, but there's a niggle about bulk wine exports, which account for almost 40 per cent of Marlborough's output, and which are not regarded as helping either quality or image. On a positive note, a long-postponed Geographical Indications Act (GI) finally came into force in 2017, guaranteeing that the names of regions (such as Auckland) and subregions (such as Waiheke Island) are reserved exclusively for wines from the stated area. New Zealand is the last significant wine-producing country to adopt a GI system. We'll see if it spurs its growers on to even greater heights.

Recent vintages

2017 A challenging vintage, with most growers battling rain before harvest. Quality-focused growers with light crops picked earlier and fared best. Central Otago more successful.

2016 Ripe, tropical fruit-flavoured Marlborough Sauv Bl. In Hawke's Bay, excellent Chard but autumn rain hit Merlot.

2015 Aromatic, vibrant Marlborough Sauv Bl. Fragrant, charming, rather than powerful, reds in Hawke's Bay.

2014 Hawke's Bay: weighty, ripe, well-rounded Chard and reds. Marlborough: those who picked early fared best.

Akarua C Ot r (p) (w) (sp) ★★★ Thriving producer of consistently outstanding Bannockburn PINOT N 16'; drink-young Rua (briefly oak-aged) 16. Stylish, creamy CHARD; off-dry RIES; full-bodied PINOT GR. Lively fizz esp complex Vintage Brut 11.

Allan Scott Marl (r) (p) w (sp) ★★ Family firm. Gently sweet RIES 17; tropical SAUV BL. Upper-tier: Generations range. Elegant, gently yeasty fizz Cecilia Brut NV.

Alpha Domus Hawk r w ★★ Family winery in Bridge Pa Triangle. Elegant The Skybolt CHARD 16; peachy VIOGNIER. Concentrated B'x-style reds esp MERLOT-based The Navigator 14 and AD CAB SAUV The Aviator 13', 15'. Generous Barnstormer SYRAH 16. The Pilot: drink young. AD is top range.

Amisfield C Ot r (p) (w) ★★→★★★★ Smooth PINOT GR 16; tense RIES (dry and medium-sweet); tangy, slightly oaked SAUV BL 16; classy Pinot Rosé, floral PINOT N 14' (RKV Res is Rolls-Royce model 13'). Lake Hayes is label to drink young.

Ara Marl r (p) w ★★ Huge v'yd in Waihopai Valley, sold 2016 to Indevin. Ara brand bought by GIESEN, now used on estate-grown, multisite blends.

Astrolabe Marl (r) w ★★ Classy wines from Simon Waghorn (ex-WHITEHAVEN). Punchy SAUV BL 17; Gd dry PINOT GR 16; dry and medium-dry RIES; peachy CHARD; crisp ALBARIÑO; lively dry rosé. Terrific dry CHENIN BL 16'. Powerful PINOT N 15'.

Ata Rangi Marl r (p) (w) ★★★→★★★★★ Highly respected family affair. PINOT N 10' 11 12 13' 14' 15' is one of NZ's greatest (1st vines 1980). Delicious younger-vine Crimson Pinot N 16. Notable Craighall CHARD 13' 14' 15' 16 (planted 1983); full-bodied, off-dry Lismore PINOT GR.

Auckland Largest city (n, warm, cloudy) in NZ with 1.1 per cent of v'yd area. Nearby wine districts: Hend, Kumeu/Huapai/Waimauku (both long est); newer (since 80s): Matakana, Clevedon, WAIH (island v'yds, v. popular with tourists). Savoury B'x blends in dry seasons 10' 13' 14', bold SYRAH 13' 14' is fast-expanding, rivals HAWK for quality; underrated CHARD 13'; promising ALBARIÑO.

Auntsfield Marl r w ★★→★★★ Consistently gd wines from site of region's 1st (1873) v'yd (replanted 1999). Intense, partly barrel-fermented SAUV BL 17'; fleshy CHARD esp single-block Cob Cottage 14'; sturdy PINOT N 13' 14'.

Awatere Valley Marl Key subregion (pronounced *Awa-terry*), with v. few wineries but huge v'yd area (more than HAWK), pioneered in 1986 by VAVASOUR. YEALANDS is a key producer. Slightly cooler/drier than WAIRAU VALLEY, with racy SAUV BL (rated higher by UK than US critics); vibrant RIES, PINOT GR; slightly herbal PINOT N.

Babich Hend r w ★★→★★★ Biggish family firm (1916). HAWK, MARL v'yds; wineries in AUCK and MARL. Age-worthy Irongate wines, from GIMBLETT GRAVELS: CHARD 13' 14' 15 and B'x-like Irongate CAB/MERLOT/CAB FR 10' 13' 14' 15. Passion-fruit/lime Marl SAUV BL biggest seller. Top red: refined The Patriarch (B'x-style) 13' 14' 15'.

Blackenbrook Nel r w ★★ Small winery with impressive aromatic whites esp Alsace-style GEWURZ 16 17; PINOT GR 16 17 and off-dry MUSCAT. Punchy, dry SAUV BL; generous CHARD 16; bold Family Res PINOT N 15. Second label: St Jacques.

Black Estate Cant r w ★★ Small Waip producer with old vines. Tight Home CHARD 16; honeyed Damsteep RIES 15; graceful PINOT N esp Damsteep 15'.

Borthwick Wair r w ★★ V'yd at Gladstone with Paddy Borthwick brand (mostly exported). Lively SAUV BL; rich, dryish RIES; toasty CHARD 16'; fleshy PINOT GR; perfumed, supple PINOT N 16'.

Brancott Estate Marl r (p) w ★★→★★★ Major brand of PERNOD RICARD NZ that replaced Montana worldwide. Top wines: Letter Series eg. fleshy "B" Brancott SAUV BL 16'; rich "O" CHARD 15; classy "T" PINOT N 15' 16. Huge-selling, value Sauv Bl 16' 17. Terroir Series: mid-tier, subregional wines. Living Land: organic. Flight: plain, low alc. Chosen Rows: v. classy Sauv Bl 13'.

Brightwater Nel (r) w ★★ Impressive whites esp weighty SAUV BL 16; medium-dry RIES 15'; gently oaked CHARD; sweetish PINOT GR 16. V. charming PINOT N 14 15. Top: Lord Rutherford (incl fleshy Sauv Bl 16).

Canterbury NZ's 5th-largest wine region; most v'yds in relatively warm n WAIP district. Greatest success with aromatic RIES (since mid-80s) and rich PINOT N. Emerging strength in Alsace-style PINOT GR. SAUV BL is heavily planted but often a minor component in other regions' wines.

Carrick C Ot r w ★★★ Bannockburn winery with organic focus. Classy RIES (dry 16', medium 16', sweetish Josephine 16'); elegant CHARD 16 esp EBM 15; partly oak-aged PINOT GR 16'; PINOT N 15, built to last. Delicious, drink-young Unravelled Pinot N 16. Top Excelsior Pinot N 13', v. fragrant, silky.

Central Otago (r) 13' 14 16 17 (w) 13' 14 16 17 Cool, sunny, high-altitude, low-rainfall inland region (now NZ's 3rd largest) in s of South Island, with many little producers. Most vines in Cromwell Basin. Crisp RIES, PINOT GR; fast-growing interest in tight-knit CHARD; famous PINOT N (over 75 per cent v'yd area) is buoyantly fruity, with drink-young charm; older vines yielding more savoury wines. V.gd Pinot N rosé and traditional-method sparkling.

Chard Farm C Ot r w ★★ Pioneer winery; fleshy, dry PINOT N 15'; tangy RIES 16'; mid-weight PINOT N (River Run: floral, single-v'yd The Tiger and The Viper more complex 14). Smooth Rabbit Ranch Pinot N. Mata-Au Pinot N is sweet-fruited, signature red 15.

Church Road Hawk r (p) w →★★★ PERNOD RICARD NZ winery with historic HAWK roots. Rich, barrel-aged CHARD 16; partly oak-aged SAUV BL 16'; Alsace-style PINOT GR 16; MERLOT/CAB SAUV 15 (all great value). Impressive Grand Res wines. McDonald Series, between standard and Grand Res ranges, offers quality, value (incl SYRAH 15', Cab Sauv 14', Merlot 14). Prestige TOM selection incl dense Merlot/Cab Sauv 14'; Chard 14' (on grand scale); v. fragrant, robust Syrah 14'.

Winemaker understatement: "challenging" 17 = two cyclones, torrential April rain.

Churton Marl r w ★★ Elevated Waihopai Valley site; weighty, bone-dry SAUV BL 16; ageable, oak-aged Best End Sauv Bl 15; creamy VIOGNIER 15; harmonious PINOT N 15 (esp The Abyss: oldest vines, greater depth 13'). Sweet PETIT MANSENG 16'.

Clearview Hawk r (p) w ★★→★★★ Coastal v'yd at Te Awanga (also drawing grapes from inland) renowned for hedonistic, oaky Res CHARD 15' 16 (Beachhead Chard is excellent junior version 15' 16); rich Enigma (MERLOT-based 15'), Old Olive Block (CAB SAUV/MALBEC/CAB FR blend 14' 15).

Clos Henri Marl r w ★★ →★★★ Founded 2001 by Henri Bourgeois of Sancerre. Weighty SAUV BL from stony soils, one of NZ's best 15'; sturdy PINOT N (on clay) 13. Second label: Bel Echo (reverses variety/soil match). Third label Petit Clos, from young vines. Distinctive, satisfying wines, priced right.

Cloudy Bay Marl r w sp ★★★ Large-volume but still classy SAUV BL (weighty, dry, some barrel-ageing since 2010) is NZ's most famous wine (17), CHARD (complex 15), PINOT N (supple 14' 15) are classy too. Also Pelorus NV sparkling. Te Koko (oak-aged Sauv Bl 14) has personality. More involvement in C OT for Te Wahi Pinot N (fleshy 14' 15'). Owned by LVMH.

Constellation New Zealand Auck r (p) w ★→★★ Largest producer of NZ wine, previously Nobilo Wine Group, now owned by Constellation Brands. Strong in US market. Strength mainly in solid, moderately priced wines (esp SAUV BL) under KIM CRAWFORD, Monkey Bay, NOBILO and SELAKS (incl Founders HAWK Chard 16', Founders MARLB Sauv Bl 16') brands.

Cooper's Creek Auck r w ★★ →★★★ Innovative medium-sized producer with gd value from four regions, incl flavoury home-v'yd MONTEPULCIANO 15' Excellent high-flavoured Swamp Res HAWK CHARD 16; gd SAUV BL, RIES; MERLOT; top-value VIOGNIER; easy-drinking PINOT N; rich SYRAH. SV (Select V'yd) range is mid-tier. NZ's 1st: ARNEIS (06), GRÜNER V (08), ALBARIÑO (11), MARSANNE (13).

Craggy Range Hawk r (p) w ★★★ →★★★★ High-profile winery with top restaurant and large v'yds in HAWK, MART. Stylish CHARD 15', PINOT N 13'; fleshy PINOT GR 15'; excellent mid-range MERLOT 14' and SYRAH 14' from GIMBLETT GRAVELS; dense Sophia (Merlot) 14' 15'; show-stopping Syrah Le Sol 14' 15'; savoury Aroha (Pinot N) 14' 15'.

Delegat Auck r w ★★ Large listed company (two million cases/yr++), still controlled by Delegat family. Owns v'yds (2000 ha) in HAWK, MARL; three wineries (incl AUCK). Hugely successful OYSTER BAY brand esp SAUV BL 17, MERLOT 16, excellent, new dry ROSÉ 17. Delegat range: citrus CHARD; full Sauv Bl; vibrant MERLOT; savoury PINOT N. (Also owns Barossa Valley Estates).

Delta Marl ★★→★★★ Partnership of winemaker Matt Thomson and UK importer David Gleave. Graceful PINOT N esp Hatters Hill (15'); weighty SAUV BL 16'.

Destiny Bay Waih r ★★→★★★ Expatriate Americans make v. classy, high-priced (but cheaper to Patron Club members) B'x-style reds, brambly and silky. Flagship is Magna Praemia 10' 13' (mostly CAB SAUV). Destinae: for earlier drinking 10' 13'.

Deutz Auck sp ★★★ Champagne house gives name to refined, great-value fizz from MARL by PERNOD RICARD NZ. V. popular Brut NV has min 2 yrs on lees, incl res wines). Much-awarded Blanc de Blancs is vivacious, piercing (14'). Crisp Rosé NV; Iharmonious Prestige (disgorged after 3 yrs), mostly CHARD 15'.

Dog Point Marl r w ★★★ Grower Ivan Sutherland and winemaker James Healy make incisive oak-aged SAUV BL (Section 94) 15'; CHARD (v. elegant, ageable) 15'; complex PINOT N 13' 14', 15, all among region's finest. Larger-volume, but v.gd unoaked Sauv Bl 16' (organic from 2017).

Dry River Mart r w ★★★ Small pioneer winery, now US-owned. Reputation for elegant, long-lived whites: savoury CHARD 13' 14 15 16'; intense RIES 13' 14' 15' 16'; sturdy PINOT GR (NZ's 1st outstanding Pinot Gr 14' 15' 16'); heady GEWURZ 16'; late-harvest whites; dense PINOT N 13' 14' 15'.

Elephant Hill Hawk r (p) w ★★→★★★ Stylish winery/restaurant on coast at Te Awanga, also draws grapes from inland. Rich CHARD 15'; crisp SAUV BL; bold MERLOT/MALBEC 14' 15; generous SYRAH 14' 15. Outstanding Res range. Top pair: Airavata Syrah (powerful 13'); Hieronymus (dense, flowing, blended red 13').

Escarpment Mart r (w) ★★★ Pioneer winemaker Larry McKenna known for savoury, dense PINOT N. Top label: Kupe. Single-v'yd, old-vine reds are esp gd. MART Pinot N is regional blend. Lower-tier: The Edge.

Esk Valley Hawk r p w ★★→★★★★ Owned by VILLA MARIA. Acclaimed MERLOT-based reds (esp Winemakers Res blend 13' 14'); excellent, mid-priced Merlot/CAB/MALBEC 14' 15 16. Supple SYRAH (Res 13' 14'). Lovely Merlot Rosé 16; barrel-fermented CHARD is superb value 15'; full-bodied dry VERDELHO 17. Striking flagship red Heipipi The Terraces: spicy, single-v'yd blend, Malbec/Merlot/CAB FR 09' 13' 14' 15'.

Fairbourne Marl ★★ NZ's only SAUV BL specialist. Tight, bone-dry wines (16'), hand-picked and partly barrel-fermented, from single v'yd on s side of WAIRAU VALLEY.

Felton Road C Ot r w ★★★★ Star winery at Bannockburn, famous for PINOT N, but RIES, CHARD notably classy too. Bold yet graceful Pinot N Block 3 (13' 14' 15' 16') and more powerful Block 5 (13' 14' 15') from The Elms V'yd; intense Ries (dr s/sw) outstanding 16'; long-lived Chard (esp Block 2 13' 14' 15'); key label is Bannockburn Pinot N 13' 14' 15, 16', blended from four v'yds. Other v. fine single-v'yd Pinot N: Cornish Point 13' 14' 15' 16' Calvert 13' 14' 15'.

Forrest Marl r (p) w ★★ Mid-size winery. Runaway success The Doctors' MARL SAUV BL, low-alc style (9.5%): delicate flavours, vague sweetness, tangy acidity. Wide range of attractive, value Marl whites; floral rosé 17; v.gd-value, silky PINOT N 15' 16'.

Framingham Marl (r) w ★★→★★★★ Owned by Sogrape (*see* Portugal). Strength in aromatic whites: intense RIES (esp organic Classic 15') from mature vines. Perfumed PINOT GR 16', GEWURZ. Vibrant, creamy CHARD 16'. Subtle SAUV BL; lush Noble Ries; silky PINOT N 15. Rare F Series wines (incl Old-Vine Ries and brilliant botrytized sweet whites), full of personality.

> **Foley's empire**
> How large will Bill Foley's NZ wine empire grow? Foley (73), an
> entrepreneurial US billionaire who built his fortune in title insurance,
> says his goal is to "bring financial discipline to the wine industry". He
> owns numerous wineries in California and Washington State. Since
> acquiring several MARL brands (Clifford Bay, Dashwood, Goldwater, GROVE
> MILL, VAVASOUR) in 2009, Foley has added two long-est MART producers,
> MARTINBOROUGH V'YD and TE KAIRANGA, and last yr acquired MT DIFFICULTY,
> high-profile C OT producer for c.$NZ55 million.

Fromm Marl r w ★★★ Swiss-owned. Distinguished PINOT N esp organic, hill-grown Clayvin V'yd 13' 14 15'. Fromm V'yd, sturdier, firmer (15'). V. stylish Clayvin CHARD 13', RIES Dry. Earlier-drinking La Strada range incl rich Pinot N 15'; tangy SAUV BL 16; fleshy, oak-aged PINOT GR 16'; excellent rosé 16'.

Gibbston Valley C Ot r (p) w ★★→★★★ Pioneer with original v'yd at Gibbston. Most v'yds now at Bendigo. Strong name for PINOT N esp smooth GV Collection regional blend 15' 16', Res 15' 16'. Silky Le Maitre 14' 15' 16', mostly from 1st vines planted in 80s. Racy, medium-dry GV RIES 17', full GV PINOT GR 17', classy CHARD (esp China Terrace 15 16). Gold River Pinot N: drink-young charm 16'.

Giesen Cant (r) w ★★ Large family winery making tangy MARL SAUV BL. Light RIES (value), distinctive new Gemstone Ries 17'. Bold The Brothers (mid-tier) Sauv Bl, barrel-fermented The August Sauv Bl. Fast-improving PINOT N. Recently leased famous Clayvin V'yd (powerful Pinot N 13'). Acquired ARA brand 2016.

Gimblett Gravels Hawk Defined area (800 ha planted, mostly since early 80s) of old river bed, mostly free-draining, low-fertility soils noted for rich B'x-style reds (mostly MERLOT-led, but stony soils also suit CAB SAUV – arguably better). And super SYRAH. Best reds world-class. Also age-worthy CHARD.

Gisborne (r) 13' 14 (w) 14' 15 NZ's 4th-largest region (biggest in 70s/80s), on e coast of North Island. Abundant sunshine but often rainy; v. fertile soils. Key is CHARD (deliciously fragrant, best mature well.) Excellent GEWURZ, VIOGNIER; MERLOT, PINOT GR more variable. Interest in ALBARIÑO (rain resistant). Top wines from MILLTON.

Gladstone Vineyard Wair r w ★★ Largest producer in n WAIR. Tropical SAUV BL (incl wooded Sophie's Choice); weighty PINOT GR 16'; v.gd medium-dry RIES 16'; creamy VIOGNIER 16'; fine-textured PINOT N under top label, Gladstone 14' 15. 12,000 Miles is lower-priced, early-drinking range.

Grasshopper Rock C Ot r ★★→★★★ Estate-grown at Alexandra by PINOT N specialist. Subregion's finest red 14' 15 16': harmonious, cherry, spice, dried-herb flavours. V. age-worthy; great value.

Greenhough Nel r w ★★→★★★ One of region's best; immaculate Apple Valley RIES 16, organic SAUV BL 16 17, consistently gd CHARD 16', PINOT N 15'. Top: Hope V'yd (organic Chard 14' 15'; old-vine PINOT BL is NZ's finest 15'; Pinot N 15').

Greystone Waip (r) w ★★★ Star producer (also owns MUDDY WATER), with rich aromatic whites (dry and medium RIES 15' 16', GEWURZ 15', Alsace-style PINOT GR 15' 16'; classy CHARD 15', oak-aged SAUV BL 15' 16'); PINOT N (fragrant 15'). Thomas Brothers is top, notably Pinot N 13' 15'.

Greywacke Marl r w ★★→★★★ Distinguished wines from Kevin Judd, ex-CLOUDY BAY. SAUV BL 16' 17; CHARD 14 15; PINOT GR 15'; gently sweet RIES 15'; PINOT N 13 14' 15'. Barrel-fermented, ageable Wild Sauv 14' 15' is full of personality.

Grove Mill Marl r w ★★ Attractive whites: punchy SAUV BL 16'; generous WAIRAU VALLEY CHARD; oily-textured PINOT GR 16'; slightly sweet RIES. Smooth PINOT N. Value, lower-tier Sanctuary brand. (Owned by Foley Family Wines).

Hans Herzog Marl r w ★★★ Warm, stony v'yd at Rapaura with dense, mature MERLOT/CAB 07' 08'; PINOT N earthy, organic 11. Creamy CHARD 13; apricot-coloured

PINOT GR 16'; oak-aged SAUV BL 15'. Classy TEMPRANILLO 13', MONTEPULCIANO 13'. Sold under Hans brand in Europe, US.

Hawke's Bay (r) 10' 13' 14' 15 (w) 14' 15 16 NZ's 2nd-largest region (13 per cent v'yd area). Long history (since 1850s) of wine in sunny, dryish climate. Classy MERLOT and CAB SAUV-based reds in favourable vintages; SYRAH (vibrant plum, pepper flavours) a fast-rising star; powerful, peachy CHARD; rounded SAUV BL (suits oak); NZ's best VIOGNIER. Alsace-style PINOT GR, promising PINOT N from cooler, elevated, inland districts esp Mangatahi and Central Hawk. *See also* GIMBLETT GRAVELS.

Huia Marl (r) w (sp) ★★ V.gd, partly oak-aged, organic SAUV BL 16'; bold GEWURZ; fleshy CHARD 15'; fragrant PINOT N 14'. Complex Blanc de Blancs 10'.

Hunter's Marl (r) (p) w (sp) ★★ →★★★ Pioneer winery with strength in whites. Classic SAUV BL 16' 17. Kaho Roa oak-aged style 16'. Vibrant CHARD 16' (new smoky Succession Chard 13'). Excellent fizz Miru Miru NV (esp late-disgorged Res 13'). RIES (off-dry), GEWURZ, PINOT GR (dry) all rewarding, value. PINOT N is easy-drinking.

Invivo Auck r w ★★ Fast-expanding young producer with strong, nettley MARL SAUV BL 17; full-bodied Marl PINOT GR; floral, savoury C OT PINOT N 16'. Recent focus on celebrity labels esp "chief winemaker" Graham Norton's Own Sauv Bl (smooth).

Isabel Marl r w ★★ Formerly distinguished SAUV BL producer. After quality and financial problems, bought by Australian supermarket giant Woolworths 2014. Classy CHARD 16' an auspicious sign.

Johanneshof Marl (r) w sp ★★ Small winery acclaimed for v. perfumed GEWURZ (one of NZ's finest 16'). Lively Blanc de Blancs fizz; v.gd RIES 16', PINOT GR 16.

Jules Taylor Gis, Marl (r) (p) w ★★ Stylish, gd value. Refined, partly barrel-aged MARL CHARD 15' 16'. Intense Marl SAUV BL 16'; fragrant Marl PINOT N 15' 16'. Complex top wines: OTQ ("On The Quiet").

Kim Crawford Hawk ★→★★ Brand owned by CONSTELLATION NEW ZEALAND. Easy-drinking (with "Res" on capsule, but not label), incl aromatic MARL SAUV BL (huge seller in US); floral PINOT GR; fruity HAWK MERLOT; generous PINOT N (blend of Marl/C OT grapes). Top range: Small Parcels, incl fragrant CHARD 16'.

Kumeu River Auck (r) w ★★★ Complex Estate CHARD 14' 15' 16 is multi-site blend; value. Single-v'yd Mate's V'yd Chard (planted 1990) is more opulent 13' 14' 15' 16; single-v'yd Hunting Hill Chard 13' 14' 15' 16 is a rising star: notably refined, tight-knit. Lower-tier Village Chard is great value 16. Floral PINOT GR.

Lake Chalice Marl (r) (p) w ★★ Medium-sized producer, now owned by SAINT CLAIR. Lightly oaked CHARD 16; dryish PINOT GR 16; punchy SAUV BL 16'. Easy-drinking PINOT N. Top range: The Raptor (incl gd-value Chard 16').

Lawson's Dry Hills Marl (r) (p) w ★★ →★★★ Best-known for intense, slightly oak-influenced SAUV BL 17 and perfumed GEWURZ 16'. Fast-improving PINOT N. Top: The Pioneer (outstanding Gewurz 14' 15'.) New Res range: weighty Sauv Bl; lightly creamy CHARD; savoury Pinot N. Lower-tier: Mount Vernon (Sauv Bl is top value).

Lindauer Auck ★ →★★ Hugely popular (in NZ), low-priced fizz esp bottle-fermented Lindauer Brut Cuvée NV. Latest batches: easy-drinking, slightly nutty and yeasty. Special Res (disgorged after 2 yrs) offers complexity, value.

Lowburn Ferry C Ot r ★★→★★★ PINOT N specialist with top reputation, bought in 2017 by US investor Brian Sheth and viticulturist Steve Smith (ex-Craggy Range). Flagship is The Ferryman Res (complex 14'). Home Block (fleshy 14' 15' 16); Skeleton Creek (not entirely estate-grown, but supple 13 14).

Mahi Marl r w ★★ Stylish, complex wines. Sweet-fruited SAUV BL (part oak-aged) 16'; gd-value CHARD (esp Twin Valleys V'yd 15'); PINOT GR 16; rosé 17; PINOT N 14 15'.

Man O' War Auck r w ★★ Largest v'yd on WAIH. Penetrating Valhalla CHARD 16; full-flavoured Paradise PINOT GR 16 (from adjacent Ponui Island); tangy SAUV BL 16. Reds incl generous MERLOT/CAB/MALBEC/PETIT VERDOT 14; delicious Death Valley Malbec 14'; spicy Dreadnought SYRAH 14'.

Marisco Marl r w ★★ Waihopai Valley producer with two brands, The Ned and Marisco The King's Series. Impressive Marisco The King's Favour SAUV BL; punchy The Ned Sauv Bl.Gd CHARD, PINOT GR, PINOT N.

Marlborough (r) 14 15 16' (w) 15' 16 NZ's dominant region (two-thirds of plantings) at top of South Island; 1st vines in modern era planted 1973 (SAUV BL in 1975.) Warm, sunny days and cold nights give v. aromatic, crisp whites. Intense Sauv Bl, from sharp, green capsicum to ripe tropical fruit (some top wines faintly oak-influenced). Fresh, medium-dry RIES (recent wave of sweet, low-alc wines); some of NZ's best PINOT GR, GEWURZ; CHARD is slightly leaner than HAWK but more vibrant and can mature well. High-quality, gd-value fizz and classy botrytized RIES. PINOT N underrated, top examples (from n-facing clay hillsides) among NZ's finest. Interest stirring in ALBARIÑO, GRÜNER V.

Martinborough Wair (r) 13' 14 15 16 (w) 13' 14 15 16 Small, prestigious district in s WAIR (foot of North Island). Cold, southerly winds reduce yields, warm summers, typically dry autumns (not in 17), free-draining soils. Success with several white grapes (SAUV BL, PINOT GR both widely planted), but esp acclaimed since mid to late 80s for sturdy, long-lived PINOT N (higher percentage of mature vines than other regions).

Martinborough Vineyard Mart r (p) (w) ★★★ Pioneer winery; famous PINOT N (Home Block 14'). Biscuity CHARD; herbaceous, partly barrel-fermented SAUV BL 16; intense Manu RIES 16'; gd-value, drink-young Te Tera range (Pinot N 14' 15). Owned since 14 by American Bill Foley. Lower-tier: Russian Jack.

Matawhero Gis r (p) w ★★ Former star GEWURZ producer of 80s, now different ownership. Unoaked CHARD; Gewurz (perfumed); rounded PINOT GR; plummy MERLOT; promising ALBARIÑO. Top range: Church House (upfront Chard 15').

Matua Auck r w ★→★★★ Producer of NZ's 1st SAUV BL in 1974 (from AUCK grapes) long known as Matua Valley. Now owned by TWE. Most are pleasant, easy-drinking. Impressive, luxury range of Single-V'yd wines, incl pure, searching Sauv Bl; v. classy ALBARIÑO; powerful CHARD; dense MERLOT/MALBEC 14'; SYRAH 14'.

Maude C Ot r w ★★ Consistently gd, scented PINOT GR 16; fine-textured PINOT N 15; outstanding, racy RIES 16', CHARD 14, Pinot N 15 from Mt Maude V'yd at Wanaka.

Mills Reef B of P r w ★★ →★★★ Easy-drinking wines from estate v'yds in GIMBLETT GRAVELS and other HAWK grapes. Top Elspeth range incl tightly structured CHARD 15'; fine-textured B'x-style reds esp CAB SAUV 15', SYRAH 13', blend Elspeth One 15'. Res range whites and reds typically gd value.

Millton Gis r (p) w ★★ →★★★★ Region's top wines from NZ's 1st organic producer. Hill-grown, single-v'yd Clos de Ste Anne range (*Chard 15, Chenin Bl 14'*, VIOGNIER 15', SYRAH 15', PINOT N 15) is characterful. Long-lived, partly barrel-fermented CHENIN BL (honeyed in wetter vintages) is NZ's finest 15' 16. Drink-young range: Crazy by Nature (gd value). Classy, new La Cote Pinot N 14 15'.

Misha's Vineyard C Ot r w ★★ Large v'yd at Bendigo. Attractively scented GEWURZ, PINOT GR 16', RIES (dry Lyric, slightly sweet Limelight); sophisticated, partly oak-aged SAUV BL; classy dry rosé 16'; PINOT N 13 (Verismo is oak-aged longer).

Mission Hawk r (p) w ★★ NZ's oldest wine producer; 1st vines 1851; 1st sales 1890s; still owned by Catholic Society of Mary. Wide range of gd-value regional varietals, with V'yd Selection next up the scale. Res range incl excellent MERLOT, CAB SAUV, SYRAH, MALBEC, CHARD, SAUV BL. Top label: Jewelstone (v. classy Chard 15' 16', Syrah 13' 14 15'). Also owns large v'yd in AWATERE VALLEY. Purchased NGATARAWA 2017.

Mondillo C Ot r w ★★ Rising star at Bendigo with scented dry RIES 15, rich PINOT N 13' 14' 15', rare, beautifully scented, silky Bella Pinot N 13'.

Mount Edward C Ot r w ★★ Small, respected producer with elegant, gently oaked CHARD, racy RIES and concentrated PINOT N. Earth's End: well-rounded Pinot N (14') for early drinking.

Mount Riley Marl r (p) w ★★ Medium-sized, gd-value family firm. Punchy SAUV BL; fine-textured PINOT GR 16', off-dry RIES 15, gently oaked CHARD, drink-young PINOT N. Top range is Seventeen Valley (v. elegant Chard 14').

Mt Beautiful Cant r w ★★ Large v'yd at Cheviot, n of Waip. Creamy CHARD 15; peachy, spicy PINOT GR 15; scented RIES 16; herbaceous SAUV BL 16'; nutty PINOT N 15'.

Mt Difficulty C Ot r (p) w ★★ →★★★ Quality producer in warm Bannockburn district, acquired by US billionaire Bill Foley 2017. Powerful PINOT N 14' 15'. Roaring Meg is slightly lighter, but still moderately complex, Cromwell Basin blend for early drinking. Single-v'yd Growers Series reds incl refined Chinamans Terrace (15'). Consistently classy whites (esp RIES, PINOT GR).

Muddy Water Waip r w ★★ Small, high-quality organic producer, owned by GREYSTONE. James Hardwick RIES (among NZ's best 15'), ageable CHARD 15'; notably complex PINOT N 15 (esp Slowhand, based on oldest, low-yielding vines 12').

Mud House Cant r w ★★ →★★★ Large, Australian-owned, MARL-based producer of South Island wines (incl Waip, C OT). Brands incl Mud House, Waipara Hills, Hay Maker (lower tier). Regional blends incl gd-value Marl SAUV BL 16' 17; scented Marl PINOT GR; medium-dry WAIP RIES 16'; charming C Ot PINOT N. Excellent Estate selection (single v'yds) and Single-V'yd range (from growers). New Sub Region Series: creamy-smooth CHARD 15'; full-bodied Pinot Gr 16'.

Nautilus Marl r w sp ★★ →★★★ Medium-sized, rock-solid range of distributors Négociants (NZ), owned by S Smith & Sons (*see* Yalumba, Australia). Top wines: weighty SAUV BL 16 17, v. classy CHARD (15'); elegant Southern Valleys PINOT N 14 15; mouthfilling PINOT GR 15' 16'; yeasty NV sparkler (min 3 yrs on lees), one of NZ's best. Excellent new GRÜNER V 16'; ALBARIÑO 16'. Lower tier: Twin Islands.

Cider now so popular in NZ that some v'yds have been uprooted, apples planted.

Nelson Nel (r) 13' 14' 15 (w) 14' 15 Smallish region w of MARL; climate wetter (v. damp in 16 17) but equally sunny. Clay soils of Upper Moutere hills (full-bodied wines) and silty WAIMEA plains (more aromatic). SAUV BL is most extensively planted, but also strength in aromatic whites esp RIES, PINOT GR, GEWURZ; also gd (sometimes outstanding) CHARD, PINOT N. Deserves more notice.

Neudorf Nel r (p) w ★★★→★★★★ Smallish winery with a big reputation. Refined Moutere CHARD 14' 15' 16' one of NZ's greatest; excellent, drink-young Rosie's Block Chard 15' 16'. Superb Moutere PINOT N 13' 14 15'; lightly oaked SAUV BL; off-dry PINOT GR 15 16; RIES (dr s/sw) also top flight. Classy new ALBARIÑO 15' 16.

Ngatarawa Hawk r w ★★ Mid-sized producer, bought by Mission 2017. Easy-drinking Stables Res range incl mouthfilling HAWK CHARD; sturdy Hawk MERLOT; generous Hawk SYRAH. Outstanding Proprietors Res selection: fragrant Chard; v. rich Merlot/CAB; firm Syrah; ravishing Noble RIES. Glazebrook: 2nd tier.

No. 1 Family Estate Marl sp ★★ Family-owned company of regional pioneer Daniel Le Brun, ex-Champagne. No longer controls Daniel Le Brun brand (owned by Lion). Specialist in v.gd fizz esp yeasty NV Blanc de Blancs, Cuvée No 1. Top end: notably harmonious Cuvée Virginie 09'.

Nobilo Marl *See* CONSTELLATION NEW ZEALAND.

Obsidian Waih r (p) w ★★ V'yd in Onetangi: v. stylish, B'x blend Res The Obsidian 10' 11 12 13' 14'; dense Res SYRAH 13' 14' 15. 2nd tier incl gd, plummy, spicy Estate MONTEPULCIANO 15 16.

Oyster Bay Marl r w sp ★★ From DELEGAT. A marketing triumph: huge sales in UK, US, Australia. Vibrant, easy-drinking, mid-priced wines with a touch of class, from MARL, HAWK. Marl SAUV BL is biggest seller, 1.5 million cases/yr (potent passion fruit/lime). Gently oaked Marl CHARD; medium-bodied, Grigio-style Hawk PINOT GR; plum/spice Marl PINOT N, smooth Hawk MERLOT, easy-drinking sparklers, impressive new rosé 17'.

Palliser Mart r w ★★ →★★★ One of district's largest and best. Excellent SAUV BL 16'; v. elegant CHARD 15'; bubbly (best in MART); v. harmonious PINOT N 13' 14 15. Top wines: Palliser Estate. Lower tier: Pencarrow (great value, majority of output).

Pask Hawk r w ★★ Mid-size winery, bought 2017 by John Benton (owns Jackson, MARL). Extensive v'yds in GIMBLETT GRAVELS. CAB SAUV, MERLOT, SYRAH well-priced, full, can be green-edged. Vibrant CHARD. Top Declaration range incl toasty Chard 15'; dark Merlot 13' 14'; complex Cab/Merlot/MALBEC 13' 14'; smooth Syrah 14'.

Passage Rock Waih r w ★★ Show-stopping, opulent SYRAH esp Res 14'; non-Res also fine value 14'. Gd B'x-style reds esp Res CAB SAUV/MERLOT 13' 14.

Pegasus Bay Waip r w ★★★ Pioneer family firm with superb range: taut CHARD 15' 16'; complex SAUV BL/SEM 13' 15'; zingy RIES (big seller) 14' 15'; exotic GEWURZ 13' 14 16'; silky PINOT N 13 14' (esp mature-vine Prima Donna 10' 11 12' 13). Lovely sweet Ries, Sem. Second label: Main Divide, v.gd value esp PINOT GR.

Peregrine C Ot r w ★★ Concentrated whites (esp RIES, dry 16, slightly sweet Rastaburn); gd, citrus, yeasty NV sparkling. Scented PINOT N 15'. Charming organic ROSÉ 17'. 2nd tier: Saddleback (classy dry PINOT GR 16').

Pernod Ricard NZ Auck r (p) w sp ★ →★★★ One of NZ's largest producers, formerly Montana Wineries in AUCK, HAWK, MARL. Co-owned v'yds for Marl whites, incl huge-selling BRANCOTT ESTATE SAUV BL 16' 17. Strength in fizz esp big-selling DEUTZ Marl Cuvée. Wonderful value CHURCH ROAD reds and CHARD. Other key brands: STONELEIGH (tropical Sauv Bl 17).

NZ now grows Arneis, Dolcetto, Fiano, Lagrein, Marzemino. Little Italy...

Puriri Hills Auck r (p) ★★ →★★★ V. classy, long-lived MERLOT-based reds (with CAB FR, CARMENÈRE, CAB SAUV, MALBEC) from Clevedon 08' 09 10' 13' 14. Res esp fragrant, with more new oak. Top: outstandingly lush Pope 10'. Second label: Mokoroa.

Pyramid Valley Cant r w ★★ →★★★ Tiny elevated limestone v'yd at Waikari, bought in 2017 by US investor Brian Sheth and viticulturist Steve Smith (ex-Craggy Range). Estate-grown, floral PINOT N (Angel Flower, Earth Smoke); citrus CHARD. Classy Growers' Collection wines (incl PINOT BL, CAB FR) from other regions.

Quartz Reef C Ot r w sp ★★ →★★★ Small, quality, bio producer with peachy PINOT GR 15' 16'; savoury Bendigo Estate PINOT N 13' 14' 15' 16'; black label esp concentrated 14' 15'. Yeasty, *racy fizz* (vintage esp gd 14').

Rapaura Springs Marl ★★ Consistently gd whites: CHARD 16, PINOT GR 17, SAUV BL 17. Esp gd-value Res range: Chard 16, Pinot Gr 16' 17, Sauv Bl 17, rosé 17.

Rippon Vineyard C Ot r w ★★ →★★★ Pioneer v'yd on shores of Lake Wanaka; arresting view and wines. Flagship is Mature Vine Rippon PINOT N 10' 12' 13', from vines planted 1985–91. Jeunesse Pinot N 13' was made with "no adjustment or additions": sense of unlocked power. Slowly evolving whites esp outstanding Mature Vine RIES 15'.

Rockburn C Ot r (p) w ★★ Crisp, full PINOT GR 16, v.gd RIES 16. Silky PINOT N 13' 14' 15 16 blended from Cromwell Basin (mostly) and GIBBSTON grapes. Second label: Devil's Staircase, cherry/plum Pinot N 17.

Rod McDonald Hawk r (p) w ★★ Highly experienced winemaker (ex-VIDAL 1993–2006). Brands: Te Awanga, Two Gates, One Off, Quarter Acre. Top CHARD, MERLOT.

Sacred Hill Hawk r w ★★ →★★★ Mid-size producer. Acclaimed Riflemans CHARD 13' 14' 15' 16', powerful but refined, from inland, elevated site. Long-lived Brokenstone MERLOT 14' 15', Helmsman CAB/Merlot 14 15' and Deerstalkers SYRAH 14' 15' from GIMBLETT GRAVELS. Punchy MARL SAUV BL 16, delicious, gd-value HAWK Merlot/Cab Sauv 15 16. Halo and Res: mid-tier.

Saint Clair Marl r (p) w ★★ →★★★ Largest family-owned producer in region, 1st vintage 1994. Acclaimed for pungent SAUV BL from relatively cool sites in lower WAIRAU VALLEY – esp great-value regional blend and strikingly aromatic Wairau

Res 16' 17. Easy-drinking RIES, PINOT GR, GEWURZ, CHARD, MERLOT, PINOT N. Res is top range; then extensive array of 2nd-tier Pioneer Block wines (incl classy Pinot N, Sauv Bl); then gd-value regional blends; 4th tier is Vicar's Choice.

Seifried Estate Nel (r) w ★★ Region's 1st and biggest winery, family-owned. Long respected for gd, medium-dry RIES 17, GEWURZ 17; value, often excellent SAUV BL, CHARD. Peachy, spicy GRÜNER V, easy-drinking Wurzer. Best: Winemakers Collection (esp Sweet Agnes Ries 16' 17, creamy Chard 15'). Old Coach Road: 3rd tier. Whites better than reds.

Selaks Marl r w ★ →★★ Old producer of Croatian origin, now a brand of CONSTELLATION NEW ZEALAND. Solid, easy-drinking Premium Selection range. Gd Res HAWK CHARD, ROSÉ, MERLOT/CAB, SYRAH. Recently revived top Founders range esp Chard 16'.

Seresin Marl r w ★★ →★★★ Quality organic producer. Sophisticated, age-worthy SAUV BL 15' 16' one of NZ's finest; generous CHARD 14'. Savoury PINOT N 14; partly oak-aged PINOT GR 16. Bone-dry sparklings. 3rd tier Momo (v.gd quality/value). Complex, fine-textured, distinctive wines.

Sileni Hawk r (p) w ★★ Large producer, strong current focus on PINOT N. Top wines: powerful Exceptional Vintage CHARD 13', SYRAH 13', MERLOT 13' 14. Mid-range Estate Selection: lush The Lodge Chard 15' 16', well-rounded Cape SAUV BL 16', fragrant Triangle Merlot 14' 15, refined Springstone Pinot N 16', then Cellar Selection (gd Merlot, Syrah, PINOT N, Chard). Smooth MARL SAUV BL (esp Straits 16').

Spy Valley Marl r (p) w ★★ →★★★ High achievers; extensive v'yds. Flavoury aromatic whites (RIES 15', GEWURZ 15' 16, PINOT GR 15' 16') are superb value; impressive SAUV BL 16, CHARD 15', PINOT N 14 15'. Satisfying Pinot N Rosé 16. Classy top selection: Envoy (Chard 14'; Alsace-style Pinot Gr 16'; dry Ries 16'; oak-aged Sauv Bl 15'; complex Outpost Pinot N 14 15').

Staete Landt Marl r w ★★ V'yd at Rapaura (WAIRAU VALLEY): refined CHARD (biscuity 15'); top-flight Annabel SAUV BL (tropical 17'); creamy PINOT GR 16', graceful PINOT N 15'. Second label: Map Maker (gd value).

Starborough Family Estates Marl (r) w ★★ Family-owned v'yds in AWATERE and WAIRAU VALLEYS. SAUV BL, deep-flavoured 16 17. Sturdy CHARD 15'. Scented PINOT GR 16. Elegant PINOT N 16'. NB: Starborough Family Estates not to be confused with Starborough brand controlled by Gallo.

Stonecroft Hawk r w ★★ Small winery. NZ's 1st serious SYRAH (1989), Res 13' 14' 15'; Serine Syrah 15'; Crofters Syrah: to drink young 16. Sturdy Ruhanui (MERLOT/CAB SAUV) 14' 15. V. intense Old-Vine GEWURZ 15'. Tropical SAUV BL 16'. NZ's only ZIN (spicy 14 15).

Stoneleigh Marl r (p) w ★★ Owned by PERNOD RICARD NZ. Based on relatively warm Rapaura v'yds. Gd large-volume MARL whites: SAUV BL 17; floral PINOT GR 16'; full-bodied RIES 16, slightly buttery CHARD 15. Top wines: Rapaura Series (esp weighty Sauv Bl 15' 16; toasty Chard 15, rich Pinot Gr 15' 16, full-bodied PINOT N 14' 15').

Stonyridge Waih r w ★★★ →★★★★ Boutique winery, famous since mid-80s for exceptional CAB SAUV-based red, Larose 10' 11 12 13' 14' 15', one of NZ's greatest. Airfield, little brother of Larose. Powerful Rhône-style Pilgrim 15'; Faithful SYRAH, made for early drinking 15. Super-charged Luna Negra MALBEC 15'.

Te Awa Hawk r w ★★ →★★★ GIMBLETT GRAVELS v'yd known since 1994 for MERLOT-based reds, now owned by VILLA MARIA and site of a key new winery. V. elegant CHARD 15' 16'; fragrant Merlot/CAB 13' 14' 15'; supple SYRAH 14. Savoury TEMPRANILLO 13' 14'. Left Field range: easy-drinking, gd value.

Te Kairanga Mart r w ★★ One of district's oldest, largest wineries, much improved since purchase by American Bill Foley in 2011. V.gd PINOT GR 16', SAUV BL 16', finely poised PINOT N 15' (value); RIES 14' 15. Runholder is mid-tier (Pinot N 14' 15'). Res is John Martin: weighty CHARD 14' 15, dense Pinot N 14' 15.

Te Mania Nel ★★ Small, gd-value produce; lively CHARD, GEWURZ, PINOT GR, RIES, racy SAUV BL (organic). Top Res range: organic PINOT N 14' and Chard 15'.

Te Mata Hawk r w ★★★ →★★★★ Prestigious winery (1st vintage 1895) run by Buck family since 1974. Coleraine (CAB SAUV/MERLOT/CAB FR blend) 10' 13' 14' 15' has rare breed, great longevity (1st 1982 vintage a lovely mouthful in 2017); much lower-priced *Awatea* Cabs/Merlot 13' 14 15' also classy, more forward. *Bullnose Syrah* 10' 13' 14' 15' among NZ's finest. Elston CHARD 13' 14' 15'. Estate V'yds range for early drinking (v.gd Chard, SAUV BL, GAMAY Noir, Merlot/Cabs, SYRAH).

Terra Sancta C Ot r (p) (w) ★★ Bannockburn's 1st v'yd, founded 1991 as Olssens, new ownership since 2011. V.gd-value, drink-young Mysterious Diggings PINOT N 15' 16'; Bannockburn Pinot N is mid-tier 14' 15; savoury Jackson's Block Pinot N 15'; outstanding, vivacious Pinot N Rosé 17' (one of NZ's finest).

Te Whare Ra Marl r w ★★ Label: TWR. Small WAIRAU VALLEY producer, some of region's oldest vines, planted 1979. Known for highly perfumed, organic GEWURZ; vibrant SAUV BL, RIES (dry "D", medium "M").

Te Whau Waih ★★ →★★★ Tiny, acclaimed coastal v'yd, restaurant, helipad. V. classy CHARD 13' 14' 15'. B'x-like, mostly CAB SAUV blend The Point 10' 12 13 14'.

Tiki Marl (r) w ★★ McKean family own extensive v'yds in MARL and WAIP. Vibrant SAUV BL esp Single V'yd 16'; fleshy PINOT GR 16'; creamy Koro HAWK CHARD 15, fragrant Koru C OT PINOT N 14'. Second label: Maui.

Tohu r w ★★ Maori-owned venture with extensive v'yds in MARL, NEL. Racy Single V'yd SAUV BL 16'; oak-aged Mugwi Res Sauv Bl 15; RIES 15; PINOT GR 16; refined Blanc de Blancs fizz 13'; increasingly complex PINOT N 15'.

Trinity Hill Hawk r (p) w ★★ →★★★ Highly regarded producer, US-owned since 2014. Refined, B'x-style blend The Gimblett 14' 15'; stylish GIMBLETT GRAVELS CHARD 14' 15' 16'. Exceptional Homage SYRAH 10' 13' 14' 15'. Impressive, plummy TEMPRANILLO 14' 15' 16. Weighty MARSANNE/VIOGNIER 16'. Lower-tier, "white label" range gd value esp drink-young MERLOT 15'.

Two Paddocks C Ot r (w) ★★ Actor Sam Neill makes several PINOT NS. Excellent regional blend 14'. Single-v'yd range: First Paddock (from cool Gibbston district 15'), Last Chance (riper, from warmer Alexandra 15'). Latest is The Fusilier 14' 15', grown at Bannockburn. Picnic: gd drink-young, The People's Pinot 14.

Two Rivers Marl r (p) w ★★ Convergence SAUV BL: classy, incisive wine from WAIRAU and AWATERE VALLEYS 17. V.gd CHARD 15'; PINOT GR 16; RIES 16. Pale, v. delicate rosé 17. Tributary PINOT N 15'. Second label: Black Cottage (gd value).

Urlar Wair r w ★★ Small organic producer with weighty PINOT GR 16'; RIES 16; oak-aged SAUV BL 15'; gently honeyed Noble RIES 15' 16'; PINOT N 16'.

Valli C Ot ★★ →★★★ Superb range of complex, single-v'yd PINOT N (Gibbston 14' 15' 16', Bendigo 14' 15' 16', Bannockburn 14' 15' 16', WAITAKI 14' 15' 16').

Vavasour Marl r w ★★ →★★★ Planted 1st vines in AWATERE VALLEY (1986). Now US-owned by Foley Family Wines. Creamy CHARD 15' (Anna's V'yd 15', from oldest vines esp elegant), best-known for nettley SAUV BL 16'; promising PINOT N.

Waitangi, 1840, made "light white wine, v. sparkling and delicious," French explorer.

Vidal Hawk r w ★★ →★★★ Est 1905, owned by VILLA MARIA since 1976. Top Legacy range: smoky, tight-knit CHARD 15' 16'; silky SYRAH 14'; superb CAB SAUV 14'; great-value mid-tier Res range: Chard 15' 16'; MERLOT/Cab Sauv 14' 15'; Syrah 14' 15'; MARL PINOT N 15' 16'. Top-value Marl SAUV BL 16' 17.

Villa Maria Auck r (p) w ★★ →★★★ NZ's largest fully family-owned winery, headed by Sir George Fistonich; his daughter Karen chairs the board. Also owns ESK VALLEY, TE AWA, VIDAL. Wine-show focus, with glowing success. Distinguished top ranges: Res (regional character) and Single V'yd (reflect individual sites); Cellar Selection: mid-tier (less oak) excellent, superb value; 3rd-tier, volume Private Bin wines can also be v.gd (esp SAUV BL **17**, also CHARD, GEWURZ, PINOT GR, RIES, VIOGNIER, rosé, MERLOT, PINOT N.) Small volumes of v.gd ALBARIÑO, VERDELHO, GRENACHE, MALBEC. New icon red, Ngakirikiri The Gravels **13**': CAB SAUV-based, v. youthful.

Waiheke Island r (w) Lovely, sprawling island in Auckland's Hauraki Gulf (temperatures moderated by sea). Pioneered by Goldwater 1978. Initial acclaim for stylish CAB SAUV/MERLOT blends; more recently for dark, bold SYRAH. Popular tourist destination; many helipads.

Waimea Nel r (p) w ★★ One of region's largest and best value producers, sold in 2017 to investment fund. Punchy SAUV BL **16**, rich PINOT GR **16**. V.gd RIES (honeyed Classic **15**), scented GRÜNER V **16**, steely ALBARIÑO **16**. Full-bodied PINOT N **14**' **15**. Spinyback is 2nd tier.

Waipara Valley CANTERBURY's key subregion, n of Christchurch; 85 per cent of region's plantings. Currently repositioning itself as "North Canterbury", after name confusion in export markets.

Wairarapa NZ's 7th-largest wine region (not to be confused with WAIP). *See* MART. Also incl Gladstone subregion in n (slightly higher, cooler, wetter). Driest, coolest region in North Island; strength in whites (SAUV BL, PINOT GR most widely planted, also gd RIES, GEWURZ, CHARD) and esp PINOT N (warm, savoury from relatively mature vines). Starting to promote itself as "Wellington Wine Country".

Wairau River Marl r (p) w ★★ Gd whites: punchy SAUV BL **16 17**, rounded PINOT GR **16**, gently sweet Summer RIES **16**, tangy ALBARIÑO **16**, delicious rosé. Res is top label: Sauv Bl **16**; VIOGNIER **15**'; CHARD **15**'; PINOT N **15**'; SYRAH **15**'.

Wairau Valley MARL's largest subregion (1st v'yd planted 1873; modern era since 1973). Vast majority of region's cellar doors. Three important side valleys to s: Brancott, Omaka, Waihopai (known collectively as Southern Valleys). SAUV BL thrives on stony, silty plains; PINOT N on clay-based, n-facing slopes. Substantial recent plantings in cooler, wetter upper reaches of valley.

Waitaki Valley C Ot Slowly expanding subregion in N Ot, with cool, frost-prone climate. V. promising PINOT N (but can be leafy), racy PINOT GR, RIES.

Whitehaven Marl r (p) w ★★ Medium-sized producer. Flavour-packed, gd-value SAUV BL big seller in US. Rich GEWURZ **16**'; citrus CHARD **16**'; oily PINOT GR **16**'; off-dry RIES **16**'; v.gd dry rosé from PINOT N **16**'; sturdy Pinot N. Top range: Greg.

Wither Hills Marl r w ★★ Large producer, owned by Lion brewery. Gd-value esp gooseberry/lime SAUV BL. Fleshy PINOT GR; gently oaked CHARD; smooth PINOT N.

Wooing Tree C Ot r (p) w ★★ Single v'yd, mostly reds. Bold PINOT N **14**' **15**' **16**' (Beetle Juice less new oak **15**' **16**'). Complex Sandstorm Res Pinot N **14**' **15**'. Creamy CHARD **15 16**'. Less "serious" wines, all from Pinot N, incl delicious dry rosé **17**', Blondie (faintly pink, off-dry white **16 17**) Tickled Pink **17**'.

Yealands Marl r (p) w ★★ NZ's biggest "single v'yd", at coastal AWATERE VALLEY site, now owned by utility company, Marlborough Lines. Partly estate-grown, mostly MARL wines. High profile for sustainability, but most wines not certified organic. Single V'yd range: SAUV BL **17**; RIES **16**'; GRÜNER V one of NZ's best, lemony **15**'. PINOT N **16**. Seductive Winemaker's Res Pinot N **16**'. Peter Yealands: top value. Other key brands: Babydoll, Crossroads, Babydoll, The Crossings.

South Africa

Abbreviations used in the text:

		Rdg/Up/V	Ridge/Upper/Valley
Bre	Breedekloof	Oli R	Olifants River
C'dorp	Calitzdorp	Pie	Piekenierskloof
Cape SC	Cape South Coast	Rob	Robertson
Ced	Cederberg	Sla	Slanghoek
Coast	Coastal Region	Stell	Stellenbosch
Const	Constantia	Swa	Swartland
Ela	Elandskloof	Tul	Tulbagh
Elg	Elgin	V Pa	Voor Paardeberg
Fran	Franschhoek	Wlk B	Walker Bay
Hem	Hemel-en-Aarde...	Well	Wellington

S outh Africa's reds are getting lighter and brighter, whites livelier and purer-fruited, pinks drier and food-friendlier. Heavy wood-derived aromas and flavours are becoming passé, and more nuanced expressions of site, soil and vine, made in old oak, clay amphoras, concrete eggs, or steel, are de rigueur. Old vines are properly appreciated, as are yesterday's grape varieties (Cinsault, Colombard, Palomino – but above all Chenin Blanc), and there is much interest in varieties suited to a warming climate, like Vermentino, Macabeo and Assyrtiko. Freshness, vitality and subtlety are the new stylistic watchwords; hence the tendency to harvest earlier and avoid the *dikvoet* (literally "thick foot") vinifications of old. New growing areas are being reconnoitred, established ones reappraised, neglected ones revitalized. There are blends being constructed from multiple origins, while others, in the newest trend, are being deconstructed, with their constituent sites/clones bottled separately. With all this in ferment, can we describe S Africa as the world's most dynamic wine region? In the running for best value too.

Recent vintages

2017 Despite 100-year-severity Cape drought, an outstanding crop, comparable with 2015.

2016 Unusually hot and dry; year for later-ripening varieties and cooler areas.

2015 Exceptional across the board, perhaps better even than stellar 2009.

2014 Challenging, needed good judgement and timing; lighter, elegant wines.
2013 Bumper harvest, in both size and quality, with bonus of moderate alcohol.

AA Badenhorst Family Wines W Cape r (p) w (sp) ★★ ·★★★★ Cousins Adi and Hein Badenhorst's winery on Paardeberg Mtn epitomizes new S Africa dynamism. Gnarled vines, ambient yeasts, old oak for mostly Med blends (red 11 **12** 13' 14 15), CHENIN BL (varietal and blended w 13 **14** 15'), heirloom varieties (CINSAULT 14' 15 16, PALOMINO 15 **16**). Exceptional-value everyday range Secateurs.

Alheit Vineyards W Cape (r) w ★★★★ Old-vine and heritage-variety specialist with multi-region CHENIN BL/SÉM Cartology 11' 12 13 **14** 15' 16, single-site Chenin Bl (Magnetic North Mtn Makstok **13**' 14 15' 16, Radio Lazarus 12' 14 15' 16), La Colline Sém 14 15', Hemelrand Vine Garden 15' 16 from HEM home farm.

Anthonij Rupert Wyne W Cape r (p) (br) w ★·★★★ Portfolio named for owner Johann Rupert's late brother, from own v'yds in DARLING, SWA, Overberg and stately home farm (and cellar-door) L'Ormarins nr FRAN. Best of the five wine ranges are flagship Anthonij Rupert and site-specific Cape of Good Hope.

Ataraxia Wines W Cape r w ★★★ Heralded CHARD 12 13 **14** 15' 16 and newer PINOT N 14 15 by grower/co-owner Kevin Grant on Skyfields farm, with remarkable chapel-like cellar-door overlooking HEM.

Babylonstoren W Cape r (p) w (sp) ★★·★★★ A C17 Cape Dutch farm nr PAARL stylishly restored by Karen Roos, ex-*Elle Decoration* editor, and media-giant husband Koos Bekker. B'x red Nebukadnesar 12 13 14 15' heads improving line-up.

Bartho Eksteen W Cape r p w sw sp ★★★ HEM-based Bartho Eksteen specializes in Rhône varieties and SAUV BL, mentors young growers/distillers under Wijnskool/ Tree of Knowledge banner.

Bartinney Private Cellar Stell r (p) w (sp) ★·★★★ Rising star on precipitous Banhoek Valley slopes, family-owned; increasingly impressive CAB SAUV 10 11 12 13 14', CHARD 12 13 **14** 15' 16. Noble Savage "lifestyle" range.

Beau Constantia Const r w ★·★★ Elegant B'x/Rhône varieties and blends from steep mtn v'yds planted by Du Preez family owners in early 2000s.

Beaumont Family Wines Bot R r w (br) (sw) ★★·★★★ Excellent handcrafted wines from charmingly rustic estate. Rare solo-botted MOURVÈDRE 10' **11** 12 13 14, elegant Hope Marguerite CHENIN BL 12' 13 **14** 15' 16', recent New Baby white 15' 16.

BEE (Black Economic Empowerment) Initiative aimed at increasing wine-industry ownership and participation by previously disadvantaged groups.

Beeslaar Wines Stell r ★★★ KANONKOP winemaker's own take on one of celebrated estate's signature grapes, PINOTAGE 12 13' **14**' 15. Refined and rather special.

Bellingham Coast r (p) w ★·★★★ Enduring DGB brand with fascinating low-volume, high-class Bernard Series (incl hen's-teeth-scarce monovarietal ROUSSANNE 14 15' **16** 17) and Homestead line, v.gd debut old-vine CHENIN BL 16.

Beyerskloof W Cape r (p) (w) (br) ★·★★★ SA's PINOTAGE champion, nr STELL. Ten versions of the grape on offer, incl varietal Diesel **09** 10 11 12 13' 14 15 16, CAPE BLENDS, Port style. Even PINOTAGE burgers at cellar-door bistro. Also classic CAB SAUV/MERLOT Field Blend 09' **10** 11 12 13 14 15.

Boekenhoutskloof Winery Coast r (p) w sw ★★·★★★★ Extraordinary quality, consistency over past quarter-century with SYRAH 09' 10 11 12' 13 14 15' 16 (now entirely SWA fruit); FRAN CAB SAUV 08' **09**' 10 **11**' 12 13 14 15 16 (also-excellent newer STELL version 14 15); *old-vines Fran Sém* 12 13 **14** 15; Med-style red Chocolate Block; gd-value Porcupine Ridge, Wolftrap lines. *See* PORSELEINBERG.

Bon Courage Estate Rob r (p) w (br) sw (s/sw) sp ★·★★★ Broad family-grown range led by Inkará reds; stylish trio of Brut MCC; aromatic desserts (RIES, MUSCAT).

Boplaas Family Vineyards W Cape r w br (sp) (sw) ★·★★★ Wine-growers Carel Nel and daughter Margaux at C'DORP. Port styles: Cape Vintage Res 08 **09**' 10 11 12'

13 14 15 and Tawny. Recently more emphasis on unfortified Portuguese grapes.

Boschendal Wines W Cape r (p) w (sw) sp ★→★★★ Famous, photogenic estate nr FRAN under DGB stewardship, noted for SHIRAZ, SAUV BL, CHARD and MCC.

Botanica Wines W Cape r (p) w (sw) ★★→★★★★ By STELL-based American Ginny Povall. Debut Mary Delany CHENIN BL 12' **13** 14' 15' 16' from old w-coast bush vines later joined by equally superlative PINOT N **12** 13 15 16 from HEM, SÉM 15' 16 (ex-ELG), VIOGNIER *vin de paille* NV (ex-Stell).

Bouchard Finlayson Cape SC r w ★★→★★★★ V. fine PINOT N grower in HEM. Galpin Peak 09 10 11 **12** 13' 15' and barrel-selection Tête de Cuvée 09 10 **12** 13. Impressive CHARD (Crocodile's Lair, ex-Ela vines, and Missionvale, both 12 13 **14** 15 16), exotic red Hannibal 10' 11' 12 13 14 15.

Breedekloof Large (c.13,000 ha) inland mostly bulk- and entry-level wine DISTRICT; pockets of high quality include Bergsig, Olifantsberg, OPSTAL, Stofberg Family.

Buitenverwachting W Cape r (p) w sw (sp) ★★→★★★ Classy family winery in CONST. Standout CHARD 12 13 **14**' 15 16, Husseys Vlei SAUV BL 12 13' 14 15 16, B'x red Christine 07 08 09' **10** 11 12. Labelled Bayten for export.

Calitzdorp DISTRICT climatically similar to the Douro and known for Port styles: Axe Hill, BOPLAAS, DE KRANS, Peter Bayly. Newer unfortified Port-grape blends, varietals.

Cape Blend Usually a red blend with PINOTAGE component. Try DAVID & NADIA, Hughes Family, Rhebokskloof, Springfontein, newcomer The Vinoneers.

Cape Chamonix Wine Farm Fran r w (sp) ★★★★ Excellent winemaker-run mtn property. Distinctive PINOT N, PINOTAGE, CHARD, SAUV BL, B'x blends (r w) and newer CAB FR, all worth keeping.

Capensis W Cape w ★★★ SA-US venture, GRAHAM BECK's Antony Beck and Jackson Family's Barbara Banke. To date, luxurious multiregion CHARD 14 **15**'.

See who in SA is certified organic/bio by visiting Biodynamicorganicwine.co.za.

Cape Point Vineyards W Cape (r) w (sw) ★★★★ Standout producer at Noordhoek on Cape Town's peninsula. Complex, age-worthy SAUV BL/SÉM Isliedh 12' **13** 14 15 16', CHARD, SAUV BL (incl new CAPE TOWN version 17 featuring some DUR fruit). Gd-value label Splattered Toad.

Cape Rock Wines Oli R r (p) w ★→★★ Area's leading boutique grower, noted for personality-packed, strikingly presented Rhône and Port-grape blends (r w).

Cape South Coast Cool-climate "super REGION" comprising DISTRICTS of Cape Agulhas, ELG, Overberg, Plettenberg Bay, Swellendam and WLK B, plus standalone WARDS Herbertsdale, Napier, Stilbaai East and Lower Duivenhoks River.

Cape Town Enlarged and renamed Cape Peninsula DISTRICT, covering Cape Town city, its peninsula and the CONST, DUR, Hout Bay and Philadelphia WARDS.

Catherine Marshall Wines W Cape r w (br) ★★★ Cool-climate (chiefly ELG) specialist Cathy M and partners focus mostly on PINOT N, MERLOT, SAUV BL, CHENIN BL. Delightful new dry, mineral RIES 16.

Cederberg Tiny high-altitude standalone WARD in Cederberg mts. Mainly SHIRAZ, SAUV BL. Driehoek and CEDERBERG PRIVATE CELLAR are sole producers.

Cederberg Private Cellar Ced, Elim r (p) w sp ★→★★★★ Nieuwoudt family with among SA's highest (CED) and most southerly (ELIM) v'yds. Elegant intensity in CAB SAUV, PINOT N, rare Bukettraube, CHENIN BL, SAUV BL, SEM, MCC, SHIRAZ (incl exceptional CWG bottling Teen die Hoog 10' 11' 12 13 14 15).

Central Orange River Standalone Northern Cape "mega WARD" (c.10,000 ha). Hot, dry, irrigated; mainly whites, fortified. Major producer is Orange River Cellars.

Charles Fox Cap Classique Wines Elg sp ★★★ Champagne-style bubbly house, complete with French consultant winemaker; four classic, delicious vintage-dated Bruts, incl new Prestige Cuvée Blanc de Blancs.

Coastal Largest REGION (c.44,000 ha), incl seaward DISTRICTS of CAPE TOWN, DARLING,

Tygerberg, STELL, SWA, but confusingly also non-coastal FRAN, PAARL, TUL, WELL.

Colmant Cap Classique & Champagne W Cape sp ★★★ Belgian family *méthode traditionnelle* sparkling specialists at FRAN. Brut Res, Rosé, CHARD and newer Sec Res; all MCC, NV and excellent.

Constantia Cool, scenic CAPE TOWN WARD, SA's first and among most famous fine-wine-growing areas, revitalized in recent yrs by GROOT, KLEIN CONSTANTIA et al.

Constantia Glen Const r w ★★★ Waibel-family-owned gem on upper reaches of Constantiaberg. Superb B'x blends (r w) and varietal SAUV BL.

Constantia Uitsig Const r w br sp ★ ·★★★ Premium v'yds and, now, cellar (vinification previously at neighbour STEENBERG) producing mostly still whites, MCC. Consistently superior SÉM 11 12' 13 14' 15'.

Creation Wines Wlk B r w ★★★ Elegant modernity in family-owned/-vinified range of B'x, Rhône and Burgundy varieties and blends.

CWG (Cape Winemakers Guild) Independent, invitation-only association of 49 top growers. Stages benchmarking annual auction of limited premium bottlings.

Dalla Cia Wine & Spirit Company W Cape r w ★★ ·★★★ Reputable 3rd-generation family vintners/distillers at STELL. Flagship: pricey "Supertuscan" Teano 11 14.

Darling DISTRICT around eponymous w-coast town. Best v'yds in hilly Groenekloof WARD. Cloof, Darling Cellars, Groote Post/Aurelia, Ormonde, Mount Pleasant, Withington bottle under own labels; most other fruit goes into 3rd-party brands.

David & Nadia Swa r w ★★★ ·★★★★ D&N Sadie follow natural winemaking principles of SWA Independent Producers. Exquisite Rhône-style blend Elpidios 11 12 13 14 15, GRENACHE, CHENIN BL (varietals and blend Aristargos 12' 13' 14' 15' 16), SEM, newer PINOTAGE 15 16, mostly from old vines.

De Krans W Cape r (p) w br (sp) ★ ·★★★ Nel family v'yds at C'DORP noted for Port styles (esp Vintage Res 08' 09' 10' 11' 12' 13' 14 15) and fortified MUSCAT. Recent success with unfortified Port grapes.

Delaire Graff Estate W Cape r (p) w (br) (sw) (sp) ★★ ·★★★★ Diamond merchant Laurence Graff's eyrie v'yds, winery and tourist destination nr STELL. Gem-encrusted portfolio headed by premium-priced, age-worthy Laurence Graff Res CAB SAUV 09' 11 12' 13' 14.

Delheim Wines Coast r (p) w sw (s/sw) (sp) ★★ ·★★★ Eco-minded family winery nr STELL. Vera Cruz SHIRAZ, PINOTAGE; cellar-worthy, best-yrs CAB SAUV-driven Grand Res 06 07' 08 13 14, scintillating Edelspatz botrytis RIES 11 12 13' 14 15'.

DeMorgenzon Stell r (p) w (sw) (sp) ★★ ·★★★★ Hylton and Wendy Appelbaum's manicured property hitting high notes with B'x, Rhône varietals and blends, CHARD, CHENIN BL. Impressive new CWG bottlings: Gravitas (r) 15 and ROUSSANNE 16.

De Toren Private Cellar Stell r ★★ ·★★★ Consistently flavourful B'x red Fusion V 09' 10 11 12 13 14 15', earlier-maturing MERLOT-based Z; light-styled Délicate (r).

De Trafford Wines Stell r w sw ★★★ ·★★★★ Boutique grower David Trafford with track record for bold yet harmonious wines. B'x/SHIRAZ Elevation 393 08 09 10 11 12, CAB SAUV 08 09 10 11 12 13 14 15, Blueprint SYRAH 11 12' 13 14 15', CHENIN BL (dry and *vin de paille*). See also SIJNN.

De Wetshof Estate Rob r w sw sp ★★ ·★★★ Famed CHARD pioneer and exponent; five versions (oaked/unwooded, still/sparkling). Top: single-v'yd The Site 12 13 14 15.

DGB W Cape Long-est, WELL-based producer/wholesaler, owner of brands like BELLINGHAM, BOSCHENDAL, Brampton, Douglas Green.

Diemersdal Estate Dur, W Cape r (p) w ★ ·★★★ DUR family farm excelling with various site/row-specific SAUV BL (incl new Winter Ferment), red blends, PINOTAGE, CHARD and SA's first/only commercial GRÜNER V.

Diemersfontein Wines W Cape r (p) w ★ ·★★★ Family wine estate, restaurant and guest lodge at WELL, esp noted for full-throttle Carpe Diem range. PINOTAGE created emulated "coffee style". BEE brand is Thokozani.

> Organic and biodynamic brands to try
> Wineries certified as organic or bio make up less than three per cent
> of the official tally of 568 cellars crushing grapes, but, with wine quality
> improving dramatically in recent yrs, they offer some of S Africa's best
> and most rewarding drinking. Some names to seek out: Avondale,
> JOOSTENBERG, Laibach, Longridge, Org de Rac, SPIER, Stellar Winery,
> WATERKLOOF, Waverley Hills, plus Elgin Ridge and REYNEKE WINES – also
> S Africa's only certified-bio producers.

Distell W Cape S Africa's biggest drinks company, in STELL. Owns or has interests in many brands, spanning styles/quality scales. *See also* DURBANVILLE HILLS, FLEUR DU CAP, JC LE ROUX, NEDERBURG WINES.

District *See* GEOGRAPHICAL UNIT.

Dorrance Wines W Cape r (p) w ★→★★★ French-toned, family-owned, with one of only two cellars in Cape Town city (reason to visit). Gorgeous SYRAH, CHARD, CHENIN BL. Entry label Simply.

Durbanville Cool, hilly WARD in Cape Town DISTRICT, known for pungent SAUV BL. Corporate co-owned DURBANVILLE HILLS, resurgent Bloemendal, many family farms.

Durbanville Hills Dur r (p) w (sw) (sp) ★→★★★ Owned by DISTELL, local growers and staff trust, with awarded PINOTAGE, CHARD, SAUV BL. V.gd newer MCC and B'x red Tangram 12 13.

Eagles' Nest Coast, Const r (p) w ★→★★★ CONST family winery with reliably superior MERLOT, VIOGNIER, SHIRAZ. Also vibrant SAUV BL, cellar-door-only Little Eagle Rosé.

Edgebaston Coast r w ★★→★★★ Finlayson v'yds and cellar nr STELL. V.gd GS CAB SAUV 08 10 11 12 13 14'; old-vine Camino Africana series; classy early-drinkers. Rare solo TEMPRANILLO under new Rough Diamond joint venture with winemaker Pieter van der Merwe, who also has own brand Sanniesrust (fine GRENACHE 16).

Eikendal Vineyards W Cape r w ★★★ Resurgent Swiss-owned property nr STELL. Historic strong suits (B'x red Classique, MERLOT, CHARD) back to form. More recent all-sorts red Charisma one to watch.

Elgin Cool-climate DISTRICT recognized for SAUV BL, CHARD, PINOT N; also exciting SYRAH, RIES and MCC. Mostly family boutiques, incl one of only two certified-bio wineries in S Africa, ELG Ridge.

Elim Sea-breezy WARD in s-most DISTRICT, Cape Agulhas, producing aromatic SAUV BL, white blends and SHIRAZ. Grape source for majors like DISTELL, up-and-comers like Trizanne Signature Wines and *garagistes*, eg. The Giant Periwinkle.

Ernie Els Wines W Cape r (p) (w) ★→★★★★ S Africa's star golfer's wine venture at STELL, driven by big-ticket B'x Ernie Els Signature (r) 09' 10 11 12 13 14. Earlier-ready Big Easy line.

Estate Wine Official term for wine grown, made and bottled on "units registered for the production of estate wine". Not a quality designation.

Fable Mountain Vineyards Coast r p w ★★★→★★★★ TUL grower and sibling of MULDERBOSCH, owned by California's Terroir Life. Exceptional SHIRAZ (varietal and blend), white blend and Rhône-grape rosé.

Fairview Coast r (p) w (br) (sw) (s/sw) (sp) ★→★★★ Dynamic, innovative owner Charles Back with smorgasbord of varietal, blended, single-v'yd and terroir-specific bottlings incl Fairview, Spice Route, Goats do Roam and La Capra.

FirstCape Vineyards W Cape r p w sp ★→★★ DYA Hugely successful export joint venture of five local co-ops and UK's Brand Phoenix, with entry-level wines in more than a dozen ranges, some sourced outside SA.

Flagstone Winery W Cape r (p) w (br) ★→★★★ High-end producer at Somerset West, owned by Accolade Wines, with impressive PINOTAGE, SAUV BL, B'x white. Sibling to mid-tier Fish Hoek and entry-level KUMALA. Winemaker Bruce Jack the driver behind his family's Overberg boutique, The Drift, for exotic reds (varietal and blended), singular Touriga Franca rosé.

Fleur du Cap W Cape r (p) w sw ★→★★★ DISTELL premium label, incl v.gd Unfiltered Collection, always-stellar botrytis dessert and B'x red Laszlo.

Foundry, The Stell, V Pa r w ★★★→★★★★ MEERLUST winemaker Chris Williams' own brand; wine-partner James Reid; v.gd Rhône varietals: GRENACHE BL 11 12' 13' **14** 15'.

Franschhoek Valley Huguenot-founded DISTRICT known for CAB SAUV, CHARD, SEM, MCC. Characterful portfolio: Grande Provence, Haute Cabrière, Holden Manz, La Bri, Maison, Paserene.

Free State Province and recently demarcated GEOGRAPHICAL UNIT. The Bald Ibis is sole producer, in e highlands.

Gabriëlskloof Bot R r (p) w (sw) (sp) ★→★★★ Having married into a shareholder family, Peter-Allan Finlayson vinifies this expanding and improving line-up, headed by Landscape Series (CAB FR, SYRAH, *Chenin Bl*, B'x white) as well as own standout Crystallum portfolio (PINOT N, CHARD).

Geographical Unit (GU) Largest of the four main WO demarcations: Eastern, Northern and Western Cape, KWAZULU-NATAL, Limpopo and new FREE STATE. The other WO delineations (in descending size): REGION, DISTRICT, WARD.

Glen Carlou Coast r (p) w (sw) ★→★★★ First-rate Donald Hess-owned winery, v'yds, art gallery, restaurant nr PAARL, hailed for B'x r styles, single/multisite CHARD.

Glenelly Estate Stell r w ★★→★★★★ Former Château Pichon-Lalande (*see* B'x) owner May-Eliane de Lencquesaing's v'yds and cellar. Impressive flagships *Lady May* (B'x r) and Estate Res duo (B'x/SHIRAZ, CHARD). Superior-value Glass Collection.

GlenWood Coast r w (sw) ★★★ Assiduous FRAN grower stepping up a level with prestige label Grand Duc (SYRAH, CHARD, botrytis SEM).

Graham Beck Wines W Cape sp ★★★→★★★★ Front-ranker focused exclusively on MCC bubbly. Seven variants led by superb Cuvée Clive (CHARD/PINOT N).

Grangehurst Stell r p ★★→★★★★ Small-batch specialist known for long bottle-ageing at cellar before release. CAPE BLEND Nikela 05 06 07' 08 and PINOTAGE 03' 05 06 07 08. Lovely dry rosé.

Groot Constantia Estate Const r (p) w (br) sw (sp) ★→★★★★ Historic property and tourist mecca in SA's original fine-wine-growing area, with suitably serious wines esp MUSCAT de Frontignan *Grand Constance* 10 11 12 13 14', reviving CONST history of world-class desserts.

Hamilton Russell Vineyards Hem V r w ★→★★★★ Admired cool-climate pioneer and Burg-style specialist. Elegant PINOT N 10 11 **12**' 13 14 15' 16 17; long-lived CHARD 11' 12' **13** 14 15' 16. Super SAUV BL, PINOTAGE and white blend under Southern Right and Ashbourne labels.

Hartenberg Estate Coast r w (sw) ★→★★★ Welcoming STELL family farm never disappoints with SHIRAZ, (several varieties and new blend, The Megan); B'x red, CHARD, RIES (semi-dry and botrytis); gd-value Alchemy blends (r w).

Haskell Vineyards W Cape r w ★★→★★★★ US-owned v'yds and cellar nr STELL receiving rave notices for trio of mono-site SYRAH, single-v'yd CHARD and red blends. V.gd sibling label Dombeya.

Hemel-en-Aarde Trio of cool-climate WARDS (Hem V, Up Hem, Hem Rdg) in WLK B DISTRICT, producing outstanding PINOT N, CHARD, SAUV BL.

Hermanuspietersfontein Wynkelder W Cape r p w ★★→★★★★ Leading SAUV BL and B'x/Rhône blend (r w) specialist; creatively markets physical and historical connections with seaside resort Hermanus. Monopoly cool site Sunday's Glen; *Die Arnoldus* is fine fresh CAB SAUV.

Iona Vineyards Cape SC r (p) w ★→★★★ Co-owned by staff, with high-altitude v'yds in ELG. Excellent blends (SHIRAZ-based and B'x white), CHARD, SAUV BL, PINOT N, newer Solace SYRAH. Wider-sourced "lifestyle" brand Sophie.

JC le Roux, The House of W Cape sp ★★ S Africa's largest specialist bubbly house at STELL, DISTELL-owned. Best labels are PINOT N, Scintilla and Brut NV, all MCC.

Jean Daneel Wines W Cape r w ★★→★★★ Family winery at Napier producing outstanding Director's Signature series esp CHENIN BL and SAUV BL.

Joostenberg Wines W Cape r w (sw) ★→★★ Ever-improving family range, organic-certified. SYRAH, CHENIN BL; some gems in experimental Small Batch Collection.

Jordan Wine Estate W Cape r (p) w (sw) ★★→★★★★ Family winery nr STELL offering consistency, quality, value, from entry Bradgate and Chameleon lines to immaculate CWG bottlings. Flagship Nine Yards CHARD 11' 12 **13** 14 15 16, B'x Cobblers Hill (r) 09 **10** 11 12 13 14 15 16.

Julien Schaal Elg, U Hem w ★★★ Alsace vigneron Julien Schaal and wife Sophie handcraft thrilling CHARD from cool-grown pockets.

Kaapzicht Wine Estate Stell r (p) w (br) (sw) ★→★★★ Family winery in STELL; widely praised top range Steytler (best-yrs Vision CAPE BLEND 08 **10** 12' 15, PINOTAGE, B'x red Pentagon, old-vines The 1947 CHENIN BL **13**' 14' 15 16') and newer Skuinsberg CINSAULT 15.

Kanonkop Estate Stell r (p) ★★→★★★★ Grand local status for three decades, mainly with PINOTAGE 08 **09**' 10' 11 12 13 14 15 16, B'x blend Paul Sauer 08 09 10 11 12 13 14' 15 and CAB SAUV. Second tier is Kadette (red, dry rosé and newer Pinotage).

Keermont Vineyards Stell r w sw ★★★ Neighbour (and supplier of some grapes to) DE TRAFFORD, on steep STELL Mtn slopes. SHIRAZ and CHENIN BL (single-v'yd and blended), new MERLOT.

Ken Forrester Wines W Cape r (p) w sw (s/sw) (sp) ★→★★★ With international drinks giant AdVini as partner, ebullient STELL-based vintner/restaurateur Ken Forrester concentrates on Med varieties and CHENIN BL (dry, off-dry, botrytis). Unputdownable budget line-up, Petit.

Klein Constantia Estate W Cape r (p) w sw sp ★★→★★★★ Iconic property, re-energized and -focused on SAUV BL, with ten different varietal bottlings, and on luscious, cellar-worthy *Vin de Constance* 08 09 11 12' 13' 14 15 (non-botrytis MUSCAT de Frontignan), a convincing re-creation of the legendary C18 CONST sweet dessert.

Kleine Zalze Wines W Cape r (p) w sw ★→★★★★ STELL-based star with brilliant CAB SAUV, SHIRAZ, CHENIN BL, SAUV BL in Family Res and V'yd Selection ranges. Exceptional value in Cellar Selection series.

Klein Karoo Mainly semi-arid REGION known for fortified esp Port-style in C'DORP. Revived old vines beginning to feature in young-buck bottlings: Ron Burgundy Wines' Patatsfontein CHENIN BL **14** 15' 16 and Le Sueur Wines' Chenin Bl 14 15 **16**.

Krone W Cape (p) sp ★→★★★ Refined and classic MCC, incl recently released RD 2001. Made at revitalized Twee Jonge Gezellen Estate in TUL.

Kumala W Cape r p w s/sw (sp) ★ DYA Major entry-level export label, and sibling to premium FLAGSTONE and mid-tier Fish Hoek. All owned by Accolade Wines.

KwaZulu-Natal Province and demarcated GEOGRAPHICAL UNIT on SA's e coast; summer rain; sub-tropical/tropical climate in coastal areas; cooler, hilly central Midlands plateau home to Abingdon Estate and resurgent Highgate.

KWV W Cape r (p) w br (sw) (s/sw) sp ★ →★★★ Formerly national wine co-op and controlling body, today one of S Africa's biggest producers and exporters, based in PAARL. Reds, whites, sparkling, Port-styles and other fortified under more than a dozen labels, headed by serially decorated The Mentors.

Lammershoek r w (br) (sp) (sw) ★→★★★ Influential in recent SWA/S Africa evolution: early emphasis on old vines, organic cultivation, "natural" winemaking, etc. Lots happening in The Mysteries range, eg. ultra-rare solo HÁRSLEVELŰ.

La Motte W Cape r w sw sp ★★★ Graceful winery and cellar-door at FRAN owned by the Koegelenberg-Rupert family. Old World-styled B'x, Rhône varietals and blends, CHARD, SAUV BL, MCC, VIOGNIER *vin de paille*.

Le Lude Méthode Cap Classique Fran sp ★★★ Celebrated and innovative sparkling-only house, Barrow family-owned. Premium-priced offering incl CHARD/PINOT N Agrafe, 1st in S Africa to undergo second fermentation under cork closure.

Le Riche Wines Stell r (w) ★★★ Fine CAB SAUV-based boutique wines, handcrafted by respected Etienne le Riche and family. Also elegant CHARD.

MCC (Méthode Cap Classique) EU-friendly name for bottle-fermented sparkling, one of SA's major success stories; c.330 labels and counting.

Meerlust Estate Stell r w ★★★★ Historic family-owned v'yds and cellar. Elegance and restraint in flagship Rubicon 09' 10' 12 13 14 15, among S Africa's 1st B'x reds; excellent MERLOT, CAB SAUV, CHARD, PINOT N.

Miles Mossop Wines Coast r w sw ★★★ Former TOKARA wine chief Miles Mossop's own brand; consistently splendid red and white blend, botrytized CHENIN BL.

Morgenster Estate Stell (p) w (sp) ★★ →★★★ Prime Italian-owned wine, olive farm nr Somerset West, advised by Bordelais Pierre Lurton (Cheval Blanc). Classically styled Morgenster Res 09 10 11' 12 13 14 and second label Lourens River Valley (both B'x blends). Old-country varieties in Italian Collection and NU Series 1.

Mount Abora Vineyards Swa r w ★★ →★★★ "SWA chic" epitomized in naturally fermented, old-vine CINSAULT, Rhône red blend and bush-vine CHENIN BL 12 13 14' 15 16', vinified by non-interventionist rising star Johan Meyer.

Mulderbosch Vineyards W Cape r p w (sw) (sp) ★★ →★★★ Highly regarded STELL winery, sibling to FABLE MTN V'YDS, owned by California's Terroir Life, with headlining 1000 Miles SAUV BL and trio of single-block CHENIN BL.

Darling district's terroir now comes wrapped as well as bottled: wine-infused toffees.

Mullineux & Leeu Family Wines Coast r w sw ★★★ →★★★★ Chris Mullineux and US-born wife Andrea with investor Analjit Singh transform SWA SHIRAZ, **Chenin Bl** and handful of compatible varieties into ambrosial blends and monovarietals based on soil type (granite, quartz, schist), CWG bottlings, and *vin de paille*. Newer, wider-sourced Leeu Passant portfolio – Dry Red and two CHARD (ex-STELL and Overberg) – equally sublime. Also California boutique brand Fog Monster.

Mvemve Raats Stell r ★★★★ Mzokhona Mvemve, SA's first qualified black winemaker, and Bruwer Raats (RAATS FAMILY): stellar best-of-vintage B'x blend, MR de Compostella 09' 11 12 13' 14 15'.

Nederburg Wines W Cape r (p) w sw s/sw (sp) ★ →★★★★ Among SA's biggest (2.8 million cases) and best-known brands, PAARL based, DISTELL owned. Excellent Two Centuries flagship (CAB SAUV 08 10' 11 12 13 14'), Manor House, Heritage Heroes, Ingenuity ranges. Small Private Bins for annual Nederburg Auction: CHENIN BL botrytis Edelkeur 09' 10' 11 12' 13 14. Low-priced quaffers, still and sparkling.

Neil Ellis Wines W Cape r w ★★★ →★★★★ Pioneer STELL-based négociant sourcing cooler-climate parcels for site expression. Masterly Terrain Specific range: Jonkershoek Valley CAB SAUV 07 09 10' 11 12 13 14 15, Pie GRENACHE 09 10 11 12 13 14.

Newton Johnson Vineyards Cape SC r (p) w (sw) ★ →★★★★ Acclaimed family winery in Up Hem. Top Family V'yds PINOT N 10' 11' 12' 13' 14' 15' 16, **Chard**, SAUV BL, Granum SYRAH/MOURVÈDRE, from own and partner v'yds; SA's 1st commercial ALBARIÑO. Lovely botrytis CHENIN BL, L'illa, ex-ROB; entry-level brand Felicité.

Olifants River W-coast REGION (c.10,000 ha). Warm valley floors, conducive to organic cultivation, and cooler, fine-wine-favouring sites in mtn WARD Pie, and, nr the Atlantic, Bamboes Bay and Koekenaap.

Opstal Estate Bre, Sla r p w (sw) ★ →★★★ Emerging as BRE's leader; family-owned, in stunning mtn amphitheatre. Fine CAPE BLEND, old-vines CHENIN BL, SEM.

Orange River Cellars *See* CENTRAL ORANGE RIVER.

Paarl Town and wine DISTRICT 30 miles+ ne of Cape Town. Diverse styles and approaches; best results with Med varieties, CAB SAUV, PINOTAGE, CHENIN BL.

Zandwijk's Kleine Draken among handful of S Africa kosher portfolios.

Paul Cluver Estate Wines Elg r w sw s/sw ★★ →★★★ Area's standard bearer, Cluver family-owned; convincing PINOT N, elegant CHARD, gorgeous GEWURZ, knockout RIES (botrytis 09 10 11' **12** 14 17 and drier version).

Porseleinberg Swa r ★★★ BOEKENHOUTSKLOOF-owned, organically farmed v'yds and cellar with expressive SYRAH 10 11 12' 13 14' 15 16. Handcrafted, incl ethereal front label, printed on-site by winemaker.

Raats Family Wines Stell r w ★★★ →★★★★ Pure-fruited CAB FR and CHENIN BL, oaked and unwooded, incl exceptional new Eden single-v'yd bottlings. Vinified by STELL-based Bruwer Raats and cousin Gavin Bruwer Slabbert, also partners in B Vintners Vine Exploration Co, unearthing vinous gems. *See also* MVEMVE RAATS.

Rall Wines Coast r w ★★★ →★★★★ Donovan Rall among original SWA "revolutionaries". Newer offerings incl CINSAULT 15 16 (ex-DAR), Ava CHENIN BL 17 (Swa), GRENACHE BL 15 16 (Pie), showing trademark understatement.

Region *See* GEOGRAPHICAL UNIT.

Reyneke Wines W Cape r w ★★ →★★★ Leading organic/bio producer nr STELL; apt Twitter handle (and newer wine brand) "Vine Hugger". Luminous SHIRAZ, CHENIN BL, SAUV BL.

Richard Kershaw Wines Cape SC r w ★★★ →★★★★ UK-born, ELG-stationed MW Richard Kershaw; top of S Africa firmament with refined, cool-climate PINOT N, SYRAH, CHARD. Constituent sites showcased in separate Deconstructed bottlings.

Rijk's Coast r w sp ★★ →★★★ TUL pioneer with multiple tiers of varietal SHIRAZ, PINOTAGE, CHENIN BL. V.gd CHARD MCC.

Robertson Valley Low-rainfall inland DISTRICT; c.13,000 ha; lime soils; historically gd CHARD, desserts; more recently SAUV BL, SHIRAZ, CAB SAUV. Major cellars eg. GRAHAM BECK and many small family concerns incl organic SOLARA.

Robertson Winery Rob r p w sw s/sw sp ★ →★★ Consistency, value throughout extended portfolio. Best: Constitution Rd (SHIRAZ and CHARD).

Rupert & Rothschild Vignerons W Cape r w ★★★ Top v'yds and cellar nr PAARL owned by Rupert family and Baron Benjamin de Rothschild. B'x red Baron Edmond 09 10' 11 12 13 14 15; CHARD Baroness Nadine.

Rustenberg Wines W Cape r (p) w (br) (sw) ★ →★★★★ Beautiful old family winery nr STELL. Flagship is CAB SAUV Peter Barlow 08 09 10 11 12' 13. Outstanding red blend John X Merriman, savoury SYRAH, single-v'yd *Five Soldiers Chard* 11 12 13 14 15, new light-textured GRENACHE.

Rust en Vrede Estate W Cape r (w) sw ★★ →★★★★ STELL owner Jean Engelbrecht's powerful, pricey offering, incl Rust en Vrede red varietals, blends; Cirrus SYRAH joint venture with California's Silver Oak; Stell Res range; Donkiesbaai PINOT N, CHENIN BL (dry and *vin de paille*); v.gd Guardian Peak wines.

Sadie Family Wines Stell, Swa, Oli R r w ★★★ →★★★★ Revered winemaker Eben Sadie's organic, traditionally made Columella (SHIRAZ/MOURVÈDRE) 08 09' 10' 11

"Natural wine" going mainstream

"Natural wine(-growing)" has no official definition in SA, and the term is used to cover everything from using ducks to manage v'yd critters to rigorously applying the precepts of bio. Generally, however, it signifies an eco-friendly approach, with an emphasis on v'yd work to allow the least possible interference in the cellar. Old vines, early or spread-harvesting, bunch-pressing, native-yeast fermentation, skin contact (for whites), restrained extraction, old or neutral oak and zero or minimal sulphur additions are some key elements associated with the natural wine movement, which in recent yrs has entered the mainstream and spread to the winelands' furthest outposts.

12 13 14 15 16, a Cape benchmark; complex, multivariety white Palladius 11' 12' 13 14' 15'; ground-breaking Old Vines series, celebrating S Africa's wine heritage.

Saronsberg W Cape r (p) w sw sp ★→★★★ Art-adorned TUL family estate with awarded B'x-blends (r), Rhône (r w) varieties, blends; newer CHARD MCC.

Savage Wines W Cape r w ★★★ Star winemaker Duncan Savage, now with cellar in Cape Town city. Thrillingly understated wines, incl new joint venture with AA BADENHORST for CWG Auction, The Love Boat; wittily named Are We There Yet? TOURIGA N from remote Malgas WARD.

Shannon Vineyards Elg r w (sw) ★★★ Top MERLOT, PINOT N, SAUV BL, SEM, rare botrytis Pinot N by brothers James and Stuart Downes, vinified at NEWTON JOHNSON.

Sijnn Mal r p w ★★★ DE TRAFFORD co-owner David Trafford and partners' pioneering venture on CAPE SOUTH COAST. Pronounced "Seine". Stony soils, maritime climate, distinctive varietals and blends, brilliant rosé. Winemaker Charla Haasbroek's partly amphora-vinified eponymous brand equally novel.

Simonsig Estate W Cape r w (br) (sw) (s/sw) sp ★→★★★ Malan family estate nr STELL admired for consistency and lofty standards. Powerful pinnacle wine The Garland CAB SAUV 08 09 10; Merindol SYRAH, Red Hill PINOTAGE; S Africa's original MCC, *Kaapse Vonkel*, remains delicious celebrator.

Solms-Delta W Cape r (p) w (br) (sp) ★→★★★ Delightfully different wines from historic FRAN estate, partly staff-owned; Amarone-style Africana (r), sparkling SHIRAZ, innovative VERDELHO/ROUSSANNE blend.

Spier W Cape r (p) w (sw) (sp) ★→★★★ Large, multi-awarded winery and tourist magnet nr STELL. Flag-bearer is brooding B'x/SHIRAZ Frans K Smit 08 09 10 11' 12 13. Creative Block, 21 Gables and Collaborative series, in particular, show meticulous wine-growing.

Spioenkop Wines r w ★★★ Ebullient Belgian Koen Roose and family on ELG estate named for Second Boer War battle zone. V.gd, individual PINOTAGE, CHENIN BL, (rare in S Africa) RIES.

Springfield Estate Rob r w ★★→★★★ Cult grower Abrie Bruwer with traditionally vinified CAB SAUV, CHARD, SAUV BL, B'x-style red, PINOT N. Quaffable white blend.

Stark-Condé Wines Stell r w ★★★ Meticulous boutique winemaker José Conde in STELL's Alpine Jonkershoek. Super CAB SAUV, SYRAH and new PETIT VERDOT in Three Pines and eponymous ranges.

Steenberg Vineyards W Cape r (p) w sp ★→★★★ Top CONST winery, v'yds and chic cellar-door, GRAHAM BECK-owned; SAUV BL, *Sauv Bl/Sém blend*, MCC, polished reds, incl rare varietal NEBBIOLO.

Stellenbosch University town, demarcated wine DISTRICT (c.13,000 ha) and heart of wine industry – Napa of SA. Many top estates, esp for reds, tucked into mtn valleys and foothills; extensive wine tasting, accommodation, restaurants.

Stellenbosch Vineyards W Cape r (p) w (sw) (sp) ★→★★★ Big-volume winery; impressive Flagship range (PETIT VERDOT, CAB FR), newer Limited Releases (GRENACHE, VERDELHO).

Storm Wines U Hem, Hem V, Hem Rdg r ★★★ PINOT N and CHARD specialist Hannes Storm expresses his favoured HEM sites with precision and sensitivity.

Sumaridge Wines U Hem r (p) w ★★→★★★ UK-owned cool-climate v'yds and cellar recently showing improved form; fine PINOT N, CHARD, Maritimus white.

Swartland Fashionable, mainly warm-climate DISTRICT; c.10,000 ha of mostly shy-bearing, unirrigated bush vines producing concentrated, hearty but fresh wines. Increasingly source of fruit for others, with many stellar results.

Testalonga Swa r w ★★→★★★ Out-there SYRAH, GRENACHE, CARIGNAN, HÁRSLEVELŰ, CHENIN BL by extreme non-interventionist Craig Hawkins under El Bandito/Baby Bandito labels. Every sip a surprise.

Thelema Mountain Vineyards W Cape r (p) w (s/sw) (sp) ★→★★★★ STELL-based pioneer of SA's modern wine revival; CAB SAUV 08 **09** 10 **11** 12 13 14, MERLOT Res, CAB SAUV/PETIT VERDOT Rabelais 08 09' **10'** 11 12 13. Sutherland (ELG) v'yds broaden the repertoire (eg. PINOT N).

Thorne & Daughters Wines W Cape r w ★★★ →★★★★ Bot R-headquartered John Seccombe and wife Tasha's single-site SÉM and multiregion blends, some from very old vines, are marvels of purity and refinement. Debut red, Wanderer's Heart, a GRENACHE-based gem.

Tokara W Cape r (p) w (sw) (sp) ★★ →★★★★ Wine, food and art showcase nr STELL. V'yds also in ELG and WLK B. Gorgeous Director's Res blends (r w); elegant CHARD, SAUV BL. Newer CAB SAUV Res 13' 14, CAB FR 12 and Chard MCC.

Tulbagh Inland DISTRICT historically associated with white, bubbly, latterly also beefy reds, some sweeter styles; c.1000 ha.

Uva Mira Mountain Vineyards Stell r w ★★★ Helderberg eyrie v'yds and cellar resurgent under owner Toby Venter, CEO of Porsche SA. Line-up incl brilliant newer SYRAH plus longtime performers CHARD, SAUV BL.

Vergelegen Wines W Cape r w (sw) ★★★ →★★★★ The 2nd governor van der Stel's mansion, immaculate v'yds/wines, stylish cellar-door at Somerset West; owned by Anglo American. Powerful CAB SAUV V 07 08 **09'** 11 12 13, sumptuous B'x blend GVB Red, perfumed SAUV BL/SÉM GVB White.

Vilafonté Paarl r ★★★ California's Zelma Long (ex-Simi winemaker) and Phil Freese (ex-Mondavi viticulturist) partnering WARWICK's Mike Ratcliffe. Superb B'x blends incl newer Seriously Old Dirt.

Villiera Wines Elg, Stell r w (sw) sp ★ →★★★ Grier family v'yds and winery nr STELL with quality/value range, esp brut MCC bubbly quintet (incl low-alc).

S Africa wine turns 360 this year: 1st harvest was on 2 February 1659.

Vondeling V Pa r (p) w sw sp ★ →★★★ UK-owned, sustainability-focused estate in Paardeberg foothills. Eclectic offering: one of SA's few *méthode ancestrale* bubblies.

Walker Bay Highly regarded maritime DISTRICT (c.1000 ha); WARDS HEM, Bot River, Sunday's Glen, Stanford Foothills. PINOT N, SHIRAZ, CHARD, SAUV BL standout.

Ward Smallest of the wo demarcations. *See* GEOGRAPHICAL UNIT.

Warwick Estate W Cape r (p) w (sp) ★★ →★★★ Tourist-cordial Ratcliffe family farm on STELL outskirts. V. fine CAB FR, opulent CHARD, newer MCC, The First Lady SAUV BL.

Waterford Estate W Cape r (p) w (sw) (sp) ★ →★★★ Classy family winery nr STELL, with awarded cellar-door. Savoury Kevin Arnold SHIRAZ 08 09 10 11 12 13, elegant CAB SAUV 08 **09** 10 **11** 12 13 14 15, intricate Cab Sauv-based flagship The Jem 07 **09** 10 11 12'. Eminently/immediately drinkable Pecan Stream trio.

Waterkloof Elg, Stell r (p) w sp ★ →★★★ British wine merchant Paul Boutinot's organic v'yds, winery and cantilevered cellar-door nr Somerset West. Top tiers: Waterkloof, Circle of Life, Seriously Cool and Astraeus MCC. Lower-priced quality under False Bay and Peacock Wild Ferment labels.

Wellington Warm-climate DISTRICT abutting PAARL with growing reputation for PINOTAGE, SHIRAZ, chunky red blends and CHENIN BL.

Wine of Origin (WO) SA's "AC" but without French restrictions. Certifies vintage, variety, area of origin. Opt-in sustainability certification additionally aims to guarantee eco-sensitive production. *See* GEOGRAPHICAL UNIT.

Winery of Good Hope, The W Cape r w (sw) ★ →★★★ STELL winery with eclectic Australian-French-SA-UK ownership. Creative, compatible blend of styles, influences, varieties and terroirs. Instant hit with newer Thirst range – juicy, lower-alc CINSAULT, Gamay, CLAIRETTE varietals. Winemaker Jacques de Klerk's SWA Reverie CHENIN BL a subtle beauty.

Worcester DISTRICT with mostly bulk-wine producers. Family-run Arendskloof/New Cape/Eagle's Cliff, Alvi's Drift, Conradie, Leipzig and Tanzanite aim higher.

Organic, biodynamic and natural wines

A pilgrim's progress?

Modern wine, like the rest of the modern world, is travelling in more than one direction. On the one hand, there is a global movement towards authenticity. We want our wine, and our food, to come from a specific place and be special because of that. We want to know that no chemicals were used, that the animal was well treated, that what is on our plate or in our glass retains a link with the earth. On the other hand, science is enabling ever-greater precision in vineyard and winery: for example, growers know how many layers of leaves a bunch of grapes needs for perfect ripeness, and where; it's not as simple as you might think. An optical grape sorter, which automatically rejects anything shrivelled or green and can check an eye-watering 10,000 berries per minute, is almost routine now in ambitious wineries.

We like the label "organic", but what does it mean? Is biodynamics another step along the same road? And if "natural" wines are natural, what are the others?

There are some definitions. Organic viticulture rejects chemicals. Biodynamism is more about prevention than cure; it is based on the application of organic preparations in homeopathic quantities according to the movements of the moon, stars and planets.

"Natural" wine is organic or biodynamic as well, and means minimal intervention in the winery – perhaps just throwing the grapes into a container and seeing what happens. There are great natural wines, and there are many great biodynamic wines. Are natural wines retrograde, or are they the future? Can growers reconcile biodynamics with science – and do they want to? These are some of the questions we'll be looking at in this supplement. (You'll find boxes scattered throughout the book pointing you to remarkable examples in different countries.) Nor will we forget the contribution of science. More understanding of ripeness and tannins (for example) in the vineyard translates into less intervention in the winery – and that, undoubtedly, is the direction of travel of great wine. Industrial wine follows its own course, but that's another matter.

The overview
Can you taste the difference?

**We are looking here at three categories
of wines: organic, biodynamic and natural.
Each is a philosophical and practical step.**

First, a bit more about the detail of what each means. "Wine from organically grown grapes" involves no use of synthetic applications in the vineyard – so no chemical herbicides, fungicides, insecticides or fertilizers. Copper sulphate is permitted because it is not considered synthetic. "Organic wine" goes further, and restricts the amount of sulphur in the winery. Be aware of the difference, because it is considerable. Both can be certified by official bodies, which vary in their strictness.

Biodynamic wine can likewise be certified. The writings of Rudolf Steiner are its starting point; the preparations used are derived from various plants and other ingredients, ideally grown on the same property, though they can be bought in. Horsetail, chamomile and others are used, as is manure buried in a cow's horn over the winter. The preparations are "dynamized" in water and sprayed on leaves, flowers or roots according to the biodynamic calendar drawn up by Maria Thun in 1962. The aim of biodynamics is for man to work in harmony with the cosmos.

Natural wine has no certification and so far no universally agreed definition. But it has lots and lots of opinions.

Is one better than another?

All viticulture was pretty much organic until the advent of chemicals after World War Two, and we all know the benefits and the problems they have brought. In the vineyard, the problems are those of dead soil, with hardly any organic life – some vineyards in Burgundy, chemically farmed, have been described as having less organic life than the Sahara. Vines farmed with chemicals become dependent on chemicals; producers who have moved suddenly from the chemical extreme to biodynamics report that the vines went into shock. But the end results are good. In Burgundy, biodynamic growers have better levels of acidity, better-balanced wines than they had before.

Given that wine-growers are generally well intentioned towards the environment, and like to cut costs on expensive chemicals where they can, the mainstream now is probably what is loosely called "sustainable" viticulture, which means fewer chemicals, and only when and where necessary. Using pheromones to keep harmful insect populations under control is mainstream, as is growing grass between the rows to adjust soil vigour and water content, and control unwanted weeds. But growers may say, "If it rains, I get mildew. Is it better or worse to go through once with a chemical systemic spray,

No more weedkiller between the rows – but choose your cover crop carefully.

or go through several times with a tractor, compacting the soil each time, to spray something organic?"

Biodynamic viticulture is expensive. It requires extra person-power and a lot of time. There is nothing in it that does harm to the environment, and it certainly seems to increase microbial life in the soil, which in turn is good for wine flavour and balance. Do you have to admire Rudolf Steiner? Do you have to believe everything its more irrational adherents say? Some say yes, some say no. Nigel Greening of NZ winery Felton Road says, "We have the best-qualified, most-motivated viticultural team on the planet. It tops a stag's bladder any day for benefits from biodynamism." But he also says that going organic and then biodynamic produces "a cascade of good consequences: things happen that we never really understood before. Everything piles up, and we see extra benefits we never knew."

But actually, can you taste the difference? The crucial point is that for wine to be great, it needs a great winemaker. It's perfectly possible to muck up even the best grapes. But if we assume a good winemaker, then to my palate, biodynamics is more likely than organics to produce a difference in flavour. Good biodynamic wines seem to have a vividness, an energy, that tastes different. But I don't think I could tell organic from non-organic, blind.

Natural wines can breed a greater tolerance of faults. If a natural wine tastes oxidized, or is fizzy when it shouldn't be, or dirty, then those are still faults, even if the winemaker says they're part of the journey of the wine. But the wines of Austrian Bernhard Ott, who throws his grapes into amphorae and leaves them to it; of Croatian Sveti Jakob, who does much the same: these wines are sublime. Like the girl with the curl in the middle of her forehead, when natural wines are good they're very, very good, and when they're bad, they're horrid.

The detail
Organics: black and white?

It's easy for organics to get lost in all the noise about biodynamics and natural wines: it seems a bit old-hat. How dull to worry about boring old copper sulphate spray when you could be out spraying biodynamic preparations by the light of the silvery moon, or ordering clay amphorae from Georgia. Organic viticulture just doesn't have the glamour, does it?

But for any grower considering abandoning chemicals and the farming model that came in after World War Two, it's a change of viewpoint. It means focusing on understanding your soil, your vines and their pests and diseases, and finding ways of helping the vineyard and combating its enemies by strengthening its resistance and encouraging a better-balanced ecosystem.

Put like that, it's hard to see why anyone wouldn't go organic, especially when different certification bodies have different rules, so you can choose what best suits you. But one reason is simple: financial risk. Go to the less profitable parts of Bordeaux, for example, and you'll see bare earth and wilting, yellow-brown weeds where the weedkiller has been at work. There's no need for it, you might think, but a lot of growers can't afford to change their ways. Organics involves more work when they can't afford to employ anybody, and it may involve losing the crop to disease when they're already in hock to the bank. When organic viticulture first took hold in Europe it was in the warmer, drier spots first. Those on the cooler, wetter western seaboard or the northern hills took a lot more convincing.

Nevertheless, Europe has proved quicker to adopt organics than much of the New World. European growers had fathers or grandfathers who had been *de facto* organic because that's what viticulture was, then. (Though ironically it was often the grandfathers who tut-tutted at what they regarded as a return to backward ways, when the grandchildren went organic.) Modern New World wine was born and raised with chemicals and regarded technology as normal. Back in the 80s many an Australian or Californian winemaker regarded soil as merely the stuff that held the vine upright. It didn't have to be looked after. (*See* p.314 from some NZ growers who have changed their ways.)

To change from conventional to organic viticulture means abandoning chemical shortcuts. It may mean creating wildlife corridors to encourage greater biodiversity, and encourage the birds that eat caterpillars and other pests; it may mean introducing specific insects to prey on specific pests, or growing specific plants that will attract the specific predators you want. But make sure you don't end up growing plants that will attract insects you don't want – those that are vectors for bacterial or viral diseases. To make a success of organic viticulture you need to understand your specific conditions in detail. What is right for one vineyard won't necessarily be right for another.

Worrying contradictions

Talking of solutions, copper sulphate is the main ingredient of Bordeaux Mixture, and a weapon against downy mildew. It's allowed in organic viticulture. But copper is a heavy metal and can build up in the soil to levels that are toxic to vines and soil micro-organisms. Arguably it's more damaging than biodegradable chemical alternatives. Organics can contain some worrying contradictions. Some would also argue, as we've seen, that repeatedly taking a tractor through a vineyard (horses are seldom viable in practice) compacts the soil. Keeping the soil directly under the vines free of weeds reduces fungal infections and frost risk. Doing it with a mechanical hoe means using a tractor, several times during the growing season. Weedkiller will probably need only a single application. Which is worse?

All the above applies to "wine from organically grown grapes". "Organic wine", though it existed elsewhere, didn't exist in the EU until 2012, and required definition of cellar practices rather than just viticultural ones. Mostly it's about sulphites: sulphites occur naturally in wine anyway, up to about 10mg/l. EU organic wine may contain up to 140mg/l; more for sweet wines. Sulphites prevent oxidation and keep wine fresh. Some people blame them for allergic reactions, however, and levels have long been falling across the board.

What all this means is that it's not a simple case of conventional = bad, organics = good. Don't assume that "conventional" growers are wicked or cynical. They may have their reasons.

Horses are fashionable, but slow and expensive.

The detail
Biodynamics: the death of reason?

The thing to remember about biodynamics is that it's not just a step onwards from organics. It requires a different mindset: an abandonment, even, of much that science tells us. It requires, in its further reaches, faith in the unproven. Some would call it superstition.

Yet it seems to work. Biodynamic wines (provided that the winemaker is competent) can have an extra dimension of depth, energy, detail. Something in biodynamics makes a difference – yet not, I suspect, always for the reasons that many of its advocates claim. Some of the reasoning is plain silly. Preparation 500, which is the cow dung buried over the winter in a cow's horn, does not work because it connects the vine to the eternal feminine. To say a stag is an astral animal and "involved with forces that are quite different to those of a cow, which are all related to the interior" (Steiner) doesn't help, either. How do they know? Who decided this, and on what evidence? Using a stag's bladder for preparation 502, yarrow, "therefore" connects the yarrow to cosmic energies and makes crops more sensitive to the cosmos. Again, who says?

Yet look at some of its practitioners: Bérénice Lurton, who studied Sciences Po at Bordeaux before taking on Château Climens, went biodynamic all at once in 2010 and says, "It's like releasing the terroir, the vines and ourselves. It's an eye-opener: a completely different way to see the vineyards... I want éclat, tension; I want to find the fruit in the terroir." At Château Smith-Haut-Lafitte the very hard-headed Florence and Daniel Cathiard went organic and biodynamic to bring the vineyard back from industrially farmed death and bring its reputation back to the very top. They're obsessive about quality.

Preparation 500 in the making.

Over in Burgundy, where biodynamics is now almost the rule at top estates, Dominique Lafon has long credited it with bringing the acidity and balance back to his wine. "I started to taste the difference after three years." Olivier Humbrecht of Zind Humbrecht in Alsace is biodynamic; so is Domaine Weinbach. In Austria, Nikolaihof is one of many. Some are certified, some are not. For something so wacky, biodynamics has attracted some clear-thinking followers. You'll find further comments, and names, on pp.53, 212, 265, 314.

The degrees of being biodynamic

Some make it a way of life. Some will even refuse conventional medicine for themselves. All stress its usefulness as a way of helping the vine protect itself: biodynamic treatments are more about prevention than cure. If you encourage grapes to have thicker skins they are less likely to rot; preparation 500 (the cow-horn one) is what one grower describes as "bug soup" and thus an obvious way to increase microbial life in your soil. Jean-Baptiste Lecaillon, the ultra-rational, ultra-clever *chef de cave* of Champagne Roederer, says "Steiner is not relevant" – a relief to those who find him more than a little worrying. "There are two kinds of doctors," he goes on. "The doctor who thinks he knows everything: that's a bad doctor. He's not empathetic; he doesn't even call you by your name but by your disease. You're a problem. And there's the empathetic kind, a family doctor, who knows who you are, where you come from. It's the same thing [with vines], and the climate and the moon." For him, it's about understanding his vines and taking care of them as individuals. He uses the preparations but doesn't honestly know if they work.

For Lecaillon, the contradictions must be dealt with by observing and then explaining. What can put people off biodynamics is being told they must believe in the irrational.

What happens in the winery matters as well, specifically when it comes to yeasts. Sorry about this, but it matters. Conventional winemaking uses laboratory yeasts proven to reach a given alcohol degree and give a predictable result. But grapes and vineyards have their own yeasts, of many different species, and not all very useful. Letting grape-must ferment in its own way and in its own time with the wild yeasts it brings in with it is risky – you don't know what off-flavours might result, or even if the fermentation might stop before you want – but it seems to give more complexity, a different texture, a more "winey" wine – something more authentic. You can use wild yeasts without being biodynamic, but no bio winemaker would dream of using anything else. It expresses the terroir better, they say. It is, I suspect, like inviting in several million tiny pets and watching them run riot. Exciting, at least.

The detail
Natural wines: back to the Garden of Eden?

Wine in its most natural state would be made without any intervention from man. This is obviously impossible, since somebody has to plant the vines, pick the grapes and put them together in a container to ferment. So, leaving aside the slightly pedantic point that there is nothing natural about a vineyard, let's look at what natural wine is and why it is being embraced around the world.

In the vineyard, as we've said, a natural winemaker will follow organic or, more often, biodynamic practices. In the winery there will be no added yeasts or sugar or acidity or enzymes. Some sulphur may be added, but if you want full brownie points (and brown here may refer to the colour of the wine) you use none. This is risky, as at the very least it means that your wine is likely to last less time in bottle. A company called Vintae makes a glorious zero-sulphur Garnacha called Le Naturel Reposado; it has a best-before date on the label.

At their best, natural wines are vivid, winey, racy and poised. They are often lower in alcohol than usual: a plus-point these days. They are seldom fruit-driven; indigenous yeasts tend not to emphasize fruit flavours in the way that commercial yeasts do. They may have a risky, walking-a-tightrope feel about them. Chenin Blanc has become a darling of natural wine aficionados, but whether it has taken off there because of the influence of Loire producers like Nicolas Joly, or whether it is because Chenin's high acidity and thick skins make it more bullet-proof than some grapes, it is hard to say.

Tasting at London's RAW WINE fair: natural-wine heaven.

If you want to take risks with sparkling wine, then go for a pét-nat – or, if you prefer, *pétillant naturel*, aka *méthode ancestrale*. What's "natural" here is that the wine is bottled before the alcoholic fermentation is complete, and the wine isn't disgorged. They're bottled with no extra SO_2, and yes, they can be idiosyncratic. Because of the lees in the bottle they may be cloudy, and often only slightly sparkling. They're being made in the Loire, in Australia and even Lambrusco (Vittorio Graziano).

The swing of the pendulum

Natural producers do not start from the point of "normal" winemaking and then remove things. They begin by asking how much manipulation is desirable. If the answer is "none", then everything you do to your grapes has to be justified. If it's not absolutely necessary, don't do it. It's the swing of the pendulum, of course, away from technical methods, and it makes us wonder again if faults are really faults – if they are, who says so? One UK importer of natural wines says that oxidation, for example, is not a fault if it's intentional.

It's perfectly true that our view of what is a fault and what is not is inconsistent. Maderization in Madeira is good; maderization in Chablis is bad. "Sweaty saddles" used to be a defining flavour of Hunter Valley Shiraz, then it became a fault. The "terroir flavours" celebrated by many a French winemaker 30 years ago are now regarded simply as dirty. Even the smell described as "petrol" and found on aged Riesling is now regarded as a fault. You have to talk about "honey" instead. So our idea of what is a fault is subject to review. Until natural wines came on the scene, that review was all in one direction: that of finding new faults to criticize. People had already begun to mutter that the end result would be perfect sterility, and that great, exceptional wines were in fact made up of low-level faults.

It's usually good when a pendulum swings; it reveals things we'd forgotten. Natural wines make us open our minds and reconsider flavours that have become unaccustomed.

But having reconsidered them, do you have to like them? The answer is no. The more extreme these wines are, the more divisive they are. There is dogmatism at both extremes, ranging from total rejection of all natural wines, however good, to total acceptance of all, however bad – not that "bad" is a concept that would be accepted here. The rational position is in the middle: there are good and bad wines and winemakers, so let's be discriminating. On p.286 you will find lists of remarkable natural wines. Whether they will frighten the horses depends on the horses.

The detail
Orange wines: skin-macerated whites

Orange wines are skin-macerated whites – it's as simple as that. White grapes have colour and tannins in the skins, but these are usually lost when the grapes are pressed before fermentation. For orange wines the juice is fermented with the skins. The colour is usually deep gold to tawny rather than the colour of clementines. But then white wines aren't white, either.

Because skins contain tannins as well as colour, orange wines have a distinct tannic grip. The idea of white wines having tannins shouldn't come as a surprise; start looking for a tannic edge in white wines and you'll find it in quite a few. It helps with the general freshness and structure of the wine. But in an orange wine, you'll spot it immediately. Macerating grapes with their skins is not a new technique. Josko Gravner and Stanko Radikon were the modern pioneers, and the wines drew on a long tradition. Their wines gained market traction only slowly. And yet suddenly orange wines are everywhere. Being a hipster staple, which they are, is enough to put some people off them, but when done well, they can be sublime.

The classic, old-as-the-hills way of making them is to take your grapes, put them into your amphora (which in Georgia, another skin-maceration hotspot, will be buried in the ground), put the lid on, seal it and go away. After three months, and perhaps not until six months, come back. Take the lid off. By that time the fermentation will have finished and all the solids will have sunk to the bottom. What is winking at you is clear, pure wine.

Or not. The potential for spoilage is obviously great. Purists take the risk, and ameliorate it with rigorous hygiene – though not sulphur, which is not considered to be playing the game. With good winemakers the results can be assured and elegant – not fruity, but substantial, textured, assured and compelling. They feel like an apotheosis of wine: the summation of the grape, the whole grape and nothing but the grape. Inevitably, there are plenty of producers now playing with the technique and absorbing it, or parts of it. Some might use steel tanks instead of, or as well as, clay amphorae, like Cullen Wines in Western Australia, whose Amber is definitely New World in style.

Skin-contact whites are popping up everywhere, from Austria (Domäne Wachau, for example) to Iberia, and are appearing even in mainstream restaurants. However, quantities are generally small – it's not something you can do on a large scale unless you adapt the techniques to modern technology. And even then, the market is still limited. How do orange wines relate to natural wines? It's clear from the above that some orange wines are natural, and some aren't. They also don't have to be organic or biodynamic. Purist examples

Macerating grapes in an amphora: this is at Kabaj Morel in Slovenia.

probably will be, but it's not a given. Think of orange wines as an addition to the repertoire, not a replacement, and remember that they are as varied as reds or whites, and that the name of the producer is probably more important than the region. On pp.168, 181, 204, 228, 257, 262, 272, 278, 286 you'll find some recommendations; do try them. And also *see* pp.334–5 for more on how these wines match food.

Red amphora wines and concrete eggs

We should put in a word here about red amphora wines, and concrete eggs. Orange wines are white wines fermented on the skins, often in amphorae; red grapes, also fermented in amphorae, make red wines, not orange ones. In Portugal's Alentejo, where reds made this way are now regulated, the grapes are often crushed first and the wine may be run off afterwards and treated quite conventionally, but the amphora (here called *talha*) fermentation does seem to give a different character to the tannins. Concrete eggs are fermentation vessels shaped like eggs and made of – yes, concrete. They stand as high as you do, and you'd be surprised at how many otherwise conventional winemakers have one or two. Their advantage is that they keep the lees in constant suspension – again, it's a textural thing, with wines made this way having extra silkiness. There's nothing intrinsically organic or biodynamic about them, though most producers in these categories will have some.

A modern mantra
Minimal-intervention wines

If they're snappy enough and press the right buttons, catchphrases can quickly become ubiquitous. "Minimal intervention" is one such. It sounds exactly right: doing as little as possible to grape juice on its journey to wine will surely produce the most pure flavours, the most healthy wine. Well, sometimes it does and sometimes it doesn't.

It's certainly a phrase you hear a lot. Few winemakers will describe themselves as "interventionist" in the winery: it's just not fashionable. As with "natural wine", minimal intervention has no definition. It might mean throwing grapes into a clay jar and forgetting about them, or it might mean a panoply of computerized optical sorting tables to select perfect grapes, and computerized fermentation tanks controllable via an app on your phone. That doesn't really matter; to announce that you believe in minimal intervention in the winery is simply to state that you believe that all the work should be done in the vineyard and that the more you as a winemaker do in the cellar the more you are likely to mess things up.

There are two kinds of intervention. There is the chemical kind, which means adding things to the wine, or taking things away. And there is the physical kind, which means pumping the wine around a lot, racking it a lot, fining and filtering it a lot.

Chemical intervention
The first thing that might be added to grapes is sulphur, to stop wild yeasts starting a fermentation before the winemaker is ready. Later yeast will be added, and it will be a yeast selected for a particular purpose: it might favour certain flavours or it might be neutral, but

Laboratory work: a necessity for most wines.

it will produce a predictable result. You might chaptalize the juice with extra sugar, or acidify it (most countries and regions have rules on this). You might add enzymes, usually to increase extraction of colour and tannins, or to increase the aroma of your wine. Enzymes occur naturally in grapes and yeasts, but you can also buy them commercially. You can add tannins if you don't think that nature has given you enough. (This happens in Ribera del Duero as well as in the Napa Valley.) You can add colour to your red wine – perhaps in the form of Mega Purple, a brand of grape concentrate extracted from a grape called Rubired, which increases colour and helps the richness and roundness a bit as well. Many a winery focused on muscle-bound reds of maximum weight keeps some Mega Purple in the cupboard. Later on you can fine with a variety of substances to ensure the clarity and stability of your wine.

Physical intervention

This often has to do with oxygen and when to allow it and when to keep it out. Keeping oxygen away from Sauvignon Blanc juice, for example, means more powerful aromas. Micro-oxygenating red means softer tannins. There's the decision on what temperature to ferment at: over 20°C (68°F) usually for reds, for colour and extraction, 15–16°C (59–61°F) or less for whites, for freshness and aroma. Skin contact (for whites, before fermentation, for extra aroma; after fermentation for reds, for tannins) is another decision, another intervention. Do you ferment in wood, stainless steel, concrete or something else? Do you put the wine into oak barrels after fermentation, and if so, what sort? Big, small, new, old, which cooper? What sort of toast? Do you rack the wine in the winery? Do you filter it?

Every one of these decisions is an intervention, and not all are bad. At the worst, the more you do the more your wine will taste exactly like everyone else's. For some consumers, and at some price points, this is quite desirable.

The point I'm trying to make is that intervention is not necessarily the big bad wolf of winemaking. Every decision is an intervention. The most interesting wines are often made with the least intervention, but they're usually made on a small scale. And things can go wrong. Wild yeasts can give more complex, compelling results, for example, but they also carry a risk of spoilage. Sulphur, overdone, is unpleasant, but used properly, it prevents wine from oxidizing and spoiling in bottle. Some of the most famous old claret vintages were chaptalized; classic Napa Valley reds were (and are) acidified. Ideally, perhaps, winemakers would only make wine from vineyards that produce perfect ripeness and perfect balance. But how much wine would that be for a thirsty world?

Wine and food
Orange with everything

Is it difficult to partner organic, biodynamic or natural wines with food? Not in the least. They're just wines.

I once heard a sommelier say, as though he meant it, that natural wines don't go with classic dishes because the wines are too complex. Sommeliers say the oddest things sometimes. The only thing that stops a natural wine going with anything you would normally match with that sort of wine is if it's faulty – in which case, don't drink it.

So the main thing to talk about here is orange wines. These, remarkably, seem to go with just about any sort of savoury food. Partly, I suspect, it's because of the much more subdued fruit flavours of orange wines. Bold, fruit-forward wines are actually not very good with food; sometimes barbecued food, which itself consists of bold, brash flavours, is the best thing. Fruit juice doesn't go with food, either. But beer goes with food, and goes very well; and those earthy bruised-fruit, dried-fruit, sourdough notes you may find in orange wines work for the same reason. Equally, many wines made from wild yeasts, with their more salty notes and less obvious fruit, are very easy to put with food. So, funnily enough, is the sort of natural wine that tastes of cider or beer. Just don't focus on how much less you'd be paying if it really was cider or beer.

Matching texture and flavour

Texture matters too. Amphora wines (which can be red) and orange wines (which are made from white grapes) are fermented with their